Money,
Banking,
and
Financial
Markets

THIRD EDITION

MONEY, BANKING, AND FINANCIAL MARKETS

ROBERT D. AUERBACH

University of California,
Riverside

MACMILLAN PUBLISHING COMPANY
New York

COLLIER MACMILLAN PUBLISHERS
London

Macmillan Publishing Company
866 Third Avenue, New York, New York 10022

Collier Macmillan Canada, Inc.

Library of Congress Cataloging-in-Publication Data

Auerbach, Robert D.
  Money, banking, and financial markets.

  Includes bibliographies and index.
  1. Money.   2. Banks and banking.   3. Finance.
I. Title.
HG221.A914   1988   332.1   87-11173
ISBN 0-02-305040-3

Printing: 2 3 4 5 6 7 8   Year: 8 9 0 1 2 3 4 5 6 7

PREFACE
FOR
INSTRUCTORS

The last three years have brought enough institutional and theoretical changes in the field of money and banking to warrant a substantial rewriting of much of this book. But those familiar with the first and second editions will still find that the basic organization is intact, with the exception of significant parts of the international aspects of money and banking. Some of the international aspects of money and banking that either have been taken out of the last part of the book or are new have been integrated into the other chapters. Examples of new material includes banking deregulation in other countries (added to Chapter 5, "Financial Intermediaries") and monetary targets in other countries (added to Chapter 27, "Targets and Instruments"). The material in the second edition on the international markets for currencies, the foreign exchange markets, has been moved to Chapter 12, "Financial Markets."

Each instructor may have his or her special interests that make the course more interesting to teach and more enjoyable to learn. This new edition is designed to allow presentation of the standard topics while also allowing flexibility in the additional institutional and theoretical material that is covered. I have based the organization of the second edition on my own experience of teaching money and banking and on the many suggestions communicated to me on the first and second editions.

Chapter 1 is a self-contained introduction to the book. This is followed by Part One, "Some Fundamentals." This part includes the subject areas that most instructors will want to cover. The three chapters in this part cover basic material and contain less detail than was covered in Part I in the first and second editions.

In Part Two, "Financial Intermediaries," more financial intermediaries are covered than has been the practice in money and banking books. This is because more financial intermediaries are now offering checking accounts and other deposits that have at least some of the properties of money. Chapter 9, "Investment and Contractual Intermediaries," can be left out in a course in which the instructor wishes to concentrate on theory. The appendices in Chapter 7, Appendix A: "The Prime Rate" and Appendix B: "History of Money and Banking in the United States to 1863," can also be deleted in those courses in which the instructor wishes to concentrate on theory.

Chapters 5, "Financial Intermediaries," 6, "Depository Intermediaries," and 7, "Commercial Banking," should probably be included in all courses, as they cover subjects that most instructors want to include, regardless of their concentration. Chapter 8, "Assets, Liabilities, and Money Creation of Depository Intermediaries," is also a basic chapter that covers accounting classifications of depository institutions together with a simple explanation of deposit creation.

In Part Three, "Financial Markets, Asset Prices, and Interest Rates," Chapter 12, "Financial Markets," concentrates on institutional details. The other chapters are mostly theoretical. Chapter 10, "Asset Prices, Income, and Interest Rates," presents compounding and discounting and the basic valuation formula that relates asset prices to their expected future income flow and to market rates of interest. Additional formulas and applications are found in the seven appendices for selection by the instructor. Chapter 11, "The Term Structure of Interest Rates," is an optional chapter that covers a dimension of interest rates that some students find difficult to grasp. Chapter 13, "Money and Stock Prices," is an elective chapter that introduces important concepts about causality and association that are important to modern money and banking theory.

Part Four, "The Federal Reserve System," describes the Federal Reserve and its influence over the supply of money. Chapter 14, "Structure and Non-monetary Functions," describes the Federal Reserve, Chapter 16, "Monetary Policy Tools," describes the way in which the Federal Reserve affects the monetary base. These two chapters should normally be covered. Chapter 15, "The Treasury, the Federal Reserve, and Monetary Base," describes the way the monetary base is changed. Courses designed to stress institutional detail can omit this chapter.

Chapter 17, "The Money Expansion Multipliers," is devoted to the relationship between the monetary base and the money supply. Instructors who wish to leave this subject in the simpler form presented in Chapter 8, "Assets, Liabilities, and Money Creation of Depository Intermediaries," can omit this chapter.

Important changes have also been made in Part Five, "Monetary Theory." The first chapter, 18, "The Demand for Money," combines material from the first introductory chapters of the first and second editions with more elaboration to form a single presentation. The main body of the chapter is straightforward and easy to read, given its theoretical content. The fall in the velocity of money in the 1980s is also discussed.

The first part of Chapter 19, "Money and Inflation, a Cash Balance Approach," which deals with the cost of inflation, is probably appropriate to most courses. The later cash balance explanation of inflation and interest rates is more complicated, and some instructors who wish to concentrate on institutional detail may wish to omit it. The two appendices further develop the relationship between nominal and real interest rates, bringing in the effect of income taxes.

Chapter 20, "The Phillips Curve and Price Expectations," brings in developments that are important to understanding how monetary policy affects inflation and how inflation is related to unemployment. Chapter 21, "Wage and Price Controls," carries the analysis of inflation into a controlled environment. Both chapters can be omitted.

Part Six, "Keynesian Expenditure Theory," begins with Chapter 22, "Aggregate Demand and Supply," presents a view of expenditure theory and simple Keynesian theory. A more sophisticated elaboration can be added by bringing in the *IS–LM* model. There is, perhaps, no other subject on which opinions are so divided and strongly held about teaching of theory in money and banking courses than whether or not to devote time to teaching the *IS–LM* Hicksian solution to macroeconomic equilibrium. Many instructors do not wish to devote as much time as mastery of this model may require in their courses. Others find the model particularly useful. If you do not wish to cover the analysis but wish to teach some expenditure theory, Chapter 22, "Aggregate Demand and Supply," has been designed for this. If you do wish to include the *IS–LM* model, all three chapters in this part of the book can be included. Three appendices in Chapter 23, "The *IS–LM* Model," can also be used to bring in additional material.

Part Seven, "Applications of Theory," presents topics of current high interest in both contemporary monetary policy and the academic literature. Chapter 25, "The Effects of Monetary and Fiscal Policy," discusses the relationships among financing government expenditures, monetary policy, and variables such as the real and nominal interest rates. Courses that are directed more toward theory may include this chapter and, if the instructor wishes, the appendix on the controversy regarding supply-side economics. Most instructors will want to include Chapter 26, "Keynesians Versus Monetarists." The appendix to the chapter is an application of the *IS–LM* model for those courses that cover this model in Chapter 23.

Part Eight, "Monetary Policy," includes the following chapters on monetary policy that should be important parts of all money and banking courses: Chapter 27, "Targets and Instruments"; Chapter 29, "Who Makes Monetary Policy?"; and Chapter 30, "Federal Reserve Policymaking and Congressional Oversight." There are two optional chapters. Chapter 28, "Selected Policies and the Record Since 1942," contains a mixture of history and some theoretical applications. Chapter 31, "Interest Rates Versus Monetary Aggregates," is an application of the *IS–LM* model to the selection of target variables.

Many instructors find it difficult to cover thoroughly (or even get to) the international finance aspects of money and banking.

Part Nine, "The International Financial System," presents a selection of subjects central to that coverage. Many instructors, including those that design courses to concentrate on institutional aspects, may wish to assign Chapter 34, "The Eurodollar Market," because there are so many misconceptions about this important market and its effects on the domestic money supply of the United States. Chapter 32, "The Balance of Payments and International Exchange Rates," and Chapter 33, "Methods of International Payments," both contain institutional description and theoretical subjects.

Pedagogical aids available in the third edition include

- Previews of key points in each chapter
- Boxed-off examples and applications
- Explanatory captions for figures and tables
- Expanded end-of-chapter questions and problems
- A glossary of key terms at the end of every chapter

The supplemental package includes a study guide written by David Klingaman of Ohio University. The instructor's manual and computer test bank have been expanded.

A NOTE OF APPRECIATION FOR THE FIRST EDITION

I am very grateful to A. Edward Day, Milton Friedman, Mark Goldman, Charles M. Place, Jr., William Poole, and Jack Rutner for helping with parts of the manuscript and to Milton Friedman for encouraging me to finish it. Former Chairman Henry Reuss and my colleagues on the staff of the Banking Committee of the United States House of Representatives receive my thanks for sharing some of their vast experience and knowledge in this area. I am indebted to my colleague at the American University, Thomas F. Dernburg, whose efforts brought me to Washington, D.C., and who encouraged me in my work. I hope that some of the insights and the perspective of those who most influenced my economic vision show through in this book. I am very grateful for the advice that the late Harry Johnson shared with me on a number of points in the early stages of the manuscript. I am also grateful to Abba Lerner for his sharp analysis during my two years of study with him, back when *saving equals investment* was considered sleight of hand, and to another of my most influential teachers, Arnold C. Harberger, whose analysis always illuminates the central core of a subject. My wife Linda assisted with parts of the manuscript and, together with Donald and Katie, made this book possible.

A NOTE OF APPRECIATION FOR THE SECOND EDITION

Many individuals have given useful suggestions for the second edition, and I would particularly like to thank Lewis Gasper, Manuel Miranda, Jr., Chip Price, Roger White, and Gregg Wilson for their contributions. I also benefited from my experience as an adivser and speech writer in the Treasury Department, working with Beryl Sprinkel, then undersecretary for monetary affairs; Carol Leisenring; and Denis Karnosky.

I was encouraged by the comments on the first edition from Robert W. Clower, Thomas F. Dernburg, Milton Friedman, and Sol S. Shalit. Also I wish to acknowledge the valuable suggestions on the second edition from Stephen M. Cross, College of the Holy Cross; A. Edward Day, University of Central Florida; David C. Klingaman, Ohio University; Gary D. Koppenhaver, Southern Methodist University; G. H. Mattersdorff, Lewis and Clark College; Emile M. Mullick, University of Texas at Arlington; James M. Rock, University of Utah, and Calvin D. Siebert, University of Iowa. I also wish to thank Hurd Hutchins, production editor at Macmillan, for his contributions to the second edition.

R.D.A.

A NOTE OF APPRECIATION FOR THE THIRD EDITION

The third edition has benefited from a number of individuals, many of whom have had extensive classroom experience with this book. I particularly want to thank James Barth, James Rock, and David L. Mengle for their help.

I am also indebted to a number of people in Washington, D.C., some of whom would welcome this public message of appreciation. Those I think would approve include Jake Lewis and Gregg Wilson of the House Banking Committee, Lewis Gasper at the Government National Mortgage Association, Carol Leisenring at the Council of Economic Advisers, Stan Wilson, and Kevin Tansey. William Barnett's presentation of the Divisia-indexed monetary series at the University of California, Riverside, in 1987 convinced me to add that development to the third edition. I also enjoyed the interesting discussions of the 1986 Western Economic Association meeting in San Francisco where Beryl Sprinkel, chairman of the Council of Economic Advisers, Milton Friedman, and William Poole took part in discussions concerning the unexpected behaviour of the income velocity of money in the 1980s. I also benefited from participating in the 1986 Eastern Economic Association meetings in Philadelphia, which used the fiftieth anniversary of the publication of Keynes's *General Theory* as its theme. Ronald Harris, the production editor at Macmillan, and Kenneth Macleod, the editor at Macmillan, made valuable contributions.

CONTENTS

CHAPTER 4
INTEREST RATES   39

PART TWO
FINANCIAL INTERMEDIARIES

CHAPTER 5
FINANCIAL INTERMEDIARIES   53

CHAPTER 6
DEPOSITORY INTERMEDIARIES   67

CHAPTER 13
MONEY AND STOCK PRICES   317

PART FOUR
THE FEDERAL RESERVE SYSTEM

CHAPTER 14
STRUCTURE AND NONMONETARY FUNCTIONS   339

CHAPTER 15
THE TREASURY, THE FEDERAL RESERVE, AND THE
MONETARY BASE   369

CHAPTER 1

AN OVERVIEW

The fields of money, banking, and financial markets have as their common subject of study pieces of paper called **financial assets**, which include **money**, **stocks**, and **bonds**. Who creates them? Why are they valuable? Where are they traded? How do they affect the economy? How should they be controlled? The answers to these questions comprise the subject matter of this book.

Throughout their lives individuals deal with money, stocks, and bonds. Whether or not they are familiar with financial assets, they will be affected in numerous ways by what happens to them. Financial assets are crucial to the efficient allocation of resources—a hollow-sounding phrase to the uninitiated. Financial assets also enable rapidly shifting funds to reach that place where they will provide the most profit.

Some financial assets are policy tools of the government. For example, the government attempts to control the quantity of money in order to influence inflation, interest rates, employment, and many other variables that affect everyone's welfare.

Financial assets have undergone great changes in the 1970s and 1980s as massive shocks hit the financial system. For example, in the 1970s, accelerating inflation, higher interest rates, and government regulations made it profitable to economize on common types of money such as currency, coin, and bank deposits. There was a search for new, higher-interest–paying types of financial assets. Financial markets broadened with the huge volume of financial assets that were traded as oil money gushed and the technology of worldwide, instant communications put the participants in constant contact.

Depository institutions—commercial banks, savings and loan associations, mutual savings banks, and credit unions—also have undergone immense changes as a result of rising interest rates and government regulations, which prevented the payment of market interest rates to their depositors, and as a result of the computer revolution. Some of the banking system was shifted out of the United States into what is called the Eurodollar market, so as to avoid government regulations.

In the late 1970s, money market funds—part of a broader class of firms dealing in financial assets, called **financial intermediaries**—benefited from the combination of high market interest rates and low interest payments allowed on deposits at depository institutions. These funds sprouted like wild mushrooms as individuals transferred their funds from deposits at depository institutions to money market funds to earn higher interest rates.

But this situation changed in 1981. On March 31, 1980, after two and a half years of hearings in the U.S. Congress and a long struggle for passage, President Jimmy Carter signed a new banking law that radically changed the structure of the U.S. banking system. The Depository Institutions Deregulation and Monetary Control Act of 1980 allowed interest-paying nationwide checking-type deposits at all depository institutions. Ceilings on the amount of interest that could be paid on those deposits were directed to be removed over a six-year period. In addition, for the first time, the requirements that all those institutions hold part of their deposits as cash reserves was made mandatory.

This move toward deregulation, begun in the Carter administration, was intensified during the Reagan administration, which began in 1981. In concept, deregulation meant that the federal government would reduce its regulations of the private sector's businesses. The deregulation of depository institutions required depository institutions to compete with one another. That is, they could bid for consumer deposits by changing the interest they paid on these deposits. This new competition, a severe recession in 1982, huge foreign loans that could not be repaid, a plunge in oil prices in the mid-1980s that suddenly reduced the incomes of many individuals in oil-producing areas (such as Texas and Oklahoma in the United States), and poor farm exports all caused more depository institutions to fail than at any time since the 1930s. Indeed, a run on one of the largest banks in the United States in May 1984 led to the takeover—the nationalization—of the bank by the U.S. government. There then were calls by federal banking regulators and members of Congress in 1985, 1986, and 1987 for new kinds of insurance for depository institutions that would mean more government control, thereby signaling a reregulation of the banking industry.

As exciting as those dramatic events since the 1970s were, they were only several data points at the end of a historical record. True, they were a social scientist's dream in that they allowed theories to be tested under hyperthyroid conditions. But understanding those events and the broader scope of relationships between other parts of the economy and financial assets requires an analytical framework.

Part I of this text describes financial assets and one of their most important characteristics, their interest rate. Money, one of the most important financial assets, is given special attention.

Part II turns specifically to financial intermediaries. Although special attention is paid to depository institutions because of the type of financial assets they can create—which are either money or very much like money—other financial intermediaries are also offering many of the same services.

The events since the 1970s and the new banking law have changed the landscape. The 1980 legislation gave all the depository institutions more uniform characteristics, and a 1982 banking law went even further. The 1980 legislation required all depository institutions to abide by similar regulatory requirements, although the phase-in period for these requirements were not completed until September 1987 (January 1993 in Hawaii).

The computer-robot revolution was felt by financial intermediaries in the form of a nationwide automatic teller machine (ATM) network, which in 1983 and 1984 began to compete actively for the financial intermediaries' business. Furthermore, the ATMs violated the rules that forbade going across state lines, which applied to most financial intermediaries. And many depository institutions themselves were invited and enticed to cross state lines and operate in many states, for the first time since the United States initiated a system of banking that, for most depository institutions, meant confinement to one state. How would the small depository institutions compete with the giants from out of state?

In addition, many new businesses began competing for deposits with the traditional depository institutions, from brokerage firms, money market mutual funds, and insurance companies to Sears, Roebuck and Company, the largest retail sales firm in the United States, which owns a brokerage firm, a savings and loan association, and an insurance company. To the owner of a financial intermediary in the 1980s, it probably seemed that old Father Time was sprinting.

Part III discusses interest rates and financial markets, beginning with the method for calculating interest rates on financial assets such as bonds and home mortgages. It explains why bonds with different final payment dates have different interest rates and describes the important financial markets, thus helping the reader understand the stock market and the relationships of stock prices and money.

The structure of the Federal Reserve System and its functions, including its control of the money supply, is described in Part IV. The Federal Reserve System is one of the most important and least understood parts of the economic system in the United States. Federal Reserve policy has more impact on the economy in many areas than does any other part of the government, even though the Federal Reserve has no constitutional authority. It was created by an act of Congress in 1913. Yet the amazing truth is that most people know little or nothing about the Federal Reserve. For example, many individuals believe that the U.S. Congress can literally appropriate money. However, the control of the money supply is the responsibility of the Federal

Reserve. If it says no to any congressional spending appropriation signed into law by the president of the United States, the appropriation must be financed by sending the U.S. Treasury into the market to sell its bonds, bills. and notes to borrow the funds.

But the Federal Reserve can directly control only part of the money supply. The rest is created by private depository institutions. Therefore, this part of the book describes not only how the Federal Reserve creates its part of the money supply but also how the depository institutions create their larger part of the money supply. An important point for government policy, discussed in the final chapter of Part IV, is how those parts of the money supply are related.

Parts V, VI, and VII offer theoretical analyses and applications. Explanations of how money, interest rates, prices, and employment are related will turn the reader—who by now should have a good knowledge of money, banking, and financial markets—toward understanding how economists analyze these important variables in the economy.

Part V examines conventional monetary theory growing out of classical monetary theory (the monetary theory that can be traced back through the centuries). In its modern version, monetary theory offers interesting explanations of inflation and a new explanation of how people base their economic behavior on what they expect will happen to the economy. Conventional monetary theory is used to analyze wage and price controls.

Part VI explains the theories of how spending affects economic activity, including the level of prices, that were first developed by John Maynard Keynes. There is an optional presentation of the most famous model in macroeconomics, the *IS–LM* model, as well as an application of this model to explaining inflation.

Part VII presents some modern applications of theory. The experiences of the 1970s and 1980s produced new evidence and new explanations. Some of these explanations now look poor; some look promising; and in some areas there is controversy that offers exciting areas for new research. All these explanations focus on important economic problems on which policies to achieve full employment, price stability, and a growing economy will be based.

Monetary policy is discussed next in Part VIII. What are its targets? What does the record of selected central bank policies since World War II show? The answers to those questions form the basis of the first two chapters of Part VIII.

Has the president of the United States determined monetary policy, even though the legal court of last resort is inside the Federal Reserve? Some evidence is presented to support this view for the period from 1953 to 1986. Has the Federal Reserve been acting as the inflation fighter it has billed itself as being? Minutes from inside the Federal Reserve, which were kept secret for five years, paint an interesting picture for the period just before President Richard Nixon's reelection in 1972.

Whether or not the hypothesis about presidential control is true, the Federal Reserve has its own interesting ritualistic method of reaching its monetary policy decisions. In addition, the U.S. Congress has, since 1975, held formal oversight hearings to question the Federal Reserve on those decisions, including the emotion-laden issue of Federal Reserve independence.

Part VIII ends with an application of a Keynesian model to an explanation of the issues in determining the best way for the Federal Reserve to conduct monetary policy.

Part IX discusses the international financial system. That it comes at the end of the book does not mean that international monetary policy is less important or can be neatly separated from domestic policy. Indeed, outside an economist's arbitrary model this cannot be done. But the separation is sometimes convenient to show the relationships among several variables without bringing in too many external influences. In any case, international analysis is treated last because it concerns the applications of many economic analyses to a more involved environment than that of a single isolated economy.

We will also discuss concepts such as the balance of payments and various arrangements for making payments between economies that have different currencies. Such arrangements include the gold standard, studied by the Reagan administration, and flexible exchange rates. We will consider the optimum size of an area to have one uniform form of money as well as arrangements for currency areas. In the last chapter in Part IX, we will turn to the Eurodollar market and the transfer to this market of domestic banking business, including deposits.

Each chapter begins with a preview of its contents along with references to previously presented material if it is extensively used. A glossary of terms introduced in the chapter is found at the end of each chapter.

Boxes are used for presenting problems and working out answers and for more detailed explanations when needed. In the first edition, much of the history before World War II was contained in one chapter. In the third edition, this history is integrated throughout the text.

GLOSSARY

Bonds. An interest-paying debt instrument, usually with a maturity of five years or more, formally offered for sale by a business or government.

Financial assets. Claims to present and future wealth and income. Stocks, bonds, and money are financial assets.

Financial intermediaries. Firms, such as savings and loan associations, that accept funds from their customers (savings and loan associations accept the funds in the form of deposits) and use them to buy income-earning assets (such as government bonds and loans to consumers).

Money. Any good used as a medium of exchange. Often the definition is extended to other goods that can be inexpensively changed into the medium of exchange.

Stocks. Ownership rights in a corporation. *Common stock* is a form of stock that enables the owner to vote regularly for the corporation's board of directors.

SOME FUNDAMENTALS

CHAPTER 2

MONEY

WHY STUDY MONEY, CREDIT, AND FINANCIAL INSTITUTIONS?

Money is a widely held good, exchanged in most transactions and stored and created by financial institutions such as commercial banks. Buying something with credit—in other words, "using the proceeds of a loan"—is also a common part of a modern society's transactions, for both consumer loans and the more formally solicited loans negotiated by business and government. Businesses and governments obtain loans by selling bonds to finance their operations.

Widespread use is an important reason for looking into the economic effects of any goods or services. But even though they are widely used, money and credit are completely different from food, drinking water, shoes, and many other common goods and services. Likewise, financial institutions that specialize in money and credit are different from other businesses in the society. That is, a shoe factory and a department store are different from a bank.

Yet different characteristics and widespread use are not sufficient reasons for spending so much time studying money, credit, and financial institutions. There are two more fundamental reasons. First, it is thought that the quantity of money and credit affects the level of output of goods and services and the prices of those goods and services. Second, it is generally believed that the government can have an important, perhaps even a pervasive, effect on the quantity and price of money and credit. Thus the government, through various policies that affect money and credit, can influence the economy, ideally toward desirable objectives such as price stability and full employment.

Because financial institutions specialize in creating money and credit, it follows that if money and credit are important, so are financial institutions. In this chapter we will talk about money, and in the next chapter we will discuss financial assets similar to money.

WHAT IS MONEY?

Money is usually thought of as something that is generally accepted as payment for goods and services and for the discharge of debt. This definition illustrates the *medium-of-exchange* function of money. But it does not nail down all the different things that may be considered money, so it is useful to look at the general functions or services that have been traditionally attributed to those goods that are called money:

1. Medium of exchange
2. Temporary abode of purchasing power
3. Store of value
4. Unit of account (sometimes called a *standard of value*)
5. Standard of deferred payment

1. A good used as a **medium of exchange** is widely accepted for the payment of debt and the purchase of goods and services. Examples are currency, coin, and checks drawn on deposits.

Some commonly used definitions of money, however, include items such as time deposits at commercial banks, which are not a medium of exchange. For example, consumer time deposits usually cannot be sold; they must be held to maturity (the termination date of the time deposit) to receive the full interest. The owner can then transfer time deposits into accounts on which a check may be written: a " checkable " deposit.

Some items that may sometimes be a medium of exchange, such as a $1,000 bill or a personal check, may not provide this service in other circumstances. That is, sellers may refuse to exchange goods and services for them. For example, a $1 bill may not serve as a medium of exchange on a bus that requires the exact fare.

Just as some items that usually serve as a medium of exchange do not always serve this function, other items that rarely serve as a medium of exchange sometimes do. For instance, common stock is sometimes exchanged for the purchase of a corporation.

Obviously, there are exceptions to the definition of money as a good that serves as a medium of exchange, although it is the core of most definitions of money. In addition, other goods that can be inexpensively changed into a medium of exchange are sometimes included in the definition of money. For example, noncheckable deposits at depository institutions can easily be transferred into deposits at the same depository institution on which a check can be written. In fact, sometimes the depository institution automatically does this when the checking account balance drops below a certain amount.

The value of the medium-of-exchange function depends both on a special kind of *uncertainty*—uncertainty about the size and timing of future receipts and expenditures—and on the reduction in the cost of making transactions.

This special kind of uncertainty can be understood by first imagining the opposite environment—complete certainty about all future receipts and expenditures. Imagine that you know for certain that you will be able to buy a bunch of turnips for $3.26 twelve years from now on July 14, after receiving your $6,379.56 paycheck on July 12. Your knowledge extends in this way through every last penny of receipts and expenditures to the moment of your death and even beyond—to the hidden ecstasy of your heirs spending your estate with tears in their eyes. Your horizon of knowledge extends far enough down the road to make even further knowledge of expenditures and receipts of negligible importance today.

Never mind the details. Ask yourself, "If everyone had this knowledge, would they need to carry checkbooks, currency, and coin?" All future transactions could be recorded in a giant computer bank, and changes in bank balances arising from here to the knowledge horizon could be cleared today. No checking accounts, currency, or coin would be needed.

The future is, however, unclear to us, but wondering about it does cause people to think in constructive ways. It pays to own a "temporary abode of purchasing power," that is, a little medium of exchange to tide you over those rough spots when you receive less than you spend.

2. The **temporary abode of purchasing power** function is thus related to the medium-of-exchange property and refers to holding money as a readily available means of negotiating future transactions. In other words, the uncertainty of receipts and payments of money requires that some money be held, even though it might not immediately be needed.

3. The **store of value** function of money is not a unique function. That is, although one way to store wealth is in the form of money, it is not the only way. Owning a house or a tract of land is also a way to store wealth.

4. A **unit of account** is a basic number in a counting system. The generally accepted practice of translating the value of all transactions, wealth, and debts into a single monetary unit of account measurement, such as a dollar, is a great convenience. One can compare a car currently valued at $1,000 with a house currently valued at $6,000 and conclude that six of the cars could be traded for the house.

However, the domestic monetary unit does not always serve as the unit of account. For example, during the colonial period, Americans frequently kept their bookkeeping records in British pounds rather than in the domestic currency. Inhabitants of countries in which foreign trade, including tourism, is a substantial part of their national income may keep their records and quote their prices in terms other than their domestic currency.

5. The **standard of deferred payment** function of money merely refers to the practice of calculating debts in terms of the unit of account used for money.

In addition to these five functions of money, it is useful to mention some of its characteristics that make it useful as a medium of exchange, such as *uniformity of appearance, ease of transport and exchange,* and *security from counterfeiting.* Ease of transport and exchange means that whatever is used as money is generally not expensive to carry around and to exchange. For example, dollar bills and checks are much easier to carry around than are bags of gold. Uniformity in appearance needs a little more explanation.

Uniformity in appearance is a characteristic of many forms of money. That is, money of the same denomination (e.g., all one-dollar bills) is usually uniform in appearance. All U.S. paper dollars look alike; this is a convenience. But the Susan B. Anthony metal dollar coin introduced in 1979 looked too much like a quarter, causing confusion. This kind of uniform similarity was a handicap.

But a money system can work without being uniform in appearance. Until 1862, currency used in the United States was mostly a heterogeneous collection of notes of varying sizes and colors, issued by private banks. Since 1862, however, the official U.S. currency has been printed by the government so that it is uniform in appearance.

Sometimes the characteristics of money are summarized by the word **moneyness,** or the degree to which the functions and characteristics of goods are similar to those of money. Such goods are said to be **near-monies**.

BENEFITS FROM THE INTRODUCTION OF MONEY

A **barter economy** is one in which goods and services are exchanged without the use of money. Goods and services are traded for other goods and services. No good's value is largely or entirely related to its medium-of-exchange services (or to the medium-of-exchange services of another good for which it can be inexpensively exchanged).

It is often held that in a barter economy, buyers and sellers are not fortunate enough to enjoy a **double coincidence** in exchange and that is why money was invented. The double coincidence occurs when both parties to a transaction wish to buy the good or service that the other party is selling, in an exact exchange. Thus in a barter economy a double coincidence would occur if a customer on a bus wanted to trade a pair of shoes for a bus ride, and the driver of the bus wanted to trade a bus ride for a pair of shoes. The problem of the double coincidence could be lessened with a triangular trade: the customer goes off to find someone who will trade the pair of shoes for a belt, which the bus driver also wants. But this is messy. The customer misses the bus, and the new driver wants a ticket to the hockey game. Because of the improbability of this double coincidence or various expeditious triangular trades, some good came into use as a medium of exchange, thereby reducing the costs of trading.

This story may not be applicable to some primitive societies, because it is not necessary to have a physical exchange of money to avoid the double coincidence and because anthropologists and archaeologists studying primitive communities have found evidence that some communities devised a unit of account before they devised a physical medium of exchange. Imagine, for example, a meeting between two primitive tribes. Each tribe has a small stack of shells or, if you like, poker chips. The tribes could mutually agree on the number of poker chips at which each commodity they wish to trade is valued. If a good valued at three poker chips were traded, each tribe could keep track of the transactions by setting three poker chips in a separate pile, to record debits and credits. At the end of the day's activities, either the tribes could make the necessary last-minute trades so that nothing was owed, or they could agree to meet again, beginning where they had stopped in trade, with one tribe owing a debt to the other tribe.[1] Thus the problem of the double coincidence would be solved without exchanging the counting pieces.

If one wants to call debt *money*, then it could be said that those tribes used some form of money. It seems more appropriate to say, however, that they developed a way of keeping track of their transactions by agreeing on a common unit of account but never found it necessary to trade their counting pieces.

Individuals in primitive communities probably could not count to even very small numbers without some device in addition to fingers and toes. Without modern implements, such as pencils, paper, and computers, the most efficient method of counting may have been the use of some homogeneous physical commodities. But the difficulty of keeping track of the values in exchange must have been great. Commodities that were fairly uniform could be used for counting purposes and became the unit of account, just as chips are used in a poker game, except that the primitive counting pieces were often not traded. The more uniform the items were, the easier they would be to understand as equal units of account. Such counting pieces may have been important ingredients for more efficient exchange and were themselves eventually traded.

When counting pieces were traded in a large number of transactions, they became a medium of exchange. They were used not only to reduce the cost of solving the problem of double coincidence but probably also because they had become objects of adoration and superstition in their record-keeping role, and because one person wanted to buy another's computer.

THE USE OF CURRENCY AND COIN IN AN ADVANCED SOCIETY

The property that originally made these counting pieces generally accepted may have been, in large part, their value in record keeping. But as technology advances, records can be kept more easily without having to carry physical counting pieces. On this basis, one could even predict a demise of the physical medium of exchange, the currency and coin of an advanced economy.

Wallets, armored trucks, change purses, cash registers, secret pockets, and currency and coin may thus become museum displays. The automated computer clearinghouse or some similar system using no physical medium of exchange is evolving, with everything done through computer terminals. The buyer's fingerprints could be his or her identification. After shopping and receiving the bill at the checkout counter, the buyer would place his or her hand in a computer on the counter and punch in his or her account number. After automatically checking the fingerprints, the computer would deduct the money from the buyer's account. If the buyer were overdrawn or had no credit, a vise would grab the finger—or in more primitive societies, would chop it off. Beggars would carry computer terminals. There would simply be no physical medium of exchange. No longer would millions of people walk the streets with pockets and purses stuffed with counting pieces, offering themselves up as hors d'oeuvres for muggers. The country would have adopted a centralized **electronic funds transfer system (EFT)**. Relative to this more modern system, the United States now has a backward form of keeping track of money and is unlikely to adopt a modern system.

In the present period—since the institution of high income tax rates and the increase in organized crime activities in the late 1930s in the United States—the demand for currency and coin compared with the total money supply has generally been robust.

Currency and coin were 20 percent of the basic money supply in 1960. That percentage grew to 27 percent in April 1986.[2] (In 1986 there was roughly $724 in cash outstanding for every man, woman, and child in the United States. Do you really think the average family of five has $3,620 in cold, hard cash?)

The reasons for this form the basis for doubting that physical counting pieces will become obsolete. Evidently, individuals do not want records of every one of their transactions, which would be recorded in a computerized payment system for all payments. For example, some people may want to avoid records of illegal transactions, such as those people violating the income tax laws or involved in illegal drug traffic and skimming proceeds from gambling operations.

NEW TECHNOLOGY AND COUNTERFEITING

As new technology is developed, it becomes less expensive for counterfeiters to copy currency and checks. Copying machines can now copy in color with fairly good results, and so the U.S. Treasury's Secret Service agents are kept busy tracking down counterfeiters. In an effort to reduce counterfeiting, the Treasury announced in 1986 the first major change in the currency in over half a century, initially scheduled to begin in 1987. The United Bureau of Printing and Engraving will print currency with new characteristics. The main difference will be a clear polyester thread in the paper of the currency that cannot be seen unless the bill is held up to the light. The thread will be to the left of the Federal Reserve seal on all denominations except the $1 bill, where it will be on the right side. Also on the $1 bill will be printed "one USA one USA" along the length of the thread. "USA" will also be printed on the threads woven into the bills. Another change will be the repeated printing—in letters so small that a magnifying glass must be used to see them—of "United States of America" around the portrait. Accordingly, the cost of the 6.5 billion $1, $5, $50, and $100 bills printed annually by the Bureau of Printing and Engraving will increase from 2.5 cents to 2.6 cents each.

But an important question arises: Will these changes be enough in the face of new technology to stop substantial counterfeiting that may threaten the supply of currency, a medium of exchange that allows privacy?

You do not, however, have to be a criminal to object to having a written record of every transaction you make: In a cashless society the government could use the records of payments to keep every citizen perpetually under a microscope. A major reason, therefore, to have currency and coin is privacy. For example, an individual may desire to keep his or her aid to a friend or a political campaign a secret.

The 1973 Watergate hearings in the U.S. Congress brought to public attention the phrase **laundered money**, or money that is transferred between individuals or businesses in such a way that it cannot be traced. In an effort to prevent narcotics traffickers from laundering money, Attorney General Edwin Meese of the Reagan administration proposed a new law in 1985, defining money laundering as a felony and including penalties of millions of dollars, forfeiture of assets, and prison terms of as much as twenty years. It would require banks to notify the government of potential violations and would also change bank privacy laws (including the Right to Privacy Act) to make it easier for government law-enforcement agencies to obtain, without notifying bank customers, bank records of alleged illegal transactions.

The proposal ignited protests from bankers' organizations and the American Civil Liberties Union. Despite the desire to stem narcotics traffic, this law would violate the right of privacy, and that right is part of the right of freedom from government surveillance and regulation, an attribute of democracies that most people want to maintain.

CONCEPTS OF U.S. MONEY

All checkable deposits in the United States were, until 1973, at financial institutions called **commercial banks**. A depositor could write out a check ordering the bank to pay a designated party a given sum of money from the depositor's account. The basic medium-of-exchange concept of money used by the U.S. government consisted of those checkable deposits, called **demand deposits**, plus all the currency and coin held by the public outside the commercial banks. Government regulations passed in the 1930s prohibited the payment of interest on those demand deposits. This concept of money is called *old M-1*.

But after 1973, other financial institutions that also offer deposits (and that, along with commercial banks, are called **depository institutions**) began to allow similar checkable accounts that could not be withdrawn by a depositor's check. (Their traditional accounts required the presentation of a passbook, either in person or by mail, to withdraw funds.) These other depository institutions include **savings and loan associations**, **mutual savings banks**, and **credit unions**. The three of them together are also called **thrift institutions**, or **thrifts**. One form of checkable account that they now offer is called a **NOW account** because depositors can withdraw their funds and order payment to a designated party with a **negotiable order of withdrawal**, which is similar to a check used at commercial banks.[3] The difference is that NOW accounts pay interest. Commercial banks then also began to offer NOW accounts so they could compete with checkable accounts that pay interest.

A new, broader concept of money, used as a medium of exchange, to fit the growth in NOW accounts was introduced by the government on February 7, 1980. The new concept includes the checkable deposits at all depository institutions plus all the currency and coin held by the public outside banks (see Table 2-1).

A still broader concept of money, called *M-2*, was introduced to include not only checkable deposits at all depository institutions but also all deposits that are **accessible on demand** plus consumer time deposits (see Table 2-1). An account is accessible on demand if the depositor can obtain his or her funds without prior notice, either by check or by presentation of a withdrawal notice

TABLE 2-1   Concepts of the United States Money Supply (Estimates are from January 1987 in billions of dollars)

M-1, M-2, and M-3 are three formal definitions of the money supply (also called **monetary aggregates**) used by the Federal Reserve, the central bank of the United States. The basic medium of exchange is M-1. Near-monies (goods that have many of the characteristics of money and are not included in M-1) that can inexpensively be changed into the medium of exchange are included in M-2 along with the components of M-1. M-3 includes M-2 plus some items that resemble bonds because they have a maturity date (a date when the bank will pay the funds due), and they can be sold to someone else before maturity.

M-1			737.7
	Currency	186.0	
	Checkable deposits	545.2	
	Travelers checks	6.5	
M-2			2,819.4
	M-1	737.7	
	Money market mutual funds	208.9	
	Savings deposits (not checkable)	376.6	
	Small time deposits	850.8	
	Overnight Eurodollars and repurchase agreements		
	Consumer time deposits and other time deposits (less than $100,000) less adjustment for retirement accounts and funds used by depository institutions to service time and savings accounts	645.4	
M-3			3,512.7
	M-2	2,819.4	
	Large-denomination time deposits and Eurodollars time deposits of U.S. citizens and	609.3	
	Money market mutual funds for institutions	84.0	

Source: *Federal Reserve Bulletin*, Board of Governors of the Federal Reserve System, April 1987, p. A13.

(sometimes a passbook is used), either in person or by mail. This concept of money includes shares in investment organizations, called **money market funds**. It also includes accounts at depository institutions that are not checkable but that can be inexpensively transferred into checkable accounts and used as a medium of exchange. Only time deposit accounts, which cannot be withdrawn until a particular date to obtain the full interest return, cannot be inexpensively transferred. The large business time deposits are therefore excluded from the concept of M-2, although consumer time deposits are included.

Other items can be defined as money under the contention that they can be inexpensively converted into money. These include (1) government bonds; (2)

available or unused consumer credit, such as that available with credit cards; (3) cash value of life insurance policies; (4) bonds issued by private corporations; and (5) common stock.

But as the list of items defined as money becomes larger, money becomes an unwieldy concept for economic analysis. It is thus probably better to break apart such a concept and define as money only those goods that serve as a medium of exchange, as well as goods that can be very inexpensively changed into the medium of exchange.

MONEY IS AS MONEY DOES

One approach to defining money uses two criteria. First, the group of goods defined as money should include only those goods referred to as money. This is the criterion of common usage. Second, a definition of money should include only goods that form a useful concept for economic analysis. For example, if knowing the quantity of M-1 allows one to predict the price level better than by using other common definitions of money, M-1 should be the concept selected. This way of defining money naturally leads to different definitions of money, depending on what one is trying to explain or predict.

This approach must be used with caution. Consider the following example: Suppose there is an economy called River City, where everyone uses River City dollars to pay for things. Obviously, dollars are the medium of exchange. However, no one can find a statistical relationship between River City dollars and anything else, least of all prices. That is, from a statistical standpoint, money does not seem to matter in River City. But it would be a mistake to conclude that there is no money in River City. Therefore, if a concept of money depends on good test results, and because tests and economic theories are imperfect, the definition may not fit the goods that people treat as money. That does not mean that one should not hope for good test results, but it does mean that the definition of money should be a group of goods that has the basic properties of money. The most important of these properties, based on the historic evolution of money, are medium of exchange and unit of account. If the concept of money is not tied to goods that either have these properties or can be inexpensively changed into goods with these properties, it would be in keeping with the historical evolution of the concept of money to call them something other than money.

COMMODITY AND FIAT MONEY

Money may be made out of a material with a valuable alternative use, such as gold. This kind of money is called **commodity money**. And if the material out of which money is made is as valuable in other uses as it is when it is used as money, it is called **full-bodied money**.

Money may also be in the form of a warehouse receipt that entitles the holder to a stated quantity of a valuable asset or group of assets, such as gold or silver held at a bank or by the government. This latter form of money is also called commodity money as long as there are 100 percent reserves of the precious metal available for conversion into the warehouse receipts.

Fiat money is made of a substance (usually paper or a bookkeeping entry in a bank account record) with negligible value. Fiat money is not convertible into a fixed quantity of physical assets, such as gold or silver held by the issuer. But fiat money may be guaranteed by the government as **legal tender**, making it acceptable under the law for the payment of taxes and all debts that arise in private transactions. All coins and currencies in the United States issued by the government were declared to be legal tender by an act in 1933 (the Thomas Amendment to the AAA Farm Relief and Inflation Act). Some forms of U.S. money officially became legal tender as far back as 1862, when a series of acts was passed called the *legal tender acts*. Virtually all of the U.S. money stock, as well as much of the money stock of other countries, is fiat money.

A money stock is partly fiat money when more units of money are issued than can be exchanged for the existing amount of physical assets, such as gold, held for convertibility. If the quantity of gold stored for conversion into a currency would be exhausted by the conversion into gold of one half of the units of money, the money stock is one-half fiat and one-half commodity money.

Commodities have been used as money for many centuries. The manufacture of coins probably began before 700 B.C. in Lydia or the Aegean Islands and in China. The use of money, whether as a medium of exchange or as counting pieces, has generated many suspicions and superstitions as well as logical explanations of its value and effects. The most important monetary invention since the introduction of money as a medium of exchange was the widespread substitution of fiat paper money for the more costly commodity money. This substitution occurred approximately 300 years ago. Fiat money produced deep emotional reactions that have not yet subsided. This general distrust of fiat money was sometimes justified on logical grounds, but it was often based on widespread, deeply felt emotional grounds.

STUDY QUESTIONS

1. What is money?
2. Describe several recent changes in the medium of exchange in the United States.
3. What is the difference between the double coincidence problem in a barter economy and the problem of trade with no physical money, just counting pieces?
4. Put yourself in the running for a Nobel Prize by thinking of a way to do away with currency and coin and still preserve privacy in a modern economy.
5. Describe the six characteristics or functions of money listed in this chapter. Are they applicable to travelers checks?

6. Under what conditions would commodity money be worth more in non-monetary uses?

7. What kind of uncertainty causes people to hold a temporary abode of purchasing power? Why would this function of money be reduced in importance or eliminated if the cost of changing other valuable things into money approached zero?

8. How could a modern society have a money system without ever physically exchanging units of money?

9. Virtually all checkable deposits in the United States were, until 1973, at commercial banks. What other depository institutions now offer checking-type accounts? What is a NOW account, and what part did it play in this change?

10. If changes in the quantity of M-1 or M-2 are a good predictor of future changes in the level of output or the price level in the economy, should that concept of money be used in economic analysis, regardless of other considerations? One of these other considerations is that individuals may be holding many types of near-monies that they can exchange for money that are not part of M-1 or M-2.

11. William Safire, a nationally syndicated columnist, stated in an article in 1986 that "money is a key weapon in the war on drugs" and suggested that the secretary of the Treasury go on television and announce that the government is recalling all $100 bills for redemption for a new blue bill.

> I'm more of a privacy nut than most, but it does not offend me to require people to "fess up" to possession of bundles of cash in sacks. If it's legit, it should be in a bank or in bonds earning interest.
> . . . Recall of C-notes [$100 bills] would complicate the criminal life enormously and sharply reduce the capital available to run drugs.[4]

The Federal Reserve estimated that two thirds of the U.S. currency is overseas or in the underground economy. And 40 percent of the $183 billion in currency is in $100 bills.

Discuss Safire's suggestion with respect to

a. Privacy.
b. Apprehending criminals.
c. Confidence in holding U.S. currency as a store of value.

GLOSSARY

Accessible-on-demand deposits. Deposits that are accessible for conversion into cash upon request during business hours under normal circumstances.

Barter economy. An economy with no money.

Commercial bank. A depository institution specifically chartered by a state or the federal government to be a commercial bank.

Commodity money. Money made out of a substance (such as gold or silver) with a significant value in alternative uses. A full-bodied commodity money would be worth at least as much in alternative uses as it is as money.

Credit union. A depository institution organized as a mutual association to accept deposits from a select group with a common bond (such as the same employer) and to make loans to its depositors, who are called *members.*

Demand deposits. A checkable deposit payable on demand, such as those found at commercial banks.

Depository institution. In the United States, commercial banks and the thrifts (savings and loan associations, mutual savings banks, and credit unions). Their common characteristic is the provision of various types of deposits for funds, many of which are accessible on demand.

Double coincidence. A condition in a transaction in which each party wants to trade exactly what the other party offers in exchange.

Electronic funds transfer system (EFT). A computerized system for payments and receipts without the use of currency, coin, or checks.

Fiat money. Money made out of a substance of insignificant value and not convertible by the issuer of money into a valuable commodity such as gold.

Full-bodied money. Money made out of a material that is as valuable in other uses as it is when used as money.

Laundered money. Money that is transferred between individuals or businesses in such a way that it is difficult or impossible to trace.

Legal tender. Money authorized by law for government and private transactions.

Medium of exchange. A good widely accepted as payment for goods and services and for the payment of debt. Such a good can be said to provide a medium-of-exchange service. Plural: *media of exchange.*

Monetary aggregate. The value of a group of items in a specific definition of money, such as M-1B or M-2.

Money. Any good used as a medium of exchange. Often the definition is extended to other goods that can be inexpensively changed into the medium of exchange. The concept of money that best predicts other variables in economic analysis is sometimes selected.

Money market fund. A mutual fund that invests in liquid, relatively risk-free short-term money market instruments. Described in Part II of this book.

Moneyness. The degree to which goods have functions and characteristics that are similar to those of money.

Mutual savings bank. A financial institution organized under state or federal charter to receive deposits and to make primarily consumer loans. Also called *savings banks.*

Near-monies. Goods that have many of the characteristics of money and can be inexpensively converted into money.

Negotiable order of withdrawal, or **NOW account.** Interest-paying consumer accounts, authorized for depository institutions, that may be drawn against with a check-type instrument called a *negotiable order of withdrawal.*

Savings and loan association. A depository intermediary organized under a state or federal charter as a stock corporation or a mutually owned association to receive deposits and to invest primarily in mortgages.

Standard of deferred payment. A function of money that provides a unit of account for recording debts.

Store of value. A service or a good that provides part of an individual's wealth.

Temporary abode of purchasing power. A service provided by money that allows a readily available means of negotiating future transactions.

Thrifts. In the United States, savings and loan associations, credit unions, and mutual savings banks.

Uniformity in appearance. A characteristic of many countries' money supply—that the different forms of money have similar appearances. For example, as of 1984, all U.S. paper currency was the same size and was made on the same type of paper, with the same green color and the same general design.

Unit of account. A numbering system used to count the size of transactions, wealth, and debts. It is based on the units of a currency.

NOTES

1. For some examples, see Paul Einzig, *Primitive Money* (London: Eyre & Spottiswoode, 1948), pp. 126–129, 366, 450; and A. Hingston Quiggin, *A Survey of Primitive Money* (London: Methuen, 1949), p. 277.

2. There have been estimates of the size of the "underground" or "subterranean" economy in which transactions are not reported (and presumably are in cash). Peter M. Gutmann estimated that the "underground" economy was approximately 10 percent of the reported gross national product in 1976, and Edgar L. Feige estimated it to be 33 percent in 1978. Peter M. Gutmann, "The Subterranean Economy," *Financial Analysts Journal*, November–December 1977, pp. 26, 27, 34. Also see Peter M. Gutmann, "Statistical Illusions, Mistaken Policies," *Challenge*, November–December 1979, pp. 14–17; and Edgar L. Feige, "How Big Is the Irregular Economy?" *Challenge*, November–December 1979, pp. 5–13. The tax law of 1986 that lowered tax rates has made it less costly to earn income that is reported to the Internal Revenue Service. This should reduce the size of the underground economy.

3. See John Wenninger and Charles M. Sivesind, "Defining Money for a Changing Financial System," *Quarterly Review*, Federal Reserve Bank of New York, Spring 1979, pp. 1–8. A discussion of the new concepts of money can be found in "The Redefined Monetary Aggregates," *Federal Reserve Bulletin*, February 1980, pp. 97–114.

4. William Safire, "Money Is a Key Weapon in the War on Drugs," *Press Enterprise* (Riverside, Calif.: August 25, 1986), editorial page.

CHAPTER 3

OTHER FINANCIAL ASSETS

CHAPTER PREVIEW

Introduction.   Financial assets are defined.

Three Types of Financial Assets.   Financial assets are classified as bonds, equities, and money.

What Are Bonds, Notes, Bills, and Stocks?   Bonds and notes are described first. Six institutional details are listed, and a special type of bond called a consol is discussed. Bills and the method of calculating their yield (which is distinctive because they are sold at a discount) are briefly discussed. Stocks are the final financial asset discussed.

Wealth, Capital, and Assets.   Attention is drawn to the equivalent meaning of these terms in most contexts and to the division of wealth into two types of assets: financial wealth and nonfinancial wealth. Three general characteristics of nonfinancial wealth are described. A few words about the meaning of the real value of wealth are presented. The differences in the same three-part classification of characteristics are highlighted by describing three important distinctive characteristics of financial wealth.

Why Does Financial Wealth Enrich a Society?   This section elaborates the benefits to society from financial assets that provide an inexpensive way in which to transfer and store wealth.

Liquidity.   This is a property of assets relating to the time and cost of exchanging them for money.

A Portfolio of Assets.   An example brings out the difference between money yield and nonpecuniary yield. The meaning of diversification is noted.

23

The Different Kinds of Risk on Financial Assets.   Three different types of risk are described.

Reducing Risk Through Intermediation.   This section serves as a means of connecting the discussion to the next part of the text on financial intermediaries.

INTRODUCTION

Bonds, notes, bills, stocks, and money, the subject of the last chapter, are all **financial assets**. Is it possible to tie this group together so that they may be useful concepts in economic analysis? Why are financial assets important anyway? They are mostly pieces of paper or a record on a computer's memory. Sometimes it is claimed, incorrectly, that those pieces of paper are just a veil. Why not lift the veil, forget it, and look at the real "guts" of the economy?

The value of financial assets to society is often misunderstood or overlooked, although those assets are an essential ingredient of a developed economy. One reason for overlooking the importance of financial assets is that no one has found an accurate way to measure their value to a society. The output of financial assets is frequently attributed to assets such as buildings, machines, and natural resources. The productivity of financial assets shows up in the form of a higher return on those assets and on labor services.

Financial assets are important components of the wealth of individuals, government, and businesses in a modern society, and they are also significant determinants of economic activity. Financial assets therefore should be at center stage in the study of interest rates, income, and inflation. John Gurley and Edward Shaw emphasized those points many years ago when they made the following observations:

> Economists have been largely preoccupied with markets for current output, real wealth and labor services. . . . One result is that books on money and banking and on monetary theory have paid insufficient attention to finance in the broad sense. . . . They have made little attempt to deal in any systematic way with financial assets, financial institutions, and financial policy generally.[1]

Whether or not economists stood guilty as accused with the preoccupation Gurley and Shaw described, such has not been the case in recent years. It is appropriate, therefore, to widen the view from money alone to all financial assets.

The formal definition of financial assets is as follows: *Financial assets are claims against present and future income and wealth.* That means that the owner of a financial asset has a claim to the income and/or wealth that someone else has at present or will have in the future. The claim is satisfied by transferring funds or items of wealth to the financial asset owner.

Having said that does not shed a great deal of light on the nature of financial assets. The discussion in this chapter of financial assets and their properties will provide much more illumination than this formal definition does. It will pave the way for understanding the introduction to the determination of interest rates in the next chapter and to the discussion of the more esoteric financial assets that are part of a revolutionary change in the characteristics of many financial markets that began in 1981. That change is discussed in Part III.

This chapter will classify the various types of financial wealth and then will describe bonds, notes, bills, and common stock. We will introduce the concepts of wealth and of the measuring rod of real values in a discussion of the broad differences and general characteristics of nonfinancial and financial wealth. Then we will present a central point of the chapter: the importance of financial assets to the economy. Their importance to society having been explained, the next step is to turn to the individual. On what grounds does the individual select his or her financial wealth? We will offer a simple analysis of considerations for selecting a portfolio of assets. This portfolio includes different types of assets. The selection process requires some consideration of the risks attached to holding financial assets, the last subject of the chapter.

THREE TYPES OF FINANCIAL ASSETS

The discussion in Chapter 2 focused on only one type of financial asset, money. The several concepts of money presented, such as M-1 and M-2, included various items that could be called money. There is also a broader group of items that have many of the characteristics of money, called *financial assets*. Financial assets can be divided into three groups, one of which is money:

1. *Bonds.*   Bonds are evidence of debt. Economists often use the term *bonds* for all debt instruments (legal evidence of debt) to simplify their analyses. There are many names for particular types of debt instruments, such as bills, notes, and bonds.
2. *Equities.*   Equities are ownership rights in businesses. Equity shares issued by corporations are called common stocks.
3. *Money.*   Money was defined in Chapter 2. (The concepts of money also include debt if deposits at financial institutions are thought of as evidence of debt to the depositor.)

WHAT ARE BONDS, NOTES, BILLS, AND STOCKS?

Bonds and Notes

A **bond** or **note** is part of a group of formally offered debt instruments. They are contracts that stipulate a series of fixed payments from the issuer to the holder of the bonds and notes. The payments are usually semiannual or once a year, sometimes quarterly. The final payment also includes the face value of the bond or note. Bonds and notes may be offered by a private corporation, a state or local government unit, the federal government, or a foreign firm or government. Most bonds and notes are **marketable**: They may be sold. Some, such as U.S. savings bonds, cannot be sold, but they can be redeemed by the original owner. Notes have shorter maturities, generally a maximum original maturity of ten years or less, whereas bonds can have any maturity. In 1986, *notes* issued by the U.S. Treasury had a minimum maturity of one year, and *bonds* issued by the U.S. Treasury had a minimum maturity of ten years.

Most bonds or notes bear the following information.[2]

1. The name of the maker (or issuer) is stated, such as "The XYZ Corporation."
2. The **face value, par value,** or simply **par,** is the amount the maker is obligated to pay when the bond matures.
3. The **maturity date** is the date of the final payment. Some bonds have provisions allowing them to be redeemed by the issuer before maturity. These provisions are called **call provisions,** and such a bond is *callable.*
4. The interest payments noted on the bond are often stated as percentage of the face value to be paid each period. This is called the **coupon rate** because the fixed dollar interest payment for each payment period is often obtained by clipping the appropriate physical coupon and exchanging it for the payment.
5. The dates at which the interest payments are to be made are indicated.
6. In the cases of bonds or notes issued by corporations, the **trustee,** usually a trust company or large bank, is named. The trustee must see that the issuer complies with the terms of the bond or note. The trustee will send interest payments upon receipt of the coupons. If the bond or note is **registered,** interest payments will be automatically sent, and no coupon will need to be mailed.

The **original term to maturity** means the time between the date of issuance and the final payment. The alternative meaning of maturity is the *time remaining from the present to the final payment.* A bond with a ten-year original term to maturity may have only a one-month maturity if the final payment is next month. Unless qualified with the term *original,* the term *maturity* is ordinarily used in this second way.

But bonds need not have a maturity. They may pay a fixed dollar amount per year forever. These bonds are called **consols** or **perpetuities** and are sold by the British government. Preferred stock, discussed later, also has the characteristics of consols.

A consol may promise to pay $5 per year forever. If the consol is sold for $50, the yield will be $5 ÷ $50, or 10 percent. Because the arithmetic involved in computing the interest is much simpler for consols than for bonds with fixed maturities, consols are frequently used in economic analysis.

Since 1967, other U.S. Treasury notes have been issued with maturities of one to ten years. Although most bonds may be issued for any maturity, Treasury bonds are currently issued with maturities of over ten years.

Bills

A **bill** usually refers to a marketable debt instrument, such as those issued by the U.S. Treasury, that matures in one year or less. They yield no interim coupon payments, only a final lump-sum payment.

The method for calculating the yield on bills is the same, in principle, as for other debt instruments. But the market convention of stating the "quoted yield" as the discount divided by the maturity value is different. For example, assume that a $10,000 one-year Treasury bill is sold at a 5 percent discount, for $9,500 (5 percent of $10,000 equals $500). When the bill matures in one year, it can be redeemed for $10,000. The yield, 5.26 percent, is simply the discount ($500) divided by the purchase price ($9,500). The market convention of describing this bill as being sold at a 5 percent discount can easily be confused as referring to yield when, in fact, the yield is different.

CALCULATING BILL YIELDS

The interest rate usually quoted on a Treasury bill is not the yield but the percentage of discount from the par value at which the bill is sold. This is sometimes a difficult concept to understand without a simple example.

The selling price of a three-month T-bill in the weekly auction of July 14, 1986, was $98.539 (per $100 of par value). Its maturity was exactly 91 days. Thus $100 − $98.539 = $1.461, which is the discount below par at which the bills were sold.

Now carefully consider what has happened. A bill was bought for $98.539, and at the end of 91 days the holder of this bill will receive $1.461 plus $98.539.

The ratio of $1.461/$98.539 is the return that will be earned on each $100 of par value. The $1.461 is the earnings, and the $98.539 is the amount paid for the T-bill. The ratio is equal to 0.014826 percent. That rate must be turned into an annual number so that it can be compared with the interest rate on other assets. If the rate were earned every day, it would be multiplied by 365 days. But here it will be earned only every 91 days. This means that 1/91 is the fraction of these days in which the interest will be earned. Thus the computation of the interest rate is as follows:

(0.014826)(365/91) = .0595, or 5.95 percent

If you understand that computation, you understand the proper interest rate for computing yields on T-bills. But there is one more obstacle to understanding the reports of activities in this market. Custom and Treasury practice does not lead to this formula. Instead, the rate on T-bills is reported on a special *discount basis*, which has two glitches: (1) The discount, $1.461, is not divided by the purchase price to obtain the exact yield; rather, it is divided by the par value, $100. (2) Instead of using 365 days in a year, 360 days are used. Thus the computation on a discount basis is

($1.461/$100)(360/91) = .0578,

or 5.78 percent

Knowing what is meant by a discount basis is important. First, when you read this number, you will know that it is not the yield. Second, you will know that it is lower than the yield. The difference between this rate and the yield widens with the length of the maturity and the level of the interest rates.

Source: Timothy Q. Cook, "Treasury Bills," in Timothy Q. Cook and Timothy D. Rowe, eds., *Instruments of the Money Market*, 6th ed., Federal Reserve Bank of Richmond, 1986, pp. 86–87.

Stocks

Stocks are ownership rights, or **equities**, in a corporation. The corporation's charter specifies the maximum authorized stock issue that can be outstanding. There are several types of stock. First, **common stock** is the basic form of ownership, allowing the holder to vote for the directors of the corporation. Usually, each share of common stock entitles the owner to one vote, but alternative systems are also used. Most votes are received by absentee ballots, each of which is called a **proxy**. Each share of common stock is a **pro rata** (in proportion to the total number of shares of common stock issued) claim against current and future earnings. Those earnings may be paid to the stockholders as dividends or retained in the corporation and invested to enhance future earnings. Until the 1986 tax law, the increase in the value of stock at the time of sale was, if it had been held long enough, taxed at a lower rate (the capital gains rate) than the tax rate that applied to dividends. But the 1986 tax law made dividends and capital gains subject to the same rate that applies to ordinary income.

Preferred stock, the second type, has no voting rights unless dividends are not paid for a number of periods, often six quarters. Preferred stock pays a fixed dividend, stipulated in the corporation charter as a percentage of the stock's par value. Each class of security has a different level of priority for claims against income and assets, with common stock generally given a priority lower than that of preferred stock or bonds. Preferred stock has the characteristic of a perpetual bond (a consol), with a fixed money income stream.

The privilege of converting preferred stock (**convertible preferred stock**) and bonds (**convertible bonds**) into common stock, at specified prices, is sometimes stipulated. Preferred stock, convertible preferred stock, convertible bonds, and **participating bonds** (which in addition to interest income may share in some of the earnings) all share some characteristics of bonds and some characteristics of equities; the line of demarcation is not clear.

WEALTH, CAPITAL, AND ASSETS

The terms **wealth**, **capital**, and **assets** all usually refer to the same things. The collection of wealth held by an individual is called his or her *portfolio* of wealth. What do you have in your portfolio? Sometimes the term refers only to financial assets. What financial assets do you own? Wealth can be divided into two parts: financial wealth and nonfinancial wealth.

Nonfinancial Wealth

Every commodity of value in an economy is part of its stock of wealth or, equivalently, its stock of capital or assets. These are factories, hotels, sidewalks, lampshades, grocery carts, and land. These are also stocks of shoes, onions, potatoes, and rhubarb. Another stock of productive resources is embedded in the population, human capital.

Wealth is valuable because it produces future services. Hotels provide housing services; lampshades produce light-deflecting services; shoes generate foot-covering services; and stocks of onion, potatoes, and rhubarb contribute nutritional services. Human capital provides labor services. Those expected future services are part of the expected *output*, or the expected future stream of goods and services from wealth.

Those examples of assets are part of the stock of **nonfinancial wealth**. Three general examples of nonfinancial wealth are important in distinguishing it from financial wealth.

1. The physical condition or form of nonfinancial wealth is important to its value. The value of a building or a machine, for example, depends on its physical condition or form.
2. The transportation costs of moving many nonfinancial assets are substantial. For example, the costs of moving a house or a machine may be large relative to its value.
3. The payments made (or estimated—adjusted for inflation) for the service from nonfinancial wealth are, under the conditions discussed here, part of the society's national income (adjusted for inflation).

The first two characteristics are straightforward, but the third characteristic requires some elaboration. Assume that a delivery truck is rented on a day-to-day basis. The delivery truck is part of nonfinancial wealth. It is a nonfinancial asset. How much are the delivery truck's services worth to society? Assume that a long-term state known as *perfect competition* exists in the market for truck services. In addition, assume that all the costs of operating trucks and all the benefits from their operation are reflected in market prices. Under some reasonable approximation of those conditions, the value of the truck services to society each period is equal to the rental price of the truck. If those conditions do not prevail, or if the truck owner also operates the truck, the appropriate market rental price can be estimated.

The essential point is that services provided by the delivery truck, valued at their perfectly competitive price, are a part of the society's income. The income for each period is called a **rental**. Adjusting all variables for inflation, the sum of all rentals from all of the wealth in an economy during a year is its *real national income*: the output of goods and services.

Measuring Wealth

Economists conventionally measure wealth in monetary units such as dollars. A newly produced truck that could be sold for $17,925.75 (in a perfectly competitive market) is valued at that amount when added to the value of total wealth.

But using **money values** or, as they are sometimes called, **nominal values** as a yardstick presents problems. First, the yardstick itself changes in dimension over time. That is, the value of a dollar, as measured by the amount of goods and services for which it can be traded, changes over time. If twice as many dollars were suddenly transferred by the government into consumers' pockets and bank accounts, consumers could be expected to bid up the price of assets. The *money* price of wealth would rise, even if the physical stock of wealth did not change.

To bypass temporarily the subject of the price indexes that are used to adjust price changes, assume that the following simple correction is made: Wealth is measured in units of **real dollars**, which are dollars adjusted as to number, so that each unit has a constant purchasing power. For example, instead of noting " adjusted for inflation," the word *real* can be used.

For example, assume that a dollar buys half as much this year as it did last year and that nothing else affecting the value of goods and services changes. This change in purchasing power is then equivalent to making things twice as expensive, to doubling the price level. Twice as many dollars are needed to measure the same unit of nonfinancial wealth in the current year as were needed last year. Under these conditions, if a machine sold for $10 last year and $20 in the current year, it is said to have the same real value.

The **real value of wealth** is thus its dollar value corrected for changes in the purchasing power of dollars.

Financial Wealth

The types of nonfinancial wealth mentioned in the previous section differ from the types of financial wealth defined here as bonds, equities, and money. Financial wealth has three distinctive characteristics:

1. Financial assets are in the physical form of paper documents, bookkeeping entries (such as bank deposit records), currency, or coins. The physical condition or form of financial assets, unlike that of nonfinancial assets, has no relationship to their value. For example, a million-dollar bond may have the same physical form as does a ten-dollar bond.
2. The transportation costs required to move a financial asset are small relative to its value.
3. The income to the owner of financial wealth, such as interest payments on bonds or dividend payments on common stock, is as valuable as is any other income to the owner. For the society as a whole, however, some income, such as interest payments, is a *transfer* of funds for which no goods or services are exchanged, and so the national income is not increased by the size of those payments.

The first two characteristics are the basis for the usefulness of financial wealth to the society. The third characteristic is the basis for much economic analysis and also for the problems in measuring the contribution of financial wealth. One way to explain the third characteristic is to note that **net wealth**— more commonly called **net worth**—is the difference between assets and liabilities. For the society as a whole, a bond issued by the private sector is an asset to the owner and a liability to the issuer. Because net wealth equals assets minus liabilities, the bond is not an item of net wealth. Having been reduced to zero on the national accounting ledger, it produces no real output from an accounting viewpoint.

Suppose, for example, that the owner of a private bond sold to him or her by the XYZ Company receives a $5 return per year in the form of interest payments. The owner's return of $5 is matched by the $5 cost to the XYZ Company. *No goods or services are thus produced at the time this transfer payment of $5 is made.* The income from this transaction to the society as a whole is not equal in value to the $5 payments. Similarly, the income from equities or from holding money may not be part of national income.

What, then, is the income to society from financial wealth?

Why Does Financial Wealth Enrich a Society?

Financial assets provide an inexpensive method for transferring and storing claims to wealth and income. If financial markets work reasonably well, financial assets will play a major role in the allocation of wealth to its best possible uses: to firms that earn higher rates of return and away from firms that earn lower rates of return. The transactions cost incurred to effect a better allocation of assets can be substantially reduced with the development of well-functioning financial markets. That is, it is much less expensive to trade and transport *claims* to physical wealth than it is to move the physical wealth itself. In addition, financial assets provide a convenient, inexpensive way for individuals and firms to store their wealth without hoarding physical resources that could be used to produce valuable output.

Imagine that a honey-making firm in a country without well-developed financial markets needs funds to finance a profitable new venture that doubles honey production by using a new strain of queen bees. The owner of the company might call his or her friends and aquaintances, place ads in newspapers, or travel to distant lands to seek funds. But other people would be reluctant to buy the firm's equities or bonds, because those potential investors would probably not be familiar with the past history of the firm or the opinions of other investors about whether this investment really is sound.

Alternatively, suppose this firm were in an advanced economy with developed financial markets. The firm may have its stock listed on a modern public stock exchange, such as the New York Stock Exchange. The price of the firm's stock conveys valuable information about the present value placed on the firm's future income. Buyers would have a ready market for selling any shares they acquired. If the owner can convince some investors of the firm's greater profitability with the new queen bees, compared with other available investment opportunities, the firm can rapidly acquire funds by selling stocks or bonds. The price of the stock in the honey-making firm may start to rise as investors take notice. More shares may be sold. The spotlight will rapidly be focused on the company's queen bees, a honey of a buy.

The transaction costs, as well as the costs of bringing information about the firm to investors, are relatively small. A phone call to a stockbroker can initiate an offer to buy the stock, often a few minutes later, on the floor of a modern stock exchange or on a computer network in the over-the-counter market.

The introduction and development of financial assets increase the efficiency with which resources are allocated. Resources that once were devoted to facilitating the transfer of wealth can be turned to other uses. This reduction in transaction costs is a major requisite for improving the allocation of resources. That is, it becomes cheaper to transfer wealth to where it is the most valuable.

The net income to society, therefore, is increased by the introduction and development of financial assets. *Financial assets do produce net additions to society's real income.* An accurate estimate, however, of the value of financial assets to society, especially the value of additional financial assets, has not been discovered.

Unlike other forms of wealth, the mere increase in the quantity of financial assets may not be associated with more real income to society. Suppose there is a doubling of the number of shares outstanding in the honey-making firm, with no change in the firm's production or earnings. The society will not necessarily receive more real income in the future.

Imperfections in the financial markets can also reduce the contribution of financial assets to the real income of society. For example, limitations on the entry into a financial market (by such means as government regulations and private agreements) may keep out participants who could make mutually beneficial exchanges of wealth. But government regulations, or at least the right to sue for damages, may improve financial markets when fraudulent financial assets—such as a worthless common stock advertised as a valuable financial asset—are sold.

Improved and more sophisticated financial instruments may increase the income from financial wealth. Computerized records of financial transactions and portfolio balances reduce transactions costs and enable information to be dispersed more rapidly.

There may be nothing produced when the shares of a firm split (two shares are exchanged for each share outstanding), but something important is produced when a new financial asset enables investors to obtain a higher rate of return and to allocate capital more efficiently than before.

Financial assets can, in general, be more rapidly developed and put into use than nonfinancial wealth can, because the costs of producing financial instruments are relatively small. For example, a legal document or piece of information in a computer's memory (such as a bank deposit balance) is cheaper to produce than is a hotel or office building. The inexpensive cost of producing financial instruments explains one of their central characteristics. They are extremely **fungible**; that is, they can readily be transformed into nearly equivalent financial instruments because they can be rapidly and inexpensively produced. Thus, attempts to prohibit legally one type of financial asset may often result in the creation of nearly equivalent financial assets.

The synchronous development of financial assets and financial markets with increases in the real value of national wealth provides rough evidence of the important contribution of financial assets. The best estimates along these lines are contained in the monumental studies by Raymond Goldsmith.[3] However, just because two events occur together, such as a huge increase in wealth and the consumption of caviar, it is not necessarily true that one causes the other. The consumption of caviar will not make you rich. It may make you poor.

LIQUIDITY

Liquidity is a property of assets relating to the time and cost of exchanging them for money. This makes money the most liquid of all assets, surpassing water in the economists' jargon.

The transactions cost of changing an asset into money is one measure of liquidity. Sometimes these transactions costs are explicit, as in a stockbroker's fee for selling a common stock. But sometimes it is difficult to separate the transactions cost.

Another way to look at liquidity is to consider the risk of not being able to trade an asset for a given sum of money at a particular time in the future. This way of looking at liquidity makes a house less liquid than a government bond, which will, in three months, be redeemed for a fixed sum of money. But who knows exactly what could happen to housing prices in three months?

A PORTFOLIO OF ASSETS

Suppose that an individual owns a Jones Corporation bond, some shares of common stock in the Smith Corporation, some money, and a group of personal assets, which will be treated as a single commodity. These items are listed in Table 3-1. Suppose also, for simplicity, that the yields on the assets are known with no uncertainty.

If the individual has no incentive to sell one of these assets and buy more of another, we can assume that each asset will give him or her the same yield, if we ignore the different kinds of risks elaborated here. First, we shall break down the yield of each of the assets into two parts. One part is the money yield. The bond has a yield of 10 percent a year. The 100 shares of common stock also yield a 10 percent rate of return. The 100 U.S. dollars are in an interest-paying NOW account from which the individual receives a 5 percent yield. The group of private items (clothing, for example) has no money yield.

The second component of the total yield on each asset is the nonpecuniary yield. The nonpecuniary yield of money is the value of the (nonmoney) services of money per dollar. Money yields many services, such as providing a temporary abode of purchasing power or a medium of exchange, which were described in Chapter 2. If we assume for simplicity that bonds and stocks yield no nonpecuniary return, then we can conclude that if the individual is in the equilibrium position of having no incentive to reduce one asset and buy another in order to increase the total yield of his or her wealth, the total yield on each asset must be the same, as shown in Table 3-1. The 100 dollars has a 5 percent nonpecuniary yield, and the group of personal items yields a 10 percent nonpecuniary yield.

What does this simple view of a portfolio illustrate? It illustrates the view that an individual can be expected to arrange the quantity of each asset held

TABLE 3-1   Equilibrium Yields on Assets in an Individual's Portfolio (in percent)*

	1 Jones Corporation Bond	100 Shares of Smith Corporation Common Stock	100 U.S. Dollars	A Group of Personal Items
Money yield	10%	10%	5%	0%
Nonpecuniary yield	0	0	5	10
Total yield	10%	10%	10%	10%

* All the different risks elaborated later in the text are ignored.

so that each has the same yield, if other considerations, noted next, are ignored. That is, if one asset has a greater yield, the individual will make some adjustments to increase the higher-yielding wealth and reduce the quantity of other assets.

As the quantity of an asset is reduced, its yield will normally rise. It thus may become unprofitable to reduce drastically one's cash balances or personal possessions, as their nonpecuniary yield will rapidly rise, for example, if one has to make do with fewer clothes or less money.

Now suppose that the assumption of certainty about the yields on the assets is removed. If the dividends on the 100 shares of Smith Corporation common stock rise so that the yield is 11 percent, will the individual sell the Jones Corporation bond, which yields only 10 percent? The answer has to do with the riskiness of the return on these assets. Given that the yield on each of these assets is uncertain, it is safer to hold a number of different bonds and stocks, so that if the yield falls on one asset, the entire portfolio of bonds and stocks may not suffer an equally unpleasant fate. This is the principle of *diversification*: Do not put all your eggs in one basket.[4]

It is also safer to hold bonds and stocks that are not in similar industries, so that a problem in one industry will not affect the entire portfolio of bonds and stocks. Diversification can lead to investments in precious commodities such as gold and diamonds, real estate, and various forms of art objects for reasons other than their expected yield.

THE DIFFERENT KINDS OF RISK ON FINANCIAL ASSETS

Suppose that Ms. Brown wants to buy a bond. She first considers the alternative types of credit instruments. Ms. Brown also must decide whether to lend her money on a short-term or a long-term basis. Suppose that she buys a $10,000 bond that will mature in six years. The bond carries a 10 percent coupon rate. Therefore, Ms. Brown can expect six $1,000 interest payments, one at the end of each year (assuming that the interest is paid annually), plus a $10,000 return of the face value at the end of the sixth year.

She faces three types of risk:

1. **Capital risk.**   If the bond is sold before it matures, the price of the bond may be unexpectedly low, or equivalently, the market rate of interest on bonds may be unexpectedly high. This is called capital risk.
2. **Purchasing power risk.**   Inflation could unexpectedly increase. This means that the real value of the income from the bond will unexpectedly decline. This is called purchasing power risk.
3. **Default risk.**   The bond may pay less than the expected nominal income. In the case of a bond that pays a fixed money return, this is called a default risk.

REDUCING RISK THROUGH INTERMEDIATION

Knowledge of these three types of risk is important not only to understanding individuals' portfolio decisions but also to explaining the existence of one of the largest group of financial businesses in a developed economy, the financial intermediaries. Financial intermediaries include commercial banks, savings and loan associations, mutual savings banks, and money market funds. They can be viewed as providing the service of reducing the risks listed in the previous section. Ms. Brown may simply put her $10,000 in an interest-paying account or share at one of the preceding financial intermediaries and let them invest directly in bonds and stocks of private corporations. There is a cost—the cost of *intermediation*—so that Ms. Brown may receive a slightly lower yield than if she invested directly. However, she may have substantially reduced the risks on her financial assets.

STUDY QUESTIONS

1. If a society produces more bonds, how will its real national income be affected?
2. List your portfolio of wealth by the categories discussed in this chapter.
3. What is meant by the statement that financial wealth is extremely fungible? Is this also true for nonfinancial wealth? Explain.
4. What is the total value of all the services from a society's wealth over a one-year period called? (The answer is a concept of income, a stream of services per unit of time.)
5. Discuss the three characteristics of financial and nonfinancial wealth explained in this chapter.
6. What are the major differences among bonds, notes, bills, common stocks and money (defined as M-1)? Place the first four assets in order of their similarity to money. Review the properties of money and the term *money-ness* enumerated in the preceding chapter.
7. Explain diversification, and use this concept in explaining one reason that an individual would hold both a U.S. Treasury bill with a 10 percent yield and a bond of a private corporation with an expected 15 percent yield.
8. What kind of risk is associated with holding currency? Explain.
9. What important function do financial intermediaries perform with respect to the riskiness of financial assets?

GLOSSARY

Assets. See **Wealth.**

Bill. A short-term debt instrument, usually with a maturity of one year or less.

Bond. An interest-bearing debt instrument, usually with a maturity of five years or more, formally offered for sale by a business or government. Sometimes it is used in economic analysis to refer to all debt instruments.

Call provisions.   Provisions of some bonds allowing for their redemption (recovery of face value) prior to maturity. Such a bond is termed *callable.*

Capital.   See **Wealth.**

Capital risk. The risk of a reduction in the value of an asset if the interest rate unexpectedly rises.

Common stock. Basic form of stock with voting rights.

Consol. A name for perpetuities sold by the British government. See **Perpetuities.**

Convertible preferred stock and **convertible bonds.**   Preferred stock and bonds that carry the privilege of conversion into specific common stocks at a specified price.

Coupon rate. The yearly interest payment on a debt instrument such as a bond, divided by its face value.

Default risk.   The risk of a failure to make a contracted payment, such as an interest payment on a bond.

Equities. Ownership rights in a business. Stocks are a form of equities.

Face value, par value, or **par.** The amount (not including any coupon payment) that the maker of a debt instrument is obligated to pay at the maturity date.

Financial assets.   Claims to present and future wealth and income.

Fungible. A property of a good, especially financial assets, that allows relatively inexpensive transformation into another form. For example, a $100,000 bond can be inexpensively changed into one hundred $1,000 bonds. *Financial*

intermediaries, discussed in Part II, perform this kind of service.

Liquidity. A property of assets relating to the time and cost of exchanging them for money.

Marketable.   Salable in the market.

Maturity date of a debt instrument.   The date on which the final payment is due.

Money or **nominal values.** Values denominated in units of money, such as $5 (five dollars) for a haircut.

Net wealth or **net worth.** Assets minus liabilities.

Nonfinancial wealth. Physical wealth—such as buildings, machines, and inventories of commodities—and human capital.

Notes.   Debt instruments, such as a U.S. Treasury note, that have a maturity between that of a Treasury bill and a Treasury bond.

Original term to maturity. The time from the date of issuance to the date of maturity of a debt instrument.

Participating bonds.   Bonds that in addition to interest income may share in some of the earnings.

Perpetuities. Bonds that do not have a maturity, that pay a fixed dollar amount per year forever.

Preferred stock. Stock with no voting rights under normal conditions. It has a constant perpetual payment stream, similar to that of a perpetuity.

Pro rata. In proportion (e.g., voting on common stock is in proportion to the total number of shares that are held).

Proxy. An absentee ballot for voting shares of common stock. Economists also use the term to denote a substitute variable in analysis.

Purchasing power risk. The risk of the loss in the real value of an asset because of an unexpected increase in the rate of inflation.

Real dollars. Dollars adjusted as to number, so that each unit has a constant purchasing power.

Real value of wealth. A measure of a good or service in units of money corrected for changes in the price level.

Registered debt instruments. Debt instruments recorded with the trustee with the location of the holder, who is mailed the payments.

Rental. The payment per period for the use of wealth. (The sum of all rentals at their perfectly competitive price in an economy—those actually paid and those estimated—in a year is *national income*.)

Trustee. The party, usually a trust company or bank, assigned to see that the issuer complies with the terms of a debt instrument—a bond or note. (The trustee administers the payments.)

Wealth, capital, assets. Usually the stock of an individual, a firm, or an entire economy of items of value at a given instant of time.

NOTES

1. John G. Gurley and Edward S. Shaw, *Money in a Theory of Finance* (Washington, D.C.: Brookings Institution, 1960), pp. 2–3.
2. Debt instruments such as bonds are rated for default risk by companies such as Moodys. The best-quality bonds have the least risk. Aaa is the best quality rating, followed in order by Aa (high quality), A (upper-medium quality), Baa (medium grade), Ba (speculative elements), B (lack desirable characteristics), Caa (poor), Ca (highly speculative), and C (extremely poor).
3. Raymond Goldsmith, *Financial Intermediaries in the American Economy Since 1900* (Princeton, N.J.: National Bureau of Economic Research, Princeton University Press, 1958); *Financial Structure and Development* (New Haven, Conn.: Yale University Press 1969); and *Financial Institutions* (New York: Random House, 1968).
4. A review of the analysis of risk in the field of finance can be found in Robert D. Auerbach, *Financial Markets and Institutions* (New York: Macmillan, 1983), pp. 191–239.

CHAPTER 4

INTEREST RATES

CHAPTER PREVIEW

Introduction.   The demand and supply of loanable funds are defined.

Real Rate of Interest.   The real rate of interest is described, with an example.

Nominal Rate of Interest.   The effect of an expected inflation on interest rates is shown.

Saving and Investment.   The concepts of saving, investment, consumption, and income are reviewed.

Rate of Return and Opportunity Cost of Investment.   The concepts of the rate of return and the opportunity cost of investment are explained.

Own Rates and Opportunity Cost of Holding Assets.   The yields and costs from holding an asset are explained.

Appendix A: The Demand and Supply of Loanable Funds.   The demand and supply schedules and some examples of the effect on interest rates of shifts in these schedules are presented.

Appendix B: The Effect of Inflationary Expectations on Interest Rates.   The loanable funds analysis is used to show the effects of the expectation of an increase in the rate of inflation on interest rates.

INTRODUCTION

Interest rates play a central role in financial markets and financial assets, tying together the stream of income from an asset and its price. Interest rates also play a central role in the allocation of resources and in decisions to save, invest, and hold assets. In addition, real and nominal rates of interest are basic to much of the analysis in money and banking.

We shall review the concepts of saving, investment, consumption, and income. We shall also explain the concepts of the rate of return on an asset, its own rate, and the opportunity cost as they are used in making decisions to invest and hold assets. The two appendices will show how the demand and supply for loanable funds can be used to analyze the determination of interest rates and the effect of inflation on interest rates.

REAL RATE OF INTEREST

Wealth is the stock of everything of economic value at a moment in time. In the last chapter we described financial and nonfinancial wealth. We defined the concept of output as the flow of goods and services from the stock of wealth.

We will first show the relationship between the stock of wealth and **income** (with real income equal to output) in an example. Suppose that a rental apartment building is valued at $100,000 and the income to the owner (after expenses) is predicted to remain at $10,000 per year. (The value of wealth and expected income have settled down to some equilibrium values.) The value of the measuring unit—a dollar—is adjusted for any expected inflation or deflation. That is, these variables are in *real* form. One could say that the $100,000 rental apartment produces output at the **real rate of interest** of 10 percent per year, as

$$(0.10/\text{year})(\$100,000) = \$10,000/\text{year} \qquad (1)$$

Thus the equilibrium real rate of interest is the rate at which real wealth produces real income.

If the only changes were inflation and the rise in the value of the rental property at approximately the same rate as the expected value of the rental income minus expenses, the real rate, 10 percent per year, would stay constant. Thus, using real values in the first place—adjusting each variable so it does not change in value with inflation—does not affect the determination of the yield from this asset.

Consider an item of financial wealth rather than nonfinancial wealth. Suppose that a consol currently selling for $100,000 pays $10,000 each year. The internal rate on this bond is 10 percent per year. The bond is not the same as the rental property in the previous example because the expected income stream is *fixed* in dollar terms. This means that an unexpected rise in the rate of inflation will reduce the expected real value in the $10,000 yearly income from the bond for as long as the inflation continues.

NOMINAL RATE OF INTEREST

A newly expected 5 percent inflation that is expected to last indefinitely will lower the real value of the income on the previously mentioned consol by 5 percent each year. (An **inflation** is a sustained rise in the price level.) That is, the $10,000 yearly interest will buy 5 percent fewer goods and services each year.

Both the buyers and sellers of these consols may well appreciate the expected decline in the real value of the income stream from these bonds and agree to trade the bonds at a lower price. To retain the same real yield, the bond would have to fall in price so that the interest payments, reduced in value by the 5 percent inflation, would still return 10 percent after the inflation adjustment.

The calculation of the required decline in the price of the bond will be simplified if a new term is introduced, nominal interest rate or nominal yield. The **nominal interest rate** is the rate of interest on the bond, which includes a premium for expected inflation. If the $100,000 bond in the example falls in price so that the individual buying the bond is exactly protected against the expected inflation, the **nominal yield** will equal

1. A 10 percent real return, as it did with no inflation, plus
2. A 5 percent extra return to cover the expected inflation

It will have a 15 percent nominal yield.

Thus, the full adjustment of the bond price will require that the nominal interest rate on the bond, i_b, equal the real interest rate, r_b, plus the expected rate of inflation, λ (the Greek letter lambda).

$$i_b = r_b + \lambda \qquad (2)$$

All three variables are in the form of percentages per year.

This calculation would explain market yields if other factors affecting the bond yields were negligible. (These other factors include the effects of the income tax, which are explained in Chapter 19.)

SAVING AND INVESTMENT

Let us next turn to a review of the relationship of two concepts from introductory economics, saving and investment.

Let Y be the dollar (nominal) expenditure on output or national income for the whole economy. The expenditures on national income are either for consumption, C, goods and services that are used up during the year, or for **investment**, I, goods that are not used up during the year. Investment goods add to the stock of wealth and produce income in the future. (This definition of investment should be distinguished from the more common and natural use of the term to mean any purchase of a financial asset, even if it does not result in the production of new capital goods, such as factories and machines. See Study Question 5.) The basic income identity is, by these definitions,

$$Y = C + I \tag{3}$$

Saving is that part of the receipts (the income) from producing the output that is not used for consumption:

$$S = Y - C \tag{4}$$

If consumption is subtracted from each side of equation (3),

$$Y - C = I \tag{5}$$

it is clear from comparing equations (4) and (5) that $S = I$. This identity reflects the fact that if income received for producing national income is greater than consumption (some is saved), some of the national income will be held for future periods (some will be invested). But investment is not always voluntary, as in the case of a car dealer who finds his or her inventory of newly produced cars is larger than desired because of poor sales.

Even though in a closed economy (no foreign trade), actual saving must always equal investment, that may not be what people want. Desired saving, S^D, may be greater or smaller than desired investment, I^D.

$$S^D \gtreqless I^D \tag{6}$$

RATE OF RETURN AND OPPORTUNITY COST OF INVESTMENT

What determines the amount of investment? What causes a society whose inhabitants could enjoy their income by consuming it instead of devoting part of it to building machines and buildings? These investment expenditures will not produce income in the present period; the inhabitants must wait for an expected future stream of income. That is, the additions to their wealth brought about by net investment will add to their income in the future.

The basic decision is how much individuals want to consume in the current period and how much in future periods. If they are willing to wait, they can reduce their current consumption by taking a larger part of the economy's output in the form of investment goods. Economists describe this willingness to postpone consumption in terms of *time preference*, a measure of individuals' preferences for future versus present consumption.

The investor may well have no knowledge of this more fundamental decision. However, his or her attempt to make the most profitable investments is one way that this kind of time preference decision is carried out in a market economy. The current or prospective business owners and managers are the *investors*. The funds for investment come in large part from the *savers*, individuals who save.[1] Savers can decide to lend their funds or buy ownership rights (purchase stock) in businesses that will use the funds to produce investment goods. Individuals' willingness to save more and consume less affects this flow of funds from the savers to the investors.

The sooner that individuals want to consume, the higher the real interest rate must be to coax them to save more and give up their current consumption. In turn, this higher interest rate will make it unprofitable for many investors to borrow to finance their investments because the yield on their investment will not be high enough to cover the cost of borrowing the funds. The result will be less investment. Thus, individuals' time preference for more current consumption affects investment. In a market economy, the demands for current consumption and investment are reflected in market prices and interest rates. The financial markets in which bonds and stocks are sold transmit these time preferences and the prospective yields on investments into the interest rates on bonds and the yields on stocks.

Thus, both the investors' income from investing and the cost of funds they will invest enter their investment decisions in the following way:

1. *Rate of return.* The value of an investment's flow of future income is compared with the cost of the investment. If the investment, as in our example of a rental apartment building, costs $100,000 and is expected to yield $10,000 per year forever, the calculation will be simple: It is $10,000/$100,000 per year, which equals .10, or 10 percent, per year. That interest rate is called the **rate of return** or **yield** from investing.
2. *Adjustment for risk.* To find an investor's risk premium, the investment can be compared with an asset that has no risk. For example, there is a substantial default risk in renting an apartment building. It could become unoccupied, and no rents would be collected for long periods of time. Therefore, given this kind of risk, the investor would want a premium higher than the yield on U.S. Treasury bond, which has no risk of default. To find how much premium is required, the investor may be asked how much yield he or she would want on the investment so as to be equally willing to buy the rental apartment building or the bonds. Suppose that the investor requires a 3 percent risk premium to make him or her indifferent.
3. *Opportunity cost.* To see whether the investment will be profitable, the rate of return on investing after this adjustment for risk is compared with the cost of the funds invested. Suppose that U.S. Treasury bonds yield a rate of return of 5 percent per year. Then 5 percent will be the opportunity cost of the funds invested in the apartment building.

Thus the investment is profitable in the sense that it brings a 2 percent higher return than do other opportunities. But suppose that the yield on U.S. Treasury bonds is 9 percent. It then would not be profitable to hold the rental apartment building rather than to sell it and buy U.S. Treasury bonds.[2]

OWN RATES AND OPPORTUNITY COST OF HOLDING ASSETS

The last section addressed the rate of return and the opportunity cost of investing. The opportunity cost of holding an asset depends on yields on other assets, while the **own rate of return** depends on an asset's own income.

Suppose that one owns an apartment building and lives in one of the apartments. The income from which the own rate of return is calculated includes the rental value of the owner-occupied apartment. The income is not in the form of money, however, but is in the form of shelter services provided by the building. It is converted into money units only in order to compute a rate of return.

Or assume that one owns money in the form of a $100 deposit in a NOW account that pays 7 percent interest per year. The money also yields services such as those described in Chapter 2 for the functions of money. These services are also part of the stream of income from holding money. The own rate of return is 7 percent plus the rate of return from these nonpecuniary services from money. The **opportunity cost of holding an asset** is the interest forgone on an alternative asset such as a (short-term) U.S. Treasury bill. The cost per dollar of holding money is then equal to the opportunity cost (equal to the rate of interest on a short-term U.S. Treasury bills) minus the direct money payments per dollar (the interest on the NOW account). If the interest on the $100 in the NOW account is 7 percent and the U.S. Treasury bill interest rate is 8 percent, the cost per dollar of holding money is 1 percent. Suppose the interest rate on U.S. Treasury bills rises to 11 percent while the NOW account interest remains at 7 percent. Then it would be more expensive per dollar to hold money and the quantity of money demanded would decline.

DIFFERENT WAYS OF EXPRESSING INTEREST RATES

In keeping straight the different ways interest rates are expressed, consider how an interest rate relates to the underlying asset and in what units the value of the asset is being measured. The own rate of return relates the income of an asset to its value. When the opportunity cost of an asset is used, the yield on another asset is related to the value of the underlying asset. In Chapter 13 yet another view of interest rates is used, relating the expected change in the value of an asset each period to its cost.

The unifying idea of the rate of interest is the average rate at which a stream of returns is tied to the value of the underlying asset that produces the income.

This note is motivated by a paper sent by James Rock that ties together different concepts of interest rates and present values.

APPENDIX A: THE DEMAND AND
SUPPLY OF LOANABLE FUNDS

The demand for loanable funds can be viewed as a desire to obtain funds by supplying financial assets. This can be accomplished by selling bonds and other securities (see Table 4-1).

The supply of loanable funds can be viewed as a desire to lend funds by demanding financial assets. This can be accomplished by buying bonds and other securities (see Table 4-1).

Although the analysis in this chapter explains one equilibrium interest rate for the economy when in fact there are many different equilibrium interest rates, this simplification allows a useful first step. It notes the complication of different interest rates for bonds issued by firms with different financial soundness. Further complications, which account for many different equilibrium interest rates on bonds of different maturities and for the rates of return on common stocks, are saved for later chapters.

Finally, although the analysis in this appendix can give valuable insights into how the expectation of inflation affects interest rates, it does not explain how different levels of prices affect interest rates. The meaning and effect of the price level will be presented in Part V.

T A B L E   4 - 1   The Demand and Supply of Loanable Funds

Name of the Demand and Supply Schedules	Indicates the Following Behavior by Individuals and Corporations	Formal Components (described later in the chapter)
Demand for loanable funds	Sale of bonds, stocks, and other securities	Desired investment plus the increase in the demand for money
Supply of loanable funds	Purchase of bonds, stocks, and other securities	Desired saving plus the increase in the supply of money

Suppose that the only supply of credit or loans to the economy was from those who saved and that those individuals supplied exactly the amount they saved. Also, suppose that the only loan demand was from people (or corporations) who invested and that this demand exactly equaled the desired investment. Then an interest rate could be found at which savers would obtain a high enough return so that they would want to save exactly what investors would want to invest. This would explain the interest rate that cleared the market for the demand and supply of loans.

However, the demand for loans in each period can be greater than the desired investment by the amount by which individuals, corporations, and governments wish to increase their holdings of money. Also, the supply of loans can be greater in each period by the amount by which the money supply increases. Therefore, the demand and supply of loanable funds must include not only desired saving and desired investment but also desired changes in money holdings and the money supply.

At some interest rate, lenders will be induced to offer the amount of loanable funds that borrowers will still find profitable to demand. This interest rate is said to be determined by the demand and supply of loanable funds, or equivalently, the demand and supply of financial assets (or securities) in each period.

The supply of loanable funds or credit consists first of any funds that individuals or corporations want to save. Second, the supply of loanable funds consists of the change in the money supply. Creation of the money supply is a major part of the subject of money and banking, and it will be explained in later chapters. Here we will simply note that both the government and the private banking system create money.

The demand for loanable funds consists, first, of desired investment and, second, of increases in the demand for money by individuals, corporations, or government.

The demand and supply of loanable funds are depicted in Figure 4-1. The supply schedule, $S_L S_L$, slopes upward on the grounds that more will be saved (at a given level of income and prices) when the reward (the interest rate) is higher. The demand schedule, $D_L D_L$, slopes downward on the assumptions that (1) with a given stock of wealth and a given level of prices, more investment opportunities will be profitable at lower interest rates and (2) there will be a greater demand to increase money holdings when interest rates on alternative assets such as bonds are lower.

FIGURE 4-1   The Demand and Supply of Loanable Funds

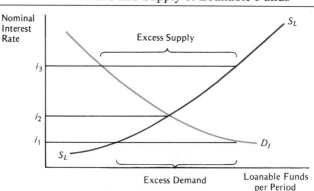

An excess supply of loanable funds is shown at nominal interest i_3 (where supply exceeds demand), and an excess demand for loanable funds is shown at nominal interest rate i_1 (where demand exceeds supply). Equilibrium (where supply and demand are equal) is at i_2.

The equilibrium interest rate i_2 in Figure 4-1 equates the amount of loanable funds supplied with those demanded. At a higher interest rate, such as i_3, there would be an excess supply of loanable funds, and the interest rate would drop. At a lower interest rate, such as i_1, there would be an excess demand, and interest rates would rise.

Other things being the same, the following changes will initially shift the demand for loanable funds $D_L D_L$ to the right and increase the nominal interest rate:

1. An increased demand for investment at each interest rate.
2. An increased demand for money at each interest rate.

Other things being the same, the following changes will also initially increase nominal interest rates by shifting the supply of loanable funds to the left:

1. A decreased demand for saving at each interest rate.
2. A decrease in the money supply because of actions by the government.

APPENDIX B: THE EFFECT OF INFLATIONARY EXPECTATIONS ON INTEREST RATES

What would happen if a 5 percent inflation were suddenly expected? This is carefully worded, with the word *suddenly* ensuring that no prior adjustments were made, as the inflation is assumed to be unanticipated.

FIGURE 4-2   The Demand and Supply of Loanable Funds Adjusting to the Expectation of More Rapid Inflation

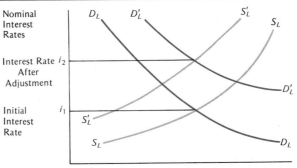

Loanable Funds per Period

With the expectation of inflation, savers will supply fewer loanable funds at each interest rate, causing the supply schedule to shift to the left. Borrowers (who can be investors) will be willing to demand more loanable funds at each nominal interest rate, causing the demand curve to shift to the right. The nominal interest rate will be higher because of the expectation of inflation. The additional role played by income taxes is explained in Part Five.

The adjustment is shown in Figure 4-2. The initial equilibrium is at an interest rate of i_1. Savers will be unwilling to lend the same amount of money at each interest rate that they were before they expected inflation. Another way of saying this is that bond buyers will demand higher interest on their bonds to cover the effect on their interest income of the expected inflation. The supply of loanable funds $S_L S_L$ will therefore shift to the left to $S'_L S'_L$.

Borrowers will also recognize the effects of inflation that will increase their money income and the amount of funds they will need to finance their investments. They will reluctantly be willing to pay more interest on the bonds they sell, and so the demand for loanable funds $D_L D_L$ will shift to $D'_L D'_L$.

A full adjustment will cause the new equilibrium interest rate i_2 to exceed the prior equilibrium interest rate i_1 by approximately the 5 percent rate of inflation that is expected. Neglecting the complications from tax laws, equation (2) provides a fairly accurate description of the equilibrium relationship of the *nominal* interest rate to the *real* interest rate.

STUDY QUESTIONS

1. What is the difference between the real and nominal rates of interest?
2. (From the appendices) Consider three possible relationships:

    a. Desired saving = desired investment.
    b. Demand for loanable funds = supply of loanable funds.
    c. Changes in the demand for money = changes in the supply of money.

    If two of these relationships hold at a given nominal rate of interest, will the third relationship be true? Explain.
3. How does the expectation of more rapid inflation affect nominal rates of interest?
4. (From the appendices) Are the following statements true, false, or uncertain?

    a. The interest rates on bonds have risen, indicating that the demand for bonds must have decreased.
    b. Inflation and high interest rates go hand in hand.
    c. If the demand for loanable funds exceeds the supply of loanable funds, nominal interest rates will tend to rise.
    d. If the supply of loanable funds exceeds the demand for loanable funds, nominal interest rates will tend to fall.

    In each case, explain your answer.
5. Distinguish two different meanings of the term *investment*, as used in the following quotations:

    a. "John invested $100 in bonds."
    b. "Sally's firm just invested $100,000 for the construction of a new office."

Notice that if the bond seller used John's money to finance the production of new investment goods, both (a) and (b) could be said to refer to a definition of investment as the payment for the production of new capital goods.

6.   What is the own rate and the opportunity cost of holding money?
7.   What is the opportunity cost of investing funds to build an apartment building?

GLOSSARY

Income. In a national income accounting sense, income is the payment for producing output. In common usage, it is the receipt of funds. Thus the common usage includes the receipt of transfer payments—payments that are not associated with the production of goods and services.

Inflation. A sustained rise in the price level.

Interest rate. A pure number per unit of time, such as .06 per year or, equivalently, 6 percent per year.

Investment. The value of the production of goods that are not used up in the current year.

Nominal rate of interest or **nominal yield.** The rate of return observed in the market for a debt instrument with a fixed payment stream.

Opportunity cost of holding an asset. The value of the next best use of the funds. It can be measured by the interest forgone on an alter-native asset such as a (short-term) U.S. Treasury bill.

Own rate of return. The rate of return that is calculated from the income an asset produces. See **Rate of return** or **yield**.

Rate of return or **yield.** The average rate at which income is expected to be earned from an asset, where both income and the value of the assets are in dollar units.

Real rate of interest. The rate (in equilibrium) at which real wealth produces real income.

Saving. Income (in the national income account sense) that is not used for consumption. The word *savings* (with an "s") is a synonym for wealth. Thus one has abundant savings because he or she has been saving.

Wealth. The stock of everything of economic value at a moment in time.

NOTES

1.   Savers need not be domestic residents. Individuals in other countries may, and do, send their savings to the United States in exchange for financial assets, because these assets provide the highest rate of return after the adjustment for risk.

2. Sometimes it would still pay to hold the house rather than the U.S. Treasury bond even if the bond paid a higher yield than the house did. One situation is when the asset owner loves risk; that is, he or she obtains pleasure (income) from taking gambles with long odds. The higher yield on the house before adjustment for risk attracts the risk lover who does not make an adjustment for risk. But perhaps most people need to be paid extra for this risk: They need a premium that is above the risk-free yield on the U.S. Treasury bond so as to entice them to buy the house. Another situation in which an individual would buy the house pertains to diversification, discussed in Chapter 3.

PART TWO

FINANCIAL INTERMEDIARIES

CHAPTER 5

FINANCIAL INTERMEDIARIES

CHAPTER PREVIEW

The Vital Connection. Financial intermediaries are described as the vital connection between saving and investment in reproducible capital.

A Definition. Financial intermediaries are defined. "Middleman"-type definitions are criticized. A "middleman"-type definition is given in note 3, and a problem concerning it is presented in Study Question 4.

Intermediation Services. Four types of services provided by financial intermediaries are described.

Types of Financial Intermediaries. Financial intermediaries are divided into three types, and each type is briefly described.

Deregulation in the 1970s and 1980s. The effects on financial intermediaries of the period of deregulation are discussed.

Financial Innovation and Deregulation in Foreign Industrial Countries. Other industrial countries besides the United States have introduced innovations and the deregulation of financial services.

Importance of Financial Intermediaries. The huge proportion (68 percent in 1982) of funds advanced in credit markets by financial intermediaries is shown.

THE VITAL CONNECTION

There is some evidence that the proportion of income saved by rich countries or rich people is not very different from that saved by poor countries or poor people. Because income saved is available for investment, it is exactly equal to investment in an economy with no foreign trade, if the national income accounting definition of investment is used. (That definition, discussed in Chapter 4, defines investment as the value of goods produced during a year that last—that is, produce services—for more than the year.) If that is the case, why do poor countries and poor people invest so little of their income? The answer may well be that they do save and do invest, but in a form that does not produce factories, machines, tractors, video cassette recording sets, or more efficient methods of farming.

In some countries in current times, individuals may invest in gold jewelry to hang around their necks. (That purchase of gold jewelry is an investment in the national income accounting sense only if it is part of the current year's output. Otherwise, it is simply a purchase of existing wealth.)

In the Middle Ages, individuals invested in beautiful, costly religious edifices such as Notre Dame Cathedral. All these things produce great psychic income, but they are not the **reproducible capital**—the factories and machines or more efficient techniques of production—that breed material wealth.

What if a poor peasant girl in a developing country who saved part of her meager income to buy a gold necklace instead placed her funds on deposit in a business called a savings and loan association? In short order the savings and loan would invest most of the money in residential housing. But this is not to be. The peasant girl in many countries would certainly not trust her money to a business over which she had no control. Why not enjoy the beauty of her jewelry rather than look forward to some future interest payment that is uncertain? So no such business exists. The handicraft industry that makes gold necklaces, as well as the gold necklace importers, may prosper. However, these recipients of funds may also fail to invest in reproducible capital.

The savings and loan association in the United States may have the nearly complete trust of its customers. It is one type of financial institution called a financial intermediary. Indeed, the very existence of numerous financial intermediaries may be the vital connection for much of the population between saving and the *form* of investment needed for a modern affluent society.

A DEFINITION

Financial intermediaries can be private firms or governmental units. They obtain funds by selling financial assets with relatively low pecuniary (money) yields, which they create and for which they are liable. Financial intermediaries use these funds to buy financial assets issued by others yielding higher pecuniary returns. The financial intermediaries receive most of their income from these assets with a higher pecuniary yield. The income covers both the cost of their operations and the payments they make on the financial assets they create. These assets are assets to the public that holds them, and liabilities to the financial intermediaries that issue them.

The financial intermediary is not in the business of managing or seeking a controlling interest in other firms, thus excluding firms called holding companies, which are not generally viewed as financial intermediaries. A **holding company**, unlike a financial intermediary, owns stock in other firms for the purpose of ownership and/or control.

Financial intermediaries should be distinguished from firms that create financial assets with special characteristics and then charge an explicit fee for those instruments.[1] Those firms earn most or all of their income from this fee rather than from financial assets issued by others, which they buy. That is, financial intermediaries provide and sell a service for which they are directly paid.

Financial intermediaries can also be thought of as taking funds from lenders (savers) and giving these funds to borrowers (investors). The financial intermediary facilitates the exchange of funds between borrowers and lenders by helping bring the borrowers and lenders together. The word *intermediary* and the general name of the services supplied by financial intermediaries, *financial intermediation*, imply this position of middleman or, more accurately, **middle participants** (to include women and corporations) in the exchange of financial assets.

The criterion of middleman sometimes turns out to be a difficult way to isolate financial intermediaries, as just about everyone is a middle participant in the flow of funds created by buying and selling financial assets.[2] From the viewpoint of the flow of funds between transactors in an economy, the middleman definition can be a circular way to designate some transactors as middlemen and others as the economic units at the beginning and end of the transfer of funds.[3] As an example, assume that a firm borrows from a bank and redeposits the money in the bank. Which is more in the middle, the firm or the bank?

INTERMEDIATION SERVICES

Why do buyers of financial assets created by financial intermediaries accept a lower yield than they would obtain by directly buying the financial assets in the financial intermediary's portfolio? The answer is that financial intermediaries provide the following intermediation services:

1. *Changing denominations.* Want to buy a $1,000 piece of a portfolio of $10,000 Treasury bills? Try a money market fund. Here the denomination is reduced; it can also be increased, allowing a large investment to be used to purchase assets of lower denomination.

2. *Changing the timing of income.* Want to invest a small sum every month and receive no return until age 65? Try a financial intermediary offering pension plans.

3. *Providing liquidity.* Want to put your funds where they can be retrieved on demand or transferred by check? Try a depository intermediary or money market fund.

4. *Reducing risks.* Pooling your assets in a large portfolio can reduce the risk of default, as compared with putting all your eggs in one company's basket. If the financial intermediary gives its customers a percentage of the income of its portfolio, capital and purchasing power risks may also be reduced. If the funds are available on demand at a fixed nominal amount, as in a demand deposit at a bank, capital and purchasing power risks can be avoided.

Thus, when the financial intermediary sells the financial assets it creates, it includes in the sale a group of services that makes the asset more valuable than is indicated from the money income of the asset alone.

When funds are deposited with financial intermediaries, it is called **intermediation**, whereas **disintermediation** refers to the withdrawal of funds from intermediaries. Disintermediation occurs, for example, when market interest rates rise sufficiently above the interest paid on deposits at savings and loan associations and the depositor withdraws his or her money to reinvest accordingly.

TYPES OF FINANCIAL INTERMEDIARIES

Financial intermediaries can be divided into three groups:

1. Depository intermediaries
2. Contractual intermediaries
3. Investment intermediaries

The size of different financial intermediaries is shown in Table 5-1.

The **depository intermediaries** consist of commercial banks and the thrifts (mutual savings banks, savings and loan associations, and credit unions). The depository intermediaries share the following characteristics:

1. They all issue deposits (credit unions call them *share accounts*) that, except for time deposits that carry specific maturity dates, are normally *payable on demand*. That means that the deposits are accessible by presentation of a withdrawal form (and sometimes a passbook) in person, by mail, or by check.

2. All are authorized to offer checkable deposits.

3. All can obtain federal deposit insurance for $100,000 of deposits for each depositor if they meet federal regulations. Some have chosen insurance funds run by their state government. Thus, deposits are relatively default-free.

TABLE 5-1 The Value of the Assets of Financial Intermediaries in the U.S. Economy, 1986 (billions of dollars)

Depository intermediaries were the largest of the three classes of financial intermediaries, and contractual intermediaries were second. The comparisons are somewhat misleading because many financial intermediaries were offering services that put them in more than one class. Contractual intermediaries, investment intermediaries, and brokerage firms (not shown) offered accounts transferable by check and were in this respect depository intermediaries.

Depository intermediaries		
1. Commercial banks	2,513.9	
2. Savings and loan associations	948.0	
3. Savings banks	216.6	
4. Credit unions	118.9	
subtotal		3,797.4
Contractual intermediaries		
1. Life insurance companies	910.7	
2. Other insurance companies	327.7	
3. Private noninsured pension plans	971.8	
4. State and local pension plans	413.7	
subtotal		2,623.9
Investment intermediaries		
1. Open-end investment companies (mutuals)	424.6	
2. Closed-end investment companies	121.7	
3. Domestic finance companies	359.6	
subtotal		905.9
TOTAL		7,327.2

Sources and computations: The available benchmark data for some of these estimates (other insurance companies, 1984; private noninsured pension plans, 1985; closed-end investment companies, 1985; and state and local pension plans, 1985) were from a previous year. The simple average yearly growth since 1983 was used to adjust these data to a 1986 estimate. The sources of depository intermediary estimates are given in the tables in the next chapter. The following estimates are taken from the *Federal Reserve Bulletin*, April 1987: Life insurance companies, p. A27, and open-end investment companies, p. A35. The other insurance companies' estimate is from the Insurance Information Institute. Pension plan estimates are from the *Life Insurance Fact Book*, American Council of Life Insurance, 1986, p. 54. The closed-end investment company estimate is from the *51st Annual Report of the Securities and Exchange Commission for the Fiscal Year Ending September 30, 1985*, 1986, p. 109.

4. The deposits of depository intermediaries have many of the properties of money. Some of these deposits are included in basic concepts of money, such as all checkable deposits in depository intermediaries, which are included in M-1.
5. All are subject to federal reserve requirements to be phased in by 1988.
6. All can purchase services from the Federal Reserve.

The **investment intermediaries** consist of investment companies and finance companies. The investment companies issue shares of ownership in their portfolios of assets, which represent different types of financial assets, such as gold or oil stocks. The **money market funds** are investment companies that specialize in buying short-term, relatively default-free debt instruments, such as U.S. Treasury bills and commercial bank certificates of deposit. The shares in the money market funds have many of the characteristics of deposits in depository intermediaries. However, unlike the deposits created by the depository intermediaries, the shares issued by investment intermediaries are not claims to a fixed nominal (money) value. Rather, they are a share in the variable value and income of the portfolio minus the management fees of the money market funds.

Finance companies are investment intermediaries that hold a portfolio of loans to consumers or businesses, on which they earn their income. They sell debt instruments and stock to raise funds.

Contractual intermediaries consist of insurance companies and pension funds. These intermediaries create credit instruments that form a contractual relationship with the buyer, such as an annuity or a pension. They hold portfolios that include bonds, common stocks, and real estate.

DEREGULATION IN THE 1970s AND 1980s

In the past, at least two factors differentiated financial intermediaries.[4] First, specialization in the management of particular types of assets and liabilities caused differences. Second, government regulations enforced the areas of specialization and created some noncompetitive barriers. Examples of the first factor are the specialization of savings and loan associations in mortgages and insurance companies in life insurance. An example of the second factor is the government limitation of checking account privileges to commercial banks until 1972.

But a number of forces eroded these differences. One such force was the rapid rise in inflation and interest rates during the 1970s. This caused depositors in depository institutions to look for alternatives to the depositories' accounts that were subject to relatively low ceiling rate regulations on the payment of interest. To the rescue came money market funds and stock brokerage firms, which began offering check-writing accounts that paid market rates of interest.

Another force reducing the differences among financial intermediaries was the vertical expansion of financial intermediaries into related fields, under the government's hands-off or look-the-other-way policies. The alternative characterizations of government actions depend on whether it is part of formal or informal policy.

The U.S. government has acknowledged and accelerated the trend toward homogenization of the financial intermediaries. The government commissioned studies on financial reform, such as the report of the Hunt Commission in 1970 and the FINE study of 1976, which suggested a number of reforms and advocated a wide range of actions to remove regulatory constraints on depository intermediaries, including the removal of deposit interest rate ceilings on deposits. But attempts to transform these suggestions into law were not successful at the time, for at least two reasons. New and more severe crises were needed to bring together all the interest groups required to pass such massive reforms. The other reason—as was apparent in the legislation that was proposed but not passed by the U.S. House of Representatives Banking Committee—was that the reforms were initially introduced together in one large bill rather than in pieces. In retrospect, that all-or-nothing approach was destined to alienate many interest groups representing the different industries involved, before the gyrating interest rates and inflation of the later 1970s made them more responsive to changes.

Legislation finally came in 1980 as high interest rates and high rates of inflation buffeted the financial intermediaries. The thrifts were in financial trouble, and the commercial banks and the thrifts watched funds flow into money market funds. (These money market funds then redeposited the funds in certain commercial banks and bought assets from certain commercial banks. There was a massive redistribution of deposits together with a sharp rise in the cost of funds that financial intermediaries use as their main input.) The Depository Institutions Deregulation and Monetary Control Act of 1980 was pushed through Congress primarily by Henry Reuss, former chairman of the Committee on Banking, Finance, and Urban Affairs. The administration under President Jimmy Carter did little to help during the two-and-a-half-year fight for this legislation, although it did set the tone for deregulation by deregulating the airline industry. The Monetary Control Act of 1980 (a short title for the legislation; technically, it applies only to the first part) went far toward reducing the regulatory constraints that restrained the homogenization of the depository intermediaries. It was the most significant banking legislation since the 1930s. The Thrift Institutions Restructuring Act of (October) 1982 broadened even further the kinds of assets that thrifts could buy, making them even more like commercial banks.

A huge push toward homogenization occurred during the beginning of President Ronald Reagan's administration, in its drive for general deregulation. The government constraints that caused barriers against homogenization were removed; the government regulators were told to pursue a deregulation policy; and a general trend toward deregulation and homogenization spread throughout financial intermediaries.

Deregulation and homogenization are not synonyms. There may be valid reasons, of the type Adam Smith described, for specialization. Indeed, a vague policy of deregulation may, through subsidies, taxes, and the remaining regulations, erode desirable types of specialization.

Government control is complicated and often misunderstood in its effects on the economy. It carries complex benefits and costs that sometimes can cause the controlled to dance to a tune that no one thought the government was playing. For example, through the discount window, the Federal Reserve often gives enormous subsidies to depository institutions when its lending rate (the discount rate) is less than the market rate. These subsidies flow not only into the depository institutions' banking activities but also into many other activities through the holding companies that own most of the commercial banks. The activities of these holding companies include insurance underwriting, mortgage banking, and consumer finance. Unfortunately, a vague policy of deregulation without substantial reform may be sauce for the goose but not for the gander. It may lead to areas of monopoly power for a favored few. That is, it may not produce a **level playing field** in which all competitors face the same regulations.

On the other side of the argument is the risk of monopoly power by the industries that are formally sheltered from competitors by government regulations. For example, the one- (or two-) bank town, where a commercial bank had monopoly power on trust activities, business loans, and checking accounts, was not uncommon in the United States from the 1930s, when one third of the banks in the country closed, until the Monetary Control Act of 1980 gave other depository intermediaries similar powers.

When analyzing financial intermediaries and their economic relationships with the rest of the economy in the 1980s, it is important to distinguish the problems of deregulation from longer-term trends. Let us explain. The phase-out of ceiling interest rates on deposits at depository intermediaries, completed in 1986, created short-term problems. From the early 1930s until this time, depository intermediaries were protected, for most types of deposits, from direct price competition. They could not raise above the legal ceiling rates the interest rate that they paid their depositors. Instead they competed in other ways, such as giving prizes for opening accounts (stuffed teddy bears, for example) and providing such services as convenient offices (which caused them to buy other depository intermediaries and/or build numerous branches, in states where this was permitted). In the 1970s with the advent of substitutes for depository intermediaries and in the 1980s with deregulation, the depository intermediaries were forced to compete for deposits based on the interest they paid. This competition was accompanied by relatively high interest rates until the middle 1980s. Many depository intermediaries did not have management personnel trained for or experienced in such competition; they could not adjust their assets to earn higher interest rates, thereby meeting the costs of their deposits; and/or they were not efficiently run (with the latest cash management and portfolio management techniques). Many depository intermediaries thus ran into trouble, with the thrift industry especially hard hit.

These problems were the effects of the deregulation period, both the deregulation itself and the high interest rates that began in the 1970s. Nevertheless, they induced responses from the government that attacked these short-run problems as if they were long-term trends in the industry. For example, many of the proposals for deposit insurance, whose premiums would be based on the condition of the depository intermediary, contained new government regulations. If enacted and signed into the law, they could reverse the 1980 trend of government deregulation for depository intermediaries. These regulations would severely limit the freedom of the managers of these depository intermediaries to develop new financial services and to manage their portfolios of assets in innovative ways. But by May 1987 none of these insurance proposals had been voted into law.

One longer-term trend that emerged from the 1980 period of deregulation was the authorization by many states and the federal government for depository intermediaries to cross state lines in offering deposit and loan services that previous laws had confined to one state. Some of the largest depository intermediaries (large commercial banks) will probably take over more and more of the depository intermediary services offered in many local areas throughout the country. Two of the questions being asked about this development are whether the supply of deposit and loan services will be dominated by a few large businesses (an oligopoly), and if so, whether this will be good or bad for depositors and those who rely on loans from depository intermediaries.

The consensus of many observers seems to be that the homogenization process, like a rolling stone, is gaining momentum and will not be stopped. It is probable, however, that like other massive changes in business, the changes are better characterized by a pendulum. Deregulation and homogenization will proceed until problems arise that reverse or arrest the process. These problems may take the form of unwanted monopoly power through the vertical integration of giant firms into many industries, the development of diseconomies of scale in some firms beyond some point of expansion, and the public's sudden awareness that it wants back some of the personalized and seemingly inefficient personal services it formerly received—leading to a revival of specialized firms.

One of the most important innovations affecting these changes is the widespread installation of home computers and word processors. The technology exists for receiving and ordering nearly all financial intermediary services from consumers' homes in a more precise and rapid manner than at present. Telephone, computer, and data-processing companies may then be able to offer many financial services through direct linkage with financial intermediaries. At some point in this development, especially in view of the traumatic effects of immense and rapid change, the public may use the government to force the pendulum back the other way.

FINANCIAL INNOVATION AND DEREGULATION IN FOREIGN INDUSTRIAL COUNTRIES

Deregulation and innovations in financial institutions have not been confined to the United States.[5] Although the forms of the innovations and deregulation differ, the following general changes occurred in many other industrial countries in the same period: a greater reliance on market interest rates, the introduction of new financial assets and markets, and increased competition among financial institutions associated with some government deregulation. The level of government regulation at the beginning of the 1970s in these countries varied from highly regulated (in Japan, West Germany, and France) to less regulated (in the United Kingdom). A high degree of regulation includes the nationalization (direct government ownership) of some banks in France and the very tight regulation of loans in West Germany. Thus the movement toward deregulation in the 1970s and 1980s has regulated some countries far more than others.

The same surge in nominal and real interest rates and inflation in the United States was also felt in many other industrial countries, beginning in 1973 (when the price of imported oil rose four-fold), and accordingly, many countries increased their money supply at more rapid rates than they had in the past. Inflation and interest rates receded later in the 1970s and then rose to new peaks in the early 1980s. This increase in interest rates widened the gap between government ceilings on interest payments at some financial institutions and market rates. In turn, this gap stimulated the adoption of new financial assets that paid competitive interest rates and also caused financial institutions to pay more competitive interest rates.

A simultaneous development that has changed the financial markets is the growing scope of international financial markets. Modern technology has enabled the industrial countries' major markets to be in constant contact. This has caused wider trading of financial assets and more competition among financial institutions. For example, commercial banks wishing to attract business deposits on which competitive interest is paid have had to compete both with other financial institutions in the United States and with those in many other countries (see Table 5-2).

Canada, West Germany, Italy, and the United Kingdom currently have no ceilings on the interest that their banks can pay on bank deposits, although there still are controls on the assets that banks can own. For example, a control known as the *corset* in the United Kingdom limits the growth of banks' interest-bearing liabilities. (A bank's liabilities include all its deposits.)

West Germany has strict regulations on financial institutions that are not banks but offer the same services as banks do. In other countries, such as the United States, these substitutes for banks have provided small depositors with competitive rates of interest. For example, in the United States, depositors can switch out of bank accounts into money market fund accounts (this will be discussed in Chapter 9) to obtain market interest rates, which has caused U.S. depository intermediaries to pay more competitive rates of interest. The regulations in West Germany have meant that small depositors are paid significantly lower rates of interest on their deposits than large depositors are. (West German money market funds cannot offer checking services.)

Banking activities in France have been tightly regulated, and the government directly determines deposit interest rates and lending rates. Credit ceilings were removed in 1985 (a step toward deregulation), but bank loans

T A B L E 5-2. Regulatory and Competitive Conditions for Banks in Selected Industrial Countries in 1985

There was some movement toward deregulation in the industrial countries induced in large part by rapid inflation and high interest rates in the 1970s and 1980s. This table shows the status of some government regulations in 1985 in six industrial countries. The nonbank financial assets are financial assets that depositors use as close substitutes for bank accounts. Postal savings in Japan allow small depositors to obtain interest on their deposits.

	Regulation		Competition	
Country	Interest Rate Controls	Balance Sheet Constraints	Other Financial Institutions	Nonbank Financial Assets
Canada	No	No	Yes*	Government bonds
France	Yes†	Credit ceilings lifted in 1985	Savings banks	Government bonds
Italy	No	No	Life	Government bonds
Japan	Yes‡	Limits on bank lending	Postal savings	Bond funds
United Kingdom	No	No	Building societies§	Government savings certificates and money market funds

* Trust and mortgage loan companies, credit unions, and insurance companies.
† Except for long-term large-denomination time accounts.
‡ Regulated except for foreign currency deposits and large time deposits.
§ Similar to savings and loan associations.
Source: J. David Germany and John E. Morton, "Financial Innovation and Deregulation in Foreign Industrial Countries," Board of Governors, *Federal Reserve Bulletin*, October 1985, p. 745.

remain under tight government control. France now has a bond market, which the government initially promoted in the 1970s to finance its deficits. In 1981, following a tightening of controls on the interest that could be paid on bank deposits, many depositors shifted their funds out of the French banks and bought the more competitive bonds. To attract the deposit back again, the banks offered more competitive accounts. The banks then used these funds to purchase bonds, and by 1984 these funds accounted for one fifth of the dollar amount of bonds purchased.

In Sweden, where the government also tightly controls the banks, there has been a development similar to that in France. A bond market has been created, spurred by the introduction in 1982 of Swedish government treasury bills.

Despite the high level of government regulation of depository intermediaries in Japan in 1970, there has been some deregulation. As in France and Sweden, a bond market was allowed to grow. Again, this market was stimulated by the Japanese government's desire to finance its government budget deficits by selling bonds. In response to competitive pressure, Japanese banks asked for and were granted the right in 1979 to offer business deposits that paid interest rates linked to competitive interest rates. All ceilings on these large deposits were removed in 1985, and liberalized interest ceilings for smaller deposits were scheduled for 1987.

Canada also has deregulated the checking accounts at its banks, thus allowing them to pay competitive interest rates to their depositors.

IMPORTANCE OF FINANCIAL INTERMEDIARIES

The introduction to this chapter illuminated the vital link between savings and investment that financial intermediaries can provide. The data for the U.S. economy presented in Table 5-3 underline this presentation. In 1986 the average credit provided by financial intermediaries was 81 percent of the funds advanced in credit markets to nonfinancial sectors. This comparison is not meant to imply that the funds raised by financial intermediaries are earmarked for nonfinancial corporations. Rather, a true picture of the flow of funds is much more complex. The comparison does indicate, however, that financial intermediaries are a major part of the credit markets and that intermediation is a major activity in the U.S. economy. Financial intermediaries are not just the vital link; they are a major part of the chain connecting saving with productive investments.

TABLE 5-3   Direct and Indirect Sources of Funds to the Credit Markets: A Comparison of Total Funds Advanced to Nonfinancial Sectors and Funds Advanced by Financial Intermediaries, Selected Years 1975 to 1986*

The importance of financial intermediaries is supported by the large proportion of credit market funds they provide.

	1975	1980	1986
1. Total funds advanced in credit markets to nonfinancial sectors	200.7	344.9	705.4
2. Credit market funds advanced by private financial intermediaries	122.5	286.2	573.0
3. Row 2 divided by row 1 times 100	61	83	81

* Rows 1 and 2 are in billions of dollars. Half-year data are at seasonally adjusted annual rates. Data in row 3 are percentages. Data for 1986 are based on the first half of the year.
Source: Federal Reserve Bulletin, March 1980, p. A45, February 1984, p. A43, and March 1987, p. A43.

STUDY QUESTIONS

1. What are financial intermediaries?
2. What do financial intermediaries do?
3. What would be the effect on investment if financial intermediaries did not develop in an economy?

4. Review note 3, which defines primary securities and indirect securities. Discuss the problems in defining financial intermediaries as firms that buy primary securities and sell indirect securities.
5. How can a financial intermediary change the timing of an income stream?
6. How can a financial intermediary reduce the risks of holding financial assets?
7. Why would massive disintermediation occur? Give a plausible example.
8. What were the underlying causes of deregulation, and was it confined to the United States? Explain.
9. What is meant by the homogenization of financial intermediaries? What is the relationship, if any, between that phenomenon and the concept of a level playing field?

GLOSSARY

Contractual intermediaries. Insurance companies or pension funds.

Depository intermediaries. In the United States, commercial banks and the thrifts. See Chapter 2.

Disintermediation. Withdrawal of funds from financial intermediaries.

Finance companies. Investment intermediaries that earn their income from a portfolio of loans to consumers or businesses.

Financial intermediaries. Firms that earn their income on the spread between the yields on the financial assets they create and the financial assets they buy. Unlike the holding companies, financial intermediaries do not buy equities for the purpose of controlling other firms.

Holding companies. Firms that buy the equities of another firm for the purpose of substantially controlling its operations.

Intermediation. An increase in the funds placed in financial intermediaries to buy the assets they create.

Investment intermediaries. Investment companies and finance companies.

Level playing field. Equal rules (laws) and regulations for all participants.

Middle participants or **middlemen.** In the flow of funds in the economy, an intermediary between two other participants.

Money market fund. A mutual fund that invests in liquid, relatively risk free, short-term money market instruments.

Reproducible capital. Capital that is used to manufacture more capital and consumption goods.

NOTES

1. There have been proposals to require banks to carry 100 percent of their deposits in reserves. If these reserves were held sterile—earning no interest—the banks would not be financial intermediaries earning their

income primarily from the spread between the interest received on the financial assets they bought and the interest paid to their depositors. Instead, they would have to charge explicit fees to cover their costs, fees that would be paid by their depositors.

2. Donald Hester noted that the "extent of middlemanness (as a measure of financial intermediation) in the economy is unknown." "Financial Disintermediation and Policy," *Journal of Money, Credit and Banking*, August 1969, p. 602.

3. John Gurley and Edward Shaw in *Money in a Theory of Finance* (Washington, D.C.: Brookings Institution, 1960) posited a middleman-type classification system in which financial intermediaries create *indirect securities*, whereas "spending units" (which include corporations producing goods and services) produce *primary securities*. Intermediaries buy primary securities and sell indirect securities. This classification is useful in a formal economic model in which the world can be simplified to illuminate certain relationships.

4. There is substantial literature on the innovation and deregulation of U.S. institutions providing financial services. Two interesting books that cover many of these areas of deregulation are George J. Benston, ed., *Financial Services, the Changing Institutions and Government Policy, Banks, Savings and Loans, Finance, Insurance and Credit Card Companies, Brokerage Houses, Mass Retailers* (Englewood Cliffs, N.J.: Prentice-Hall, 1983); Kerry Cooper and Donald R. Fraser, *Banking Deregulation and the New Competition in Financial Services* (Cambridge, Mass.: Ballinger, 1986). Also see Federal Bank of Chicago, *Economic Perspectives*, September–October 1985, especially the articles by Douglas D. Evanoff, Herbert Baer, Diana Fortier and Dave Phillis, Paul L. Kasriel, Robert D. Laurent, Randall C. Merris and John Wood, and Donna C. Vandenbrink.

5. J. David Germany and John E. Morton, "Financial Innovation and Deregulation in Foreign Industrial Countries," Board of Governors, *Federal Reserve Bulletin*, October 1985, pp. 743–753; and for Japan, see Barbara Cassasus, "Deregulation Makes Its Impact," *The Banker*, January 1986, pp. 63–69.

CHAPTER 6

DEPOSITORY INTERMEDIARIES

CHAPTER PREVIEW

Introduction. The four types of depository intermediaries are listed by the size of their total assets, and a characteristic common to all four, the creation of liabilities included in the money supply, is noted.

Short Guide to Federal Regulators. The federal regulators of depository intermediaries are discussed. The Federal Reserve System is described in more detail in Part IV.

Market Rates and Ceiling Rates. This section explains what happens when the maximum rate that depository institutions can pay depositors is less than the interest rates on other financial assets sold in financial markets.

The Era of Deregulation. This is the story of what happened when rising interest rates and low ceiling rates made it profitable to find new ways to evade the ceiling rates. This economic condition led to the era of deregulation (1980–1983).

Savings Banks. A depository intermediary originally serving the small depositor is described.

Savings and Loan Associations. A depository intermediary that specializes in single-family home mortgages is described. This section also contains some history of mutual savings banks and savings and loan associations.

Credit Unions. The most numerous and smallest depository intermediary that is formed around a common bond is described.

A Turbulent Period for Thrifts. This section discusses the adverse financial conditions during the turbulent period for thrifts in which rising interest rates, beginning in the 1970s, and deregulation, in the 1980s, significantly affected the industry.

An Increased Number of Thrift Holding Companies. Three out of every four thrift holding companies were formed after 1981 by large firms in and out of the thrift industry, supplying funds to an industry in need of capital. Is this a trend for the future structure of the thrift industry?

INTRODUCTION

All depository intermediaries share an important characteristic. They create liabilities that either are included in common concepts of money or are only one step away and have many of the properties of money. The number and the amount of deposits of the depository intermediaries are shown in Table 6-1. Commercial banks dominate this group, with 66.2 percent of the combined

T A B L E 6-1   Number and Assets of Depository Institutions (beginning of 1986)

The data on the value of assets show commercial banks to be dominant, with over 66 percent of the assets. Savings and loan associations are a large group, with nearly 25 percent of the assets. Credit unions (though numerous) and savings banks are relatively small, with a little over 3 percent and nearly 6 percent of the assets, respectively. The total assets of the largest commercial bank (by asset size) is roughly 1.5 times the total value of the assets in all credit unions.

Type	Number*	Total Assets (billions of dollars)	Percentage of Total Assets
All Commercial Banks	15,119	2,513.9	66.201
Savings and Loan Associations	3233	948.0	24.964
Savings Banks	370	216.6	5.704
Credit Unions	17,230	118.9	3.131
Total	35,952	3,797.4	100.000

* The numbers of financial institutions are not exactly comparable to the asset values, as only federally insured institutions are included in the asset values. In addition, not all data are for the same date. Collecting these numbers by calling all the agencies was an interesting experience, as the numbers were rapidly changing because of failures, mergers, and changes on the form of charter under which institutions were operating at the end of 1985 and the beginning of 1986.

Source: "Commercial Banks, Savings and Loan Associations, and Credit Union Assets," *Federal Reserve Bulletin*, Board of Governors, July 1986, pp. A18, A26; assets and number of Savings and Loan Associations, Federal Home Loan Bank Board statistics release, 1985, p. 4. Numbers of federally insured credit unions are from the National Credit Union Administration; numbers of nonfederally insured credit unions are from the Credit Union National Association; and numbers of savings banks and savings and loan associations are from the National Council of Savings Institutions.

assets of all four types, although the relatively small credit unions are most numerous.

This chapter will describe three types of depository intermediaries, known as the thrifts. By itself, this introduction may appear to be dull reading, but it should not be—the 1970s and 1980s were turbulent years for the thrifts.

Economic and political forces have buffeted these institutions, as has the advent of technological developments, such as the introduction of nationwide teller machine networks in 1983.

Before beginning the story, however, the reader is asked to review a short guide to federal regulators. Although this request may smack of memorizing a directory in the lobby of a federal office building, it is a good way to meet the federal bureaucracy.

The discussion will begin with a review of market and ceiling rates, a subject that explains much of what has happened to the thrifts. Then we will examine the era of deregulation. The term *deregulation* might engender a view of relieving the thrifts of onerous federal regulations. But they—the owners and managers of thrifts—never saw it that way. Most of the thrifts were humming along, protected by regulation that allowed them to pay one fourth of a percentage point more interest on their savings deposits than the commercial banks were allowed to pay. True, the commercial banks could offer checking services and the thrifts could not. Nevertheless, the differential looked too good to trade for check privileges. The thrifts would be forced to compete with banks, and there was uncertainty as to how that competition would affect them. And then it happened. Market interest rates rose substantially above the rates that the savings and loan associations could pay on their accounts. The era of deregulation, caused in large part by this phenomenon, was a painful one for the thrifts, and so they were given substantial aid. The thrift industry is still in trouble, now competing with commercial banks, and the consumer is the beneficiary of much of this competition.

Beside reviewing the history of the thrifts, the reader should read about attempts to help them and try to answer the question, "What would have been the best way to help them?"

A GUIDE TO ABBREVIATIONS FOR REGULATORY AGENCIES FOR DEPOSITORY INSTITUTIONS

CLF, Central Liquidity Facility (for credit unions)

DIDC, Depository Institutions Deregulation Committee

FDIC, Federal Deposit Insurance Corporation

FFIEC, Federal Financial Institutions Examination Council

FHLBB, Federal Home Loan Bank Board

FRB, Federal Reserve Board (of the Federal Reserve System)

FSLIC, Federal Savings and Loan Insurance Corporation

NCUA, National Credit Union Administration

SHORT GUIDE TO FEDERAL REGULATORS

At this point we shall mention the federal regulatory agencies that are discussed in this chapter. First is the Federal Reserve System, which is described in greater detail in later chapters. The Federal Reserve is the central bank of the United States. It has direct control of the monetary base and also has regulatory powers over many depository institutions. The Federal Reserve headquarters in Washington, D.C., is called the Board of Governors of the Federal Reserve System. Associated with it are twelve regional Federal Reserve banks (nominally organized as private organizations) and their branches throughout the United States. The Comptroller of the Currency regulates commercial banks that have a federal charter and are called national banks.

The Federal Home Loan Bank Board (FHLBB) supervises savings and loan associations and savings banks, which are its members. Savings banks can also become members of the Federal Reserve System.

The National Credit Union Administration (NCUA) supervises member credit unions. The Central Liquidity Facility (CLF) for credit unions, which is under the aegis of the National Credit Union Administration, borrows funds from the private sector, which it in turn can lend to credit unions.

Regulation is also administered by federal agencies that provide deposit insurance. The Federal Deposit Insurance Corporation (FDIC) provides insurance for deposits in commercial banks and savings banks. The Federal Savings and Loan Insurance Corporation (FSLIC) provides insurance for deposits in savings and loan associations and savings banks. The National Credit Union Administration supplies Federal Share Insurance for credit union deposits. The deposit insurance from these three federal agencies was raised from $40,000 to $100,000 for each depositor in 1980.

The Federal Financial Institutions Examination Council (FFIEC), set up in 1978, coordinates information found by examiners of the various federal bank regulatory agencies. This is important, as many of the commercial banks and thrift institutions are examined by examiners from more than one federal regulatory agency. In order to guard and preserve exclusive jurisdiction to an agency's area of control, sometimes referred to in Washington as "turf," agency personnel may be tempted to hold information for their own action, when in fact it could be combined with information found by other regulatory agencies into something more useful. In addition, of course, the FFIEC can save other agencies and the taxpayers the cost of obtaining the same information services. The coordinating council should alleviate this problem for bank examination.

The Depository Institutions Deregulation Committee (DIDC) was set up in 1980 to phase out ceiling rate regulations on deposits at depository intermediaries.

MARKET RATES AND CEILING RATES

The Banking Acts of 1933 and 1935 prohibited the payment of explicit **pecuniary** (money) **interest** on demand deposits by Federal Reserve member banks and nonmember banks. The words *explicit pecuniary* should be stressed, because "free" services, including convenient branch banks and "gifts" for demand depositors, have partially substituted for money interest payments. Regulation Q of the Federal Reserve Act allows the Board of Governors, the governing body of the Federal Reserve System, to set maximum rates that may be paid on all time deposits of both member (effective 1933) and insured nonmember (effective 1936) banks and for the savings depositories owned and operated by the federal government in the Postal Savings System, which were run by your friendly neighborhood post offices from 1911 until they were closed in 1966.

The Federal Reserve's setting of maximum interest rates on deposits has had a number of predictable effects. Assume that the federal government were to set a maximum price of 10 cents a pound on flour for sale to millers. When the market price is 9 cents, no one would be concerned. If the demand for bread were to increase, so that millers would be willing to pay 15 cents per pound, they would rejoice because they would not have to pay more than 10 cents, and they would gain profit, at least in the short run, until farmers shifted into other grains. But what if other firms that were not covered by the price control started buying the flour at 11 cents a pound and the millers ran short of flour? Now the millers would complain and ask that either the price controls be made to cover everyone or that they be abandoned.

When interest rates were low in the depression of the 1930s, Regulation Q was not an effective constraint. In the post–World War II period, when market rates were sufficiently above ceiling rates, there was massive disintermediation from savings and time deposits in commercial banks and thrifts.

The reader may ask why the regulations prohibiting the payment of interest on demand deposits were enacted. One reason is that if banks were allowed to pay any interest, they would attract more funds than they could "safely" handle. This argument might also be restated as an argument against price competition that could be applied to any industry.

In the 1950s and 1960s, market interest rates frequently went above the ceiling rates payable on time deposits at commercial banks, as shown in Figure 6-1. Interest payments on demand deposits at commercial banks were prohibited.

In 1966, interest rate limitations were extended to savings and loan associations and savings banks, although at a higher level than those for commercial banks. From 1973 to 1980, the difference was one quarter of a percentage point on most savings and time deposits. In 1973, 1974, and again after 1977, market rates soared above ceiling rates. In the first episode, 1973–1974, there was a massive drain of funds, or disintermediation, out of depository intermediaries.

FIGURE 6-1   Selected Market Interest Rates and Ceiling Rates on Commercial Bank
Time Deposits, 1934–1980

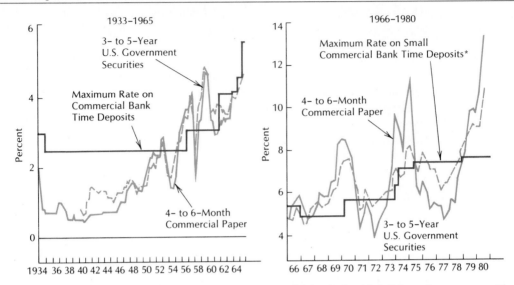

As can be seen, ceiling rates (maximum rates on commercial bank deposits) did not become a problem
from the implementation of these regulations in the 1930s until the 1950s. During the late 1950s and early
1960s, the ceilings were raised to reduce the spread between the market interest rates and the ceilings.
That spread became a problem in the late 1960s and in the 1973–1974 period of high interest rates. None
of these events compares with the rise in interest rates after 1978.

* Except for "wild card" certificates in 1973 and some floating-rate certificates after June 1978. "Wild card" certificates
was the name applied to CDs with denominations of $1,000 or more and maturities of four years or more.
Source: Scott Winningham and Donald Hagan, "Regulation Q: An Historical Perspective," *Economic Review,* Federal
Reserve Bank of Kansas City, April 1980, pp. 4, 7.

In the 1978–1980 period, the depository intermediaries were allowed to offer
consumer time deposits with yields that were tied to market rates (called
money market certificates), and disintermediation was not quite as serious for
the depository intermediaries, except for the shift to money market funds.

To understand the role played by money market funds and the lifting of
ceiling rates (which occurred most dramatically at the end of 1982 and the
beginning of 1983), one must understand the events around the general
reduction of regulations on depository intermediaries. These events leading up
to and including the rapid deregulation of depository intermediaries in the
1980s is a fascinating story (of rising interest rates), forcing political action that
has had far-ranging consequences for the country's system of money and
banking (see Table 6-2).

T A B L E 6 - 2   Selected Regulatory Changes Affecting Thrifts from 1932 to 1987

1932

The Federal Home Loan Bank, FHLB, was established to provide a central credit system for S&Ls financing home mortgages.

1934

The Federal Deposit Insurance Corporation, FDIC, was authorized in 1933 and created in 1934. Its insurance provisions are less liberal for S&Ls than for commercial banks insured under the FDIC.

1966

The Stevens Act granted to the FHLBB the power to fix the maximum rates on different types of accounts. Up until then the interest rates paid had not been controlled by law. The FHLBB had used "moral suasion" in 1962 and 1963 to try to hold down rates and in 1965 had announced that S&Ls that did not abide by its suggested ceilings would be restricted in their borrowing from the FHLBB's regional offices.
Federal insurance of S&Ls was made nearly equivalent to FDIC coverage.

1980

The Depository Institutions Deregulation and Monetary Control Act was signed on March 31, 1980, giving all depository institutions the right to offer interest-paying consumer checking accounts (NOW accounts); Federal Reserve requirements were placed on some accounts (including all checkable accounts) at all depository institutions, interest rate ceilings that gave a one fourth of a percentage point higher ceiling interest rate that could be paid to depositors at thrifts (compared with commercial banks) were scheduled to be phased out by 1986; and thrifts were given expanded powers, such as the right to make loans to businesses. FSLIC members were also allowed to make real estate loans without regard to geographic area (they had been confined to the local area) and to exceed the former limitation on the size of these loans of 90 percent of the value on one- to four-family properties.

1981

All Savers Certificates were authorized for depository institutions. These were tax-free securities that had one-year maturities and could not be issued after January 1, 1983. The interest rate that could be paid on them was fixed at 70 percent of the one-year T-bill rate.
Nationwide NOW accounts were introduced.
Regulations were liberalized to permit mutually chartered institutions to convert to stock-type organizations.
Adjustable-rate mortgages, ARMs, were authorized. ARMs allow the mortgage rate to change according to some criterion, such as a change in the Treasury bill rate, with limitations on the amount of adjustment in one year.
The FHLBB and the FSLIC created income capital certificates which institutions could acquire and sell to the FSLIC in exchange for a promissory note (a contract of indebtedness) for the purpose of boosting the value of the institution's net worth

TABLE 6-2 *(continued)*

under special creative accounting rules known as *regulatory accounting principles (RAP)* (as opposed to *generally accepted accounting principles, GAAP*). When the institution became profitable, the certificates would be redeemed.

1982

The Garn–St Germain Depository Institutions Act, DIA, was signed into law on October 15, 1982. The DIA authorized (the emergency acquisitions provisions) depository institutions to buy troubled state depository institutions in other states. The DIA also authorized depository institutions to issue new accounts with more competitive rates of interest (super NOW accounts and money market accounts). The DIA authorized both the FSLIC and the FDIC to acquire Net Worth Certificates from qualifying weak institutions.

Appraised equity value adjustments were allowed so as to increase net worth. The FHLBB authorized FSLIC-insured institutions to make a one-time adjustment to their net worth, increasing the reported value of their buildings and land by the difference between the market value and the book value. As of mid-1984, one fourth of the FSLIC-insured institutions had used the method to increase their net worth.

Money market deposit accounts were implemented in December 1982.

Federal SBs could obtain federal mutual or stock charters while keeping their FDIC insurance.

The net worth requirement was reduced from 5 to 3 percent of liabilities.

1983

California led the way in giving state authorization to broaden the thrifts' powers, by passing the Nolan bill, allowing state-chartered thrifts to expand the types of assets they could own.

Super NOW accounts allowed by the Garn–St Germain bill were introduced in January.

The Federal Home Loan Bank, FHLB, permitted advances to its members for terms of up to twenty years (was ten years).

Minimum capital requirements were raised, and other restrictions were imposed on institutions seeking FSLIC insurance.

1984

Federal associations were allowed to establish finance subsidiaries to issue securities for the parent institution.

1985

The Federal Reserve Bank of Cleveland lent funds to Ohio institutions experiencing runs. These institutions were insured by the private fund, Ohio Deposit Guarantee Fund, ODGF. On March 15, 1985, the governor of Ohio ordered the closing of all ODGF-insured institutions. This was the first "banking holiday" since President Franklin Roosevelt closed all the banks in the country in 1933. The FHLBB agreed to consider issuing FSLIC insurance to qualified ODGF institutions, and the institutions were gradually reopened, some with a withdrawal limit of $750 per account per month.

Runs in Maryland were limited by a withdrawal limit of $1,000 (imposed by the governor). These runs occurred at institutions insured by a private fund, Maryland

T A B L E   6 - 2   *(continued)*

Savings–Share Insurance Corporation, MSSIC. MSSIC was replaced by the Maryland Deposit Insurance Fund, which was given state backing.

1986

GAO reports on the thrift industry (including *Cost to FSLIC of Delaying Action on Insolvent Savings Institutions*) that 582 insolvent thrifts that were "warehoused," as well as estimates that the FSLIC could be down to $1 billion at the end of the year, spurred rescue proposals in both houses of Congress for expected final passage in 1987.

1987 (through August)

GAO declared the FSLIC fund to have been insolvent since the beginning of March 1987. Congress passed 10.8 billion recapitalization bill. Stricter accounting rules to be put in place on January 1, 1988, could put many more thrifts on the insolvent list.

THE ERA OF DEREGULATION

Before 1972, only commercial banks and a few thrifts (with state deposit insurance) offered third-party payment services—checking accounts. A thrift institution (savings and loan associations, mutual savings banks, and credit unions) would, upon presentation of a passbook—in person or by mail—issue a check drawn on its account at a commercial bank. The thrift did not offer the depositor the opportunity to withdraw and transfer his or her funds by check. The thrifts paid interest on their deposits, and it was presumed to be illegal to offer checking services for these deposits.

Or was it? In July 1970, a mutual savings bank (MSB) in Massachusetts proposed a plan to the state banking commissioner to allow checking-type accounts by means of third-party "negotiable orders of withdrawal," or NOW accounts. Those accounts would pay interest, just as other savings accounts do, but would be accessible by check. Since September 1970, savings and loan associations have been permitted by the Housing Act of 1970 to make pre-authorized transfers from savings accounts for household-related bills, but NOW accounts were a clearly broadened power, and the Massachusetts state banking commissioner said no to the proposal. However, in May 1972, the Massachusetts Supreme Judicial Court unanimously allowed MSBs in Massachusetts to offer NOW accounts. Then in September 1972, a savings bank in New Hampshire began offering NOWs. The NOW account cat was out of the bag, and the U.S. Congress gave chase when in August 1973 all depository institutions in Massachusetts and New Hampshire except credit unions were authorized by federal law to offer NOWs. In 1976, federal legislation authorized NOW accounts in Connecticut, Maine, Rhode Island, and Vermont; and the Financial Institutions Regulatory Act allowed them in New York in 1979.

Legislation submitted by the Carter administration for the Federal Reserve in the 95th Congress (1977 and 1978) would have extended NOW accounts nationwide. Unfortunately for the success of this provision, the proposal also contained authority for the Federal Reserve to pay interest on the reserves it required of its 5,628 member banks. This additional ornament—intended to help the Federal Reserve hold on to its member banks—did not win the necessary support from a budget-minded Congress. It died in the Senate, and hearings were never held in the House of Representatives.

Despite federal legislation confining NOWs to New England and New York, checking deposits and remote cash-dispensing machines began to spread. In January 1974, First Federal Savings and Loan of Lincoln, Nebraska, installed automatic terminal facilities (ATFs) or remotes in two supermarkets, allowing remote cash withdrawals from savings accounts. Other savings and loan associations also adopted such systems.

Also in 1974, money market mutual funds began offering their shareholders withdrawals by check. And in 1974, some federal credit unions began offering checking accounts, called share drafts.

As interest rates rose in 1978 and 1979, as shown in Figure 6-2, there was a huge flow of money into money market funds. Although these funds were

FIGURE 6-2   Monthly Interest Rates of Three-Month U.S. Treasury
Bills, 1951–1987

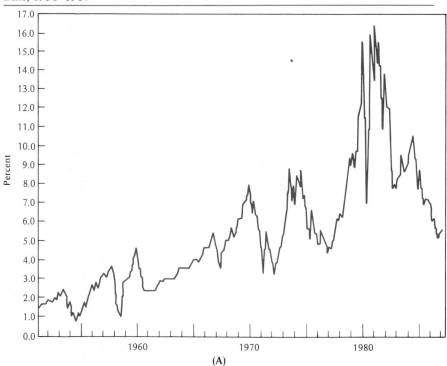

(A)

FIGURE 6-2   (*continued*)   Differences Among Interest Rates on
Three-Month U.S. Treasury Bills Each Month, 1951–1987

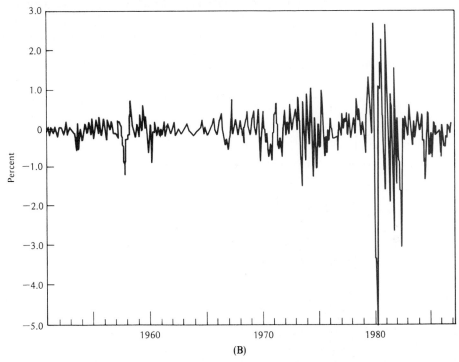

(B)

Interest rates have generally risen since 1950, as shown by the interest rates on three-month Treasury bills in Figure A. The data for the early 1970s, late 1970s, and early 1980s reveal especially large variations in these interest rates, as illustrated in Figure B.

Source: Cambridge Planning and Analytics, Inc., Boston.

redeposited into the banking system, so that there was no overall decline in deposits, the distribution of deposits among depository institutions changed dramatically, and many institutions were severely affected. In addition to this development, many commercial banks left or threatened to leave the Federal Reserve System and become nonmember state banks, so as to avoid posting reserves with the Federal Reserve. These federal required reserves earned no interest, and in a period of high interest rates, the Federal Reserve requirements looked very expensive. Could the Federal Reserve continue to control the money supply if it could not impose reserve requirements on banks? We hope that you will become an expert on the answer to that question as you proceed through this book. At the time—1978 and 1979—the question was often asked amid dire threats of a crumbling banking reserve system and a runaway money supply.

The Federal Reserve—under pressure from these compelling forces in the economy and still without a successful bill in Congress that would authorize nationwide NOW accounts—authorized a new type of account. On November 1, 1978, commercial banks were authorized to offer savings accounts that could be automatically transferred to checking accounts (automatic transfer service, or ATS, accounts) whenever funds were needed to cover a check. Although large minimum balances were imposed by the private banks on these ATS accounts, they were a means of paying interest on checking accounts.

On April 20, 1979, the U.S. Court of Appeals in Washington ruled that all interest-paying checking accounts, except those specifically authorized by Congress to operate in the six New England states and New York, were illegal. All ATS accounts, share draft accounts at credit unions, and the remote cash-disbursing units of savings and loan associations (ATFs) would be illegal. The court delayed the effective date of its ruling until January 1980, to give the Congress a chance to act.

An excerpt from the *Washington Star* of April 21, 1979, explains this decision. It also captures part of the scramble in the thrift and commercial banking industries to obtain favorable government regulations while at the same time dodging the existing regulations, such as the prohibition against interest payments on demand deposits (page A6, a jump from a page 1 story):

> The decision covers three different suits. In each one, a section of the industry is trying to take away the interest-bearing checking account from another while at the same time trying to keep its own account.
>
> The American Bankers Association, which represents commercial banks and benefits from the automatic transfer account, sued the National Credit Union Administration in an effort to take away the share draft account.
>
> The United States League of Savings Associations, which represents the savings and loan industry and has the remote service unit, sued the Fed and the FDIC to take away the automatic transfer.
>
> And the Independent Bankers Association of America, which could benefit from the new accounts, sued the Federal Home Loan Bank Board, which regulates the savings and loan industry, to take away the remote service unit.
>
> In its decision, the court recognized the narrowing of differences among financial institutions and said it was a change that should be addressed by Congress.
>
> "Three separate and distinct types of financial institutions created . . . to serve different public needs have now become . . . three separate but homogeneous types of financial institutions offering virtually identical services to the public, all without the benefit of congressional consideration."

Congress reacted with a three-month extension—until April 1980—that also contained a provision that gave NOW accounts to New Jersey. Then at the last moment, March 31, 1980, after two and a half years of hearings in both the House of Representatives and the Senate and a prolonged battle among interest groups, a major bill was passed and signed into law. The Depository Institutions Deregulation and Monetary Control Act of 1980 (or simply, Monetary Control Act of 1980, although technically this name applies only to Title 1 of the act) authorized nationwide NOW accounts. The law also extended the types of assets that the thrifts were authorized to buy, moved toward eliminating state usury ceilings, and imposed Federal Reserve requirements on all depository institutions that offered checkable deposits or business certificates of deposits with maturities of less than four years. It increased federal deposit insurance from $40,000 to $100,000 per depository at a financial depository.

The Depository Institutions Deregulation and Monetary Control Act of 1980 also directed that over a six-year period the ceiling rate limitations be eliminated on consumer NOW accounts and share draft accounts. Exhibit 6-1 shows the first press release of the Depository Institutions Deregulation Committee (DIDC), which was set up by this 1980 legislation "to provide for the orderly phaseout of interest rate ceilings over the six-year period and eventually provide depositors with a market rate of return on their savings." Table 6-3 begins to tell the story of a disorderly phaseout. Additional information is provided in Chapter 8.

The DIDC, although encouraged by Donald Regan, then secretary of the Treasury, to begin its task by raising ceiling interest rates, could not get a majority vote for this course of action. Under the prodding of Richard T. Pratt, then chairman of the Federal Home Loan Bank Board, and with the support of Chairman Paul Volcker of the Federal Reserve, the DIDC chose essentially to retain (or only slowly to remove) the ceilings. It was thought that the thrifts, already hurt by the high mortgage interest rates that they had to pay for some of their funds (when they held mortgages in their portfolios that yielded the lower interest rates of years past) would be doubly hurt if they were forced to pay higher rates on their deposits.

The DIDC was finally forced into rapid action by the U.S. Congress via the latter's passage of the Garn–St Germain Depository Institutions Act of 1982. That legislation completely removed the ceiling rate on two types of short-term deposits that required a $2,500 minimum balance. The largest and fastest flow of funds in the history of the U.S. banking system began almost immediately, an episode described in Chapter 8. The disorderly phaseout of ceiling rates produced these huge surges in funds plus a tangled web of new regulations for the many new instruments that the DIDC created. A question for further research is whether or not two other alternative methods of deregulation, on net (considering the general welfare of the public and the special problems of the thrift industry), would have produced better results. The two alternatives are the immediate lifting of ceiling rates in 1980 or an orderly phaseout.

As mandated in the Depository Institutions Deregulation and Monetary Control Act of 1980, all interest rate ceilings under the direction of the Depos-

EXHIBIT 6-1

DEPOSITORY INSTITUTIONS DEREGULATION COMMITTEE
PRESS RELEASE

COMPTROLLER OF THE CURRENCY
FEDERAL DEPOSIT INSURANCE CORPORATION
FEDERAL HOME LOAN BANK BOARD
NATIONAL CREDIT UNION ADMINISTRATION
TREASURY DEPARTMENT

For immediate release   May 7, 1980

The Depository Institutions Deregulation Committee today
announced that at its first meeting it elected Paul A.
Volcker, Chairman of the Federal Reserve Board, as Its
Chairman. Irvine H. Sprague, Chairman of the Federal
Deposit Insurance Corporation, was named Vice Chairman.

The Committee was created by the Depository Institutions
Deregulation and Monetary Control Act of 1980, signed on
March 31. Title II of that Act transferred to the newly
formed Committee the authority to set interest rate
ceilings on deposits of commercial banks, mutual savings
banks and savings and loan associations. The
Committee's assignment under the Act is to provide for
the orderly phase-out of interest rate ceilings over a
six-year period and eventually to provide depositors
with a market rate of return on their savings.

Members of the Committee are the Secretary of the
Treasury and the chairmen of the Federal Home Loan
Bank Board and the National Credit Union Administration
Board. The Comptroller of the Currency serves as a
nonvoting member.

In its first substantive action, the Committee requested
comment by June 9 on a proposal to prohibit any premium
or gifts given by an institution upon the opening of a
new account or an addition to an existing account.
Premiums are now limited to $5 (at wholesale, exclusive
of packaging and shipping costs) for deposits of less
than $5,000 and to $10 for deposits of $5,000 or more.

In addition, the Committee proposed to limit any
finder's fees to third parties to cash payments and to
regard any finder's fees as interest to the depositor.

Comment was requested on this proposal, also by June 9.

The Comptroller of the Currency serves under the secretary of the Treasury, both of
whom were on the DIDC. The others on the DIDC are independent agencies. The
"orderly phaseout of interest rate ceilings" that was supposed to take place was not
achieved.

T A B L E 6 - 3   Depository Institutions Deregulation Committee Changes in Interest Rate Ceilings on Deposits, 1980–1983

This is the record of the Depository Institutions Deregulation Committee from 1980, when it started, until 1986. Both the Money Market Deposit Accounts and the super-NOW account were mandated in the Garn–St Germain Depository Institutions Act of 1982. These two deposits are described in Chapter 8, along with reserve requirements. One important aspect of the DIDC should be clear from this table. The phaseout was not an orderly one in which deposit ceilings were lifted in a smooth process. By March 1983, three years after the DIDC was set up, ceilings on NOW accounts under $2,500 were virtually unchanged. (Note that a basis point is 1/100 of a percentage point.)

Effective Date of Change	Type of Deposit	Nature of Change
June 2, 1980	Small savers certificates (time deposits with maturities of 30 months or more, no minimum denomination)	*Prior ceilings:* Commercial banks were permitted to pay the yield on 2.5-year Treasury securities less 75 basis points, and thrift institutions were permitted to pay 25 basis points more than commercial banks were. The maximum interest rates permissible, however, were 11.75 percent at commercial banks and 12 percent at thrift institutions. *Changes:* Ceiling rates relative to yield on 2.5-year Treasury securities raised 50 basis points. Ceiling rates will not fall below 9.25 percent at commercial bank or 9.5 percent at thrift institutions. The maximum ceiling rates of 11.75 and 12 percent are retained.
June 5, 1980	Money market certificates (time deposits in denominations of $10,000 or more with maturities of 6 months)	Raised the ceiling rate from the discount yield on 6-month Treasury bills established at the most recent auction to that rate plus 25 basis points at both commercial banks and thrift institutions.*
December 31, 1980	NOW accounts	Set the ceiling rate on NOW accounts at 5.25 percent for commercial banks, mutual savings banks, and savings and loan associations. The ceiling rate on interest-bearing checkable deposits was 5 percent until December 31, 1980.
August 1, 1981	Small savers certificates	Eliminated caps on these ceiling rates of 11.75 percent at commercial banks and 12 percent at thrift institutions. With the caps lifted, thrift institutions may pay the yield on 2.5-year Treasury securities, and commercial banks may pay 25 basis points less.
October 1, 1981	All Savers Certificates	Adopted rules for All Savers Certificates specified in the Economic Recovery Act of 1981.
November 1, 1981	Money market certificates	Depository institutions are now permitted to pay the higher of the discount rate on 6-month Treasury bills at the most recent auction, plus 25 basis points, or the average auction rate in the past four weeks, plus 25 basis points.
December 1, 1981	IRA/Keogh accounts (see glossary)	Created a new category of IRA/Keogh account with minimum maturity of 1.5 years, no regulated interest rate ceiling, and no minimum denomination.

TABLE 6-3 *(continued)*

Effective Date of Change	Type of Deposit	Nature of Change
May 1, 1982	Time deposits with maturities of 3.5 years or more	Minimum balance requirements removed.
May 1, 1982	91-day time deposits with $7,500 minimums	Based ceiling on Treasury bill rate.
September 1, 1982	7- to 31-day time deposits with $20,000 minimums	Imposed ceiling at Treasury bill rate and no ceiling after January 5, 1983.
December 14, 1982	Money market Deposit Accounts	Described in Chapter 8.
January 5, 1983	Super-NOW Accounts	Described in Chapter 8.
October 1, 1983	Most time deposits; all time deposits of more than 7 days and Money Market Deposit Accounts	Ceiling rate limitations abolished, provided that the $2,500 minimum balance is maintained. Also a 5.25 ceiling rate was imposed on savings accounts not deregulated, such as one of these accounts with less than $2,500.
January 1, 1984	Eliminated rate differential between commercial banks and thrifts on passbook savings accounts and 7- to 31-day time deposits of less than $2,500. All depository institutions may now pay a maximum of 5.5 percent. Maximum denominations on MMDAs, super-NOW accounts, and 7- to 31-day ceiling–free time deposits reduced to $1,000.	
January 1, 1986	Eliminated maximum denomination on MMDAs, super-NOW accounts, and 7- to 31-day ceiling–free time deposits.	
March 31, 1986	All interest rate ceilings terminated on all deposit accounts, except for demand deposits, under the direction of the Depository Institutions Deregulatory Committee.	

* Other changes in the ceiling rate on money market certificates are relevant when the yield on 6-month Treasury bills falls below 8.75 percent.

Source: Jan G. Loeys, "Deregulation: A New Future for Thrifts," *Business Review*, Federal Reserve Bank of Philadelphia, January–February 1983, p. 23; and R. Alton Gilbert, "Will the Removal of Regulation Q Raise Mortgage Interest Rates?" *Review*, Federal Reserve Bank of St. Louis, December 1981, p. 7, updated for October 1983 change.

itory Institutions Deregulation Committee were eliminated on March 31, 1986. There was no authorization in the law to remove ceilings on checking accounts that businesses may use, called *demand deposits*. Demand deposits continue to pay no money interest directly.

SAVINGS BANKS

Savings banks, or SBs, are chartered in seventeen states and Puerto Rico and are concentrated in New England and the Middle Atlantic States. In 1986 there were 370 SBs, of which 326 were organized as mutual associations (and are sometimes called *mutual savings banks* or *MSBs*).[1] This was the only form of organization until the 1980s. Forty-four of these SBs are organized as stock-owned corporations. Before 1981, SBs were eligible to join the Federal Reserve System and to purchase FDIC deposit insurance, just as commercial banks can. All the SBs are formed by obtaining charters from their individual states. In 1980, the federal regulatory entity for savings and loan associations, the

Federal Home Loan Bank Board, or FHLBB, opened its doors to SBs. The FHLBB offered its own federal insurance (FSLIC) to SBs as well as the opportunity to obtain directly from the FHLBB a federal charter to operate. This is what happened when the two government agencies both tried to regulate the same entity. FDIC insurance was in effect for 355 SBs, and FSLIC was in effect for 13 SBs. Most (336) of the SBs continued to operate under state charters. The FHLBB began offering federal charters to SBs in 1980, and by 1986, 34 SBs had federal charters.

The history of SBs up to the 1980s is a history of mutual savings banks, or MSBs. The original purpose for MSBs was to provide a safe depository for small savers. MSBs create short-term financial assets that take the form of very liquid savings deposits. Some of these accounts are checkable. These accounts, as well as the regular passbook savings accounts at all MSBs, earn interest. The profits earned by the MSBs are divided among the depositors on the basis of the size of their deposits, but not exceeding any ceiling regulations on interest payments. The Federal Deposit Insurance Corporation insures eligible deposits of MSBs and commercial banks up to $100,000 for each depositor at a bank.

MSBs' experience with substantial declines in the value of their investments in mortgages during the deep depressions of the 1930s caused them to reduce their holdings of higher-interest mortgage loans and to increase their holdings

TABLE 6-4   Assets and Liabilities of Mutual Savings Banks, January 1986 (in billions of dollars)

Assets	$216.7
Loans	
Mortgages	108.3
Other	31.8
Securities	
U.S. government	12.6
Mortgage-backed securities	21.4
State and local government	2.3
Corporate and other	20.8
Cash	5.6
Other assets	13.2
Liabilities	$216.7
Deposits	186.3
Regular	182.4
Ordinary savings	32.4
Time and other	104.4
Other	3.9
Other liabilities	17.1
General reserve accounts	12.9

Source: Federal Reserve Bulletin, July 1986, p. A26.

of government securities. Since the late 1940s, they have again increased their holdings of mortgages, until in November 1983, mortgage loans constituted 50 percent of their financial assets, as indicated in Table 6-4.

SAVINGS AND LOAN ASSOCIATIONS

Savings and loan associations (S&Ls) are found in every state, in the District of Columbia, and in Puerto Rico and Guam. There were 3,573 S&Ls in November 1986. S&Ls are the third largest private financial intermediaries (after commercial banks and insurance companies) and the second largest depository institution, with $948 billion in assets as of 1986. The original purpose for their development was mortgage finance, rather than as a safe depository for savings, as was true of SBs. They are the principal source of first-mortgage residential loans for residences in the United States, with 60.9 percent of their assets invested in mortgages, mostly single-family residences, as indicated in Table 6-5.

Of the 3,573 S&Ls in 1986, 1,852 operated under state charters, and 1,721 had federal charters from the FHLBB. The S&Ls have traditionally been organized as mutuals, and in 1986, 2,486 S&Ls were mutuals. The stock form of organization has been adopted by a growing number of S&Ls, reaching 1,087 in 1986.

Home-financing organizations have been reported as existing in ancient Egypt, China, and the South Sea Islands. The Birmingham Building Society, established in 1781, was the first firm recorded, which rose in reponse to the need for small-home financing in Great Britain. The English building societies were a product of the rapidly growing mine and factory towns in Great Britain's period of early industrialization.

The Birmingham Building Society was organized in a pub, where its founders and owners were also its sole participants. Members were fined if

TABLE 6-5   Assets and Liabilities of Federally Insured Savings and Loan Associations, January 1986 (in billions of dollars)

Assets		Liabilities	
Total assets	$1,069.8	a. Savings capital	$852.3
a. Mortgages	651.8	b. Borrowed money	151.0
Mortgage-backed		FHLBB*	82.6
securities	111.6	Other	68.2
b. Cash and investment		c. Other	24.2
securities	139.8	d. Net worth	47.2
c. Other	103.9		

* These are advances from the Federal Home Loan Bank.
Source: Federal Reserve Bulletin, July 1986, p. A26.

they did not show up at the "Fountain" in Cheapside on the first Monday of every month with half a guinea for each share they owned. When the fund became large enough, a lottery was held to determine who would obtain the first home loan. The recipient would repay the loan plus interest. Then another member would be granted a loan. When all the members had repaid their loans, the funds were divided among the shareholders, and the Birmingham Building Society was terminated.

The Oxford Provident, organized in 1831 in the small factory town of Frankfort, Pennsylvania, was the first such building and loan society in the United States. Its operation was similar in many ways to the Birmingham Building Society. It was operated with the sole purpose of providing loans to its members. No depositor could withdraw funds unless he or she terminated membership in the association, gave one month's notice, and paid a penalty fee. The loans were allocated in a different manner from those given by the Birmingham Building Society. When the fund reached $500, a loan was made to the member who agreed to pay the highest interest rate.

During the early history of banking in the United States there were several important differences between the MSBs and the S&Ls that influenced their growth. Initially, the MSBs offered small-deposit accounts, which could not be readily obtained from other financial intermediaries. Early commercial banks did not encourage small accounts. (Some commercial banks still discourage small accounts.) The practice precipitated a rapid growth of MSBs from 10 banks and $1 million in deposits in 1820 to 620 banks and $819 million in deposits by 1880. Then came the banking panic of 1873, which was followed by 123 suspensions of savings banks from 1875 to 1879. This setback ended the period of greatest growth for MSBs.

MSBs operated under *permanent charters*, which allowed depositors to enter or leave the association at any time. S&Ls first used *terminating charters*, which opened membership only to original members. After 1854, *serial charters* allowed new groups of members to enter the associations under separate loan plans. Slowly, the S&Ls adopted permanent charters. They continued to emphasize regular savings, with fines and withdrawal fees for delinquents.

The more liquid deposits of MSBs were a major factor in their more rapid growth to the 1920s. In 1910, MSBs and commercial banks had approximately equal amounts of saving deposits. By 1920, commercial bank savings deposits had grown much more rapidly than had either MSB deposits or those of the smaller S&L industry.

The post–World War I building boom caused a rapid expansion of S&Ls, which the MSBs did not experience. In 1929, there were 3,709 more S&Ls than MSBs in 1930, with more than three times the amount of assets. Then came the depression of the 1930s. In 1929, the 12,342 S&Ls had $8.7 billion in assets, which included 24 percent of all nonfarm residential mortgages outstanding in the United States.

In 1935 and 1936, real estate owned outright by S&Ls from mortgage foreclosures amounted to 20 percent of their assets, compared with 2 or 3 percent in the 1920s. Most of this was sold at a profit during the 1940s. Mortgage loans could not rapidly be converted into cash when S&Ls were hit by large withdrawals. In addition, most cash reserves of S&Ls were held as deposits at commercial banks, many of which failed. By 1940, there were 4,821 fewer S&Ls than in 1929, a decline of 39 percent. The S&Ls held $5.7 billion in assets in 1940, which was a decline in money terms of nearly $3 billion, or 34 percent. The decline in real terms, adjusted for a decline in prices, was much less: roughly 7 percent.

Was this a bad record? Kroos and Blyn claimed that "No other financial intermediary, not even the commercial banking system, was more hard hit by the depression than the savings and loan industry."[2] Another analyst stated, "Depressions in the 1890s and especially in the 1930s caused lapses in its overall growth and a fair number of failures, but, on the whole, S&Ls survived the depressions very well. In fact, they survived better than banks."[3]

The extremely rapid growth of S&Ls in the 1920s and in the post–World War II decades was largely a result of the residential housing booms of the post–World War I and II periods. During the 1930s, the loss of 4,821 S&Ls and the default of many S&L accounts made that decade a catastrophic period for the owners and depositors of many S&Ls.

The S&Ls emerged from the 1930s with unprecedented federal supervision and assistance. The Reconstruction Finance Corporation had given $18 million to failing S&Ls. The Home Owners Loan Corporation gave $3 billion in mortgage credit between mid-1933 and mid-1936, with the S&Ls directly receiving $800 million. The Federal Home Loan Bank was established in 1932 to supervise and provide credit to S&Ls for mortgages. The Federal Savings and Loan Insurance Corporation was created in 1934 to issue deposit insurance to S&Ls. Federal chartering of S&Ls began with the federal government authorized to invest $1 million in each new S&L so chartered. All federally chartered S&Ls have federal insurance. Three fourths of the state-chartered S&Ls are members of the FHLB and have federal insurance.

The Federal Home Loan Bank has its headquarters, which is called the Federal Home Loan Bank Board, in Washington, D.C. It is controlled by a three-person board, employing approximately 1,200 people throughout the country. It controls twelve district Federal Home Loan Banks, which supervise the S&L industry. Each of the twelve district banks is a separate corporation nominally owned by stockholders, which are mostly S&Ls. The approval of the FHLBB in Washington is required before any major action can be taken.

CREDIT UNIONS

Credit unions are consumer cooperatives that provide loans and a means of regular savings to their members. The officers of a credit union are members who serve without compensation, except for the treasurer in some instances.[4]

Business managers are often hired to run the credit union. Savings are deposited as shares, and interest is returned to the members as dividends. Credit unions operate under state and federal charters. In 1986 there were 17,230 state and federal credit unions (57.6 percent being federal).

All federally chartered credit unions and 42.4 percent of credit unions with state charters have federal deposit insurance. The National Credit Union Administration provides federal insurance up to $100,000.

Credit unions' members must have a **common bond**, such as a common place of employment. However, the restriction of a common bond can be mitigated. For example, the Cincinnati-based Everybody's Credit Union was organized to serve the poor in nineteen counties. There are credit unions for hairdressers in Connecticut; for inmates of Oregon State Penitentiary; for individuals with the last name of Lee in San Francisco; for the owners of Arabian horses in Burbank, California; and a credit union called "Alaska US," with branches throughout Alaska and a service center in Denver, Colorado. Credit unions generally are small compared with commercial banks. This was emphasized in Table 6-1, which noted that the commercial bank with the most assets had 1.5 times the assets of the entire credit union industry. Nevertheless, there are some relatively large credit unions, with over $1 billion in assets, as shown in Table 6-6.

T A B L E 6 - 6   Largest Credit Unions in the United States in 1985 (by asset size in millions of dollars)

Although most credit unions are small financial institutions, these five credit unions are relatively large, with the top three having over $1 billion in assets.

Rank	Name of Institution	Asset Size
1	Navy FCU	$1.908
2	Pentagon FCU	1.180
3	State Employees CU	1,002
4	United Air Lines Employees CU	860
5	Alaska USA FCU	598

Source: The American Banker, December 2, 1985, p. 1.

Credit union deposits are usually called **shares**, and their checkable deposits are called share drafts (see Table 6-7). Where are the member shares invested? Most of the assets are loans back to the credit union members. These loans are for durable goods such as automobiles, furniture, home furnishings, and household appliances. Loans are also made to consolidate debts; to finance vacations; and to pay medical, dental, and funeral expenses.

Credit unions originated in the nineteenth century in Germany. They were closely connected with moral and humanitarian goals and were frequently organized in and supported by churches. They emphasized self-help for the

TABLE 6-7   Assets and Liabilities of Federally Insured Credit Unions, January 1986 (in millions of dollars)

The ratios of shares and deposits to assets for state- and federally chartered credit unions reflect the credit unions' reliance on deposits for funds (not active in financial markets such as the federal funds market) and the use of those funds for loans to members.

Total assets	$118.9	Savings	$107.2
Federal	78.6	Federal	
State	40.3	(shares)	72.2
Loans outstanding	73.5	State (shares	
State	48.1	and deposits)	35.1
Federal	25.5		

Source: Federal Reserve Bulletin. February 1984, p. A28.

impoverished. Credit unions first started in the United States in 1909, but they did not develop rapidly until after 1930. Edward Filene, part-owner of a department store in Boston, was one of the most important credit union promoters until his death in 1937. It is estimated that he spent $1 million supporting the work of the Credit Union National Extension Bureau, which promoted credit union formation. In the 1920s, credit unions paid as much as an 8 percent return to their members to attract funds. They did well during the depression of the 1930s, increasing in number and in total assets. In 1934, federal charters were granted. By 1940, there were 3,756 federally chartered credit unions and 5,176 operating under state charters. The total number of credit unions declined during World War II to 8,615 in 1945; however, they grew rapidly in the postwar period. In 1965, credit unions had 16.8 million members. Credit unions were the third largest source of consumer credit in the United States, with 15.7 percent of the market, compared with 4 percent in 1950.

The expansion of credit unions has been due in large part to favorable government actions such as the tax-exempt status; the higher interest payments that credit unions were allowed to pay on their deposits before deregulation; their new power to make mortgage loans up to thirty years for one- to four-unit residential property; the extension to twelve years on the maximum time allowed on unsecured loans; the allowance to participate in loans with other credit unions; the ability to offer checkable accounts; and the Corporate Credit Union Network, to be described. Credit union checks, or share drafts, were begun by the National Credit Union Administration in October 1974.

Liquidity has been an ever-increasing problem for credit unions. Many credit unions receive deposits from their customers throughout the fall, winter, and spring and then suffer massive withdrawals in the summer as the members of the credit union go on vacation. Federal credit union liquidations (closings) rose to 326 in 1980. Government regulators forced 258 of these into involuntary liquidations, mostly because of insolvency (21 percent of the 258 were due to plant closings).

One of the most interesting structures of any U.S. industry is the network of private—not government—organizations that service the credit unions in the United States. A network of 42 corporate credit unions is, in turn, connected to the Corporate Credit Union Network, with U.S. Central (located in Overland Park, Kansas) at the center, as shown in Figure 6-3. In 1986, this system serviced 15,500 credit unions. The Credit Union National Association, CUNA, 52 State Leagues, 50 League Service Corporations around the country, and 42 Corporate Credit Unions are also part of this private system that services credit unions.

The Corporate Credit Union Network provides the following services for its member credit unions: lines of credit, loans, a depository for money and securities, advice and information on investments, services for transferring funds, check processing and collecting, and access to the Federal Reserve System. The U.S. Central borrows funds in the markets and lends these funds to credit unions.

FIGURE 6-3 The Private Corporate Network That Services Credit Unions

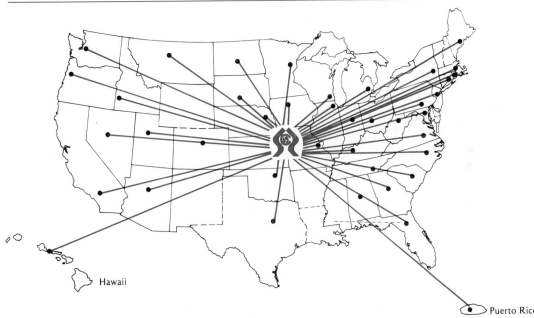

The Corporate Credit Union Network is the credit union movement's primary source of financial and payment services. The network consists of U.S. Central and 42 regional corporate credit unions whose functions are to provide financial and payment systems services to their nearly 15,500 member credit unions and their consumer constituency. U.S. Central's role in the network is one of a financial intermediary between the corporates and credit unions and the remainder of the financial community. (*Corporate Credit Union Network. A Review of the Credit Union Financial System: History, Structure, Status & Financial Trends.* Published by U.S. Central Credit Union, 1986.)

Source: U.S. Central 1984 Annual Report, accompanying brochure, "The Corporate Credit Union Network," p. 3.

To provide for more efficient interlending among credit unions, every state has at least one credit union league. These are nonprofit cooperatives of individual credit unions fully financed by member dues. Fifty-seven of these in 35 states are called *centrals*. They lend funds to individual credit unions and provide a clearinghouse for interlending among credit unions. In addition, the National Credit Union Association opened the U.S. Central Credit Union in 1974 to provide for interstate lending and to allow U.S. centrals to borrow more easily from outside the credit union industry.

An important legislative victory for the credit union industry, which enabled credit unions to obtain more funds, occurred with the passage of the Financial Institutions Regulatory Act in the dying hours of the 95th Congress in 1978. The Central Liquidity Facility, or CLF, is authorized to provide more funds for credit unions. The CLF can borrow from the public and lend the funds to the credit union industry. It is administered by the National Credit Union Administration, a federal regulatory agency.

The supervision of credit unions has an interesting history. The Federal Credit Union Act was passed in 1934 "to establish a Federal credit union system, to establish a further market for securities of the United States and to make more available to people of small means credit for provident purposes through a national system of cooperative credit, thereby helping to stabilize the credit structure of the United States." The act was first administered by the Farm Credit Administration. In 1942, the administration was transferred to the Federal Deposit Insurance Corporation. In 1948, Congress transferred the administration to a Bureau of Federal Credit Unions, which became one of the program bureaus of the Social Security Administration subject to the direction of the Commissioner of Social Security. The National Credit Union Administration Act of 1970 established an independent agency, the National Credit Union Administration, directed by an administrator appointed by the president with the advice and consent of the Senate. An advisory board was set up with six members, one from each of the six regions with the indicated headquarters city: Boston, Harrisburg, Atlanta, Toledo, Austin, and San Francisco. Finally, the Financial Institutions Regulatory Act of 1978 established a three-member board to supervise insured credit unions, to be appointed by the president and approved by the Senate, replacing the single administrator, and called the National Credit Union Board.

A TURBULENT PERIOD FOR THRIFTS

The savings and loan industry had severe problems in the 1980s. Four experts associated with the Federal Home Loan Bank Board, FHLBB, presented a well-documented assessment of conditions in the industry in the middle 1980s.[5] They pointed out that from 1980 to 1984, 511 thrift institutions insured by the Federal Savings and Loan Insurance Corporation, FSLIC, had failed. A record 252 institutions failed in 1982. Approximately 434 institutions had a zero or negative net worth (were insolvent), and 856 institutions had a low net worth. Even though an unprecedented number of institutions had been closed from 1980 to 1984, the number of insolvent institutions still operating had grown. Indeed, in 1984 the combined assets of the nearly insolvent and the insolvent institutions represented 45 percent of all assets in FSLIC-insured institutions.

The causes of these conditions in the thrift industry began in the 1970s and intensified in the early 1980s, with generally rising and highly erratic interest rates, as shown in Figure 6-2. The savings and loan associations were especially hard hit because they had sold mortgages that paid an interest income lower than the cost of their money at the rates prevailing in the late 1970s and early 1980s. The difference between mortgage rates contracted twelve years previously and current Treasury bond rates is shown in Figure 6-4.

FIGURE 6-4   The Interest Rate Squeeze: Interest on Business Time Deposits and Mortgage Interest Rate Twelve Years Earlier

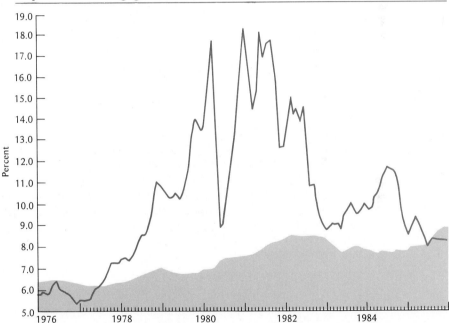

The continuous line shows the interest rate on business time deposits (called certificates of deposit) sold by depository institutions. This is one rough (and incomplete) measure of the cost of funds at the "average" S&L. The shaded area at each date shows the mortgage rate on mortgages contracted twelve years earlier. The difference between the top of the shaded area and the line is the interest rate spread that became negative for many savings and loan associations that held mortgages from these prior lower interest rate periods. This measure of the spread is shown to have turned negative in the middle of 1977, and it did not become positive again until 1985.

Source: Cambridge Planning and Analytics, Inc., Boston.

FIGURE 6-5   The Number of Savings and Loan Associations in the United States, 1930–1985

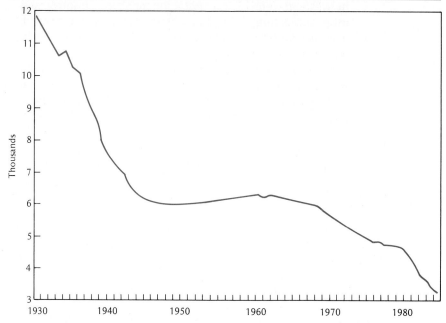

The data plotted indicate the severe decline in the industry during the 1930 depressions. The post–World War II prosperity was good for the housing industry and for the savings and loan associations that sold mortgages. The decline in the number of S&Ls halted, and the industry grew rapidly for three decades. Adjusting for the rise in the price level, the real value of assets was 14.5 times higher in 1974 than in 1941. The 1970s was a period of further decline, as interest rates generally rose and became more variable. The early 1980s was a period of rapid decline similar to that of the 1930s.

Source: Savings and Loan Associations, Federal Home Loan Bank Board statistics release, 1985, p. 4. The data show fewer (approximately 340 fewer for 1985) total credit unions than do the estimates by the National Council of Savings Institutions, which include some noninsured S&Ls not depicted in the above data.

Figure 6-5 shows the severe decline in the S&L industry during the depressions of the 1930s. After World War II, the housing industry mushroomed, which was good for the savings and loan associations that sold mortgages to finance residual housing. Accordingly, the decline in the number of S&Ls halted, and the industry grew rapidly for three decades, their total assets rising from $6.049 billion in 1941 to $294.906 billion in 1974. Adjusting for the rise in the price level, the real value of assets was 14.5 times higher in 1974 than in 1941. But the 1970s was a period of further decline, as interest rates generally rose and became more variable. The early 1980s was a period of rapid decline similar to that of the 1930s.

During 1981 and 1982 there was increasing concern that many S&Ls would be mortally wounded by the interest rate squeeze that had gripped the industry since 1979. S&Ls had made long-term mortgage commitments at rates considerably lower than the market rates of interest in that period. Their income from mortgages did not cover their expense for the new money that was bought at higher current market rates.[6]

Richard Pratt, who was then chairman of the Federal Home Loan Bank Board, fought to keep passbook savings account ceiling rates from rising even to 6 percent in 1981, when short-term market rates were near 15 percent. He did this by either gaining or joining a majority of the six members of the DIDC.

In 1981, Congress authorized savings certificates—the *All Savers Certificates*—for depository intermediaries that could pay up to $1,000 ($2,000 on a joint tax return) on tax-free interest. These tax-free certificates had one-year maturities and could not be issued after January 1, 1983. The rate of interest was fixed at 70 percent of the one-year Treasury bill rate. The Reagan administration accepted the provision for the All Savers Certificates with reluctance because it was tied to its main tax bill in 1981. Whether the All Savers Certificate was of any help to thrifts in trouble is a matter for further testing. It did provide a substantial inflow of funds to commercial banks, which were not the target for assistance. It also reduced the demand for **tax exempts** (see the glossary), driving up their yield at a time that federal aid to states and cities was being reduced.

No aid (or, as it was called, the bailout bill) for S&Ls and MSBs had passed the U.S. Congress by February 1982. Early in the Reagan administration, House Banking Committee Chairman Fernand St Germain met with Paul Volcker, chairman of the Federal Reserve, and Richard T. Pratt, then chairman of the FHLBB. They supported a bill to assist troubled thrifts, but President Reagan announced his opposition to a bailout, and action in the House of Representatives ceased at that time. In February 1982, Chairman St Germain, a Democrat, proposed a $7.5 billion emergency fund, the Home Mortgage Capital Stability Fund, for the FDIC, the FHLBB, and the National Credit Union Administration (NCUA), "to administer a program of direct capital assistance for home mortgage lending institutions whose net worth slips below two percent of assets." Although that proposal did not succeed, a different one initially passed the House Banking Committee. On May 11, 1982, the House Banking Committee passed a St Germain bill (by a 25-to-15 vote) that would give federal guarantees of net worth to thrifts that had a net worth valuation of less than 2 percent of assets. The thrift industry supported the legislation thinking that it would do away with forced mergers. A bill with this provision was passed by Congress in September 1982 and was called the Garn–St Germain Depository Institutions Act of 1982.

The law allows one depository institution to take over another, even though the institutions are not in the same state. Thrifts in trouble can, subject to the regulators' approval, be purchased by a more prosperous depository institution, a "white knight," as the acquiring firm is sometimes called. Priority is given to institutions of the same type in the same state. The FDIC and the FSLIC also are allowed to assist troubled thrifts and commercial banks even before they fail. (The FDIC and the FSLIC had expended almost $2 billion in aid to troubled banks and S&Ls over the previous twenty months, which had been a major catalyst for the bill.) Regulatory agencies are even allowed to give troubled institutions **Net Worth Certificates** that they can add to their statement of net worth. Their happier appearance should help keep them in business and prevent them from being taken over. The acquisition provisions and the Net Worth Certificates were to last only three years. In legislative language, they were subject to **sunset** in three years (see Figure 6-6).

An important part of this law is the complete removal of ceiling rates on new short-term deposits that require a $2,500 minimum balance. This provision was implemented at the end of 1982 and in January 1983. The thrifts had a huge inflow of deposits. (Details of these deposits are given in Chapter 8.)

FIGURE 6-6   Government Regulators of Thrift Institutions

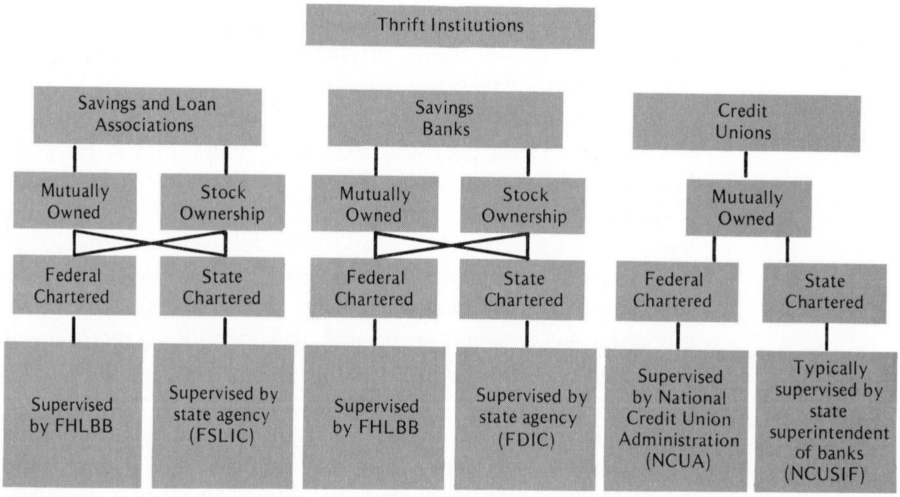

The Garn–St Germain Depository Institutions Act of 1982 made it easier for commercial banks to convert to savings and loan associations. But between 1982 and 1986, only two of the thirteen requests for conversion were approved and completed. There may be more because of inducements such as fewer prohibitions on S&Ls' branching across state lines. Bad conditions in the thrift industry in the 1980s apparently convinced some thrifts to convert to commercial banks. Six such conversions were completed between 1982 and 1986.

Source: Sylvester Johnson, Jr., "The Thrift Charter—A Valuable Alternative for Commercial Banks?" *Economic Review*, Federal Reserve Bank of Atlanta, October 1985, p. 27.

The rush of funds into the thrifts in 1983 raised questions about the band-aid approach of the administrators and the members of Congress to helping the thrifts during a period of high interest rates. Would it not have been better for the country and for the thrift industry to have simply phased out the ceiling rates rapidly and at a fairly uniform rate so that they could compete effectively for funds? Was it wise for Chairman Pratt to delay the lifting of ceiling rates at the DIDC meetings and, instead, seek various kinds of direct aid?

It is all too easy to say that the thrifts would have had even less trouble if Chairman Pratt had not led the way to defeat Treasury Secretary Donald Regan's modest proposal to raise the ceilings on the thrifts' passbook accounts to 6 percent in 1981 and then let that ceiling continue to rise. More funds would have been moved into the thrifts and might have done more good than did the direct-aid methods. However, it is probably impossible to be an elected official (a member of Congress, for example) or the head of a federal regulatory agency and withstand the pressures of dire predictions of massive failures and hundreds of individuals from financial institutions clamoring for help as they perceive the possibility of their businesses' failing. It might have been a kami-kaze mission for most members of the U.S. Congress, who found their offices filled with the chief operating officers of troubled financial institutions, to pro-claim that they would get no help, only the right to pay higher interest to their depositors. There is a lesson here. Do not allow an industry to adjust to price controls that will make it uncompetitive. This can be done by never imposing such controls.

Both the S&Ls and SBs showed negative income from 1981 to 1982, a period during which there was a severe recession with over 10 percent of the labor force unemployed, and there were high interest rates until the middle of 1982.

On February 15, 1983, the emergency acquisitions provision of the Garn–St Germain Institutions Act of 1982 was first used. First Tennessee National Corporation acquired the failed United American Bank of Knoxville, the fourth largest commercial bank to collapse in U.S. history. This was an important event in the removal of state laws that prevented depository institutions from crossing state boundaries and is discussed in the next chapter.

By 1983, the SBs reported substantially more profits, but federally insured S&Ls only broke even. The S&Ls continued to improve after that, although many continued to have serious problems. Credit unions grew rapidly after this period, partly because of the higher interest they paid to their depositors. In mid-1986 their average rate on regular savings shares was 7.3 percent, whereas the average rate paid by other thrifts was 5.5 percent. In 1984, the ceredit unions had 9.2 percent of the thrift industry's assets and 9.9 percent of its deposits. In 1986, just two years later, the credit unions had increased their market share to 10.4 percent of the industry's assets and 11.5 percent of its deposits.[7]

Dealing with Troubled Thrifts in the Last Half of the 1980s

Between 1980 and 1985, many FSLIC-insured thrifts closed or were merged into other institutions, as shown in Table 6-8. But these failed thrifts were only some of the insolvent (with negative net worth) thrifts. At the end of 1985, 107 thrifts that had become insolvent before 1982 were still insolvent, and an additional 585 thrifts that had became insolvent after December 1982 were still insolvent.[8] Nonetheless, these institutions remained open, because

1. The FSLIC did not have enough personnel to close the insolvent thrifts. It is an expensive and lengthy process to close an institution efficiently. Either the institution's assets may have to be sold (liquidation of assets), or the institution must merge with a healthy institution.
2. There were not enough funds in the FSLIC fund in 1986 to close all the insolvent FSLIC-insured institutions and reimburse the depositors.

In September 1986 an official of the FHLBB was quoted as saying that the FHLBB

> can keep a thrift afloat for an indefinite period of time. . . . We have $7 billion of cases we could solve today, but with the $4 billion we have [in reserves for the FSLIC insurance fund], we would go into a negative position and come into conflict with the antideficiency law.
>
> We could go three or four months at the pace we are at now before the funds are down to dangerously low levels.[9]

T A B L E 6 - 8 Reductions in Number of FSLIC-insured Thrifts, 1980–1985

The second and third columns show the number of failed FSLIC-insured institutions between 1980 and 1985. Failing FSLIC-insured institutions could be closed and their assets sold, could be merged with other institutions, or could have a new management put into place by the FSLIC (called *management consignment*). Some institutions were merged without the FSLIC's help, and some institutions did not fail but merged with other institutions.

Year	FSLIC-assisted Failed Institutions	Failed Institutions Without FSLIC Assistance	Nonfailed Attrition (voluntary mergers)	Total
1980	11	24	82	117
1981	28	53	206	287
1982	70	182	262	514
1983	52	49	107	208
1984	28	14	33	75
1985	59	11	47	117

Source: James R. Barth, Dan Brumbaugh, Jr., and Dan Sauerhaft, "Failure Costs of Government-regulated Financial Firms: The Case of Thrift Institutions," June 1986, by correspondence.

The antideficiency law referred to here prohibits federal agencies from spending more than they are budgeted to spend. The official said that a dangerously low level for the FSLIC fund would be about $1 billion.

The thrifts that were insolvent but had not been closed were said to have been "warehoused." In his presentation at the Western Economic Association in 1986, Ed Kane used the term *zombie S&Ls* and *the living dead* for the thrifts that were being kept alive but could not be rescued even by a fall in interest rates.[10]

But it also was expensive to allow the insolvent institutions to remain open. They carried the full $100,000 federal account insurance that enabled them to hold and attract depositors. And they had an incentive to make riskier-than-average investments that paid a higher rate of interest—if they succeeded—in order to try to regain their profitability. In other words, they lost nothing and had a small chance of recovering if they adopted an investment strategy of "go for broke." But by letting them continue to attract deposits and make such investments, the costs to the FSLIC of liquidating them went up even more, according to estimates at the time. At the end of 1986 the General Accounting Office (GAO), a federal investigative body used by the U.S. Congress, reported a warning about the costs of warehousing thrifts:

> Our simulations predict that FSLIC may lose over $1.4 billion from warehousing 367 thrifts from December 1985 to December 1987 if interest rates do not change over this period. Moreover, even modest increases in interest rates result in substantially higher costs to FSLIC.[11]

Is it desirable to keep businesses alive even after they are insolvent? This question applies not only to the insolvent FDIC-insured thrifts but also to the Continental Illinois Bank, a commercial bank that was in effect nationalized (taken over by the government). Would it have been preferable for the Congress to have acted rapidly, replenishing the FSLIC funds, hiring more personnel, and closing the insolvent institutions?

What about the creative accounting that made many thrifts appear to be in better health than they really were? As of mid-1984, 93 FSLIC-insured institutions and 24 FDIC-insured savings banks had Net Worth Certificates, representing 10 percent of the industry's assets. One (incomplete) piece of evidence on the effectiveness of this creative accounting in saving institutions with negative net worth was whether they did return to profitability. As of the second quarter of 1984, 31 of the 93 FSLIC-insured and 4 of the 31 FDIC-insured institutions reported a positive net income. But the reason for such a change may well have been the fall in interest rates, not the creative accounting.

The success of the Net Worth Certificates is uncertain. They did camouflage the net worth statistics for those not familiar with the regulatory accounting principles' creative accounting methods. This camouflage also allowed the insurance regulators to look the other way at a time when they did not have enough personnel to supervise the closing of all the institutions that should have been closed, according to their unaltered balance sheet reports. But camouflaging the balance sheets of depository institutions contradicts the government's requirement of truth in labeling. The government simultaneously enforces such truth-in-lending laws so as to reduce deception. And so allowing government-sponsored cosmetics on the thrift's balance sheet can only diminish the public's trust in government examination. Furthermore, if the public that uses S&Ls and SBs learns that the regulatory agencies are deliberately hiding a failing institution, it may not trust the regulators to provide accurate information about any institution.

Some thrifts do not have federal deposit insurance; they are shown by state in Table 6-9. These institutions may, however, have state or privately issued deposit insurance. These types of deposit insurance use an insurance fund maintained by assessments on the insured institutions.

Although the percentage of non-FSLIC-insured S&Ls is very small, *runs* (masses of depositors running to the bank to withdraw their deposits) on these institutions can threaten many other institutions. This is because a frightened public may not distinguish from the healthier institutions this small group of S&Ls that cannot make the necessary cash withdrawals to prevent or stop a run.

In 1985, there were runs on non-FSLIC-insured thrifts in two states. On March 6, 1985, there was a run on the Home State Savings Bank in Ohio after news that it would incur large losses from the failure of a securities dealer in Florida. The institution was one of seventy insured by the private Ohio Deposit Guarantee Fund, ODGF. It was soon expected that the losses to the Home State Savings Bank would exceed the ODGF's funds. Runs on other ODGF-insured institutions ensued. The Federal Reserve Bank of Cleveland lent money to the affected institutions to keep them operating, and on March 15, 1985, the governor of Ohio ordered all ODGF-insured institutions to close. This was the first "banking holiday" since President Franklin Roosevelt closed all the banks in the country in 1933. The FHLBB agreed to consider issuing FSLIC insurance to qualified ODGF institutions, and the institutions were gradually reopened, some with a withdrawal limitation of $750 per account per month. Later, the Home State Savings Bank was purchased and reopened by three Ohio banking organizations.

Only two months later, in May of 1985, runs began on two Baltimore institutions, Old Court Savings and Loan Association and Merritt Commercial Savings and Loan Association, 2 of the 102 institutions insured by the private Maryland Savings–Share Insurance Corporation, MSSIC. The losses of the two institutions exceeded the MSSIC's resources. There also were runs limited by a withdrawal of $1,000 (imposed by the governor) at other MSSIC-insured institutions. Finally, the MSSIC was replaced by the Maryland Deposit Insurance Fund, which was given state backing.

The depositors' loss of confidence in these insurance funds confirmed for many observers the need for a strong federal fund. A strong federal fund would require that the troubled FSLIC be promptly recapitalized. The Com-

T A B L E 6 - 9   Non-FSLIC-insured Savings and Loan Associations,
December 31, 1985

Although the percentage of non-FSLIC-insured S&Ls is very small, runs (masses of depositors running to the bank to withdraw their deposits) on these institutions can threaten many other institutions. This is because a frightened public may not distinguish from healthier institutions this small group of S&Ls that cannot make the necessary cash withdrawals to prevent or stop a run.

State	Number of Associations	Total Assets (thousands of dollars)	Percentage of Assets of All Associations	Percentage of Assets Held in Each State
Delaware	8	5,130	.001	4.34
Florida	1	7,661	.001	.01
Georgia	6	144,057	.015	1.40
Illinois	1	5,136	.001	.01
Indiana	5	2,019		.02
Iowa	5	5,035	.001	.07
Maryland	49	1,736,300	.183	9.44
Massachusetts	100	5,943,968	.627	73.40
Missouri	1	809		
Nebraska	1	1,729		.02
New Jersey	25	16,563	.002	.04
New York	1	583,526	.062	2.95
North Carolina	6	454,240	.048	2.56
Ohio	8	253,990	.027	.63
Oklahoma	1	144		
Pennsylvania	64	261,230	.028	.79
South Dakota	1	284		.02
Texas	2	598,736	.063	.65
Utah	1	209		
Virginia	1	3,644		.02
West Virginia	1	2,174		.13
Wisconsin	1	57,016	.006	.37
United States	289	10,083,800	1.064	

Source: Savings and Loan Associations, Federal Home Loan Bank Board statistics release, 1985, p. 30.

petitive Equality Banking Act of 1987 gave the FSLIC authority to borrow 10.8 billion.) Deciding on the best form of federal insurance was also a concern in this period. Should the institutions pay insurance premiums on federal deposit insurance based on their financial condition? Should the government regulators supervise more closely the insured institutions? The proposals made during this period for new types of deposit insurance are discussed in the next chapter.

A call for more government regulation followed these episodes and was expressed in some of these deposit insurance proposals. It is an interesting turn in direction toward more regulation from what started in the early 1980s as a period of deregulation.

AN INCREASED NUMBER OF THRIFT HOLDING COMPANIES

Since the end of 1981, there has been a large increase in the number of holding companies that have bought thrifts. These so-called thrift holding companies are firms with a controlling interest in a thrift. The largest thrift holding companies include firms such as Citicorp (also the largest commercial banking holding company), Sears, Roebuck (also an operator of department stores and the owner of a commercial bank), and Gulf & Western (also the owner of a movie studio).

At the end of 1985, three fourths of the thrift holding companies had acquired thrifts after 1981. The main reason for this surge in the number of thrift holding companies was a lack of capital in the thrift industry, and those large firms, shown in Table 6-10, have access to investment funds.

TABLE 6-10   Largest Thrift Holding Companies in the United States, December 1985 (billions of dollars)

Since 1981 there has been a large increase in the number of holding companies that have bought thrifts. The reason is a lack of capital in the thrift industry, and these large firms have access to investment funds. Will the thrift industry be dominated by large firms, and is this desirable?

Rank	Type/Name	Assets
	Depository Institutions Holding Companies	
1	Citicorp	$173.6
2	Financial Corp. of America	27.4
3	H. F. Ahmanson & Co.	27.4
4	Great Western Financial Corp.	25.5
5	CalFed, Inc.	19.0
	Total	272.9
	Diversified Holding Companies	
1	Sears Roebuck & Co.	66.4
2	Ford Motor Co.	31.6
3	Household International Inc.	11.9
4	American Financial Corp.	7.1
5	Gulf & Western	4.5
	Total	121.5
	Grand Total	394.4

Source: The American Banker, November 12, 1986, p. 1.

Will the thrift industry be dominated by large firms, and is this desirable? Consider two aspects of the 1970s and 1980s that point to larger firms in the thrift industry rather than to the generally smaller firms that characterized it in the past. (1) The age of deregulation authorized firms to buy thrifts across state lines. (2) The problems of thrifts in the 1970s and early 1980s with high and variable interest rates point to the desirability of more diversification of assets in thrifts. This diversification cannot be attained with a small thrift that holds mostly mortgages, but it can be attained by large holding companies. But will the large firms gradually edge out the smaller firms so that some areas will no longer have a number of competitors offering mortgage loan services?

The holding companies also present a problem of regulation. Should examiners regulate only the large companies' subsidiary depository institutions, or should they examine the entire company? These questions arise when assessing the deposit insurance, whose premiums are based on the institution's stability. For example, is the efficiency of Gulf & Western's movie studios related to its thrifts' operations? Should the FSLIC examine all the accounting records of these firms? These questions suggest one way in which the age of deregulation may turn into the age of increased government regulation.

STUDY QUESTIONS

1. What are the differences among the depository institutions discussed in this chapter?
2. How do you think each of the types of depository intermediaries will change after the early 1980s period of deregulation? Will they become more alike or more different? What will they look like in 1990?
3. Is competition a good thing for depository intermediaries? Review the 1980–1983 episode of thrifts in trouble in formulating your answer. Is direct aid preferable to unfettered competition in such an episode?
4. Why were the S&Ls at a disadvantage during the periods of high interest rates in the 1970s and 1980s? Your attention should center on their large holdings of mortgages.
5. What is a common bond, and will it survive?
6. Why do many S&Ls want to convert to stock companies? Will the depositors be helped, hurt, or not affected by this change?
7. When did ceiling rates on deposits injure (a) the depositors and (b) the owners of depository intermediaries? What is the argument for ceiling rates? Assess that argument.
8. What has happened to the growth of checking account services among financial intermediaries since 1972? Trace the history of this change and assess its benefits to (a) depositors and (b) owners of financial intermediaries.
9. What are the consequences of warehousing thrifts?

GLOSSARY

Common bond. The characteristic, such as the same place of employment, that is required for membership in a credit union.

Net Worth Certificates. The Garn–St Germain Depository Institutions Act of 1982 gave regulatory agencies the authority to increase depository institutions' net worth with Net Worth Certificates in an amount up to 70 percent of their operating losses. To qualify, an institution must have at least 20 percent of its loan portfolio in residential mortgages and must have incurred operating losses during the two previous quarters. It is subject to sunset in 1985. (The portfolio requirement tended to limit the eligibility to S&Ls, an example of tilted, not level playing field, rules.)

Pecuniary interest. Interest paid in the form of money rather than gifts or services (these were common when ceiling rates effectively reduced or eliminated the pecuniary interest payments on deposits at depository intermediaries).

Shares and **share drafts.** Shares are deposits at credit unions; share drafts are check-type instruments offered by credit unions.

Sunset. A federal law subject to sunset at a specific date will no longer be valid after that date unless it is again passed by the Congress.

Tax exempts. Debt instruments such as bonds issued by cities (called *municipals*) and states pay interest that is free from federal income tax.

NOTES

1. Information on mutual savings banks can be found in George J. Benston, "Savings Banking and the Public Interest," *Journal of Money, Credit and Banking*, February 1972, pp. 133–266; Alan Teck, *Mutual Savings Banks and Loan Associations: Aspects of Growth* (New York: Columbia University Press, 1968); Benton E. Gup, *Financial Intermediaries, An Introduction* (Boston: Houghton Mifflin, 1976); and Herman E. Kroos and Martin R. Blyn, *A History of Financial Intermediaries* (New York: Random House, 1971).
2. Kroos and Blyn, *A History*, p. 191.
3. Thomas Marvell, *The Federal Home Loan Bank Board* (New York: Praeger, 1969), pp. 7–8. This provocative history of the regulation of S&Ls contains a number of case studies. See also Gup, *Financial Intermediaries*; and Kroos and Blyn, *A History*.
4. See Olin P. Pugh's "Credit Unions: From Consumer Movement to National Market Force," *Bankers Magazine*, January–February 1980, pp. 19–27. See also Gup, *Financial Intermediaries*; and Kroos and Blyn, *A History*.

5. See James R. Barth, Dan Brumbaugh, Jr., Dan Sauerhaft, and George H. D. Wang, "Insolvency and Risk-Taking in the Thrift Industry: Implications for the Future," *Contemporary Policy Studies*, Fall 1985, pp. 1–6. The quotations are from pp. 1 and 4. The authors were associated with the FHLBB and present candid and well-documented assessments of adverse financial conditions at federally insured S&Ls. Barth, a professor of economics at George Washington University, was a visiting scholar at the FHLBB, Brumbaugh was the deputy chief economist at the FHLBB, Sauerhaft was a financial economist at the FHLBB, and Wang was a senior econometrician at the FHLBB. In reading reports about the conditions of S&Ls, one must be careful when accounting practices are labeled *RAP* (*regulatory accounting practices*) instead of *GAAP* (*generally accepted accounting practices*).

6. See George J. Benston, "Interest on Deposits and the Survival of Chartered Depository Instititions," *Economic Review*, Federal Reserve Bank of Atlanta, October 1984, pp. 42–55; L. Michael Cacace, "Credit Unions Win Bigger Share of Thrift Market," *The American Banker*, December 2, 1985, p. 1; William N. Cox and Pamela V. Whigham, "What Distinguishes Larger and More Efficient Credit Unions?" *Economic Review*, Federal Reserve Bank of Atlanta, October 1984, pp. 34–41; Diana Fortier and Dave Philis, "Bank and Thrift Performance Since DIDMCA," *Economic Perspectives*, Federal Reserve Bank of Chicago, September–October 1985, pp. 58–68; Robert E. Goudreau, "S&L Use of New Powers: Consumer and Commercial Loan Expansion," *Economic Review*, Federal Reserve Bank of Atlanta, December 1984, pp. 15–33; Robert E. Goudreau and Harold D. Ford, "Changing Thrifts: What Makes Them Choose Commercial Lending?" *Economic Review*, Federal Reserve Bank of Atlanta, June–July 1986, pp. 24–35; Michael C. Keeley, "The Health of Banks and Thrifts," *FRBSF Weekly Letter*, Federal Reserve Bank of San Francisco, February 21, 1986; and Patrick J. Mahoney and Alice P. White, "The Thrift Industry in Transition," *Federal Reserve Bulletin*, Board of Governors, March 1985, pp. 137–156.

7. Cacace, "Credit Unions Win Bigger Share of the Thrift Market," p. 1. The estimates of market share are from *The American Banker*'s annual survey of the top 100 credit unions. The estimates of interest rates paid are from the Credit Union National Association (CUNA).

8. U.S. Government Accounting Office, *Thrift Industry, Cost to FSLIC of Delaying Action on Insolvent Savings Institutions*, September 1986, Briefing Report to the Chairman [Doug Barnard, Jr.], Subcommittee on Commerce, Consumer and Monetary Affairs, Committee on Government Operations, House of Representatives.

9. This quotation is attributed to Robert J. Sahadi, acting director of policy and research, FHLBB, and is found in Robert M. Garsson, "Shaky S&Ls May Stay Open to Keep Funds Afloat," *The American Banker*, September 15, 1986, p. 10.

10. Ed Kane, "The Dangers of Capital Forbearance: The Case of FSLIC and the Zombie S&Ls," Western Economic Association, San Francisco, July 4, 1986. Distributed outline with presentation.

11. U.S. Government Accounting Office, *Thrift Industry*, p. 4.

CHAPTER 7

COMMERCIAL BANKING

CHAPTER PREVIEW

Introduction. Commercial banks had 66.2 percent of the assets of depository institutions in 1986.

Structure of Commercial Banking. The general government role and the meaning of national and state commercial banks are described.

Characteristics of Banks by Location and Size. Large money center banks, small rural banks, banks in the nation's capital, and banks in the Hawaiian Islands all have special characteristics related to their location. Size itself is related to location, with the largest banks in the country (the nine largest) located in four cities.

Correspondent Banks. The services that banks provide to other banks are discussed.

Branch Banking. Branch banking has been confined to the state in which the parent bank is located, but the state walls may be tumbling down.

Bank Holding Companies. Over 83 percent of U.S. commercial banks operate as holding companies, which allows them to offer many nonbank services and to buy nonbank subsidiaries that are not restricted to a single state.

The Walls Have Tumbled Down. For the first time since the United States was founded, nationwide banking became prevalent in the 1980s. Deregulation is characterized by a maze of new state and federal laws and regulations concerning interstate banking and including the new widespread phenomenon, nonbank banks.

Nonbank Banks. The formation of nonbank banks as a means of interstate banking proceeded rapidly from 1984 to 1986. Over 300 federal banking charters were issued to form nonbank banks, although judicial proceedings put them in a state of limbo awaiting action by Congress, which deliberated the issue in 1987.

Competition for Banking Services. Competition was affected by (1) the decrease in the number of depository institutions and (2) the increase in the number of branches and/or subsidiaries across state lines. The effects of nationwide banking cannot easily be judged by U.S. history, as it is a new phenomenon. Foreign experience, however, provides a basis for future predictions.

Economies of Scale in Banking. The efficiency of large nationwide banking firms relative to smaller banking firms depends largely on economies of scale. The evidence is mixed and does not definitely show that large banks can offer all kinds of services at a lower price just because they are large.

Federal Deposit Insurance Corporation. The FDIC's deposit insurance stopped the widespread runs on banks in the 1920s and 1930s. Despite the many bank failures beginning in 1983, there have been few runs, at least up to 1987. But the increased number of bank failures in 1980 and the way the FDIC handled the bank run on the failing Continental Illinois National Bank and Trust Company of Chicago promoted several proposals for reforming FDIC insurance.

Proposals to Reform Deposit Insurance and Raise Capital Requirements. Proposals for increasing banks' capital-to-assets ratios for risk-based premiums for deposit insurance, and for changing the coverage of deposit insurance are discussed.

An Example of a Bank Failure with Some Perplexing Questions. A view of a failed bank and the Federal Reserve's loans to keep it operating for a short period produce some challenging questions about how failing commercial banks should be treated.

Bank Credit Cards. Bank credit cards are a way to make short-term unsecured consumer loans profitable to banks, thereby producing a popular service to customers.

Assets, Liabilities, and Income of U.S. Commercial Banks. Business loans comprise the commercial banks' largest category of assets, and the interest income on loans is their largest source of income.

Foreign Loan Problems. U.S. banks have a significant number of foreign loans in poor countries that have had difficulty repaying them. Some observers date the near-banking crisis to be in 1982, when Mexico announced that it could not repay its loans. The Baker proposal of 1985 is a short-term controversial remedy that raises a number of questions about helping both poor countries and large U.S. commercial banks.

Appendix A: The Prime Rate. Below-advertised prime rate lending is discussed. What does it mean for the economy, the banking system, and the borrower?

Appendix B: History of Money and Banking in the United States to 1863. The early theories of money and banking, the theories growing out of the cessation of convertibility by the Bank of Engalnd in 1797, and U.S. banking history to the National Banking Act in 1863 are presented.

INTRODUCTION

Commercial banks are a vital financial intermediary that supplies many services. These may be using a bank credit card, sending or receiving a check drawn on a commercial bank, or negotiating for a business loan. In 1986, commercial banks accounted for 66.2 percent of the depository intermediaries' assets. Commercial banks have gone through immense changes in the 1980s. Their near monopoly in providing checking account services began to collapse in 1973 and then was destroyed with the age of deregulation in the 1980s. Deregulation brought a totally different type of banking, with the removal of the interest rate ceiling on deposits, a wave of bank failures, a bank run on the seventh largest bank, which was effectively nationalized in 1984, and problems with foreign loans that some observers contend nearly caused a banking crisis in 1982.

STRUCTURE OF COMMERCIAL BANKING

Banking institutions associated with commercial banks that are operated by the government should be distinguished from the private part of the banking system. There is a little confusion because of the Federal Reserve System. The Board of Governors of the Federal Reserve in Washington, D.C., and the 12 regional Federal Reserve banks and their branches are essentially run by the government. The purist must note that the 12 regional Federal Reserve banks are nominally organized as private corporations. They are, however, supposed to operate with national goals rather than for profit maximization.

Private commercial banks and mutual savings banks can join the Federal Reserve System. In addition to the option of membership in the Federal Reserve System, private commercial nonmember banks may purchase and member banks must purchase federal insurance for their depositors from the Federal Deposit Insurance Corporation (FDIC). The FDIC is a federal agency that provides insurance and regulation for insured banks. Over 95 percent of all commercial banks have this insurance.

TABLE 7-1   Number of Commercial Banks in the United States and in Each State by Status in 1985: Member or Nonmember of the Federal Reserve, National or State Charter, and Federally Insured or Noninsured

There were over 15,000 commercial banks. More had state than federal charters and less than one half of 1 percent had no federal deposit insurance.

| State | Total | Member | | Nonmember | |
		National	*State*	*Insured*	*Noninsured*
United States	**15,072**	**4,968**	**1,085**	**8,380**	**639**
Alabama	240	54	26	160	0
Alaska	16	6	0	9	1
Arizona	61	14	10	28	9
Arkansas	262	82	5	172	3
California	536	171	30	282	53
Colorado	577	241	68	162	106
Connecticut	58	17	1	39	1
Delaware	39	15	3	18	3
District of Columbia	22	18	0	1	3
Florida	433	182	56	187	8
Georgia	374	54	15	304	1
Hawaii	26	3	0	19	4
Idaho	26	7	3	16	0
Illinois	1,297	400	68	767	62
Indiana	374	110	41	220	3
Iowa	626	111	37	477	1
Kansas	625	168	20	436	1
Kentucky	335	78	7	248	2
Louisiana	303	71	6	225	2
Maine	25	8	2	15	0
Maryland	91	25	5	60	1
Massachusetts	122	58	2	55	7
Michigan	361	119	81	158	3
Minnesota	739	212	34	489	4
Mississippi	148	33	3	110	2
Missouri	679	126	37	511	5
Montana	173	55	42	73	3
Nebraska	459	121	9	324	5
Nevada	19	6	1	10	2
New Hampshire	64	24	3	34	3
New Jersey	128	71	10	45	2
New Mexico	98	45	6	45	2
New York	416	104	39	52	221
North Carolina	65	17	0	46	2
North Dakota	181	43	6	130	2

TABLE 7-1 (*continued*)

State	Total	Member		Nonmember	
		National	*State*	*Insured*	*Noninsured*
Ohio	323	144	69	107	3
Oklahoma	542	231	22	282	7
Oregon	76	8	13	46	9
Pennsylvania	330	184	17	112	17
Rhode Island	30	6	0	10	14
South Carolina	74	20	5	49	0
South Dakota	138	25	26	87	0
Tennessee	294	58	10	221	5
Texas	1,951	1,058	70	808	15
Utah	62	7	16	36	3
Vermont	26	12	0	13	1
Virginia	169	46	82	41	0
Washington	113	24	3	71	15
West Virginia	219	97	27	94	1
Wisconsin	582	119	22	435	6
Wyoming	116	59	25	31	1
Puerto Rico	23	1	2	10	10
Virgin Islands	6	0	0	0	6

Source: *Annual Statistical Digest 1985*, Board of Governors of the Federal Reserve System, October 1986, p. 76.

Individuals who wish to open a bank must receive a charter from either a state government or the federal government. Prior to the Civil War, the federal government granted only a few charters to private commercial banks. The First Bank of the United States (1791 to 1811) and the Second Bank of the United States (1816 to 1836) operated under federal charters and served as the primary banker for the federal government. Other commercial banks operated under state charters until the passage of the National Banking Act of 1863, which allowed private commercial banks to operate under federal charters. (The historical development of money and banking to 1863 is presented in Appendix B. The reader may gain an interesting historical perspective by reading that appendix now.) The federal charters are issued by the Comptroller of the Currency, whose office supervises the national banks. The Comptroller of the Currency is part of the Treasury Department. Federally chartered private banks are referred to as **national banks**, whereas private banks operating under state charters are referred to as **state banks**. National banks can be identified by the word *national* in their name or instead of the word *national*, the letters *NA* are added to indicate *national association*.

All national banks must be Federal Reserve members, and all Federal Reserve member banks must carry FDIC insurance. Most state banks are not Federal Reserve members, as shown in Table 7-1.

CHARACTERISTICS OF BANKS BY LOCATION AND SIZE

The *geographical area* in which a bank operates may be related to the type of service it offers. Rural banks may offer many services to the farming industry, such as agricultural loans. A rural bank will normally carry a greater percentage of its deposits in the form of vault cash (cash on the bank premises) because of the longer time required for the delivery of cash. Vault cash is necessary for daily business needs, but excess amounts of currency and coin are normally deposited in another bank or at the Federal Reserve. This practice is safer and also enables the bank to transfer funds more rapidly when it buys assets. Rural banks often receive their currency and coin by registered U.S. mail, so that several days may be needed for delivery. A city bank that is a member of the Federal Reserve in a city with a Federal Reserve regional bank or branch bank may obtain a cash delivery by armored truck with little delay. A Federal Reserve member bank or a nonmember bank in a large city may obtain currency and coin from another commercial bank where it has a deposit.

As with many general statements of this type, there are important exceptions. For example, banks in the Washington, D.C., area carry substantial vault cash for city banks. Although the Washington, D.C., area is a large metropolitan area and although it is an important hub for the transfer of federal government checks, it has no Federal Reserve bank or branch. Therefore, the cash for its commercial banks is delivered each day from the Baltimore, Maryland, branch of the Richmond, Virginia, Federal Reserve. In all of the cities of similar size, the Federal Reserve has either a regional bank or a branch of a regional bank that can make frequent deliveries to the banks in the area.

A POLITICAL RAILROAD JUNCTION

Question: Why does not Washington, D.C., a large metropolitan area that is the central location of the federal government (with a large flow of checks) have a Federal Reserve facility for handling checks or cash?

Answer (suggested): In the past the Treasury building across from the White House had some cash facilities for commercial banks, but that was stopped. The reason seems to be that the capital city does not have full representation in the U.S. Congress. It has no senators and only one representative, who is not allowed to vote on the floor of the House of Representatives, although he or she can vote in committee votes on the committees on which he or she serves. Without a vote, new Federal Reserve facilities were not built in Washington, D.C.; instead, they were built in Richmond, Virginia, and in Baltimore, Maryland. Does this mean that the Federal Reserve is strongly influenced by political pressures? Yes, it does. (See Part VIII.)

Another exception in the fifty states to the observation that city banks carry less vault cash is found on the Hawaiian Islands. When the Hawaiian Islands were a territory, from 1900 to 1959, all banks were chartered as national banks and were, after 1913, members of the Federal Reserve System. However, there is no Federal Reserve branch on the islands. When Hawaii was admitted to the Union in 1959, these banks continued to be national banks for some time. But after ten years and long experience with poor central bank service in such areas as check clearing and the provision of currency and coin, most of the Hawaiian banks gave up their national charters. They became state banks, dropped their membership in the Federal Reserve, and were freed (temporarily) from their Federal Reserve requirements. Their distance from the continental United States, as well as the absence of a Federal Reserve branch of the regional San Francisco Federal Reserve Bank to hold cash in the Hawaiian Islands, requires these Hawaiian banks to carry larger-than-average amounts of vault cash.

The largest banks in the United States are located in New York City, San Francisco, Los Angeles, and Chicago, as shown in Table 7-2. In general, large banks that receive deposits from other smaller banks and carry on extensive business outside their locale are called *money center banks.* Just how large these banks must be, how many interbank deposits they must have, and how much business outside their locale they must have to qualify as money center banks is not clear. One indication of the line of demarcation between money center banks and other banks comes from the reserve requirements that the Federal Reserve formerly calibrated at a special level for money center banks. Wherever the line is drawn between money center banks and all other banks, it is clear that the twenty banks in Table 7-2 are money center banks. Those twenty largest banks had $1.07 trillion in assets on June 30, 1986, which was 42.5 percent of the assets of all commercial banking institutions in the United States.

Larger banks in larger cities often specialize in particular ancillary services in addition to the bank deposit services they supply (see Table 7-3). They may have foreign branches in order to provide banking services in particular foreign countries. Large banks may sell consumer credit card services; that is, they may allow individual banks to join their credit card network. They may be brokers in the federal funds market, a market for short-term loans in which commercial banks participate. Banks may specialize in handling trust agreements. Large banks often provide many of these services for their depositors as well as sell these ancillary services to other banks. This provision of services to other banks is called *correspondent banking.*

The degree of competition in the market for banking services may be related to the number of depository intermediaries in a particular locality. For example, if there is one commercial bank and no thrifts in a small town in a remote area, most of the residents will probably deposit their funds in the local bank. If there are no financial intermediaries offering similar services, such as business loans, the local bank may supply most of these loans. In most areas, other financial intermediaries and nearby banks compete for loan business.

TABLE 7-2 Location of the Twenty Largest Commercial Bank Holding Company Offices in the United States, by Asset Size, June 30, 1986 (in millions of dollars)

The largest bank holding companies' main offices in the United States are concentrated in New York City and California (San Francisco and Los Angeles). Chicago and Dallas have two of the twenty largest, and Boston, Buffalo, Pittsburgh, and Charlotte, N.C. each have one. These are only the main offices, and these holding companies can have offices (supplying various services, including taking deposits and making loans) in the same state, in other states, and in other countries. Chicago has been considered the third largest banking center in the United States, but with the reduction in the size of the Continental Bank following its failure and "nationalization" in 1984, Dallas is not far behind.

Citicorp was not the largest bank in the world at the end of 1986. Dai-ichi Kangyo Bank Ltd. in Japan had assets worth $207 billion in U.S. dollars, based on the exchange rate at that time (177 yen to the dollar in March 1986), and the ranking could change if the yen falls in value.

Rank	Locations/Name	Asset Size
	New York	
1	Citicorp, New York	183,388.00
3	Chase Manhattan	90,610.38
4	Manufacturers Hanover Corp., New York	75,574.32
5	J. P. Morgan & Co., New York	72,664.00
6	Chemical New York Corp.	56,899.83
8	Bankers Trust, New York Corp.	52,400.00
16	Marine Midland Banks, Inc., Buffalo, N.Y.	24,532.33
19	Irving Bank Corp., New York	22,242.40
	Northeast	
13	Bank of Boston Corp.	30,434.24
	Mid-Atlantic	
12	Mellon Bank Corp., Pittsburgh	36,178.75
	Southeast	
17	NCNB Corp., Charlotte, N.C.	23,875.77
	Midwest	
11	First Chicago Corp.	39,369.87
14	Continental Illinois Corp., Chicago	29,079.00
15	First Bank System, Inc., Minneapolis	27,156.02
	West: California	
2	BankAmerica Corp., San Francisco	117,314.00
7	Security Pacific Corp., Los Angeles	53,634.00
9	First Interstate Bancorp, Los Angeles	49,230.20
10	Wells Fargo & Co., San Francisco	43,563.48
	West: Texas	
18	RepublicBank Corp., Dallas	22,494.17
20	MCorp., Dallas	21,705.00
	Total	1,072,345.75

Source: The American Banker, September 30, 1986, p. 22.

TABLE 7-3   Services Offered by U.S. Banks According to Deposit Size (percentage of banks performing this service)

This table shows the results of a study of the percentage of banks with different-sized deposits offering particular services. The study shows that all services are supplied by at least some of the banks in each category. More of the larger banks ($50 million and larger) offer all the services, with a few exceptions such as telephone-bill paying (payment of customers' bills by telephone authorization). The results do not differentiate the way that the services are offered (how much individual attention, and the like) or the costs (including convenience) of the services.

	Deposit in millions				
Services intended to attract:	*Under $10*	*$10–$25*	*$25–$50*	*$50–$100*	*Over $100*
A. Consumer deposits					
1. Automatic bill paying	35.7%	31.0%	31.9%	21.5%	44.1%
2. Automatic deposit transfer	71.9	72.2	84.8	91.1	88.4
3. Automatic loan payment	94.8	93.0	93.8	96.2	92.6
4. Planned savings program	53.1	77.3	86.5	89.9	81.4
5. Trust powers	20.7	41.5	70.3	81.6	97.1
a. Trust services	22.4	40.9	69.6	80.0	97.1
6. Customer parking facilities	84.5	89.9	97.3	96.2	98.6
7. Drive-up windows	78.4	92.2	99.1	100.0	98.6
8. Deposit by mail	100.0	100.0	100.0	100.0	100.0
a. Self-service envelopes	97.2	96.1	99.1	97.7	95.7
b. Postage fees prepaid	31.4	40.3	50.9	47.6	53.0
9. Special no-minimum checking accounts	38.1	40.8	55.4	54.4	66.2
10. Automatic savings bond purchases (new)	43.6	62.1	79.8	74.7	75.4
11. On-the-job customer services (new)	4.3	7.0	5.4	12.7	12.5
12. Revolving charge card (new)	24.5	35.2	50.5	68.4	78.3
B. Business deposits					
1. Night depository	83.5	97.7	99.1	98.7	98.6
2. Automatic payroll deposit	59.8	65.6	75.9	78.2	85.3
3. Leasing capital assets (new)	11.5	13.0	25.0	32.0	66.2
4. Special check services for business	36.5	50.0	75.2	76.3	95.5
a. Data processing	33.3	46.0	55.6	56.1	68.2
b. Payroll services	72.2	77.8	85.2	89.4	84.9
c. Locked box services	13.9	27.0	42.0	39.4	74.2
C. Consumer and business deposits					
1. Foreign exchange service	41.7	47.6	60.2	64.1	79.7
2. Telephone bill paying	23.7	11.8	3.6	2.5	11.8
3. Safe-deposit services	94.8	99.2	100.0	100.0	98.6
4. Overdraft privileges (new)	29.9	35.2	50.2	68.4	78.3

Source: Douglas Evanoff and Diane Fortier, "Geographic Expansion in Commercial Banking: Inferences from Intrastate Activity," in Federal Reserve Bank of Chicago, *Toward Nationwide Banking, a Guide to the Issues*, 1986, p. 50; from a study by Rose Kalari and Kenneth Riener, "A National Survey Study of Bank Services and Prices Arrayed by Size and Structure," *Journal of Bank Research*, Summer 1985, pp. 72–85.

Larger loans made to larger local businesses may not be supplied solely by banks in the local area. Unlike the cost of transporting physical property, the cost of transporting money by check is negligible. *The capital market, the market for borrowed funds, cannot easily be subdivided by geographical areas.* This consideration makes measuring the competition for large-loan business in a geographical area a difficult problem.

CORRESPONDENT BANKS

Commercial banks that supply services to other commercial banks are called **correspondent banks**. The correspondent bank is paid indirectly, in the form of income from deposit balances maintained by its bank customers, as well as by direct money payments. Small banks may have five or six correspondent banks, which provide many services: bookkeeping services (especially those that require large computers); assistance in the sale or purchase of assets (including the consolidation of purchases with other buyers); and the provision of information about capital markets (including the sale of equity shares in their banks). Large banks may have as many as thirty corresponding banks that provide services and representation in other localities (including foreign countries) and specialized services that the correspondents can offer at a smaller cost.

Until 1981 the Federal Reserve provided free check-clearing facilities to its members, but nonmember banks relied entirely on correspondent banks to clear their checks. The correspondent banks often clear nonmember banks' checks through the Federal Reserve. The total amount of checks debited against all insured banks in October 1982 (adjusted to an annual basis) was $93.5 trillion, of which 42 percent was from New York banks. Private clearing houses owned by groups of banks handled a large amount and so did the Federal Reserve, which began charging for that service.

BRANCH BANKING

All states have some form of branch banking. A **branch bank** is defined as a structure separate from a bank's main office. It mainly accepts deposits but may offer such services as extending loans.

Table 7-4 presents a three-part classification for state banking laws in the fifty states. Lawyers may squirm because they know that the states' laws are complex and nearly always different in some way. The laws may govern the number and type of branches a bank may have and the types of services that these branches may provide. Forty-eight percent of the states allow statewide banking, and 52 percent have restrictions for branch banking. The meaning of these restrictions with the advent of nationwide automatic teller machine networks and the authorization in 1982 to cross state lines to buy troubled depository institutions is unclear, but the regulations will have to be changed.

TABLE 7-4   Branch Banking Laws, 1984

Statewide Branching	Limited Branching	Severe Restrictions
Alaska	Alabama	Colorado
Arizona	Arkansas	Illinois
California	Georgia	Kansas
Connecticut	Indiana	Missouri
Delaware	Iowa	Montana
Florida	Kentucky	North Dakota
Hawaii	Louisiana	Texas
Idaho	Michigan	Wyoming
Maine	Minnesota	
Maryland	Mississippi	
Massachusetts	Nebraska	
Nevada	New Mexico	
New Hampshire	Ohio	
New Jersey	Oklahoma	
New York	Pennsylvania	
North Carolina	Tennessee	
Oregon	West Virginia	
Rhode Island	Wisconsin	
South Carolina		
South Dakota		
Utah		
Vermont		
Virginia		
Washington		
Total number	24	18	8
Percentage of states	48%	36%	16%

Column 1 of Table 7-4 lists the states with the most unrestricted branching rules. These are sometimes called **statewide branching** states. *Limited-branch* states are listed in column 2. These are states with less stringent regulations. The so-called **unit banking** states have the strictest rules, approaching the requirement that full banking services can be offered only at the main office.

National banks were prohibited from having branches (branching) by the National Bank Act of 1864. (The banking acts of 1863 and 1864 established the national banking system, the federal chartering of commercial banks.) The Pepper–McFadden Act of 1927 (or the McFadden Act), as amended by the Banking Act of 1933 (one section of which is called the Glass–Steagall Act), gave national banks the same branching rights as state chartered banks had, except that it forbade branching across state lines. Finally, the Douglas amendment to the Bank Holding Company Act of 1956 gave states the power to regulate the interstate (between-state) expansion of bank holding companies. What all this adds up to is that individual states can govern both the branching in their own state and the entry of banks from other states. Commercial banks also can establish corporations with other commercial banks across state lines for the purposes of international trade.[1]

Laws regulating the number and type of branches may affect the amount of deposits a bank can obtain, as well as the type of local competition it faces from other banks and financial intermediaries. When branch banking is limited, substitutes for branch banks are created. The currency exchange found, for example, throughout the Chicago area is one such substitute that provides services for transferring funds. Currency exchanges cash checks, sell money orders and travelers checks, and provide other associated services.

Bank of America, located in California where branching is allowed, had 1,069 branches in 1983. The Continental Illinois National Bank and Trust Co. and the First National Bank, the two largest banks in Illinois, had no branches outside the downtown Chicago area, as Illinois has tight restrictions on branches.

The use of *automatic teller machines (ATMs)* for depositing and withdrawing money offered a new method for banks to obtain branches. Initially the regulations for teller machines were more favorable for thrift institutions, but by 1982 the rush was on to form nationwide and regional networks of ATMs.

There was a large increase in automatic teller machines in the early 1980s, with shipments of new ATMs reaching about 14,000 per year in 1983.[2] Then the sale of new machines fell to under 9,000 per year by 1986. There had been predictions of as many as 150,000 ATMs by 1990, but experts in the industry lowered their optimistic projections to 100,000. In 1986 there were approximately 60,000 ATMs in operation in the United States.

The reduction in the shipments of new ATMs and the lowering of projections of the number of ATMs by 1990 occurred for the following reasons:

1. The ATMs have been very successful, and the choice locations for busy corners in cities have already been taken.
2. ATMs placed in convenience stores and supermarkets have generally not been profitable. Olivetti USA, an ATM manufacturer, said that on the average, the cost of maintaining an ATM in such a location was 2 percent greater than its revenue.
3. Although 48 percent of bank customers responding in a survey used ATMs, only a third reported using them regularly.
4. In 1986 the purchase of a new ATM cost around $30,000. Yearly maintenance costs about $12,000 a year and, for some locations, far more.
5. Expensive advertising campaigns must sometimes be conducted to persuade customers to use ATMs.
6. ATMs offer a number of services, including dispensing cash for different accounts, transferring funds between accounts, accepting deposits, and providing balance information. This has made the operation of ATMs complex for some customers, especially those who only want cash and do not wish to stand in line waiting for those individuals who spend a lot of time completing their transactions.

Two avenues that future innovations in ATMs may take are

1. Cheaper and less complex machines can be built that will concentrate on dispensing cash.
2. More complex machines can be built that offer more banking services.

Based on the preceding reasons for the decline in new ATM sales, the first option appears likely for the immediate future. When consumers gain more experience with computer technology, more advanced ATM technology may be feasible. The use of telephone lines for the more advanced technology would be appealing if problems of theft (of both funds and private deposit information) could be overcome.

The installation of remote terminal networks has completely muddied the concept of what a branch is. It is possible, for example, for an individual to use his or her telephone as a remote bank terminal for many kinds of bank business. The telephone could be plugged into a computer at the bank by dialing a particular number (the personal identification number, or PIN), and the individual could punch a code into the telephone along with appropriate instructions. A telephone call could, for example, be used to transfer money to a food market's account. Separate calls need not be placed if the food store rented lines and the customer merely placed an identification card (and punched in a secret number) in a terminal permanently in service. In this way, the food market could instantly be paid for its sale of food to the customer without waiting for a check to clear.

It is also feasible to have financial consulting booths positioned next to ATMs that individual customers could enter and communicate their financial messages via a video camera. Their messages would be processed by a central computer, and an answer would be transmitted on a video screen. If the individual's financial problems were especially severe, an arm would be extended to pat the individual's back while soft violin music was played.

BANK HOLDING COMPANIES

Banks, through their holding company organizations, buy other facilities not only in their host state, but also throughout the country, facilities that do not receive deposits. These may take the form of loan offices; consumer credit card facilities; or, in Washington, D.C., an office for lobbying and gathering information on laws and regulations relevant to the bank. In addition, holding companies may control a number of banks in a single state. Although these **subsidiary banks** have different names, many in the field would view them as similar to branches, especially in analyses of competition among depository institutions.

A **bank holding company** is a company that holds controlling stock in one or more commercial banks. *By 1978, bank holding companies had become the predominant organizational form of commercial banking in the United States, with*

71 percent of all domestic bank deposits in holding company banks. In 1983 there were 5,409 bank holding companies, and they held 83.8 percent of total commercial bank deposits.

The Banking Act of 1933, which also established deposit insurance, provided mild regulation for bank holding companies. A bank holding company was defined in that law as "any corporation, business trust association or similar organization which owns or controls directly or indirectly either a majority of the shares of the capital stock of a member bank or more than 50 percent of the number of shares voted for the election of directors of any one bank at the preceding election or controls in any manner the election of the majority of directors of any one bank." This act covered only those holding companies that own Federal Reserve member banks.

The Banking Act of 1935 provided an exemption for most one-bank holding companies, that is, holding companies that own only one bank.

Pressure mounted for some legislation, including a plea by President Franklin Roosevelt in a special message to Congress in 1938. This pressure did not produce federal legislation until the Bank Holding Company Act of 1956 was passed. This act set a new standard for a bank holding company as an organization owning 25 percent or more of the stock of two or more banks. It gave the Federal Reserve the power to supervise bank holding companies and to approve or disapprove their acquisition of additional banks, whether or not the banks were members. Existing interstate holding companies were allowed to retain their subsidiary banks. This practice is known as **grandfathering in existing structures** and explains why some holding companies own banks in more than one state. The act required that future interstate acquisitions be subject to specific authorization by individual state law. Such authorization did not exist in any state, and so the formation of nationwide bank holding companies was halted.

As the number of multibank holding companies grew rapidly, new amendments were passed in 1970, which allowed the Board of Governors to determine that a corporation is a bank holding company if it controls a bank, even without owning 25 percent of the stock.

Meanwhile, the number of one-bank holding companies was growing rapidly, from 550 in 1965 to 1,440 at the end of 1970. Favorable tax treatment and ease in raising funds were important reasons for this growth. Bank investors found that by forming a one-bank holding company to own their bank, the bank could circumvent the ceiling interest rates that could be paid on deposits and raise money directly by having the bank holding company sell debt instruments, which had the advantage of no ceiling rate and the disadvantage of no FDIC insurance. In addition, nonbank activities of one-bank holding companies, such as loan agencies, could cross state lines and expand throughout the country. Representative Wright Patman, former chairman of the House Banking Committee, introduced a bill that was enacted into law at the end of 1970, which finally brought one-bank holding companies under the regulatory apparatus of the Federal Reserve.

One of the primary reasons for forming holding companies, other than the obvious reason of acquiring chains of additional banks, is to engage in certain activities that are not allowed to banks. These activities include mortgage banking and the development of out-of-state consumer finance companies. A 1956 law allowed multibank holding companies to operate safe depository companies, to liquidate property acquired by subsidiary banks, to own and manage holding company property, and to provide services to subsidiary banks. The Federal Reserve Board was permitted to allow or deny other nonbank activities, such as the operation of an insurance company, if these activities were closely related to the business of banking.

The era of deregulation begun in 1980 included the weakening of the prohibitions on banks from engaging in the brokerage business (the sale and purchase of stock and bonds for customers). Banks were prohibited from engaging in these activities by the Banking Act of 1933, more commonly known as the Glass–Steagall Act. Senator Carter Glass, who had been a principal architect of the law setting up the Federal Reserve in 1913, wanted to separate banks' activities that posed a conflict of interest. For example, banks make loans to corporations and can conceivably influence the value of a corporation's stock by granting or failing to grant such a loan. Fifty years after the passage of the Glass-Steagall Act, the Federal Reserve Board of Governors issued a press release asking for public comment on allowing bank holding companies to buy discount brokerage businesses. (Discount brokerage businesses buy and sell securities on a commission basis. The commission rates are lower than are those that most brokerage firms charge, although these latter firms provide customers with a wider range of services. See Exhibit 7-1 for the press release.)

Holding companies are allowed to engage in many nonbank activities, which are listed in Table 7-5. The Bank Holding Company Act as amended in 1970 [under Section 4(c)8] allows bank holding companies to acquire shares of any company doing business that the Board of Governors of the Federal Reserve System allows as proper for the bank holding company to engage in. The companies thus acquired are called 4(c)8 subsidiaries, and they can be purchased across state lines (because they are not banks and are not directly subject to restrictions on banks). The second column of Table 7-5 shows the allowable activities for these 4(c)8 companies. The third column lists the activities that they were denied.

This expansion of commercial banks into other fields can be viewed as part of a process of making banks more like other financial intermediaries, a process induced by the desire to compete more effectively. The process is not unidirectional. Other financial intermediaries, such as brokerage houses, which originally made their income on commissions from buying and selling securities, are becoming more like banks, as some of them offer services that closely resemble bank deposit services.

On October 15, 1982, President Ronald Reagan signed into law the Banking Affiliates Act of 1982 (which was part of the Garn–St Germain Depository Institutions Act of 1982). The law was designed to prevent the

EXHIBIT 7-1   Federal Reserve Press Release

FEDERAL RESERVE press release

For immediate release   February 22, 1983

The Federal Reserve Board today proposed for comment an amendment to Regulation Y — Bank Holding Companies -- to add discount securities brokerage and securities credit lending to the list of nonbanking activities permissible for bank holding companies.

The Board asked for comment by April 8, 1983.

In January, the Board approved the application of BankAmerica Corporation to acquire The Charles Schwab Corporation and thereby engage in discount securities brokerage and securities credit lending activities. These activities have not yet been approved for all bank holding companies. In light of the extensive record developed in the Schwab application, the Board has asked whether these activities should be added to the list of permissible nonbanking activities in Regulation Y.

Discount securities brokerage in the context of the proposal means buying and selling securities solely as agent for the account of customers; it specifically excludes securities underwriting activities and the provision of investment advice or research services. Securities credit lending means extending credit for the purchase or carrying of securities by nonbank sub— sidiaries of bank holding companies pursuant to the Board's Regulation T — Margin Credit Extended by Brokers and Dealers.

The Board's notice in this matter is attached.

-0-

Attachment

Bank of America was one of the leaders in the commercial banking industry in acquiring brokerage facilities. As a footnote to this particular acquisition, it should be added that because of a need to raise funds to alleviate financial problems, Bank of America had to offer this brokerage for sale at the end of 1986.

TABLE 7-5 Permissible Nonbank Activities for Bank Holding Companies by Subsidiaries, November 1984

The Bank Holding Company Act as amended in 1970 [under Section 4(c)8] allows bank holding companies to acquire shares of any company doing business that the Board of Governors approves as proper for the bank holding company to engage in. The companies thus acquired are called 4(c)8 subsidiaries, and they can be purchased across state lines (because they are not banks and thus are not directly subject to restrictions on banks).

The first column shows activities generally approved for all holding companies, and the second column shows the results of case-by-case approvals of the 4(c)8 activities authorized by the Board of Governors. Activities denied by the Board of Governors are listed in the third column.

Activities Permitted by Regulation	Activities Permitted by Order	Activities Denied by the Board
1. Extensions of credit[2] Mortgage banking Finance companies: consumer, sales, and commercial Credit cards Factoring	1. Issuance and sale of travelers checks[2,6]	1. Insurance premium funding (combined sales of mutual funds and insurance)
2. Industrial bank, Morris Plan banks, industrial loan company	2. Buying and selling gold and silver bullion and silver coin[2,4]	2. Underwriting life insurance not related to credit extension
3. Servicing loans and other extensions of credit[2]	3. Issuing money orders and general-purpose variable denominated payment instruments[1,2,4]	3. Sale of level-term credit life
4. Trust company[2]	4. Futures commission merchant to cover gold and silver bullion and coins[1,2]	4. Real estate brokerage (residential)
5. Investment or financial advising[2]	5. Underwriting certain federal, state, and municipal securities[1,2]	5. Armored car
6. Full-payout leasing of personal or real property[2]	6. Check verification[1,2,4]	6. Land development
7. Investments in community welfare projects[2]	7. Financial advice to consumers[1,2]	7. Real estate syndication
8. Providing bookkeeping or data processing services[2]	8. Issuance of small denomination debt instruments[1]	8. General management consulting
9. Acting as insurance agent or broker primarily in connection with credit extensions[2]	9. Arranging for equity financing of real estate	9. Property management
10. Underwriting credit life, accident, and health insurance	10. Acting as futures commissions merchant	10. Computer output microfilm services
11. Providing courier services[2]	11. Discount brokerage	11. Underwriting mortgage guaranty insurance[3]
12. Management consulting to all depository institutions	12. Operating a distressed savings and loan association	12. Operating a savings and loan association[1,5]
13. Sale at retail of money orders with a face value of not more than $1000, travelers checks, and savings bonds[1,2,7]	13. Operating an Article XII Investment Company	13. Operating a travel agency[1,2]
	14. Executing foreign banking unsolicited purchases and sales of securities	14. Underwriting property and casualty insurance[1]
	15. Engaging in commercial banking activities abroad through a limited purpose Delaware bank	15. Underwriting home loan life mortgage insurance[1]
	16. Performing appraisal of real estate and real estate advisor and real estate brokerage on nonresidential properties	16. Investment note issue with transactional characteristics
		17. Real estate advisory services

TABLE 7-5 *(continued)*

Activities Permitted by Regulation	Activities Permitted by Order	Activities Denied by the Board
14. Performing appraisals of real estate	17. Operating a Pool Reserve Plan for loss reserves of banks for loans to small businesses	
15. Issuance and sale of travelers checks		
16. Arranging commercial real estate equity financing	18. Operating a thrift institution in Rhode Island	
17. Securities brokerage	19. Operating a guarantee savings bank in New Hampshire	
18. Underwriting and dealing in government obligations and money market instruments	20. Offering informational advice and transactional services for foreign exchange services	
19. Foreign exchange advisory and transactional services		
20. Futures commission merchant		
21. Options on financial futures		
22. Advice on options on bullion and foreign exchange		

[1] Added to list since January 1, 1975.

[2] Activities permissible to national banks.

[3] Board orders found these activities closely related to banking but denied proposed acquisitions as part of its "go slow" policy.

[4] To be decided on a case-by-case basis.

[5] Operating a thrift institution has been permitted by order in Rhode Island, Ohio, New Hampshire, and California.

[6] Subsequently permitted by regulation.

[7] The amount subsequently was changed to $10,000.

Source: David D. Whitehead, "Interstate Banking: Probability or Reality?" Federal Reserve Bank of Atlanta, *Economic Review*, March 1985, p. 10.

misuse of a bank's resources resulting from financial transactions between the bank's subsidiaries in a holding company, called **sister bank subsidiaries**, or between a subsidiary and the parent company. The law grew out of a review in the mid-1970s by the banking committees of the U.S. Congress and the federal bank supervisory authorities. The review was prompted by the discovery that several large banks had been adversely affected by transactions with their affiliates. The best-known case was the Hamilton National Bank of Chattanooga, which failed after having purchased several low-quality mortgages from a mortgage banking subsidiary of the bank's parent company. The act allows unrestricted transfers among domestic holding company banks that are at least 80 percent owned by the parent (a liberalization of earlier law); however, low-quality assets cannot be purchased from a sister bank.

THE WALLS HAVE TUMBLED DOWN

The United States' banking system began with only state-chartered banks, as described in Appendix B. These banks operated in one state, although the First (1791–1811) and Second (1816–1836) Banks of the United States conducted nationwide banking business because they had the federal government as their major customer.

The banking laws of 1863 and 1864 set up the national banking system, a system for federally chartering banks. The McFadden Act of 1927 (amended in 1933) prohibited federally chartered banks—national banks—from branching across state lines—that is, *interstate branching*. They were allowed to branch within a state—that is, *intrastate branching*—only if the state's banks were also permitted this right. But because state banks were chartered in a single state and could not cross state lines, the McFadden Act effectively limited any domestic bank from doing business across state lines.

Nonetheless, there were exceptions, as some banks had operated across state lines before the McFadden Act was passed, and the law could not be made retroactive. (In general, laws cannot make prior actions illegal, as these actions transpired when they were legal.) These banks' right to operate across state lines thus is said to have been "grandfathered in" before such actions were prohibited. Among the bank holding companies that have operated across state lines because they were grandfathered in, the following used this right from 1980 to 1985 to acquire banks in states other than the one in which they have their main office:

First Interstate Bankcorp in Los Angeles, California, acquired a bank in the state of Washington.

General Bankshares Corp. of St. Louis, Missouri, acquired banks in Illinois and Tennessee.

NCNB Corp. of Charlotte, N.C., acquired banks in Florida.

Norwest Corp. in Minneapolis acquired banks in Nebraska.[3]

The door to interstate banking was opened wider by the Bank Holding Company Act of 1956, which allowed bank holding companies to acquire banks across state lines if the relevant state law permitted it. As of the end of 1985, 24 states and the District of Columbia had a state banking law permitting full interstate banking, as shown in Table 7-6. The new state bank laws allowing interstate banking also introduced new jargon, defined in Table 7-7, such as opt-outs and anti-leapfrogging provisions. Finally, a summary of the state banking laws is presented in Table 7-8.

As a step toward permitting their states to have full interstate banking, some states (as of the end of 1985) adopted regional banking provisions, which allowed interstate banking from the nearby region. In June 1985 the U.S. Supreme Court upheld these state regional banking laws, and in the same month the House Banking Committee passed a bill permitting a five-year phase-in of nationwide banking, beginning in 1990.

T A B L E 7 - 6   State Laws Permitting Full Interstate Banking (effective 1978–1988)

The rush to allow interstate banking is shown by this list of states and the District of Columbia that developed these laws. Maine was the first in 1975, and Michigan was the last state as of the end of 1985. Regional reciprocal agreements (RRO) allow interstate banking within a region. **De novo** branches, or subsidiaries of banks, are new branches or subsidiaries.

California passed legislation in September 1986 opening entry from banks in eleven western states in July 1987 and nationwide banking on January 1, 1991. Governor George Deukmejian was expected to sign the proposed law.

State	Date Enacted	Date Effective	Provisions
(Branching status)*			
Maine	June 18, 1975	Jan. 1, 1978	Nationwide reciprocal
(S)	Feb. 7, 1984	Feb. 7, 1984	Reciprocal provision dropped
New York	June 28, 1982	June 28, 1982	Nationwide reciprocal
(S)			
Alaska	July 1, 1982	July 1, 1982	Nationwide, no reciprocal provision
(S)			No *de novo* entry permitted
Massachusetts	Dec. 30, 1982	July 1, 1983	Regional reciprocal (region consists of five other New England states)
(S)			Permits entry through merger or *de novo* branching
			Anti-leapfrogging provision†
			Applicable to banks and savings and loan associations
Connecticut	June 8, 1983	June 8, 1983	Regional reciprocal (region consists of the five other New England states)
(S)			Anti-leapfrogging provision†
			Applicable to banks and savings and loan associations
Rhode Island	May 17, 1983	July 1, 1984	Regional reciprocal (region consists of the five other New England states)
(S)		July 1, 1987	Nationwide reciprocal (trigger); amended from previous date of July 1, 1986
Georgia	April 5, 1984	Jan. 1, 1985, if two contiguous states in region have interstate laws;	Regional reciprocal (region consists of Alabama, Florida, Kentucky, Louisiana, Mississippi, North Carolina, South Carolina, Tennessee, Virginia)
(L)			No *de novo* entry permitted
		otherwise, July 1, 1985	Anti-leapfrogging provision†
Utah	April 6, 1984	April 15, 1984	Regional reciprocal (region consists of Alaska, Washington, Oregon, Idaho, Wyoming, Montana, Colorado, New Mexico, Arizona, Nevada, Hawaii)
(S)			Applicable to banks and savings and loan associations
Kentucky	April 7, 1984	July 15, 1984	Regional reciprocal (region consists of Illinois, Indiana, Missouri, Ohio, Tennessee, Virginia, West Virginia)
(L)			No *de novo* entry permitted
		July 15, 1986	Nationwide reciprocal (trigger)
South Carolina	May 21, 1984	January 1, 1986	Regional reciprocal (region consists of Alabama, Arkansas, District of Columbia, Florida, Georgia, Kentucky, Louisiana, Maryland, Mississippi, North Carolina, Tennessee, Virginia, West Virginia)
(S)			

TABLE 7-6 *(continued)*

State	Date Enacted	Date Effective	Provisions
Florida (S)	May 22, 1984	July 1, 1985, or when states with over 20% of region's deposits have interstate laws in effect	Anti-leapfrogging provision† No *de novo* entry permitted Regional reciprocal (region consists of Alabama, Arkansas, District of Columbia, Georgia, Louisiana, Maryland, Mississippi, North Carolina, South Carolina, Tennessee, Virginia, West Virginia)
North Carolina (S)	July 7, 1984	Jan. 1, 1985	Anti-leapfrogging provision† No *de novo* entry permitted Regional reciprocal (region consists of Alabama, Arkansas, District of Columbia, Florida, Georgia, Kentucky, Louisiana, Maryland, Mississippi, South Carolina, Tennessee, Virginia, West Virginia)
Oregon (S)	March 12, 1985	July 1, 1986	Regional nonreciprocal (region consists of Alaska, Arizona, California, Hawaii, Idaho, Nevada, Utah, Washington) No *de novo* entry permitted
Idaho (S)	March 21, 1985	July 1, 1985	Anti-leapfrogging provision† Regional reciprocal (region consists of contiguous states: Montana, Nevada, Oregon, Utah, Washington, Wyoming) No *de novo* entry permitted Applicable to banks and savings and loan associations
Virginia (S)	March 24, 1985	July 1, 1985	Regional reciprocal (region consists of Alabama, Arkansas, District of Columbia, Florida, Georgia, Kentucky, Louisiana, Maryland, Mississippi, North Carolina, South Carolina, Tennessee, West Virginia) No *de novo* entry permitted
Arizona (S)	April 18, 1985	Oct. 1, 1986	Nationwide nonreciprocal Applicable to banks and savings and loan associations *De novo* entry permitted beginning 7/1/92
Indiana (L)	April 18, 1985	Jan. 1, 1986	Regional reciprocal (region consists of contiguous states: Illinois, Kentucky, Michigan, Ohio) Ceiling on control of statewide deposits 10% before 7/1/86; 11% before 7/1/87; 12% after 6/30/87 No *de novo* entry permitted Opt-out provision ends 6/30/87‡
Tennessee (L)	May 1, 1985	July 1, 1985	Regional reciprocal (region consists of Alabama, Arkansas, Florida, Georgia, Indiana, Kentucky, Louisiana, Mississippi, Missouri, North Carolina, South Carolina, Virginia, West Virginia) No *de novo* entry permitted
Washington (S)	May 16, 1985	July 1, 1987	Nationwide reciprocal No *de novo* entry permitted
Maryland (S)	May 21, 1985	July 1, 1985 July 1, 1987	Regional reciprocal (region consists of Delaware, District of Columbia, Virginia, West Virginia) Region expands to include Alabama, Arkansas, Florida, Georgia, Kentucky, Louisiana, Mississippi, North Carolina, Pennsylvania,

TABLE 7-6 (*continued*)

State	Date Enacted	Date Effective	Provisions
			South Carolina, Tennessee
			Applicable to banks and savings and loan associations
			De novo entry permitted beginning 7/1/89, with certain economic concessions
Nevada (S)	June 13, 1985	July 1, 1985	Regional reciprocal (region consists of Alaska, Arizona, Colorado, Hawaii, Idaho, Montana, New Mexico, Oregon, Utah, Washington, Wyoming)
			Applicable to banks and savings and loan associations
		July 1, 1990	*De novo* entry permitted
			Regional provision expires; trigger effective
Ohio (L)	July 18, 1985	Oct. 17, 1985	Regional reciprocal (region consists of Delaware, District of Columbia, Illinois, Indiana, Kentucky, Maryland, Michigan, Missouri, New Jersey, Pennsylvania, Tennessee, Virginia, West Virginia, Wisconsin)
			Applicable to banks and savings and loan associations
			De novo entry permitted as allowed by reciprocal state
			Anti-leapfrogging provision†
			Ceiling on control of statewise bank and savings and loan deposits of 20%
		Oct. 17, 1988	Nationwide reciprocal (trigger)
District of Columbia (S)	Oct. 8, 1985	Nov. 22, 1985	Regional reciprocal (region consists of Alabama, Florida, Georgia, Louisiana, Maryland, Mississippi, North Carolina, South Carolina, Tennessee, Virginia, West Virginia)
			No *de novo* entry permitted
Illinois (U)	Nov. 25, 1985	July 1, 1986	Regional reciprocal (region consists of Indiana, Iowa, Kentucky, Michigan, Missouri, Wisconsin)
			No *de novo* entry permitted
			Anti-leapfrogging provision†
			Opt-out provision ends 7/1/88‡
			Acquirers must have ratio of total capital/total assets of at least 7%
Michigan (L)	Dec. 5, 1985	Jan. 1, 1986	Regional reciprocal (region consists of Illinois, Indiana, Wisconsin, Ohio, Minnesota)
			De novo entry permitted
		Oct. 10, 1988	Nationwide reciprocal (trigger)

* Refers to state restrictions on bank branching: S = statewide branching, L = limited branching (e.g., within county boundaries), and U = unit banking state.

† This provision prevents banks from outside the reciprocal region from entering a state within the region that has no regional restrictions and from their entering the state with regional reciprocal constraints.

‡ This provision grants immunity from acquisition to banking organizations that do not wish to be participants in interstate banking, for a specified term.

Note: Iowa and Illinois permit continued expansion by bank and trust company subsidiaries that had entered those states prior to 1956. Before May 22, 1984, Florida allowed continued expansion by those that had entered before year-end 1972.

Delaware, Nebraska, and South Dakota permit *de novo* interstate banking only, subject to minimum capitalization and employment levels. These banks must operate in a manner not likely to attract customers from the general public.

Source: Federal Reserve Bank of Chicago, *Toward Nationwide Banking, a Guide to the Issues,* 1986, App. 1, pp. 85–87.

TABLE 7-7 The New Lexicon of 1980s State Banking Laws Allowing Interstate Banking

	Common Provisions in Interstate Banking Laws	
Provision	*Definition*	*State Examples*
Reciprocity	Requires that banking laws governing out-of-state banks seeking entry into home state allow entry to banks from the home state on equivalent terms	Nationwide: NY, WA Regional: MA, CT, RI, GA, UT, SC, FL, NC, ID, VA, IN, TN, NV, MD, OH, DC, IL
Institutional coverage	Eligibility of foreign banks, savings and loan associations, mutual savings banks, industrial savings banks, and trust companies for participation in interstate banking may vary.	Foreign bank entry prohibited by: FL, Savings & loan associations included in: AZ, OH, MA, CT, UT, ID, MD
Form of entry	Means by which out-of-state banks are allowed to enter home state, e.g., by acquiring an existing bank, by chartering a new bank (*de novo* entry), or by branching.	*De novo* entry forbidden by AK, GA, KY, SC, FL, OR, ID, VA, IN, TN, WA Entry by branching prohibited by all.
Design by region	May be based on geography, economic similarities, interstate trade patterns, or arbitrary political boundaries.	
Anti-leapfrogging	In regional agreements, prevents banking firm whose principal place of business is outside region from entering state by acquiring a bank in another state that is part of the region.	MA, CT, GA, SC, FL, OR
Nonseverability	Included in regional agreements prior to *Northeast Bancorp.* decision upholding regional interstate banking; protects transactions consummated prior to decision.	
Phase-in or "trigger"	Specifies a time limit or sequence of events which must occur in order for provision for national entry to become effective, i.e., "triggered."	ME, RI, KY, MD, NV, OH, MI
Opt-Outs	Allows home state banks to declare themselves immune from interstate banking—either from acquiring or being acquired—for a specified period.	IN

Source: Larry A. Frieder, "The Interstate Landscape: Trends and Projections," in Federal Reserve Bank of Chicago, *Toward Nationwide Banking, a Guide to the Issues,* 1986, p. 3.

Interstate banking became a reality in the 1980s for the first time since the establishment of the United States. The outlook for the rest of the 1980s is for the continuation of interstate banking. Indeed, the question is no longer whether interstate banking will be permitted but, rather, how soon interstate banking will be nationwide. The U.S. Supreme Court's 1985 decision removed the legal barriers for regional banking so that the state legislatures that have not acted for fear of legal prohibitions will now feel free to do so. States that do not act will be pressured by competition from nearby states that do permit

TABLE 7-8   Summary of Interstate Banking Laws at the End of 1985

Some banks' holding companies were grandfathered in, as they existed before the passage of the McFadden Act (column 1). Some state laws limited the functions of out-of-state banks (column 2). Some banks were allowed to purchase if they were in trouble (column 3). Some states required reciprocity—equal access to their banks in the other state—before allowing a purchase from an out-of-state bank (column 4). Some had unrestricted legislation, unrestricted after a phase-in period, and reciprocity confined to a region (columns 5, 6, and 7, respectively).

	(1) Grandfather Laws	(2) Limited-Purpose Laws	(3) Troubled-Institution Laws	(4) National Reciprocity Laws	(5) National Unrestricted	(6) Nationwide Phase-in	(7) Regional Reciprocity Laws
Alaska					×		
Arizona					×		
Connecticut							×
Delaware		×					
District of Columbia							×
Florida	×						×
Georgia							×
Idaho							×
Illinois	×		×				×
Indiana							×
Iowa	×						
Kentucky						×	
Maine					×		
Maryland		×					× *
Massachusetts							×
Michigan						×	
Nebraska	×	×					
Nevada		×				×	
New York				×			
North Carolina							×
Ohio			×			×	
Oregon			×				× †
Rhode Island						×	
South Carolina							×
South Dakota		×					
Tennessee							×
Utah			×				×
Virginia		×					×
Washington			×	×			
Subtotals (12/5/85)	4	6	5	2	3	5	15

* Although Maryland has a regional statute, it has enacted separate legislation that has allowed Citicorp and Chase to enter.

† Oregon's regional statute is nonreciprocal.

Source: Larry A. Frieder, "The Interstate Landscape: Trends and Projections," in Federal Reserve Bank of Chicago, Toward Nationwide Banking, a Guide to the Issues, 1986, p. 8.

bank holding companies with extensive nationwide operations. In addition, the leaders of many states and cities want to attract the best banks from the United States and, in many cases, from around the world.

NONBANK BANKS

The story of nonbank banks is a continuation of the breakdown of the limitations on interstate banking. Even more than did the story of the growth of interstate branching, it turned into a legal seesaw between regulators trying to retain their control of depository institutions, state officials wanting to increase the banking facilities in their states, and managers of firms wanting to establish nonbank banks. Congress was caught in the intersection of competing interests regarding the rather esoteric subject of nonbank banks. This subject was not of much, if any, concern to their constituents; rather, it was a struggle of special interests. This left the judicial system to referee the contest until Congress acted.

For nearly thirty years, bank holding companies have had nonbank subsidiaries in states other than the state of their main office. In addition, for a number of years, a few firms that were not in the banking business have offered deposit services. For example, Control Data, Dreyfus, Prudential Insurance, and Parker Pen Company purchased banks and then sold the lending business but retained the deposit business. These firms' deposit operations are called **nonbank banks**. The Bank Holding Company Act defines a bank as a firm that takes in deposits and makes commercial loans. Firms that offer only one of these services—such as taking in deposits—are not legally classified as banks.

Nonbank banks have even been able to obtain regular federal bank charters, and if they do, they also are required to have federal deposit insurance (FDIC) insurance. This insurance is a great asset for depository institutions and makes, to depositors, these nonbank banks indistinguishable from regular national banks. The first nonbank bank was given a federal bank charter in 1980, when the federal office that grants bank charters, the Comptroller of the Currency, allowed Gulf & Western Industries to acquire Fidelity National Bank of Concord, California. The Comptroller approved a few nonbank banks over the next three years. When Dimension Financial Corp. filed in 1983 with the Comptroller of the Currency for new charters for 31 nonbank banks in 25 states, questions were raised about the interstate implications for the entire banking system. The Comptroller of the Currency then announced a moratorium on the issuance of charters to nonbank banks.

Nonbank banking firms were specifically authorized for bank holding companies by the Bank Holding Company Act as amended in 1970 under Section 4(c)8. Subsidiaries of bank holding companies operating under this law are called *4(c)8 subsidiaries*. In addition to those bank holding companies whose principal business is that of a depository institution, some bank holding companies owning nonbank banks are not primarily in the banking business.

The Federal Reserve tried to stop these firms that were not primarily in the banking business from operating nonbank banks. At the end of 1982, Paul Volcker, chairman of the Board of Governors of the Federal Reserve, said he would ask Congress to close a loophole in the law that allows nonbank businesses to get into the banking business in this manner. The following excerpt is from the Federal Reserve's reluctant approval for the Comptroller's charter for a nonbank subsidiary in Florida. It indicates the Federal Reserve's desire to introduce more regulation and to limit or end deregulation. It seems likely that Congress will eventually close the nonbank loophole in the Bank Holding Company Law for firms not in the banking business.

> If the nonbank concept, particularly as expanded by the interpretation of demand deposits adopted by the Tenth Circuit, becomes broadly generalized, a bank holding company, or commercial or industrial company, through exploitation of an unintended loophole, could operate "banks" that offer NOW accounts and make commercial loans in every state, thus defeating congressional policies on commingling of banking or commerce, conflicts of interest, concentration of resources, and excessive risk, or with respect to limitations on interstate banking. Congressional action thus is urgently needed to ensure that the policies of the Act are maintained.[4]

But Christine Pavel and Harvey Rosenblum came to a different conclusion:

> When attention began to focus on nonbank competitors—such as Sears, American Express, General Motors, Prudential, and Merrill Lynch—early in the 1980s, their new competitive thrusts seemed to represent a real and immediate danger to the banking industry. With the benefit of hindsight and the research discussed in this and our previous studies, we conclude those fears are unwarranted, although some nonbank firms have gained substantial market shares in some product lines and are increasing their presence at a very fast pace.[5]

Nonbank banks acquired before December 1982 (such as Boston Safe Deposit and Trust Co., owned by Shearson/American Express Company) were to be eligible to apply for a "hardship extension" from the new legislation sought by the Federal Reserve. Although the Federal Reserve failed to obtain legislation at that time, it later sought to expand the kinds of activities that would cause a firm to be considered a bank under Regulation Y.

In 1984 the Federal Reserve granted the right to the U.S. Trust Company of New York to convert its Florida trust company into a firm that accepted deposits but did not offer commercial loan services. This firm was a nonbank bank. Because Congress did not act, the Comptroller of the Currency revoked the moratorium on granting charters to nonbank banks.[6] Between 1984 and 1986, 300 nonbank bank applications for charters were filed with the Office of the Comptroller of the Currency. Then in May 1985, the Eleventh U.S. Circuit Court of Appeals overturned the U.S. Trust Company of New York decisions, thus leaving the legality of nonbank banks in limbo. Congress deliberated the issue in 1987.

The basic question is whether to allow firms that are not primarily in the banking business to open nonbank banks. This harks back to a principle established in the 1930s of separating firms selling brokerage services (buying financial assets such as stocks and bonds for customers) from banking firms. This principle was stated in the Glass–Steagall Act (the Banking Act of 1933). But in 1987 it appeared that even all the king's men could not put Humpty Dumpty together again. The wall between these different types of firms had already come tumbling down, because of two actions: (1) Bank holding companies were allowed to acquire brokerages, and (2) brokerage firms had begun to offer checking account services, as we will point out in Chapter 9.

COMPETITION FOR BANKING SERVICES

An analysis of how these changes in the 1980s have affected competition among firms supplying banking services should take into account the following:

1. The number of depository institutions fell, as high and rising interest rates in the early 1980s drove many toward insolvency and collapse.
2. The number of subsidiaries and branches of depository institutions increased, as some depository institutions were encouraged to acquire failing depository institutions in other states; many states passed interstate branching laws; and the number of nonbank subsidiaries operating across state lines rose.

Because of these changes, there will be fewer independent depository institutions nationally but more competitors in many local areas where local and state banking institutions will compete with out-of-state branches. There may eventually be fewer competitors in many local areas where there is competition or predatory pricing (in which some firms lower prices until the other firms go out of business). In judging these effects on competition, it is helpful to try to imagine the composition of the banking industry after it has settled down into a new equilibrium. It appears that there will indeed be fewer depository institutions, but with more branches and subsidiaries and with the broader powers for the thrifts that have already been legislated. The effects of this change, however, cannot easily be related to the historical record of the United States' banking system because the 1980s has been a new era of nationwide banking never before experienced. Other countries that have had nationwide banking for many years are therefore useful to examine.

Herbert Baer and Larry Mote analyzed the historical records of the banking industries in Canada, France, West Germany, Japan, and the United Kingdom, and they concluded:

The existence of nationwide banking does not fully explain the extremely high levels of concentration observed in some foreign countries. The explanation for high concentration appears to lie in regulations that limit the availability of new bank charters, restrict the ability of foreign banks to compete in the domestic market, and prevent thrifts from offering a broad array of banking services. Based on the German and British experiences, the removal of restrictions on branch banking would cause the five firm concentration ratio [the percentage of services offered by the top five firms] in the commercial segment of the market to settle somewhere between 25 and 50 percent. If thrift lending powers were broadened, commercial market concentration would probably be somewhere between 20 and 40 percent. The Canadian, German, and Japanese experience suggests that elimination of bank branching restrictions would cause concentration in retail banking [consumer deposits and consumer loans] to rise to somewhere between 20 percent and 30 percent.[7]

In other words, the experience of other countries shows that the high concentration ratios of some other countries have been due more to banking restrictions than to the presence of nationwide banking. But nationwide banking still permits a high level of competition with a number of competitors, as viewed from the interesting but limited vantage point of the percentage of business done by the top five firms.

Nationwide banking may also discourage the following practices that impair competition:

1. Several bank holding companies may acquire a large proportion of the banks in a locale or in a state.
2. In single-bank towns (or those with only a few banks), the small independent hometown banker may gain monopoly power through favors to friends rather than freely allocating services according to market prices.

Nationwide banking may bring about the following practices that impair competition:

1. The small profitable bank that offers specialized personal services that large banks cannot efficiently provide may disappear because large bank branches and/or subsidiaries will be able to undercut the small bank's prices (i.e., offer deposits that pay a higher interest and make loans at lower rates) until the smaller bank goes out of business.
2. The smaller number of banking concerns may be able to maintain more easily a uniform advertised prime rate, as discussed in Appendix A.
3. A few very large banking firms may acquire enough political power to influence banking legislation and regulation in their favor. That is, the frequently opposing views of small and large banks that have typified lobbying in the federal government may be eclipsed by the agendas of a few large banks.

The main benefit of nationwide banking—if the end result is not a sufficient reduction in the number of banking firms and the domination by a few firms (called *oligopoly*)—is likely to be the following:

> More banking services for consumers and businesses will be provided in many locales around the country where branches and subsidiaries of out-of-state banks are permitted.

Much of the argument of whether a few large banks with many branches and/or subsidiaries are more efficient than many small independent banks all rests on the question of whether larger banks can offer less expensive banking services. And this is a question about economies of scale.

ECONOMIES OF SCALE IN BANKING

The existence of many small banks has been attributed to the legal prohibitions that prevented bank deposit business across state lines, a prohibition that may now be circumvented. Will these small banks survive in competition with the large banks in the era when state walls are tumbling down? Some studies claim that there are economies of scale, and so the answer from these studies appears to be no.[8]

This view leads to the conclusion that larger banks are more profitable because they can provide more services at a smaller cost per unit than can smaller banks providing the same number of services. There is much more to say for this argument, but the supporting evidence is not clear. Many small banks offer specialized services, such as loans to agriculture, which are not handled by large banks. Furthermore, the evidence of economies of scale is weak, perhaps even flawed.[9]

A special issue of the *Economic Review* of the Federal Reserve Bank of Atlanta (November 1982) published the results of studies of economies of scale in banking.[10] The major conclusion was

> With remarkable consistency, the studies reported here suggest that large size does not seem to give a financial institution significant competitive advantage.[11]

What about the ability to buy a sophisticated computer system? Will not a large bank be better able to afford (i.e., find it profitable) to purchase the new technology, such as ATM networks?

Paul F. Metzker, who did one of the studies in the *Economic Review* issue just cited, replied:

> A large bank is likely to be heavily committed and heavily invested in a software/hardware system that becomes prematurely obsolete.[12]

If these studies are correct, why do bank holding companies continue to buy banks? There are several plausible reasons that both acquisitions by large bank holding companies continue and new small banks are opening. The 1980–1986 period was part of an adjustment period to different levels of government regulations, and the entire 1970s was part of an adjustment period to historically high and fluctuating interest rates and rates of inflation. There is considerable uncertainty as to what the nature of the banking industry will be after the dust settles. Small-bank entrepreneurs may think that they can take advantage of a new portfolio of assets, untied to past interest rates. That is, they see a good chance for future profits. Owners of large bank holding companies may think that economies of scale will develop with more acquisitions and, perhaps, that a larger size offers monopoly power and profits. In other words, uncertainty gives rise to differing expectations.

Another guess is that large holding companies and small banks can exist side by side with both offering slightly different services. But the nature of those services is not clear. One is tempted to say that small banks offer more personal services. However, branches and/or subsidiaries of large banks may also offer these personal services. But the larger organizations may fall short in the quality of these personal services. For example, in a small bank, customers may talk directly to the individuals who have major authority for running the bank. But in a branch or subsidiary of a large bank, employees' responses to customers' questions are likely to be less personal. Efficient and thorough training can program individuals with "personal" stock answers, but the customer may sometimes wish more than this veneer. For example, he or she may want to know whether a policy can be changed.

FEDERAL DEPOSIT INSURANCE CORPORATION

The FDIC, an independent federal agency (not operating under the aegis of another agency or department), was established by the Banking Act of 1933. The FDIC insurance on bank deposits, originally limited to a maximum of $2,400, was first issued on January 1, 1934. The maximum insurance was increased a number of times, reaching $100,000 per private depositor at each insured bank in 1980. All commercial and mutual savings banks that are members of the Federal Reserve System are required to carry FDIC insurance. Nonmember commercial banks and mutual savings banks may obtain FDIC insurance, but they must first satisfy the general requirements of the FDIC.

The premiums that banks must pay for FDIC insurance were set by statute at one twelfth of 1 percent of total "assessable deposits." The banks pay half this premium twice a year on their average assessable deposits in the preceding half-year. The assessable deposits are approximately equal to a bank's total deposits, plus uninvested trust funds and minus some deductions.

The FDIC was formed as a corporation, with its entire income consisting of assessments on insured banks. The corporation is authorized to use, but never has used, borrowing privileges of up to $3 billion from the U.S. Treasury.

The FDIC has powers to examine insured banks, to prescribe various rules and regulations, and, in some cases, to pass on mergers or consolidations. It has the power to subpoena any officer or employee or any books or records of insured banks that are relevant to its investigations. In addition, the Financial Institutions Regulatory Act of 1978 gives to financial institution supervisory agencies, such as the FDIC, other powers, such as civil money penalties, cease-and-desist orders, the power of removal and suspension of insiders (those who own a significant portion of the stock in the bank), and the power to approve or disapprove of foreign branches of state nonmember banks.

It is interesting that the Banking Act of 1933 also prohibited interest on demand deposits and ruled that the FDIC police this regulation for nonmember insured banks and enforce ceiling rates of interest on time and savings deposits. The legislation passed in 1980 to remove ceiling rates over a six-year period included the chairman of the FDIC on the five-member deregulation committee. The phase-out was completed in March 1986.

The most important results of the creation of the FDIC have been the virtual elimination of bank runs and the substantial reduction in the number of bank failures until the 1980s. Between 1934 and 1980, there was an average of only 12.3 insured bank failures per year. But this statistic gives a somewhat misleading picture, as bank failures tapered off from a high level in the 1930s. In the post–World War II period, from 1947 to 1980, there was an average of only 6.4 failures per year. Of the 568 banks that failed from 1934 to 1980, most (551) were small, with total assets under $100 million, except for 10 banks. The 2 largest banks that failed in the post–World War II period, with total assets over $1 billion, were United States National Bank of San Diego, California (failed October 18, 1973, with total assets of $1.3 billion), and the Franklin National Bank of New York City (failed October 8, 1974, with total assets of $3.7 billion).

The establishment of the Federal Reserve at the end of 1913 did not stop bank suspensions; they kept growing until 1934, when FDIC insurance first was issued. Indeed, the presumed function of the Federal Reserve as the lender of last resort may have caused some banks to reduce their reserves and other liquid assets below the level that ordinarily would have been considered prudent. The bankers thought the Federal Reserve stood ready to help them in time of bank runs, but in the period of the greatest number of banks runs, 1930–1933, the Federal Reserve failed to lend the banks much money. One third of the banks closed permanently during this period.

During the early 1980s also, the financial conditions of many commercial banks in the United States deteriorated. The main reasons seem to have been the following:

1. There were two recessions in the early 1980s, with the worst in 1982. Many firms had loans from commercial banks at rates of interest tied to the prime rate (floating-rate loans) when the prime rate rose above 20 percent. (The prime rate and floating-rate loans will be described later in this chapter.) Deteriorating financial conditions in many firms and the large number of

business bankruptcies were reflected in the financial conditions of many commercial banks—the primary lenders to small and medium-sized businesses—by an increase in "problem" loans, including those in default (or, as they are sometimes called, *nonperforming loans*).

2. Some of the assets in the commercial banks' portfolios turned out to be poor investments. These included many foreign loans, agricultural loans (a decline in the price of agricultural goods in the 1980s severely hurt U.S. farms), oil exploration loans (after the price of oil dropped from $30 to near $10 a barrel in the middle 1980s), and some real estate loans (during a period of excess supply of office buildings, largely in response to tax laws that were finally changed in 1986).

3. The deregulation of interest rates on deposits and automatic teller machines, ATMs (approximately 60,000 by 1986), made unprofitable many elaborate branches and/or subsidiaries of commercial banks. Such banks as the Bank of America with over a thousand branches (usually in expensive buildings with large staffs), which had been a convenient service for depositors during the five decades when money interest on checking deposits could not be paid, found many of their branches to be losing money in an age of ATMs and money interest payments that took the place of other services offered to depositors.

4. From the early 1930s until the 1980s, commercial banks were prohibited by law from paying money interest on checking accounts. Money interest on savings accounts had low ceiling limits, a sort of *cartel* arrangement (a pricing arrangement applicable to a number of firms) imposed by the government. It was efficient when interest rates rose and no other depository institutions offered checking account services. Many of the smaller depositors simply received no money interests for their deposits, and the services supplied by the commercial banks were not an adequate compensation. Although some experts have held that the prohibition on paying interest on checking deposits was largely circumvented by gifts and by discounts on loans, it is doubtful whether this prohibition was inexpensively and completely circumvented for nonbusiness depositors. When the deposit ceiling was removed (phased out from 1981 until 1986), enough depositors began shopping for higher rates in NOW accounts to compel the commercial banks to be more competitive in the interest they had to pay. No longer were deposits, an important input in the banking business, as inexpensive as they had been. The loss of a sometimes-valuable cartel arrangement and the need for new management skills probably imposed higher costs on many commercial banks.

These conditions caused financial problems for many commercial banks, and as a result, many failed.

No failure was as large as that of the Continental Illinois National Bank and Trust Company of Chicago, a commercial bank that had a good reputation and was considered to be on the way to becoming one of the largest commercial banks in the United States. But in May 1984 there was a run on the bank: depositors withdrew $9 billion in one week. Continental Illinois had been in trouble since the failure of Penn Square Bank, NA, in 1982, because Continental Illinois had extended loans to Penn Square, which had in turn relent the funds to energy-related businesses that defaulted. Continental Illinois reported $2.3 billion in problem loans in the first quarter of 1984.

Former FDIC Chairman William M. Isaac announced that all Continental Illinois depositors and general creditors would be fully protected, not just those covered by the $100,000 FDIC deposit insurance maximum. The bailout funds peaked at $13.7 billion on August 13, 1984. The rescue package included funds from fifteen of the largest banks in the United States. A thirty-day line of credit was set up for Continental Illinois by the largest U.S. banks, led by Lewis Preston, chairman of Morgan Guaranty in New York, and Irvine H. Sprague, a former FDIC director.[13] A $2-billion note for Continental Illinois, of which $1.5 billion was supposed to be from the large banks, was issued after the chairman of the Federal Reserve, Paul Volcker, visited Morgan Guaranty. During a banking crisis no bank management would enjoy having the chairman of the Federal Reserve stride through the front door, especially the conspicuous six-foot, seven-inch Volcker. Indeed, he was asked to use a side entrance of Morgan Guaranty to avoid being seen. Sprague claimed that what really happened is that the FDIC put up the original $2 billion note, and the banks later bought a quarter of it. Apparently the managements of the large banks were in close contact with the regulators that bailed out Continental Illinois.

The FDIC had handled 32 failures up to the Continental Illinois run in 1984, 48 in 1983, and 42 in 1982, all of which were administered in the customary way, with a guarantee of only the standard deposit insurance. However, when Continental—with $40 billion in assets—ran into trouble, it became apparent that the $100,000 deposit insurance would not be sufficient, as the larger institutional depositors and foreign depositors were withdrawing their accounts (by their refusal to buy new large certificates of deposits, CDs, to replace maturing ones) that were in excess of $100,000. Later, in May 1984, rumors circulated about similar troubles at large commercial banks in New York City, Texas, and California that were known to have large problem loans.

This full protection of all deposits was prompted by the regulators' desire to protect the banking system as a whole by not letting a big commercial bank fail and possibly causing runs on other commercial banks. But many experts disagreed with this stance, claiming that it would have been better to let Continental Illinois be treated in the same way as were the other failed commercial banks. The implied message from the FDIC's action at Continental Illinois was clearly the following:

> If a big commercial bank fails, it is likely that all deposits will be protected. But smaller commercial banks will receive only the customary $100,000-limit protection.

Thus the FDIC policy had the effect of encouraging depositors with deposits over $100,000 to use large commercial banks. This undesirable result of the FDIC's action could hurt small commercial banks and violate a principle of law and regulation that all must be treated equally. The reply to this kind of criticism is that the FDIC may have had no other choice at the time, given the nature of the deposit insurance system and its available resources. The FDIC's fund reserves were 1.2 percent of insured deposits in 1985. The FDIC thus may have felt constrained from announcing any plan for other commercial banks similar to the one for Continental Illinois, whose failure might have led to other commercial bank runs.

Attempts to find a "white knight," a healthy commercial bank that wanted to buy Continental Illinois, failed, and so the FDIC took over the administration of Continental Illinois. New managers were installed, and Continental Illinois National Bank and Trust Company of Chicago continued to operate as the fourteenth largest commercial bank in the United States (with $29 billion in assets, as shown in Table 7-2). The government, in effect, nationalized Continental Illinois National Bank and Trust Company of Chicago.

The number of failing commercial banks increased significantly in 1982 to 42, in 1983 to 48, and in 1984 to 79, as shown in Table 7-9. In 1985 the FDIC had 1,140 commercial banks on its problem list, and 120 commercial banks failed. In 1986 there were 138 bank failures and 1,484 banks on the problem list. Banks concentrating on agricultural loans were jolted by the poor financial condition of many American farms; indeed, 51 percent of the bank failures in 1985 were of agricultural banks.

Despite these problems, the FDIC's insurance fund grew from $16.5 billion to $17.9 billion from revenues in 1985. Over half of the FDIC's income comes from investments—primarily in U.S. Treasury debt instruments—and most of the rest comes from premiums.

The data in Table 7-9 on bank failures also include some savings banks that are insured by FDIC. The case of the Bowery Savings Bank in New York City is an example of an alternative to paying off depositors. In 1985 the FDIC paid $273 million so that a group of private depositors could buy the bank. A payoff by the FDIC would have cost it $620 million, and so the managers of the FDIC could say that they were saving money by their actions. There is a question here for students of money and banking about the objectives of government policy. Should private stockholders be subsidized if the FDIC can save money by doing so? It may well have been in the public interest—for the optimum allocation of resources—to pay the larger amount out of the FDIC fund, by paying off insured depositors, recouping some of the funds from the sale of the savings bank's assets, and closing the bank. That is, these actions may have been preferable to rewarding investors for buying an asset that would not yield the market rate of return. It is a principle of the optimum allocation of resources that society will benefit if funds are invested in assets that yield the highest rate of return. It is generally agreed among economists and a matter of public policy (with some prominent exceptions, such as a

TABLE 7-9   Total Number of Bank Suspensions in Selected Years, 1865–1986*

Year	Total Number of Suspensions	Total Number of Insured Bank Suspensions	Total Number of Noninsured Bank Suspensions
1865	6	.	6
1875	28	.	28
1885	46	.	46
1895	124	.	124
1905	80	.	80
1915	152	.	152
1925	618	Before	618
1926	976	FDIC	976
1927	669	Insurance	669
1928	499	.	499
1929	659	.	659
1930	1,352	.	1,252
1931	2,294	.	2,294
1932	1,456	.	1,456
1933	4,004	.	4,004
1934	61	9	52
1935	32	26	6
1936	72	69	3
1937	83	76	7
1938	80	73	7
1939	72	60	12
1940	48	43	5
1950	5	4	1
1960	2	1	1
1969	9	9	0
1975	14	13	1
1976	17	16	1
1977	6	6	0
1978	7	7	0
1979	10	10	0
1980	10	10	0
1981	10	10	0
1982	42	42	0
1983	48	48	0
1984	79	79	0
1985	120	120	0
1986	138	138	0

* These figures include mutual banks and commercial banks, both of which were insured by the FDIC. There were 1,807 noninsured and 14,150 insured banks in 1934.

Source: Historical Statistics of the United States: Colonial to 1957 (Washington, D.C.: U.S. Government Printing Office, 1960), pp. 633–637; FDIC, *1985 Annual Report*, p. 61.

guaranteed loan to Chrysler automotive manufacturers) that subsidies should not be given to failing businesses.

In 1986 the FDIC had acquired approximately $11 billion in assets of failed banks. Some of these assets were rather bizarre forms of collateral from the borrowers of failed banks who had defaulted, such as an Arkansas social club, 200 boxes of toilet lids, a bag of gold teeth, a live lion, and an 8-foot-tall, 200-pound electronic gorilla that swayed back and forth.[14]

Although after 1982 there was a record number of bank failures per year for any year since the 1930s, there were no widespread runs on federally insured commercial banks, even though as many as seven banks failed in one day (May 31, 1985). The FDIC insurance carried out the valuable function of keeping depositors' confidence in the safety of domestic deposits up to $100,000 in insured commercial banks in the United States. Still, a large question lurked in the background. What if one or more large banks failed and they were not fully guaranteed, as was Continental Illinois? Should the FDIC continue to protect depositors in large institutions but not depositors in small institutions?

Partly in response to these questions and to questions about making the healthier depository institutions pay the same deposit insurance rate as the ailing ones did, there were calls for a reform of deposit insurance.

PROPOSALS TO REFORM DEPOSIT INSURANCE AND RAISE CAPITAL REQUIREMENTS

When the FDIC deposit insurance began in 1935, there was a $5,000 limit that covered 35 percent of deposits in insured banks. In 1984 there was a $100,000 limit that covered 63 percent of the deposits. In the middle 1980s, many banks were in trouble or had failed, and so there were many proposals for insurance reform and for increasing the banks' capital requirements.

The central feature of most of these proposals was the establishment of a *risk-based premium system* rather than the flat one twelfth of assessable deposits in effect in 1987. The premiums for most private insurance are based on the probability of an insured event (the risk of a payoff) and the expected size of the payoff. There has been a wide range of academic opinion on the size and type of deposit insurance premiums. Some observers believe that the FDIC set the insurance premium below the market value so as to encourage banks to remain insured and under the insurance regulations. Others believe that the deposit insurance may have been overpriced.[15]

According to a principle of rewarding rather than penalizing those banks that are prudently managed, a risk-based premium is desirable. There are, however, many problems with such a system:

1. At present there are not enough trained personnel to rate adequately the portfolios of insured institutions. The regulators in the FDIC and the

FSLIC were not able to predict accurately many of the specific bank failures, including those resulting from gross negligence. A huge army of examiners would be required to go through the massive loan and investment portfolios of the depository institutions that want to be insured. And the end result would not be a uniform system of examination, as there are no precise standards for evaluating the risks of different types of loans.

2. The announcement of a low rating for a particular commercial bank and the requisite increase in its premiums could itself provoke a run on the bank, especially by those with uninsured deposits. Only nearly 100-percent deposit insurance could guarantee against this destabilizing effect.

3. Most observers cite externalities (or neighborhood effects) from deposit insurance. These are benefits that exceed the value of the insurance to the insured. For example, it pays each banker to have other banks insured because a run at other banks can precipitate a run at his or her bank. Thus there is an argument for subsidizing deposit insurance and not fully penalizing a bank with a risky portfolio. This leaves open the question of how the owners of a bank should be discouraged from making risky investments that they would not make if there were no such subsidy.

4. Finally, how would the risk classes be determined and phased in, given the diversity of insured depository institutions and their political power to change the rating system to benefit their portfolios and to hurt their competitors?

Partly because the proposals for risk-based deposit insurance pose a number of problems that have not been resolved, another approach has been used, the imposition of capital requirements, or the ratio of capital to total assets. In 1985 the Cabinet Council (the cabinet of the U.S. government plus other top officials, such as the chairman of the council of economic advisers) and the FDIC proposed higher capital requirements. In 1986 the Federal Reserve, working with other government bank regulators, proposed a risk-based capital requirement to supplement existing capital requirements.

Consider the principles behind the capital requirements:

Viewpoint of regulators: Imposing higher capital requirement, the ratio of capital to total assets, is a way to protect deposits by providing more discipline for banks in managing their portfolio.

Viewpoint from finance for unregulated firms: The objective of a business, consistent with the optimum allocation of resources in the economy, should be to maximize the firm's present value. This means that a corporate mangement should be guided by the desire to make the value of the firm's stock as high as possible. The value of the stock is held to be equal to the present value of all expected future profits. One action that frequently promotes this objective is trying to increase the value of assets relative to the invested capital, as given by the value of the stock. Therefore, a low capital-to-asset ratio can mean an efficiently run firm.

Add a subsidy in the form of subsidized deposit insurance: If the deposit insurance for commercial banks is subsidized (the premiums are less than would be charged under competitive conditions), it will encourage firms to try to hold more assets and/or to buy riskier assets that have a higher yield. But the imposition of increased capital requirements may not be the most efficient way to offset these effects of the subsidy, as we shall show.

First, consider what is meant by capital and what capital requirements have been used. The Federal Reserve counts as capital what it terms primary capital and secondary capital. Generally, **primary capital** is the value of common stock, perpetual preferred stock, surplus and undivided profits, and reserves held for capital services. **Secondary capital** is the value of limited-life preferred stock and some debt instruments such as unsecured long-term debt. In 1983, the minimum capital ratios for banks—even the largest banks that were not formerly subject to capital requirements—were set at 5 percent and in 1984 were raised to 5.5 percent. In 1985 the ratio of capital to total assets for all commercial banks was 7.49 percent, having steadily climbed from 1980, when it was 6.65 percent.

The Cabinet Council recommended a capital ratio of 8 to 10 percent (one third of which could be met by certain debt instruments), and the FDIC recommended an increase to 9 percent. An attempt to raise all this new capital would impose many problems for commercial banks. As of December 31, 1984, 8,101 banks (55 percent of all insured commercial banks, with 82 percent of the assets) were below the 9 percent level. Approximately $50 billion in additional capital would have been needed to bring these banks into compliance with such a requirement. Generally the value of bank stock has been declining since 1974, and in 1985 the market value of many bank stocks was near the banks' book value (their net worth). An attempt to sell more stock to raise capital may so dilute the ownership of stock that there may be large declines in its value, thereby reducing the capital-to-asset ratios. Another way to raise capital ratios would be to sell assets, thereby reducing the banks' size. How would the increased capital ratios affect the banks' failure rate? The evidence is mixed. There is some evidence that requiring a 9 percent capital ratio may lead to fewer bank failures and insurance fund losses. However, if the public loses confidence in a bank's ability to allow withdrawal of its deposits, a capital ratio of 9 percent will have little effect. In addition, this may mean a huge cost to the banking system for raising capital (which may be much more costly than raising premiums on deposit insurance) to achieve some perceived level of safety. Because the commercial banks are the primary lenders to small and medium-sized businesses, this cost would have widespread impacts and may not improve the failure rate in the banking over what it would have been without this stiff reregulation of the banking system.

After the General Accounting Office gave this information on the huge costs of raising capital requirements to the FDIC for review, before its publication in September 1986, the chairman of the FDIC, L. William Seidman, discarded the FDIC's suggestions for increased capital requirements, adding that increased capital requirements would have been needed only if the banking industry were suffering from "undercapitalization":

> With respect to capital requirements, the GAO report focuses on the implications of raising minimum standards to nine percent (the figure used as an example in an earlier FDIC capital proposal). After subsequent consideration of this proposal, however, we believe that industry standards should be increased if there is evidence of industry undercapitalization. Such evidence is lacking.[16]

This rejection of the previous proposal to raise capital requirements, which apparently was based on the perceived undercapitalization of the banks, illuminates the difficulty in putting much meaning into the term undercapitalization, as used here.

Four proposals for changing deposit insurance coverage have been suggested:

1. Scale back the deposit insurance's coverage. This was recommended in the FDIC's 1983 report to Congress. Some proposals would reduce the coverage to $50,000. Depositors with accounts over this amount would deposit at their own risk. One problem with this plan is that checking account money would not be safe, and it is the principal medium of exchange in the United States. Deposits therefore would be diversified, and other goods might be substituted—such as short-term Treasury instruments—for use as media of exchange. Remember that many retail stores, such as grocery stores in suburban shopping centers, can easily deposit more than $50,000 for a single day's receipts. Should the armored truck company that picks up the cash deposit these funds in many different banks, so as to take advantage of the safety of government insurance, the main reason for deposit insurance—to prevent bank runs—may be defeated.

2. Another strategy is to extend the deposit insurance's coverage, with some proposals suggesting 100-percent coverage while at the same time limiting to the very safest the assets that the banks could buy. This insurance coverage would stabilize the country's payments system and prevent bank runs. The asset requirement would inhibit innovations, put U.S. banks at some disadvantage compared with banks in countries with fewer restrictions, and cause a transfer of banking business to other countries that allowed banks to buy a broader range of assets.

3. A third proposal is to extend the insurance's coverage, possibly to even 100 percent, and let the banks diversify their assets. The banks' safety would be guided by government-imposed rules concerning allowable loans and investments and diversification activities. This would allow the banks to compete worldwide and might even result in a safe portfolio of assets for many banks. But the rules would be difficult to establish, as they would be based on an assessment of risk, which would differ among bank examiners

and agencies. Finally, there are not enough examiners to enforce the rules, as banks make millions of loans and investments each year.

4. The fourth proposal is to extend the insurance's coverage, possibly to even 100 percent, and to let the banks diversify but to close them as soon as they become insolvent (that is, their net worth becomes zero or less). If the insurance coverage is not near 100 percent, as was the case in 1987 with the $100,000 limit, a run could be started by large depositors, as happened at Continental Illinois National Bank and Trust Company of Chicago in May 1984. If the coverage had been near 100 percent, there would not have been a run in the first place.

Most of the proposals for risk-based premiums, changes in deposit insurance coverage, and changes in capital requirements carry with them extensive supervision authority for the regulators. They would, in large measure, end the 1980 period of deregulation and impose stiff new regulations on the insured depository institutions.

AN EXAMPLE OF A BANK FAILURE WITH SOME PERPLEXING QUESTIONS

When an insured bank fails to close, either voluntarily or by an order from a regulator, the FDIC steps in to repay the insured deposits. The FDIC often attempts to arrange a marriage of a failing bank with a healthy bank, keeping all the deposit claims intact. But sometimes a willing suitor cannot be found, and so the FDIC assumes the liquidated bank's assets and tries to sell them to cover as many claims against the bank as it can.

The FDIC can also form a new corporation to take over a failing bank if it perceives that there is a large volume of claims against the bank. It had done so only twice in its fifty-year history before Penn Square Bank, NA, of Oklahoma City was closed on Monday, July 5, 1982. For that bank, the FDIC formed the Deposit Insurance National Bank, and the new corporation assumed the $460 million of its deposits. At 9 A.M., one day after federal regulators closed Penn Square, the new corporation opened and began paying out the insured deposits in what was expected to be the largest payout in FDIC history.

Since at least 7:05 P.M., Monday, July 5, 1982, when C. T. Conover, Comptroller of the Currency, declared Penn Square Bank to be insolvent and named the FDIC to be receiver (the entity that takes over the bank), there had been concern about and investigations into the fourth largest bank failure in FDIC history up till then. Penn Square had about 80 percent of its portfolio in energy loans (such as oil and gas production) and had sold more than $2 billion in participations (by other lenders on loans that the originating bank does not fully finance) to several large lenders. (One of these lenders was Continental Illinois.) This practice is called **selling loans upstream** to bigger banks. It illustrates the interconnected nature of some banking business. Investigations were launched because of alleged improper banking practices and because the federal regulators appeared to be uncoordinated. Penn Square was able to borrow $20 million from the Kansas City Federal Reserve bank two business days before it closed. That amount was repaid, and an additional $5.7 million was lent on July 2. In the bank's last days, at least one large depositor was able to draw out a deposit of over $20 million, and the Federal Credit Union of Albuquerque, New Mexico, deposited an additional $700,000 (on July 1), making the uninsured part of its deposits (those above $100,000) equal to $900,000. The failing bank managed to garner deposits from as far away as the credit union for the U.S. House of Representatives (the Wright Patman credit union). There are some questions concerning the federal regulators:

1. Will the Federal Reserve know about a bank's expected demise even if other regulators have this information? The Federal Institutions Examination Council was set up in 1978 precisely to coordinate and dispense information among federal regulators. If the Federal Reserve has information of an expected bank closing, should it lend such a bank additional funds to keep it open a little longer?
2. Should the Federal Reserve temporarily keep open a failing bank? It may be possible for large depositors to pull out their uninsured deposits, especially if they get some hint, possibly from inside information. And it may be possible for large depositors who are unaware of the situation to deposit large uninsured amounts. All this could be done in the "grace period" afforded by the Federal Reserve's loans.
3. Do you think it would be a good idea to streamline federal bank regulations by combining all regulatory functions under one regulatory agency? This suggestion has been made frequently.

BANK CREDIT CARDS

Bank credit cards were first issued in the United States in 1952 by the Franklin National Bank of New York.[17] They have characteristics similar to those of the nonbank credit cards of Diners Club, first issued in 1950, and American Express Company and Hilton Credit Corporation, which began issuing credit cards in 1958. Both bank and nonbank credit cards allow card holders to purchase goods and services and to obtain loans with preauthorized credit from specified retailers. The credit card company repays the merchant the amount charged minus a discount. The discounts are typically from 2 to 5 percent. In addition, a bank that issues a nationwide bank card, Visa or MasterCard, pays an assessment to the credit card corporation. For example, MasterCard International, Inc., announced in 1986 that beginning in 1987:

MasterCard members worldwide will pay the association 95 cents for each $1,000 of MasterCard sales volume instead of the current $1.20 for each $1,000 of volume.

The assessment fees cover about 80 percent of MasterCard's budget, so about $135 million of the organization's $169 million annual budget comes from these levies.[18]

Bank credit card interest charges on unpaid balances were a matter of controversy in the middle 1980s because they had not fallen after 1981 with other rates, as shown in Figure 7-1. In 1985 Congressman Mario Biaggi of New York introduced a usury bill in the House of Representatives that would have limited credit card interest to five percentage points above the 90-day commercial paper interest rate (discussed in Chapter 12). At that time, approximately half the states had usury laws on credit card interest. Some were as high as 22 percent, and New Jersey had a 30-percent ceiling. Connecticut, Arkansas, Washington, and Texas enacted a ceiling of 15 percent.

FIGURE 7-1   Interest Rates Charged on Credit Card Balances and Other Interest Rates

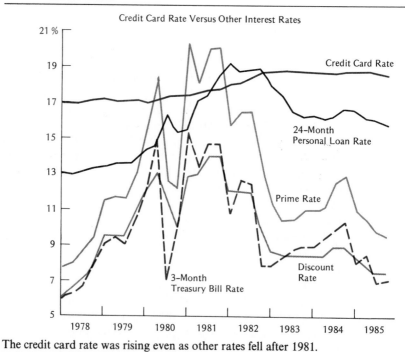

Credit Card Rate Versus Other Interest Rates

The credit card rate was rising even as other rates fell after 1981.

Source: Anthony W. Cyrnak, "Credit Card Controversy," Federal Reserve Bank of San Francisco, *Weekly Letter*, December 27, 1986, p. 3.

From 1982 to 1986, credit card debt increased by 47 percent to approximately $122 billion, despite the high interest that many lenders charged on unpaid balances. Approximately 162 million U.S. residents carried credit cards in 1986, with an average of seven credit cards for each person. The average credit card balance in 1986 was estimated to be $1,650.00.[19]

The yield on loans for merchandise is substantial. Assume that the retailer pays a 5 percent discount on credit card purchases. If the retailer does not absorb the discount, the credit card holder will pay $100 in 25 days for $95 worth of merchandise. The actual loan is $95. The simple daily interest rate is $5/$95 divided by 25 days, or .2105 percent. The simple yearly interest rate is .2105 percent times 365 days, or 76.8 percent. If the card holder does not pay until the second billing period, the credit card lender will receive $5 plus one month's interest of, say, $1.50 on a $95 loan of 60 days' duration. This is a simple yearly interest rate of 41.6 percent. The interest rate will fall if the loan is for a longer period.

Small personal loans with short maturities were formally unprofitable for most banks. Although the preceding yields appear to be relatively high, costs associated with checking credit and bookkeeping formed a high percentage of those small loans. The computerized central bookkeeping techniques of credit card loans have allowed some banks to lend their money profitably for small loans. However, credit card operations have not been consistently profitable for many banks. In late 1979 and early 1980, when market interest rates rose above legal ceiling interest rates on consumer credit, credit card loans were especially unprofitable for banks.

A consumer with an unused line of credit on his or her credit card account may make retail purchases without presenting a demand deposit check or cash. **Unutilized credit card credit** is used instead. The line of unutilized credit available to card holders may be a good candidate for inclusion in the definition of money. These credit lines serve as a medium of exchange for the purchase of a wide variety of goods and services. Lines of unutilized credit card credit are similar to unutilized demand deposit overdraft facilities, which allow customers to issue checks for more money than they have on deposit. Overdrafts, which have long been used in Great Britain or Canada, are now widely used in the United States, often against bank credit card credit.

The range of transactions that may be included in computerized credit card transactions is large. Taxicabs, newspaper stands, vending machines, public transportation, street vendors, and highway toll stations, to name but a few places where cash is used, all could be outfitted with small machines that store information about purchases. These data sources could be linked into computer terminals at convenient locations or could be entered synchronously with the purchase through centralized communication networks. A centralized electronic funds transfer system could even instantaneously charge the purchases against the buyers' bank accounts and credit the funds to the sellers' bank accounts.

ASSETS, LIABILITIES, AND INCOME OF U.S. COMMERCIAL BANKS

Business loans (commercial and industrial) and loans for real estate comprised 37.9 percent of commercial bank assets in 1986, as shown in Table 7-10. Investments comprise 16.9 percent of assets, and the largest category of investments is U.S. government securities.

TABLE 7-10   Assets and Liabilities of U.S. Banks, April 1986 (billions of dollars)

Business loans (commercial and industrial) and loans for real estate comprised 37.9 percent of commercial bank assets. The principal liabilities are deposits. Checkable accounts include all kinds of deposits (including NOW accounts, which are technically classified as savings acocunts) on which checks can be drawn. Time deposits, the largest category of deposits, are issued for a given length of time and have the characteristics of a debt instrument. Residual is the name given to the Federal Reserve Accounts to a measure of net worth.

Assets	
Loans and securities	2,106.0
Investment securities	423.6
U.S. government securities	252.4
Other	171.2
Trading account assets	27.9
Total loans	1,654.5
Interbank loans	151.4
Other loans	1,503.1
Commercial and industrial	510.7
Real estate	442.1
Individual	295.7
Other	254.6
Total cash	211.1
Reserves with the Federal Reserve	25.6
Vault cash	22.3
Other	163.2
Other cash assets	196.8
Total assets and liabilities	2,513.9
Liabilities	
Deposits	1,789.4
Checkable accounts	540.3
Savings accounts	465.5
Time deposits	783.5
Borrowing	387.4
Other liabilities	177.6
"Residual" (assets and liabilities)	159.5

Source: Board of Governors of the Federal Reserve System, *Federal Reserve Bulletin*, July 1986, p. A18.

TABLE 7-11   U.S. Commercial Banks Consolidated Statement of Income, End of 1984 (billions of dollars)

The major source of income, 72.2 percent of revenue, is interest on loans. The fees and service charges, such as those applied to small accounts, are less than 10 percent of revenue. The major operating expense, 65.9 percent of operating expenses, is the interest paid on deposit and on borrowed funds.

Revenue	
Interest on loans	200
Interest on investments	50
Fees and service charges	27
Total revenue	277
Operating expenses	
Deposit insurance	1
Salaries, building, and other	73
Interest on deposits and borrowed funds	168
Loan loss provision	13
Total operating expenses	255
Net pretax income	221

Source: FDIC Consolidated Reports of Condition and Income, December 31, 1984, as reported by the GAO, *Deposit Insurance, Analysis of Reform Proposals*, September 30, 1986, vol. 2, p. 23.

The U.S. commercial banks' greatest liability (71 percent) is deposits. Accounts that can be accessed by check are 30 percent of deposits. Checkable accounts include all kinds of deposits (including NOW accounts, which are technically classified as savings accounts) on which checks can be drawn. (When the Monetary Control Act was written, these accounts were named *transactions accounts*, as they include regular checking accounts plus the new NOW accounts.) Time deposits, the largest category of deposits (43.8 percent), are issued for a given length of time and have the characteristics of a debt instrument.

The main source of income (72.2 percent of revenue) is the interest on loans, as shown in Table 7-11. The fees and service charges, such as those applied to small accounts, are less than 10 percent of revenue. The major operating expense (65.9 percent of operating expenses) is the interest paid on deposits and borrowed funds. Premiums for deposit insurance were only .4 percent of their operating expenses.

FOREIGN LOAN PROBLEMS

A crisis atmosphere developed in the early 1980s regarding loans by U.S. banks to poorer countries, sometimes collectively called the Third World. It appeared to many that there could be defaults and runs on many of these banks, which could cause the collapse of many large U.S. banks. Some observers date the beginning of this crisis as August 19, 1982, when Mexico's finance minister, Jesus S. Herzog, walked into Citibank in New York City to tell its management that he would announce to all bankers on the following day that Mexico could not repay its foreign loans.

Much of the non-oil-producing Third World suffered extreme financial problems when **OPEC (Organization of Petroleum Exporting Countries)** raised its oil prices during the 1970s. There were three huge shocks in the world economy from changes in the price of oil in the thirteen years up to 1986. The first two, in 1973 and 1979, were an increase in the oil price, and the third, in 1985 and 1986, was a fall in the oil price, as shown in Figure 7-2. Nominal oil prices tripled from 1973 to 1974 and then rose 30 percent in the next four years. A second round of price increases began in 1979, causing another threefold increase in the price of oil, from $13 a barrel in 1978 to $33 in 1982. These price increases hurt the oil-importing countries and benefited the oil producers.

FIGURE 7-2   Crude Oil Prices, 1973 to 1985

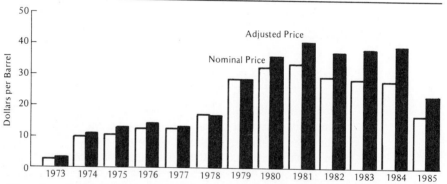

There have been three huge shocks in the world economy from changes in the price of oil in the thirteen years up to 1986. The first two, in 1973 and 1979, were caused by an increase in the oil price, and the third, in 1985 and 1986, was caused by a fall in the oil price. Nominal oil prices tripled from 1973 to 1974 and then rose 30 percent in the next four years. A second round of price increases began in 1979, causing another threefold increase in the price of oil, from $13 a barrel in 1978 to $33 in 1982. Oil prices started falling sharply in 1985 and 1986. In April 1986 the spot price of oil fell for a short time below $10 a barrel, one third of the $30 price that existed in November 1985.

Between 1978 and 1982, the adjusted price of oil, a *real price* computed by adjusting the nominal price by the exchange value of the dollar, rose by even more than did the nominal price. However, from 1982 to 1985, as the nominal price of oil fell, the real price was steady. The 16-percent rise in the price of oil was offset by a 15 percent decline in the value of the dollar. Then in 1986 the real price fell sharply.

Source: Ramon Moreno and Bharat Trehan, *Weekly Letter,* Federal Reserve Bank of San Francisco, June 6, 1986, p. 3, using Saudi Arabian benchmark prices; and Normal S. Fieleke, "The Decline of the Oil Cartel," *New England Economy Review,* Federal Reserve Bank of Boston, July–August 1986, p. 33.

Then oil prices began to fall. Although Mexico benefited from the higher price of oil, its economy was already in poor condition when it was struck a double blow, the recession of 1982 and declining oil prices. Oil prices dropped sharply in 1985 and 1986. In April 1986, the spot price of oil fell for a short time below $10 a barrel, one third of the $30 price that had prevailed for the previous six months.

The Third World countries had borrowed to support their programs for development and to pay their bills. Thus their external debt grew from $340 billion in 1978 to $640 billion in 1982, when they were hit by a worldwide recession and the accompanying decrease in demand for their exports. Their short-term debt—that calling for quick repayment—rose from 17.6 percent to 25 percent of their total debt in the same four-year period.

In 1982, U.S. banks had $100 billion in loans to these countries (including some countries such as Mexico that are oil producers). Although there was only a small growth in the number of these loans, they remained large. The total to non-OPEC developing countries (poor countries that are not members of the OPEC cartel) stood at $105 billion at the end of 1985 (see Table 7-12). The "exposure" of five large U.S. banks to loan problems in five

TABLE 7-12 U.S. Banks' Foreign Claims, December 31, 1985 (billions of dollars)

According to these estimates, U.S. banks had $369 billion in foreign claims, which amounted to 17.56 percent of their combined total assets (using the asset estimates in Table 7-10). These claims mostly were in the form of loans.

The G-10 countries are those that have adhered to the IMF's General Arrangements to borrow. These countries are Belgium, Canada, France, West Germany, Italy, Japan, the Netherlands, Sweden, Switzerland, the United Kingdom, and the United States.

Country Group	Amount
Non-OPEC developing countries	105.5
Argentina	8.9
Brazil	25.7
Mexico	23.9
South Korea	9.5
All others	37.5
OPEC countries	21.8
Eastern Europe	4.2
Smaller developed countries	30.5
G-10 countries	150.5
Offshore banking centers	67.2
Others and unallocated	17.2
Total	396.9

Source: Rodney H. Mills, "Foreign Lending by Banks: A Guide to International and United States Statistics," Board of Governors, *Federal Reserve Bulletin*, October 1986, p. 693. These particular estimates are made by the Board of Governors. This source also reports on other estimates, including the frequently used data from the Bank for International Settlements.

TABLE 7-13 Latin American Exposure of Five Large U.S. Banking Companies, December 31, 1985 (millions of dollars)

	Citicorp	Bank-America	Chase Manhattan	Manufacturers Hanover	Chemical New York
Argentina	1,400	a	920	1,400	402
Brazil	4,700	a	2,820	2,200	1,434
Chile	500	a	a	791	369
Mexico	2,800	2,709	1,680	1,800	1,471
Venezuela	1,200	1,450	1,250	1,100	714
Reported exposure	10,000	6,958	6,670	7,291	4,021
Reported nonperforming	1,575	510	485	199	137.2
Exposure as percentage of equity	130%	153%	175%	205%	143%

Note: Nonperforming loans is the term used for loans that have defaulted.
"a" indicates that the exposure is less than 1 percent of total loans and other investments.
Source: Gordon Matthews, "Big Banks' Latin American Exposures Decline Noticeably but Remain Large," *The American Banker*, May 25, 1986, pp. 1, 8.

Latin American countries is shown in Table 7-13. From 1983 to 1986 **nonperforming loans**—loans that had defaulted—dropped as a percentage of loans to these Latin American countries. But they nonetheless remained large debts, and another major recession that reduced their exports could worsen the situation.

Why did the banks lend money to these countries? One reason is that it seemed to be a profitable move. Another reason is that banks were encouraged to do so by the U.S. government and international organizations such as the International Monetary Fund (IMF). The United States is one of the principal contributors to the IMF (which represents more than 20 percent of quota resources), and its sister organization, the World Bank. The Reagan administration, however, sought to cut back the United States' contributions (more precisely, to reduce substantially its additional contributions).

The Banking Committee of the House of Representative has at times threatened to hold up appropriations for the IMF and the World Bank. In December 1982, Chairman Fernand St Germain of the Banking Committee sent letters to Federal Reserve Board Chairman Paul Volcker and then Secretary of the Treasury Donald Regan asking whether assistance to the IMF was not tantamount to a bank bailout and whether weak bank regulations had contributed to the current loan situation. Poland, Mexico, Argentina, Brazil, and Romania had already defaulted on their debts and were asking (and usually receiving) additional loans to enable them to make their interest payments. Poland even listed $3 billion of its 1983 debts, which it would not repay, as a saving in its current budget. Was the U.S. government bailing out countries so that it could repay the U.S. banks via its contributions to the IMF? That would certainly be a roundabout bailout procedure!

The U.S. banks were encouraged even further to lend to Third World countries in the "Baker plan," announced in October 1985 in Seoul, South Korea, at the joint annual meeting of the World Bank and the IMF. U.S. Treasury Secretary James Baker requested an agreement—which became known as the Baker plan—among commercial bankers in many countries. This plan asked banks to increase their lending to fifteen major debtor nations by $20 billion over the next three years, which would be a 2.5 percent annual increase in their lending. The plan also called for increased lending by government and international agencies, amounting to approximately $29 billion in additional funds for nations such as Brazil, Mexico, and the Philippines. Harold Meyerman, an executive vice-president of First Interstate Banking Corporation, said that banks would be "happy to look at the plan positively if there are some comfortable backstops."[20] U.S. Treasury officials continued to ask banks to lend more money to Third World nations. At the next annual meeting of the World Bank and the IMF, a substantial increase was reported in World Bank loan disbursements, from $2.7 billion in 1982 to $3.9 billion in 1985 to an expected $5.5 to $5.7 billion in 1986. But there were indications initially that the private banks were not eager to increase dramatically their loan exposure without guarantees and that the Baker plan was mostly a plan to increase the funds lent by governments through the international organizations.

Is the Baker plan just a short-term remedy, a loan of money to troubled debtor nations to cover their current interest payments, thereby pushing the underlying debt problem farther into the future? Will such action merely aggravate the problem?

Experience has shown that trying to change the system of support for Third World countries is difficult. That system includes making loans through international organizations such as the World Bank and the IMF and "encouraging" private banks to make loans (some consider this encouragement to imply guarantees of assistance to the lender if there is a default). The system also sometimes includes increasing the size of loans to cover the interest payments of debtor nations that otherwise may not have been paid. Some proponents of the current system mix the need to help solve the problems of the Third World with the issue of making sure that the bank loans are repaid, so as to prevent a general banking collapse. This is where the implied guarantee to private banks comes in: There are other ways of helping U.S. banks that find themselves in financial straits because of poor foreign loans. They may borrow from the Federal Reserve, a service of the Federal Reserve that will be described in Part IV. No U.S. bank need collapse if the Federal Reserve wants to lend it sufficient funds to continue to operate.

Although the banking crisis that many had predicted (including those who continually predict the doomsday for banking) did not materialize, it may have given support to the status quo and to the plans to help Third World countries, such as the Baker plan. Nonetheless, fundamental questions still remain:

1. Should the Federal Reserve bail out banks in trouble because of foreign loans? Are these loans a proper risk for the stockholders who invested in the banks?
2. Should the U.S. government give funds to the IMF and World Bank or directly to countries so that the loans from U.S. banks can be repaid? Should these funds be in the form of more loans, or should they be outright grants?
3. Are the IMF and other international organizations the best vehicles for dispensing aid? (Much of the aid goes to countries to which the United States would not directly give aid because of political considerations.)
4. Are plans such as the Baker plan helping the problem of poor bank loans, encouraging banks to worsen their foreign loan exposure positions, and/or placing additional responsibility on the U.S. government to bail out banks that follow Baker's advice?

The Reagan administration changed its policy between a meeting in Toronto in 1982 and its meeting with the **Group of Ten (G-10)** in January 1983. From an initial response of giving modest additional funds to the IMF, the administration later decided to increase the United States' quota by about 50 percent. Federal Reserve Chairman Volcker applauded the new appropriation and commented that for the first time, any one of the 146 members of the IMF could borrow funds, "but only when the borrower has agreed to a major adjustment program and when there is deemed to be a threat to the stability of the international monetary system."[21]

Volcker's criterion for lending—"the stability of the international monetary system"—can be interpreted in many ways. Language such as this and predictions of "banking collapse" can lead to many short-term solutions such as increasing loans to help debtor nations pay the interest on their outstanding loans. This may be a desirable action, as the Third World may be able to improve its export position and be better able to pay off its debts. But given the state of forecasting and the immense problems faced by the Third World— including its rapidly increasing populations and in some cases, severe food problems—such predictions must be made cautiously. Would it be better to allow investors in banks to operate without any implied government guarantees for high-risk foreign loans? Should poorer countries be helped by direct grants from wealthier countries or by direct lending to private concerns in the Third World rather than by funds funneled through governments? Although the banking crisis over private bank loans to Third World countries temporarily receded in the middle 1980s, it has not been resolved, and fundamental questions are not being publicly discussed by government officials. In 1987 Brazil defaulted on its foreign loan payments. A number of large New York City banks reported significant declines in earnings as they placed their Brazilian loans on a nonperforming status.

APPENDIX A: THE PRIME RATE

Commercial banks have a range of rates for loans to borrowers, ostensibly hinged to their prime rate. The **prime rate** has been defined in money and banking books, in literature throughout the banking industry, and in the media as the lowest rate charged on short-term business loans. Sometimes that definition is stated as the rate charged to the most creditworthy business customers, presumably on the assumption that the most creditworthy business customers would receive the lowest rate. A question asked by many borrowers after a report was published by Congress in April 1981 was, "Is the advertised prime rate of banks their lowest short-term business lending rate?" The first part of that report is presented in Exhibit 7-2. It was submitted as a staff report by Fernand St Germain, chairman of the Committee on Banking, Finance, and Urban Affairs of the House of Representatives.

This report was used subsequently in connection with a number of legal proceedings concerning the prime rate. The *Wall Street Journal* changed its definition of the prime rate after the report was published. You might want to look at the new definition in the *Journal*'s box listing interest rates, which is printed daily.

The Federal Reserve conducts quarterly surveys of bank lending practices. The surveys include approximately 20,000 loans at over 340 banks. Exhibit 7-3 presents one page from the forms sent to banks participating in this survey. Notice the definition of the prime rate that the banks are given. After reading this definition, you may wonder how banks can give discounts below the prime if the prime is defined as the "nominal rate charged on short-term loans to your most creditworthy customers" when it seems likely that the most creditworthy customers generally receive the lowest rate.

Nevertheless, these surveys indicate a sharp increase in the already extensive practice of below-advertised "prime rate" lending in 1980. The 48 large banks hit a high of 94 percent of their short-term business loans at rates below the "prime rate" in November 1984. See Table 7-14, which shows the percentage of gross loan extensions made at rates below the prime. The average spread between the rates charged on short-term business loans and the advertised prime in basis points has also been reported for some periods. (A basis point is one one hundredth of a percentage point.) In August 1980, the spread was 212 basis points, or 2.12 percentage points. The average advertised prime rate in August was approximately that given in the Federal Reserve's published records, 11.12 percent. The average loan rate actually charged on below-"prime" loans, according to the survey results, was, therefore, 11.12 percent minus 2.12 percent, or 9 percent. That is only an average discount. Loans were evidently extended at much lower rates. On December 19, 1980, the advertised prime rate hit a record 21.5 percent, and on May 22, 1981, it rose again near the record, to 20.5 percent. The average actual prime rate at the 48 largest banks probably never came near these heights. That is, the average actual lowest business lending rates that the 48 large banks generally used for short-

EXHIBIT 7-2   Staff Report of the Committee on Banking, Finance, and Urban Affairs

[COMMITTEE PRINT 97-2]

AN ANALYSIS OF PRIME RATE LENDING PRACTICES AT THE TEN LARGEST UNITED STATES BANKS

HOLD FOR RELEASE UNTIL

APR 3 0 A.M.

STAFF REPORT FOR THE

COMMITTEE ON BANKING, FINANCE AND URBAN AFFAIRS HOUSE OF REPRESENTATIVES

97th Congress, First Session

APRIL 1981

Printed for the use of the
Committee on Banking, Finance and Urban Affairs

This report has not been officially adopted by the Committee on Banking, Finance and Urban Affairs and may not therefore necessarily reflect the views of its members

U.S. GOVERNMENT PRINTING OFFICE

77-468 O   WASHINGTON : 1981

For sale by the Superintendent of Documents, U.S. Government Printing Office
Washington, D.C. 20402

EXHIBIT 7-2 *(continued)*

> "When I use a word," said Humpty Dumpty in a
> rather scornful tone, "it means just what I
> choose it to mean -- neither more nor less."
>
> -- <u>Alice In Wonderland</u>

INTRODUCTION

For decades, the phrase "prime rate" has been regarded as the very best interest rate available to the most creditworthy commercial customers of the nation's commercial banks.

So common has the phrase become that Webster's New Collegiate Dictionary has defined the prime rate as:

> "An interest rate at which preferred customers
> can borrow from banks and which is the <u>lowest</u>
> <u>commercial interest rate available at a</u>
> <u>particular time.</u>" (Emphasis added)

The news media, in particular, has consistently through the years referred to the prime rate as the lowest business borrowing rate, often trumpeting the changes in prime rates as major headline news.

The Wall Street Journal has made its designation of "prime rate" so formal that it includes it in a daily listing of "Money Rates" and defines the prime as, "The charge by large U.S. money center banks to their best business borrowers" -- a definition fully consistent with Webster's understanding of the term.

On May 7, 1980, the prime rate dropped from 18 percent to 17 percent. At that time, the New York Times informed its readers:

> "The prime rate is what banks charge their most
> creditworthy corporate customers. Rates for
> other business borrowers typically are scaled
> upward from the prime rate."

The Washington Post on the same date reported:

> "The prime rate is the interest banks charge
> their most creditworthy corporate customers."

And so it went in newspapers across the nation and on the evening network news shows.

77-468 O - 81 - 2

1

EXHIBIT 7-2 *(continued)*

The American public, including prospective borrowers, had every reason to believe that, indeed, the lowest possible interest rate that could be expected on a commercial loan at U. S. banks was 17 percent on May 8, 1980.

Months later -- on July 17, 1980 -- the Federal Reserve Board cast serious doubt on these news reports and assumptions, replying to a request from the Banking, Finance and Urban Affairs Committee with a survey which showed that 60.7 percent of commercial loans granted by large commercial banks in New York during May of 1980 were below the publicly announced prime rate.[1/] In fact, the Federal Reserve reported to the Committee that at these large New York City banks, the average discount from the prime rate was 4.26 percentage points.

In May of 1980, was the prime rate 17 percent as announced by the commercial banking industry, or was it less than 13 percent as determined by the average commercial rate revealed in the Federal Reserve study?

THE SURVEY

In an effort to clarify the growing confusion over the prime rate, Chairman Fernand J. St Germain of the Banking, Finance and Urban Affairs Committee wrote the chief executive officers of the nation's ten largest banks on February 12, 1981, asking a series of questions about the credibility gap between the announced "prime rate" and actual commercial lending practices. (Copy of Chairman St Germain's request to the banks in Appendix on Page 28). The staff analysis was conducted under the direction of Dr. Robert D. Auerbach, economist for the Committee.

---

1. The phrase "prime rate" took on a formal meaning in 1933 when the industry adopted a 1 1/2 percent rate for its most preferred customers, a move prompted, in part, by efforts to stabilize the industry and to dampen what some felt could be excessive efforts to compete for the limited number of truly "prime" customers remaining in the economy. Prior to 1933, many banks did post "prime rates" but these were not publicized and tended to vary across the nation.

For 17 years, the prime remained at the depression-era 1 1/2 percent. The prime continued to be an extremely stable rate through the 1950's and the first half of the 1960's. Since that time, the rate has been much more volatile with large and frequent changes. In the late 1970's and in the first part of the present decade, it has not been unusual for prime rate announcements to occur on a week by week basis.

2

EXHIBIT 7-2 *(continued)*

Surveyed were:

Bank of America NT S&A, San Francisco;
Citibank, N.A., New York City;
Chase Manhattan Bank, N.A., New York City;
Manufacturers Hanover Trust Company, New York City;
Morgan Guaranty Trust, New York City;

Chemical Bank, New York City;
Continental Illinois National Bank, Chicago;
Bankers Trust Company, New York City;
First National Bank of Chicago;
Security Pacific National Bank, Los Angeles.
(Ten largest banks listed in order of deposits as of December 31, 1980 as published in the American Banker on March 6, 1981.)

The results of the survey establish that the once clear barometer of interest rates has become a murky, ill-defined term that rarely reflects the lowest rates available to corporate customers.

Two of the banks, in fact, insisted that they had no "prime rate". Instead, they had what they described variously as a "base rate" or a "corporate base rate".

Obviously keeping Humpty Dumpty's declaration in mind, Morgan Guaranty Trust of New York -- the nation's fifth largest bank -- provided this enlightenment:

"The 'Bank's Prime Rate' shall mean the rate of interest publicly announced by the Bank in New York City from time to time as its Prime Rate."

Whatever the term and whatever the definition provided, all ten banks conceded that some business customers did, indeed, borrow at less than the announced prime.

MERELY SEMANTICS?

The prime rate is clearly more than an interesting news item for the business pages of the daily newspapers or an intriguing indicator of how imprecise the banking community can be in describing its lending practices.

Thousands of loan contracts, particularly those entered into by small and medium-sized businesses, are tied specifically to the prime rate. According to documents furnished the Committee by small business persons, many of these loan contracts carry interest

3

EXHIBIT 7-2 *(continued)*

rates several points above those charged the biggest and most
creditworthy customers by the big banks, moving up and down with
each prime rate announcement. But, if the prime is not the prime,
and if the prime customers are receiving a lower rate, just what is
the small business person's contract tied to at his or her local bank?

Even in those situations where the contract is not tied specifically
to the prime rate, the confusion over what is the "best" rate creates
havoc. Lacking the research capabilities of big corporations, the
small business person often uses the prime rate as the benchmark for
negotiations with lenders. The small business firm assumes it is doing
very nicely if it receives an interest rate close to what the news
media announces as the prime rate. But the firm is being sadly misled
if it believes that this means their rate is anywhere near the best rate
charged the big creditworthy customers.

In addition to skewing business judgments, the impreciseness of
what constitutes the best lending rate impacts throughout the
economy.

For the public at large, the highly visible prime rate is
an important economic indicator, and artificially high prime rate
announcements that are not truly reflective of interest rate
conditions add to inflationary expectations.

While the prime rate refers to commercial loans, there is an
indirect effect on other lending activity. Local mortgage lenders,
seeing the prime hanging at high levels, are less likely to modify
terms or to make new commitments. Consumer rates, while less
volatile than other rates, do not escape the trickle down from
what is perceived as the prime rate, thus affecting both cost and
availability.

4

EXHIBIT 7-3   Quarterly Survey of Bank Lending Practices

FR 2028A-s
OMB No. 7100-0061
Approval expires May 1985

PRIME RATE SUPPLEMENT TO
SURVEY OF TERMS OF BANK LENDING TO BUSINESS

for the week of _____ 19, ____ .

This report is authorized by law [12 U.S.C. §248(a) and 12 U.S.C. §248(i)]. Your voluntary cooperation in submitting this report is needed to make the results comprehensive, accurate, and timely.

Please report below the prime rate at your bank for the days covered by the survey. For purposes of this report, the prime rate is defined as the nominal rate charged on short-term loans to your most credit-worthy customers, without regard to size.

The rate should be entered to three decimal places. For example, a rate of 8 1/2 percent should be reported as 8.500.

Date (Month, day)	Prime Rate (Percent)
_____	_____ . _____
_____	_____ . _____
_____	_____ . _____
_____	_____ . _____
_____	_____ . _____

_____
Name and Address of Respondent Bank

_____

_____

_____
Person to be contacted concerning this report

_____
Telephone number

Please return one copy to _____

_____ by _____

TABLE 7-14   Percentage of Below-advertised Prime Rate Loan Amounts for Large and Other U.S. Banks

Since 1978, the percentage of below-advertised prime rate lending on short-term (a year or less) business loans from U.S. commercial banks generally grew. The figures for the large banks indicate that the dollar volume of loans at rates of interest at the advertised prime or higher generally fell to low levels, less than 10 percent in many periods.

Year	Percentage of Large Banks	Percentage of Other Banks
1978	16.4	11.2
1979	32.9	26.4
1980	47.1	18.9
1980 (Aug.)	64.7	16.4
1980 (Nov.)	20.3	16.2
1981 (Feb.)	71.5	23.2
1981 (May)	38.0	31.2
1981 (Aug.)	75.0	27.4
1981 (Nov.)	85.0	30.5
1982 (Feb.)	62.3	36.6
1982 (Aug.)	91.0	38.0
1984 (Feb.)	88.9	42.7
1984 (Nov.)	94.0	55.6

Source: The figures up to February 1982 are from "Survey of Terms of Bank Lending of the Board of Governors," Federal Reserve System, May 1982 release. The figures from August 1982 through the preliminary figures for the last observations in November 1984 are from Thomas F. Brady, "Changes in Loan Pricing and Business Lending at Commercial Banks," *Federal Reserve Bulletin*, January 1985, p. 3.

term loans were substantially lower. But the wrong number is in the record books; the nation was given worse interest rate information than what actually prevailed; and many borrowers who thought that their loans were tied to the lowest rate on short-term business loans were misled.

In the early 1970s, many businesses signed floating-rate contracts with banks. These contracts held that the business loan rate would be changed whenever the bank changed its prime rate. (Some banks used the term *base rate*, a rate generally equal to the advertised prime rate prevailing at other banks.) Their loan rates could be changed, without notice, to any level that the bank announced as the prime. Many borrowers thought that rate was tied to the lowest short-term business lending rate at the bank. They did not understand it to be a contract with no limits on remuneration. If the prime rate no longer means the lowest rate, then borrowers should be told to what their loan rate is tied. Floating rates make business loans very short term, as the loans can be changed at a moment's notice, even though they may be carried on the books as 90-day renewable loans. Thus the evidence in the survey about how many below-"prime" rate loans are for very short terms is somewhat misleading. Of course, there is one conclusion that *cannot* be drawn from this evidence: all banks advertise or notify their customers of a "prime rate" that does not reflect their lowest lending rate. That conclusion is not justified; there may be many banks that do not operate in this manner.

Why do the banks follow this practice rather than simply lower their prime? One possible answer from price theory is that the banks are practicing price discrimination, or charging different prices for the same commodity because of the banks' ability to separate classes of customers according to their demand curves (more precisely, according to their different elasticities of demand). Price discrimination is however, a form of monopolistic pricing that injures certain groups (those with less elastic demands). The two aforementioned groups of bank customers are those that rely solely on banks for credit and those that have alternatives. Alternative sources of loans include other domestic banks and banks and branches overseas that have rates that are tied to market rates. One such rate is the London interbank lending rate. It is called the London interbank offered rate or, more commonly, the LIBOR rate. Larger firms with individuals who can be assigned to shopping for good credit terms are either given competitive rates such as a loan rate close to LIBOR or they can take their business elsewhere.

Price discrimination can also occur because of incorrect information about prices in a market. For example, some smaller bank customers believe that the advertised prime rate is the lowest rate in the bank and notice that almost all banks post nearly the same—often exactly the same—advertised prime rate. They do not have the information to shop elsewhere. The information in this discussion would help them, but the banks themselves should supply accurate information about their lowest lending rate.

Some people believe that because *they* are familiar with the banks' prime rate lending practices, the managers of small and medium-sized businesses should also have this information. But even if the managers of small and medium-sized businesses were familiar with bank lending practices, they would not know the actual prime rate for the United States, because it is not published. That is, the banks could still practice price discrimination because many people would not know the exact discount from the advertised prime rate that the large banks are offering. And even if they did have this information, these lending practices lead to the following questions: What is the meaning of the floating-rate contract that ties the borrower's loan rate to the prime rate? How does one define the advertised prime rate in terms other than that it is a rate announced from time to time by a given bank?

One answer is that the advertised prime rate is a short-term money market rate. But although money market rates are determined in competitive markets, the advertised prime rate is not. Figure 7-3 charts the advertised prime rate, and Figure 7-4 shows the difference between the prime rate and the three-month business certificate of deposit, or CD, rate. This is a time deposit claim with a three-month maturity. The data in Figure 7-4 are from the yields from the sale in the competitive market of CDs that the commercial banks have already issued. The difference between the advertised prime rate and the three-month CD rate is shown to be highly variable, indicating that there is no simple close relationship between money market rates, such as the CD rate, and the advertised prime rate.

A new advertised prime rate is generally announced by a trend-setting bank, usually one of the large banks in New York City, and the other banks follow suit. In the 1970s, Citibank, then the second largest bank in the country, often played the role of the bellwether bank for advertised prime rate changes. Before 1979, Citibank's advertised prime was generally set equal to the average rate on prime commercial paper of the previous four weeks, plus an additional amount, which ranged from three fourths to one and a fourth percentage points. In 1979, Citibank substituted the four-week average rate on three-month business certificates of deposit and made the "spread" between that average and its advertised prime rate equal to one and a half percentage points. But this spread was not always adhered to because of other considerations, and in 1980 (when advertised prime rates peaked), the formula for setting the advertised prime was dropped.

FIGURE 7-3　The Advertised Prime Rate, 1951–1987

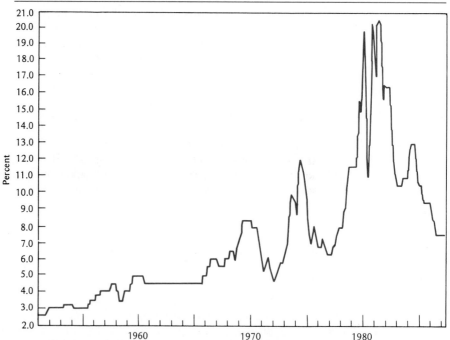

Compared with its later performance, the advertised prime rate was relatively low, with periods of stability up to 1967. This monthly series shows spikes in many months which caused interest rates tied to the prime, such as floating-rate loan rates for businesses, to suffer huge increases that were unlikely to have been anticipated.

Source: Cambridge Planning and Analytics, Inc., Boston.

FIGURE 7-4   The Difference Between the Three-Month Certificate of
Deposit Rate and the Advertised Prime Rate, 1970–1986

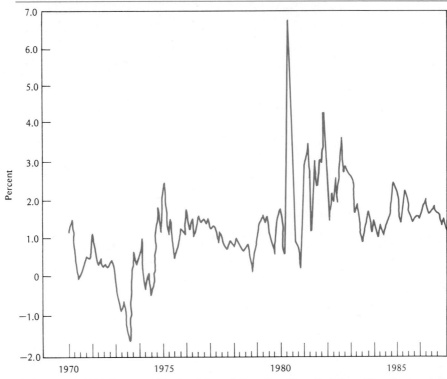

A three-month business certificate of deposit is a time deposit claim with a three-month
maturity. The data are from the sale of these instruments, which are closely related to
the cost of funds for larger commercial banks. The difference between the advertised
prime rate and the three-month CD rate is shown to be highly variable, indicating that
there is no simple close relationship between money market rates, such as the CD rate,
and the advertised prime rate.

Source: Cambridge Planning and Analytics, Inc., Boston.

APPENDIX B: HISTORY OF MONEY AND BANKING IN THE UNITED STATES TO 1863

This appendix relates the history of money and banking until the National
Banking Act of 1863. A continuation of this history is found in Part IV, in
which the formation of the Federal Reserve and the record to the end of
World War II are explained. We shall begin with some early theories of
money and banking as background for the U.S. history.

Early Theories

The theories of the nineteenth century concerning both private banks and government-owned banks were primarily related to the type and quantity of the medium of exchange that a country should provide. The theories centered on two questions: How should money be supplied? What are the determinants of its value? Those ideas were widely discussed in England and the United States by economists, politicians, and bankers. The debate about money and banking was heated, prolonged, and far from being a mere academic curiosity, as the banking laws and regulations in the United States were based in large part on these theories. Indeed, many of the ideas that developed from these theories persist in one form or another, often in a rather disguised version.

Bank of England Ceases Convertibility and Debate Ensues

The Bank of England, a central government bank founded in 1694, issued paper money, which it agreed to exchange, on request, for specie (precious metal such as gold). But in 1797, the Bank of England had insufficient reserves of specie to continue this convertibility.

Two opposing explanations of why the cessation of convertibility by the Bank of England was necessary may be generalized from the extensive debate that followed.[22] The **bullionist** or **hard-money view** blamed the Bank of England for issuing too much paper money. The **antibullionist view** was that overissue was impossible as long as money was lent to finance the legitimate needs of trade.

Views in the United States about paper money were influenced by the value of Continentals, the paper money issued in excessive quantities to finance the Revolution. Congress issued $250 million at face value, which fell in real value to one fortieth of this amount by 1780.

The opposing views—bullionist or hard money versus antibullionist—were used to interpret not only the actions of the central bank but also the actions of private banks that issued bank notes, a form of money, in excess of the value of their reserves of specie. Private banks, operating in an industry to which entry was limited, could earn monopoly profits from printing and issuing bank notes. Long-held prejudices against interest payments were used to depict banking loan operations as immoral practices. Those views were held especially among farmers and skilled workers who depended on private banking for financing. During the 1840s, these convictions were voiced through political movements in the United States, such as the Locofocos.

Locofocos and Hard-Money Views in the United States

The Locofocos were a faction of the Democratic party, taking their name from the popular name for the new friction matches.[23] In a meeting in New York's Tammany Hall in 1835, this faction lit candles with their locofocos matches after the gas lights in the room had been turned out to prevent the insurgents from nominating their own slate of candidates. Although the Locofocos (also called the Equal Rights party) were vehement in their denunciations of banks, some northern Locofocos thought that banks were not necessarily evil and that they could be corrected by state regulation. The southern Locofocos movement wished to abolish banks gradually and to impose strict regulations immediately.

The farmers, whose business usually required them to borrow funds, favored hard money and thought that banks were an institution of the devil. Presidents Thomas Jefferson and John Adams, although opponents on other issues, both were adamant in their denunciation of banks. Jefferson said that banks were "maniacal inventions of ruinous tendencies," and Adams asserted that "every bank of discount, every bank by which interest is paid or profit is made, is downright corruption."

Antibullionists, the Banking School, and the Currency School

The antibullionist view, that overissue of paper currency was impossible as long as the new money was used to finance the needs of trade, was incorporated into a theory of banking whose adherents were labeled as members of the **banking school**. (Some early banking school theorists also believed in the convertibility of paper money into gold—essentially a gold standard—which will be discussed in Part IX. They were in this respect bullionists, and their views on bank money logically followed.) The views of the banking school still surface in many contexts. For example, they were influential in the design of banking legislation, such as the important National Banking Act of 1863 (which launched the federal chartering of banks—national banks). And the Federal Reserve has frequently used these views to explain its policy decisions.

This central idea of the banking school is referred to as the **real bills, needs of trade**, or **commercial loan doctrine**. The real bills doctrine holds that short-term loans by banks for increased trade (e.g., to purchase inventories) cannot produce inflation because more goods, which require financing, are brought into the market by the additional bank-created money. (Bank-created money is discussed in Part IV.) The increase in goods is simultaneous with the increase in money, so that "there are not more dollars chasing the same (or fewer) goods." Inflation is, therefore, held to be an unlikely result. But this is a flawed doctrine because it neglects the multiplier effects that take place after the borrower spends the new money. That is, the additional money passes through many hands, creating more total spending than the nominal value of the new money issue.

The **currency school** opposed the views of those in the banking school. The currency school wished to strictly regulate currency, whereas the banking school saw no need for such regulations as long as convertibility was maintained.

The general distrust of paper money contained in the hard-money views that surfaced into significant political pressures, such as those from the Locofocos movement, also affected government regulation of banking. Initially, Arkansas, Texas, and Iowa forbade the formation of private banks. But the actions of President Andrew Jackson temporarily eliminated paper money as a means of paying debts to the government. In recent times, the call to restore gold as the universal international currency can be traced to the bullionist view.

Commercial Banks

The first commercial bank in the United States, the Bank of North America in Philadelphia, was established in 1782. Ten years later, there were only 14 banks, but by "1816 there were 260 banks with $82 million in capital and $200 million in bank notes, credit, and bank paper in one shape or other."[25] In the first 27 years of commercial banking (1782 to 1809), no bank failed. Bank charters were issued by special acts of various state legislatures until 1838. The Farmers Bank of Annapolis, Maryland, in 1804 was the first bank in the United States to pay interest on demand deposits.

The Medium of Exchange

Bank notes were a major form of currency used as a medium of exchange before the Civil War.[26] The circulating media of exchange in the United States up to the Civil War were a hodgepodge of varied forms of bank notes, demand deposit checks, paper money issued by local governments and business firms, and metal coins. Few casual observers today would judge this mess to be a workable form of money.

Bank notes were similar to modern travelers checks, except that bank notes did not require the bearer's signature for validation. Bank notes circulated until some bearer (often another bank) returned them to the issuing bank for conversion to specie. The quality of bank notes depended on the soundness of the issuing bank, whereas the bank deposit checks required additional information on the bearer's credit.

Without rapid, inexpensive communication and check-clearing systems, the bank deposit checks imposed higher transaction costs than did the bank notes. That is, bank notes were less expensive to use as a medium of exchange outside a local area because of the smaller transactions cost to the seller, just as modern travelers checks are less costly to use in foreign countries. Banks in large cities, such as New York City, issued relatively few bank notes before the Civil War.

In addition to bank notes and checks on demand deposits, gold and silver coins were circulated. Under the leadership of Alexander Hamilton, the first secretary of the Treasury, a bimetallic standard was adopted in 1792, with the original official valuation of 1 ounce of gold equal to 15 ounces of silver. Under bimetallism, the government attempted to fix the relative prices of gold and silver money, through a standing offer to buy or sell the gold and silver coins at a fixed relative price. Gold was undervalued relative to its world market price and did not circulate domestically as money. That is, at the price fixed by the government, gold was worth more in some use other than as money. The bimetallic standard was abandoned during the Civil War, and paper money in denominations as low as 3 cents was issued. A specie standard was not resumed until 1879.

Few coins were produced by the United States mint. U.S. half-dollars and Spanish silver dollars were the main larger denomination coins. Paper money issued by local governments and business firms also circulated.

Operating a Bank and Early Bank Failures and Runs

Often the individual state government would be an investor in a bank or would require a bank either to purchase a substantial quantity of state bonds or to finance particular state projects. Persons seeking to open a bank often had to declare a stated purpose for the bank. Robert Morris (financier of the American Revolution) said that his bank, the Bank of North America, would help supply the armies of the United States. Aaron Burr (vice-president, 1801 to 1805, who killed Alexander Hamilton in a duel) asked for a bank charter for the Manhattan Company to finance the water supply for New York. The early state banks, protected from competition by these severe entry restrictions, were very profitable, paying dividends of 9 to 12 percent a year.

Early bank charters, following the Bank of England's practice, limited a bank's liabilities to a multiple (usually 3, 4, or 5 to 1) of its equity. In 1837, the state of Virginia changed the limitation on liabilities into a ratio of *reserves* to liabilities. Thus began general government reserve requirements in the United States.

The first bank failure occurred in 1809. The Farmers Exchange Bank in Gloucester, Rhode Island, failed with "no deposits to speak of, but it had note liabilities of $800,000 and—when it was ripped up—according to a contemporary, it had only 'some odds of forty dollars in its vaults.'"[27]

When Washington, D.C., was occupied by the British in 1812, there were bank runs. Most banks experiencing bank runs did not close but simply refused to make specie payments: The public could continue to use the bank notes, but they could not be exchanged for commodity money. There were additional bank panics and suspensions of specie payments in 1837, 1857, and 1861.

The First and Second Banks of the United States

Alexander Hamilton, the secretary of the Treasury under George Washington (president, 1789–1797), proposed the establishment of a semipublic bank that would carry out many of the central banking functions needed by the new country. In his *Report on a National Bank* (1790), Hamilton described a central bank as a vehicle by which convertible paper money could be expanded to two or three times the value of the specie base. Hamilton showed great insight in understanding the operation of fractional reserve banking and in perceiving the additional confidence and convertibility of bank notes that would be brought about by a federally chartered bank.

The First (1791–1811) and Second (1816–1836) Banks of the United States were operated on a fractional reserve basis (reserves amounted to only a fraction of deposits) and were in most respects no different in their operations from other commercial banks, except for the large volume of business with their largest customer, the federal government. The First and Second Banks of the United States assumed some of the powers of the central bank. They affected the proportion of reserves held by other commercial banks through their policy of frequently presenting other commercial banks with their notes for convertibility. Banks therefore needed to carry ample reserves against the bank notes they issued, which might be returned as fast as a horse could travel back, should these notes be deposited in the First or Second Bank of the United States. However, the First and Second Banks of the United States were not charged with any particular responsibilities for increasing or decreasing the money supply; rather, they were managed primarily for the profitability of their investors. Some episodes in the colorful history of the Second Bank of the United States illustrate this point.

The Second Bank of the United States had 25 directors, 20 of whom were elected by the shareholders and 5 by the president of the United States. William Jones was elected as the first president by the stockholders. In an excellent and well-documented history, George Rogers Taylor commented on William Jones:

> That this man who during the war had shown notorious incompetence as the Secretary of the Navy and the Acting Secretary of the Treasury should have been chosen for this key position is difficult to understand. Apparently his contemporaries regarded him as a loyal political follower and a trustworthy individual. At any rate, he at once adopted a loose expansionist policy for the bank, seemingly with the purpose of maximizing profits for stockholders.[28]

A byproduct of this action may be viewed as a desirable monetary policy in terms of present-day goals, but Taylor does not attribute Jones's policies to these objectives.

The bank opened branches in the larger cities and rapidly bought interest-earning assets. Difficulties in the management of the bank soon developed. The Baltimore branch of the bank "fell into the hands of a ring of unscrupulous operators who easily robbed it of more than a million dollars before they were exposed and the branch was forced into the hands of a receiver.[29] Members of the bank's parent board of directors "speculated in the bank's own stock, and Jones himself accepted a present of $18,000 which his officers of the bank had 'earned' for him from this kind of speculation."[30]

In January 1819, President Jones was allowed to resign, and Langdon Cheves, a lawyer from South Carolina, became president. The expansionist policy was reversed, loans were called in, and a contraction followed in which there was a wave of bank and business failures, especially in the West and South. As soon as Cheve's management resulted in reduced dividends, stockholders sought different leadership.

Nicholas Biddle, the third and most famous president of the Second Bank, was elected following Cheves's resignation in the fall of 1823. Biddle slowly expanded the bank's operations emphasizing commercial loans of short maturity. The bank began to pay dividends of 7 percent per year and continued to do so until the bank lost its federal charter in 1836.

The fluctuations in the supply of money in the United States, induced by the policies of the three presidents of the Second Bank of the United States, appear to have been related in large part to the adoption of policies that would maximize the returns to either the bank's stockholders or, in the cases cited during Jones's administration, to some of the operators of the bank. The First Bank of the United States was also intended to earn most of its income by carrying on regular commercial banking business. It paid substantial dividends to its owners.[31]

In 1833 Andrew Jackson began to withdraw government money from the Second Bank of the United States, during a famous quarrel with Nicholas Biddle. President Jackson deposited the money in various state banks, called his "pet banks" by his critics, because they were supposedly selected on the basis of their management affiliations with the Democrats. Roger Taney, who was appointed the secretary of the Treasury in 1833 by President Andrew Jackson, succeeded two secretaries of the Treasury who had failed to distribute federal funds as ordered. Taney was unable to find enough well-managed banks that were run by party faithfuls and did in fact put government funds in banks with Whigs (another major political party that disappeared in the 1850s) on their boards of directors.

The Independent Treasury

Jackson's successor, Martin Van Buren, placed the government's money in government vaults, which were completely independent of the banking system. This vehicle for storing government funds was called the *Independent Treasury*. An Independent Treasury Act was passed in 1840, repeated in 1842, and then passed again in 1846. The Independent Treasury system included subtreasuries in various parts of the country, which served as vaults for government money. The government held no bank money under Van Buren's plan; it carried out all transactions in specie stored in Treasury offices. In 1863, the National Banking Act was passed, and government deposits at private banks were again authorized, but the Treasury continued to store some of its funds in its own vaults. The system was finally officially ended in 1920, after the establishment of the Federal Reserve System.

Free Banking and State Bank Regulations

In 1838, New York passed the first *free banking law*, which allowed charters to be issued without a special act of the legislature, upon compliance with the provisions of the law. Essentially, any *free bank* could be formed if the minimum capital requirements were met and the founders agreed to follow the procedures for issuing notes. By 1860, half the states had free banking laws.

Each free bank could obtain bank notes printed by the state government by purchasing special eligible bonds, which had to be given back to the state government as collateral for the note issue. Reserve requirements were imposed on the free banks but were not always effectively enforced.

The collateral requirements varied, but we may assume, for illustration, that an equal amount of eligible bonds, valued at par, was required to be exchanged for the state bank notes. If the eligible bonds sold at par, the state bank could buy $100 in eligible bonds and exchange them for $100 in state-issued notes. The free bank in this example would keep some of the $100 in notes as reserves and use the remainder to buy income-earning assets. At times, the eligible bonds sold substantially below par, enabling a bank to obtain state bank notes that were more valuable than the eligible bonds it bought.

Free banking worked well in New York, but many of the western states that tried to adopt this system after 1840 created banks that used poor banking practices. Bray Hammond described this experience, which has been called the period of *wildcat banking*:

> In Michigan the same law was enacted. . . . Within two years, more than 40 free banks had been established and had failed. Wisconsin and Indiana, carried away with the democratic ideal of free banking and the hope of making something out of nothing, followed Michigan's example. Speculators bought bonds, issued notes to pay for them, and eluded their debtors by taking to the woods among the wildcats. Notes were issued by banks with no known place of business and no regular office hours; and kegs of nails with coin lying on top were moved overnight from "bank" to "bank" to show up as cash reserves just ahead of the bank examiners.[32]

Not until 1837 did any state government enact clear regulations concerning reserve requirements. Rules in earlier bank charters had limited the ratio of a bank's liabilities to its capital, but the meanings of capital and liabilities were vague. Sometimes liabilities was taken to mean bank notes in circulation only and not total deposits. In 1837, Virginia required a cash reserve equal to 20 percent of a bank's note circulation. In 1842, Louisiana made the reserve requirement a percentage of bank notes as well as deposits. By the time of the passage of the National Banking Act in 1863, twelve states had initiated reserve requirements, nine of which were applied against bank notes only and three against deposits plus bank notes.

Louisiana adopted stringent banking laws in 1842, which contrasted with the less severe provisions of the free banking laws. During a recession all the Louisiana banks were suspended, and a group of stringent banking regulations, called the "forestall system," was instituted. Loans of deposits were limited to 90 days, with no renewals. Louisiana banks continued to make specie payments in the 1850s when many other banks suspended these payments. At the beginning of the Civil War, the Louisiana banks even remitted funds to their correspondent banks in New York.

In 1824, the Suffolk Bank of Boston agreed to accept bank notes from high-quality country banks at par (without an added charge) in return for compensating balances. The Suffolk Bank would return the bank notes of other banks for redemption in species. This "Suffolk plan" limited the bank note expansion of New England banks.

In New York, a "safety fund system," begun in 1829, created an insurance fund for bank notes and deposits. Deposit protection was discontinued after substantial failures in the 1840s. Participating banks paid the premiums.

The Suffolk plan in New England, the safety fund system in New York, and free banking are examples of the different types of banking practices that arose in the pre–Civil War period. Banks took many forms. A bank owned by the state of Indiana was the only bank in the state until free banking laws were passed. Interbank liability systems in Ohio, Indiana, and Iowa, operating under the supervision of boards of governors, required banks in the system to redeem the notes of any bank in the system that failed. Land banks were formed in the South by investors who pledged mortgages but invested no cash.

A Necessary Condition for the Circulation of the Hodgepodge Money Supply

The paper currency in the United States before the Civil War included an almost unbelievable hodgepodge of different sizes, shapes, and colors of notes drawn on banks, state governments, the federal government (which printed currency during the Revolutionary War and the War of 1812), private firms, and counterfeiters. The transaction costs of using such a medium of exchange were large, compared with the costs of using a more uniform currency issued by the government. There were regularly published guides on the discounts given on different bank notes. The expense of returning them to the issuer kept them circulating at a discount.

Given the transaction costs of this currency and the lack of understanding and general distrust of the paper currency and of those who "manipulated" it, why were all the different types of paper currency, as well as gold, actively circulated as media of exchange?

A necessary condition for different types of money with different market values but with fixed face values, to be simultaneously used as a medium of exchange, is the freedom to exchange them at their market value, rather than at their face value. **Gresham's law** asserts that "bad" money drives out "good" money. The "law" is true only if the exchange value between the different types of currency is fixed at a rate that will not clear the market. For example, assume that there are two types of currency: notes printed by a state government and XYZ Bank notes. Both notes are denominated in $1.00 units, but the state notes are thought to be of higher value than are the XYZ Bank notes. If they both can be exchanged for only $1.00 in goods and services, people will try to use the XYZ notes for exchange and will hoard as many of the state notes as they can. Gresham's law describes this phenomenon. If, however, the XYZ notes can be bought and sold at their market value, say, $.75, there will be no advantage in using them instead of the state notes. "Bad" money will not drive out "good" money if the exchange rates between different currencies are allowed to fluctuate. This was probably the case in the period before the Civil War, except for gold and silver, whose relative prices were fixed by the government.

GRESHAM'S LAW

Gresham's law is a principle named after Thomas Gresham (1519?–1579), an English merchant and financier who acquired a large private fortune and was the royal financial agent in Antwerp after 1551. After Queen Elizabeth became the Queen of England, he spent most of his time in London. Gresham observed that when two metals, such as gold and silver, are used as money, the cheaper metal becomes the dominant medium of exchange, and the more expensive metal is hoarded, sold abroad, or melted down and sold domestically. It has been shown that Gresham was not the first to state the principle, that it was stated long before his name was associated with it, and he did not formulate it.

The National Banking Act

The National Banking Act of 1863 (modified by a new law in 1864) established the conditions under which private commercial banks could obtain a federal charter and issue their own money, *national bank notes*. National banks were given the right to issue currency if they deposited special eligible bonds as collateral with the Treasury, in much the same manner as occurred under the free banking laws in the individual states. The issuance of state bank notes was eliminated by a prohibitive 10 percent tax on state bank note issue, which went into effect in 1866.

National bank notes were printed by the federal government for the issuing bank and were almost perfect substitutes for other U.S. currency, except that national bank notes could not be counted as reserves by national banks. The privilege of note issue was given to the national banks in order to provide an elastic currency in the tradition of the banking school's real bills doctrine.

Although Philip Cagan estimated that the national banks could have earned as high as a 31.2 percent return in 1879 and a 10.5 percent return in 1896 in their note issue, national bank notes were never fully expanded to their legal limit.[33] In 1935, when the privilege of issuing bank notes by national banks was terminated, there were in circulation $704 million worth of national bank notes, out of $5,567 million worth (12.6 percent) of currency.

STUDY QUESTIONS

1. What are the major similarities and differences among commercial banks, savings and loan associations, and credit unions?
2. What are the differences and similarities among a branch bank, a correspondent bank, and a subsidiary bank in a holding company?
3. What is the prime rate?
4. How do commercial banks earn most of their income?
5. What is the significance of nationwide automatic teller machine networks for branch banking and insterstate banking?
6. What are the remedies for the U.S. banks' foreign debts problems? Should country limits be put on these banks that would limit loans to a given amount authorized by the regulators? Can the capital market be segregated by country boundaries?
7. What are the advantages of organizing a bank holding company if the holding company owns only one bank?
8. Describe the era of deregulation in the 1980s. What do you think the future holds for the commercial banking system? Will it become more concentrated? Is there a place for small and large banks?
9. Are there significant economies of scale in banking in such inputs as deposits, so that the lowest costs per unit of service (somehow measured) will be found in the largest banks?
10. Given all the problem loans of large banks, should not the FDIC insurance premiums be based on the riskiness of a bank's portfolio?
11. Should the Federal Reserve or the FDIC help a failing bank keep going a little longer? What criteria should be used?
12. Under what conditions is a 76.8 percent (simple) interest connected with bank credit cards? Calculate the interest for yourself.
13. Is unutilized bank credit a good candidate to be included in the official concepts of money?
14. How is the real price of oil related to the financial condition of large banks in the United States?
15. If U.S. banks are owed $105.5 billion by non-OPEC developing countries (as of December 31, 1985), will the real income of the United States be higher if

    a. Banks with foreign loans in default lend additional funds to the borrowers to ensure future payments or

b. The U.S. government or an international organization that uses U.S. contributions send funds to the country where the borrower is located?

There is no simple answer. What are the important considerations? After stating them, give a plausible answer based on your assumptions.

16. What is a wildcat bank?
17. What is the National Banking Act, and what did it provide?
18. Write a brief description of the nature of the U.S. money supply and the banking system up to the Civil War. In what major way has the banking system changed since then?

GLOSSARY

Antibullionist view. The view that the overissue of paper money was impossible as long as it was lent to finance the legitimate needs of trade.

Bank holding company. A company that holds controlling stock in one or more commercial banks.

Banking school. A school of thought that included the belief that short-term loans by banks to purchase inventories and the like, so as to increase trade, and which also increased bank-created money, are not inflationary. This belief is called the *real bills doctrine.*

Bank notes. A form of currency created primarily by banks and similar to modern bank travelers checks except that no signature was required (they were good to the bearer). Used extensively before the Civil War.

Branch banks. Structures separate from a bank's main office. Branches mainly accept deposits but also may offer such services as extending loans.

Bullionist (or **hard-money**) **view.** The view of those who, following the cessation of convertibility of the Bank of England in 1797, advocated convertibility of money into gold bullion.

Correspondent bank. A bank that performs one or more services for another bank, the *respondent bank.*

Currency school. A view arising after the Bank of England suspended convertibility in 1797, that only currency should be strictly regulated.

De novo. (Latin) Anew. *De novo* branches or subsidiaries of banks are new branches or subsidiaries.

Grandfathering in existing structures. A law outlawing a practice such as ownership by a bank holding company of banks in more than one state that leaves intact any arrangements existing at some date prior to enactment (as when the law is proposed).

Gresham's law. A principle named after Thomas Gresham (1519?– 1579). Gresham observed that when two metals, such as gold and silver, are used as money, the cheaper metal becomes the dominant medium of exchange, and the more expensive metal is hoarded, sold abroad, or melted down and sold domestically. It is sometimes stated as the principle that bad money drives out good money. It depends on the condition that the monetary price for money is different from the price that would prevail in a free market.

Group of Ten (G-10). The following nations have met to discuss problems in the world and new IMF quotas: Belgium, Great Britain, West Germany, France, Italy, the Netherlands, the United States, Japan, Canada, and Sweden. Switzerland is an associate member. The Group of Ten also met in January 1982 to increase other resources available to the IMF under an arrangement known as the General Agreement to borrow (GAB). They wished to raise these resources from $7.1 billion to $19 billion.

National bank. A commercial bank operating under a federal charter from the Comptroller of the Currency.

Nonbank banks. Firms that either take in deposits or make commercial loans, but not both.

Nonperforming loans. Loans that have defaulted.

Organization of Petroleum Exporting Countries (OPEC). An organization founded in 1960. The 13 members of OPEC in 1986 were Algeria, Ecuador, Gabon, Indonesia, Iran, Iraq, Kuwait, Libya, Nigeria, Qatar, Saudi Arabia, United Arab Emirates, and Venezuela.

Primary capital. The value of common stock, perpetual preferred stock, surplus and undivided profits, and reserves held for capital services.

Prime rate. The lowest business lending rate on short-term (generally a year or less) loans at commercial banks. See Appendix A for the difference between the prime rate and the advertised prime rate.

Real bills doctrine, needs of trade doctrine, or **commercial loan doctrine.** See **Banking school.**

Secondary capital. The value of limited-life preferred stock and some debt instruments such as unsecured long-term debt.

Selling loans upstream. Refers to when a smaller bank originating a loan sells part of the loan to a larger bank (called a *loan participation*).

Sister bank subsidiaries. Banks in bank holding companies, not including parent or main bank.

State bank. A commercial bank operating under a state charter.

Statewide branching. Refers to laws of a state that permit the opening of branch banks throughout the state.

Subsidiary bank. A bank in a bank holding company that is not the main office.

Unit banking. Refers to laws of a state with strict regulations against branch banking. States classified as unit banking states may permit some form of branching, such as a branch within a given number of yards of the main office or in the same county or metropolitan area. The prohibitions may be largely academic. See "The Walls are Tumbling Down."

Unutilized credit card credit. The unused remainder of the line of credit on a credit card.

NOTES

1. Edge Act corporations are formed by banks that join together to conduct foreign business. One Edge Act corporation contains 17 banks. The authorization of these entities dates back to 1919 and an act sponsored by Senator Walter Edge. Edge Act corporations are not allowed to receive deposits from U.S. corporations or to make loans to them unless the loans or deposits are directly related to foreign business. They can buy equity in foreign businesses, an activity not allowed to domestic banks. The impetus for many Edge Act corporations in recent years has been their ability to open offices outside the home state of the parent bank or banks. In 1979 there were over 100 Edge Act corporations in operation, with assets of more than $12 billion.

2. Most of the information in this paragraph is from Paul Duke, Jr., "Bank Machine Makers Rethink Strategy," *The Wall Street Journal*, June 5, 1986, p. 6.

3. Federal Reserve Bank of Chicago, *Toward Nationwide Banking, a Guide to the Issues*, 1986, App. 2, p. 91. Another exception is the presence of foreign banks in more than one state. For example, it is common for foreign banks to have operations in both California and New York City.

4. From the March 23, 1984, order by the Board of Governors of the Federal Reserve that reluctantly gave the Comptroller of the Currency permission to give a charter to the subsidiary in Florida, as reprinted in Janice M. Moulton, "Nonbank Banks: Catalyst for Interstate Banking," *Business Review*, Federal Reserve Bank of Philadelphia, November–December 1985, p. 6.

5. Christine Pavel and Harvey Rosenblum, "Banks and Nonbanks: The Horse Race Continues," in *Economic Perspectives*, Chicago Federal Reserve, May–June 1985, p. 15.

6. Janice M. Moulton, "Nonbank Banks: Catalyst for Interstate Banking," p. 5.

7. Herbert Baier and Larry R. Mate, "The Effects of Nationwide Banking on Concentration: Evidence from Abroad," in Federal Reserve Bank of Chicago, *Toward Nationwide Banking, a Guide to the Issues*, 1986, p. 37.

8. See Robert Coates and David E. Updergraff, "The Relationship Between Organization Size and the Administrative Component of Banks," *Journal of Business of the University of Chicago*, October 1973, pp. 576–588.

9. See Robert Auerbach, "The Measurement of Economies of Scale: A Comment," *Journal of Business of the University of Chicago*, January 1976, pp. 60–61; see also the Coates–Updergraff rejoinder immediately following.

10. See "Economies of Scale in Banking," *Economic Review*, Federal Reserve Bank of Atlanta, November 1982, with studies by George J. Benston, Gerald A. Hanweck, David B. Humphrey, James E. McNulty, David D. Whitehead, Robert L. Schweitzer, B. Frank King, Jan Lujytes, and Paul F. Metzker.

11. Ibid., p. 4.

12. Paul F. Metzker, "Future Payments System Technology: Can Small Financial Institutions Compete?" ibid., p. 64.

13. Irvine H. Sprague, *Bail Out, an Insider's Account of Bank Failures and Rescues* (New York: Basic Books, 1986); Robert Trigaux, "Former Chairman Sprague's Candid Account of What the FDIC Does When It Rides to the Rescue," *The American Banker*, September 25, 1986.

14. See the *1985 Annual Report*, Federal Deposit Insurance Corporation, August 1, 1986; and later *Annual Reports* for data on the FDIC. Kit Frieden reported on some of the FDIC's assets in "Bank Failures Leave FDIC Holding Odd Bag," *Press Enterprise*, September 29, 1986, p. B-10.

15. See U.S. Government Accounting Office, *Deposit Insurance, Analysis of Reform Proposals*, September 30, 1986, 2 vols.; Stephen A. Buser, Andrew H. Cohen, Edward F. Kane, "Federal Deposit Insurance, Regulatory Policy, and Optimal Bank Capital," *Journal of Finance*, March 1984, pp. 51–60; Kenneth Scott and Thomas Mayer, "Risk and Regulation Banking: Some Proposals for Federal Deposit Insurance Reform," *Stanford Law Review*, May 1971, pp. 857–902; Fisher Black, Merton Miller, and Richard Posner, "An Approach to the Regulation of Bank Holding Companies," *Journal of Finance*, July 1978, pp. 379–412; and Alan J. Marcus and Israel Shaked, "The Valuation of FDIC Deposit Insurance Using Option Pricing Estimates," *Journal of Money, Credit and Banking*, November 1984, pp. 446–460. For a bibliography on this subject and some analysis of how to measure the value of deposit insurance, see James B. Thomson, "The Use of Market Information in Pricing Deposit Insurance," August 1986, which can be ordered as long as copies are available, from the Federal Reserve Bank of Cleveland, as Working Paper #8609. For a more recent analysis, see Huston J. McCullock, "Interest-Risk Sensitive Deposit Insurance Premia: Stable ACH Estimates," *Journal of Banking and Finance*, July 1981, pp. 103–115; and Paul M. Horvitz, "Why Risk-related Insurance Premiums Are No Answer," *The American Banker*, May 26, 1983, pp. 4, 6.

16. Letter from L. William Seidman, chairman of the FDIC, to William J. Anderson, director of the General Government Division, U.S. General Accounting Office, *Deposit Insurance, Analysis of Reform Proposals*, September 30, 1986, vol. 1, p. 165.

17. Dennis W. Richardson, *Electric Money: Evolution of an Electric Funds-Transfer System* (Cambridge, Mass.: MIT Press, 1970). The Franklin National Bank failed in 1974, but not because of this meritorious action in the history of bank credit cards.

18. Michael Weinstein, "MasterCard Announces 21% Levy Cut.," *The American Banker*, September 11, 1986, p. 1; and Monica Langley, "Proposed Federal Rules May Limit Interest on Credit Cards," *The Wall Street Journal*, September 27, 1985, p. 31.

19. These data are taken from industry estimates published in Marc Adams,

"Tax Break Loss Unlikely to Stem Credit Cards," *Washington Times*, September 2, 1986, pp. 1A, 8A.

20. Jonathan Friedland, "Baker Urges $20 Billion Boost in Bank Lending to 3rd World," *The American Banker*, October 9, 1985, p. 2.

21. Paul A. Volcker, Board of Governors of the Federal Reserve System, statement before the Committee on Banking, Finance, and Urban Affairs of the U.S. House of Representatives, February 2, 1983, p. 23.

22. The classic description of this subject is found in Jacob Viner, *Studies in the Theory of International Trade* (New York: Harper and Bros., 1937).

23. Arthur Schlesinger, Jr., "The Rise of the Locofocos," in *The Age of Jackson* (Boston: Little, Brown, 1945), Chap. 15.

24. Herman Kroos and Martin Blyn, *A History of Financial Intermediaries* (New York: Random House, 1971), p. 13.

25. The quotation is from Mathew Carey, *Essays on Political Economy* (Philadelphia, 1822), p. 231, found in the Remsen Papers in the manuscript collection, New York Public Library. It is reprinted in Kroos and Blyn, *A History of Financial Intermediaries*, p. 22. Much of the information in this section is taken from Kroos and Blyn's book, as well as the following studies: Kroos, with an introduction by Paul Samuelson, *Documentary History of Banking and Currency in the United States*, vol. 1 of 3 vols. (New York: McGraw-Hill, 1969); and Bray Hammond, "Banking Before the Civil War," in Deane Carson, ed., *Banking and Monetary Studies* (Homewood, Ill.: Richard D. Irwin, 1963) pp. 1–14.

26. Jack L. Rutner estimated that the values of deposits and specie both exceeded the value of bank notes by the early 1850s, in his "Money in the Ante-Bellum Economy," Ph.D. diss., University of Chicago, 1974. Edward J. Stevens's estimates show that the value of specie used as currency and coin was less than the value of bank notes plus bank deposits in every estimate from 1843 to 1859. Commodity money included copper cent and half-cent pieces, gold coins, and coins with some silver content. Domestic silver coinage was authorized by the original coinage law of 1792. Although the United States was formally on a bimetallic standard, the official price of silver was too low to be used profitably in coins after 1834, until the silver content was sufficiently lowered in 1853. See Stevens, "Composition of the Money Stock Prior to the Civil War," *Journal of Money, Credit and Banking*, vol. 2, February 1971, pp. 86–87. The 1834 law set a new official federal ratio of 16.002 ounces of silver to 1 ounce of gold (adjusted to 15.988/1 in 1837) in an attempt to rectify the undervaluation of gold. Silver became relatively more undervalued after the California gold discoveries and those in Australia in the 1850s. The U.S. mint increased the coinage of gold, alleviating the shortage of domestic coins. The premium on silver was small, and there were actually imports of silver from Mexico from 1834 to 1843. The Subsidiary Coinage Act of 1853 lowered the silver content of half-dollars, quarters, dimes, and half-dimes so that these coins were more valuable as money than in alternative uses, and the silver coinage in circulation increased.

27. Hammond, " Banking Before the Civil War," p. 5.
28. George Rogers Taylor, *The Transportation Revolution 1815–1860*, vol. 4 of *The Economic History of the United States* (New York: Harper & Row, 1951), p. 303.
29. Ibid., p. 303.
30. Ibid.
31. Ross N. Robertson, *History of the American Economy* (New York: Harcourt Brace, 1964), p. 158.
32. Hammond, " Banking Before the Civil War," p. 9.
33. Philip Cagan, *Determinants and Effects of Changes in the Stock of Money, 1875–1960*, Nationwide Bureau of Economic Research (New York: Columbia University Press, 1965), Table 13, p. 88; see also Cagan, "The First Fifty Years of the National Banking System—An Historical Appraisal," in *Banking and Monetary Studies* (Homewood, Ill.: Richard D. Irwin, 1963), pp. 15–42.

CHAPTER 8

ASSETS, LIABILITIES, AND MONEY CREATION OF DEPOSITORY INTERMEDIARIES

CHAPTER PREVIEW

Introduction. The important concepts of private banking, including the creation of money, are presented.

Deposits. The adjustments to obtain the amount of deposits held by the nonbank public are discussed. Then different types of deposits are described.

Reserves. Reserves are the assets of depository institutions that may be directly exchanged for a depositor's withdrawal claims.

Required Reserves. The wild and woolly mess of reserve requirements before 1981, state reserve requirements, and the dual banking system are described.

Required Reserves After 1980. The Monetary Control Act, part of the Depository Institutions Deregulation and Monetary Control Act of 1980, made the reserve requirements more uniform and, for the first time, applied them to all depository institutions operating in the United States. In 1982 the very small institutions were excused from these requirements.

Super-NOWs and MMDAs, Part of the Uneven Process of Deregulation. After a slow process of lifting ceiling rates with special newly created types of deposits, the Depository Institutions Deregulation Committee (DIDC) was ordered by Congress to drop all ceiling rates on two new types of deposits, resulting in the most massive flow of funds in U.S. history into these new accounts in the first part of 1983.

Float.   An explanation is given of the double counting of money because records are not simultaneously changed when a check is used to make a payment.

The Managed Liabilities.   There are four kinds of liabilities that depository institutions can rapidly buy or sell to adjust their reserve position.

The Federal Funds Market.   One important class of these managed liabilities is federal funds. Another closely related type is repurchase agreements.

Money Creation.   The chapter ends with a description of how the private depositories create money.

Appendix: How Much Money Can the Entire Banking System Create?   The discussion under "Money Creation" is restated in algebraic form.

INTRODUCTION

This chapter discusses the important concepts of private banking, including the creation of money. Countless times, individuals—from representatives in the U.S. Congress and members of the media to otherwise well-informed observers—have asked, "Could you tell me how the private banking system can create money? Is this a figment of economists' imaginations? All depository institutions do is make loans and buy investments, so how can you claim that they make money?" Even one of the country's leading newspapers, in an article presented to inform the policymakers and others in Washington, D.C., incorrectly explained that private banks cannot make much money in a recession because there would be fewer people to whom to lend money. (The writers of the article had omitted the banks' ability to buy investments.) All this could be solved by reading and learning the material contained in this chapter.

In this chapter, we present a general discussion of deposits followed by three sections on the nature of reserves and required reserves. These three discussions bring out the relationships between deposits and reserves. Then we review the "mess" that occurred during the 1980–1983 period of deregulation. This requires a knowledge of both the nature of deposits and the function of reserves, which have been described previously. The next three sections examine important topics associated with deposits and reserves. The first section, on float, presents an interesting problem associated with the double counting of both reserves and deposits. The next two sections describe the ways in which depository institutions manage their reserve positions. The final section shows how depository institutions use reserves literally to make more deposits, that is, to expand the money supply. The appendix restates this example in algebraic form and derives the limit to the expansion of the money supply.

DEPOSITS

Deposits are *claims* against depository institutions by depositors. Estimates of these deposits must be adjusted to fit into the common concepts of money. These concepts attempt to restrict the concept of money to the holdings of the *nonbank* public. Therefore, it is necessary to adjust gross deposits to the deposits recorded on the books of the nonbank public. The following three aggregates must be deducted to obtain the deposits on the books of the nonbank public.

1. Federal government deposits
2. Interbank deposits
3. Bank float

Federal government deposits in private commercial banks are substantial. They are mostly deposits of income tax withheld by employers, in special accounts of the U.S. Treasury called **tax and loan accounts**. In April 1986, for example, U.S. government deposits at commercial banks amounted to $3.5 billion in demand deposits and another $22.9 billion held in the form of special note balances from the Treasury.

Interbank deposits are the deposits of one depository institution in another. Each interbank deposit is entered as a liabilility for the receiving bank and an asset for the depositing bank. For the banking system as a whole, the net value of domestic interbank deposits is zero. Domestic interbank deposits are subtracted out to prevent double counting for the banking system as a whole.

The third deduction from gross demand deposits is bank float. The estimate of bank float is made by the Federal Reserve and is called the **Federal Reserve float**.

Commercial bank deposits, including demand deposits, are subject to immediate withdrawal during regular banking hours at the request of the depositor, with the exception of certain time deposits, discussed in this section. Demand deposits may be withdrawn in the form of currency or coin, or they may be transferred to another account at any commercial bank. Demand deposits at commercial banks can be transferred by bank check and are sometimes called *checking accounts*. No money interest is paid on demand deposits. Checkable NOW accounts, or share drafts at credit unions, which are available to consumers but not business depositors, pay interest. Technically, they are savings accounts that are accessible by a negotiable order of withdrawal.

Savings deposits at commercial banks and thrifts can usually be withdrawn as currency or coin, or as a cashier's check of the bank (a check drawn against the issuing bank); or they may be transferred into the depositor's demand account at the same bank, although technically the bank may refuse to withdraw or transfer a savings account for 30 days.

Time deposit accounts with specified maturities are exceptions to the convention that commercial bank deposits should be convertible to cash on demand. Before the date of maturity, the bank may refuse to exchange such a time deposit claim or may impose a penalty fee. The time deposit pays interest, giving it one of the characteristics of other private bonds.

Before 1976, a savings deposit at a commercial bank could be held only by a private individual or certain nonprofit organizations. But since 1976, corporations also may have savings accounts of $150,000 or less. Ownership of savings account claims is sometimes evidenced by passbooks, which may be presented during regular banking hours for immediate withdrawal of the depositor's funds, although the bank may legally delay payment for 30 days. But a bank would never, unless absolutely necessary, invoke such a waiting period, as it would seriously harm its deposit business.

Corporations and private firms, as well as some wealthy individuals, have, in an increasing volume since 1961, deposited their money in special time deposits, for which large-denomination marketable **certificates of deposit (CDs)** (over $100,000) with specified matures are given as evidence of their claims. CDs are negotiable, which means that they can be sold to others before their maturity date, and they pay market-determined rates of interest. The popularity of CDs was partly a result of the prohibition until 1976, and then the limitation, of savings accounts held by businesses.

Consumer or personal time deposits include CDs in denominations of less than $100,000. They are nonnegotiable; that is, they cannot be sold and must be returned to the issuing bank by the original purchaser. Until 1976, there were effective ceilings on interest payments. In 1978, consumer CDs, or **money market certificates**, were first authorized, with ceiling interest yields closer to market interest rates. Consumer CDs' interest payments have been allowed to vary without any restrictions since ceiling rate limitations were removed in 1986.

Also, in 1982, banks started making arrangements with money market funds to offer depositors the following service, called a money fund *sweep* service. That is, money is transferred automatically back and forth into a money market fund so as to maintain a given minimum balance in a NOW account.

RESERVES

In the broadest sense, reserves of depository intermediaries are the assets a bank holds that may be exchanged for depositors' withdrawal claims. It is conceivable that a depositor who had originally deposited money would take an asset other than money. For example, a bank could return a bond or any good not included in the concept of money in exchange for a depositor's claim.

The depositor generally, however, expects currency or coins, or a check that can be deposited in another bank account in return for his or her claim. These expectations are reinforced by government regulations for domestic bank deposits. The depositor may appear at the teller's window and request currency and coins, or he or she may sign an instrument such as a check or a negotiable order of withdrawal (NOW), which orders the bank to transfer funds to another bank. The bank must be ready with cash assets to meet demands for withdrawals that exceed deposits. Therefore, bankers store money on their premises (**vault cash**), and they also hold "clearing balances," either as part of their reserves at the Federal Reserve or as correspondent balances at other banks.

Depository intermediaries store funds in other depository intermediaries. Those interbank deposits disappear from the total reserves of the entire banking system when the reserves of all banks are aggregated according to conventional accounting practices. This is because the depository to which an interbank deposit is due has an asset exactly equal to the deposit liability of the depository from which the deposit is due. That is, the interbank deposit liabilities exactly cancel the interbank assets for the banking system as a whole.

There are close substitutes for reserves in a bank's portfolio. Other non-money assets that may be converted into reserves at little cost are excluded from the definition of reserves used here. For example, an overnight loan to another financial depository is an asset considered to be a very close substitute for money reserves.

REQUIRED RESERVES

Reserve requirements specify the type and amount of reserves that banks must hold in order to fulfill government regulations. The type of reserves that may be used to fulfill Federal Reserve requirements are called *legal reserves*. Legal reserves are equal to reserves on deposit at the Federal Reserve banks and all vault cash. (Correspondent balances of banks that are passed through, dollar for dollar, to the Federal Reserve also qualify as legal reserves under the Monetary Control Act of 1980.) The **required reserve ratio** is a fraction, with the required reserves in the numerator and the deposits in the denominator, or *RR/D*. Multiplying this ratio by 100, one obtains the percentage of required reserves.

The Federal Reserve in the past has imposed a set of reserve requirements on all its member banks, as indicated in Table 8-1. Notice especially the last footnote to this table, which details the supplementary and marginal reserve requirements imposed during 1978 and 1979, when President Jimmy Carter switched from an antirecession to an anti-inflation program, which included higher reserve requirements.

As of March 31, 1980, the reserve requirements of all of the more than 42,000 depository institutions in the United States were a wild and woolly mess. The nonmember state commercial banks were subject to different reserve requirements in every state. Unlike the Federal Reserve, which required that reserves be held as vault cash or deposits at the Federal Reserve, state regulations allowed reserve requirements to be satisfied by the holding of vault cash, by interbank deposits, and by the holding of securities of the U.S.

TABLE 8-1   Federal Reserve Member Bank Reserve Requirements Prior to March 31, 1980* (phased out by September 1, 1983)

The Federal Reserve requirements listed here were part of the wild and woolly mess of reserve requirements, which included fifty different reserve requirement arrangements for the nonmember banks in each of the fifty states.

Type of Deposit and Deposit Interval (millions of dollars)	Requirements in Effect February 29, 1980		Previous Requirements	
	Percent of Deposits	*Effective Date*	*Percent of Deposits*	*Effective Date*
Net demand†				
0–2	7	12/30/76	$7\frac{1}{2}$	2/13/75
2–10	$9\frac{1}{2}$	12/30/76	10	2/13/75
10–100	$11\frac{3}{4}$	12/30/76	12	2/13/75
100–400	$12\frac{3}{4}$	12/30/76	13	2/13/75
Over 400	$16\frac{1}{4}$	12/30/76	$16\frac{1}{2}$	2/13/75
Time and savings†,‡,§				
Savings	3	3/16/67	$3\frac{1}{2}$	3/2/67
Time‖				
0–5, by maturity				
30–179 days	3	3/16/67	$3\frac{1}{2}$	3/2/67
180 days to 4 years	$2\frac{1}{2}$	1/8/76	3	3/16/67
4 years or more	1	10/30/75	3	3/16/67
Over 5, by maturity				
30–179 days	6	12/12/74	5	10/1/70
180 days to 4 years	$2\frac{1}{2}$	1/8/76	3	12/12/74
4 years or more	1	10/30/75	3	12/12/74

	Legal Limits	
	Minimum	*Maximum*
Net demand		
Reserve city banks	10	22
Other banks	7	14
Time	3	10
Borrowings from foreign banks	0	22

* For changes in reserve requirements beginning in 1963, see the Board's *Annual Statistical Digest, 1971–1975*, and for prior changes, see the Board's *Annual Report* for 1976, Table 13. *Note:* Required reserves must be held in the form of deposits with Federal Reserve banks or vault cash.

† (a) Requirement schedules are graduated, and each deposit interval applies to that part of the deposits of each bank. Demand deposits subject to reserve requirements are gross demand deposits minus cash items in process of collection and demand balances due from domestic banks.

(b) The Federal Reserve Act specifies different ranges of requirements for reserve city banks and for other banks. Reserve cities are designated under a criterion adopted effective Nov. 9, 1972, by which a bank having net demand deposits of more than $400 million is considered to have the character of business of a reserve city bank. The presence of the head office of such a bank constitutes designation of that place as a reserve city. Cities in which there are Federal Reserve banks or branches are also reserve cities. Any banks having net demand deposits of $400 million or less are considered to have the character of business of banks outside reserve cities and are permitted to maintain reserves at ratios set for banks not in reserve cities. For details, see the Board's Regulation D.

(c) Effective Aug. 24, 1978, the Regulation M reserve requirements on net balances due from domestic banks to their government, as well as those of the states and local governments. In Alaska and California, gold served as a reserve. Louisiana specified that in addition to cash reserves of at least 20 percent, banks were required to hold up to 80 percent of demand deposits in bills of exchange or discounted paper maturing within one year, or U.S., state, and local securities. New York had one reserve requirement for New York City, Albany, and Buffalo and another reserve requirement for the rest of the state. Some states based reserve requirements on their populations. Some states allowed cash items collected in ten days to be counted to meet reserve requirements. The examples of state reserve requirements can be extended on and on until the reader receives the full view of the collage. The reader may name the composite either a "hodgepodge" or a "tribute to the dual banking system."

The **dual banking system** is the name applied to the concept of regulation that allows some of the banking system to be regulated by the states and some to be regulated by the federal government. Proponents of the dual banking system see the composite as a striking example of the kind of innovation and regulation needed in a free society. Opponents argue that it interferes with the control of the money supply and is, for that reason, inferior to a system of more uniform reserve requirements.

REQUIRED RESERVES AFTER 1980

To rationalize and simplify the reserve requirement structure and to make the required reserve ratios more uniform for all depository institutions, a new system of reserve requirements was signed into law (the Monetary Control

---

foreign branches and on deposits that foreign branches lend to U.S. residents were reduced to zero from 4 percent and 1 percent, respectively. The Regulation D reserve requirement on borrowings from unrelated banks abroad was also reduced to zero from 4 percent.

(d) Effective with the reserve computation period beginning Nov. 16, 1978, domestic deposits of Edge Act corporations are subject to the same reserve requirements as are deposits of member banks.

‡ Negotiable order of withdrawal accounts and time deposits such as Christmas and vacation club accounts are subject to the same requirements as savings deposits.

§ The average reserve requirement on savings and other time deposits must be at least 3 percent, the minimum specified by law.

‖ Effective Nov. 2, 1978, a supplementary reserve requirement of 2 percent was imposed on large time deposits of $100,000 or more, obligations of affiliates, and ineligible acceptances.

Effective with the reserve maintenance period beginning Oct. 25, 1979, a marginal reserve requirement of 8 percent was added to managed liabilities in excess of a base amount. Managed liabilities are defined as large time deposits, Eurodollar borrowings, repurchase agreements against U.S. government and federal agency securities, federal funds borrowings from nonmember institutions, and certain other obligations. In general, the base for the marginal reserve requirement is $100 million or the average amount of the managed liabilities held by a member bank, Edge Act corporation, or family of U.S. branches and agencies of a foreign bank for the two statement weeks ending Sept. 26, 1979.

Source: Federal Reserve Bulletin, February 1980, p. A9.

Act) on March 31, 1980. It was to be phased in over a four-year period for member banks and an eight-year period (ending September 3, 1987) for other depository institutions (except for nonmember commercial banks in Hawaii, which will not be completely phased in until January 7, 1993).

The new reserve requirements, shown in Table 8-2, apply only to checkable accounts and business certificates of deposit. All other deposits will have no reserve requirements. The reserve requirements (to be in full effect after the phase-in) on checkable deposits were initially 3 percent on the first $25 million in checkable deposits and 12 percent above that amount. This $25 million was the *breakpoint* for switching from 3 percent to 12 percent reserve requirements. Subsequently, the first $2 million in deposits were exempted from reserve requirements. The $2 million amount is the *minimum cutoff* for reserve requirements on checkable deposits. This was done to eliminate the burden on very small depository institutions.

The Federal Reserve was given authority to vary the reserve requirements on checkable deposits over the breakpoint, from 8 to 14 percent. The Federal Reserve is required to change the breakpoint each year (determined as of June 30 for implementation at the end of each year) according to the growth in checkable deposits. The adjustment every year is by 80 percent of the growth in total checkable deposits for the previous year. For example, if checkable deposits grow by 10 percent in a year, then the breakpoint will be increased by 80 percent of that amount, or by 8 percent. The Federal Reserve is also required to increase the minimum cutoff by 80 percent of the percentage change in total deposits, subject to reserve requirements (not just checkable deposits). In 1986 these computations led to a breakpoint of $31.7 million for checkable accounts and a $2.1 million minimum cutoff. These computations keep the percentage of deposits subject to reserve requirements somewhat (given the 80 percent changes) the same from year to year.

The regular reserve requirement on business CDs with maturities of less than two and a half years is 3 percent, with authority given to the Federal Reserve to vary this requirement between 0 and 9 percent.

In addition, the Federal Reserve may impose supplementary reserve requirements on all checkable accounts, provided that at least the amount of reserves that could be raised at the previously mentioned initial reserve requirements levels is being held.[1] Unlike the regular reserve requirements, which can be satisfied by holdings of vault cash or deposits at a Federal Reserve bank, the supplemental reserve requirements must be held at a Federal Reserve bank. The Federal Reserve may vary the supplemental reserve requirement from 0 to 4 percent. Unlike the regular reserve requirements, the Federal Reserve is authorized to pay interest to the depository intermediaries for reserves held under the supplementary reserve requirements.

The Board of Governors of the Federal Reserve may impose any reserve requirements in a national emergency situation, under the authorization of the Monetary Control Act of 1980. It must consult with the "appropriate committees of the House and the Senate" and promptly issue an explanatory

TABLE 8-2   Reserve Requirements on Domestic Deposits Authorized by the Depository Institutions Deregulation and Monetary Control Act of 1980 (As Amended) for All Depository Institutions in the United States (to be totally phased in by 1993)

These are the fully phased-in reserve requirements. Nonmembers and thrifts were fully phased up to the Federal Reserve requirements (that they never had before) on September 3, 1987. For member banks and nonmembers that once were members but jumped off the Federal Reserve ship after July 1, 1979, their reserve requirements were fully phased down by October 24, 1985. The exception is Hawaii, which gets a reprieve until 1993, as most of its banks became state-chartered nonmember banks when Hawaii became a state and its lobbyists were able to convince the Congress that a faster phase-in would be too costly to the banks and the economy in Hawaii.

	Initial Level	Legal Limits
1. Regular reserve requirement percentages with no interest payments satisfied by vault cash or deposits at a Federal Reserve bank*		
a. Checkable accounts†		
From $2.1 million to $31.7 million	3	No variation
Over $31.7 million	12	8 to 14
b. Nonpersonal time accounts of less than 1.5 years maturity‡	3	0 to 9
c. Eurocurrency liabilities	3	
2. Supplemental reserve requirements with interest paid on reserves satisfied by deposits at Federal Reserve banks only*,§		
a. Checkable accounts	0	0 to 4

* "Federal Reserve bank" means a regional or branch Federal Reserve bank, not a private member bank. However, a nonmember bank may meet reserve requirements by an interbank deposit at a member bank if the member bank passes on these deposits, dollar for dollar, to a Federal Reserve bank. These pass-through accounts can also be maintained at a Federal Home Loan Bank or the National Credit Union Administration Central Liquidity Facility.

† Checkable accounts are called *transactions accounts* in the legislation. The Board of Governors of the Federal Reserve was given discretion in determining which accounts are accessible by a check-type instrument. In 1981, these transactions accounts included demand deposit accounts, share-draft accounts, NOW accounts, ATS accounts, and telephone transfer accounts that are accessed more than three times a month. The $31.7 million cutoff and $2.1 million minimum (effective in 1986) will be changed each year by 80 percent of the change in checkable deposits of all depository institutions.

‡ These are business certificates of deposit. Individual accounts of less than 2.5 years' maturity that are transferable to checking accounts will also bear 3 percent reserves, if such accounts arise. The 2.5-year criterion became effective March 31, 1983. In addition, there was a 3 percent reserve requirement on all Eurocurrency liabilities, effective November 13, 1980.

§ The interest rate will be no higher than the average interest rate on the Federal Reserve's own portfolio of financial assets.

Source: Federal Reserve Bulletin, October 1983, p. A8.

report to the Congress. This emergency reserve requirement action may not be extended for more than 180 days without the vote of at least five of the seven members of the Board of Governors.

Reserve requirements were first introduced by the state of Virginia in 1837. However, until March 31, 1980, there had never been mandatory federal reserve requirements on depository institutions located in the states. Bank managers could decide whether or not they wanted to belong to the Federal Reserve System, which did impose reserve requirements. Even the management of a national bank, which must be a Federal Reserve member bank, could opt to change to a state charter and drop Federal Reserve membership and, with it, Federal Reserve requirements. Only national banks in Washington, D.C., or in the U.S. possessions had no such option, as state charters were not available to them. Those banks were required to belong to the Federal Reserve and thus had mandatory Federal Reserve requirements.

High interest rates made Federal Reserve requirements especially burdensome in the late 1970s. That is, the higher the market interest rate was, the higher also was the opportunity cost of interest forgone on sterile reserves. Member banks thus began jumping from the Federal Reserve ship, and a large exodus was predicted. For this reason, the historic legislation that was passed to remedy this problem, by imposing mandatory reserve requirements, was frequently called the Membership Bill. That is, it made the membership problem largely irrelevant by keeping membership voluntary, while imposing the same reserve requirement schedule on all nonmember depository institutions.

The process of deregulation accelerated in the 1980–1983 period as the DIDC began to remove ceiling interest rate regulations on the payment of interest on deposits.

SUPER-NOWs AND MMDAs, PART OF THE UNEVEN PROCESS OF DEREGULATION

The Depository Institutions Deregulation Committee was, until the very end of 1982, slow and uneven in removing ceiling rates on deposits, at which time the U.S. Congress stepped in with the Garn–St Germain Depository Institutions Act of 1982. Among other things, it authorized new types of deposits at depository institutions that would be competitive with money market funds.

Two new accounts were set up by the DIDC in compliance with the law:

1. A **money market deposit account (MMDA)**, established on December 14, 1982, requires a $2,500 minimum average monthly balance. (Depository institutions generally advertise a $2,500 minimum, which is perfectly legal, as the limitation established by law is a floor, not a ceiling.) There is no ceiling interest rate. No more than six preauthorized payments, of which no

more than three can be by check, are allowed. (A telephone transfer is classified as a preauthorized transfer.) But the depositor can come to the bank in person, or send in a request by mail, to withdraw funds an unlimited number of times. The distinctions drawn are supposed to make this new creation look more like a savings account than a checking account. For reserve requirement purposes, it is treated as a savings account.

2. **Super-NOWs**, established on January 5, 1983, also have an average $2,500 monthly minimum balance. And they also have no ceiling limitation on interest payments. They are different in that they allow unlimited checking privileges. For this reason, they are treated, for reserve requirement purposes, as checking accounts. They have higher reserve requirements than do MMDAs, and so depository institutions offer less interest on them than they do on MMDAs.

The horse race was on at full gallop with the money market funds. Depository institutions raised the interest on MMDAs above the rates paid on money market funds, which were tied to market rates. With money market funds paying a little over 8 percent at the beginning of 1983, depository institutions advertised rates on MMDAs of approximately 10 percent. With that spread and with the added features of MMDAs, of a guaranteed nominal amount (rather than a share of a portfolio that varies in value, as do the money market funds) and with federal insurance, MMDAs surged. Starting with $8.8 billion by mid-December 1982, they grew to over $200 billion by mid-January 1983, a month later. By March 1983, the new accounts created in mid-December 1982, including several other types (discussed next), had attracted over $300 billion.

The DIDC had sprung forward after the Garn–St Germain Act. With super-NOWs and MMDAs, it had removed ceiling rates from short-term deposits that maintained a $2,500 average minimum balance. In early 1983 it also took the ceiling rates off time deposits of three and a half years or more. It announced that in April 1983 the ceilings would come off time deposits of two and a half years or more and that those with maturities of from one and a half to two and a half years would be given "liberalized" ceilings. If you are confused by this intricate web of different types of deposits with different types of regulations, you are sharing the feelings of an informed depositor or a manager of a depository institution at the time. To further your experience of a deregulatory process that went forward by fits and starts, study Table 8-3 and read its lengthy footnotes.

Having studied Table 8-3, you are now ready to take on the important topics concerning reserves and deposits that managers of depository institutions deal with every day. First, there is the interesting problem of float. It not only complicates the planning of reserve and deposit positions in an individual depository institution; it also makes it more difficult for the central bank to manage the money supply. On a more positive note, you will also discover that some people are very fond of float because it increases their available funds.

TABLE 8-3 Time, Savings, and Repurchase Agreements at All Insured Commercial Banks and All Mutual Savings Banks, November 30, 1982, December 29, 1982, and January 26, 1983 (in millions of dollars, not seasonally adjusted)[1]

This table describes various types of time and savings accounts at insured commercial banks and mutual savings banks during the adjustment period at the end of 1982 and the beginning of 1983.

There were some anxious moments during the adjustment period. It looked to many as if the money supply could never again be defined or controlled. However, the rush into money market funds in 1978 and 1979 was probably just as startling to those who did not realize that a significant part of the population responds quite rationally to price changes, as they did again in the scramble to get funds into the new higher-interest-paying money market deposit accounts at depository institutions in 1983.

Liability Categories	Insured Commercial Banks			Mutual Savings Banks		
	Nov. 30	Dec. 29	Jan. 26P	Nov. 30	Dec. 29	Jan. 26P
Super-NOW accounts	—	—	12,136	—	—	528
(standard error of the estimate)[2]			(257)			
Money market deposit accounts[3]	—	61,944	136,737	—	8,352	18,081
(standard error of the estimate)		(202)	(856)		(22)	(120)
7- to 31-day money market certificates[4]	14,714	9,714	6,698	831	369	205
(standard error of the estimate)	(726)	(644)	(689)	(68)	(22)	(14)
91-day money market certificates[5]	7,322	7,280	6,300	916	819	630
(standard error of the estimate)	(194)	(182)	(171)	(32)	(31)	(25)
6-month money market certificates[6]	226,682	218,657	203,975	47,519	45,728	40,620
(standard error of the estimate)	(2,030)	(1,895)	(1,894)	(843)	(717)	(757)
2.5 year and over variable ceiling certificates[7]	86,968	86,607	87,655	26,506	25,634	25,270
(standard error of the estimate)	(1,812)	(1,770)	(1,768)	(535)	(503)	(517)
3.5-year ceiling-free time deposits in[8]	2,760	3,269	3,757	426	485	547
Fixed-rate accounts	2,614	3,125	3,600	397	455	515
(standard error of the estimate)	(221)	(263)	(307)	(26)	(32)	(36)
Variable-rate accounts	146	144	157	29	30	32
(standard error of the estimate)	(61)	(63)	(84)	(6)	(7)	(7)
All IRA/Keogh plan deposits[9]	17,272	18,096	19,763	6,199	6,347	6,396
Ceiling-free IRA/Keogh Time Deposits in:	10,420	11,224	12,837	1,592	1,694	1,867
Fixed-rate accounts	8,276	8,963	10,190	1,313	1,387	1,532
(standard error of the estimate)	(340)	(367)	(411)	(75)	(83)	(92)
Variable-rate accounts	2,144	2,261	2,647	279	307	335
(standard error of the estimate)	(137)	(143)	(164)	(29)	(32)	(35)
All other IRS/Keogh time and savings deposits	6,852	6,872	6,926	4,607	4,653	4,529
(standard error of the estimate)	(356)	(371)	(383)	(190)	(192)	(191)
Retail repurchase agreements[10]	7,677	5,937	4,581	2,576	1,472	807
(standard error of the estimate)	(772)	(683)	(533)	(460)	(279)	(153)

[1] Estimates are based on data collected by the Federal Reserve from a stratified random sample of about 550 banks and 90 mutual savings banks.

[2] NOW accounts containing an agreement between depositor and depository so that, provided certain conditions—including a $2,500 minimum balance—are met, some or all funds deposited are eligible to earn more than 5.25 percent.

[3] Deposits with a $2,500 initial and average balance requirement, no required minimum maturity, but institutions must reserve the right to require at least 7 days' notice prior to withdrawal, no restrictions on depositor eligibility, or limitations on the amount of interest that may be paid unless the average balance falls below $2,500 during which

FLOAT

Float occurs because the records of the money balances of the parties to a transaction are not simultaneously adjusted to show the transfer of money. That is, there is a delay between the time that the recorded money balances of the person or firm receiving the money are increased and the time that the recorded money balances of the person or firm paying the money are reduced.

Total float is composed of two parts: mail float and bank float. *Mail float* occurs when an individual or firm mails or delivers a check to another individual or firm before the check is deposited in a bank. Mail float increases the recorded money supply because the individual's deposit at the bank is not yet reduced, even though the individual has used part of that deposit to make a payment. Likewise, the bank cannot bring its books up to date until it receives the check. When the bank receives the check, there is still a problem of float until the check finds it way to the checkwriter's bank. That second part of float is discussed next.

Bank float arises when one bank is credited with a deposit, but the deposits of the bank on which the check was drawn have not yet been reduced. The funds that must be collected through the check-clearing system are called **uncollected cash items** or **items in the process of collection**. A rise in bank float increases bank reserves and deposits.

---

period the NOW account rate ceiling applies; such accounts may allow up to six transfers per month, no more than three of which may be by draft and may permit unlimited withdrawals by mail, messenger, or in person.

[4] Nonnegotiable time deposits that require a minimum daily balance of $20,000, but less than $100,000, and have an original maturity or required notice period of at least 7 days but no more than 31 days. The maximum permissible rate of interest is tied to the discount yield (auction average) on the most recently issued 91-day Treasury bill.

[5] Negotiable or nonnegotiable time deposits issued in denominations of at least $7,500, but less than $100,000, with original maturities of exactly 91 days for which the maximum permissible rate of interest on new deposits is tied to the discount yield on the most recently issued 91-day (13-week) Treasury bill (auction average).

[6] Nonnegotiable time deposits in denominations of $10,000, but less than $100,000, with original maturities of exactly 26 weeks for which the maximum permissible rate of interest on new deposits related to the discount yield on the most recently issued 6-month Treasury bill (auction average).

[7] All 4-year and over variable ceiling accounts having no legal minimum denomination issued between July 1 and December 31, 1979 and all 2.5-year and over variable ceiling accounts issued since January 1, 1980.

[8] All negotiable or nonnegotiable time deposits in denominations of less than $100,000 with original maturities of 3.5 years or more that were authorized beginning May 1, 1982. Fixed-rate accounts pay one rate of return over the life of the instrument, whereas variable-rate accounts pay a rate of return that may vary over the life of the instrument. Excludes IRA/Keogh accounts.

[9] Deposits of less than $100,000 with original maturities of 1.5 years or more were authorized beginning December 1, 1981. Fixed-rate accounts pay one rate of return over the life of the instrument, whereas variable-rate accounts pay a rate of return that may change periodically over the life of the instrument. All other IRA and Keogh plan time and savings deposits include all IRA/Keogh time deposits, regardless of maturity or ceiling rate.

[10] Retail repurchasing agreements are in denominations of less than $100,000 with maturities of less than 90 days that arise from the transfer of direct obligations of, or obligations fully guaranteed as to principal and interest by, the U.S. government or an agency thereof.

P – Preliminary.

TABLE 8-4 The Creation and Elimination of $100 of Federal Reserve Float

	Riggs N.B.		Federal Reserve		Bank of America	
	Assets	*Liabilities*	*Assets*	*Liabilities*	*Assets*	*Liabilities*
Period 1 Zero Federal Reserve float	$100 deferred availability cash items	$100 Memorabilia deposit	$100 uncollected cash item from B of A	$100 deferred availability cash item to Riggs	$100 reserves and income-earning assets	$100 Nancy West deposit
Period 2 $100 Federal Reserve float	$100 reserves and income-earning assets	$100 Memorabilia deposit	$100 uncollected cash item from B of A	$100 deposit to Riggs (if withdrawn, Federal Reserve notes will be increased or the deposits will be credited to another bank)	$100 reserves and income-earning assets	$100 Nancy West deposit
Period 3 Zero Federal Reserve float	$100 reserves and income-earning assets	$100 Memorabilia deposit	0	0	0	0

* Federal Reserve notes are regular U.S. currency, which is a liability of the Federal Reserve. The assets and liabilities of the Federal Reserve are explained in a later chapter.

Here is how the bank float works. On a visit to Washington, D.C., Nancy West of California buys a picture of the White House for $100 from Memorabilia Souvenirs. Her check is drawn on Bank of America in California. The seller deposits the check in his account at Riggs National Bank in Washington, D.C. This first step is shown in the T-accounts in Table 8-4 for period 1. There is as yet no Federal Reserve float because the Federal Reserve has not yet allowed Riggs to use the reserves. Riggs has put the check on an armored truck, which carries it to the Baltimore, Maryland, branch of the Richmond, Virginia, Federal Reserve Bank.

The Federal Reserve thus has a $100 liability—a **deferred availability cash item**—that is an asset to Riggs. This is because Bank of America still credits Nancy West with $100 in her account, and Bank of America still has $100 to use as reserves or to use to buy income-earning assets. The check is being cleared, sorted electronically, and put aboard an airplane under private contract to the Federal Reserve.

The Federal Reserve gives Riggs credit for the $100, say, two days later. The deferred availability cash item is changed at the Federal Reserve to a $100 deposit to Riggs. This is shown in period 2 of Table 8-4. Now there is $100 in bank float. Riggs has full use of the funds, to keep as reserves or to use to buy income-earning assets. At the same time, Bank of America also has the use of the funds. Even Nancy West, if she illegally practices what is called "kiting," can use the $100 if she is careful to redeposit it before the check clears.

Where is that—expletive deleted—check? Is it winging its way in an airplane to the San Francisco Federal Reserve Bank? Somehow, until the middle 1980s it took five days. Federal Reserve float stood at $7.7 billion at the end of February 1980, or 24 percent of all member banks' reserve deposits at the Federal Reserve (see Table 8-5). Federal Reserve float was just under $1 billion in August 1983.

Five days later, Nancy West's check is cleared through the San Francisco Federal Reserve Bank. The uncollected cash item is removed from the Federal Reserve T-account in period 3. The $100 in Federal Reserve float has been eliminated.

The bank float for checks cleared by the Federal Reserve up until the phase-in of charges in 1984 was regarded as an interest-free loan to member banks, against which checks had been drawn and credited but not yet collected. Legislation passed in March 1980 required the Federal Reserve to begin, within 18 months, charging an interest fee on float. Finally, in April 1981, the Federal Reserve began charging depository institutions for a small portion of float. From that time until April 1984 additional portions of Federal Reserve float were allowed to carry charges. The result, as Table 8-5 and Figure 8-1 indicate, is that float has continued to fall from its peak in the late 1970s.

A form of deliberately planned float, by which an individual can increase his or her money balance, is called **kiting**. This illegal activity is as follows: you pay a bill with a check drawn on, for example, Southwest National Bank. Just

T A B L E   8 - 5   Federal Reserve Bank Float for December of Selected Years, 1939–1986 (in millions of dollars)

Year	Average of Daily Figures
1939	83
1941	170
1945	652
1050	1,117
1960	1,665
1965	2,349
1966	2,383
1967	2,030
1968	3,251
1969	3,235
1970	3,570
1978	7,521
1979	6,499
1980	5,797
1982	3,136
1986 (Feb.)	1,056

Source: Federal Reserve Bulletins, Table 1.18, recent issues. For data before 1961, *Supplement to Banking and Monetary Statistics*, Board of Governors, January 1962, pp. 14–19.

before the check reaches Southwest National Bank, you make a deposit to cover the check. This deposit is a check drawn on another bank. It sounds simple, but the house of cards can rapidly fall if the Southwest National Bank refuses to credit your check until it clears, that is, if the bank puts your deposits on a **collection basis**. An elaborate kiting scheme may involve many banks, even though the depositor's total balance, if all checks were cleared instantly, would be smaller than his or her current recorded deposits.

Is kiting a national pastime? This important question can be phrased in a gentler form: Do individuals and firms treat float as part of their money balances? The answer is probably yes for many individuals and businesses. For some individuals, overdraft protection is a partial safeguard against bad timing. For example, in recent years, banks have commonly provided overdraft lines of credit, sometimes on one of the national credit cards. The risk of having a check returned marked "insufficient funds" from a miscalculation of the time in which the check will clear is thus eliminated, and the practice is perfectly legal unless the line of overdraft credit is exceeded.

The market rates of interest on alternative liquid assets and the lower rates on bank accounts make the float a profitable investment for many. Many business firms use cash management arrangements whereby the bank is instructed to maintain zero balance accounts (all funds are withdrawn each day) and to forward any excess funds for immediate investment. Short-term

FIGURE 8-1   Federal Reserve Float, 1915–1985

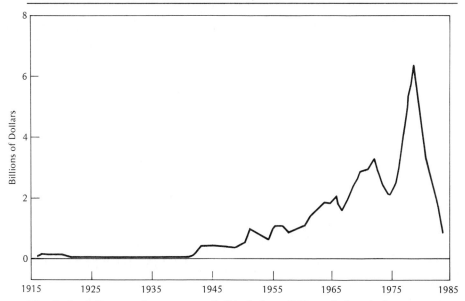

The Federal Reserve float was negligible before 1939, and then it began to grow rapidly. The Federal Reserve took various administrative steps to hasten check clearing. The Monetary Control Act of 1980 directed the Federal Reserve to begin charging depository institutions for float, and such charges were phased in between April 1981 and April 1984. The float has continued to fall from its peak in the late 1970s.

Source: John E. Young, "The Rise and Fall of Float," *Economic Review*, Federal Reserve Bank of Kansas City, February 1986, p. 31.

financial assets can be sold to cover any deficiencies. For accounts payable, some firms use checking accounts in banks that are distant from the places to which the checks are sent, in order to increase the check-clearing time and increase the float. The float on the checks issued can be a substantial asset. Arrangements such as these lead to the suggestion that float (or a proportion of float) should not be subtracted from deposits but, rather, should be included in deposits, to obtain an estimate of what the nonbank public treats as its supply of money.[2]

The existence of varying amounts of float can complicate the process of estimating reserve positions and deposit levels for both the managers of depository institutions and the central bankers who are given responsibility for controlling the money supply. Changes in deposits and reserves can occur for many reasons, such as the sudden withdrawals of deposits or a correction in a depository institution's reserve position of a mistake by the central bank in adjusting float positions. Depository institutions then turn to the managed liabilities to adjust their reserve positions.

THE MANAGED LIABILITIES

Of special importance to the process by which depository institutions adjust their reserve position are the **managed liabilities**.[3] These are

1. Negotiable certificates of deposit over $100,000.
2. Eurodollar borrowings, including overnight deposits at Caribbean branches of U.S. banks, included in M-2. (This subject is discussed in Part IX.)
3. Federal funds borrowings.
4. Short-term repurchase agreements.

These managed liabilities have the following characteristics:

1. They pay market rates of interest.
2. They have reserve requirements different from those for checkable accounts (unless they are defined by the Board of Governors as checkable deposits subject to the same requirements).
3. The depository institutions can, rapidly and at small expense, change the amount of their managed liabilities.

For example, if checkable deposits decline, drawing down reserves, a depository institution can attract funds by immediately increasing its managed liabilities. Even if managed liabilities, such as federal funds borrowings, are not included in the concept of money, such changes can cause erratic movements in the money supply. This is because of the different reserve requirements for managed liabilities and for checkable deposits.

This problem is vividly illustrated by the advent in the 1970s of the equivalent of overnight borrowings from nonbank depositors to banks. Some large nonbank depositors made the following arrangements: Their deposits were regularly drawn out of their accounts shortly before the bank closed each day. The bank then sold a Treasury bill to the depositor and agreed to buy it back at the same price in the morning, when the funds were replaced in the depositor's account. This repurchasing agreement arrangement allowed the depositor to receive market interest on his or her bank account. Because reserve requirements were calculated on the closing balances, the bank needed to carry no required reserves against these deposits. And the depositor's funds were safe overnight, as the ownership of the Treasury bill was passed to the depositor.

Although the amount of these automatic arrangements was believed to be relatively small, large corporate and local government customers who made specific arrangements early in the day had much larger amounts in overnight repurchase agreements. Indeed, overnight domestic repurchase agreements amounted to $142.3 billion in March 1986. This amount is not included in the estimates of M-1; it is added to M-2.

THE FEDERAL FUNDS MARKET

The Fedwire, the communication system of the Federal Reserve, is an important part of the payment mechanism for transactions between banks involving federal funds. This communication system is discussed in Chapter 14. Federal funds are immediately available funds that can be transferred through the Fedwire. The federal funds market is a short-term loan market with the important function of allocating reserves to banks that need them.

Some federal fund loans are made directly between commercial banks; other federal funds loans are arranged with money market dealers who also maintain a position in the market. Private corporations, mutual savings banks, and foreign banks may also enter the market, although the market has been primarily made up of domestic commercial banks and New York money market dealers.

A number of the aspects of the federal funds market explain its widespread use by commercial banks for short-term adjustments in their reserve position. Federal funds loans are a way for banks to obtain funds and legally to pay market rates of interest. Since 1964, member banks can borrow not only from other members but also from savings and loan associations, agencies of the U.S. government, and nonbank securities dealers.

Federal funds are payable "immediately"; that is, there is same-day clearing. In contrast, ordinary checks drawn on individuals, banks, or other business firms take at least one day to clear and to be made available to member banks for meeting their legal reserve requirements. But banks in the federal funds market can use federal funds and obtain same-day clearing for immediate additions to their reserve position.

A common type of federal funds transaction is a one-day overnight loan between member banks, in which the Federal Reserve debits the lender's account and credits the borrower's account on the same day. No collateral is exchanged. The loan is considered an unsecured loan and is limited by bank regulations to a percentage of the lending bank's capital plus surplus. Some federal funds are secured with government securities. However, the large size of this market in unsecured, uninsured loans raises the possibility of injury to the banking industry if a large bank were to have financial problems and be unable to honor its federal funds borrowings. Presumably, the Federal Reserve would come to the rescue.

Banks also use **repurchase agreements (RPs)** to obtain short-term funds. In an overnight repurchase agreement, a security, such as a U.S. Treasury bill, might be sold to another bank, with the agreement to repurchase it at the same price the following day. (Repurchase agreements are discussed further in Chapter 12.)

The rate of interest on federal funds—the *funds rate*—is closely watched at the trading desk of the Federal Reserve Bank of New York, as a signal of the reserve position of the banking system. Market dealers and banks that participate in the federal funds market may post slightly different and varying rates during the day. All depository institutions with federal reserve requirements end their reporting period and must come up with their required reserves by the close of business on alternate Wednesdays. A perceived surplus in the system sends the federal funds rate plummeting downward, and an expected shortage sends the rate shooting upward, with perceptions sometimes shifting rapidly on some Wednesday afternoons. The federal funds rate is, therefore, very erratic and unstable on alternate Wednesdays, because of the **Wednesday scramble** in and out of reserves.

Now all the material in this chapter on reserves and deposits will be tied together in a fascinating story of how depository institutions literally create money.

MONEY CREATION

Fractional Reserve Banking

Fractional reserve banking is the practice of keeping only a fraction of deposits in the form of reserves. Depository institutions (commercial banks, savings and loan associations, mutual savings banks, and credit unions) are able to do this because only a small fraction of their depositors is expected to turn up during any given day or week to withdraw their deposits. The bulk of deposits is invested in financial assets, from which the depository institutions earn most of their income.

Those income-earning financial assets range from bills, notes, and bonds issued by private corporations and by the federal, state, and municipal governments to mortgage loans for housing. Each type of financial institution has a different type of portfolio of assets, which reflects its area of special expertise in managing financial assets.

To demonstrate how depository institutions create money under the current system of fractional reserve banking, we will use a hypothetical example of a commercial bank, Southwest National Bank. We will assume that federal regulations require Southwest National Bank to hold a percentage of its deposits in the form of cash reserves, or the reserve requirement. The reserves may be held in the form of currency and coin on the premises, a form of reserves called vault cash. Or they may be held in a deposit at a regional Federal Reserve bank.

Assume that the Southwest National Bank management, taking into account the reserve requirement and the projected amount of withdrawals and deposits, decides to keep 20 percent of its deposits in reserves.

The Southwest National Bank Creates Money

Under a fractional reserve banking system, banks create money. The money creation story begins when John Jones deposits $1,000 in currency in the Southwest National Bank.

The Southwest National is no charity. It is a profit-maximizing institution that can be expected to look eagerly for ways to earn income on the 80 percent of John Jones's deposit that it does not want to hold. Alvin Bly comes to the bank with a loan application. Southwest National Bank makes an automobile loan for $800 to Mr. Bly. Mr. Bly gives the check drawn on the Southwest National Bank to an automobile retail dealer, Selma White. John Jones believes that his deposit of $1,000 is in the bank, and Selma White, the automobile dealer, also believes that she has a valid check for $800. In this way, fractional reserve banking has allowed the Southwest National Bank to create an additional $800.

Money Creation in Accounting Form

It is customary to show how banks create money by using simple T-accounts and double-entry bookkeeping. The following presentation is deceptively simple, but it helps explain the principle of deposit expansion. Some important complications will be disregarded. The time it takes for bankers to adjust their portfolios so that they hold their desired reserves will be ignored. The value of the currency and coin held by the public outside depository institutions is assumed to be constant. At first, we will also assume that Southwest National Bank is the only available depository institution, so that all checks drawn on the bank will be redeposited in the same bank.

Tables 8-6 and 8-7 display simple T-accounts for the Southwest National Bank. Each T-account shows

1. The sum of the value of all *assets* (claims on future income and other commodities of value held by the bank) listed in the left-hand column of each T-account, which is exactly equal to
2. The sum of the value of all *liabilities* plus the owners' equities.

The equality of assets and liabilities plus the owners' equity is equivalent to the statement that everything of value in the bank belongs to someone.

TABLE 8-6   Initial Deposit

Assets	Liabilities
(2) $1,000 cash	(1) $1,000 deposit by John Jones

TABLE 8-7 $800 Is Created

Assets	Liabilities
(2) $1,000 cash	(1) $1,000 deposit by John Jones
(3) −$800 cash*	
(4) $800 auto loan to Alvin Bly	

TABLE 8-8   Redeposit of the New Money

Assets	Liabilities
(2) $1,000 cash	(1) $1,000 deposit by John Jones
(3) −$800 cash	(5) $800 deposit by auto dealer, Selma White
(4) $800 auto loan to Alvin Bly	
(6) $800 cash	

There are two types of claims on assets:

1. *Equities*, claims of the owners of the banks.
2. *Liabilities*, claims of persons or firms who are not owners of the bank, for example, deposits, which are claims of depositors on the bank.

The process of creating money is illustrated step by step in the T-accounts for the bank in Tables 8-6 through 8-10. The time-honored rules of double-entry accounting are followed, which require that all entries be made at least twice.

In comes John Jones with a $1,000 deposit, which is represented as both a $1,000 liability (1) and a $1,000 cash asset (2) in Table 8-6. The bank wants to maintain a 20 percent reserve ratio, so that $800 is available to purchase an income-earning asset. In comes Alvin Bly for an $800 automobile loan. The loan is made, causing a reduction in cash of $800 (3) and a new asset (4), the automobile loan shown in Table 8-7. In this step, $800 is created, as Alvin Bly has $800 that did not exist before. Selma White, the automobile dealer, deposits the $800 (5), adding $800 to the bank's cash assets (6), as shown in Table 8-8.

The bank now has $1,800 in deposits and $1,000 in reserves. The management wants to keep 20 percent of its deposits, $360, as reserves and use the remainder of its reserves, $640, to purchase income-earning assets. Therefore, the bank management decides to lend $640 to K Corporation. This loan reduces the bank's cash assets by $640 (7) to acquire the new business loan asset (8), as shown in Table 8-9. In this step, $640 is created, as K Corporation has $640 that it did not have before.

TABLE 8-9   Second Money Creation

Assets	Liabilities
(2) $1,000 cash	(1) $1,000 deposit by John Jones
(3) −$800 cash	(5) $800 deposit by auto dealer, Selma White
(4) $800 auto loan to Alvin Bly	
(6) $800 cash	
(7) −$640 cash	
(8) $640 business loan to K Corporation	

TABLE 8-10   Hypothetical Creation and Redeposit of $1,440 by Southwest National Bank

Assets	Liabilities
(2) $1,000 cash	(1) $1,000 deposit by John Jones
(3) −$800 cash	(5) $800 deposit by auto dealer, Selma White
(4) $800 auto loan to Alvin Bly	(9) $640 deposit of the K Corporation
(6) $800 cash	
(7) −$640 cash	
(8) $640 business loan to K Corporation	
(10) $640 cash	

K Corporation redeposits the $640, creating a new deposit (9) and adding $640 to the bank's cash assets (10), as shown in Table 8-10. The total cash reserves of the Southwest National Bank are still $1,000. Its total deposits are now $2,440. Because the desired reserve ratio is 20 percent, the desired reserve level is now $488, and the bank will want to purchase $512 in additional income-earning assets. This process of creating money can continue if each income-earning asset purchased is redeposited at the Southwest National Bank.

APPENDIX: HOW MUCH MONEY CAN THE ENTIRE BANKING SYSTEM CREATE?

In our example, the amount of desired reserves grows from $200 after the first deposit of $1,000, to $360 after the second deposit of $800, and to $488 after the third deposit of $640. The desired reserves increase while the total reserves remain constant at $1,000. Eventually, the Southwest National Bank will have created so many deposits that all of the $1,000 will be wanted for reserves, and no additional earning assets will be purchased. The T-account example may be pursued to find the limiting amount of deposits for the original deposit of $1,000 on currency. But a more convenient method that employs a few symbols may be used to find the answer to the question, How much money can the entire banking system create? To generalize the result of the entire banking system (all depository institutions), the Southwest National Bank is replaced by the entire banking system. Instead of requiring redeposits in the Southwest National Bank, redeposits in similar accounts at any depository institutions will allow the money expansion process to proceed.

Let d be the average desired ratio of reserves to deposits, which in the previous example is .2. Then $1 - d$ $(= .8)$ is the desired proportion of deposits that an average bank management uses to buy income-earning assets. Let $L = 1 - d$.

If new deposits currently are $1, the bank will purchase L times $1, or L of earning assets. The sum of L is redeposited in a bank, which lends L times that amount, or L^2. This process is repeated a large number (N) of times resulting in the following series:

$$S = \$1(1 + L + L^2 + \cdots + L^N) \tag{1}$$

The sum (S) of the numbers in the parentheses is the total dollar value of deposits that banks can create with an initial deposit of $1 in currency. Dropping the dollar sign for convenience, equation (1) becomes

$$S = 1 + L + L^2 + L^3 + \cdots + L^N \tag{2}$$

Now we will use a simple trick to find the value of this series of L's. The equality in equation (2) is not altered by multiplying each side of the equation by L:

$$LS = L + L^2 + L^4 + \cdots + L^{N+1} \tag{3}$$

Subtract equation (3) from equation (2) to obtain

$$S(1 - L) = 1 - L^{N+1} \tag{4}$$

The fraction L approaches zero as it is multiplied by itself a great many times, so that L^{N+1} is approximately zero. This leaves (after substituting d for $1 - L$)

$$S = \frac{1}{1 - L} = \frac{1}{d} \tag{5}$$

This shows that the sum of the value of deposits (new money) of the entire banking system, D, created by an initial $1 deposit of currency, is

$$D = \frac{\$1}{d} \tag{6}$$

If $d = .2$, D will be $5. If, as in the example, the initial deposit of currency is $1,000, D will be $5,000. In more general form, the preceding equation may be written as

$$D = \frac{R}{d} \quad \text{or} \quad d = \frac{R}{D} \tag{7}$$

where R represents the total cash reserves of the banking system.

The example and the derivation of equation (6) are intended to give you an intuitive feeling for how the private banking system creates money. This description will be modified by Chapter 17 to take account of varying amounts of cash held by the nonbank public. If, for example, Mr. Bly demanded his $800 loan in the form of currency that he then put in a safety deposit box, there would have been no further expansion of money by the Southwest National Bank, because most loans are made by increasing a depositor's account rather than in cash. Nevertheless, our analysis does explain the fundamental principle of the private depository institution's expansion of the money supply.

STUDY QUESTIONS

1. Why and how are depository intermediaries' checkable deposits adjusted to obtain an estimate of the nonbank public's deposits?
2. What happened to Federal Reserve requirements in 1980? Describe Federal Reserve requirements before and after 1980.
3. What is float? Why is it important?
4. What are the managed liabilities of banks? How do banks use these managed liabilities? What part do interest rates play in selecting a portfolio of managed liabilities? What part do reserve requirements play in selecting managed liabilities? Are managed liabilities money?
5. What is the federal funds market?
6. How does a federal funds loan differ from an overnight repurchase agreement between banks?
7. How does a private depository institution create money? Can it create money if no one asks for a loan? Explain.
8. What is fractional reserve banking? Suppose that the desired (or required) reserve ratio is 100 percent. How will private depository institutions be paid for their services? How would that differ from the present form of their income?

GLOSSARY

Bank float. See **Float**.

Certificates of deposit or **CDs.** Consumer and business time deposits. Business time deposits are negotiable (salable) and in denominations of $100,000 or more. Consumer time deposits are nonnegotiable and in smaller denominations.

Collection basis. On this basis, deposits are credited to an account only after sufficient time has elapsed to allow the deposited check to be returned, if there are insufficient funds.

Deferred availability cash items. Reserves due a bank by the Federal Reserve for a check deposited in that bank, drawn on another bank, and cleared through the Federal Reserve. After the reserve account of the bank where the check was deposited is credited, those reserves can be used to buy income-earning assets, even though the check has not yet been deducted from the bank on which it is drawn. (It is an *uncollected cash item.*) Until the check clears, therefore, the bank can earn interest on this interest-free loan.

Dual banking system. The regulatory system in which banks operate under state and federal law, freely choosing to operate under either federal or state charter. The Depository Deregulation and Monetary Control Act of 1980 increased federal regulation (with reserve requirements on all depository institutions) and reduced state regulation of the banking system. Thus, it was seen by some as an attack on the dual banking system.

Federal Reserve float. The difference between uncollected cash items and deferred availability cash items.

Float. The sum of *bank float* plus *mail float*, or *total float*. The amount of checks used for transactions (to pay bills) that has not yet been entered into the banking system's books is called mail float. Once the checks reach the banking system, they must be sent from the bank in which they are deposited to the bank on which they are drawn. Bank float is equal to the amount of these uncollected cash items. To obtain Federal Reserve float, subtract the deferred availability cash items from these uncollected cash items. See note 2 for the reasoning behind these last two concepts of float.

Fractional reserve banking. The practice of keeping only a fraction of the deposits of depository institutions as cash reserves.

Kiting. Deliberately planned float by which an individual increases his or her recorded money balances.

Mail float. See **Float**.

Managed liabilities. Liabilities that a depository institution can rapidly buy and sell. They include business CDs, Eurodollar borrowings, federal funds, and short-term repurchase agreements.

Money market certificates. Generally, consumer time deposits. In the tangled web of ceiling rate phaseout creations, they are time deposits for consumers in denominations of $10,000 or more with maturities of six months (established June 5, 1980).

Money market deposit accounts (MMDA). Accounts at depository institutions requiring a $2,500 monthly average minimum balance and offering up to six preauthorized transfers, up to three of which can be checks (established December 14, 1982). As of March 1983, these accounts have been treated as savings accounts for reserve requirement purposes.

Required reserve ratio. The ratio of required reserves to a specific category of deposits, specified as the minimum ratio of required reserves that must be held.

Repurchase agreement (RPs). An agreement to purchase a financial asset, such as a Treasury bill, at the same price. It is a vehicle for a short-term loan in which ownership of a security is temporarily switched to the lender.

Reserve requirements. Specifications of the type and amount of reserves that banks must hold in order to fulfill government regulations.

Super-NOWs. NOW accounts requiring a $2,500 monthly average minimum balance, offering unlimited checking privileges, and, as of March 1983, classified as a checking account for the purposes of reserve requirements. Established January 5, 1983.

Tax and loan accounts. U.S. Treasury accounts at private depositories used for the reception of tax receipts such as income tax withheld by corporations from their payrolls.

Time deposit. A deposit at a depository institution that cannot be redeemed without a penalty at that institution until a specified date.

Total float. See **Float**.

Uncollected cash items (or items in the process of collection). The total value of checks deposited at one bank but not yet deducted from the records of the banks on which they are drawn.

Vault cash. Cash reserves of depository institutions held on the premises.

Wednesday scramble. The scrambling in and out of reserves by depository institutions that must come up with their Federal Reserve requirements on Wednesday of each week.

NOTES

1. The reason for this provision is that both chairmen of the banking committees, Henry Reuss in the U.S. House of Representatives and William Proxmire in the Senate, did not want the Federal Reserve to pay interest on reserves to the commercial banks, as is allowed under the supplemental reserves requirements. That is, they did not want the Federal Reserve to lower the reserve ratios to the bottom of the allowable range and substitute a supplemental requirement that allowed those interest payments. The Monetary Control Act of 1980 further requires the affirmative vote of at least five of the seven members of the Board of Governors and consultation with other regulators before the supplemental reserve requirements can be imposed. Furthermore, they can be imposed only to enhance monetary policy and not as a means of reducing the cost burden of the basic reserve requirements.

2. The subtraction of deferred availability cash items on the Federal Reserve records to obtain a concept of Federal Reserve float is important for bank reserves but may be incorrect for demand deposits. Suppose that money is defined as the "nonbank" public's holdings of commercial bank demand deposits and currency and coin. An "increase" in "uncollected cash items" means that there is an increase in the value of checks that have been deposited in one bank and not yet deducted from the account on which they are drawn at another bank. Nancy West in our example may well know that she has, say, four days before she must cover her check in California—illegal though that practice may be. The existence of "deferred availability cash items" is a deduction she does not make.

3. For reference, see Thomas D. Simpson, *The Market for Federal Funds and Repurchase Agreements*, Staff Studies, Board of Governors of the Federal Reserve System, July 1979.

CHAPTER 9

INVESTMENT AND CONTRACTUAL INTERMEDIARIES

CHAPTER PREVIEW

Introduction. Investment and contractual intermediaries are entering more and more of the same areas as the depository intermediaries.

Investment Intermediaries. Investment companies, stockbrokers, and finance companies are discussed, with special attention given to money market funds.

Contractual Intermediaries. Life insurance companies, private and government pension plans, and personal trust funds are discussed.

INTRODUCTION

The immense changes in the investment and contractual intermediaries during the 1970s and early 1980s cannot easily be comprehended. Imagine the birth and growth of the money market funds, which grew to $180 billion in assets by 1982, starting from zero in 1972. In addition, pension funds, trust funds, finance companies, investment companies, stock brokerage houses, and other insurance companies are entering more and more of the same areas as the depository institutions.

INVESTMENT INTERMEDIARIES

The major financial intermediaries classified as **investment intermediaries** are investment companies and finance companies. Brokerage firms that offer money market funds and checkable accounts may also be considered an investment intermediary. The major financial assets created by investment companies are pro rata (in proportion to) shares in their portfolio of financial assets. The major financial assets created by finance companies are debt instruments, often short-term commercial paper. These financial assets created by investment intermediaries are very liquid; some (money market shares) are even included in the definition of money (M-2).

Investment Companies

Investment companies sell shares to their customers and purchase income-earning financial assets issued by others. Each shareowner has a pro rata share in the investment company's assets. An investment company's income-earning portfolio of financial assets either may be limited to the particular assets in which it specializes, or it may be diversified, with many types of financial assets. In either case, unlike holding companies, investment companies do not acquire equities with the primary objective of ownership or control. For example, they may purchase financial assets in only one industry, such as gold mining or oil, or they may buy more conservative securities, such as government bonds. Some specialize in municipal bonds in order to receive preferential tax treatment. Others may invest in equities with reliable dividends to ensure continuous income, or they may invest in equities with little or no dividends in order to obtain income only from the lower-taxed capital gains.

Investment companies may be classified as follows:

1. The **fixed** or **fixed-trust investment companies** offer certificates for a proportional part of their portfolio (a *unit* of the portfolio). The portfolio is selected by the promoters and remains virtually intact, with little discretionary management.
2. The **open-end** or **mutual funds investment companies** constantly offer to sell

new shares. The shares are sold directly by the companies (or by a broker-dealer or underwriter). The mutuals continually adjust their portfolio of assets.

3. The **closed-end investment companies** issue a "limited' number of shares of common stock, which are traded in regular financial markets. They may also issue marketable bonds or borrow limited amounts from other firms.

Money Market Funds

A giant investment company suddenly appeared on the scene in 1978: the money market mutual funds, or as they are more commonly called, the money market funds (MMFs). The MMFs are mutual funds that specialize in a portfolio of very liquid short-term debt instruments, such as U.S. Treasury bills and certificates of deposits from large domestic and foreign banks. A customer may purchase a share in these funds for a minimum investment, such as $500, $1,000, or $5,000. These funds may then be withdrawn from the MMFs by mail, by telephone, or, in many cases, by a check for $500 or more.

By November 1983, the giant group of MMFs had grown to over $241.6 billion in aggregate shares.[1] The first MMF had begun to offer shares only a few years earlier, in 1972, and by the end of 1977, the total value of MMF assets was a comparatively small $3 billion to $4 billion. Growth began to accelerate in 1978 and then to boom in 1979. In 1982 there were approximately 150 MMFs, each with $100 million or more in assets.[2]

The explosion in MMFs is not hard to explain. Market interest rates shot up in 1978 and 1979, and the interest rates on checking accounts and passbook savings accounts at depository intermediaries were held down by government regulation. The **spread** between the yields at the five largest MMFs and the passbook savings account ceiling at the thrift intermediaries is shown in Figure 9-1. Superimposed on this figure is the value of the monthly change in the MMFs. The spread rose from the middle of 1977 until the end of 1978, with the most rapid increase at the end of 1978. Investment in MMFs also rose after a slight lag and then, in the beginning of 1979, with a huge jump. In March 1980, MMFs were temporarily required to hold a 15 percent reserve at the Federal Reserve on any new deposits, as part of President Jimmy Carter's program to restrain credit.[3]

A number of similar investment intermediaries also grew during the 1970s.[4] They all invested primarily in short-term money market securities. Along with money market funds they are called **short-term investment pools (STIPs)**. They include short-term tax-exempt funds (which invest in short-term tax-exempt securities), a Treasury bill pool, short-term investment funds (which are pooled accounts of bank trust departments that invest mostly in commercial paper). All these STIPs resemble MMFs and grew for the same reasons.

In 1983 the Federal Reserve combined tax-exempt funds with taxable money market funds and included that combined total in M-2. Previously only taxable money market funds were included in M-2.

FIGURE 9-1   Change in the Size of Money Market Funds and the Spread Between Their Yield and the Ceiling Rate on Passbook Savings Accounts at Thrifts, 1975–1979 (in millions of dollars)

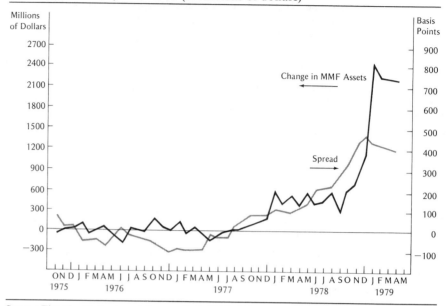

Source: Timothy Q. Cook and Jeremy G. Duffield, "Money Market Mutual Funds: A Reaction to Government Regulation or a Lasting Financial Innovation?" *Economic Review*, Federal Reserve Bank of Richmond, July–August 1979, p. 27.

MMFs can be divided into three groups: (1) *Institutional funds* are available only through institutional investors. Noninstitutional MMFs, available to all investors, are divided into two groups. Some are available through (2) *stockbrokers* and *dealers*. Others are available to all investors, and these are (3) *general-purpose MMFs.*

Are MMFs a temporary phenomenon? No, they are probably not temporary unless they are ended by government regulation. They would be injured slightly if they were prohibited from offering withdrawals by check, and they would suffer to a larger extent if reserve requirements were permanently imposed. Many individuals, attracted by the large spread in 1978 and 1979, learned how to hold a portfolio of high-grade debt instruments, including negotiable certificates of deposit with minimum denominations of $100,000, by buying shares in MMFs. Brokers and their customers have learned to transfer money to brokerage-house MMFs when cash accumulates in the customer's accounts. The services provided by MMFs were evidently so attractive that during 1976, when the spread shown in Figure 9-1 was negative, there was still growth in MMFs during some months.

And then, on December 12, 1982, came the money market deposit accounts (MMDAs), described in the last chapter. Money market funds had reached a high of $241.6 billion in November 1982. They fell slightly to $229.7 billion in December. By January 26, 1983, they had fallen by $19.0 billion more, to $210.7 billion, and the new MMDAs had surpassed them in total deposits. By October 1983, MMFs had fallen to $177.6 billion, $64.0 billion less than their November 1982 peak, whereas MMDAs had reached $366.6 billion.

In April 1985, $265.9 billion was invested in MMFs. This was 10.1 percent of M-2. It thus appeared that MMFs were well in place, although they were smaller than they would have been if the Monetary Control Act of 1980 had not provided nationwide interest-paying checking accounts for depository institutions that have federal deposit insurance.

Typically, MMFs clear their checks (legally called *drafts*) through a commercial bank. There have been many complaints that deposits are held too long before the funds are made available to the customer. In 1986 *The Wall Street Journal* reported,

> Paine Webber Inc. has its Cashfund, and Dean Witter Reynolds Inc. has a Liquid Asset Fund. But at times neither money-market mutual fund is very liquid or easily converted to cash.
>
> As is true with most money-market funds, including those tied to brokerage firms' cash management accounts, customers who make deposits by check sometimes don't have access to their money for about two weeks.[5]

The depository intermediaries guarantee the depositor a fixed nominal sum, whereas the MMFs promise only a pro rata share (based on the relative size of the share) of the value of their total portfolio, which can vary. Precisely because MMFs offer a different type of asset, one that can vary in nominal value and therefore can pay a slightly greater rate of return on average, some MMF shares should be demanded.

Are accounts at MMFs money? They are included in M-2 in the United States. They are limited as a medium of exchange (because of the usual $500 minimum check size), with a capital risk of getting back a smaller nominal amount than that invested. Tests may determine whether some measure of the value of shares in MMFs or shares in any of the STIPs allow better predictions of the price level and other variables to justify including them in the concept of money.

Stockbrokers

Many firms buy and sell securities for customers on a commission basis. Some medium-sized regional firms often closely follow the equities of the firms in their region.[6] Some firms specialize in a single market, such as tax-exempt bonds. Some firms are called *discounters* because they offer minimal service and research, but their fees are usually less than half of those charged by the full-service firms.[7] And some firms are geared to dealing only with institutions and individuals of wealth, those with six- and seven-figure portfolios.[8] These firms include large firms, often with offices in major cities. Many of the firms limited to large investors offer a broad range of services, such as underwriting or, as it is also called, investment banking.

The very large brokerage houses offering a wide range of services to the public include American Express/Shearson; Prudential-Bache; Dean Witter Reynolds; E. F. Hutton; Paine Webber; Smith Barney Harris Upham; Drexel Burnham Lambert; Kidder Peabody; and the largest, Merrill, Lynch, Pierce, Fenner & Smith, Inc. (often called simply Merrill Lynch).

Stockbrokers also offer pension plans: Keogh and IRA plans and Simplified Employee Pension Plans (SEPs)—IRA plans. These investments make stockbrokers part-contractual intermediaries.

Merrill Lynch also offers a special type of account accessible by check, which it calls a *cash management account.* (Other large brokerage businesses, including Shearson/American Express, Prudential-Bache, and E. F. Hutton, have similar plans.) In a cash management account, the investor selects his or her portfolio of financial assets, including Merrill Lynch MMFs. A check may be written on Bank One of Ohio. The check is drawn against the value of the cash assets (such as MMF shares) plus the unused margin on securities in the Merrill Lynch cash management account. The portfolio must be valued at $20,000 or more. (One regional brokerage planned a minimum of only $1,000.) This device allows market rates of interest to be earned on deposited funds, and it reduces the transactions costs of shifting from securities into a medium of exchange and back again.

The cash management accounts make Merrill Lynch partly a depository intermediary, and the mutual funds it manages makes it partly an investment company.

Finance Companies

Finance companies held $332.5 billion in financial assets in 1986 (see Table 9-1).

Finance companies raise funds by borrowing from other financial intermediaries, and by selling their own credit instruments in the financial markets. They lend to businesses and consumers. They are licensed and supervised by diverse state laws. Domestic finance companies had $134.7 billion in consumer loans and $192.7 billion in business loans and real estate in the second quarter of 1986. The finance companies had borrowed $106.4 billion from the commercial banks and had raised $101.8 billion throught the sale of long-term bonds.

Finance companies have been affected by the general movement toward deregulation and the expansion into new financial services, beginning in the late 1970s. Some finance companies have established nationwide computer facilities to transfer funds. For example, Beneficial Corporation developed a revolving loan system in about half the states, where the law permits. It operates through regular checkable accounts at a commercial bank, which Benefi-

TABLE 9-1   Domestic Finance Companies, Second Quarter 1986 (in billions of dollars)

Finance companies borrow from banks and sell debt instruments to raise funds to make business and consumer loans.

Assets	$332.5	Liabilities	$193.9
Accounts receivable, gross		Bank loans	22.9
Consumer	134.7	Commercial paper	106.4
Business and real estate	192.7	Debt	
Total	327.5	Short term	20.9
Less: Reserve for unearned		Long term	101.8
income and loans	47.0	Other	40.4
Accounts receivable, net	280.4	Capital, surplus,	
Other	52.1	and undivided profits	40.2

cial acquired for that purpose. Household Finance purchased a savings and loan in California, and Gulf & Western Associates bought a consumer credit card operation in California.

CONTRACTUAL INTERMEDIARIES

The major contractual intermediaries, with the value of their financial assets in 1984, are as follows:[9]

1. Life insurance companies	$772.97
2. Other insurance companies	264.7
3. Private pension funds other than life insurance companies	623.3
4. State and local government pension funds	323.5
5. Federal civilian employees	129.5
6. Federal railroad retirement	3.7
7. Social security: Old-age survivors and disability insurance	31.3

The data for the life insurance companies' assets are not directly comparable with the pension funds' assets because of some overlapping assets in the pension funds run by life insurance companies. But the data do show that the life insurance companies hold most of the assets of these entities, that is, if one does not count the assets of the U.S. government, which presumably will fund the social security retirement funds and the two other federal·pension plans. Whether or not one wishes to classify these government pension funds as financial·intermediaries depends on the objectives of one's analysis.

Contractual intermediaries create credit instruments that form a contractual relationship with the buyer, such as an annuity or pension. The terms of payments by the buyers and the obligations of the issuer vary according to the contract. Under stipulated conditions at specified times, these instruments can be converted into an exact amount of money and/or a specified share of earnings or a loan at a specified interest rate. The claims against contractual inter-mediaries provide the holder with an asset that can be very liquid, often at a distant date.

Contractual intermediaries directly sell services such as life and property insurance. The administrative costs of operating expenses added to a premium are called the *load factor*. If the premiums just cover these costs plus the actu-arial cost of the insurance, there will be no financial intermediation. Services are sold for a fee. However, the premiums are invested and earn income, which allows a portion of the insurance companies' income to come from the spread between the return on their portfolio and the return they pay on the financial assets—insurance policies that they create. Insurance policies may be viewed from an economic viewpoint as a debt instrument, with the interest contingent on specific events, such as a fire (casualty insurance), a death (life insurance), or the attainment of a particular age (savings plan or, in the 1800s, a tontine). These types of insurance policies will be discussed in the next two sections.

Insurance companies also create financial assets other than insurance poli-cies. They create pension and annuity plans and also have money market funds, making them partly investment intermediaries.

After 1981 many types of contractual and investment intermediaries began offering **Individual Retirement Accounts (IRAs)**. Mutual funds and brokerage firms advertised vigorously for this business, and the depository institutions also joined in. All these financial intermediaries, therefore, were partly in the classification of contractual intermediaries. To understand IRAs and the answer to Study Question 9, here is a brief explanation.

In 1962, the Self-employed Individuals Tax Retirement Act (Keogh Act) per-mitted self-employed individuals to set up retirement programs, or **Keogh plans**, to which they can make contributions that are deductible from their taxable income. (They pay taxes on the later payouts from the pension plan.) The Keogh Act programs are allowed to invest in a special series of govern-ment bonds, certain life insurance contracts, special trust accounts at banks, and mutual funds. Many mutual funds began offering Keogh plans, which puts them partially in the pension business, along with the contractual inter-mediaries.

The 1981 tax act (the Economic Recovery Act of 1981) allowed deductible contributions for employed individuals already in qualified pension plans, up to $2,000 for an individual ($2,250 if a nonworking spouse is included). The individual retirement accounts had not previously been allowed for individuals already in pension plans. Until 1987, not only were the contributions deduc-tible from taxable income, but the earnings on the invested funds were also tax free if they were not withdrawn. The earliest age at which the funds can be withdrawn without a special tax penalty is age $59\frac{1}{2}$. At that time payouts are treated as regular taxable income. But the 1986 tax act cut back on IRA deductions from taxable income. After 1986, the IRA deduction was allowed only for persons below specified income levels who are not active participants in an employer pension plan.

Life Insurance Companies

Life insurance companies had financial assets of $844.0 billion in 1986. Their assets are listed in Table 9-2.

Despite stringent regulations affecting life insurance companies' portfolios in each of the fifty states, their aggregate portfolios contain a slightly wider range of assets than do those of commercial banks, MSBs, and S&Ls. Life insurance companies own a substantial amount of common and preferred stock for pension funds as well as corporate bonds. They invest in both residential and commercial mortgages and own substantial real estate. They also hold securities from federal and local government units and from foreign governments.

Life insurers are the major source among institutional investors (followed by pension funds and other insurance companies) that supply long-term funds.

A key distinction between life insurance companies and depository intermediaries is that the life insurance companies grew under individual state laws. The decision of the U.S. Supreme Court in *Paul* v. *Virginia* in 1869 held that "issuing a policy of insurance is not a transaction of commerce" and "such contracts are not inter-state transactions, though the parties may be domiciled in different states." For a long time, this decision blocked federal regulation, which means both costs and benefits (such as the discount window and free services—before 1981—from the Federal Reserve). Thus a vague call for deregulation, leaving some financial intermediaries under federal supervision, may not produce the level playing field discussed in Chapter 5.

Life insurance companies' incomes are already taxed at a lower rate than are the nonfinancial corporations' incomes. Therefore, tax-free lower-yield municipal obligations have had less appeal to these insurance companies.[10]

In addition, the policyholders' difficulty in paying their premiums during the depression of the 1930s, as well as the reduction in the real value of these

TABLE 9-2   Assets of Life Insurance Companies, March 1986 (in billions of dollars)

Securities	
Government	79.5
U.S.	55.7
State and local	10.1
Foreign	13.8
Business	434.7
Bonds	349.3
Stocks	85.4
Mortgages	173.4
Real estate	29.5
Policy loans	54.2
Other assets	57.4
Total assets	844.0

Source: Federal Reserve Bulletin, October 1986, p. A27.

hard-won savings due to inflated post–World War II prices, caused many investors to shift to other assets. Therefore the size of life insurance companies, relative to that of other financial intermediaries, declined, although life insurance companies themselves continued to grow.

And then came the 1970s. "Change has been whirling through the life insurance business, converting it to something far different from what it was five years ago," wrote Carol Loomis in 1980.[11] Rising rates of inflation and interest rates, as well as the rapid increase in employer insurance plans as a fringe benefit, brought many changes. The rate of return on policyholders' savings was estimated to average under 5 percent in the policies of 100 companies examined.[12] In this respect, policyholders paid a high opportunity cost by not having their savings invested in assets that were more in line with the rising market interest rates. However, policyholders benefited from policy loan rates, which were also low. The policy loans stood at $53 billion in September 1982, 9 percent of the life insurance companies' assets and a rise from 4.8 percent in 1965. These interest rate squeezes are examples of the effects of rapid inflation and the accompanying high interest rates of the 1970s and early 1980s on long-term contracts made on the basis of the lower levels of inflation and interest rates that existed in all earlier peacetime periods in the United States.

When interest rates fell after 1982, life insurance companies benefited. In addition, the Tax Reform Act of 1984 completed the revision of the life insurers' reform, which relieved them of some of the adverse effects of a 1959 tax law that based their tax revenues on the difference between the rate of return on their portfolios and the rate set by state insurance commissioners. By 1983, 86 percent of American families owned an average of $63,000 in life insurance from regular U.S. legal reserve life insurance companies. Life insurance companies received 24.9 percent of their income from life insurance premiums, 20.8 percent from selling annuities, 19.7 percent from selling health insurance, and 28.7 percent from their investments. These investments in life insurance and annuities are evidence that U.S. families wish to leave a large part of their wealth to their heirs, an important point that will be used in our analysis in Chapter 25.

Private, Federal, State, and Local Government Pension Plans

Private pensions provide a huge source of funds for the financial markets. In 1984, private pension funds amounted to more than $916 billion. Thirty-seven percent of these private pension funds were managed by life insurance companies and so are called **insured pension plans**. Nearly all the remaining pension plans, or **noninsured pension funds**, are operated as trusts by commercial banks. Pension funds held 47.2 percent of their assets in equities, or $432 billion in equities, a giant participant in the stock markets.

After 1940, pension plans expanded, with a Supreme Court decision in 1949 contributing to this rapid growth. Employers generally had provided pension plans on a selective basis. But the Supreme Court, by declining to review a

National Labor Relations Board rule, let stand the decision that required Inland Steel Company to bargain with its employees over wages and other conditions of employment, including pension benefits. Pension plans thus became part of the fringe benefits for which labor unions bargained, together with higher wage rates. In the twenty years following World War II, more than half the workers in private employment were covered by private pension plans.

The extensive pension reform legislation that took effect between 1957 and 1981 was contained in the Employee Retirement Income Security Act of 1974 (ERISA), which covered regulations regarding vesting time (the length of time that one must work before being entitled to receive retirement benefits). Employers were required to choose one of three plans for vesting: (1) An individual could be vested with full entitlement to benefits after 10 years of service. (2) An individual could be vested after 5 years of service, starting with entitlement to 25 percent of the pension plan and working up to 100 percent of the pension plan by 15 years of service. (3) The third plan is known as the "Rule of 45." An employee is entitled to 50 percent vesting when his or her age plus number of years of service (employment) add up to 45. Thus, if an individual is 45 years old, he or she will immediately receive 50 percent vesting. The Rule of 45 allows for 10 percent vesting for each succeeding year until full vesting is achieved.

Private pension plans compete with state, local, and federal government pension plans. State laws authorizing pensions for the handicapped were adopted in a number of states after 1900. In 1920, the retirement system for federal civil service employees was established. But these plans were small compared with the old age "insurance" program of the federal government enacted into law in 1935 in the Social Security Act. In 1982 there were 160.6 million employed persons covered by old age, survivors, and disability insurance under social security.

The Social Security Administration does not have the characteristics of a financial intermediary, in general, or a pension and insurance fund, in particular. Within the Social Security Administration and to some extent in Congress, the label of insurance is cherished and tightly held.[13] It also provides a rationale for raising employment taxes. That is, the workers' reactions would be less adverse if individuals thought that their contributions were an actuarially correct payment for their insurance and annuity benefits; that a sound trust fund was being built up so that future generations of workers would not need to face unexpectedly higher tax rates. But that is not the case, as Edwin L. Dale, Jr., assistant director of the Office of Management and Budget for public affairs during the Reagan administration so vividly described:

> As everyone knows and acknowledges, the main Social Security trust fund, the one that pays old age and survivors' benefits, is technically bankrupt. The solution to the problem, for the short run at least, is to have this fund borrow from the disability and Medicare trust funds so that the checks can go out on time and in the full amount due.

The administration and Congress agreed on that solution last year. But the legislation permitting the interfund borrowing expires at the end of 1982. There is no doubt that it, or an alternative means of keeping the checks flowing, will be passed this year, but it still has to be identified in the budget as proposed legislation.[14]

In 1982 President Ronald Reagan appointed a commission chaired by Alan Greenspan to recommend a solution to the Social Security Administration's financial problems. A compromise plan that decreased benefits and raised contributions, but with no fundamental changes, was signed into law in March 1983.

Under the present system, if prices rise and real private consumption per capita does not rise, there will be a redistribution of real income among social security recipients. This could occur, for example, with an imported oil price rise. Internal prices would rise, and the oil price rise would act as an external tax, tending to reduce real income. Social security payments thus should be indexed on an aggregate such as nominal private consumption per capita, to maintain the share of output going to recipients.[15]

Despite the competition from government pension plans, private plans have grown rapidly, much more rapidly than have nominal national income. They have also been combined with profit sharing and tailored to a wide variety of needs.

Why do people prefer this method of holding corporate credit instruments? Why not invest in one of the large mutual funds that has a similar widely diversified portfolio? Employees could purchase a portfolio of similar assets without the mandatory pension contributions and the bias in most pension plans against employees who leave or retire before they are vested. In some company plans, high employee turnover means an increase in the forfeited benefits that increase the costs of changing jobs. Why not bargain for higher wages rather than equivalent employer outlays for pension funds?

The primary reason for the post–World War II surge in private pension fund growth appears to be the increase in personal and corporate taxes and the preferential tax treatment given to pension funds. Employees therefore have an incentive to take their pay in forms other than highly taxed money wage income. Favorable tax treatment is given to both contributions and income earned from assets invested by pension funds.

Personal Trust Funds

Personal trust funds (including managed estates) are assets placed in the care of administrators (formerly called *fiduciaries*) who are often employed by financial intermediaries in their trust departments. The administrators of trust funds are very close in concept to investment companies and therefore are sometimes treated as financial intermediaries. Commercial banks provide trust services. In 1980, the value of assets in personal trust funds and estates managed by commercial banks was $229 billion, as shown in Table 9-3. For

TABLE 9-3 Personal Trusts and Estates Administered by Banks 1969–1980* (asset holdings at year-ends; in billions of dollars)

	1969	1970	1971	1972	1973	1974	1975	1976	1977	1978	1979	1980
1. Total assets	132.761	135.411	159.678	183.104	170.640	142.615	164.862	192.750	189.575	179.325	200.564	228.992
2. Deposits + credit market instruments	34.145	36.926	42.000	45.532	49.632	51.916	57.124	66.168	71.381	69.016	76.926	79.948
3. Total deposits	3.478	3.808	4.858	5.710	5.917	6.235	5.938	7.022	7.665	6.936	7.123	7.217
4. Demand deposits	1.748	1.681	1.694	1.843	1.898	1.795	1.594	1.614	1.563	1.849	1.880	1.881
5. Time + savings accounts	1.730	2.127	3.164	3.867	4.019	4.440	4.344	5.408	6.102	5.807	5.243	5.336
6. Credit market instruments	30.667	33.118	37.142	39.822	43.715	45.681	51.186	59.146	63.716	62.080	69.803	72.731
7. U.S. government securities	8.860	9.566	8.803	8.628	10.012	11.623	14.094	15.753	17.021	15.713	19.154	21.287
8. State and local government securities	10.953	11.879	14.033	15.208	16.184	15.046	16.494	19.986	22.108	21.278	22.750	20.994
9. Other short-term obligations†	.0	.0	.0	.0	.0	.0	.0	.0	.0	9.071	12.294	14.446
10. Other securities	8.662	9.354	11.884	13.527	14.938	16.069	17.752	20.443	21.618	13.149	12.399	12.070
11. Mortgages	2.192	2.319	2.422	2.459	2.581	2.943	2.846	2.964	2.969	2.869	3.206	3.934
12. Corporate equities												
—common	88.438	87.199	104.899	123.835	107.200	76.120	91.350	109.611	100.284	92.700	104.244	124.765
—preferred	2.900	3.018	3.543	3.748	2.727	2.012	2.923	2.656	2.234	2.449	1.859	1.967
13. Real estate	5.473	6.210	6.814	7.450	8.151	9.158	10.141	10.820	11.883	12.183	13.830	18.347
14. All other assets	1.805	2.058	2.422	2.539	2.930	3.409	3.324	3.495	3.793	2.977	3.705	3.965

* Coverage:
1968–1977 All insured commercial banks; total trust assets.
1978 Insured commercial banks and eight Federal Reserve member noninsured trust companies; trust assets over which bank has investment discretion. Omission of nondiscretionary trusts beginning 1978 makes the totals not comparable with earlier years.
1979–1980 Insured commercial and mutual savings banks, Federal Reserve member trust companies, nonmember nondeposit trust companies owned by bank holding companies. Discretionary assets only. Mutual savings banks and trust companies introduced in 1979 held about 2 percent of total 1979 assets.

† Included in line 10 before 1978.

Source: Flow of Funds Accounts, Assets and Liabilities Outstanding 1975–80, Board of Governors of the Federal Reserve System, September 1981, p. 58.

comparison, consider that the income of the Old Age and Survivors Insurance Trust Fund for 1980 was only 44 percent of that amount; the assets of all noninsured pension funds in 1979 amounted to $223 billion, also less than that amount; and the total assets of life insurance companies was 2.2 times larger. In addition, since the 1981 legislation on personal IRA funds, described previously, there has been a rapid growth in IRA and Keogh accounts that commercial banks hold in trust. These holdings amounted to $29.2 billion in October 1982. (Thrift institutions held $37.7 billion, and money market funds held $5.1 billion.)

The amount of common stock managed in these trust funds, $125 billion, makes the banks the major institutional participants in the stock markets. The banks manage these investment funds in their trust departments.[16]

Funds are frequently placed in trust under agreements that have the characteristics of pensions or life insurance claims. The agreements often stipulate payments to the individual after his or her retirement or to his or her heirs. Income from these trusts is frequently taxed at a lower rate. In addition to this stimulant to the formation of trust agreements, trusts provide continuous "responsible" management of an estate according to the directions of the agreement. In fact, it allows the management of an estate to be under the direction of its founder even after his or her death. Because the estate's beneficiaries may be inexperienced in handling the estate, they may benefit from the managerial services of the trust officer.

Administrators of trust funds, such as commercial banks, manage vast amounts of securities, often with considerable latitude. But there may be a conflict of interest, in that commercial banks can lend money at favorable terms to firms in which they hold substantial equities in their trust department.

STUDY QUESTIONS

1. Some insurance companies offer money market funds that are checkable. Will insurance companies therefore become more like banks?
2. If a bank lends money to a corporation and simultaneously trades in the stock of that corporation for its trust accounts, can a conflict of interest arise? If so, how should it be resolved?
3. What similar services do credit unions and stockbrokers offer to the public?
4. Why did money market funds grow so rapidly, and what does the future hold for them?
5. Do finance companies borrow money from banks and then lend it to consumers? Why do not the consumers go directly to the banks? Answer the question by explaining intermediation services.
6. Is the social security system in the United States a financial intermediary? Is its pension plan an old age annuity or "insurance" plan whose premiums are based on actuarial projections of the expected payouts?

7. How did the high interest rates of the 1970s and early 1980s affect insurance companies' profits?

8. How should the concepts of the *level playing field* and *deregulation* be applied to investment and contractual intermediaries? Should these concepts be applied as a matter of policy? Does this mean equal federal regulation for all financial intermediaries? What about nonbank banks?

9. On February 11, 1983, the Board of Governors of the Federal Reserve adjusted the money supply series as follows: Tax-exempt, general-purpose and broker/dealer money market funds were included in M-2, whereas tax-exempt, institution-only money market funds were added to M-3. Each of these tax-exempt funds had previously been excluded from the monetary aggregates. IRA/Keogh accounts at depository institutions and those held in money market mutual funds were removed from M-2 and M-3. IRA/Keogh accounts were held to be less liquid than were other components of M-2 and M-3 because of the relatively high penalty for withdrawing funds from these accounts before age $59\frac{1}{2}$. Do you agree with the rationale behind these changes? If so, explain your reasons. If not, explain what you would have done, and why.

GLOSSARY

Closed-end investment companies. Investment companies that issue a limited number of shares that are traded in financial markets.

Contractual intermediaries. Financial intermediaries that create credit instruments that form a contractual relationship with the buyers, such as an annuity or pension.

Finance companies. Companies that borrow funds from other financial intermediaries and sell their own credit instruments in the financial markets and lend these funds to consumers and businesses.

Fixed or **fixed-trust investment companies.** Investment companies whose portfolios remain virtually intact. They offer certificates for a proportion of the portfolio, or a unit of the portfolio.

Individual Retirement Accounts (IRAs). Individual pension funds deposited in special accounts.

Insured pension funds. Pension funds administered by insurance companies.

Investment companies. Companies that sell shares to their customers and buy income-earning financial assets issued by others.

Investment intermediaries. Financial intermediaries, which include investment companies and finance companies.

Keogh plans. Individual retirement plans for self-employed persons.

Mutual funds. See **Open-ended investment companies.**

Noninsured pension funds. Usually separate entities managed by a committee appointed by a sponsoring organization, which in turn uses the services of a financial intermediary.

Open-end investment companies (or mutual funds). Investment companies that constantly offer to sell new shares (or to redeem outstanding shares) and constantly adjust their portfolios to the available level of funds.

Short-term investment pools (STIPs). Mutual funds that have a portfolio of short-term money market assets.

Spread. The difference between two interest rates, such as the difference between the average ceiling rate on savings deposits and the average rate paid by money market funds in 1978 and 1979, when MMFs grew rapidly.

NOTES

1. The $241.6 billion included MMFs that invested in taxable assets and those that invested in tax-exempt assets. In 1983 they were combined by the Federal Reserve and became a component of M-2. See Chapter 2.

   The estimate of aggregate shares is published by the Federal Reserve Board each week. This estimate is from Board of Governors of the Federal Reserve System, *Federal Reserve Statistical Release*, March 4, 1983, p. 3, Table 3.

2. The number of MMFs with at least $100 million in assets is from *Donoghue's Money Fund Report* (Holliston, Mass.), as reported by *The New York Times*, February 14, 1982, p. F-11.

3. For a further description of the Credit Control Act of 1969, under which this action (reserve requirements for MMFs) was taken, see Chapter 14.

4. Timothy Q. Cook and Jeremy G. Duffield, "Short-Term Investment Pools," *Economic Review*, Federal Reserve Bank of Richmond, September–October 1980, pp. 3–24.

5. Monica Langley, "Holds on Checks Annoy Investors in Money Market Funds," *The Wall Street Journal*, November 11, 1986, p. 39.

6. The classification and name of brokerage articles are taken from Laurence J. De Maria, "How to Pick a Stockbroker," *The New York Times*, February 21, 1982, p. 14. His names for the classifications are the *survivors* (medium-sized regional firms), the *discounters*, the *Guccis* (firms specializing in large investors), the *specialty houses* (firms specializing in specific markets), and the *outsiders* (firms that are not members of the New York Stock Exchange or other exchanges).

7. Ibid.

8. Ibid.

9. The data for the life insurance companies are not directly comparable with the data for the pension funds because some of the life insurance companies' funds come from private pension funds and from state and local pension funds that the life insurance companies manage. The total value of life insurance assets can be found in the *1985 Life Insurance Fact Book* (Washington, D.C.: American Council of Life Insurance, 1985), p. 68. Data on pension fund assets can also be found in this book, on p. 22. Information on other insurance companies can be found in *Insurance*

Facts, 1985–86, Property/Casualty Fact Book (New York: Insurance Information Institute, 1986), p. 18.

10. Herbert E. Dougall, *Capital Markets and Institutions* (Englewood Cliffs, N.J.: Prentice-Hall, 1965), p. 5.

11. Carol J. Loomis, "Life Isn't What It Used to Be, and Neither Are the Inflation-buffeted Insurance Companies That Sell the Product," *Fortune*, July 14, 1980, p. 86.

12. The study, conducted by Consumers Union, is reported in ibid, p. 88.

13. This is in keeping with the original principles of social security legislation accepted by President Franklin Roosevelt and by Congress. James H. Schultz summarized the six principles involved, including this one: "Social security benefits were to be a matter of right; there was to be no *means test*. Workers were to earn their benefits through participation and contribution to the program. The system was to be self-supporting through those worker contributions, together with so-called employee contributions." [*The Economics of Aging* (Belmont, Calif.: Wadsworth, 1980), p. 95]. The employer's contributions are partly and perhaps substantially borne by the worker, given that the demand for labor is sloping downward.

14. Edwin L. Dale, Jr., "Stockman Didn't Slash That Much," *The Washington Post*, February 16, 1982, p. A19.

15. Jack Rutner suggested indexing payments to GNP minus 3.5 percent (the average expected rise in real GNP). There is no perfect index that will maintain the recipients' proportion of real income to the private sector. It is not even clear what constant proportion of real income they should receive. Should they share in capital gains that accrue to the private sector? Should they share only in labor income, indexing on wage income?

16. The size of these fixed income funds for 1981 is reported in the daily banking newspaper, *The American Banker*, February 25, 1982, pp. 10, 12, 13. The classification of all trust department business as either contractual or investment intermediaries is not meaningful; they are both.

PART THREE

FINANCIAL MARKETS, ASSET PRICES, AND INTEREST RATES

CHAPTER 10

ASSET PRICES, INCOME, AND INTEREST RATES

CHAPTER PREVIEW

Introduction. The arithmetic connection among the price of assets, their yield, and their expected income, as given by the basic valuation formula, is fundamental to much analysis.

Compounding Once a Year. All the formulas follow from the compound interest formula presented in this section.

Discounting Once a Year. The present value of a stream of income is discussed.

The Basic Valuation Formula. The basic valuation formula is the present value of future income; it is used for stock prices.

Internal Rate of Return. If the expected income and the price of an asset are known, the unknown variable will be the internal rate of return.

The appendices present extensions of the basic computations in the chapter.

INTRODUCTION

The price of an asset and its expected income are related by its interest rate (also called the yield or rate of return). But whereas the price per unit of an asset has the dimension of dollars, the expected flow of income has the dimension of dollars per unit of time. The **rate of interest**, or **yield**, is a pure number per unit of time, such as 5 percent a year. The interest rate shows the time dimension of an asset. To illuminate this view of the interest rate, consider its reciprocal, the **year's purchase**. The reciprocal of 5 percent a year is 1/.05/year, or 20 years. This means that a dollar invested at 5 percent interest will be repaid (at simple interest) in 20 years.

Interest rates thus measure the connecting link between the **stock variable** of assets and their expected **flow variable** of income (or payment stream). Learning the arithmetic of relationships between interest rates and these stocks and flows is a necessary step for fruitful analysis.

There are a number of important statistics used to describe financial assets, including their price, the size of their payment stream, and their yield. These statistics can often be found in bond and annuity tables, provided that the characteristics of the financial asset conform to the table's assumptions. Tables are certainly useful and should be used, just as a cashier making a retail sale uses a sales tax chart or a programmed calculation in the cash register. But understanding the nature of financial assets requires knowing the underlying computational procedures. These underlying computations reveal the relationship among the income, market value, and yield on a financial asset. The best way to become familiar with these relationships is to examine the underlying formulas and, most important of all, actually to calculate the statistics for different types of financial assets. It is possible to stare for a long time at a formula that gives the present value of a bond without understanding it. But substituting in the actual values for a bond's income stream and yield and actually calculating the present value is, like a picture, worth a thousand words.

That learning experience can be more rewarding and enjoyable than can many other trips to the land of mathematics, because the versatile hand computer takes almost all the drudgery out of the tedious arithmetic calculations. Multiplying 1.0675 by itself 25 times—as is required for a bond maturing in 25 years with a 6.75 percent yield—is a headache if you use only pencil and paper. But on many calculators you punch in 1.0675, the Y^x button, 25, and then the = (equals) key. In a second, the answer, 5.119141, appears. The drudgery is gone. Only the satisfaction of learning the practical skills of computing statistics for financial assets on a modern calculator remains.

But it is necessary to have a calculator that contains at least the following features: (1) a Y^x key for raising a number to a higher power or for taking a root and (2) several memories, including a summation memory. If you wish to learn continuous compounding, your calculator should have natural logarithms. Business calculators programmed for the formulas in this chapter should not be used to learn these procedures.

The price of an asset such as corporation's stock, the income it is expected to produce, and its yield (or, equivalently, its rate of return or interest rate) all are tied together by the basic valuation formula. That formula will be presented after we explain the arithmetic involved in calculating the relationship.

The concepts in this relationship are from the fields of finance and economics and are often overlooked, with embarrassing results. For example, a large bank's research department reported, "The market looked good today; both bond prices and bond yields rose." It is hoped that when you complete this chapter, you will find that statement to be a joke.

COMPOUNDING ONCE A YEAR

Suppose that the interest payment on a savings account is to be calculated and added to the account once a year. This is called **compounding** once a year (annually). If $100 were initially deposited and the interest rate were 5 percent per year, $5 interest would be paid at the end of the first year. This would increase the deposit balance to $105. During the entire second year, the deposit would have amounted to $105; the account would be paid 5 percent of that, or $5.25, on the last day of the second year. Interest would be earned on the interest earned in previous periods. At the end of the second year, the account would have a balance of $110.25 at the compound interest rate of 5 percent.

This example of compound interest can be put into a more general form. If $100r$ is the (percentage) interest rate and R_1 is the value of the deposit at the end of the first year, then

$$PV(1 + r) = R_1 \qquad (1)$$

where PV is called the present value or, in equilibrium, the *market price* of R_1. If R_1 is compounded for another year,

$$R_1(1 + r) = R_2 \qquad (2)$$

where R_2 is the value of the deposit at the end of the second year. This process can be repeated for any number of years. Rather than write this long expression, the terms can be collected into a simpler general statement:

$$PV(1 + r)^Y = R_Y \qquad \textit{Compound Interest} \quad (3)$$

where Y is the number of years and R_Y is called the **return** at the end of the Yth year. This is the **compound interest** or **future value** formula. It is a basic formula from which every formula in this chapter can be derived.

Returning to the mathematical example, suppose that $100 is left on deposit for three years at a 5 percent interest rate. The deposit grows to $105 at the end of the first year. Five percent of that plus the $105 equals $110.25, the value of the deposit at the end of the second year. Five percent of that is $5.5125, so that the deposit is $115.7625 at the end of the third year. If equation (3) is used, the same result will be obtained. First, multiply 1.05 by itself three times, which equals 1.157625. Multiply this product by the original principal, $100, and $115.7625 is obtained. This is the value of $100 compounded once a year, for three years, at 5 percent.

PRACTICE PROBLEM: COMPOUNDING

Suppose that $752.39 is deposited in a savings account on January 1, 1929. How large would the balance be on March 4, 1988, if interest had been paid at a rate of 3.5 percent compounded and payable on December 31 of each year? Repeat for 10.5 percent interest.

Answer: The last compounding will have been on December 31, 1987, which would have been the fifty-ninth yearly compounding. The compounding factor is unity plus the interest rate, 1.035. Taking the compounding factor up to the fifty-ninth power, it equals 7.611682. Multiply this amount by the original deposit, $752.39, to obtain the answer, $5,726.95; at 10.5 percent, the answer is $272,155.69.

DISCOUNTING ONCE A YEAR

The terms in equation (3), the compound interest formula, can be rearranged so that they appear as

$$PV = \frac{R_Y}{(1 + r)^Y} \quad \textit{Discounting or Present Value} \quad (4)$$

This is called the **discounting** or **present value** formula. The present value of future income discounted once a year, at the end of the year, at a rate of r is given by the discounting formula. In the previous example, the $110.25 expected at the end of the second year will have a present value of $100 if it is discounted at 5 percent. If R_Y is expected in the Yth year, the present value can be obtained if the interest rate is known.

PRACTICE PROBLEM: DISCOUNTING

If John's rich aunt leaves him $100,000, payable ten years after her death, what will be its present value at the time of her death using a 7 percent interest rate (and assuming that the bequest is not taxed)? The answer is obtained by discounting $100,000 back ten years at 7 percent.

Answer:

$$\frac{\$100,000}{(1.07)^{10}} = \$50,834.93$$

PRACTICE PROBLEM: DISCOUNTING

Wilma suddenly remembers a savings account she opened 70 years earlier. She finds that it currently contains a balance of $146.06. How much did she originally deposit if the interest rate was 3 percent for the first 40 years and 5 percent for the last 30 years?

The answer is found by first discounting $146.06 back 30 years at 5 percent:

$$\frac{\$146.06}{(1.05)^{30}} = \$33.795$$

Then that sum (saving the integers to the right of the decimal point for the accuracy needed for high powers—repeated compounding) is in turn discounted back 40 years at 3 percent.

Answer:

$$\frac{\$33.795}{(1.03)^{40}} = \$10.36$$

PRACTICE PROBLEM: DISCOUNTING A STREAM OF INCOME

Suppose that a three-year bond has a coupon payment of $70.00 each year, a 7 percent coupon rate, and an annual (December 3) payment date. In the third year, the owner of the bond receives the $70.00 coupon payment plus the $1,000 face value of the bond. The present value of $70.00 one year in the future will be $65.42 if the interest rate is 5 percent:

$$\$65.42 = \frac{\$70}{1 + r}$$

If $r = .05$, the present value of the three-year bond will be

$$\$1,054.47 = \frac{\$70}{1.05} + \frac{\$70}{(1.05)^2} + \frac{\$1,070}{(1.05)^3}$$

Now take out your calculator, clear it, and solve for the present value. Here are some hints that are useful for most calculators. First, enter 1.05 on the calculator. If the calculator has a memory, store this in the memory; then divide by $70.00. Then take the reciprocal, $1/x$.* This should equal

$66.6667. If the calculator has a summation memory, push the summation button. If it does not, record the number. Now recall 1.05 from the memory and square it. Divide it by $70.00 and take the reciprocal. Again, if the calculator has a summation button, sum this number into the summation memory; if it does not, record the number. Recall 1.05 from the memory and cube it; that is, take it up to the power of 3. This is 1.1576. Divide by $1,070.00 and take the reciprocal. This is $924.30. Again, sum it into the memory or record it. Next, either recall the three amounts summed into the memory or add them up from the record you are keeping, to obtain the present value, $1,054.47, rounding to the nearest penny.

* For many students, it is more natural to divide the numerator by 1.05 to the appropriate power. However, it is simpler on a calculator to take the denominator to the appropriate power first and then to divide and take a reciprocal.

The discounting formula can be put in general terms for a stream of income R_1, R_2, and so on, to R_N: a rate of discount r and an initial present value PV.

$$\text{PV} = \frac{R_1}{1 + r} + \frac{R_2}{(1 + r)^2} + \cdots + \frac{R_N}{(1 + r)^N} \quad \begin{array}{l} \textit{Present Value of an} \\ \textit{Income Stream} \end{array} \quad (5)$$

This formula says that the present value is the discounted value of expected future returns. The time periods can begin in the present period, 0, and continue to the termination of income in period N. The income stream in equation (5) begins with an annual payment one year in the future.

THE BASIC VALUATION FORMULA

Another name for equation (5) is the **basic valuation formula**. It says that the present value of wealth, PV, is the discounted value of future income, R_1, R_2, and so on, discounted by using the rate of interest, r. To see how it works, consider the following example in which it is applied in general terms to evaluating a corporate stock.

The value of corporate stock may be viewed as the **present value** of the future profits of the corporation. The stock price, SP, of a share of stock can be inserted for the present value, and the expected profits can be used for the income stream. The size of future profits is a rough estimate, often made with a great deal of uncertainty. One way to express these expected profits that takes into account this uncertainty is to call on probability theory. But for simplicity, this call is not made; the complication is bypassed, except for a note.[1]

The expected profits in the years one, two, three, and so on are R_1, R_2, R_3, and so on. Then

$$SP = \frac{R_1}{1 + r} + \frac{R_2}{(1 + r)^2} + \frac{R_3}{(1 + r)^3} + \cdots \quad (6)$$

where $\cdots$ means "and so on" and r is the rate at which the individual discounts the future.

If the future becomes more uncertain, say, because of the threat of war, r will rise and stock prices will fall. The rate of discount will rise because an income payment far in the future—say, 5, 10, or 20 years away—becomes less valuable. There is a shift in preferences toward present consumption ("live it up today") rather than future income from stock purchases ("tomorrow is a lifetime away"). Notice that *a change in preference toward income today instead of income in the future may lower the price of stock, even though there is no change in the expected stream of profits.*

INTERNAL RATE OF RETURN

In most cases, the buyer of a financial asset knows its present value, its present price on the market. The buyer also knows, or can estimate, the payments stream. The unknown variable is the interest rate or yield or, as it is sometimes also called, the **internal rate of return**.

The value of the internal rate of return is found through a trial-and-error hunt called **iteration**. Iteration merely amounts to trying different interest rates in equation (5) until one is obtained that is consistent with the present value, the price of the financial asset in the market. Some business calculators can find this internal rate of return merely by being given the price and the dated payment pattern. Programmable calculators with enough memory and program steps can be programmed to look for the correct yield. If you have the time, you can insert different interest rates into the discount formula, solve for the present value for each interest rate, and, correcting each time in the right direction, see if you can sail into port in this more tedious blindfolded navigational feat.[2]

APPENDIX A: EQUATIONS FOR REFERENCE

An Approximation for the Rate of Return on a Bond

Suppose that a bond pays a *coupon* of $110 per year, payable on the last day of the year. The bond will mature in three years. This means that there are three coupons left, and on the last payment, there is a return of the *face value*, or an additional $1,000.00. So the final payment is $1,110. The bond is currently selling for $1,050.63. What is its yield?

The formula for this problem is equation (5). Substituting the values just given,

$$\$1,050.63 = \frac{\$110}{1+r} + \frac{\$110}{(1+r)^2} + \frac{\$1,110}{(1+r)^3}$$

The problem is to find the value of r. One shortcut approximation that often works is given by the following formula:

$$r \approx \frac{\text{coupon rate} + \left(\dfrac{\text{face value} - \text{purchase price}}{\text{number of years to maturity}}\right)}{(\text{face value} + \text{purchase price})/2} \tag{7}$$

where r is the approximate annual yield on a bond held to maturity.

Substituting in the values from this example,

$$r \approx \frac{\$110.00 + (\$1,000.00 - \$1,050.63)/3}{(\$1,000.00 + \$1,050.63)/2} = 9.08\%$$

The 9.08 percent approximation is very close to the actual value of 9 percent.

If bond tables are available, they can be consulted. But the problem posed is often in a slightly different form than that in the bond tables or that given for equation (7). In these cases, one must iterate. This can be time-consuming without a computer program, and if done manually, you must explain to friends that you cannot visit them because you are iterating.

Perpetuities

Equation (5) can be simplified if the same income is received in every future period; that is, $R_1 = R_2 = R_3 = \cdots = R_{N-1} = R_N$, where N is a very large number. Equation (5) becomes

$$PV = \frac{R}{r} \qquad \textit{Consol or Perpetuity} \quad (8)$$

where the return R is expected to be constant over time. Equation (8) can be used for a bond with a constant (and therefore perpetual) income stream. It is called a *perpetuity* or, in the case of such bonds sold by the British government, a *consol*.

Suppose that a consol pays $5 a year forever and the market rate of interest is 10 percent. What is the price of the bond? Insert these values into equation (8). The ratio of $5/.1 is $50, the price of the bond. If the bond has a maturity date, equation (5) should be used.

Compounding More Than Once a Year

Suppose that a depository intermediary compounds quarterly to calculate interest payments on deposits. Therefore, instead of paying r interest each quarter, it pays $r/4$, or one fourth of the yearly interest each quarter. Also instead of compounding Y times in Y years, it compounds $4Y$ times.

More generally, suppose that the interest is compounded N times a year. Then r/N interest is paid each compounding time, and compounding occurs NY times in Y years.

It is easy to substitute these new values in equation (3) for compounding N times a year:

$$PV\left(1 + \frac{r}{N}\right)^{NY} = R_Y \qquad (9)$$

It turns out that equation (9) is not only useful in calculating quarterly (four times), semiannually (two times), and other discrete values of N; it is also a step toward continuous compounding when N approaches infinity. Luckily, this does not require punching the keys on a calculator at rapid speeds for an entire year. A simple formula is available.

Continuous Compounding and Discounting

Continuous or instantaneous compounding and discounting formulas are valuable tools for a number of reasons, including the following two: First, many growth processes are fairly continuous. That is, compounding takes place at nearly every instant in time. It is the inability to gather data continuously that causes these processes to appear as discrete changes from the available estimates. Second, many depository institutions that have been subject to ceilings on the interest they pay their depositors have used continuous compounding. This has allowed them to pay slightly higher interest amounts.

Suppose that a bank pays 5 percent interest on its accounts and pays that interest only once, on the last day of the year. A $1,000,000 deposit would therefore receive an interest payment of $50,000. If the bank compounded at every instant of time at the same 5 percent yearly interest rate, a $1,000,000 deposit would receive $51,271 in interest payments over the year. At the end of the second year, the size of the deposits for annual and continuous compounding would be, respectively, $1,102,500 and $1,105,171 (which is .2 percent larger). At the end of 50 years, the size of the deposit would be $11,467,400 with annual compounding and $12,182,494 (or 6.2 percent larger) with continuous compounding.

The basis of continuous compounding and discounting is **Euler's** e. Leonard Euler (1707–1783) discovered that if M in the following equation is given larger and larger values, the right-hand value will approach a constant number, which has been named Euler's e. Suppose M rises all the way up to infinity; then

$$\text{limit of } (1 + 1/M)^M = 2.7182818284 \cdots = e \tag{10}$$

as M approaches infinity (where $\cdots$ means "and so on"). Euler's e can be approximated by 2.718 for most purposes. This degree of accuracy will be attained if M is equal to 10,000. Take the reciprocal of 10,000 ($= .0001$), add 1, and raise this sum to a power of 10,000 to obtain 2.718.

To show how Euler's e can be used, suppose that a bank compounds N times during the year. The appropriate compound interest formula is then equation (9). As N becomes larger (that is, the number of compoundings each year increases), the instantaneous rate of compounding is approached. Suppose that N approaches infinity. Euler's e enters the analysis. Let $1/M = r/N$ so that equation (9) can be written as

$$PV[(1 + 1/M)^M]^{rY} = R_Y \tag{11}$$

As N approaches infinity, M approaches infinity, and the expression in brackets in equation (11) approaches Euler's *e*. Equation (11) then can be rewritten as

$$PVe^{rY} = R_Y, \qquad \text{or } PV(2.718 \cdots)^{rY} = R_y \quad \textit{Continuous Compounding} \quad (12)$$

The interest rate, *r* in equation (12), is referred to as the **instantaneous** or **continuous rate of interest**.

Stating interest in continuously compounded form yields a smaller number than does stating interest in a discretely compounded form. If a $100 deposit grows to $105 in one year, the discrete rate of interest for compounding once a year on the last day of the year will be 5 percent. Continuous compounding of $100 at 4.88 percent for one year also will produce a deposit at the end of the year of $105.00.[3] Generally, the continuous interest rate is labeled the same as the corresponding interest rate under discrete compounding. These two types of interest rates can usually be differentiated by the way they are used.

Compound Interest Approximation

An approximation for equation (12) is handy for those who do not carry a calculator. It allows one to calculate rapidly compound interest rates on the back of an envelope or in one's head without resorting to tables or calculators. The expression e^{rY} in equation (12) is approximated as follows:

$$e^{rY} = 1 + rY + \frac{(rY)^2}{2} + g \qquad (13)$$

where *g* is the remainder (the error in the approximation which is less than .024 when *rY* is as large as .5. The error is smaller with smaller values of *rY*. In words, equation (13) requires the following four simple steps to obtain e^{rY}:

1. Multiply the number of years by the interest rate.
2. Square the number found in step 1, and divide it by 2.
3. Add the number found in step 2 to the number found in step 1.
4. Add 1 to the number in step 3 to find the answer.

Now try a problem. What is the value of a $100 deposit earning 5 percent continuous interest at the end of four years? The values for the four steps are

1. $4 + .05 = 0.2$

2. $\dfrac{(0.2)^2}{2} = 0.02$

3. $0.2 + 0.02 = 0.22$
4. $1 + 0.22 = 1.22$

So $e^{4(.05)}$ equals 1.22. Because $100 was deposited, multiply $100 by 1.22 to obtain $122, the answer.

The correct value of $e^{4(.05)}$ rounded to two decimals is found by looking in Table 10-1. It is also 1.22.

TABLE 10-1 Continuous Interest Rates of Discounts for Selected
Years (Y) and Interest rates (r)

Suppose that $500 is compounded continuously at 10 percent interest for five years. What is its future value? In this case, $rY = .5$. Find .5 in the first column of the table. The multiple for this compounding (e^x) to five decimal places is 1.64872. Multiplying this number by $500 gives $824.36, the value of $500 continuously compounded at 10 percent for five years.

How much will the present value be of $100 to be received 40 years in the future if it is continuously discounted at 6 percent? In this case, $rY = 2.4$. Find that number in the first column of the table. The multiple for this compounding (e^{-x} or $1/e^x$) is found in column 3 of the table. It is, to five decimal places, .09071. Multiply this number of $100 to obtain $90.71, the present value. (For values of rY between the values in column 1, simple interpolation will give a fairly close answer.)

Check all computations on your calculator. The table provides more decimal places than can be obtained on most hand calculators and can be used as a check for calculations done on the calculator for an open-book examination in which calculators are not permitted.

$rY(=X)$	Multiple for Future Value e^x	Multiple for Present Value $1/e^x$
0.0	1.00000 00000 00000	1.00000 00000 00000 00000
0.1	1.10517 09180 75648	.90483 74180 35959 57316
0.2	1.22140 27581 60170	.81873 07530 77981 85867
0.3	1.34985 88075 76003	.74081 82206 81717 86607
0.4	1.49182 46976 41270	.67032 00460 35639 30074
0.5	1.64872 12707 00128	.60653 06597 12633 42360
0.6	1.82211 88003 90509	.54881 16360 94026 43263
0.7	2.01375 27074 70477	.49658 53037 91409 51470
0.8	2.22554 09284 92468	.44932 89641 17221 59143
0.9	2.45960 31111 56950	.40656 96957 40599 11188
1.0	2.71828 18284 59045	.36787 94411 71442 32160
1.1	3.00416 60239 46433	.33287 10836 98079 55329
1.2	3.32011 69227 36547	.30119 42119 12202 09664
1.3	3.66929 66676 19244	.27253 17930 34012 60312
1.4	4.05519 99668 44675	.24659 69639 41606 47694
1.5	4.48168 90703 38065	.22313 01601 48429 82893
1.6	4.95303 24243 95115	.20189 65179 94655 40849
1.7	5.47394 73917 27200	.18268 35240 52734 65022
1.8	6.04964 74644 12946	.16529 88882 21586 53830
1.9	6.68589 44422 79269	.14956 86192 22635 05264
2.0	7.38905 60989 30650	.13533 52832 36612 69189
2.1	8.16616 99125 67650	.12245 64282 52981 91022
2.2	9.02501 34994 34121	.11080 31583 62333 88333
2.3	9.97418 24548 14721	.10025 88437 22803 73373
2.4	11.02317 63806 41602	.09071 79532 89412 50338
2.5	12.18249 39607 03473	.08208 49986 23898 79517
2.6	13.46373 80350 01690	.07427 35782 14333 88043
2.7	14.87973 17248 72834	.06720 55127 39749 76513

TABLE 10-1   *(continued)*

$rY(=X)$	Multiple for Future Value e^x	Multiple for Present Value $1/e^x$
2.8	16.44464 67710 97050	.06081 00626 25217 96500
2.9	18.17414 53694 43061	.05502 32200 56407 22903
3.0	20.08553 69231 87668	.04978 70683 67863 94298
3.1	22.19795 12814 41633	.04504 92023 93557 80607
3.2	24.53253 01971 09349	.04076 22039 78366 21517
3.3	27.11263 89206 57887	.03688 31674 01240 00545
3.4	29.96410 00473 97013	.03337 32699 60326 07948
3.5	33.11545 19586 92314	.03019 73834 22318 50074
3.6	36.59823 44436 77988	.02732 37224 47292 56080
3.7	40.44730 43600 67391	.02472 35264 70339 39120
3.8	44.70118 44933 00823	.02237 07718 56165 59578
3.9	49.40244 91055 30174	.02024 19114 45804 38847
4.0	54.59815 00331 44239	.01831 56388 88734 18029
4.1	60.34028 75973 61969	.01657 26754 01761 24754
4.2	66.68633 10409 25142	.01499 55768 20477 70621
4.3	73.69979 36995 95797	.01356 85590 12200 93176
4.4	81.45086 86649 68117	.01227 73399 03068 44118
4.5	90.01713 13005 21814	.01110 89965 38242 30650
4.6	99.48431 56419 33809	.01005 18357 44633 58164
4.7	109.94717 24521 23499	.00909 52771 01695 81709
4.8	121.51041 75187 34881	.00822 97470 49020 02884
4.9	134.28977 96849 35485	.00744 65830 70924 34052
5.0	148.41315 91025 76603	.00673 79469 99085 46710

Source: U.S. Department of Commerce, National Bureau of Standards, *Handbook of Mathematical Functions with Formulas, Graphs, and Mathematical Tables*, eds. Milton Abramowitz and Irene A. Stegun (Washington, D.C.: Superintendent of Documents, U.S. Government Printing Office, June 1964), p. 136.

The Rules of 70 and 72

The following is another useful approximation for continuous compounding that requires no calculator. How long will it take $1 to double (to become $2) at a compound interest rate of r? Using equation (12) (with units of dollars),

$$1 \cdot e^{rY} = 2 \tag{14}$$

For those who know logarithms, transform equation (14) into

$$rY = \ln 2 \quad \text{or} \quad Y = \frac{\ln 2}{r} \approx \frac{.70}{r} \tag{15}$$

Because $\ln 2 = .693$, which will be approximated as .70, divide .70 by the interest rate. The **rule of 70** is *to divide 70 by the interest rate (in percentage form) to determine the number of years for doubling the value.*

For example, if the interest rate is .05, one dollar will double in approximately $70/5 = 14$ years. If the interest rate is 7 percent, one dollar will double in approximately $70/7 = 10$ years. At a 10 percent inflation rate, college tuition should double every 7 years.

For compounding once a year, instead of continuous compounding, the number 72 is divided by the percentage interest rate. In the example, using 5 percent, the approximate time period for doubling would be $72/5 = 14.4$. This can be checked by inserting these values in equation (3):

$$\$1(1.05)^{14.4} = \$2.02$$

This is the **rule of 72**.

APPENDIX B: COMPOUND INTEREST ANTICS

The possibilities for enormous growth with compounding are easily illustrated. Suppose that when Peter Minuit of the Dutch West India Company bought Manhattan Island from the Indians in 1626 for $24 (in trinkets), the Indians had invested this sum. At 10 percent interest, the Indians would have had, at the end of 1980, with continuous compounding, $56,785,297,000,000,000. Had they placed their investment with a depository, compounding only once a year, they would have had much less by 1980—$10,794,979,000,000,000. The difference is $45,990,318,000,000,000, enough to buy New York City and the rest of the world.

APPENDIX C: MORTGAGES AND ANNUITIES

Suppose that Walter Johnson began working at age 21 for the United Tool Company, which invests $100 for Walter each month at a 7 percent annual yield. How much would Mr. Johnson receive, in addition to the customary gold watch, at age 65, when he rose to speak at his retirement party? This method of saving is embodied in a contract called an **annuity**.

The solution begins by noticing that Mr. Johnson receives one month's interest rate on the last payment, one month before he retires. That amount is $P(1 + r)$, where P is the $100 monthly payment and r is the monthly interest rate (.07 per year/12). Two months before retirement, the $100 payment would yield two months' interest at retirement, $P(1 + r)^2$, and so on, backward in time to his first payment, which was made one month after he started. If N is the number of months Mr. Johnson worked at United Tool, that first month's payment will, at age 65, amount to $P(1 + r)^{N-1}$. Mr. Johnson will have worked 44 years, which (times 12 months) is 528 months, the value of N.

The sum, S, of the values of these monthly payments at age 65 can be painlessly computed from a formula derived as follows. For ease in notation, let $L^i = (1 + r)^i$, where i takes values from 1 (on the final payment) to $N - 1$ (on the first payment). Then

$$S = 1 + L + L^2 + \cdots + L^{N-1} \tag{16}$$

This series can be simplified. Multiply each side of equation (16) by L and then subtract the resulting equation from equation (16). Then solve for S and substitute $(1 + r)^i$ back in the equation for L^i.

The symbol S is the value of the annuity if $1 is invested each month. If P dollars are invested each month, the value of the annuity after N periods, R_N, is then found by multiplying by P to obtain

$$R_N = P\left[\frac{(1 + r)^N - 1}{r}\right] \tag{17}$$

From this equation, the value of an annuity at age 65 can easily be calculated to be $352,535.39. The present value of this annuity at age 21 can be found by dividing equation (17) by $(1 + r)^Y$, where r is an annual rate of interest. In this case, if 7 percent is also the annual rate used to discount future income, the present value at age 21 will be $17,960.42 (using yearly discounting periods).

Suppose that a homeowner wants to find out how much is owed on a mortgage. If the owner borrowed $50,000.00 at 8.5 percent 9 years (108 months) ago and has been making a payment of $384.46 each month (excluding other payments for taxes, insurance, and so on), the annuity formula, equation (17), can be used in a new formulation to compute the balance. If no payments had been made on the mortgage, the balance would be found simply by inserting the original amount borrowed in the compound interest formula, equation (3) with N (the number of months instead of Y, the number of years). But because the homeowner has made monthly payments in the same form as an annuity, the annuity formulation in equation (17) becomes an offsetting amount. The balance B_N after N months is

$$B_N = B_0(1 + r)^N - P\left[\frac{(1 + r)^N - 1}{r}\right] \tag{18}$$

where B_0 is the original amount borrowed and r is the monthly rate of interest. It is .085/12 in this example. According to this formulation, the homeowner still owes $45,110.84. On a more positive note, he has paid off $4,889.16 of the loan, which, together with the down payment and capital gain, may make his net assets larger than they were 9 years before.[4]

STUDY QUESTIONS

1. Using compounding once at the end of the year, quarterly, and continuously at interest rates of 1 percent, 5 percent, and 20 percent, to what amount will $100 grow in ten years?

2. What are the differences between compound and simple interest?
3. What is the present value of each of the three following three-year bonds with the following indicated income stream at an interest rate of 6 percent?

	Year 1	Year 2	Year 3
a.	$70	$70	$1,070
b.	50	50	1,050
c.	60	60	1,060

4. What is the value of a perpetuity paying $4.50 a year forever if the interest rate is 10 percent?
5. How big are the payments on a 30-year mortgage for $100,000 at 9 percent interest?
6. What is the present value of the perpetuity in study question 4 if it is not inherited for two years? Use an 8 percent annual rate for discounting. [*Hint:* The present value of $X that is to be received in two years is $X/(1 + r)^2$.]
7. Approximately how long will it take $5,000 to double if it is invested at a 1 percent interest rate? Describe the rule of 70 approximation for this answer.
8. If a three-year bond costing $973.27 has the following future income stream, what will be its yield?

Year 1	$ 50
Year 2	50
Year 3	1,050

GLOSSARY

Annuity. A financial instrument with a series of payments (such as every month for N years) up to a given date (often retirement) and then a series of returns (such as every month for X years) or a lump-sum return. There are many variations of this instrument.

Basic valuation formula. See Present value.

Compounding. Adding the compound interest to a balance.

Compound interest. An interest rate computed on the accumulating balance.

Continuous (or instantaneous) rate of interest. Compound interest rate in which the number of compoundings per year approaches infinity.

Discounting. Finding the present value of an expected income stream.

Euler's e. The base for the continuous rate of interest calculation. (More formally, it is the value of the limit in equation (10) as M goes to infinity.) To four decimal places, it is equal to 2.7182.

Flow variable. A variable, such as income, with the dimensions of an amount per unit of time.

Future value. See **Compound interest.**

Internal rate of return. The interest rate at which an expected income stream is discounted to obtain a given present value. (It may not have a unique value.)

Iteration. Finding a solution by trial and error that essentially plugs in different values until one that is consistent with the given values in an equation is obtained.

Present value. The present value of a future income stream. Using the present value formula, it is obtained by discounting an expected income stream.

Rate of interest. A pure number per unit of time, such as .06 per year. It is used to translate an expected income stream into a present value. The yield and rate of return are usually used as synonyms for the rate of interest, although the rate of return is a name often reserved for problems in which the present value and the expected income stream are known and the rate of return is unknown.

Return. The amount received, or expected to be received, in the payment stream from an asset. (Unfortunately, it is also used in the finance literature as the rate of return.)

Rule of 70. An approximation for estimating the time it takes for an asset to double in value if it is subject to continuous interest rates.

Rule of 72. An approximation for estimating the time it takes for an asset to double in value if it is subject to compounding once a year.

Stock variable. A variable, such as the stock of particular assets, that has the dimension of dollars, such as $11 trillion or $.50.

Years' purchase. The reciprocal of the interest rate. It shows the years required to return the cost of an investment at simple interest rates.

Yield. See **Rate of interest.**

NOTES

1. Essentially, this would require all possible profits or losses (entered as a negative) in each period to be weighted by a fraction indicating the probability of each possible outcome. The fractions would be constructed so that they would sum to unity. The weighted alternative profit possibilities for each period would be added together, and the sum for each period would be the expected profit for the respective period. The computations become somewhat more complex if the profit in one period is dependent on the profit for another period.

2. There is the possibility of getting more than one answer for this problem; in fact, there are as many answers as there are years to maturity, although most are not positive real numbers. For this problem of multiple roots and a number of other problems that have made the field of finance turn to a criterion other than internal rate of return for selecting the most profitable investments, see Robert D. Auerbach, *Financial Markets and Institutions* (New York: Macmillan, 1983), Chap. 13.

3. By dividing an amount by e^{rx} (or, equivalently, multiplying by e^{-rY}, the present value in the Yth year can be found. The values of e^{-rY} are found in the lower triangles of Table 10-1.

4. The present value of the annuity, when N equals the total number of periods in the loan, gives the amount borrowed. Divide equation (18) by $(1 + r)^N$, and to simplify, assume that the balance is zero (when $N = 360$ in the example). Then the original amount borrowed, B_0, is given by

$$B_0 = P\left[\frac{(1 + r)^N - 1}{r(1 + r)^N}\right] \tag{19}$$

This is a useful formulation for finding the original amount borrowed, or by solving equation (19) for P, the monthly payments can be found if their size is unknown:

$$P = B_0\left[\frac{r(1 + r)^N}{(1 + r)^N - 1}\right] \tag{20}$$

where again N is the total number of periods in the loan.

CHAPTER 11

THE TERM STRUCTURE OF INTEREST RATES

CHAPTER PREVIEW

Introduction. The yield curve and the term structure of interest rates are described.

The Pure Expectations Hypothesis. Long rates (rates of interest on debt instruments with more distant maturities) are averages of one-year rates expected each year up to the date of maturity.

Finding a Single Implied Forward Rate. The method of finding the interest rate expected in a future year from today's interest rate is shown.

The Capital Risk Hypothesis. A premium must be added to the implied forward rates to cover the increased capital risk that buyers assume for longer-term bonds.

Market Segmentation. Markets are disconnected so that rates in one market, say, the mortgage market, need not be related to rates in any other market, say, the one-year Treasury bill market.

Interpreting Yield Curves. Factors affecting the real interest rate (such as different levels of uncertainty) and factors affecting the nominal rate (such as different expectations of inflation) are shown to determine the shape of the yield curve according to the liquidity preference and pure expectations theories.

The Rapid Increase in Financial Instruments of the Term Structure. New financial assets discussed in the next chapter can be used to reduce the uncertainty of transactions necessary to take advantage of expected profits from rates that do not conform to the pure expectations hypothesis.

INTRODUCTION

In speaking about interest rates, it is common practice to speak of "the interest rate" as if there were only one. Usually, what is meant is the rate on a one-year government debt instrument (a U.S. Treasury bill) with no risk premium for default. (A default risk premium is an addition to the rate of return to cover the possibility that part of the payment stream will not be paid.) There is also another dimension. There are bonds of all different maturities, and the relationship among the yields on these bonds of different maturities is called the **term structure of interest rates.** The use of bonds of similar default risk, such as all U.S. Treasury debt instruments or all top-rated corporate debt instruments, simplifies the view of the term structure of interest rates.

The term structure of interest rates can be pictured as in Figure 11-1. The bonds are arranged by maturity on the horizontal axis, and their respective yields are plotted against the vertical axis. A curve showing the term structure is called a *yield curve*. Three different hypothetical yield curves are depicted in Figure 11-1.

FIGURE 11-1   Three Hypothetical Yield Curves

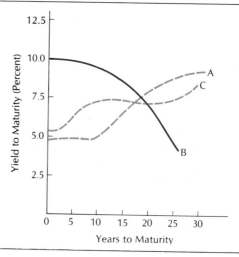

There are many theories of the term structure of interest rates.[1] Several are built on the basis of the pure expectations hypothesis, whereas others contradict it. The pure expectations hypothesis explains the term structure of interest rates under specific conditions, that is, it explains the *shape* of the term structure.

Two alternative explanations of the term structure interest rates are also covered in this chapter, the capital risk (or *liquidity preference*) and the market segmentation hypotheses.

THE PURE EXPECTATIONS HYPOTHESIS

Suppose that the rate of interest on a one-year default-free bond is 2 percent. The rate of interest that is expected to prevail on such one-year bonds in the following year is 7 percent. Then the rate of return on a two-year default-free bond sold at present might be expected to yield a return equivalent to the yield on a sequence of one-year bonds. Thus the one-year yields expected during each of the next two years would be related to the yield on the two-year bonds currently observed in the market. The view that such a relationship exists is called the **pure expectations hypothesis**.[2]

Assume that there is available a list of current yields on default-free bonds, bonds that differ only by their maturity—say, U.S. Treasury bills, notes, and bonds. These current rates are sometimes called **spot rates**. The published rates of interest reflecting observable current market prices—the spot rates—are S_1, S_2, S_3, ..., S_N for one year, two years, three years, and so forth, all the way out to a distant maturity of N years.

Now consider the one-year rates that are *expected* to prevail during the N years on one-year bonds in each of these years. The yields expected on these one-year bonds are sometimes call **expected** or **implied forward rates**. Let i_1, i_2, i_3, ..., i_N be the respective implied forward rates.

Refer to the compound interest formula (3) in the last chapter. If \$1 is invested in a one-year bond, it will grow in value to $\$1(1 + S_1)$ in a year. This is the same amount as is obtained for the first year using the expected rates, $\$1(1 + i_1)$. The one-year interest that clears the market for one-year bonds is a reflection of what individuals expect that rate to be. So, for the first year,

$$1 + S_1 = 1 + i_1 \quad \text{or} \quad i_1 = S_1 \tag{1}$$

If funds are to be lent—that is, bonds are to be bought—there are two choices: (1) buy a two-year bond or (2) buy a series of two one-year bonds. If there are negligible transactions costs for buying and selling the bonds and the same rate of return can be earned by either choice, then the return on the two-year bond $(1 + S_2)^2$ will be equal to the combined return on the two one-year bonds $(1 + i_1)(1 + i_2)$:

$$(1 + S_2)^2 = (1 + i_1)(1 + i_2) \tag{2}$$

or

$$1 + S_2 = \sqrt{(1 + i_1)(1 + i_2)} \tag{3}$$

The pure expectations hypothesis holds that this relationship between observable market rates of interest on bonds and the implied or expected forward rates is approximated in the bond markets.

The justification for this can be seen with an example. Suppose that the market rate on two-year bonds is 11 percent and that the market rate on one-year bonds is 10 percent. The values of the symbols are then $S_2 = .11$ and $S_1 = i_1 = .10$. From equation (2) we find that $i_2 = .12009$ is the consistent value for the expected one-year rate in year 2.

Suppose that this were not true and that a rate of 15 percent were expected on one-year bonds during the second year. In that case, some individuals who held this expectation would sell two-year bonds, paying 11 percent on the loan. They would then buy a series of two one-year bonds earning 10 percent the first year and, if their expectations are correct, 15 percent the second year. The two-year return would be 12.472 percent, a 1.472-percentage-point profit. They could eliminate the risk by simultaneously making contracts with borrowers (who also expect no less than 15 percent interest in the second year) to buy their bonds during the second year at 15 percent. This is called a *futures contract* and is discussed in the next chapter. If no such futures contract exists, there will be uncertainty about the one-year rate in the second year.

Suppose that the markets are working perfectly in the sense that individuals can borrow funds at a rate at least as low as their lending rate. That is, they can borrow at 11 percent and relend for a profit. They would merely be borrowing and relending for a profit and would cease performing these transactions when there was no more expected profit in the transactions. This would occur when the equality, in equation (3), between the observable market rate on two-year bonds is equal to the average of the implied forward rates.[3]

Using the same type of reasoning, a formula for the implied forward rates for a bond of any maturity can be stated. Suppose that the observable market yield on an N-year bond is S_N. Then

$$1 + S_N = \sqrt[N]{(1 + i_1)(1 + i_2) \cdots (1 + i_N)} \qquad (4)$$

This is the general relationship in the pure expectations hypothesis between the expected forward rates and the corresponding observable market rate or spot rate.

FINDING A SINGLE IMPLIED FORWARD RATE

If the conditions for the equality in equation (4) hold, the implied forward one-year interest rates can easily be calculated from a series of observable market interest rates for each period. The calculation can be illustrated by looking at relationships with observed two- and three-year rates. The two-year relationship is

$$(1 + S_2)^2 = (1 + i_1)(1 + i_2) \qquad (5)$$

The three-year relationship is

$$(1 + S_3)^3 = (1 + i_1)(1 + i_2)(1 + i_3) \qquad (6)$$

Now suppose that the rate observed on two-year bonds, S_2, is 4 percent and the rate observed on three-year bonds, S_3, is 5 percent. What is the implied rate during the third year? To find the answer, divide equation (6) by equation (5):

$$\frac{(1 + S_3)^3}{(1 + S_2)^2} = 1 + i_3 \qquad (7)$$

Substituting in the values for S_3 and S_2, the value of $1 + i_3$ can be found easily. It is 1.07. The forward rate implied by the current observable rates on two- and three-year bonds is 7 percent.

In a more general form for any maturity, say, for bonds of N and N minus one year's maturity, equation (7) becomes

$$i_N = \frac{(1 + S_N)^N}{(1 + S_{N-1})^{N-1}} - 1 \qquad (8)$$

EXAMPLE: FINDING AN IMPLIED FORWARD RATE

Here is an example of how equation (8) can be used. The management of a firm decides to increase its inventory for one year, to take advantage of an expected increase in sales two years in the future. The firm needs $1 million in funds at that time. How does it arrange to borrow the funds at today's interest rates if it does not need these funds for two years, and then only for a one-year loan? It would sell $1 million in three-year bonds; that is, it would obtain a three-year loan from bond buyers. The management of the firm would also simultaneously buy $1 million in two-year bonds. For the first two years, it would pay out the interest it receives on the two-year bond that it owns to cover the interest on the three-year bond that it sold. At the end of the second year, the two-year bond will mature, and the firm will have $1 million to spend on inventory for one year. At the end of the third year, it must pay back the holders of the three-year bonds.

What rate will the firm pay on this one-year loan? It is given by equation (8). If three-year bonds currently have a 10 percent interest and two-year bonds have a 12 percent interest, i_N in equation (8) will be 6.1 percent.

THE CAPITAL RISK HYPOTHESIS

The **capital risk** or **liquidity preference hypothesis** of the term structure asserts that the future rates implied from equation (4) are a *combination* of the expected rates and a liquidity premium. The liquidity premium pays for **capital risk**, the risk that the bond will fall in value and a loss will be incurred if it is sold prior to maturity. In addition, it is asserted that more distant rates have larger liquidity premiums. Curve AA in Figure 11-2 is a yield curve that is consistent with expected future rates, according to the pure expectations hypothesis. Curve $A'A'$ includes liquidity premiums in keeping with the liquidity preference hypothesis.

The liquidity preference hypothesis can be depicted in equation (4) by adding a capital risk premium to each of the implied forward rates. The farther the rates are in the future, the larger the risk premium will become.

FIGURE 11-2   The Capital Risk Hypothesis Yield Curve *A′A′* Compared with the Expectations Hypothesis Yield Curve *AA* for the Same Series of Expected Forward Rates

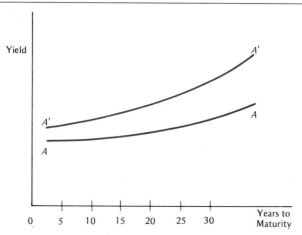

If individuals demand a risk premium that is higher on bonds with more distant maturities, then instead of curve *AA*, implied by the pure expectations hypothesis, the yield curve will look like *A′A′*.

The liquidity preference proponents claim that the " risk aversion of lenders makes them value the stability of the principal more than the stability of income."[4] That is, the desire to have ten years of risk-free money income from bonds is less important than is the fear of a decline in the bond's value during the ten-year period. The market is alleged to have a *congenital weakness* on one side, so that more risk is attached to ten-year bonds than to nine-year bonds.[5]

Although the yield curve has frequently sloped upward, there is little decisive evidence on the size of the risk premiums, but that does not mean that they do not exist.

MARKET SEGMENTATION

Suppose that from a position of equilibrium, the yields on 20-year mortgages remain constant as the yields on 5-year U.S. Treasury notes double. One explanation is that each instrument is sold in somewhat unrelated markets. Market participants are not selling sufficient quantities of mortgages in one market and not buying sufficient quantities of Treasury notes in another market to bring the rates in line with equation (4), after allowance is made for differences in the default risk. There are various hypotheses regarding this type of phenomenon, called **market segmentation hypotheses**.[6]

Numerous frictions can produce market segmentation, including legal restrictions, the lack of a homogeneous debt instrument that can be sold easily on a national market, crisis conditions that cause wild gyrations in yields, the absence of free markets with enough volume to provide continuous spot prices to prospective buyers and sellers, uncertainty about default risks, transactions costs, and a lack of knowledge. A market is said to be **thin** if there are relatively few sales. In such a market, participants—bond brokers with inventories of a particular bond—may post prices that are not precisely consistent with the market prices that would prevail if sales were being made.

The profits that can be earned by overcoming these frictions can be substantial. The modern technology for instantaneously communicating the price and yield on financial assets to traders all over the world makes a lack of knowledge a minor problem for many bonds. The ease of changing the form of financial assets to avoid some legal restrictions can make some of these frictions ineffective.

INTERPRETING YIELD CURVES

The three hypothetical yield curves in Figure 11-1 are averages of the implied forward rates for bonds of the various maturities listed along the horizontal axis. If one believes the expectations hypothesis, these curves will reveal the bond traders' expectations of the future one-year rates.

Curve A reveals a belief in rising rates over the next 30 years; curve B indicates a belief in falling rates over the same period. Curve C indicates expectations of rising rates for 15 years, then falling rates for 5 years, a trough, and then rising rates again.

What determines these interest rates? One explanation is that an observable market rate of interest on bonds is a real rate, r_b, plus the expectation of inflation λ (neglecting income tax effects), which is called the nominal interest rate, i_b.

$$i_b = r_b + \lambda \tag{9}$$

For example, if the real rate of interest is 10 percent, that will be the rate of interest that would be observed on bonds if there were no inflation. If people expect a sudden 5 percent rise in prices (an inflation rate of 5 percent), the coupon and return of face payments on the bond will buy 5 percent fewer goods and services each year. That is, the bond will not be worth as much to them, and they will require an additional 5 percent yield to cover the cost of inflation. This formula says that they would buy bonds if the interest rate were 15 percent. (In Part V, this explanation is repeated, and the effects of income tax rates are taken into account in a broader discussion of this topic. At this point, the discussion here is all that is needed to understand what the pure expectations hypothesis has to say about the shape of yield curves.) If real interest rates are assumed to be fairly constant, a yield curve such as A in

Figure 11-1 will mean that increasing rates of inflation are expected over the next 30 years, whereas a curve such as *B* will mean that decreasing rates of inflation (and then increasing deflation) are expected in that period.

If rising rates of inflation and economic expansion are held to be tied together, and falling rates of inflation are thought to be tied to a recession, curve *C* can be interpreted as follows: The peak of an expansion is expected in 15 years, and the trough of a recession is expected in 20 to 25 years.

The real rate of interest may also vary widely. For example, suppose that there is an increase in uncertainty about the general economic outlook for the future, so that payment streams on bonds undergo a change in default, purchasing power, or capital risk. This is one plausible explanation for the leap upward of long-term rates in the United States in the fourth quarter of 1979, after they had fallen. There was increased uncertainty about future economic conditions in that period, following an announcement by the Federal Reserve that it would concentrate on slowing money growth. Uncertainty about the future further increased in November 1979, when the staff of the American Embassy in Iran was taken hostage, and a major crisis ensued.

Commenting on this period, the Federal Reserve Bank of St. Louis presented the following hypothesis of how yield curves change with the business cycle:

> In general, the shape of the yield curve changes over a business cycle. At the beginning of an economic expansion, the yield curve is upward-sloping—short-term rates are lower than long-term rates. As the expansion proceeds, short-term rates tend to rise faster than long-term rates, so the yield curve shifts upward and flattens out. Near the business cycle peak, the yield curve can become downward-sloping or inverted—short-term yields are higher than longer-term yields. Then, as economic activity declines, short-term interest rates decline faster relative to longer-term rates and the yield curve again flattens out, eventually becoming upward-sloping again before the next expansion begins.

Then the 1979 and 1980 changes in the yield curve, depicted in Figure 11-3, were described as follows:

> The shape of the yield curve for the U.S. Treasury securities has changed dramatically between March 14, 1980, and May 5, 1980. Short-term yields are currently about the same as intermediate- and long-term yields, resulting in a flat yield curve. This contrasts with the downward-sloping yield curves that existed since late 1978. The last time such a change in the yield curve's shape occurred was during the 1974–75 recession. Current yields on short-term Treasury securities are at about the same levels as prevailed in March 1979. Current long-term yields, on the other hand, remain 100 to 150 basis points higher than they were a year ago.[7]

The evidence presented in Figure 11-3 is consistent with the view that the yield curves change over the business cycle. However, if market participants could

FIGURE 11-3   Yield Curves in 1979 and 1980 on U.S. Government Securities

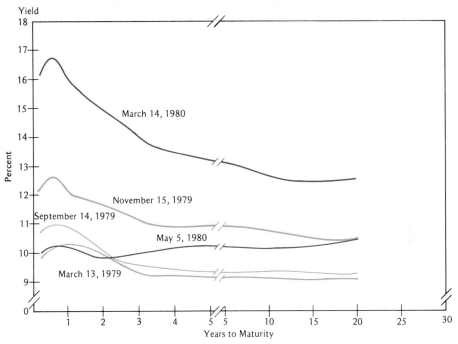

The changing yield curves are an indication that expectations about the future have significantly changed.

Source: U.S. Financial Data, Federal Reserve Bank of St. Louis, May 7, 1980.

predict these changes over business cycles, the expected rates would already indicate cyclical movements, as in yield curve *C* in Figure 11-1. The current time period would merely move to the right in Figure 11-1. Long-term rates would change slightly, according to the expectations hypothesis, as each current year's rate dropped into history. The longer-term rates would then be averages of a slightly different set of forward rates. The phenomena described by the St. Louis Federal Reserve could occur only under an expectations hypothesis if the phases of the business cycle changed future expectations. Perhaps 1979 was a year of fundamental changes in long-term expectations, or perhaps there were changes in risk, as the preceding comments suggest. The interesting Catch-22 of the expectations hypothesis is that the changes depicted in Figure 11-3 could not happen if the expectations embodied in previous yield curves were maintained, or at least they would not change significantly. If the yield curves dramatically shift, it will be an indication that the public is changing its views of the future, reducing the value of a single yield curve as an indication of expectations.

FIGURE 11-4   Three Yield Curves in 1986

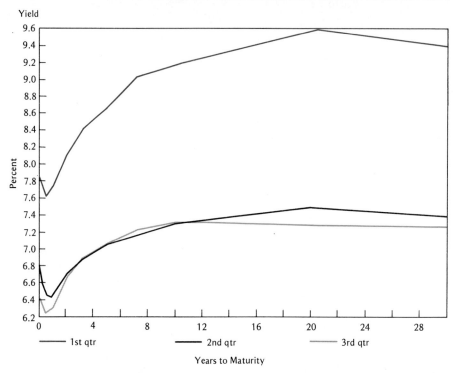

These three yield curves are obtained from plotting the spot interest rates on U.S. government securities of different maturities. As interest rates fell during 1986, the yield curves also fell. Yet the shape of the yield curves indicates that there was an expectation of higher interest rates.

Source: Cambridge Planning and Analytics Inc., Boston, with reformulations by Gary Mitchell.

Yield curves sometimes show that individuals hold expectations that do not conform to recent experience, which was evidently the case in 1986. The three yield curves shown in Figure 11-4 were obtained from plotting the spot interest rates on U.S. government securities of different maturities. As interest rates fell during 1986, the yield curves also fell. The yield curve in the first quarter is steeper, indicating that the expectations of higher interest rates and the rate of the expected renewed inflation may have been lowered as the year progressed. Yet the yield curves' upward sloping shape indicates that there was an expectation of higher interest rates. Individuals apparently were using other information besides the recent changes in interest rates to predict the course of interest rates for about ten years in the yield curves during the second and third quarters of 1986.

THE RAPID INCREASE IN FINANCIAL INSTRUMENTS OF THE TERM STRUCTURE

Beginning in the 1980s, there has been a rapid increase in the number of financial assets and a massive increase in the volume of financial assets that allow trading on future asset prices and rates of return. This subject is discussed in the next chapter, but it is important to note these developments in connection with the pure expectations hypothesis of the term structure.

It is now possible, for example, to buy a contract that allows the owner to purchase a 90-day Treasury bill at a specified price and yield on a given date in the future. Thus the rate to be earned on a three-month Treasury bill next year can be nailed down in advance. The kind of risk in buying a series of one-year loans, as an alternative to buying a two-year bond, is removed. The risk, and therefore the cost, of achieving equilibrium accurately reflecting future expectations is reduced.

STUDY QUESTIONS

1. Plot the current term structure, using the yields on U.S. Treasury securities.
2. Explain the following hypotheses of the term structure of interest rates: the pure expectations hypothesis, the liquidity preference hypothesis, and the market segmentation hypothesis.
3. How could a firm borrow $2 million three years from now for two years by buying and selling bonds in the current period?
4. Suppose that bonds with no default risk have the following spot yields: a three-year bond yields 7 percent, and a four-year bond yields 8 percent. What is the implied forward rate during the fourth year?
5. What does a rising yield curve mean?
6. What does a falling yield curve mean?
7. What does a shifting group of yield curves for successive time periods mean?
8. What would the yield curve look like if individuals planned for only five years in advance?

GLOSSARY

Capital risk. The risk that a bond will fall in value and a loss will be incurred if it is sold prior to maturity.

Capital risk hypothesis (or liquidity

preference hypothesis). Hypothesis holding that there is a premium on implied future rates that increases with more distant maturities.

Expected or **implied future** or

forward rates. Rates implied in the pure expectations hypothesis for future years.

Market segmentation hypothesis. Hypothesis holding that markets for different financial assets are not sufficiently interrelated to allow prices or yields to be described by a theory such as the pure expectations hypothesis. An alternative definition that may be used (after *arbitrage* is described in the next chapter) is the following: There is incomplete arbitrage among debt instruments in different markets and with different maturities.

Pure expectations hypothesis. Hypo-

thesis holding that rates on debt instruments are an average of the rates expected in each year up to the date of the maturity of the debt instrument.

Spot rates. Current market rates.

Term structure of interest rates. The relationship among the yields of debt instruments of different maturities.

Thin market. A market with few enough sales so that there are significantly long periods when no sales are made. Posted prices or prices of previous transactions may not reflect current market prices.

NOTES

1. Lester Telser in "A Critique of Some Recent Empirical Research on the Explanation of the Term Structure of Interest Rates," *Journal of Political Economy*, August 1967, Supplement, *Issues in Monetary Research*, pp. 546–561. The classic statement of the expectations hypothesis is found in David Meiselman, *The Term Structure of Interest Rates* (Englewood Cliffs, N.J.: Prentice-Hall, 1962). Some of the important books that include different explanations of the term structure of interest rates are J. R. Hicks, *Value and Capital, An Inquiry into Some Fundamental Principles of Economic Inquiry*, 2nd ed. (Oxford, England: Clarendon Press, 1946); Ruben A. Kessel, *The Cyclical Behavior of the Term Structure of Interest Rates*, National Bureau of Economic Research, Occasional Paper 91 (New York: Columbia University Press, 1965); John Maynard Keynes, *The General Theory of Employment, Interest and Money* (New York: Harcourt Brace, 1936), pp. 202–204; Meiselman, *Term Structure*; Burton Malkiel, *The Term Structure of Interest Rates: Expectations and Behavior Patterns* (Princeton, N.J.: Princeton University Press, 1966); and Friedrich A. Lutz, *The Theory of Interest Rates* (Chicago: Aldine, 1968). A bibliography of books and articles can be found in Terence C. Langetieg, "A Multivariate Model of the Term Structure," *Journal of Finance*, March 1980, p. 97; and in Robert J. Shiller, "The Volatility of Long-Term Interest Rates and Expectations Models of the Term Structure," *Journal of Political Economy*, December 1979, pp. 1217–1219.

2. The equation for this relationship was developed by Hicks in *Value and Capital*, Chap. 11, especially Part 3, pp. 144–145.

3. This is a *geometric* average. To compute the common arithmetic average, *N* numbers are added together and divided by *N*, whereas a geometric

average is obtained by multiplying the numbers together and taking the Nth root. The arithmetic average of 7, 8, and 9 is 8, and the geometric average is 7.96, slightly lower.

4. Telser, "A Critique," p. 546. The need for borrowers to pay risk premiums that grow larger as the maturity becomes farther away was called "normal backwardation" by John Maynard Keynes in 1930 in *A Treatise on Money* (New York: Harcourt Brace, 1930), Vol. 2, pp. 142–144.

5. The meaning of *congenital weakness* can best be analyzed as if the market were dominated by the lenders' side of the market; that is, the lenders are averse to risk but are more averse to longer loans, according to Meiselman, *Term Structure*, p. 14. However, Meiselman contended that many borrowers, such as life insurance companies and pension funds, keep the demand for long-term bonds high enough to offset any congenital weakness. The market need not have a congenital weakness in the sense described; there can be a sudden increase in uncertainty about the future, which will cause implied real interest rates in the future to have an uncertainty premium. This effect on the real rate of interest is covered in Robert D. Auerbach, *Financial Markets and Institutions* (New York: Macmillan, 1983), Chap. 9 and p. 172.

6. A leading proponent of this view is John M. Culbertson; see "The Term Structure of Interest Rates," *Quarterly Journal of Economics*, November 1957, pp. 485–517. The view is described by Malkiel in *The Term Structure of Interest Rates*, Chap. 6, pp. 144–180. Culbertson's theory is called the *hedging-pressure hypothesis*, which holds that market participants, such as large institutional investors, prefer particular maturities and will not change. Changes in expectations do not specifically enter into this theory of the term structure.

The *preferred habitat* is a variant of the hedging-pressure theory. See Franco Modigliani and R. Sutch, "Debt Management and the Term Structure of Interest Rates: An Empirical Analysis of Recent Experience," *Journal of Political Economy*, August 1967, pp. 569–589; and Franco Modigliani and R. Shiller, "Inflation, Rational Expectations and the Term Structure of Interest Rates," *Economica*, February 1973, pp. 12–43.

The preferred habitat refers to definite holding periods for transactors who lend or borrow forward. The hedgers are held to dominate the market with their fixed preferences for particular periods for holding bonds or for borrowing. Risk premiums arise because of the composition of these preferred holding or borrowing periods. The risk premiums do not necessarily increase in size with more distant maturities. (Hedging is explained in the next chapter.)

Some economists have subjected the theory to statistical tests, not all of which support it. The test results that were viewed favorably have been questioned. See Douglas Fisher, "The Term Structure of Interest Rates," in Richard S. Thorn, ed., *Monetary Theory and Policy* (New York: Praeger, 1976), p. 531.

7. Federal Reserve Bank of St. Louis, *U.S. Financial Data*, May 7, 1980, p. 1.

CHAPTER 12

Financial Markets

CHAPTER PREVIEW

Introduction. The importance of financial markets is discussed.

Types of Financial Markets. Several ways of viewing the term markets and several types of markets are described.

Market Participants. Four kinds of market participants are described, although a single individual could conduct trading in a way that places him or her in more than one of these classifications.

The Money Market. The money markets, their functions, and five of the instruments traded are described.

The Stock Markets. The stock markets, the New York Stock Exchange, and the relationship of stock market prices to economic conditions are discussed.

The Corporate Bond Market. The market for trading private corporate bonds is described.

The Financial Asset Options Market. This relatively new market allows traders to take positions with limited risk of loss (limited to the value of the option) and in relatively small amounts compared with buying the underlying financial asset itself.

Commodity Futures Markets. A simple example is given of how commodity futures trading works.

Financial Asset Futures Markets. Markets for trading contracts for future financial assets are discussed.

Functions of Futures and Options Markets. The allocation of commodities over time, the bearing of risks of unfavorable future interest rates and price movements, and hedging are three important functions provided by futures markets.

The Secondary Mortgage Market. Government-directed and -sponsored intervention in this market has funneled huge amounts of funds into building single-family dwellings in the United States and away from other investments.

The Foreign Exchange Market. Foreign currencies and internationally accepted monies (media of exchange such as gold and monies issued by international organizations such as the IMF) referred to as foreign exchange are traded in the markets described.

INTRODUCTION

The financial markets play a vital role in allocating funds to the activity where they will achieve the highest rate of return. The financial markets therefore reflect the underlying state of the economy. The prices of equities, the financial assets of the corporations' ownership in the economy, and instruments of debt—such as bonds, bills, and notes—are derived from these underlying conditions. Changes in the prices of assets that can be traded on financial markets affect the economy because these assets represent a major portion of society's wealth.

There have been major changes in the financial markets during the 1980s, with the massive increase in trading instruments such as repurchase agreements and the introduction of options and futures contracts on financial assets.

Understanding the massive financial markets, including the pervasive changes of the 1980s, is essential to understanding how the economies of the United States and other developed countries function. In addition, perhaps you can make a little money on the side. But whether you profit or lose, your understanding would be greatly enhanced, and your attention would be more sharply focused, by the purchase of a few options on financial assets.

TYPES OF FINANCIAL MARKETS

There are two general ways in which the term **market** is used in economics. First, a market is thought of as a formal or informal organization of buyers and sellers who conduct trades in particular commodities or services. The market may be located at a particular geographical meeting place, such as your friendly neighborhood bookstore or shopping center (a retail market). Or a market may be organized over wide areas connected through phones or computer terminals. Although the trading room of the New York Stock Exchange is located in New York City, buyers and sellers who actively participate in this market may conduct their trades from distant locations. This description is the *institutional* way of looking at a market.

The second meaning of the word *market* is used in formal economic models. Here the equations that explain the demand and supply of a commodity such as money are sometimes grouped together. Although money is traded on all markets, the reasons for *supplying* and *holding* money are thought to be specific enough to warrant separate equations. This is an *abstract* way to think of the money market, and it is not used in this chapter.

New financial assets are traded in **primary markets**. Financial assets that are resold are traded in **secondary markets**. Firms that specialize in trading either new or reissued financial assets are called **primary** and **secondary dealers**, respectively. Both new and reissued securities are traded in many markets, such as the U.S. money market. The New York Stock Exchange, however, is a secondary market.

Sometimes markets are classified according to the maturity of the instruments traded. Short-term debt instruments are traded in the **money market**, and longer-term securities, such as stocks and bonds, are traded in the **capital markets**.

MARKET PARTICIPANTS

Participants in financial markets can be classified into four groups according to their market behavior: speculators, hedgers, arbitragers, and investors. Although these market participants can be distinguished in a hypothetical model, in which they are limited to a particular activity, such a distinction is difficult, if not meaningless, in most financial markets. That is, most individuals who fit one classification also fit some or all of the other classifications. Nevertheless, it is useful conceptually to separate these activities so that the actions of the market participants can be better understood.

Many individuals and firms buy financial assets primarily for the income they receive from holding the assets. This income may be in the monetary form of dividends and interest payments. These individuals and firms are **investors**. There is not always an operational way, short of psychoanalysis, to separate individual investors from other financial asset holders, called **speculators**, who would be willing to sell their holdings any time they could make a large enough profit.

Speculation occurs when an asset is held for resale at a higher price or is sold short for purchase at a lower price. Many individuals purchase assets over which they have property rights and, perhaps, dreams of resale at a profitable price. They are speculators. A professional speculator trades frequently and in large amounts, making his or her income primarily from this activity. The frequency of trades and the primary income characteristics could be used to differentiate the professional speculators from other speculators, although the distinctions are not clear-cut.

Some firms and individuals hold financial assets in order to hedge. **Hedging** occurs when two or more assets are held with the expectation that they will have offsetting price movements because of some nonrandom relationship between them. This differs from **diversification**, in which there is an expectation of offsetting price movements caused by random fluctuations. An individual diversifies because he or she expects that if the price of one asset falls from some expected level, another asset in the portfolio will have an offsetting price movement as a matter of random chance.

Many hedges have a simple *mechanical relationship*, such as the simultaneous purchase of both a stock and a put option on that stock. (A **put option** is a contract to sell a stock at a specified price on a future date.) Two or more assets are perfectly hedged if, regardless of price fluctuations, their aggregate value is expected to remain the same because of a mechanical relationship. If an asset is not hedged by another asset, the asset holder may be a speculator. He or she is gambling on a rise (or fall) in the value of the assets. But he or she may not be a *voluntary* speculator. Assets that would act as perfect hedges for his or her portfolio may not exist or may be too expensive to purchase. An individual's budget may not be large enough to obtain a hedge, or he or she may not consider the cost of the hedge to be worth the increase in protection.

Still another type of financial market participant is the **arbitrager**, who performs *arbitrage*. One form of arbitrage, *simple arbitrage*, takes place when an asset is bought and simultaneously sold at a higher price. For example, if a stock is bought for $5.00 on the Paris Bourse (stock exchange) and simultaneously sold for $5.25 on the New York Stock Exchange, the transaction is known as arbitrage. An arbitrager must usually carry an inventory because all his or her sales cannot be made simultaneously with purchases. The arbitrager, therefore, holds a speculative inventory ("takes a position") and cannot be easily distinguished from a speculator. The underlying mechanism for keeping the term structure of interest rates in line is arbitrage.

All three types of trading in financial assets (speculation, hedging, and arbitrage) perform useful functions. Hedging allows individuals who do not wish to take unnecessary gambles, or who are unfamiliar with the market information they deem necessary for successful speculation, the opportunity to buy insurance. For example, farmers can ensure in advance a price for their grains by buying a contract that guarantees them a specific price in the future from buyers who also want to ensure against unfavorable price changes. Farmers can then concentrate on farming rather than on speculating in grain prices.

Under normal conditions, speculation reduces the amplitude of fluctuations in the prices of financial assets. That is, speculators try to buy when the asset is low in price, thus bidding its price upward. They try to sell when the price of the asset is high, thus forcing the price downward. They reduce extreme price fluctuations in commodities such as food by storing more when food is abundant in summer and using this inventory when it is scarce in winter.

Arbitragers help maintain consistent prices for the same or "related" financial assets. This reduces the search costs of other traders who wish to buy or sell assets on the best possible terms.

Arbitrage cannot, even in principle, be separated from hedging or speculation if the following types of transactions are considered to be arbitrage: An asset with a lower rate of return is sold, and an asset of equal value with a higher rate of return is purchased. In this sense, every trader may be thought of as attempting to arrange his or her trades so that he or she arbitrages the rates of return.

THE MONEY MARKET

The term *money market*, as in the "New York money market" or the "U.S. money market," is used to designate a group of markets in which low-default-risk, very liquid, large-denomination debt instruments are traded. New York and London have been the leading market centers for the past century. Although much of the money market is devoted to short-term debt instruments, the dealers in the money market also trade in longer-term debt instruments, such as U.S. Treasury bonds that are part of what is known as the capital market. The U.S. money market can best be understood by the government regulations that govern it and by the activities of the primary dealers and nonprimary dealers.

Securities trading was regulated by state law until the depressions of the 1930s. Then in 1933 and 1934, federal laws were passed that authorized regulations for corporate debt and stocks. The Securities and Exchange Commission was established as the federal regulator. In 1986 there were a number of regulators with jurisdiction over the many types of securities in the firms that they were authorized to regulate. These regulators include the banking and thrift regulators, the Federal Reserve, and the Commodities Futures Trading Commission. All firms that trade securities or act as brokers (arranging sales for others) in these securities are also subject to regulation. But Treasury securities are exempted from most federal regulations because the U.S. government guarantees them. In addition, certificates of deposit (CDs), short-term bankers' acceptances, commercial paper, and municipal securites are exempt from the registration requirements of the Securities and Exchange Commission.

The Federal Reserve, the central bank of the United States, authorizes dealers to be primary dealers in the government securities market. These dealers are expected to trade directly with the Federal Reserve in its daily auctions. The designation as a primary dealer by the Federal Reserve is an advantage, as it confers upon the recipient the stamp of extremely good credit.

This is useful in the automated market for dealers when trading is done through a computer system in what is called a "blind" basis because no participating dealer knows the identity of the other party in a transaction and the brokers offering the automated service usually do not guarantee the trade. In other words, both parties depend on the good faith of the other that the payment for the securities will be made. In 1974, automated brokerage services were offered to primary dealers from brokers called *screen brokers*. Such services provide continually updated quotes for nearly fifty dealers. Deals are made by phone on the basis of these prices. In 1986, nine screen brokers provided this service, and seven limited their service to primary brokers. The Federal Reserve monitors the primary dealers, and as a result nearly all the government data regarding the money markets come from the primary dealers. Federal Reserve operations in the government securities markets are the primary vehicle for the government's control of the United States' money supply, as will be explained in Chapter 16, together with a further description of primary dealers. It was estimated in 1985 that these primary dealers conducted 75 percent of the volume in the government securities market.[1] The total number of nonprimary dealers is not known but was estimated by the Federal Reserve to have been between 200 and 300 in 1985.

The U.S. money market is a collection of these primary and nonprimary dealers that both trade and arrange trades for others. The size of this trading can be seen in Table 12-1, which lists the positions (the amount of securities held) and the financing of primary dealers. The primary instruments of the money market are Treasury securities. Direct positions in these securities with maturities of one year or less were reported by the Federal Reserve to have been $31.4 billion on an average day in July 1986. These securities are held indirectly through the most popular money market instrument, repurchase agreements. The financing for repurchase agreements by primary dealers on an

TABLE 12-1   Positions and Financing of Selected Money Market Instruments, July 1986 (millions of dollars)

All but the repurchase agreements and federal funds are primary dealers' holdings of money market instruments on an average day in July 1986. The data for repurchase agreements are estimates of the financing of daily transactions by primary dealers. Federal funds transactions by commercial banks plus their repurchase agreements for short-term funds were $72.686 billion on July 21, 1986.

U.S. Treasury Bills (1 year or less)	31.455
Federal agency securities	29.237
Certificates of deposit	9.866
Bankers' acceptances	5.809
Commercial paper	5.806
Federal funds	72.686
Repurchase agreements (and reverse repurchase agreements)	444.924

Source: Federal Reserve Bulletin, October 1986, pp. A5, A32.

TABLE 12-2 The Number of Primary Dealers and Their Average Daily Transactions in Government Securities, 1970–1985

In 1985 the average total daily amount of transactions in government securities of primary dealers was $86.968 billion, and the total amount of transactions was $18 trillion. That large total does not include sales and purchases of repurchase agreements and forward transactions. This is a major portion of the huge engine that transmits interest rates in the U.S. economy and throughout the world where this trading and the interest rates derived have major influence.

Year Ended	Dealers	Treasury Securities		Federal Agency Securities	Total
		Bills	*Notes and Bonds*		
			(millions)		
1970	20	NA	NA	463	2,976
1975	29	$ 3,886	$ 2,130	$ 1,049	$ 7,065
1980	34	11,227	6,705	3,102	21,034
1981	36	14,649	9,875	3,291	27,815
1982	36	18,392	13,841	4,134	36,367
1983	37	22,393	19,742	5,576	47,711
1984	36	26,035	26,743	7,846	60,624
1985	36	32,898	42,430	11,640	86,968

Source: U.S. General Accounting Office, *U.S. Treasury Securities, the Market's Structure, Risks, and Regulation.* Briefing Report to the Chairman, Subcommittee on Domestic Banking, Finance and Urban Affairs, House of Representatives, August 1986, p. 24.

average day in July 1986 amounted to $444.9 billion. The total volume of repurchase agreements is not known.

The number of primary dealers and their transactions in Treasury Securities and other federal government securities are shown in Table 12-2 for selected years from 1970 to 1985. In 1985 the average total daily amount of transactions in government securities by primary dealers was $86.968 billion, and the total amount of transactions was $18 trillion. That large total does not include sales and purchases of repurchase agreements and forward transactions.

These huge estimates of trading show that the money markets are a major mechanism for transmitting interest rates in the U.S. economy and throughout the world. But the lack of good estimates of the volume and prices in money market trading, the barriers to entry as a primary dealer into the market, and the focus of nearly all of the research in finance on other markets for which there are good data leave unanswered many questions about the money markets: How competitive are the prices for each of the instruments traded? Is there enough information for each of the instruments traded? Is there enough information publicly available so that all potential participants can have reasonably accurate knowledge, or is there a closely guarded network that receives special information and higher-than-normal profits from use of this information?

Functions

The money markets provide an efficient way for large firms, including large financial intermediaries, to

1. Economize on their cash balances by lending money for short periods at prevailing yields when they temporarily have excess cash.
2. Economize on their cash balances by having a ready market for short-term borrowing, which enables them to hold less money for temporary unexpected cash drains.
3. Reduce brokerage fees, search costs, and other transactions costs incurred in buying and selling short-term debt instruments.
4. Finance long-term needs through *rollovers* (continuous renewal of loans).

Short-Term Interest Rates

The short-term interest rates for money market instruments are shown in Figure 12-1. The central and most important instrument of the U.S. money market is the rate on U.S. government debt instruments. The three-month U.S. Treasury bill rate—the T-bill rate—is derived from worldwide trading. The price paid for three-month U.S. Treasury bills is not determined by a small group of traders and is not fixed by the U.S. government, but is the product of trading in many markets all over the world, including the huge volume in the domestic money markets in the United States. It is a market-determined rate, in sharp contrast with the advertised prime rate that we discussed in Chapter 7.

The T-bill rate has the least amount of default risk, as it is guaranteed by the U.S. government, which can also print the money to pay it. The prime commercial paper rate is very close to the CD rate, with the CD rate slightly higher in most of this period. The business CDs are for denominations of $100,000 or more, so that part of their redemption value at the issuing depository institutions is not insured by federal deposit insurance. Evidently, the market participants rate the default risk on these CDs slightly higher than that on the prime commercial paper, and thus there is a higher interest on the CDs to cover this risk. The interest rate on bankers' acceptances is very close to the commercial paper rate shown.

Business Certificates of Deposit

The market for large **business certificates of deposit** or **negotiable certificates of deposit (CDs)** in denominations of $100,000 or more has been active since 1961. It is a money market specializing in the sale of marketable, interest-yielding deposit certificates with specified maturity dates, issued by four types of financial intermediaries: domestic CDs, issued by U.S. banks; Euro CDs, or dollar-denominated CDs issued by banks outside the United States; Yankee

FIGURE 12-1   Short-Term Interest Rates, 1976–1986

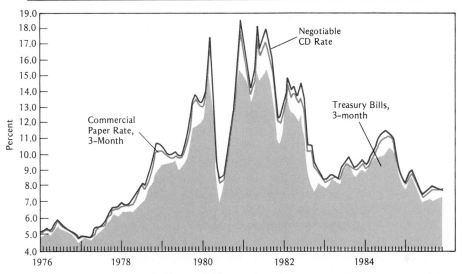

The shaded area shows the three-month U.S. Treasury bill rate (T-bill rate). One line is the three-month business certificate of deposit rate (CD rate) sold in secondary markets after the depository institutions have issued them. The other line is the three-month prime (highest-quality) commercial paper rate.

   The T-bill rate has the least amount of default risk, as it is guaranteed by the U.S. government, which can also print the money to pay it. The prime commercial paper rate is very close to the CD rate, with the CD rate slightly higher in most of this period. The business CDs are for denominations of $100,000 or more, so that part of their redemption value at the issuing depository institutions is not insured by federal deposit insurance. Evidently, the market participants rate the default risk on these CDs slightly higher than that on the prime commercial paper, and thus there is a higher interest on the CDs to cover this risk. The interest rate on bankers' acceptances is very close to the commercial paper rate shown.

Source: Cambridge Planning and Analytics Inc., Boston.

CDs, or CDs issued by U.S. branches of foreign banks; and thrift CDs, CDs issued by domestic thrifts.

   Large CDs, in denominations of $1 million or more, are issued by the largest banks. Large CDs grew rapidly from the mid-1970s to 1982, as they were a primary asset of the money market funds that also grew in that period.[2] In 1986, the CDs of approximately 25 U.S. banks, 15 foreign banks operating in the United States, 20 London banks, and 10 thrifts were traded in the secondary market. The transactions' sizes, called *round lots*, varied from $5 million to $10 million.

   Federal Reserve regulations limit the minimum maturity of a CD to seven days to prevent its being used as a demand deposit. The shortest maturities of large CDs are normally fourteen days, and they typically have maturities of from one to twelve months. In 1986 the average maturity was five months.

In 1986, 15 percent of all newly issued large domestic CDs were variable-rate CDs. The total maturity of these CDs is divided into equally long periods, called *legs* or *roll periods*. The rate in each period is some fixed spread above some market rate. Banks are willing to pay higher rates on variable-rate CDs because CDs with maturities of one and one-half years or more are exempt from reserve requirements.

Euro CDs, or Eurodollar CDs, are issued in denominations from $250,000 to $5 million and usually have maturities of from one to twelve months. Some are issued with floating rates tied to the *London interbank offered rate*, or *the LIBOR rate*. This is an important international money market rate showing the going rate for short-term loans among depository institutions in England.

Certificates of deposit from thrifts—thrift CDs—are sold in the U.S. markets, but few thrifts are large enough to sell their CDs in international markets. The thrift CDs in denominations of $100,000 are frequently sold through brokers—*brokered CDs*—and are appealing to investors, as they are fully insured by the $100,000 federal deposit insurance.

The CD is an instrument that allows the depository intermediaries to raise funds at competitive market rates. It is called one of their *managed liabilities*. Because they lend funds at the CDs' lending rates, they normally keep their advertised prime rate above the CD rate. The prime rate formula that Citibank used set the prime one and one-half points above the previous three-week average of 90-day (three-month) CDs sold in the secondary market. But this formula was dropped in 1980 as interest rates soared. Its use by Citibank, a bellwether bank that often set the standard for the national advertised prime rate, is an indication that the banks' lending rates are related to the cost of funds that banks must pay by selling CDs.

As we noted, the yield on three-month CDs is usually higher than that on three-month T-bills, but Treasury bills have a lower default risk than do CDs. In addition, the interest on T-bills is exempt from state and local taxes.

Bankers' Acceptances

Bankers' acceptances often arise in foreign trade.[3] A business buying goods from abroad where it is not well known and does not have other credit arrangements will first obtain a letter of credit from its own bank. This letter will authorize the foreign seller to draw a draft on the company's bank. A *draft* or *bill of exchange*, as it is sometimes called, is a debt instrument. It can be made payable on sight, that is, upon presentation, payable upon arrival of the merchandise, or payable in a fixed number of days. A draft can be made payable in, say, 30 days after it is presented to the bank against which it is drawn. This draft can be discounted at the seller's bank so that the seller receives immediate payment. If this is done the draft can be sent via correspondent banks back to the domestic bank against which it is drawn. The domestic bank can then buy the draft, a short-term loan agreement to be paid by the company buying the goods abroad. But this action ties up bank funds. Alternatively, the bank can stamp the draft "accepted," with the appropriate signature, thereby indicating that the bank guarantees the draft, and then sell it in the secondary market, through one of approximately fifteen dealers.

The volume of bankers' acceptances grew rapidly in the 1970s. But in the early 1980s, major banks offering acceptance services were unable to accommodate customers because of statutory limits on the size of the acceptances they could offer. Remedial legislation in 1982 increased the limit, and then the volume of bankers' acceptance rose for a few years. But in the middle 1980s the volume of bankers' acceptances began to shrink again. The reason may be the declining role of U.S. banks as providers of short-term credit. Indeed, more borrowers obtained funding directly from domestic and foreign nonbank investors in the commercial paper market and the Eurodollar market. (The Eurodollar market is discussed in Chapter 34.)

Commercial Paper

The **commercial paper** market is a market for short-term, low-risk debt instruments issued by many different types of borrowers.[4] Large finance companies, bank holding companies, utilities, trust funds, college endowment funds, and other large commercial institutional investors are participants in this market. In 1980 savings and loan associations and mutual savings banks also were given permission to invest in commercial paper. Some firms sell directly in the market. Other participants sell first to dealers, who then sell the commercial paper. There are six major commercial paper dealers but no secondary markets. Commercial paper may sometimes be redeemed early if there is an urgent need for funds, but this practice is discouraged.

This specialized part of the money market offers a rapid way to meet short-term needs for money or to economize on money balances with short-term loans, frequently of less than 30 days' duration, which are called *weekend paper*. Many firms have different demands for cash during different seasons of the year. They can make loans and borrow in this market according to their seasonal demands.

In 1970 the Penn Central Transportation Co. defaulted, with $82 million of commercial paper outstanding. Since that shock to the commercial paper market, most commercial paper carriers have been rated. Five services evaluate commercial paper: Moody's Investors Service, Inc., Standard and Poor's Corporation, Fitch Investors Service, Duff and Phelps, Inc., and McCarthy, Crisanti & Maffei, Inc. The first four charge the issuer a fee (around $5,000 for the initial listing and an annual fee of from $5,000 to $25,000 a year). The fifth rating company charges the investors a fee to subscribe to the service. From highest to lowest quality, commercial paper ratings are

Moody's: Prime-1 (P-1), Prime-2 (P-2), Prime-3 (P-3).

Standard and Poor's: A-1, A-2, A-3.

Fitch: F-1, F-2, F-3.

Duff: Duff-1 +, Duff-1, Duff-2, Duff-3.

McCarthy, Crisanti & Maffei: MCM 1 through MCM 6.

Approximately four fifths of the rated issues are in the top category, P-1 or A-1, or **prime commercial paper**. If an issuing firm is not so rated, it must pay a higher interest to cover the risk premium that investors will demand. Many issuers have a line of credit from a bank to back their commercial paper.

Some companies that consistently have millions of dollars of commercial paper outstanding hire their own sales force and sell their own commercial paper so as to avoid dealer commissions. Other companies work through dealers. In 1986 there were about seventy dealers who arranged sales in commercial paper. Dealers charge a commission for selling commercial paper of around $3.00 per $1 million. Almost no commercial paper is traded among dealers, and the commercial paper market is less active than is the market for other money market instruments such as Treasury bills. The typical investor is a bank, often the trust department or on behalf of a corporate customer. Most commercial paper is held to maturity and is not resold.

In the late 1970s, money market funds bought large amounts of commercial paper. Banks issuing large CDs thus had to offer rates that were nearly the same as the commerical paper rate. The cost of funds to banks includes the need to put funds aside for reserve requirements (3 percent reserve requirement on CDs with maturities of one and one-half years or less). Thus the banks found it difficult to lend at the commercial paper rate, and so companies that were large enough to issue their own prime commercial paper found it more profitable to issue paper than to obtain bank loans. This "reserve requirement tax" on banks, which may drive them out of the market for financing large corporations' short-term financing, could be remedied by paying interest on bank reserves.

Commercial paper continued to grow rapidly in the 1980s, partly because of the use of interest rate swaps.

Interest Rate Swaps

An **interest rate swap** consists of two holders of debt instruments exchanging the instruments' interest payments when these payments are different. For example, one may be a fixed-rate interest stream, and the other may be a floating-rate interest stream, tied to some market rate. If the two holders want each other's stream, they exchange the rights to the interest stream without exchanging any capital; that is, they swap interest rate streams.

An example shows how a company can use the commercial paper market to hedge against interest rate changes in a swap arrangement that provides a less expensive way to raise long-term funds. The company enters into a swap agreement in which it agrees to make fixed payments to an investor in return for a stream of floating-rate payments. Notice that no capital is involved, only the risk that the floating-rate receipts will be less than the fixed-rate payment that the company must make. These floating-rate payments can be tied to the commercial paper rate or, most frequently, to the LIBOR rate. There is one more step in the financing process. The company issues short-term commercial paper and rolls over (reissues) the paper as it matures. It thus pays the current interest rate for its money received from the commercial paper it issues. If interest rates fall, it will receive less from its floating-rate swap agreement, but this will be offset by the lower interest the company must pay on the funds it invested in the commercial paper market. The company now has a fixed-rate interest stream to pay, which is the same kind of interest rate stream that it would pay if it issued long-term bonds to finance its operations. It also has two offsetting floating-rate streams (the floating-rate receipts in the swap and the stream of interest payments that must be made on its commercial paper.) Thus the commercial paper market serves as a hedge against interest rate changes.

Repurchase Agreements

Repurchase agreements, or repos, are

1. The major debt instrument that the Federal Reserve buys and sells to carry out the U.S. government's monetary policy.
2. The main way in which money market dealers finance their inventories.
3. A major vehicle for investing the cash of large corporations and state and municipal governmental bodies.
4. A common way by which commercial banks manage their cash positions.

A **repurchase agreement**, or **repo**, is a debt instrument through which the borrower sells securities to the lender with the agreement that the borrower can repurchase the securities at a stipulated price. From the lender's viewpoint, the debt instrument is called a **reverse repurchase agreement**, or **reverse repo**. The repurchase price of overnight repos often has added to them the accrued interest. Separate interest charges can be charged if the agreement calls for a repurchase price that is the same as the price at the initial sale. The repurchase price is often lower than the purchase price for longer-term repos, in addition to any interest charged to protect the lender against any change in the securities' price. The difference is called a *margin* or *haircut*. In 1986, haircuts ran from approximately one eighth of a point to 5 percent.

Repurchase agreements can be tailored to any short time period; they can be secured by a number of relatively default-free securities, usually Treasury securities; and they provide a vehicle for relatively default-free loans. There is no established central market in repos: They are negotiated between individual parties and therefore can be made in many different forms. Large formal markets require homogeneous financial instruments so that round lots—100 shares of stock—of the asset can be traded.

The maturities of repos are often overnight or standard maturities such as one, two, or three weeks or months. The repos' maturities generally are the following:

1. *Overnight:* one-day repos.
2. *Open* or *continuing contract:* a series of overnight repos that either party can terminate.
3. *Term repos:* contracts for a specified time period, usually not exceeding 30 days.

Overnight contracts are often made in amounts of $25 million or more. The smallest denomination is $1 million. The Federal Reserve trades in repos and reverse repos in maturities up to 15 days.

Some repos were negotiated before the 1960s, but they were not even a significant money market instrument before that time. In the 1980s they have grown rapidly, from $111.7 billion in 1981 (annual averages at primary dealers) to $320.8 billion in 1985, a 287 percent increase.

Although short-term repo rates are negotiated and set at Federal Reserve auctions, they are closely related to other short-term rates. This relationship has not been precisely measured, however, because repos have no central markets. Even the Federal Reserve auctions do not produce market-clearing prices for repos, as all bids or offers on one side of a cutoff level are accepted. And data on the accepted bids or offers at these Federal Reserve auctions are not generally available.

Although the safety of repos is uncertain, they are regarded as one of the safest money market instruments. Unlike federal funds, in which loans are made between banks and other participants on the basis of faith, repos carry with them collateral that is generally of very high quality, most often Treasury securities. For this reason, the interest rate for repos is generally lower than that for federal funds.

The demand for T-bills and other Treasury securities is partly a derived demand by those dealers who need them for repurchase agreements. For example, usually every morning the Federal Reserve of New York meets with the money market participants to disucuss the general conditions of the market. If the dealers think that they will be selling repos to the Federal Reserve in the auction that day, they then need to increase their inventories of Treasury securities to use in these transactions.

Besides using repos to finance their operations, dealers also arrange repos for other parties. Because the dealer can act on both sides of the transactions, arranging both the repos and the reverse repos, he or she keeps a *matched book* to make sure that the funds arranged have been matched. That is, in order to lock in favorable rates, a dealer may not have perfectly matched the maturities of the repos and reverse repos, which would put the dealer at risk.

The securities underlying under most repos are Treasury securities, often T-bills. However, one advantage of repos is that a large variety of instruments can be used, including Treasury securities, Federal Home Loan Mortgage

Corporation securities, Government National Mortgage Association securities, CDs, and bankers' acceptances. The legal status of the securities underlying a repo has been disputed. Outwardly they appear to have been sold to the lender, which is very good security. But in practice, the securities are often not delivered; just the good faith of the borrower is assumed. Indeed, sometimes the borrower does not have the underlying securities and would have to buy them if they were demanded.

The failure in the 1980s of some repo dealers caused considerable losses to investors, including depository institutions, and thereby prompted a call for government regulation. The first failures occurred in 1982 when Lombard–Wall failed in August and Drysdale failed in May. In 1985, E. S. M. Government Securities Inc. and Bevill, Bresler and Schulman Inc. failed with losses of more than $500 million to investors. In addition, the failure of E. S. M. Government Securities Inc. triggered runs on state-insured thrifts in Ohio and the temporary closing of seventy thrifts. The reason? The dealers used customer-owned securities held in connection with repos for other transactions.

These problems emphasize the need to observe care when entering repo contracts. Often the dealer or the bank that arranges or takes part in lending funds on a repo contract may already have the securities in storage, a *custodial arrangement*. This saves the customer funds in a continuing relationship with the repo lender. However, when the Mount Pleasant Bank and Trust Company failed in 1982, the customers found that their securities—backing $350,000 worth of repos—were denied priority status under an FDIC ruling that the bank had failed to identify the securities adequately as customer property. In 1984 Congress passed the Bankruptcy Amendments Act, which exempted repos in Treasury and government agency securities, certain CDs, and bankers' acceptances from the bankruptcy law's automatic stay provisions. These automatic stay provisions prevent creditors from trying to enforce a lien against the property of a bankrupt estate. But this legislation does not resolve the problem of whether a repo is a sale of the security—thereby transferring the ownership rights of the underlying securities in the repo contract— or a secured piece of collateral to be included with other assets in the liquidation of a failed company during bankruptcy procedures.

Without a custodial arrangement, lenders may ask for delivery of the underlying securities if they are not fully confident of the borrower. The transaction costs of such an action, a *delivery repo*, are not insignificant. For example, consider an overnight repo using a Treasury security that is registered with the government, a book entry that does not require paper to change hands. The book entry must be changed for one day to the lender and then changed again back to the borrower. The fees include use of a wire system to notify the Treasury and the parties of the changes. For a $1 million–delivery round trip between the borrower and the lender and back to the borrower, the transactions costs of a delivery repo would be around $50 to $60.[5] This cost would be substantial for a continuing overnight repo that is renegotiated every day for several months. Lenders may also demand large haircuts on term repos. Of course, the desire to continue a profitable relationship with their borrowers may persuade lenders to increase the risk of repo arrangements.

In general, the transactors in the market have top credit ratings. The primary dealers must be approved by the Federal Reserve, and none of them have yet failed. Such dealers are also controlled by federal regulators unless they trade exclusively in securities that are exempt from regulation, such as Treasury securities. The depository institutions' dealers have their own depository institution regulators, and corporations must register with the Securities and Exchange Commission. The Dealer Surveillance Unit of the New York Federal Reserve Bank was organized in 1982 to monitor primary dealers more closely, and the Federal Reserve drew up voluntary capital adequacy guidelines for nonprimary dealers who are not subject to federal oversight. Haircut standards were also suggested for term repos.

There are many questions concerning the repo market, but there are few data to help answer them. Here are some of those questions:

1. Is the repo market always highly competitive?
2. Is there a significant amount of inside information that is not publicly available?
3. Do the barriers to entry as a primary dealer afford monopoly profits?
4. The business of dealing in repos can be considered a subset of the underwriting business, or the selling of new securities, because repos are tailor made, and therefore each negotiation is a new instrument. The underwriting market is, from casual evidence, one in which huge monopoly profits are made. As soon as the stocks and bonds are traded in the secondary markets, such as the New York Stock Exchange, these profits diminish or disappear. Monopoly profits in the main instrument of the money market—repurchase agreements—may also severely impair the allocation of funds in this country. And they may limit the availability of funds to smaller (than the largest corporations) businesses that cannot participate in the repo market. More government regulations added to the existing cobweb of regulations and different government regulators thus may not produce a better allocation of funds. What, then, is the best kind of regulation or deregulation for the repo market?

Treasury Securities

The U.S. Treasury sells large quantities of government securities to finance government operations and to refinance maturing debt (see Chapter 2 for a description of bills, notes, and bonds and the method of calculating the yield on a bill, and Table 12-3 for a further description of Treasury securities). Treasury open-market activities are sometimes labeled **debt management**. The Treasury can issue new government debt instruments and sell them to the public. The Federal Reserve cannot issue new debt instruments; it can buy and sell only existing government securities.

TABLE 12-3 Marketable Treasury Securities

Individuals can purchase marketable Treasury securities from local financial institutions, such as banks or securities dealers, or in person or by mail from Federal Reserve banks or the Department of the Treasury. If purchased through a financial institution or a brokerage firm, the procedure and the collection and payment method will be determined by that institution. Listed here is basic information on purchasing Treasury bills, notes, and bonds directly from the Treasury or Federal Reserve banks and branches. A new book-entry system, designed primarily for individuals, was scheduled to become operational in mid-1986.

Bills	Notes and Bonds
Issuance	*Issuance*
Treasury bills are issued by book-entry form (i.e., on computer records).	Treasury notes and bonds are issued in book-entry and registered (i.e., paper certificates) form. After mid-1986 all new notes and bonds will be issued in book-entry form only.
Bills may be obtained directly from the Treasury or through a Federal Reserve bank or a financial institution.	If in book-entry form, notes and bonds can be obtained only through a financial institution. If registered, they can be obtained through the Treasury, a Federal Reserve bank, or a financial institution. After mid-1986, book-entry notes and bonds may be purchased only at the Treasury or a Federal Reserve bank.
Bills are issued at a discount. The investor pays the face value when submitting a bid and sends a check for the discount as set by the auction when the bill is issued and the face value is returned at maturity.	Notes and bonds are issued at face value or at a premium or discount from face value as determined by auction. The investor pays the face value when the bid is submitted and sends a check for the discount or a letter requesting premium payment when the notes or bonds are issued.
Denomination	*Denomination*
Bills are bought in denominations of $10,000 minimum, thereafter in multiples of $5,000.	Treasury notes and bonds, whether book-entry or registered, are purchased in denominations of $1,000, $5,000, $10,000, and $1,000,000, with the exception of notes with terms of less than four years, which have a $5,000 minimum denomination.
Terms	*Terms*
Bills have terms of 3 months (13 weeks), 6 months (26 weeks), and 1 year (52 weeks).	Notes have a term of at least 1 year but not more than 10 years. Bonds have terms of more than 10 years.

TABLE 12-3 (continued)

Bills	Notes and Bonds
Issuance	*Issuance*
Sales	*Sales*

Treasury bills are sold by an auction process. Three-month and six-month bills are auctioned every Monday unless Monday is a holiday, in which case they are auctioned on the following Tuesday. One-year bills are usually auctioned every four weeks, on a Thursday. The usual deadline for submission of tenders is 1:00 P.M. Eastern time on the day of the auction. Noncompetitive tenders submitted by mail will be considered timely if they are postmarked no later than the day before the auction and are received by the issue date.

Although the schedule for the sale of notes and bonds may vary, in recent years the Treasury has generally observed the following financing schedule:

1. Two-year notes are usually issued at the end of each month.
2. Four-year notes are usually issued every three months, in late March, June, September, and December.
3. Five-year, two-month notes are usually issued every three months, in early January, March, July, and October.
4. Seven-year notes are usually issued every three months, in early January, April, July, and October.
5. The Treasury usually issues a three-year note, a ten-year note, and a thirty-year bond on the fifteenth day of February, May, August, and November.

Tenders must be received at Federal Reserve banks or branches, or at the Treasury, by the deadline established in the public announcement, usually 1:00 P.M. Eastern time. Noncompetitive tenders submitted by mail will be considered timely if they are postmarked no later than the day before the auction and are received by the issue date.

Interest	*Interest*

The price and the discount rate are not known before the auction as they are determined by competitive bidding. Refund (discount) checks are mailed on the issue date, usually the Thursday following a Monday auction. The discount represents interest to the owner at maturity.

The price and the coupon rate are not known before the auction, as they are determined by competitive bidding.

TABLE 12-3 *(continued)*

Bills	Notes and Bonds
Issuance	*Issuance*
Interest	*Interest*
If purchased through a Federal Reserve bank, the Federal Reserve bank will mail the check.	Interest is paid semiannually by the Federal Reserve bank and passed through by a financial institution holding book-entry accounts. Interest for registered securities is paid by mailed checks.
If purchased through a Federal Reserve bank, the Federal Reserve bank will mail the check.	
For bills purchased by investors under the proposed Treasury Direct Book-Entry Security System, discount payments are made by electronic fund transfer to the customer's bank account.	For notes and bonds purchased by investors under the proposed Treasury Direct Book-Entry Security System, interest payments are made by electronic fund transfer to the customer's bank account.
	A semiannual interest check for definitive issues is mailed automatically from the Treasury.
Principal Payment	*Principal Payment*
The principal on Treasury bills is paid on the maturity date through a check to the owners of record on the Treasury's book-entry system.	The principal on Treasury notes and bonds is paid on or after the maturity date upon presentation of the definitive security. After receipt and examination of the securities, a check is mailed to the owner. For notes and bonds purchased by investors under the proposed Treasury Direct Book-Entry Security System, principal payments are made by electronic funds transfer to the customers' bank account.
Taxes	*Taxes*
Income in most cases is not considered earned until the bill has matured or unless it is sold before maturity.	Income is considered earned each year.
Bills are exempt from state and local income taxes but are liable for federal taxes.	Notes and bonds are exempt from state and local income taxes but are liable for federal taxes.

Source: U.S. General Accounting Office, *U.S. Treasury Securities, the Market's Structure, Risks, and Regulation,* Briefing Report to the Chairman, Subcommittee on Domestic Banking, Finance and Urban Affairs, House of Representatives, August 1986, Appendix 3, pp. 84–87.

The Federal Reserve acts as the agent for the Treasury in the sale of Treasury bills, notes, and bonds. Auctions are conducted through each of the Federal Reserve banks and the main Treasury building in Washington, D.C., to sell Treasury bills, often every week. Predominantly financial institutions, but also anyone else who has the minimum amount of funds, usually $10,000, necessary to buy the smallest denomination issued may place a **tender offer**.

Exhibit 12-1 is a sample tender for Treasury bills. The buyer may enter a "noncompetitive tender offer," in which he or she agrees to buy the bills at the average price of the accepted competitive bids. The signed and filled-out tender offer, plus a cashier's check or a certified check, must be received by a Federal Reserve bank or by the Treasury in Washington, D.C., by a specific time. When the auction ends, the tender offer with the highest competitive bids, plus the noncompetitive tender offers, are accepted.

In recent years, longer-term maturities—notes and bonds—have been offered mostly through auctions to the highest bidder, although some fixed-price sales have been held. In the past, these securities were sold on a subscription basis, with a preannounced price and coupon rate. Auctions have been held on the basis of price or the equivalent yield (*price auction* or *yield auction*). In these auctions, all accepted bids pay the price submitted on each bid. Sometimes a single price equal to the lowest accepted offer is uniformly applied to all accepted bids. (See Table 12-4 for a description of the markets for Treasury securities.)

The Treasury Department switched to weekly auctions of Treasury bills on a *discount basis*, rather than on a price basis, with the April 18, 1983, weekly auction. This means that the discount given from the face value is used for auction purposes. The method of converting that discount into an interest rate was shown in Chapter 3. Competing bidders submit bids to two decimal points, such as a 6.84 percent discount. The calculation of prices of accepted bids is carried to three decimal places in the form of price per hundred dollars or a percentage of the face value. The Treasury Department said that the change would conform the bidding in Treasury auctions to market pricing conventions and simplify the submission of tenders. Unfortunately, this is true only for those experienced in such markets. Many others will continue to confuse the discount with the yield.

Treasury bills are the main debt instruments in the money market. From 1929 until 1934, maturities of 30, 60, and 90 days were offered. Then 182- and 273-day maturities were offered to reduce the number of refundings. Ninety-one-day bills were used after 1937 and were supplemented in 1958 with 6-month bills and in 1959 with 1-year bills. A 9-month maturity was tried and discontinued in 1972. From 1972 to 1982, the maturities were 91 days, 6 months, and 1 year. A 13-week maturity was issued in 1982.

U.S. Treasury securities are widely held, as shown in Table 12-5, and are the debt of the federal government. The federal debt consists of all the securities issued by the Treasury and a small amount of debt issued in the past by executive branch agencies. The Treasury debt is subject to a statutory limit

EXHIBIT 12-1   Sample Tender for Treasury Bills

FORM PG 4432-2
Dept. of the Treasury
Bur. of the Public Dept.

**TENDER FOR TREASURY BILLS
IN BOOK-ENTRY FORM AT THE
DEPARTMENT OF THE TREASURY
26-WEEK BILLS ONLY**

MAIL TO:

☐ Bureau of the Public Dept. Securities Transactions Branch
Room 2134, Main Treasury, Washington, D. C. 20226

☐ Federal Reserve Bank or Branch
of your District at: _____

**BEFORE COMPLETING THIS FORM READ THE
ACCOMPANYING INSTRUCTIONS CAREFULLY**

Pursuant to the provisions of Department of the Treasury Circular, Public Dept Series No. 27-78, the public announcement issued by the Department of the Treasury, and the regulations set forth in Department Circular, Public Dept Series No. 26-76. I hereby submit this tender, in accordance with the terms as marked, for currently offered U.S. Treasury bills for my account. (Competitive tenders must be expressed on the basis of 100, with three decimals. Fractions may not be used.) I understand that noncompetitive tenders will be accepted in full at the average price of accepted competitive bids and that a noncompetitive tender by any one bidder may not exceed $500,000.

TYPE OF BID
NONCOMPETITIVE ☐   or   COMPETITIVE ☐   at: Price_____

AMOUNT OF TENDER $ _____
(Minimum of $10,000. Over $10,000 must be in multiples of $5,000.)

ACCOUNT IDENTIFICATION: (Please type or print clearly using a ball-point pen because this information will be used as a mailing label.)

Depositor(s) _____

_____

_____

Address _____

_____

_____

DEPOSITOR(S) IDENTIFICATION NUMBER

SOCIAL SECURITY NUMBER

FIRST NAMED ☐☐☐ - ☐☐ - ☐☐☐☐   OR   EMPLOYER IDENTIFICATION NO. ☐☐ - ☐☐☐☐☐☐☐

SOCIAL SECURITY NUMBER

SECOND NAMED ☐☐☐ - ☐☐ - ☐☐☐☐

DISPOSITION OF PROCEEDS

The per amount of the account will be paid at maturity unless you elect to have Treasury reinvest (roll-over) the proceeds of the maturing bills. (See below)

☐ I hereby request noncompetitive reinvestment of the proceeds in book-entry Treasury bills.

METHOD OF PAYMENT

TOTAL
SUBMITTED $ _____   Cash $ _____   Check $ _____   Maturing Treasury Securities $ _____

DEPOSITOR'S AUTHORIZATION

Signature _____   Date _____   Telephone Number During Business hours (_____)
Area Code

FOR OFFICIAL USE ONLY

Received by _____   Date _____

STATEMENT OF ACCOUNT		Issue Discount Price $		Amount of Discount $		
Date	Transaction	Per Amount Transacted		Account Balance	Authority Reference	Validation
		Decrease	Increase			
		$	$	$		

A: DEPARTMENT OF THE TREASURY COPY

TABLE 12-4   Structure of the Treasury Securities Market

The securities issued by the U.S. Treasury are sold by the Federal Reserve. The secondary market consists of the direct sale of these securities and as the underlying security in repos. These transactions comprise the "cash" or "spot" market for Treasury securities. Derivative markets for future delivery of Treasury securities include the markets for futures contracts, options for the right to buy or sell these securities, and options to buy or sell the future contracts. In addition, there are both commitments by dealers to buy Treasury securities that will be issued and forward contracts to purchase these securities in advance.

Market Component		Annual Activity (1985 unless noted)
I. Cash Markets		
A. Debt Auction Market	The Treasury, through the Federal Reserve System (principally the Federal Reserve Bank of New York) acting as the Treasury's fiscal agent, sells new securities to the public to raise new funds and refinance existing debt.	Almost $1.2 trillion debt sold in 1985.
B. Secondary Markets		
1. Outright purchase and sale	Dealers buy and sell securities in an over-the-counter market, with transfers made through clearing banks and the Fedwire network. The market is used by the Federal Reserve for open-market conduct of monetary policy.	Over $75 billion in average daily transactions (through primary dealers). About $22 billion in net purchases by Federal Reserve System in 1985.
2. Repurchase agreements	Dealers obtain financing and securities from and for customers in an over-the-counter market. Also used by the Federal Reserve Open Market Committee for conduct of monetary policy.	About $31 billion on an average daily basis reported by primary dealers. About $8 billion gross purchases and sales on an average daily basis reported by Federal Reserve open market account in 1985.
II. Derivative Markets		
A. When-issued Commitments	Over-the-counter market used by dealers to lock in purchase and sale orders for securities announced but not yet issued—used to take or hedge position risk.	N/A
B. Forward Commitments	Over-the-counter market used by dealers to lock in purchase and sale orders at least 5 days in advance of delivery—used to take or hedge position risk.	Total unknown—$1.3 billion in average daily transactions reported by primary dealers.
C. Futures	Exchange market organized by the Chicago Board of Trade and Chicago Mercantile Exchange used by dealers to lock in purchase and sale orders in advance of delivery—used to take or hedge position risk.	46,448,064 contracts in 1985.

TABLE 12-4 *(continued)*

Market Component		Annual Activity (1985 unless noted)
	II. Derivative Markets	
D. Options	Exchange market organized by the American Stock Exchange (for bills and notes) and the Chicago Bond Options Exchange (bonds) used by dealers to purchase the right to buy or sell securities at a given price for a set period of time—a hedging tool.	437,959 contracts in 1985.
E. Options on Futures	Exchange market organized by the Chicago Board of Trade (notes and bonds). Dealers purchase the right to buy or sell futures contracts at a given price for a set period of time.	12,078,408 contracts in 1985.

Source: U.S. General Accounting Office, "How Repurchase Agreements Work," *U.S. Treasury Securities, the Market's Structure, Risks, and Regulation,* Briefing Report to the Chairman, Subcommittee on Domestic Banking, Finance and Urban Affairs, House of Representatives, August 1986, p. 19.

that must be approved by Congress and consists of all the negotiable Treasury debt. (Savings bonds sold to consumers in small denominations, sometimes from payroll savings, are not negotiable and must be redeemed by the original purchaser or his or her heirs.) In March 1986, Treasury debt subject to statutory limitation stood at nearly $2 trillion ($1,973.3 billion). That is an estimate of its par value, not its present market value.

The government's total public debt includes these Treasury securities plus state and local government debt. In a consolidated statement of government debt, the securities held by the government, including the Federal Reserve, would be subtracted.

The biggest change has been the large increase in the foreign holdings of public debt, from 4 percent in 1970 to a high of 15.7 percent in 1978; it then fell to 11.5 percent in 1985. There was a large increase in state and local government debt in 1981, the first year in which the Reagan administration was in office and advocated a policy of turning many governmental functions from the federal to the state and local governments.

THE STOCK MARKETS

After a stock is sold to the first group of purchasers in the primary market it is traded on one of the many *secondary stock markets*. The best-known secondary stock market is the New York Stock Exchange, located on Wall Street in New York City. There are many other secondary markets throughout the

TABLE 12-5   Percentage Ownership of U.S. Government Securities, 1970–1985

The federal debt consists of all securities issued by the U.S. Treasury and a small amount of debt issued in the past by executive branch agencies. In a consolidated statement of government debt, the securities held by the government, including the Federal Reserve, would be subtracted. The government's total debt includes state and local government debt.

The biggest change has been the large increase in the foreign holdings of public debt, from 4 percent in 1970 to a high of 15.7 percent in 1978 and then to 11.5 percent in 1985. There was a large increase in state and local government debt in 1981, the first year in which the Reagan administration was in office and advocated a policy of turning many governmental functions from the federal to the state and local governments.

End of Fiscal Year	Total*	U.S. Government Accounts	Reserve	Foreign and International	Private Financial Institutions†	Corporations	Individuals	State and Local Governments	Other‡
1970	100.0	25.7	15.6	4.0	16.8	3.0	22.2	6.6	6.2
1971	100.0	25.8	16.4	8.2	17.7	2.5	19.6	5.4	4.3
1972	100.0	26.1	16.7	11.5	16.7	2.2	17.2	6.3	3.3
1973	100.0	27.0	16.4	13.0	15.0	2.1	16.6	6.3	3.7
1974	100.0	29.1	17.0	12.0	13.0	2.3	17.0	6.0	3.7
1975	100.0	27.3	15.9	12.4	14.9	2.6	16.3	6.0	4.7
1976	100.0	24.1	15.2	11.3	17.5	4.0	15.5	6.3	6.1
1977	100.0	22.4	15.0	13.7	17.2	3.3	14.9	7.6	6.1
1978	100.0	21.8	14.9	15.7	15.0	2.8	14.2	8.8	6.9
1979	100.0	22.7	14.0	15.1	13.8	2.7	14.0	8.1	9.7
1980	100.0	21.8	13.3	13.9	14.8	2.9	13.6	8.5	11.3
1981	100.0	20.9	12.5	13.1	15.2	1.8	11.0	10.0	15.6
1982	100.0	18.9	11.8	12.3	16.7	1.9	10.1	10.7	17.5
1983	100.0	17.4	11.3	11.6	18.1	2.6	9.4	10.9	18.8
1984	100.0	16.7	9.9	11.2	16.2	3.0	9.4	N/A	N/A
1985	100.0	17.3	9.3	11.5	12.0	3.1	8.3	N/A	N/A

* Totals may not add to 100.0 because of rounding.
† Includes commercial banks, mutual savings banks, and insurance companies through 1980. From 1981 on, excludes mutual savings banks but includes money market funds.
‡ Includes S&Ls, nonprofit institutions, credit unions, corporate pension trust funds, dealers and brokers, certain U.S. government deposit accounts, and U.S. government–sponsored agencies. From 1981 on, also includes mutual savings banks.
N/A = Not available.
Source: U.S. General Accounting Office, *U.S. Treasury Securities, the Market's Structure, Risks, and Regulation*, Briefing Report to the Chairman, Subcommittee on Domestic Banking, Finance and Urban Affairs, House of Representatives, August 1986, Appendix 2, p. 82.

world. In 1986, there were many exchanges that were registered with the Securities and Exchange Commission operating in the United States, as shown in Table 12-6. Those exchanges in the United States outside New York City are sometimes called *regional exchanges*. They provide *continuous auction markets* and are organized under formal rules for trading. Trading on the New York Stock Exchange accounts for most of the total dollar volume on all exchanges. Approximately 2,200 stocks are traded on the New York Stock Exchange. These securities markets operate at one location. They receive orders from around the world through a network of brokers and dealers who are members of the exchange. Private stockbrokerage businesses, in turn, act as agents for the public in buying and selling stocks and bonds. The stockbrokerage firms hold stock on account for customers and lend money to customers to purchase stocks " on margin."

In addition, there are active secondary stock markets that are not centred in one geographical location. The over-the-counter market in the United States includes 30,000 to 40,000 different common stocks, most of which are not actively traded. On February 8, 1971, part of the over-the-counter market was tied into a computer system called NASDAQ, an acronym for the National Association of Securities Dealers Automated Quotations. At the end of 1984 approximately 4,723 stocks were listed by NASDAQ. Dealers and brokers all over the United States were able to receive information instantly from their computer terminals.

There are many indexes of the prices of financial assets. The most famous stock price index is the Dow Jones and Company, Inc., index of 30 industrial stocks that are published daily in the largest-circulation newspaper in the United States, Dow Jones's *The Wall Street Journal*. Standard & Poor's index of 350 stocks is used for tests in Chapter 13. The New York Stock Exchange Index of stocks on that exchange is a broader index.

Many **block trades** are negotiated, which are sometimes traded in the third market. The **third market** is a market for stocks listed on the New York Stock Exchange that is not conducted through the New York Stock Exchange. Stocks sold in the third market are said to be sold *off the Board*. Before 1975, when fixed commissions on the New York Stock Exchange were ended, the high commission fees caused increased trading volume off the Board.

In addition to the third market, the large institutional block traders often bypass both stockbrokers and stock exchanges and negotiate among themselves. This is called the **fourth market**. There are apparently no data on the size of the fourth market. Desktop computer terminals link approximately 150 institutional traders in the fourth market by a system called *Instinet*.

Another important development in stock trading is the *National Market System*, mandated by Congress in 1975 and established by the Securities and Exchange Commission as an electronic computer system that integrates all stock exchanges, the over-the-counter market, and the fourth market. This single computer system enables all market participants, regardless of the stock exchange in the United States from which they are receiving quotes, to have

TABLE 12-6 Formal Markets for Securities in the United States and Canada, with Selected Items Traded in 1986

Stock Exchanges

New York Stock Exchange

National Association of Securities Dealers (NASD or over-the-counter trading). The NASDAQ system used for trading is the "National Association of Securities Dealers Automated Quotation" computer network system.

American Stock Exchange (AMEX)

Boston, Midwest, Pacific, Philadelphia, Montreal, and Toronto

---

Bond Trading

New York Stock Exchange Bond Room

American Exchange

Future Markets

Commodities

Chicago Board of Trade: corn, gold—kilo, silver, soybean meal, soybean oil, soybeans, wheat

Chicago Mercantile Exchange: cattle—feed, cattle—live, pork bellies, wood, hogs

Commodity Exchange, New York: aluminum, copper, gold, silver

Coffee, Sugar, and Cocoa Exchange, New York: cocoa, coffee, sugar—domestic, sugar—world

New York Cotton Exchange: cotton, orange juice, propane

Kansas City Board of Trade: wheat

MidAmerica Commodity Exchange: cattle—live, corn, gold, hogs—live, silver, soybean meal, soybeans, wheat

Minneapolis Grain Exchange: wheat

New York Mercantile Exchange: crude oil—light sweet, gasoline—unleaded, heating oil no. 2, N.Y. gasoline (regular, unleaded), platinum, palladium, potatoes—cash

Winnipeg Commodity Exchange: barley, flaxseed, oats, rapeseed, rye, wheat

---

Financial

Chicago Board of Trade: GNMA (Government National Mortgage Association), Major Market Index, Muni Bond Index, Treasury notes, Treasury bonds, 500 Times Index

Chicago Mercantile Exchange: Standard and Poor's 250 Index, Standard and Poor's 500 Index

Coffee, Sugar, and Cocoa Exchange, New York: CPI-W futures (also called *inflation futures*, a consumer price index)

International Money Market at Chicago Mercantile Exchange: European currency units, bank CDs, British pounds, Canadian dollars, Eurodollars, Japanese yen, Swiss francs, Treasury bills, West German marks

Kansas City Board of Trade: Mini Value, Value Line Index, 500 Times Index

MidAmerica Commodity Exchange: British pounds, Japanese yen, Swiss francs, Treasury bills, Treasury bonds, West German marks

New York Futures Exchanges, unit of New York Stock Exchange: New York Stock Exchange Index

New York Futures Exchange, unit of the New York Stock Exchange: stock composite index

TABLE 12-6 (*continued*)

Futures Options

Chicago Board of Trade: corn, soybeans, Treasury bonds, Treasury notes
Chicago Mercantile Exchange: Standard and Poor's 300 Stock Index, British pounds, cattle—live, Eurodolllars, hogs—live
Coffee, Sugar, and Cocoa Exchange, New York: sugar—world
Commodity Exchange, New York: gold, silver
International Money Market at Chicago Mercantile Exchange: Treasury bills, Japanese yen, Swiss francs, West German marks
New York Cotton Exchange: cotton

Options

Index Options

American Exchange: major market index, computer technology
Chicago Board of Trade: Standard and Poor's 100 Index, Counter 250 Index, oil index, airline index
National Association of Security Dealers: NASDAQ 100 Index
New York Stock Exchange: NYSE Index, NYSE Double Index, Options National Over-the-Counter Index
Pacific Exchange: technology index
Philadelphia Exchange: gold/silver index; Value Line Index; Standard and Poor's 500 Index, Standard and Poor's Over-the-Counter Index

---
Interest Rate Options

Chicago Board Options Exchange: U.S. Treasury bonds, 5-year U.S. Treasury notes

---
Stock Options

American Exchange
Chicago Board of Trade
New York Exchange
Philadelphia Exchange

---

the same information about stock prices. This system also removes the price differences between the domestic exchanges and lowers the transactions costs of trading, thereby ending *market fragmentation.* It is no surprise that the New York Stock Exchange (NYSE), with a virtual domestic monopoly in trading many of its listed stocks, did not support the idea. The NYSE forbids its members from trading stocks listed on the NYSE in any place other than the NYSE. These provisions are called *off-board trading restrictions.* In 1982, almost 90 percent of the trading volume was on the NYSE, and millions of dollars in commissions were made by specialists trading on the floor of the NYSE. The NASDAQ, which began in 1971, became an important challenger to the NYSE by 1982 when it equaled the American Stock Exchange in trading volume (17 percent of all trading on the domestic exchanges). The 150 institutional brokers hooked into Instinet by 1982 and trading in the fourth market also challenged the NYSE.

The development of the National Market System was, in any case, slowed by the pressures from the NYSE. In 1980 the Securities and Exchange Commission lifted the off-board restrictions and ruled (Rule 19c-3) that any stocks listed on the NYSE after April 1979 must also be listed on the National Market System. By 1986 the National Market System stocks comprised a large group of stocks, covering more than a full page in *The Wall Street Journal.* The computer system provides simultaneous quotes, and dealers may trade through the system. But despite this, the NYSE is still the principal trading market for stocks.

The New York Stock Exchange

A group of New York City brokers who had been trading securities under a buttonwood tree on Wall Street in 1792 drew up the first agreement in the history of the New York Stock Exchange.[6] The Buttonwood Agreement increased the importance of brokers relative to that of auctioneers. At first, government stocks were traded at the Tontine Coffee House. In 1817, a more formal organization, the New York Stock and Exchange Board, was organized under a constitution. In 1863, its name was changed to the New York Exchange, sometimes called the **Big Board**. Regular trading sessions were scheduled, officers were elected, and the rules for the induction and regulation of members were formalized. But as late as 1835, no industrial stock was traded, rather, the New York Stock and Exchange Board handled government, utility, and transportation bonds. By 1856, fewer than twenty different industrial stocks were traded.

Until 1840, the markets for financial assets in other parts of the country were as important as those in New York City. State Street in Boston and Chestnut Street in Philadelphia were as influential as Wall Street. Nevertheless, the seeds of New York's prominence and the dominance of the New York Stock Exchange were planted early. With the opening of the Erie Canal (1823), New York enjoyed increased trade. Commercial paper to finance trade was handled in increasing amounts by New York banks. The New York banks also received more deposits, which allowed them to increase their *call loan* business to finance the sale of securities. The banks considered these loans to be desirable, since they were very liquid short-term loans.

The volume of business on the New York Stock Exchange reached 700,000 shares on a record day in 1879, and 1 million shares per day were traded in 1886. A new high of over 3 million shares traded in one day was reached in 1901, and this record was not surpassed until 1916. In the following decades the exchange suffered from the publication of reports of fraudulent practices such as the sale of phony stock issues. Annual reports were not always informative or available. When the exchange asked a railroad for its report shortly after the Civil War, the company replied that it makes "no reports and publishes no statements—and has done nothing of the sort for the last five years."[7] The exchange began to regulate itself with stock registration and, eventually, required public financial reports of listed stocks.

With public confidence restored and a "new era" of great expectations, trading volume rose from 173 million shares in 1921 to more than a billion in 1929. Stock prices reached a peak of 254 on September 7, 1929 (on the Standard & Poor's index of 90 common stocks). At first there was an orderly decline in stock prices, then a short rally, and finally a plunge, beginning on October 23. The day of greatest panic, "Black Tuesday," was October 29, on which the Dow Jones Industrial Average of stocks fell 12 percent (60 percent below its September 29 peak) and 16.4 million shares were traded (compared with the daily September average of slightly more than 4 million shares). The Dow Jones Industrial Average fell from 381 on September 3, 1929, to its low of 36 in 1932 and did not regain its 1929 peak for 25 years. During 1929, American Telephone & Telegraph Company stock dropped from a high of $310\frac{1}{4}$ to $199\frac{1}{2}$; General Electric dropped from $396\frac{1}{4}$ to $168\frac{1}{8}$; and White Sewing Machine, which had been selling at $48, closed at $11 on Black Tuesday, with a block of stock reportedly bought at $1 by an employee on the stock exchange floor.

The belief that the October crash produced many suicides has been challenged on the grounds that the suicide rate was relatively low in the United States in October and November of 1929, but for many the results were indeed painful.

> One of the worst victims was Clarence Birdseye, who started Birdseye Foods on a pittance, sold it to General Foods for $30 million, and put the entire sum into the market not long before the crash. His fortune was obliterated. Another big victim was William C. Durant, the founder of General Motors. After his fortune was wiped out, Mr. Durant ended up running a bowling alley in Flint, Michigan.[8]

The 1929 stock market crash had momentous effects throughout the country and much of the world. It has been the subject of many books which characterize the 1930s as the aftermath of the stock market crash of 1929. This type of analysis, however, is mostly wrong. The country was already in an economic decline, although this decline was certainly accelerated by the stock market's negative impact on investment and on the value of the public's stock of wealth. Moreover, the stock market is but one market among many. The economy did not fall into two depressions in the 1930s solely or even primarily because of the October 1929 stock market crash. The severe business contraction, which had begun before October, would have ended in late 1930 or 1931 if additional events had not occurred. The most important of these were the collapse of a large number of commercial banks and the accompanying huge decline in the quantity of money in circulation—it decreased by fully one third.

Beginning at the end of World War II, volume again grew in the securities markets. Trading volume and the composite index of New York Stock Exchange prices from 1966 to 1986 are shown in Figure 12-2.

The New York Stock Exchange went through a number of crises in the late 1960s and early 1970s. There was a record volume that was difficult to handle

FIGURE 12-2 Trading Volume and the Composite Index of Prices of Shares on the New York Stock Exchange, 1967–1986

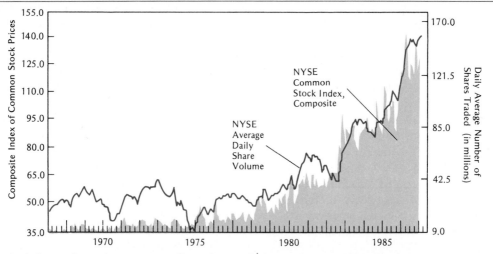

The shaded area shows the average trading volume, which went up over 100 million shares on the average day in the 1980s. The stock price index was lower in the middle 1970s (during a recession) than in 1967. The level of the index did not rise above its average in 1967 until the early 1980s, a period of about 14 years of poor stock price performance. Then it began to rise rapidly except for the period around the two recessions in 1980 and 1982 and a brief fall in 1984.

Source: Cambridge Planning and Analytics, Inc., Boston.

and a record number of failures to complete transactions by delivery of the stock that had been offered (called *fails*). The third and fourth markets (arrangements for sales outside the formal exchanges), which were not subject to the New York Stock Exchange's arbitrary commission schedule, were created, and the number of members of the New York Stock Exchange dropped.

Beginning on May 1, 1975, the fixed commission rate schedule of the New York Exchange was completely abandoned in favor of competitive rates set by the stockbrokers.

Because of the failure of a number of brokerage houses hit by rising volume and increased costs, Congress passed the Securities Investor Protection Act of 1970, which created the Securities Investor Protection Corporation (SIPC). The SIPC insures customers of member brokers against the losses incurred if a broker goes bankrupt. The SIPC has no direct funding from the government but can borrow up to $1 billion from the U.S. Treasury.

In 1986 and 1987, stock market trading was under attack because of allegations of widespread **inside trading**, trading on the basis of information not available to the public. The meaning of inside information and its relevance to the theories of markets are examined in the next chapter.

Also in the middle 1980s as the stock price indexes rose rapidly and sometimes fell by large amounts, as shown in Figure 12-3, there were a number of new effects. First, the giant institutions that dominate much of the stock market sometimes do their trading through computerized programs that are programmed to sell off giant blocks of stock if the market price indexes fall by a prescribed amount. This kind of trading is called *programmed trading,* and the models used for this trading are called *filters* in finance theory. Its effects on stock market prices have not been rigorously researched, in part because the computer programs are not public information.

Another new effect of trading in the 1980s occurs on the last hour of those days on which three types of financial assets based on stock prices (stock options, stock index futures, and stock index options) all expire simultaneously. This hour is called the *triple witching hour,* during which there is a substantial increase in stock market volume. (During the triple witching hour on Friday, September 19, 1986, 25 percent of the day's trade was transacted.) It is likely that the presence of all these financial assets based on stock prices increases the competitiveness of the market and the number of participants who may trade. Whether or not the triple witching hour interferes with stock market trading so that it does not respond to underlying demand and supply conditions is a matter for continued research.

At the end of 1984, there were 1,458 different issues traded on the New York Stock Exchange, which is an organization of *member* firms and individuals. The number of available *seats* for members on the Exchange has been 1,366 since 1953. In addition, there are *allied members* (such as a general partner in a member firm who is not a member) and *approved persons* (such as a director of a member corporation). Seats on the New York Stock Exchange sold for prices that varied from $515,000 to $200,000 in 1969, then fell in the 1970s; a seat sold for $45,000 in October 1977 and $90,000 in October 1978. In 1929, the "bad old days," seats varied from $550,000 to $625,000.

The exchange is run by twenty directors: ten public representatives and ten brokers. In addition, there is a full-time paid chairman of the board.

Members trade on the floor of the New York Stock Exchange in one or more of the following capacities:

1. **Commission brokers** act on orders from the public relayed through brokers.
2. **Specialists** buy and sell particular stocks that are assigned to them. They keep a list of limit and stop orders and take a position by buying, selling, and holding the stocks they are assigned. They attempt to provide more continuous trading in a stock at prices that are closer to their concept of normal. Thus a stock that has been selling for $10 might be bought by a specialist for $9.75 rather than letting it fall to $9 if he or she believes that most trades will take place around $10. An attempt is made to prevent prices in successive transactions from being conducted at more than one eighth of a dollar per share difference. The specialist must make an "effective execution of commission orders" and provide "maintenance,

FIGURE 12-3   The Nominal and Real Values of Stocks Listed on the New York Stock Exchange, 1966–1986

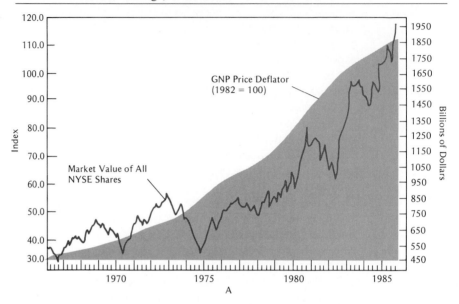

A

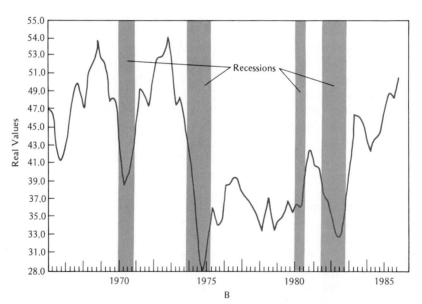

B

The amount of wealth held from 1966 to 1986 in the form of listed stocks is plotted in Figure 12-3A. From $34 billion in 1966 it grew to over $1.8 trillion in 1986. The price index for all goods and services in GNP (the GNP deflator with the base year as 1982) is also plotted. To obtain the real value of the shares listed on the New York Stock Exchange, divide the market value by the price index. The interesting result is shown in insofar as reasonably practicable, of a fair and orderly market on the Exchange" in the assigned stocks (Rule 108). The specialist can act as an agent for other brokers or as a dealer for his or her own account, carrying out his or her functions. The approximately 400 specialists are evaluated quarterly by the floor brokers they serve.

3. **Odd-lot dealers** buy and sell stocks for which they have received orders for less than the standard 100-share multiples.
4. **Floor brokers** trade for other members, on a commission basis. They are popularly known as $2 brokers, the standard commission formerly paid for executing a 100-share order.
5. **Registered traders** trade primarily for themselves. (There are approximately 100 registered traders.)
6. **Bond brokers** trade bonds in the exchange's Bond Room.

The huge volume of stocks actively traded on the Big Board makes it a fairly competitive market, which precludes any substantial collusive action or sustained domination by a small group of traders.

Some practices probably reduce the degree of competition. For example, the limitation on membership can be reflected in monopolistic prices for seats on the exchange. It therefore might be advantageous to allow more specialists in single stocks. This is because the specialist in a single stock has special information and also has schedules for a particular stock for all limit and stop orders. These orders are entrusted to the specialist by other exchange members. The orders specify a *floor* or *ceiling* price (**limit orders** to sell or buy, respectively) and/or directions to buy or sell if a given price is reached (**stop loss orders**). For example, a limit order might instruct the specialist to sell XYZ for $50 or better, whereas a stop loss order would instruct the specialist to sell XYZ if the price fell below $50. The specialist therefore has important information for predicting the future price of stocks that is not available to other market participants.

There are similar participants in the over-the-counter markets. Many firms or individuals can act as specialists in a security by actively buying, selling, carrying an inventory of the stock, and accepting some type of limit orders. Limited numbers of specialists on the Big Board (no more than one in each stock) may reduce the competition in providing these services. The specialist, however, is probably prevented by other traders from making substantial

---

Figure 12-3B, in which the peaks and troughs of recessions are shown by bars. The decline in the real value of stock during the 1974–1975 recession was very large and the most striking part of this series in Figure 12-3B. The stock market's real values had not recovered their 1973 highs by 1986. It thus appears from this casual evidence that the plunge in real value of equities did have substantial wealth effects.

Source: Cambridge Planning and Analytics Inc., Boston.

monopoly profits on the Big Board. If other traders suspect that a market is being made around prices that differ from their concept of normal, they will rapidly adjust their bids and offers to the new information.

The Stock Market and the Economy

Stock prices are sometimes said to be a symptom or a reaction, to either past conditions or expected future conditions in the economy. This may be true in large part, but the size of the stock market reaction may well change these future conditions. For example, if it is thought that the economy is going into a recession, so that the profits of companies with stocks sold on the New York Stock Exchange will take an unexpected dive the following year, stock prices may immediately fall. And if the stock prices fall by a huge amount, this reaction could make the recession bigger than expected. This is because people who own stocks will suffer significant decline in their wealth. If this decline is thought to be long term, these individuals may dramatically reduce their spending.

A huge amount of wealth is held in the form of stocks that can be traded on the New York Stock Exchange, as shown in Figure 12-3A from 1966 to 1986. From $34 billion in 1966 it grew to over $1.8 trillion in 1986. The price index for all goods and services in the gross national product (GNP) (the GNP deflator with the base year as 1982) is also shown. To obtain the real value of the shares listed on the New York Stock Exchange, divide the market value by the price index. The interesting result is shown in Figure 12-3B, in which the peaks and troughs of recessions are indicated by bars. Notice that in the 1970, 1974–1975, and 1982 recessions, the real value of stock declined substantially, but that this did not happen in the short recession in 1980.

Changes in the value of wealth held in stocks can affect individuals' spending and investment plans. If they regard a drop in the real value of this wealth to be temporary, it should have little effect on their spending. For example, stock may be bought quickly if stock prices fall. That is, some people may start spending their money furiously to buy up the stock of companies at this new low price, creating chains of new spending, which would somewhat offset the stock market decline. But if the declining value of the stock market wealth is considered to be for a longer term, as apparently happened in 1975, then spending plans can be cut back for long periods, beginning a chain of declines in expected income and accompanying declines in the demand for goods and services.

The drop in the real value of stock during the 1974–1975 recession was very large and the most striking part of this series. The stock market's real values had not recovered their 1973 highs by 1986, and in addition, there was a long period of high unemployment. It thus appears from this casual evidence that the plunge in the real value of equities did have substantial wealth effects. The 1975 recession occurred when the price of imported oil was susbstantial; the OPEC countries stopped selling oil to the United States; and the Nixon administration implemented price controls that prevented the price system from rationing the reduced oil supplies. Conversely, the decline in the real value of stocks listed on the NYSE during the 1970 and 1982 recessions was substantial but short-lived.

Investment in new plants and equipment may be curtailed by low stock prices. That is, it is less expensive to buy capital in another company by buying its stock at a low price than it is to build or rent the capital.

Can we predict recessions by looking at stock market price indexes or the real value of equities? The stock prices shown in Figure 12-2 indicate that they fell in the recessions, but they also fell in other periods, such as the end of 1978. For example, after September 8, 1978, the popular Dow Jones index of 29 leading industrial stocks fell 15.2 percent in ten weeks, but no recession ensued. Apparently Paul Samuelson, a winner of the Nobel Prize in economics, was right when he reminded us that "the market has forecast nine of the last five recessions."

It may well be that one of the reasons for a stock market decline is the attempt to sell off stocks in order to invest funds in other parts of the economy, such as the home building industry, in which case the market's decline may to some extent be the result of another sector's expansion. Economists blandly call this a *portfolio adjustment*; those with long positions in the stock market may call it murder.[10] Portfolio adjustments and changes in the prices of stocks and their real values are also related to many other variables in the economy, including the expected profits of the underlying business. In one view, the stock market is a transmission mechanism by which these underlying conditions affect the rest of the economy. However, the stock market is more than a reflection of underlying conditions. In addition, changes in the real value of stocks feed back on the economy by changing people's wealth, that is, stock both directly owned and indirectly owned through institutions such as pension funds.

THE CORPORATE BOND MARKET

New corporate bonds are sold to the public in two ways. In *private placements*, bonds are placed directly with particular lenders. Life insurance companies often acquire bonds by this method. The decline in private placements from about one half between 1953 and 1964 to one third in 1977 reflects the life insurance companies' reduced share of bond acquisitions.[11]

The other and more common method of selling corporate bonds is by a public offering handled by underwriters (investment banking firms). During the 1920s, most public offerings were handled by commercial banks. The Glass–Steagall Act (the Banking Act of 1933) terminated the banks' underwriting of corporate bonds. Investment banking firms have been the major underwriters since that time.

The secondary market for corporate bonds is sometimes considered rather thin because most corporate bonds are purchased by large institutional buyers. However, secondary bond markets, such as those found in the New York Stock Exchange Bond Room, appear to be competitive and an efficient market.

The bond market changed after the last quarter of 1979. The interest rates on the composite indexes of long-term U.S. Treasury bonds and long-term AAA (highest-grade) corporate bonds are shown in Figure 12-4 to have had increased volatility beginning at the end of 1979. There were a number of events at the end of the 1970s and in the early 1980s that caused great uncertainty, which was reflected in the greater variation in long-term interest rates.[12] Long-term nominal rates depend on the real rate of interest plus a premium for expected inflation, as explained in Chapter 4. The real rate of interest may rise with greater uncertainty about the future. That is, it requires a higher real rate of return to persuade investors to invest funds when they are more uncertain about the future. In the period to which we just referred, the following events caused increased uncertainty: United States embassy personnel were taken as hostages in Iran in 1979. The Federal Reserve announced that its monetary policy would place more emphasis on controlling the money supply, and the actual policy caused increased variability in the nation's money supply. The largest banking deregulation bill in U.S. history was signed

FIGURE 12-4　Interest Rates of Long-Term U.S. Treasury Bonds and Long-Term AAA Corporate Bonds

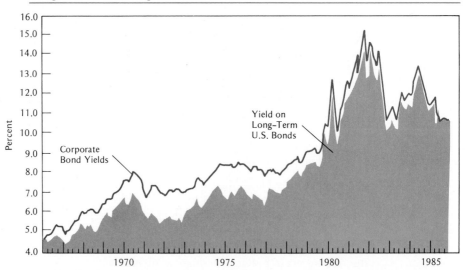

The interest rates on the composite indexes of long-term U.S. Treasury bonds and long-term AAA (highest-grade) corporate bonds had increased volatility beginning at the end of 1979.

Source: Cambridge Planning and Analysis Inc., Boston

into law in March 1980, and depository institutions were faced with a difficult period of adjustment. And there were recessions in 1980 and 1982, with over 10 percent of the labor force out of work in the second recession.

As Figure 12-4 shows, in 1986, long-term nominal interest rates were still high by historical standards. Their high level and great volatility helped create new financial assets that provided ways to hedge against interest changes and to profit from the variability. These new financial assets were options and futures contracts on financial assets.

THE FINANCIAL ASSET
OPTIONS MARKET

A **financial asset option** gives the owner the right to buy or sell a financial asset at a particular price before a specified date. The terms used in the option market are as follows:

1. An option to sell is a **put**.
2. An option to buy is a **call**.[13]
3. The price at which the option owner can buy or sell the stock is the **exercise price**, the **striking price**, or the **strike price**.

Before 1973, options were offered by private dealers, who charged a premium for them. Options for some financial instruments are now heavily traded on the formal exchanges. The formal trading options began with options on sixteen stocks on the Chicago Board Options Exchange (C.B.O.E.) on April 23, 1973. There are now hundreds of different stock options traded on a number of formal exchanges, including the Chicago C.B.O.E., the American Stock Exchange in New York, the Philadelphia Stock Exchange, and the Pacific Stock Exchange. If you have never traded options, the entire subject probably sounds complicated and even boring. A small position in options would clarify these problems rapidly, but in place of that some oversimplified examples may do.

Bill Frank owns 100 shares of common stock in General Wheel, which he believes will not significantly rise in price in the next six months. If a call option for General Wheel is traded on an exchange, Bill Frank might try to make some extra money without selling his stock. He would take his 100 shares of General Wheel to a broker and write a call option on them for sale on an exchange. The price of a share of General Wheel is $60 on the day in January that the call is written. An April call on 100 shares of General Wheel has a striking price of $65 and is called an *April 65 call*. The call option on 100 shares is currently selling on an exchange for $3.25 a share, or $325 for 100 shares. Bill Frank receives $325 (minus brokerage fees) on a call option that expires at the end of the second week in April.

Tom Pass believes differently. He buys the call option for $325 because he expects the price of General Wheel to rise significantly. If the price of General Wheel does rise above $65, the call option will be said to be **in the money**.

Suppose the price of General Wheel rises to $75. Then the April 65 call will rise to at least $10 a share (or higher if a further rise is expected and the expiration date is not at hand). Why has the call risen in price to $10 or higher? Because the owner of such a call can exercise it and buy a share of General Wheel for $65 and then turn around and sell the same share at its current market price of $75, making a $10 profit minus brokerage fees. In this situation, Tom Pass, like most stock options market participants, would not exercise his call; he would instead sell it in the market.

If the price of General Wheel does not rise to $65 before the end of the second week in April, Bill Frank will make his profit on selling the call, and he will not be forced to sell his 100 shares at $65 each. Instead, he will retain ownership of the 100 shares.

A put may be bought in place of a riskier short sale. A common stock may be *sold short* in anticipation of a price decline. Or an individual may sell short a stock that he or she does not currently own. Think of this transaction as a loan of stock from the stockbroker that the short seller must return within a stated time period. The short sale is riskier than a put is in terms of the limits on the possible loss. That is, the possible loss on a short sale theoretically has no limit if the stock keeps rising, but the put owner can lose only the cost of the put plus brokerage fees.

Assume, for example, that an individual, Mr. Williams, expects XYZ stock to fall in price from $15 to $5 per share. Williams does not own this stock but sells the stock short at $15 per share for 90 days by borrowing the stock from the broker. If he sells 100 shares, he will receive $1,500. If the stock falls to $5 per share before 90 days have passed, Williams will repay the dealer by buying the stock for $5 and returning it to the broker. He then will make a profit of $1,000 minus the brokerage fees. If the stock were to rise to $20 a share, Williams would lose $500 plus brokerage fees.

Rather than sell short, Mr. Williams may simply buy a put for the stock. Assume that a put with a $10 striking price is available. The put costs $1.75 a share, or $175 for 100 shares. Then if the price of the stock falls to $5, Williams can exercise his put and make at least $500, minus the $175 cost of the put and the brokerage fees. If the stock price rises, Williams can lose only $175 plus the brokerage fees.

Stock options are financial assets that allow individuals to take a position on stocks at a small fraction of the cost of the stock. They also offer a way to hedge against unfavorable price changes on stocks.

In 1982, proposals were made to trade *options* on debt instruments and indexes of stocks. By 1986, options on many debt instruments and stock index options were traded, as shown in Table 12-6. These options on the future stock indexes allow a position to be taken on the general level of the stock market. Unlike future contracts for these assets, which expose the buyers to the possibility of large losses, options buyers can only lose the price of the options (plus the brokerage fee).

COMMODITY FUTURES MARKETS

A **commodity futures contract** is a legal instrument by which an individual agrees to buy or sell a commodity at a fixed price in the future. The futures contract may call for delivery as long as eighteen months in the future. But few of these purchase orders result in deliveries; rather, roughly 90 percent of all futures contracts are settled by offset rather than delivery, as explained in the example. *Buy* contracts are purchased if prices are expected to rise, and *sell* contracts are purchased if prices are expected to fall.

The following hypothetical example illustrates the general mechanics of futures contracts. Assume that Jones has entered a futures contract to buy a given quantity of commodity X at $1,000 six months hence. Jones expects the price to rise above $1,000. This is called a **long position**. The other party to the futures contract, Smith, agrees to sell a given quantity of commodity X at $1,000 six months hence. Smith expects the price to fall. This is called a **short position**. Smith does not own commodity X but must deliver cash equal to the value of the commodity if he wishes to terminate his contract. (Parties to a contract need not actually trade with each other in the future; long and short positions are matched through clearinghouses such as the Chicago Board of Trade Clearing Corporation.) Now assume that the price of a contract on commodity X, scheduled for the same delivery date, rises in price to $1,200. Jones may decide to take his profit and so sells his contract for $1,200. Smith, fearing a higher price and a bigger loss, wishes to terminate his short position. In effect, Smith pays off the owner of a buy contract, Jones, by delivering $1,200 rather than actually delivering commodity X. The original contract is canceled, with a loss of $200 to Smith and a gain of $200 to Jones, neglecting brokerage fees.

In this manner, most futures contracts do not result in the delivery of the commodity. Thus many more people than those actually interested in taking future delivery on a commodity are able to act on the market in an attempt to predict future prices.

Commodity futures trading began with the establishment of the Chicago Board of Trade on April 3, 1848. It grew rapidly in the 1970s. Approximately fifty different commodity futures contracts are currently traded.[14]

FINANCIAL ASSET FUTURES MARKETS

A major innovation in the history of financial markets occurred in the United States in 1981. Although contracts for the future delivery of currencies used in international trade had long been traded, and three-month U.S. Treasury bill futures contracts had been traded since 1978, the change in the financial markets in 1981 was huge. That is, the government authorized many new financial asset futures contracts to be traded, and volume surged.

The pressure to start trading these financial assets grew out of the extremely variable (by historical standards) interest rates in the 1970s and early 1980s. Financial asset futures allow lenders, for example, to reduce the risk of an unforeseen rise in interest rates. Suppose, for instance, that a bank agrees to make a loan at 8 percent for two years. But when the borrower comes in to exercise his or her agreed option to borrow at that rate, rates have risen to 12 percent. The bank is caught in the middle. It has to borrow at 12 percent (or forsake 12 percent investments) to lend at 8 percent. In these situations, many financial institutions simply stop agreeing to make such commitments, and this has a detrimental effect on investment. For example, if one is planning to put up a shopping center in six months, it is necessary to arrange the financing in advance. Financial futures contracts allow the bank to make such a commitment with little or no interest rate risk. That is, potential borrowers can buy a financial futures contract that will rise in value with a rise in interest rates, and the bank will not lose by such an unforeseen circumstance.

AN EXAMPLE OF THE USE OF A FINANCIAL FUTURES CONTRACT BY A BANK

The following example of a bank's use of financial futures was suggested by Barbara Bennett of the Federal Reserve Bank of San Francisco:

For example, suppose a bank on last May 6 funded a $10 million six-month bullet loan (principal and all interest due at maturity) with 90-day CDs and wanted to preserve a 300 basis point spread on the difference between the going CD rate of 8.31 percent and the loan rate of 11.31 percent. The bank was open to the risk that when the 90-day CDs matured on August 4 and had to be rolled over for another 90 days at a new rate, the CD rate could have risen, thus reducing its earnings spread over the six-month life of the loan. To protect itself against this risk, the bank could have sold ten CD futures contracts (which are traded in $1 million lots) on May 6 for delivery in September, the contract delivery date closest to the roll-over date of its CDs. Using data on the actual closing price of the September CD futures contract that was quoted in the *Wall Street Journal* on May 6, 1983, the bank would have acquired its short position at the going price of 91.43, or a discount rate of 8.57 percent. It would then have closed out its position on August 4 when it issued the new CDs. According to the *Wall Street Journal*, the closing price of the September CD contract on August 6 was 89.84 for a discount rate of 10.16 percent. The bank's profit on this transaction, then, would have been 159 basis points because, as interest rates rose and securities prices fell, the bank could, in essence, have met the terms of its original contract to deliver CDs at a price of 91.43 by purchasing those securities at 89.94, and then selling them at the higher price. Thus, while the CD rate had risen from 8.31 to 9.88 percent over that time, the bank would have still earned a spread of 301 basis points over the six-month term of the loan.

Unhedged, the bank's spread would have averaged only 221 basis points.

A basis point is one one-hundredth of a percentage point. For example, a change from 5.01 percent to 5.02 percent is an increase of one basis point. A spread is the difference between interest rates. A rollover means the refinancing of a given debt.

Source: Barbara Bennett, *FRB SF Weekly Letter*, Federal Reserve Bank of San Francisco, November 25, 1983, pp. 2–3.

Futures contracts for Ginnie Maes (Government National Mortgage Association–guaranteed wholesale mortgages), Treasury bonds, and Treasury bills are traded on the Chicago Board of Trade. Futures contracts for commercial bank CDs (certificates of deposit) are traded on the International Monetary Market of the Chicago Mercantile Exchange.

Futures contracts based on stock indexes were first approved for trading on the Chicago Board of Trade and the Commodity Exchange Inc. in New York City in 1982. On February 24, 1982, the Kansas City Board of Trade began selling futures contracts on an index of stocks. More than 2,000 were traded the first day. The first-day volume in these stock index futures was double the normal volume in futures for hard, red winter wheat, for which it was the biggest market.

Three *stock index futures* contracts were approved in 1982. The Standard & Poor's 500 futures index is traded on the Chicago Mercantile Exchange; the New York Stock Exchange futures index is traded on the New York Futures Exchange; and the Valueline Futures Index is traded on the Kansas City Board of Trade.

Stock index futures rise and fall with the stock market averages. Holders of sell contracts will benefit if the price of the composite bundle of stocks falls below the contract price, because the price of the bundle in the contract is fixed. Theoretically, the bundle can be bought at the lower market price and sold at the contract price if the contract is executed. Instead, transactors usually sell off their contracts at a profit. Holders of buy contracts will benefit if the price rises above the contracted price of the bundle. Theoretically, they can buy at a lower contracted price if they exercise the contract and sell at the higher market price. Instead, transactors usually sell off their buy contracts at a profit. They will lose if prices move in the other direction than indicated in these two examples.

Why buy stock index futures? First, they offer an opportunity to make profits on changes in the stock market or turns in the business cycle—so far as they are reflected in the stock market—if one believes that the present price of a stock future index contract does not correctly reflect these future events. Second, stock index futures are hedges against general economic or stock market changes. For example, suppose that an investor holds a broad portfolio of stocks and fears a business downturn but does not wish to sell off his or her position. The investor may want to take advantage of possible lower rate taxes by holding the stock a bit longer (one year for the lower capital gains tax rate). As insurance, sell contracts can be taken in a stock futures contract. If business conditions turn sour and the market falls, the sell contracts will rise in price, tending to offset the loss in stock values in the portfolio. As another example, assume that an individual wishes to invest in shopping centers but wants to be protected in case of a general business downturn. Stock futures index contracts may provide the insurance desired.

Such hedges can be used for more risky investments that depend on general business conditions and in this way promote innovative technologies. Once the mechanics become familiar, they will be an important vehicle for reducing investment risk.

FUNCTIONS OF FUTURES AND OPTIONS MARKETS

Futures and options markets perform valuable functions. One is to improve the allocation of the commodity over time. For example, without futures contracts, individuals might store an insufficient amount of food in the summer for use the following winter. But there might not be enough food in the winter if there were no way for the price system adequately to reflect next winter's expected food prices during the summer, when food is abundant. Speculators also would not be tempted to buy food in the summer and store it for the winter. But it is this kind of speculation that brings down winter prices and raises summer prices of food, provides a better allocation of food over the seasons, and leads some individuals to specialize in the storage of food in a manner that is more efficient than if each household provided separate storage.

Futures and options traders also perform the important function of bearing the risks of unfavorable future interest rate and price movements. Some producers and buyers of commodities or financial assets (such as loan commitments by banks) may be reluctant to gamble on future prices and may lack knowledge or funds to speculate on market conditions six months in the future. Futures trading, however, allows the risk to be borne by those in the futures market who agree to buy or sell at a particular price, months before the commodity or financial asset is delivered.

An example of this second function can be found in the futures markets for currency. Suppose that American Wheel, Inc., wants to buy some merchandise in West Germany for delivery 60 days later. The merchandise may already be on order, so that it must be paid for in West German marks. But rather than speculate on the price of German marks 60 days later, American Wheel may acquire a contract for the delivery of West German marks in 60 days at a stipulated price. This is a **forward contract**, or buying West German marks forward. The seller of the contract, perhaps a professional speculator, bears the risk of unfavorable increases in the price of West German marks.

Futures and options markets also allow hedging, examples of which were given in the last two sections.

THE SECONDARY MORTGAGE MARKET

The *secondary mortgage market* is a market in which mortgages that have already been negotiated are traded. The secondary mortgage market is sometimes included in the markets referred to as the money market. However, mortgages are long-term debts and might be more appropriately classified with long-term bonds in the conventional bond markets or classified separately because of their distinctive features.

The private participants in the secondary mortgage market include private investors and mortgage brokers who buy and sell mortgages. The federal or quasifederal participants are huge and operate nationally. The story of the secondary mortgage market is the story of its giant participants.

The Federal National Mortgage Association (FNMA), also known as "Fannie Mae," is the largest single supplier of funds for residential housing. Fannie Mae is a government-sponsored mortgage investment corporation nominally owned by its stockholders with a portfolio of residential mortgage loans (see Table 12-7). Its stock is sold on the New York Stock Exchange.

Fannie Mae is not a primary lender. It lends money to institutions such as savings and loan associations, which themselves negotiate mortgage loans directly with homeowners. Homeowners continue to send their monthly payments to the original lenders and are not aware that Fannie Mae owns the mortgage. In 1981, Fannie Mae acquired approximately one in every twenty mortgages written in the United States.[15] It lost money in the early 1980s, reflecting the general interest rate squeeze in the thrift industry. Fannie Mae announced plans to buy **adjustable-rate mortgages**—ARMs (mortgages that tie their interest return to a market rate between specific limits)—and bought some *second mortgages* (mortgage loans that are subordinate to first mortgages in case of default). Fannie Mae was tracking 75 different types of ARMs in 1982. One problem in buying different types of mortgages is that the uniformity needed for competitive auctions with many participants can be impaired.

Fannie Mae is run by a board of fifteen directors, five of whom are appointed by the President of the United States. There is federal supervision in addition to the requirement that five appointments be made by the president. The secretary of Housing and Urban Development (HUD) can at times fix the aggregate amount of dividends that Fannie Mae pays in a year. The secretary of HUD can also require that a reasonable proportion of the corporation's

T A B L E 1 2 - 7 Mortgage Debt Outstanding, Fourth Quarter, 1985 (millions of dollars)

All holders	**2,248,501**	Federal Housing and Veterans Administration	4,903
1- to 4-family	1,467,231		
Multifamily	202,891	1- to 4-family	2,246
Commercial	471,279	Multifamily	2,657
Farm	107,100		
		Federal National Mortgage Association	98,282
Selected financial institutions	1,385,530		
Commercial banks[1]	423,003	1- to 4-family	91,966
1- to 4-family	214,340	Multifamily	6,316
Multifamily	22,906		
Commercial	174,336	Federal Land Banks	48,129
Farm	11,241	1- to 4-family	2,829
		Farm	45,300
Savings banks	177,193		
1- to 4-family	122,136	Federal Home Loan Mortgage Corporation	13,244
Multifamily	23,236		
Commercial	31,743	1- to 4-family	11,208
Farm	78	Multifamily	2,036
		Mortgage pools or trusts[3]	413,913
Savings and loan associations	587,045	Government National Mortgage Association	212,145
1- to 4-family	430,876		
Multifamily	66,467	1- to 4-family	207,198
Commercial	89,126	Multifamily	4,947
Life insurance companies	167,887	Federal Home Loan Mortgage Corporation	99,088
1- to 4-family	13,499		
Multifamily	19,453	1- to 4-family	98,182
Commercial	122,925	Multifamily	906
Farm	12,010		
		Federal National Mortgage Association	54,987
Finance companies[2]	30,402		
		1- to 4-family	54,036
		Multifamily	951
Federal and related agencies	166,764		
Government National Mortgage Association	1,473	Farmers Home Administration	47,693
		1- to 4-family	22,186
1- to 4-family	539	Multifamily	6,675
Multifamily	934	Commercial	8,189
		Farm	10,643
Farmers Home Administration	733	Individual and others[4]	282,294
1- to 4-family	183	1- to 4-family	165,405
Multifamily	113	Multifamily	45,294
Commercial	159	Commercial	44,801
Farm	278	Farm	26,794

1. Includes loans held by nondeposit trust companies but not bank trust departments.
2. Previously included in "Individuals and others." Assumed to be entirely 1- to 4-family loans.
3. Outstanding principal balances of mortgages backing securities insured or guaranteed by the agency indicated.
4. Other holders include mortgage companies, real estate investment trusts, state and local credit agencies, state and local retirement funds, noninsured pension funds, credit unions, and other U.S. agencies.

Note: Based on data from various institutional and governmental sources, with some quarters estimated in part by the Federal Reserve. Multifamily debt refers to loans on structures of five or more units.

Source: Federal Reserve Bulletin, April 1986, p. A39.

mortgage purchases be "related to the national goal of providing adequate housing for low- and moderate-income families, but with reasonable economic return to the corporation." The secretary of HUD must approve offerings of stock and debt obligations, and the secretary of the Treasury must approve the issuance of various forms of debt securities.

With all this government supervision, it is quite evident that Fannie Mae is unlike the normal private corporation. It is, in large part, a government-created and government-organized corporation that has moved substantial amounts of capital funds out of other sectors into the housing market.

Fannie Mae has relatives. Freddie Mac, the Federal Home Loan Mortgage Corporation (FHLMC), was established on July 24, 1970, by the Emergency Home Finance Act, to purchase residential mortgages. Its board of directors is the three members of the Federal Home Loan Bank Board, whose chairman is also the chairman of the FHLMC. The corporation is technically privately owned through the sale of nonvoting common stock issuable only to the twelve Federal Home Loan banks.

Fannie Mae was originally chartered under the National Housing Act of February 1938 as the National Mortgage Association of Washington. In 1968, it was partitioned into two corporations, Ginnie Mae (the Government National Mortgage Association) and the new Fannie Mae, just described. Ginnie Mae is the corporation entirely within the government; it is in HUD, under the direct supervision of the secretary of HUD.

All these agencies either raise money by selling debt instruments in the private financial markets or guarantee the debt raised by private lenders. Ginnie Mae fully guarantees borrowings by private mortgage lenders. These debt instruments can often be especially attractive to investors who want investments with little default risk. Because the government either directly owns, or in large part supervises, these corporations, it is expected that the federal government will keep them from suffering a default. Ginnie Mae–guaranteed "loan certificates" are advertised as follows:

> The certificates are sold by GNMA dealers or by mortgage originators in face values as low as $25,000. The purchaser of a GNMA certificate receives a standardized, highly marketable instrument with interest payments comparable to, or higher than, those for other debt instruments. The purchaser is guaranteed timely payments of principal and interest by the Government National Mortgage Association even if the individual homeowner or GNMA issue defaults. GNMA certificates are backed by the full faith and credit of the U.S. government.[16]

The question arises as to whether a dollar spent from funds borrowed by the Mae sisters and cousin Freddie is a government or a private expenditure. Is there a difference between an expenditure in the housing industry financed by the U.S. Treasury or Fannie Mae (or any of her relatives) and selling a bond to the public? In both cases the allocation of funds to the housing industry is largely determined by the federal government.

THE FOREIGN EXCHANGE MARKET

There also are markets for parties in different countries. Accordingly, the payments for these international transactions usually involve parties that use different currencies. Thus foreign transactions must include arrangements to exchange the currency of the buyer or investor for that of the seller. To do so, an **exchange rate**—the price of a unit of the foreign money relative to the price of a unit of the domestic money—must be determined.

Foreign currencies and internationally accepted monies (media of exchange such as gold and monies issued by international organizations such as the IMF) are sometimes referred to as **foreign exchange**. Foreign exchange must be obtained by buyers or investors making international transactions. It is held by central banks and is traded in foreign exchange markets. The banks in financial centers that serve as the brokers and dealers for foreign exchange comprise the center of the foreign exchange market. Large foreign exchange markets are found in London, New York, Frankfurt, and Tokyo. The center for mark–dollar transactions is Frankfurt; Tokyo for yen–dollar transactions; and London for sterling–dollar transactions. New York is a secondary center for all foreign exchange. Banks communicate with one another by telephone and telex (which records messages on word processors). Firms and banks that conduct international transactions generally have their phone number and their telex number on their stationery. Funds and transactions can thus be rapidly transferred between foreign exchange markets by means of this communication technology.

The dealers at the foreign exchange markets list buy and sell quotes of various foreign exchange rates for their customers, the difference in the rates being the *bid–ask spread*. Trading in foreign exchange occurs continuously, as the markets are located around the world in different time zones.

The U.S. foreign exchange market was described by Patricia Revey as follows:

> The United States foreign exchange market consists of a network of commercial banks—located principally in New York and, to a lesser extent, in other major cities—which buy and sell bank deposits ("exchange") in another currency, and of several organized exchanges, which trade foreign exchange futures contracts. Except for the currency futures market, there is no central marketplace where participants meet to trade. Instead trading is over the counter, with dealers communicating directly by telephone and telex or indirectly through foreign exchange brokers who serve as agents, bringing together buyers and sellers for a fee.
>
> While most banking institutions are prepared to offer their customers a service in foreign exchange, there are only about 80–100 banks that actively trade foreign exchange for their own account. Of these, relatively few act as market makers by standing ready to quote fresh prices and execute business up to recognized amounts. At the same time, foreign

exchange brokers in the United States number less than a dozen. Thus, the heart of the market is comparatively small.

The overwhelming bulk of all transactions occurs in the interbank market, where banks seek to hedge or manage their exchange risk and to anticipate exchange and interest rate movements. Their operations give the market liquidity and make possible the smooth transaction of customer business. The customer or retail market, which accounts directly for as little as 10 percent but indirectly for perhaps as much as 50–60 percent of all exchange deals, consists of multinational corporations, nondealing banks, other nonbank financial institutions, and individuals.

Roughly two thirds of all foreign exchange transactions are conducted spot, that is, at current exchange rates. . . . Another 30 percent of all transactions are swaps involving the simultaneous purchase and sale of a specified amount of foreign currency for two different maturities. Swaps are most commonly used to fund exchange positions, to take a view on interest rate differentials between two currencies, and in borrowing and lending operations. Only 6 percent of total exchange transactions are outright forwards involving a single purchase or sale of foreign currency for a value date more than two days in the future.

Foreign exchange trading in the United States is highly competitive. No one bank or single group of banks commands a dominant share of turnover in such major currencies as the German mark, Japanese yen, Canadian dollar, or pound sterling. However, in other currencies, such as the Belgian franc and Italian lira where the strength of commercial, financial, and speculative demand does not support an active market, trading is relatively more concentrated among a few banks.

In the United States, foreign exchange trading is not regulated, though bank examiners review exchange transactions as a normal part of routine bank supervision. Commercial banks operate under self-imposed internal controls that cover most aspects of their involvement in the market. Issues related to foreign exchange trading, operations, and technical practices are discussed on the institutional level in the forum of the Foreign Exchange Committee, established in 1978 under the sponsorship of the New York Federal Reserve Bank. The Foreign Exchange Committee consists of representatives from east coast, regional and foreign banks, brokerage firms, and as observers members of the FOREX Association of North America. The FOREX brings together as individuals a large number of traders and brokers from 220 banking and 19 brokerage offices around the country.[17]

STUDY QUESTIONS

1. Describe the U.S. money market and the functions it performs.
2. There is interest in holding down federal government expenditures by adopting a law or a constitutional amendment setting some arbitrary

limits on government spending. If one views government expenditures in the wide perspective of government allocation of expenditures, how will the following three transactions differ?

a. The Treasury borrows $100 and gives it to an S&L (savings and loan association).

b. One of the Mae sisters borrows money and lends it to an S&L, saving the S&L $100 over what it would cost the S&L to raise these funds elsewhere.

c. A law is passed affecting reserve requirements at savings and loans, allowing an S&L to make an additional $100 profit.

3. Do the Mae sisters or cousin Freddie Mac change the allocation of resources? Can a case be made that the bedroom suburbs of the middle class were heavily subsidized, whereas the inner city was further deprived, by the allocation of huge amounts of funds to thrifts by these sisters and their cousin?

4. Does a significant decline in stock prices affect economic activity? Note that it is helpful here to differentiate declines that are expected to persist from those that are expected to be temporary. With respect to cycles of expansion and contraction in the economy, is the stock market a reflection of them, a cause of them, or both?

5. Can the same person be a hedger, an arbitrager, and a speculator? Explain.

6. What are the differences in concept among a money market in an economic model, the market for skis in Denver, and the market for fish at Fisherman's Wharf in San Francisco? Where is the counter in the over-the-counter market for stock?

7. Look up the prices and striking prices of a put and call option (where both are traded) and then look up the price of the corresponding stock. Do the option prices reveal any information about market participants' expectations?

8. Find the futures price for U.S. Treasury bills (reported daily in *The Wall Street Journal*). What information does this market convey about future short-term interest rates?

9. Savings and loan associations do not hold all the mortgages they originate. The home buyers who originated mortgages at S&Ls continue to send their monthly payments to the S&Ls. How do you explain this?

10. How can one hedge with a New York Stock Exchange futures index contract? What effects will financial futures contracts have on investment?

11. What is meant by "selling foreign exchange forward"?

GLOSSARY

Adjustable-rate mortgages (ARMs). Mortgages whose interest rate is tied, within specified limits, to the movements of market interest rates.

Arbitrager (or arbitrageur). One who simultaneously buys an asset on one market and sells it in another for profit.

Banker's acceptance. A short-term liquid debt instrument that has been guaranteed by a bank as signified by a notation, such as "accepted by the XYZ Bank," on the debt instrument.

Big Board. An unofficial name for the New York Stock Exchange.

Block trade. A very large transaction in one stock.

Bond brokers. Those who arrange bond sales and purchases, such as the New York Stock Exchange bond traders operating in the exchange's Bond Room.

Business certificates of deposits or **negotiable certificates of deposit (CDs).** Marketable, interest-yielding deposit certificates in denominations of $100,000.00 or more, with specified maturity dates, issued by U.S. banks, foreign banks, U.S. branches of foreign banks, and U.S. thrifts.

Call option. An option that gives the holder the right to buy (stock) at a fixed price.

Capital markets. Markets for longer-term securities, such as stocks and bonds.

Commercial paper. Short-term marketable debt instruments issued by commercial and institutional enterprises.

Commission brokers. Brokers who buy and sell on orders from the public.

Commodity futures contract. A contract to buy or sell a commodity such as wheat or a Treasury bill at a specific future date at a fixed price that is not negotiated by the buyer or seller, traded on formal exchanges. That fixed price remains constant while the present price of the futures contract fluctuates in the futures market. See also **Forward contract**.

Debt management. The issuing, refinancing, and management of the debt of an individual, business, or government. (For the U.S. Treasury, debt management also includes the regulation of the term structure of the national debt.)

Diversification. A strategy of reducing the risk of a decline in the average price of a portfolio of assets by buying a number of assets in which there is an expectation of offsetting price movements caused by *random* fluctuations.

Exchange rate. The price of a unit of one country's currency being traded for a unit of another country's currency.

Exercise price. See **Striking price**.

Financial asset options. Options that give the owners the right to buy or sell a financial asset at a fixed price before a specified date.

Floor broker. A trader on a stock exchange who trades for other members on a commission basis.

Foreign exchange. Foreign currencies and internationally accepted monies (media of exchange in international trade, such as gold and monies issued by international organizations like the IMF).

Forward contract. A contract for the future delivery of an asset in which the future delivery price is negotiated by the buyer and seller so that the current price at the time the contract is negotiated of the forward contract is zero (plus transactions costs). See also **Commodity futures contract**.

Fourth market. Trades in stock between large institutional investors that take place outside a stock exchange and without stockbrokers.

Hedging. A strategy in which two or more assets are held that have offsetting price movements because of a *nonrandom* relationship between the prices. For contrast, see **Diversification.**

Inside trading. Engaging in profitable trading of securities on the basis of information "not available to the public." The precise meaning of "not available to the public" seemed to include (in 1986 and 1987 legal proceedings) confidential information about a company's activities that can be used to make profits on the securities of the company. Refraining from trading the company's securities on the basis of this information was generally not considered.

Interest rate swap. An agreement in which two holders of debt instruments exchange the instruments' interest payments when these payments are different.

In the money. A situation that occurs when the market price of the financial asset underlying an option is higher than the striking price if it is a call or lower than the striking price if it is a put.

Investors. In the classification used in this chapter, the market participants who buy an asset and hold it for income (dividends or interest income).

Limit orders. Orders specifying a maximum price at which to buy or a minimum price at which to sell stock, options, or other financial assets.

Long position. The ownership of an asset, such as a common stock, whose value is increased by a rise in its price.

Market. A formal or informal organization of buyers and sellers who trade particular commodities or services. This is the *institutional* definition. In economics, a market is sometimes thought of part of an economic model describing the demand and supply of a particular good or service. This is the *abstract* way of viewing markets.

Money market. A market with traders who buy and sell short-term liquid financial assets such as prime commercial paper and certificates of deposit.

National market system. A system whereby stocks are listed on the New York Stock Exchange, NASDAQ, and regional exchanges.

Odd-lot dealers. Dealers who combine small orders of stock into 100-share multiples for purchase or sale.

Primary dealers. Dealers who negotiate the sale of new financial assets.

Primary markets. Markets for new assets.

Prime commercial paper. The highest-quality commercial paper.

Put option. A stock option to sell.

Registered trader. Traders (as on the New York Stock Exchange) who trade primarily for themselves.

Repurchase agreement (repo). A debt instrument by which the borrower sells securities to the lender with the agreement that the borrower can repurchase the securities at a stipulated price. See also **Reverse repurchase agreement (reverse repo).**

Reverse repurchase agreement (reverse repo). A repurchase agreement from the lender's viewpoint. See **Repurchase agreement (repo).**

Secondary dealers. Dealers who

negotiate the sale of financial assets that have previously been issued.

Secondary markets. Markets for financial assets that have previously been issued.

Short position. The position resulting when an asset such as a stock is borrowed and sold. A decline in price will result in a profit because the loan can be repaid with a stock that costs less, assuming that the transactions costs are covered.

Stop loss orders. Orders that become market orders once a predetermined price is reached (e.g. to sell if the price drops to a specified price).

Specialists. Traders who buy, sell, and maintain an inventory in particular stocks. They provide a more continuous trading in a stock than would occur with sporadic buyers and sellers alone.

Speculation. Acquiring a position with the intention of liquidating it for a profit. The term covers short and long positions.

Speculators. Individuals who speculate. See **Speculation.**

Striking price (or strike price or exercise price). The price, specified in an options contract, at which the option holder is entitled to sell or buy the underlying asset.

Tender offer. An offer to buy a security, such as a U.S. Treasury bill.

Third market. A market for stocks that are listed on a stock exchange but are not traded through a stock exchange.

NOTES

1. U.S. General Accounting Office, *U.S. Treasury Securities, the Market's Structure, Risks, and Regulation*, Briefing Report to the Chairman, Subcommittee on Domestic Banking, Finance and Urban Affairs, House of Representatives, August 1986, p. 26. Knowing that newly derived estimates have a life of their own, this conjecture is presented with some reluctance, yet it does give the impression that primary dealers have more than half.

2. Rob J. M. Willemse, "Large Certificates of Deposit," in Timothy Q. Cook and Timothy D. Rowe, eds., *Instruments of the Money Market*, 6th ed., Federal Reserve Bank of Richmond, 1986, pp. 36–52.

3. Frederick H. Jensen and Patrick M. Parkinson, "Recent Developments in the Bankers Acceptance Market," *Federal Reserve Bulletin*, January 1986, pp. 1–12.

4. Timothy D. Rowe, "Commercial Paper," in *Instruments of the Money Market*, pp. 111–125.

5. Recent information on repurchase agreements can be found in the following: Gary Haberman and Catherine Piche, "Controlling Credit Risk Associated with Repos: Know Your Counterparty," in "Repurchase Agreements: Taking a Closer Look at Safety," *Economic Review*, Federal Reserve Bank of Atlanta, September 1985, pp. 28–34; Stephen A. Lumkin, "Repurchase and Reverse Repurchase Agreements," in *Instruments of the Money Market*, 1986, pp. 65–80; Bobbie McCrackin, A. E.

Martin, III, and William B. Estes III, "State and Local Governments' Use of Repos: A Southwestern Perspective," in "Repurchase Agreements: Taking a Closer Look at Safety," pp. 20–27; Don Ringsmuth, "Custodial Arrangements and Other Contractual Considerations," in "Repurchase Agreements: Taking a Closer Look at Safety," pp. 40–47; Richard Syron and Sheila L. Tschinkel, "The Government Securities Market: Playing Field for Repos," in "Repurchase Agreements: Taking a Closer Look at Safety," pp. 10–19; Sheila L. Tschinkel, "Overview," in "Repurchase Agreements: Taking a Closer Look at Safety," pp. 5–9; Sheila L. Tschinkel, "Identifying and Controlling Market Risk," in "Repurchase Agreements: Taking a Closer Look at Safety," pp. 35–48; and U.S. General Accounting Office, *U.S. Treasury Securities, the Market's Structure, Risks, and Regulation,* Briefing Report to the Chairman, Subcommittee on Domestic Banking, Finance and Urban Affairs, House of Representatives, August 1986, app. 6, pp. 101–118.

6. For a broad historical view, see Lance Davis, Jonathan Hughes, and Duncan McDougall, *American History* (Homewood, Ill.: Richard D. Irwin, 1965), Chap. 13.

7. *Understanding Financial Statements* (New York: New York Stock Exchange, March 1981), p. 1.

8. The suicide rate is discussed by John Galbraith, *The Great Crash, 1929* (New York: Time Inc.: 1961), pp. 131–132. The quotation is from William G. Shepherd, Jr., "Recollections of Some Who Were There," *The New York Times,* September 23, 1979, p. F9.

9. *Newsweek,* November 11, 1978, p. 90. It turned out that rate of growth of the real gross national product was negative for the second quarter of 1979. However, using the rule of thumb that a recess is a period in which at least two consecutive quarters have negative real growth, this period did not qualify as a recession.

10. A *long position* involves the ownership of stock, whose value is reduced by a fall in stock prices. A *short position* ("selling short") involves the sale of stock that in effect is lent to the seller for a given period (on which interest must be paid). The short seller can replace the stock at a profit if the price of the stock *falls* by enough to offset his or her transactions costs.

11. Burton Zwick, "The Market for Corporate Bonds," *Quarterly Review,* Federal Reserve Bank of New York, Autumn 1977, p. 29.

12. "Bonds and Beyond: Long Term Get Tougher," *Business Week,* March 1, 1982, p. 47. Some experts hold that changes in *bond duration* and yield volatility are the best measure of a bond's price volatility. Bond duration is the length of time before a stream of payments from a bond generates one half of its present value (Jess B. Yarvitz, "The Relative Importance of Duration and Yield Volatility on Bond Price Volatility," *Journal of Money, Credit and Banking,* February 1977, pt. 1, pp. 97–102.

13. A warrant is an instrument similar to a call except that it is issued by the

corporation that also issues the stock. It also has an exercise price and a maturity. The maturities are generally much more distant than those of calls, which do not normally exceed one year. Warrants are sold on regular stock exchanges.

14. *The ABC's of Commodities* (New York: New York Merchantile Exchange, 1980), p. 8.

15. Some of the information in this and the following paragraph are from Clyde H. Farnsworth, "Trying to Stem Fannie Mae's Losses," *The New York Times*, May 16, 1982, p. 6. Farnsworth described the Fannie Mae headquarters as a building that "looks like an English manor—an elegantly proportional, Williamsburg-styled, red brick mansion" that is not in the down town Washington, D.C., area. Despite these cosmetic differences, as well as its sale of stock and different salary schedule, it is a government-created and government-sponsored corporation.

16. *There's More to Ginnie Mae Than Meets the Eye* (Chicago: Chicago Board of Trade, January 25, 1980), p. 1.

17. Patricia Revey, "Evolution and Growth of the United States Foreign Exchange Market," *Quarterly Review*, Federal Reserve Bank of New York, Autumn 1981, pp. 34–35.

CHAPTER 13

MONEY AND STOCK PRICES

CHAPTER PREVIEW

Introduction. The discussion of the relationship of money and stock prices requires some understanding of the correctness of the efficient market hypothesis.

Yield and Stock Values. The basic valuation formula from Chapter 10 and stock yields are presented.

Efficient Markets. This discussion defines efficient markets and their workings and what they mean for stock prices.

Inconsistent Evidence and Theoretical Doubts. The efficient market hypothesis has been subjected to an enormous amount of testing, most of which has shown no substantial deviations from the hypothesis. Nonetheless, there is enough contradictory evidence and plausible analysis to raise some serious doubts about the efficient market hypothesis as it has been applied to formal markets for financial assets; the October 1987 decline is an example.

Introduction of Money and Stock Prices. The common belief that stock prices can be predicted simply by prior changes in the money supply is examined.

Problems in Relating Money to Stock Prices. Important statistical problems that are applicable to much of macroeconomics, money, and banking are related to money and stock prices.

Causation. Do money supply changes cause stock price (or stock yield) changes, or is it the other way around?

Further Tests. Stock yield changes have some synchronous and future effects on the money supply.

INTRODUCTION

This chapter will examine the relationship of money and the value of stock. The manner in which stock prices are formed must be understood before the relationship of stock values to changes in the money supply will have any meaning. We will begin by opening the curtain on the efficient market hypothesis, which has won wide support among economists and specialists in the field of finance. Although it explains a great deal about how formal markets for financial assets, such as bonds and stocks, function, a number of inconsistencies have been shown in recent research, and these inconsistencies point toward a reformulation of efficient market theories. Some evidence supports the view that changes in the value of stocks are statistically related to current and future money supply changes, and also the view that changes in the money supply may immediately (synchronously) affect the value of stock.

If nothing else, the reader should leave the chapter with the warning against rushing out and losing funds in the market on the basis of some simplistic scheme. Of course, if the reader makes a profit, it can always be said, as a sour grapes protest, that it was not worth the risk.

YIELD AND STOCK VALUES

The basic valuation formula and its application to stock prices were presented in Chapter 10. To review it and to put it in more compact form, the **basic valuation formula** means that the value of a share of stock—its price—is equal to the discounted value of all future profits (and, for precision, the salvage value of any assets sold by the corporation):

$$PV_{SP} = \sum_{i=1}^{N} \frac{R_i}{(1 + r)^i} \tag{1}$$

where PV_{SP} is the present value of a stock and $\sum$ (sometimes defined as the capital Greek letter sigma) is the summation sign, meaning "add up all profits to the corporation from time 1 to N." This formula has been the basis for many statistical tests of stock prices noted in this chapter.

The owner of a stock receives his or her return from the stock in two ways: expected dividends and changes in the price of the stock. This return compared with the price of the stock is a measure of the **stock yield** or the **rate of return** from the stock. The stock price change is divided by the price of the stock to obtain the percentage change in the price of the stock. Add to this the expected dividend divided by the expected price of the stock to obtain a measure of the rate of return or stock yield to the owner of the stock.

In symbols, the stock yield, r_{SY}, is the expected dividend, D, plus any expected gain in the price of the stock, ΔSP, during the year, divided by the price of the stock, SP:[1]

$$r_{SY} = \frac{D + \Delta PV_{SP}}{PV_{SP}} \tag{2}$$

For example, if the dividend is expected to be $10 per year and the stock that currently sells for $60 is expected to rise in value by $14 during the year, the expected stock yield will be

$$r_{SY} = \frac{\$10/\text{year} + \$14/\text{year}}{\$60} = .40/\text{year} \tag{3}$$

or 40 percent per year.

Equation (2) is often calculated in the form of an event that has occurred: last year's dividend and capital gain. This is because investors may have had very different expectations of what their dividends and capital gains will be in the future when they decided to buy, hold, or sell a stock. It is those beliefs that ideally should be estimated in explaining their behavior.

EFFICIENT MARKETS

An explanation of stock prices that won widespread support in the economics and finance fields is the **efficient market hypothesis**.[2] Financial markets are said to be efficient if the prices of the securities traded fully reflect available information. But this is a rather weak, vacuous statement unless it is better specified. What is "available information," and how does one know when prices "fully reflect" it? The finance literature has developed rigorous and sophisticated testable hypotheses to put meat on the bones of this definition of efficient markets. A simplified example will bring out many of the points involved.

Suppose that there is free access to all information about the XYZ Corporation. No inside information is available to particular investors who could use it to advantage. Suppose that the price of XYZ stock is currently $50 per share. Suddenly a new, cheaper method is found to make the products produced by the XYZ Corporation, and so, given this new information, traders now believe that the stock is worth $60. Even if they all do not have identical beliefs, assume that a dominant number of traders do generally believe this.

Now assume that the transaction costs of changing one's portfolio of financial wealth are negligible: approximately zero brokerage fees. Will traders be willing to sell XYZ stock for $50, $55, $58, or even $59, given this new information? No, they would be foolish if they did because other traders are willing to buy the XYZ stock for $60. The price of the XYZ stock will thus instantaneously rise to $60, as there are no transactions costs of buying and transferring it rapidly.

Only new information can affect the price of XYZ stock under these assumptions, as old information is instantaneously reflected in (or discounted into) the price. What if new information were not randomly generated? Would not the price of XYZ stock change in a nonrandom way? Nonrandom information is information that follows a predictable pattern. Such a pattern would already be known in a world of free access to all information. Nonrandom information is already discounted into the price and thus is not new information. Of course, a change in the interpretation of old information can affect stock prices.

The sequence of past *changes* in the price of a stock contains no information about future price changes. Future price changes are random, or not predictable. A series of numbers in which the changes, or differences among the numbers, are random is called a **random walk**.

The *level* of the stock price is not random. If a stock is selling at $60 per share, the best guess of tomorrow's price is $60 plus the daily rate of interest. However, the *change* in the price of the stock is random. The use of charts and graphs of past prices or past information about the corporation to predict such changes has zero value under these assumptions.

The requirement that stocks behave as a random walk was found to be an unnecessarily stringent requirement for the existence of efficient markets. Furthermore, stocks do not precisely follow a random walk, although day-to-day fluctuations are close to being a random walk. Instead, the stock market can be described as a **fair game** (see the end-of-chapter glossary). The fair-game explanation of efficient markets allows general trends in prices, but it holds that no one can benefit from knowing more about a stock than its price. Given only the current public knowledge, no trading system or any public information can increase the expectation of profits above that conferred on market participants who only know the stock's current prices.

INCONSISTENT EVIDENCE AND THEORETICAL DOUBTS

Many observers would say that the efficient market hypothesis describes formal financial asset markets—markets such as the New York Stock Exchange—well enough to justify the general conclusion that it plausibly explains most price movements, even though it is only approximately, not perfectly, correct. Perhaps the most important lesson of the efficient market hypothesis is that it is difficult to do better than the stock market average without some *inside information*, information not publicly available. This is because the hypothesis tells one only what to say when an individual offers some tips based on *public information*. For example, suppose one is told that General Motors has had an increase in profits and therefore it is a good time to buy its stock. The reply should be, "You are too late to benefit from that kind of information, as it almost surely was discounted into the price of GM stock long ago."

The efficient market hypothesis has been subjected to an enormous amount of testing, most of which has shown no substantial deviations from the hypothesis. The efficient market hypothesis has been an essential assumption of many sophisticated theories in finance. For example, the theory known as the *capital asset pricing model, CAPM*, has been a centerpiece of much of the finance theory. It provides a theory for pricing assets and for analyzing and pricing risk premiums, the extra yield over and above the "normal" rate of return, which just covers the likelihood that the income flow from the asset will be less than expected.

In an efficient market, all stocks earn the same return after an adjustment for risk. (The adjustment for risk is studied in the field of finance. The yield is higher on those stocks for which the future earnings stream is more uncertain.) If the rate of return adjusted for risk on one stock is higher than the others, it is said to yield an *abnormal return*.

What has made the efficient market hypothesis so interesting is the rather extreme assumption that formal markets for financial assets adjust almost instantaneously. An *inefficient market* is characterized by the failure of market prices to register the underlying market-clearing price between demand and supply over significant periods of time. Inefficient markets thus cannot function as an allocative device between suppliers and demanders nor as a signal of the market participants' valuation of an asset. That is, deviations from efficient markets are possible in markets that adjust slowly.

The efficient market hypothesis can be used as a starting point when analyzing financial markets in which deviations from the hypothesis, if applicable, are viewed in terms of how they change the results. That is one way to look at the following empirical evidence and theoretical doubts, which are inconsistent with the efficient market hypothesis.

Some researchers have found enough contradictory evidence and plausible analysis to raise some serious doubts about the "extreme" forms of the efficient market hypothesis as it has been applied to formal markets for financial assets. In the 1980s, more and more test results of the efficient market hypotheis justify some questioning of its foundations and even some reformulation of it.

One occurrence that has frequently been tested is called the *January effect*.[3] The January effect is the change in the price of small companies' stocks during the first days of each year so that most of these stocks' rate of return for the year will accumulate in these days in January. Some researchers believe that the January effect is related to tax effects. That is, to claim losses on the current year's taxable income, stocks that have accumulated losses must be sold before the end of the year. Thus they may fall in value at this time and then rise again in January if they are repurchased. But this does not satisfactorily explain the January effect, as it existed before U.S. tax laws prompted end-of-year selling to acquire losses, and it also exists in other countries where the tax year (the accounting period for income taxes) either does not end on December 31 or does not encourage end-of-year selling.

According to Robert Haugen, the January effect may be caused by mutual fund managers' "cleaning up" their portfolio of small nonperformers at the end of the year so that their reports of performance will not contain such stocks. They then buy back these stocks at the first of the year. The January effect thus may be thought of as a seasonal event that has a high probability of occurring each year at about the same time. But this January phenomenon contradicts the efficient market hypothesis, as some of the stocks causing the January effect earn 90 percent of their rate of return in the first few days of January. Conversely, an efficient market explanation would be the following: Market participants would observe this phenomenon and discount this information into the stock long before January arrived. No seasonal event of this type can occur in an efficient market.

Another recent test of financial asset markets also found inconsistencies in the efficient market hypothesis. Richard J. Sweeney tested prices in the international exchange market where U.S. dollars and currencies from countries such as Canada, West Germany, the United Kingdom, the Netherlands, Japan, and Switzerland are traded.[4] He conducted the tests after March 1973, when governments first attempted to manage the prices of their currencies under a system in which the prices were free to change. (Further discussion of the foreign exchange market and the period of floating exchange rates is found in Part IX.) The international currency prices were controlled by the government's buying and selling their currencies in order to keep the prices at a target level (or within a target range) with respect to other currencies. If the governments pushed the prices of their currencies far from their market-clearing levels, there would be profit opportunities for private traders who thought the prices would eventually return to the market-clearing prices. The test results showed great inefficiency in this strategy, and Sweeney found that substantial unexploited profits have continued to exist in this market.

If these potential profits can be explained by varying the risk premiums placed on the underlying assets, then the results can be viewed as consistent with the efficient market hypothesis. In other words, suppose the price of a currency indicates that substantial profits could be made by buying and selling it after a given period of time. However, the risk of doing so is so great that after adjusting for this risk, there will be no profit above the normal rate of return. Then the profit opportunity will yield only the normal rate of return, which is consistent with the efficient market hypothesis. However, if the risk premium is nearly constant over time and does not change, the observed larger profits that Sweeney found will violate the efficient market hypothesis. A plausible argument and some tentative evidence support the view that risk premiums do not vary enough to explain the extra profit opportunities. The test results thus are consistent with the hypothesis that intervention by a large trader can keep a financial asset market from achieving market-clearing prices for a significant period of time.

The literature is full of tests of the efficient market hypothesis that show deviations from it. Such deviations show the existence of abnormal profits. In an efficient market, the market participants would immediately sell their stocks and buy the stock yielding the abnormal return. In the process, the price of the stock yielding the abnormal return would rise until it yielded the same return as did all the other stocks, that is, the normal return, after adjustment for risk. Finding persistent abnormal rates of return, therefore, contradicts the efficient market hypothesis.

Besides sophisticated evidence, there also has been casual evidence of trading on insider information. If insider information is fully exploited by those who know it, so that the market price incorporates this information, the market can be efficient in the sense that prices do reflect information. It is, of course, not fair to those who do not have access to this information, but as this discussion will indicate, it is not clear where to draw the line between public and insider information. Suppose that there are many items of insider information but few are fully exploited. Then the market will not include this information in its prices. If this is a common practice, then public information will not be accurately discounted into the prices, because they reflect some of the partially exploited items of insider information. But the insider information also is not fully discounted into the prices. In this situation, the markets would have significant inefficiencies.

The use of insider information to make huge profits in trading financial assets was underscored in 1986 with the allegations that Ivan Boesky had used such inside information to make millions on the stock market. Boesky was known as the "King of Arbitrageurs," trading stock to take advantage of opportunities to make substantially more than the normal rate of return. The Securities and Exchange Commission reportedly settled for the following penalty in return for Boesky's cooperation in identifying others who used insider information: He was directed to pay a fine of $100 million, to quit trading by April 1, 1988, and agree to plead guilty to one felony count.[5]

The kind of insider information that many observers think should be and apparently is regulated is information that is to be kept confidential as a condition of one's employment. Therefore, giving away such information is similar to stealing an asset, such as a machine, from the company.

The attempt to make insider trading illegal illustrates how slippery the meaning of insider trading is. Suppose that Edward worked in a company where he has access to the management's intentions. Edward learns that in six months, the management is going to accept a takeover offer, at an inflated price, from another company. Edward had been planning to sell his holding of the company's stock because he thought—on the basis of public information—that the takeover offer was likely to be turned down. But then, based on this insider information, Edward decides not to sell his stock in the company. Insider information can thus also be used to keep people *from* trading. Needless to say, *not* trading is nearly impossible to detect.

This difficulty with detecting no trading on the basis of insider information is only one of the problems of insider trading. In addition, there are many degrees of insider information and no clear line to draw between public information and insider information, as the following two examples illustrate: (1) Information may be useful only to experts. That is, information means different things to different people, depending on their level of expertise. What appears to be new information to one trained observer may be incomprehensible to others. Suppose someone mentions that his employer has just hired a new accountant and the trained observer knows that the accountant's firm specializes in bankruptcy law. The observer may then sell her stock short. (2) For a trained expert, a seemingly insignificant piece of information may be quite informative, and furthermore, publication of this information may bring legal action. For example, the repeated visits of a bank examiner to a commercial bank may indicate trouble in the bank. This kind of information cannot be published, as the bank may take legal action against someone who points out that this is happening and that it indicates problems in the bank and, in the process, may start a run on the bank.

Or suppose that the insider information is widely known but that the people who have this information do not fully exploit it. They may fail to take advantage of their insider information because they do not want to reveal that they know it. That is, to exploit the information, these people may have to borrow money from others, which may cause the insider information to be leaked to someone who would make it public. But if the insider information is not fully exploited, the market will then have inefficiencies.

Next we will present five more reasons for doubting that formal markets for financial assets are exactly explained by the efficient markets hypothesis.

First, there is the existence of a huge volume of assets created by financial intermediaries. If the efficient markets hypothesis is true, individual investors should be equally able to select their own portfolios. Many investors buy assets from financial intermediaries, undoubtedly because they value the decision-making services that these intermediaries provide. If efficient markets require rational, informed behavior, then it is somewhat inconsistent and fatuous to classify as either irrational or uninformed all investors who highly value the financial intermediaries' services. Rather, their actions could be justified under an efficient market explanation, as a payment for diversification. For a small investment, the financial intermediary gives these investors a broad portfolio of assets. It seems likely, however, that many individuals buy assets created by financial intermediaries to employ experts to manage their funds.

Second, many traders on the floors of the stock exchanges make a living by trading stock for themselves. They even pay large sums for a seat on a stock exchange. Their success cannot be dismissed as a random run or a lucky exception if it is sustained over a number of years.

Third, decision making is expensive. Events, especially significant events such as the beginning of a war, the imposition of price controls, or an oil boycott, may impose especially large decision costs that require a long period of portfolio adjustments. Those who have some insight into this adjustment process may reap better-than-average profits. For example, the downward fall of stock prices in October 1987, with a one-day decline (October 19) of nearly 25 percent, did not have the characteristics of instantaneous adjustment to new information.

Fourth, if all economic data were reported daily, most would look random. The reasons are that it takes time for people to adjust to new conditions and that there are innumerable disturbances that affect to some extent their day-to-day behavior. In addition, it is impossible to distinguish a random from a nearly random series. Special care should be taken in calling a process efficient because it cannot be explained statistically on the basis of prior changes. As more observations become available—say, in fifty years—trends and cycles may become clear that could not easily be discerned earlier with the data available.

Fifth, when new information about a stock does become known, random though it may be, a number of individuals must attempt to buy or sell the stock to take advantage of the new information, so that it does get discounted into the price of the stock. For them, the price changes are not random. The adjustment process may not be smooth, and so there may be undershooting and overshooting from which the smart trader can profit. "Selling into good news" about a corporation can be profitable if overshooting is expected.

INTRODUCTION TO MONEY AND STOCK PRICES

Having reviewed the efficient market hypothesis, we can now investigate the interesting relationship between money and stock prices. It is frequently argued that movements in the aggregate indices of common stock prices can be predicted from prior changes in the money supply.[6] This belief was supported by a number of statistical studies that appeared during the 1960s and early 1970s. Those studies purported to show that changes in the quantity of money have a strong influence on movements in future stock prices. But more recent evidence, as well as the work done on the efficient market hypothesis, raises doubts about the accuracy of this simplistic linkage between money and future stock prices.

The remainder of the chapter will explore the relationship between money and stock prices. The next section will briefly review and comment on some of the earlier studies that dealt with this relationship. The following section will offer evidence regarding the relationship, in an attempt to correct some of the deficiencies of earlier studies. The results presented there indicate that although money is statistically related to stock prices, the relationship is much weaker than that claimed in some earlier studies. Also, and perhaps more important, changes in stock prices are found to be statistically related to both current and future changes in the money supply, but not to past changes in money. *Thus, the common belief that stock prices can be predicted simply by prior changes in the money supply appears to be unfounded.*

PROBLEMS IN RELATING MONEY TO STOCK PRICES

Early studies and much common sense on and off Wall Street viewed an increase in the money supply as a stimulant to future stock price changes. After all, an increase in the money supply can be expected to stimulate spending and, eventually, the demand for stocks. This will drive up the prices of stocks at some point in the future.

In an influential book, *Money and Stock Prices*, Beryl Sprinkel compared the level of an *index of stock prices* with a moving average of *rates of changes in the money supply*.[7] He then compared selected turning points in each of these two series with turning points in the business cycle. He observed that changes in both money and stock prices led business cycle turning points. He also found that changes in money had a longer lead time before business cycle turning points than before stock price changes. Hence, money supply changes appeared to lead stock price changes. From these observations, Sprinkel concluded that

> the average lead of changes in monetary growth prior to the business cycle peak is about 19 months compared to a 4-month average lead of stock prices. Changes in monetary growth lead cyclical upturns by an

FIGURE 13-1   Rates of Change in Stock Prices, 1967–1985

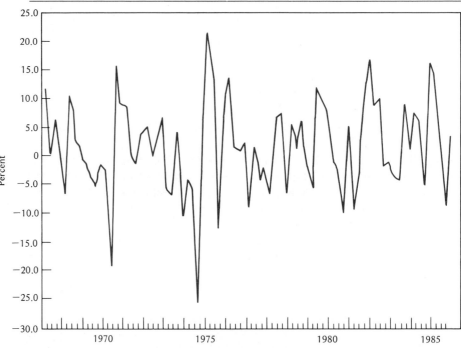

The levels of stock prices can be misleading in finding periodic variations, variations that have a "consistent" probability of repeating themselves. Rates of change remove some of the apparent trends that impair statistical tests. The rates of change in the Standard & Poor's index of 500 industrial stocks are shown here. But it is difficult from this information to find periodic variations just by looking at the data.

Source: Cambridge Planning and Analytics, Inc., Boston.

FIGURE 13-2   Hypothetical Series on Per Capita Miles Jogged in Idaho and Average Rainfall in Brazil, with Turning Points Labeled to Show Association

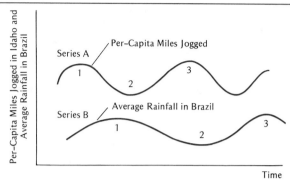

As a matter of arithmetic, it is always possible to compute an average lag time between turning points in two series that do not have synchronous turning points. In this figure, the judicious labeling of the turning points can be wrongly interpreted to show that running faster in Idaho can make it rain more in Brazil.

average period of about 7 months, whereas stock price upturns occur about 5 months prior to business upturns on average. Therefore, changes in monetary growth lead changes in stock prices by an average of about 15 months prior to a bear market and by about 2 months prior to bull markets.[8]

There are three fundamental problems with Sprinkel's technique for relating money to stock prices and the business cycle. First is the problem of determining which movements in the time series of data on money and stock prices are significant turning points. Visual inspection of the data, as Sprinkel used, is less exact than are other statistical techniques. Some idea of this problem can be seen in the rates of change in stock prices from 1976 to 1986 in Figure 13-1.

The second problem is determining whether it is money or stock prices that change first. It is not clear, as the evidence presented here shows, that the money supply changes always precede the related stock changes.

The third problem pertains to using averages, which raises the following question: Are the average time lags between the change in one variable and the change in the second variable stable time lags? Stability means that over repeated episodes these lags will approach the same average time period.

As a matter of arithmetic, it is always possible to compute an average time lag between turning points in two series that do not have synchronous turning points. This is displayed in Figure 13-2, in which, by judiciously labeling the turning points in two hypothetical series, one can show that running faster in Idaho can make it rain in Brazil. However, it is not the existence of such a lag between turning points in two series but, rather, the stability of the lag that supports the view that the two series are related.

In view of these problems, later researchers used other statistical techniques to examine the relation between money and stock prices. These studies used the standard present value approach, presented earlier, to explain stock prices. This formulation holds that the price of a share of common stock is equal to the present discounted value of the corporation's expected profits.

Variations of equation (1) were examined in statistical tests with surprisingly good results. The results were suspect, however, because of the statistical methods that were used. That is, the tests suffered from a problem that often arises when one attempts to find a relationship among variables from a time series (a series of observations from successive periods) that have common trends and/or common movements during business cycles. One must take account of these common trends and cycles in the variables; otherwise, statistical tests may support a close relationship among the variables, even though they are basically unrelated.

Most economic series have risen during the post–World War II period and would, in most cases, show a fairly strong association with one another if they were tested without adequately accounting for their common rising trend. There are numerous examples of such faulty tests. It therefore is necessary both for conventional statistical testing and for validating underlying economic relationships to fully account for the trend.

To state the matter more emphatically, no causal relation is implied by a finding that the quantity of grain harvested in one country is highly correlated with the application of fertilizer in another country on the basis of data that shows both series increasing along a common trend.

Removing a trend is not enough! Cycles or periodicities in each variable must be accounted for or removed. **Periodicity** (or in the statistician's jargon, *autocorrelation*) in a variable is the association among the values of the variable in different periods. The presence of such periodicities allows some of a variable's future values to be predicted from the variable's own past history. Tests for causality can produce spurious results if these periodicities are left in the data. This problem is illuminated with three examples.

1. Every morning before the sun rises, roosters crow. This periodicity indicates a strong statistical relationship, but it does not prove that the rooster's brain makes the sun shine. Only the *irregular* event—say, when the roosters are sick and do not crow—tends to support or contradict the relationship. The variables—sun rises and rooster crows—follow each other, so that there is no meaning to the concept of causality. (This is similar to the question of which came first, the chicken or the egg.) Each variable, sun rises and rooster crows, has a precise repeating periodicity over time. Only the part of the change in either variable that is *not* part of this periodicity—the irregular event—can be used to test for an underlying causal relationship.

2. Many variables go up and down during business cycles, but this does not necessarily mean that they are related. For example, during most inflationary expansions, income taxes rise, whereas miles jogged may decline (because of

higher employment and more overtime). This association does not support the notion that higher taxes take your breath away, impeding jogging.

3. Suppose that in a coin-tossing experiment, two heads are always followed by two tails, which are again followed by two heads. Larger samples from this experiment indicate that on average heads comes up almost exactly half the time, with the precision improving as the number of tosses increases. This last test result, taken by itself, is evidence that it is a fair coin with no bias toward heads or tails. However, the periodicity in the outcomes of the tosses, with the sequence of two heads followed by two tails, and so on, invalidates this conclusion. It shows that each toss has a perfect bias towards heads or tails, depending on the outcome of the previous toss. This is not a fair coin, and conventional statistics has nothing to say about future tosses. Again, only with the irregular events—in which a head or tail deviates from this periodicity—can conventional statistics be used. For example, if the irregular event is random, the chance of heads may be predicted from the data using conventional statistics.

To illustrate the problems that can arise when no attention is paid to trends and periodicities, an artificial series having no economic significance was constructed by adding a trend onto a series of random numbers. This artificial series was then used in the same tests that were used in some studies to explain the quarterly levels of stock prices (measured by the Standard and Poor's index) from 1959 through 1974. The results show that this single artificial variable was able to explain 86 percent of the change in stock prices.[9] The finding that such an artificial variable can explain nearly as much of the variation in stock prices as reported in the previous studies underscores the possibility, when trends in the data are ignored, of producing results that are statistical illusions.

CAUSATION

A further problem with the earlier studies is that they tested a one-way statistical association with money related to future changes in stock prices. They did not consider that changes in stock prices could be related to future changes in the money supply. If, for example, the stock market is as efficient as the efficient market hypothesis holds, stock prices will be determined by market participants on the basis of all available information. If the public "expected" a change in the money supply to occur that would ultimately affect price levels, corporate profits, and so on, the public would immediately buy and sell stocks at prices that would take account of the expected effects. That is, the expected changes in the money supply would immediately be discounted into the prices of stocks. Consequently, if subsequent changes in the money supply were to occur as expected, the stock prices would change before and not after observed changes in the money supply.

Another aspect of the efficient market hypothesis involves an "unexpected" change in the money supply. In this case, the efficient market hypothesis holds that when the public observes an unexpected monetary change, it will immediately discount this information into stock prices. Hence, an unexpected money supply change would produce a synchronous statistical relationship.[10]

Richard Cooper examined the leads and lags among rates of change of money supply and the stock *yield* described previously.[11] Cooper related the stock yield to the current percentage change in money to past percentage changes in money for up to twelve months and to future percentage changes in money for up to six months. He used monthly data for the period between 1947 and 1970, as depicted in Figure 13-3. On the basis of his tests, Cooper concluded that it was difficult, with the type of statistical tests used in earlier studies, to assess the significant lead and lag relationships among rates of change in the money supply and stock yields. A new statistical test by Cooper produced results that were consistent with the hypothesis that the market was efficient. In addition, there was some support for a statistical association between stock yields and future changes in his money variable.

FIGURE 13-3   Monthly Stock Yields, 1947–1970 (Standard & Poor's common stock indexes)

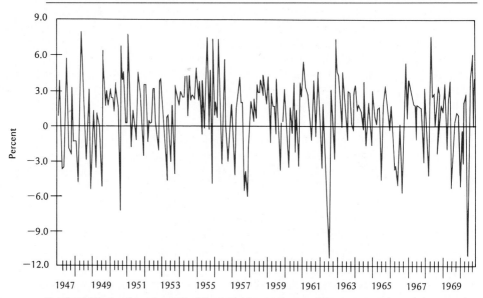

Stock yields in the test period look fairly random, without a trend, and test results support this observation.

Source: Robert Auerbach, "Money and Stock Prices," *Monthly Review*, Federal Reserve Bank of Kansas City, September–October 1976, p. 9.

FURTHER TESTS

Results of additional tests on the relation between money and stock prices are presented in this section.[12] As in Cooper's study, the tests examine the lead–lag relation between the stock yield and the rate of change in the money supply.

Two modifications were made in Cooper's approach. First, the data for the variables were examined for evidence of trends and cycles. This examination revealed that both variables contained trend and cycle elements that could bias the tests. The trend and cycle components of each variable thus were removed, and a cleansed series was tested to make sure it was free of trends and cycles. Second, the degree of association between the rates of change or the money supply and the stock yield was measured by a statistic called a **correlation statistic**, which is a measure of the degree to which two variables are related. It can vary from +1 to −1. If two variables display little or no association, the correlation will approach zero. If there is a perfect positive association, the correlation will be +1. With perfect negative association, the correlation will be −1.

The correlation was computed between the current stock yield and the current money variable. Next, correlations were calculated between the current stock yield and the money variable in each of sixty prior monthly periods. Finally, to test whether stock yields lead money, the variables were reversed, and correlations were computed between the current money variable and the stock yield in each of sixty prior monthly periods. These tests also were conducted using monthly data for the period between 1947 and 1970.

As shown in Table 13-1, the correlations between the current stock yield and the sixty prior values of the money variable were not statistically significant. Only the synchronous correlation was statistically significant, at a value of .18. When the variables were reversed to test whether the stock yields led the money, the synchronous correlation was equal to .18, as expected. Correla-

TABLE 13-1   Correlations Between the Money Supply and the Stock Yield After Both Series Are Cleansed of Trends and Cycles, 1947–1970

Period	Current Stock Yield with Percentage Change in M-1	Current Percentage Change in M-1 with Stock Yield
Synchronous	.18*	.18*
1 month prior	−.03	.12*
2 months prior	.07	.20*
3 through 60 months prior	None significantly different from zero	None significantly different from zero

* Significantly different from zero.
Source: Robert Auerbach, "Money and Stock Prices," *Monthly Review*, Federal Reserve Bank of Kansas City, September–October 1976, p. 9.

tions between the current money variable and the stock yields in each of the previous two months also were found to be statistically significant. Stock yields one and two months in the past had significant correlations with the current percentage change of money of .12 and .20, respectively. Taken together, the current stock yield and the two prior stock yields serve to "explain" about 8.7 percent of the variation in the current percentage change in money.[13]

These findings can be explained by the efficient market hypothesis and the belief that the public is knowledgeable about a relationship between money and other variables—such as the price level—as Cooper suggested.[14] If the public is able to predict some money supply changes, it will discount this information into stock prices one or two months before the money supply changes. Unanticipated money supply changes are discounted into stock prices in the same months that the monetary change occurs.

One reservation about this explanation of the results concerns the public's ability to forecast the monetary variable in advance. Because trends and periodicities have been removed from the money series in these tests, the public is required to predict deviations from the trend and past periodicities. Earlier values of the money supply series provide no useful information for this forecast. It is questionable whether anyone can predict more than a very minor component of these monetary changes. Thus, there may be other explanations of these results.

An alternative explantion is that the relationship between prior and synchronous stock yield changes and the current rates of change in money is the result of actions taken by the Federal Reserve. Suppose, first, that the Federal Reserve uses stock yields, or some variable related to stock yields, as an indicator of business cycle fluctuations. Suppose further that the Federal Reserve acts to partially accommodate increased business activity by increasing the money supply. Under these conditions, stock yields will increase slightly earlier and synchronously with monetary expansion, and one will observe the findings reported in these tests.[15]

STUDY QUESTIONS

1. If an increase in profits of a corporation is not distributed in dividends, why should the price of a stock or the stock yield rise? First define the stock yield.
2. Suppose that each one of a group of stocks is equally risky. That is, the chance of the expected profit stream's occurring is the same for each. Explain how diversification needs may cause some investors to buy stocks with lower yields.
3. Why is it that the best guess of the price of a stock tomorrow is today's price plus the daily rate of interest, using the efficient market hypothesis?

4. What are the pitfalls in using a series of money data to predict changes in a series of stock price data?
5. What are the explanations for finding a relationship between stock yields and current or future money supply changes?
6. Why would an individual "hire" an expert, as in a financial intermediary, to manage a portfolio of assets in which the individual buys a share? Can an expert be expert according to the efficient market hypothesis?
7. What do you think of the conclusion that the efficient market hypothesis is approximately true, if not precisely correct? Explain. What conditions must be present before the efficient market hypothesis is valid?
8. How does inside information affect stock prices?
9. Can financial market inefficiencies affect the entire economy? Explain.

GLOSSARY

Basic valuation formula. The equation relating the price of a stock to the discounted value of all future profits and the future salvage value of any assets. Because *profits* and *salvage values* are imprecise terms, it is more accurate to measure the discounted value of all future net cash flows—cash inflows minus outflows each period.

Correlation statistic. A measure of the degree to which two variables are related.

Efficient market hypothesis. A hypothesis that applies to a market in which all available information is immediately discounted into the price of the goods that are traded.

Fair game. For stock markets, the condition in which no information other than the price of the stock will improve one's chance of predicting future stock prices.

Periodicity. The value of a series of numbers that can be predicted from previous numbers in the series. The statistical measure of this association is called the *autocorrelation*.

Random walk. A series of numbers in which the differences among the numbers form a random series.

Stock yield (or rate of return). The sum of the dividend plus the change in the price of a stock divided by the price of the stock in a period of time.

NOTES

1. The Greek letter Δ (delta) means "the change in."
2. For a review of this hypothesis, see Eugene F. Fama, "Efficient Capital Markets: A Review of Theory and Empirical Work," *Papers and Proceedings of the Twenty-eighth Annual Meeting of the American Finance Association, Journal of the American Finance Association,* May 1970, pp. 383–416; Eugene Fama and Merton Miller, *The Theory of Finance* (New York: Holt, Rinehart and Winston, 1972), pp. 335–340; and C. W. J.

Granger and O. Morgenstern, "Spectral Analysis of New York Stock Market Prices," in Paul Cootner, ed., *The Random Character of Stock Market Prices* (Cambridge, Mass.: MIT Press, 1964).

3. Recent research and a bibliography on the "January effect" can be found in K. C. Chan, "Can Tax-Loss Selling Explain the January Seasonal in Stock Returns?" *Journal of Finance*, December 1986, pp. 1115–1128. Information was also obtained from the presentation (at the University of California, Riverside, November 25, 1986) by Robert Haugen—who collected extensive worldwide evidence regarding the January effect.

4. Richard J. Sweeney, "Beating the Foreign Exchange Market," *Journal of Finance*, March 1986, pp. 163–182.

5. "True Greed," *Newsweek*, December 1, 1986, p. 52.

6. See Robert D. Auerbach, "Money and Stock Prices," *Monthly Review*, Federal Reserve Bank of Kansas City, September–October 1976, pp. 3–11.

7. Beryl W. Sprinkel, *Money and Stock Prices* (Homewood, Ill.: Richard D. Irwin, 1964). He used M-1 as the concept of money. His "Monetary Growth As a Cyclical Indicator," *Journal of Finance*, September 1956, pp. 333–346, also presents a similar methodology.

8. Sprinkel, *Money and Stock Prices*, p. 119.

9. The artificial series is denoted by X. It contains a trend variable at an annual rate of 2.5 percent. The equation estimated was

$$SP = -49647.3 + 0.11X$$

with a correlation coefficient (squared)—a measure of association where 1 is perfect association—equal to .86. See Auerbach, "Money and Stock Prices," note 8, p. 6.

10. Transactions and decision-making costs may produce lags between monetary changes and changes in stock prices. But except for momentous events, these lags should be short.

11. Richard V. L. Cooper, "Efficient Capital Markets and the Quantity Theory of Money," *Journal of Finance*, June 1974, pp. 887–908. Cooper used sophisticated spectral techniques to examine the relation of money and stock prices. These results showed that stock returns led money changes but did not lag money changes. On this basis, he felt his results supported the concept of market efficiency. See p. 898.

12. These tests were conducted by R. Auerbach and reported in "Money and Stock Prices."

13. Squaring and adding these correlations produce a statistic equal to .0868, which in concept is rougly equivalent to a squared multiple correlation coefficient in regression analysis, as explained in note 9.

14. It cannot be emphasized too strongly that the statistical tests presented in this section look only at the irregular movements in money and stock yields. That is, movements in money and stock yields are cleansed of trends and periodicities. This is not a serious problem for stock yields or

rates of change in stock prices, as these variables have little trend or periodicity (see Figure 13-1). But what about the trend in the money supply or the trend in the rate of change of the money supply? These trends may be and probably are used by the public to forecast future stock prices and the prices of goods and services.

The problem is that conventional statistical tests are biased when the level of a series depends on time (it is time dependent), as occurs with a trend or periodicity. This does not mean that the trends and periodicities should be discarded. On the contrary, they convey valuable information. See the last part of Robert Auerbach, "A Convergence of Views," *The Federal Reserve Authorities and Their Public Responsibility* (Rochester, N.Y.: University of Rochester, Center for Research in Government Policy and Business, 1980).

15. If the public also uses stock yields or a related variable to signal business cycle fluctuations in the same way that the Federal Reserve does, the public will be able to forecast monetary changes, and this alternative explanation will not differ from the first explanation. That is, the public is discounting this information into stock prices.

PART FOUR

THE FEDERAL RESERVE SYSTEM

CHAPTER 14

STRUCTURE AND NONMONETARY FUNCTIONS

CHAPTER PREVIEW

Introduction. The locus of power for controlling the money supply in the United States is not the U.S. Congress, which can vote expenditures but cannot literally appropriate money. Rather, it is the Federal Reserve that has primary responsibility for controlling the monetary base.

The Board of Governors. The ruling body of the Federal Reserve is composed of seven members who legally serve fourteen-year terms but can serve longer (as explained in the text).

The Federal Open Market Committee. The Federal Open Market Committee formulates monetary policy in the United States.

The District Banks. Twelve district banks organized to look something like private corporations are important parts of the Federal Reserve bureaucracy.

The Thrift Institutions Advisory Council. This is the first official presence of thrift executives in the Federal Reserve (with the exception of mutual savings banks' representatives who can be members).

Nonmonetary Functions. Bank supervision, the regulation of certain types of credit, and the maintenance of a payments system are the three types of nonmonetary functions.

Appendix: History of the Federal Reserve System from the Banking Panic of 1907 to World War II. The Federal Reserve was born out of banking panics, and it floundered when it was needed in the deep depressions of the 1930s, at which time it was reorganized in its present form.

INTRODUCTION

The locus of power for controlling the money supply of the United States is not the U.S. Congress. It is not the U.S. Treasury. Although the president of the United States can exert substantial, perhaps even decisive, pressure and although he or she has the power to make some new appointments to the group that does control the money supply, legally the president does not control the money supply.

Rather, a small group of twelve people, the members of the Federal Open Market Committee, FOMC, of the Federal Reserve has the primary responsibility for controlling the country's money supply. They have the power to expand or contract, by huge amounts in a short period of time, the monetary base of the nation's money supply. The **monetary base** is the currency and coin held by the nonbank public and the cash reserves of the banking system. (See the end-of-chapter glossary for a more detailed definition.)

The Federal Reserve is the central bank of the United States, and its functions are similar to those of central banks in many other countries. It controls the money supply, regulates substantial parts of the banking system, and intervenes in the international markets for currencies.

Even some history books continue to depict the U.S. Congress as the body that controls the nation's money supply. It is still generally thought that Congress can literally appropriate money, when in fact all it can do is vote expenditures. When bills requiring expenditures are signed into law, the secretary of the Treasury can borrow the money by selling U.S. securities and adding to the national debt. But he or she has little power to create money. The Federal Open Market Committee has the ultimate authority to abstain or to finance, with new money issue, the expenditures of the federal government. It is a sad commentary on the general knowledge of the U.S. economy that so little is known about who controls the money supply and about the functions of the Board of Governors and the Federal Open Market Committee of the Federal Reserve System. The problem is not only a widespread lack of information but also widespread misinformation.

In this chapter, we will discuss the structure and the nonmonetary functions of the Federal Reserve. These nonmonetary functions include the provision of a payments mechanism, including a wire transfer service, which is one means for the transfer of funds between banks. The federal funds market that uses this service is the final subject in the chapter. The monetary base and the tools of the Federal Reserve are discussed in Chapters 15 and 16, and the relationship between the monetary base and the total money supply is examined in Chapter 17.

THE BOARD OF GOVERNORS

The most important structural changes in the Federal Reserve came in the 1930s, after it had failed to prevent the worst series of banking panics in the nation's history. Much, although not all, power was taken away form the regional Federal Reserve banks and was centralized in a seven-member Board of Governors, who now dominate most of the decisions made by the Federal Reserve (see Figure 14-1).

The headquarters of the Federal Reserve is in Washington, D.C. The United States is divided into twelve Federal Reserve districts, each with a Federal Reserve bank. These Federal Reserve banks and their 25 branches—in 25 additional cities—are shown on the map in Figure 14-2 and in Table 14-1. (Twelve Federal Reserve facilities that are not classified as branches are also listed in Figure 14-2.) The Federal Reserve has over 22,000 employees, including approximately 500 economists in the research departments at the Board and the twelve regional Reserve banks.[1]

The Board of Governors is composed of seven members, each of whom is appointed by the president of the United States, subject to Senate confirmation. The term of office is fourteen years. Appointment dates are staggered, so that only one appointment is made every two years unless a member leaves the Board before the end of his or her term. Thus, a president can appoint two members during a four-year term of office if no member leaves before the end of his or her term.

The chairman and vice-chairman of the Board of Governors of the Federal Reserve System also are appointed by the president, subject to consent by the Senate, to serve a term of four years (see Table 14-2). They are part of the seven-member Board of Governors and may finish the remainder of their fourteen-year terms as ordinary Board members when their four-year terms end.

The members of the Board of Governors are required to devote their entire time to the business of the Board and are not allowed to be officers, directors, or stockholders in any banking institution, trust company, or Federal Reserve bank. No more than one Board member may be selected from each district. But this rule can easily be stretched so that the term of residence may be at any prior time. This rule may be invoked when a member is appointed mainly because of knowledge of the Board's work.

No member of the Board of Governors who has served a full 14-year term may be reappointed. However, this law can be circumvented by means of a trick with the calendar. For instance, if a member knows that he or she will be reappointed, the member can tender a resignation just before the end of his or her term. Because a full 14-year term has not been served, the member can be reappointed for another 14-year term. In this manner, one governor, M. S. Szymczak, served 28 years, the record. But the practice of extending a tenure past the 14-year term has not been important since William McChesney Martin, Jr., left in 1970, after serving nearly 19 years as chairman. In recent

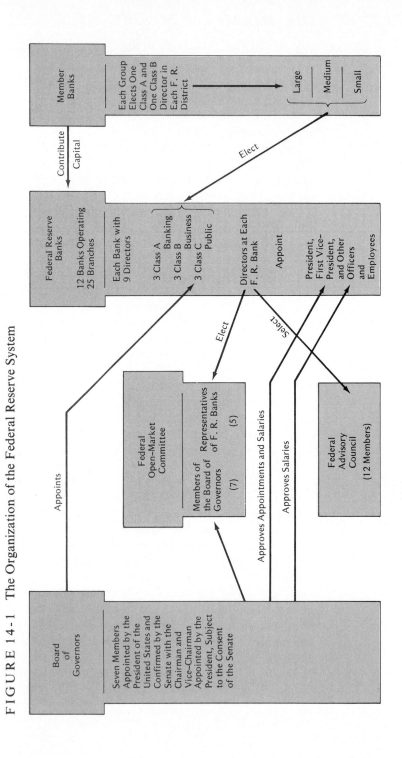

FIGURE 14-1   The Organization of the Federal Reserve System

FIGURE 14-2   Boundaries of Federal Reserve Districts and Their Branch Territories*

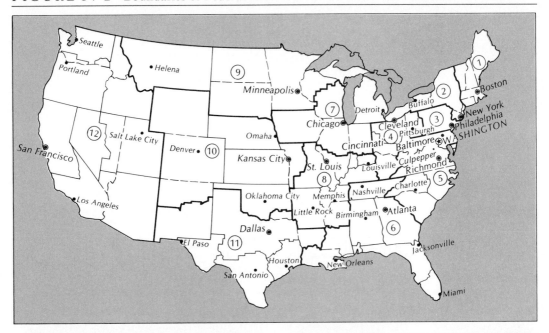

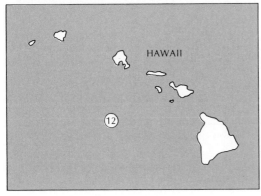
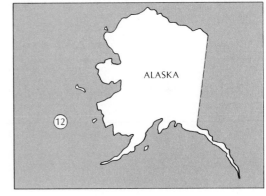

—— Boundaries of Federal Reserve districts

⊙ Federal Reserve bank cities

—— Boundaries of Federal Reserve branch territories

• Federal Reserve branch cities

⊛ Board of Governors of the Federal Reserve System

· Federal Reserve bank facility

Approximately 22,000 individuals and $853.9 million in land, machinery, and buildings (GAO estimate for 1980), with the Board of Governors in Washington, D.C., 12 regional Federal Reserve banks, 25 branch banks, and 12 additional facilities (including check-clearing centers) add up to a large bureaucracy constituting the world's most influential and powerful central bank, the Federal Reserve System.

* Additional offices of these banks are located in Lewiston, Maine; Windsor Locks, Connecticut; Cranford, New Jersey; Jericho, New York; Utica at Oriskany, New York; Columbus, Ohio; Columbia, South Carolina; Charleston, West Virginia; Des Moines, Iowa; Indianapolis, Indiana; and Milwaukee, Wisconsin. The Federal Reserve no longer uses the communications and record center in Culpepper, Virginia.

Source: Federal Reserve Bulletin, August 1982, p. A78.

TABLE 14-1 Addresses and Phone Numbers of the Federal Reserve Banks and the Board of Governors

Federal Reserve Bank of	Address and Phone number
BOSTON	600 Atlantic Avenue, Boston, Massachusetts 02106—(617) 973-3800
NEW YORK	33 Liberty Street (Federal Reserve P.O. Station), New York, New York 10045—(212) 791-5823 (Telephone 24 hours a day, including Saturday & Sunday)
Buffalo Branch	160 Delaware Avenue (P.O. Box 961), Buffalo, New York 14240—(716) 849-5046
PHILADELPHIA	100 North Sixth Street (P.O. Box 90), Philadelphia, Pennsylvania 19105—(215) 574-6580
CLEVELAND	1455 East Sixth Street (P.O. Box 6387), Cleveland, Ohio 44101—(216) 579-6580
Cincinnati Branch	150 East Fourth Street (P.O. Box 999), Cincinnati, Ohio 45201—(513) 721-4787, ext. 333
Pittsburgh Branch	717 Grant Street (P.O. Box 867), Pittsburgh, Pennsylvania 15230—(412) 261-7864
RICHMOND	701 East Byrd Street (P.O. Box 27622), Richmond, Virginia 23261—(804) 643-1250
Baltimore Branch	114-120 East Lexington Street (P.O. Box 1378), Baltimore, Maryland 21203—(301) 539-6552
Charlotte Branch	401 South Tyron Street (P.O. Box 30248), Charlotte, North Carolina 28230—(704) 373-0200
ATLANTA	104 Marietta Street, N.W., (P.O. Box 1731), Atlanta, Georgia 30301—(404) 586-8657
Birmingham Branch	1801 Fifth Avenue, North (P.O. Box 10447), Birmingham, Alabama 35202—(205) 252-3141, ext. 215
Jacksonville Branch	515 Julia Street, Jacksonville, Florida 32231—(904) 354-8211, ext. 211
Miami Branch	3770 S.W. 8th Street, Coral Gables, Florida 33134 (P.O. Box 847), Miami, Florida 33152—(305) 448-5732
Nashville Branch	301 Eighth Avenue, North, Nashville, Tennessee 37203—(615) 259-4006
New Orleans Branch	525 St. Charles Avenue (P.O. Box 61630), New Orleans, Louisiana 70161—(504) 586-1505, ext. 230, 240, 242
CHICAGO	230 South LaSalle Street (P.O. Box 834), Chicago, Illinois 60690—(312) 786-1110 (Telephone 24 hours a day, including Saturday & Sunday)
Detroit Branch	160 Fort Street, West (P.O. Box 1059), Detroit, Michigan 48231—(313) 961-6880, ext. 372, 373
ST. LOUIS	411 Locust Street (P.O. Box 442), St. Louis, Missouri 63166—(314) 444-8444
Little Rock Branch	325 West Capitol Avenue (P.O. Box 1261), Little Rock, Arkansas 72203—(501) 372-5451, ext. 270
Louisville Branch	410 South Fifth Street (P.O. Box 899), Louisville, Kentucky 40201—(502) 587-7351, ext. 237, 301
Memphis Branch	200 North Main Street (P.O. Box 407), Memphis, Tennessee 38101—(800) 238-5293, ext. 225
MINNEAPOLIS	250 Marquette Avenue, Minneapolis, Minnesota 55480—(612) 340-2051
Helena Branch	400 North Park Avenue, Helena, Montana 59601—(406) 442-3860
KANSAS CITY	925 Grand Avenue (Federal Reserve Station), Kansas City, Missouri 64198—(816) 881-2783
Denver Branch	1020 16th Street (P.O. Box 5228, Terminal Annex), Denver, Colorado 80217—(303) 292-4020
Oklahoma City Branch	226 Northwest Third Street (P.O. Box 25129), Oklahoma City, Oklahoma 73125—(405) 235-1721, ext. 182
Omaha Branch	102 South Seventeenth Street, Omaha, Nebraska 68102—(402) 341-3610, ext. 242
DALLAS	400 South Akard Street (Station K), Dallas, Texas 75222—(214) 651-6177
El Paso Branch	301 East Main Street (P.O. Box 100), El Paso, Texas 79999—(915) 544-4730, ext. 57
Houston Branch	1701 San Jacinto Street (P.O. Box 2578), Houston, Texas 77001—(713) 659-4433, ext. 19, 74, 75, 76
San Antonio Branch	126 East Nueva Street (P.O. Box 1471), San Antonio, Texas 78295—(512) 224-2141, ext. 61, 66
SAN FRANCISCO	400 Sansome Street (P.O. Box 7702), San Francisco, California 94120—(415) 392-6639
Los Angeles Branch	409 West Olympic Boulevard (P.O. Box 2077, Terminal Annex), Los Angeles, California 90051—(213) 683-8563
Portland Branch	915 S.W. Stark Street (P.O. Box 3436), Portland, Oregon 97208—(503) 228-7584
Salt Lake City Branch	120 South State Street (P.O. Box 30780), Salt Lake City, Utah 84127—(801) 355-3131, ext. 251, 270
Seattle Branch	1015 Second Avenue (P.O. Box 3567), Seattle, Washington 98124—(206) 442-1650

Board of Governors of the Federal Reserve System   Washington, D.C. 20551—(202) 452-3000

TABLE 14-2   The Chairmen of the Board Since Its Inception*

These relatively few men have had the major responsibility for running the Federal Reserve System, especially since 1935 when authority was centralized at the Board of Governors. Since 1951, they have been the most important single individuals for economic policy in the central government, outside the president of the United States.

1. Charles S. Hamlin	Aug. 10, 1914–Aug. 9, 1916
2. W. P. G. Harding	Aug. 10, 1916–Aug. 9, 1922
3. Daniel R. Crissinger	May 1, 1923–Sept. 15, 1927
4. Roy A. Young	Oct. 4, 1927–Aug. 31, 1930
5. Eugene Meyer	Sept. 16, 1930–May 10, 1933
6. Eugene R. Black	May 19, 1933–Aug. 15, 1934
7. Marriner S. Eccles	Nov. 15, 1934–Jan. 31, 1948
8. Thomas B. McCabe	Apr. 15, 1948–Mar. 31, 1951
9. William McChesney Martin, Jr.	Apr. 2, 1951–Jan. 31, 1970
10. Arthur F. Burns	Feb. 1, 1970–Jan. 31, 1978
11. G. William Miller	Mar. 8, 1978–Aug. 6, 1979
12. Paul Volcker	Aug. 6, 1979–Aug., 1987
13. Alan Greenspan†	Aug. 1987–

* Designated "governor" before August 23, 1933.
† Nominated June, 1987.

years, most governors have failed to serve their full terms, primarily because they have resigned and returned to a position in the private sector.

The Board has the final word on all major decisions inside the Federal Reserve except those pertaining to the control of the money supply through open market operations, which are handled by the FOMC. The Board sets reserve requirements within the legal range and may implement the supplemental reserve requirements described in Chapter 8. The Board must approve changes in the rate of interest charged on loans to depository institutions, called the *discount rate*. In practice, the Board sets the discount rate; the New York bank adopts it; and the boards of directors of the regional banks rubber-stamp their agreement, with an occasional recalcitrant regional Reserve bank delaying for several weeks.

"Subject to the approval of the Board" is the refrain heard throughout the Federal Reserve System. The budgets of the twelve regional banks and their branches; the approval of the presidents of the twelve regional Reserve banks, who are selected by the boards of directors of the individual banks; much of the research and publications of the regional banks; the purchase of property for additional office space; all building and remodeling; the security systems of the regional banks; and all legal actions pertaining to commercial bank mergers and acquisitions (for all member banks and all banks in holding companies, members and nonmembers)—all are subject to the Board's approval.

Even though this kind of centralization is necessary and proper for efficient management, the preceding statement would not be accepted by many people in the Federal Reserve, in which there is some ceremonial bowing to the pretense of a rather complete diffusion of power, with each regional bank being a center for decision making. This diffusion of power was written into the Federal Reserve Act of December 1913, but it was largely, though not entirely, ended in 1935, with legislation that centralized authority in the Board and the Federal Open Market Committee.

Because the five presidents of the regional banks always vote on the FOMC, in addition to the seven members of the Board, the regional banks still do exert some decision-making power. The presidents of the regional banks must, however, be approved every five years by the Board, and their salaries, the budgets of their regional banks, and most of the important decisions they must make are subject to the Board's approval. Since 1935, there have been some presidents, such as Darryl Francis, former president of the St. Louis Federal Reserve Bank, who have been known to differ consistently with the Board of Governors, but the fact is that the Board holds most of the control over the system.

Within the Board, the chairman has major control. He or she runs the meetings, including the important FOMC meetings, in which he or she has always been elected chairman of the FOMC. The chairman also keeps in close contact with the president of the United States, the secretary of the Treasury, and the Congress.

Arthur Burns, G. William Miller, and Paul Volcker (the prior three chairmen) were very expert in another activity of the chairman, that of keeping close working relationships with members of Congress and lobbying for the legislation that they desired and against the legislation they disliked. Although their styles differed, all were skilled negotiators and were familiar figures hurrying to appointments through the halls of the House of Representatives and the Senate. (The chairman normally represents the Federal Reserve as a witness at most important hearings before the U.S. Congress.)

The Board's congressional liaison staff is of central importance to the Board's relationship with Congress. The chief liaison and his or her staff keep in close contact with members of Congress and their staffs. The liaison staff provides Congress with information about the Federal Reserve operations, the voluminous money and banking statistics collected by the Federal Reserve, and the numerous reports, many of which are requested by the Congress. The liaison staff assists the chairman in lobbying and reporting to Congress and in keeping informed of the views of banking industry associations and banking industry lobbyists.

The staffs of the banking committees of the House of Representatives and the Senate often have daily contact with the liaison staff or with the top economists at the Board. These two congressional committees oversee the Federal Reserve for Congress. Additional information on this relationship and the relationship of the Federal Reserve and the president of the United States is presented in Part VIII.

THE FEDERAL OPEN MARKET COMMITTEE

The Federal Open Market Committee (FOMC) is one of the most powerful economic policy groups in the government. It formulates Federal Reserve's open market policy and, by doing so, affects the supply of money, interest rates, inflation, the level of economic activity, and the international exchange value of the U.S. dollar.

The FOMC is composed of the seven members of the Board of Governors plus five representatives of the Reserve banks, who may be either Federal Reserve bank presidents or vice-presidents. The president or vice-president of the New York Federal Reserve Bank is always on the FOMC. Each of the other four Reserve bank members is from one of the following four groups, which send a member to the FOMC on a rotating basis for one-year terms beginning on March 1: (1) Boston, Philadelphia, and Richmond; (2) Cleveland and Chicago; (3) Atlanta, Dallas, and St. Louis; and (4) Minneapolis, Kansas City, and San Francisco.

The FOMC meets formally nine or ten times a year. It determines the policy for the purchase and sale of securities by the Federal Reserve. These transactions, which create or contract the monetary base, are called **open market operations**. The New York Federal Reserve Bank executes all open market operations for the system.

Open market operations were not mentioned in the original Federal Reserve Act of 1913, nor were they understood by the original Federal Reserve officials. Rather, the FOMC was originally organized as an informal committee in the 1920s and was invested with its present statutory powers in 1935. Traditionally, the chairman of the Board of Governors is selected as the chairman of the FOMC committee, and the vice-chairman is the president of the Federal Reserve bank of New York. Each of the Reserve banks usually sends a president or an alternate to each of the meetings, even if he or she is not currently a voting member. The FOMC receives reports from the staff at the Board and from the manager of the System Open Market Accounts. The FOMC votes and gives its directive to the manager of the System Open Market Account. The System Open Market Account manager supervises open market operations at the New York Federal Reserve Bank's "trading desk," sometimes referred to as "the desk." The directive is not made public for approximately 30 days. Before 1975 the delay was 90 days. The records of the policy actions of the FOMC are then published in the *Federal Reserve Bulletins*. The reason sometimes given for the 30-day secrecy is that a more "orderly market" is attained through this secrecy. If, for example, the public knew that the FOMC had instructed the New York Federal Reserve Bank to expand the money supply, the public might take action that would cause bond prices to fluctuate in a "disorderly" way.

On the other hand, it is argued that ignorance of what is happening in the market or of what the government intends to do may well cause financial market participants to react to rumors, which causes wider oscillations in the prices of stocks and bonds than would have occurred if the information had immediately been made public. Secrecy also makes it profitable for insiders to act on information that is not available to the public.

The manager of the System Open Market Account carries out the open market activities in the New York bank. The manager may at times ask for a special conference telephone meeting of the FOMC, even when it is not in session.

The formal directives to the FOMC have often been somewhat vague as to what exactly its actions should be. The following is an excerpt from the August 19, 1986, Federal Open Market Committee directive, issued as a press release on September 26, 1986. Also included are the dissenting views of Thomas C. Melzer, president of the St. Louis Federal Reserve Bank, and Henry C. Wallich, former member of the Board of Governors:

> The Federal Open Market Committee seeks monetary and financial conditions that will foster reasonable price stability over time, promote growth in output on a sustainable basis, and contribute to an improved pattern of international transactions. In furtherance of these objectives the Committee agreed at the July meeting to reaffirm the ranges established in February for growth of 6 to 9 percent for both M2 and M3, measured from the fourth quarter of 1985 to the fourth quarter of 1986. With respect to M1, the Committee recognized that, based on the experience of recent years, the behavior of that aggregate is subject to substantial uncertainties in relation to economic activity and prices, depending among other things on the responsiveness of M1 growth to changes in interest rates. In light of these uncertainties and of the substantial decline in velocity in the first half of the year, the Committee decided that growth of M1 in excess of the previously established 3 to 8 percent range for 1986 would be acceptable. Acceptable growth of M1 over the remainder of the year will depend on the behavior of velocity, growth in the other monetary aggregates, developments in the economy and financial markets, and price pressures. Given its rapid growth in the early part of the year, the Committee recognized that the increase in total domestic nonfinancial debt in 1986 may exceed its monitoring range of 8 to 11 percent, but felt an increase in that range would provide an inappropriate benchmark for evaluating longer-term trends in that aggregate.
>
> For 1987 the Committee agreed on tentative ranges of monetary growth, measured from the fourth quarter of 1986 to the fourth quarter of 1987, of 5-1/2 to 8-1/2 percent for M2 and M3. While a range of 3 to 8 percent for M1 in 1987 would appear appropriate in the light of most historical experience, the Committee recognized that the exceptional uncertainties surrounding the behavior of M1 velocity over the more recent period would require careful appraisal of the target range at the

beginning of 1987. The associated range for growth in total domestic nonfinancial debt was provisionally set at 8 to 11 percent for 1987.

In the implementation of policy for the immediate future, the Committee seeks to decrease slightly the existing degree of pressure on reserve positions, taking account of the possibility of a change in the discount rate. This action is expected to be consistent with growth in M2 and M3 over the period from June to September at annual rates of about 7 to 9 percent. While growth in M1 is expected to moderate from the exceptionally large increase during the second quarter, that growth will continue to be judged in the light of the behavior of M2 and M3 and other factors. Somewhat greater or lesser reserve restraint might be acceptable depending on the behavior of the aggregates, the strength of the business expansion, developments in foreign exchange markets, progress against inflation, and conditions in domestic and international credit markets. The Chairman may call for Committee consultation if it appears to the Manager for Domestic Operations that reserve conditions during the period before the next meeting are likely to be associated with a federal funds rate persistently outside a range of 4 to 8 percent.

Votes for this action: Messrs. Volcker, Corrigan, Angell, Guffey, Heller, Mrs. Horn, Messrs. Johnson, Morris, Rice, and Ms. Seger. Votes against this action: Messrs. Melzer and Wallich. Absent and not voting: None.

Messrs. Melzer and Wallich were in favor of maintaining the existing degree of reserve pressure. Mr. Melzer continued to be concerned about the impact of further easing on inflationary expectations and the value of the dollar in foreign exchange markets. In addition, he noted that during the intermeeting period the outlook for real economic activity in the second half of 1986 and in 1987 had not deteriorated and perhaps even had improved slightly. Mr. Wallich emphasized that the implementation of unchanged reserve conditions would improve the prospects for significant slowing in monetary growth, thereby reducing the potential for inflation.

THE DISTRICT BANKS

Each of the twelve **Federal Reserve banks** was organized as a separate corporation and should be distinguished from private commercial banks, which may or may not be members of the Federal Reserve System. Every national bank must join the Federal Reserve System. State banks may elect to join.

Each member bank must subscribe to stock in the Reserve bank corporation. It must buy an amount of stock equal in value to 3 percent of the value of its capital, plus any surplus (from profits) in the bank, with another 3 percent subject to call by the Reserve bank. These funds collected from member banks are put in an account called *paid-in surplus*. The stocks held by the member banks are different from the stocks issued by private banks. The stocks receive a fixed return, currently 6 percent, and do not give their owners proprietary rights (that is, the legal rights of ownership and control that normally belong to stockholders).

The member banks in each district elect six of the nine members of the board of directors of the Reserve bank in their district. The directors of each of the reserve banks are classified into three groups, consisting of three members each.

1. *Class A directors* must be members of the stockholding banks.
2. *Class B directors* must be members "with due but not exclusive consideration to the interests of agriculture, commerce, industry, services, labor and consumers," provided they are not officers, directors, employees, or stockholders of any bank. The Federal Reserve Reform Act of 1977, quoted here, broadened the representation of Class B directors from an earlier limitation to "commerce, agriculture or some other industrial pursuit."
3. The three *Class C directors* are chosen by the Board of Governors and cannot be officers, directors, employees, or stockholders of any bank. The same language for Class B directors applies to those eligible to be Class C directors.

Directors of Reserve banks and branches are limited to one or two full three-year terms. The Federal Reserve Reform Act of 1977 also requires that all directors be chosen "without discrimination on the basis of race, creed, color, sex, or national origin." The August 2, 1977, House Banking Committee report on the bill noted (p. 6): "the virtual exclusion of women, blacks, and representatives of labor unions, consumer interest organizations and non-managerial and non-producer interest groups. Currently, for example, out of 108 Reserve Bank directors only 4 are women and only 3 are minority persons."

The chairman and deputy chairman of each Reserve bank's board of directors are appointed by the Board of Governors from the three Class C directors. Class A and B directors are elected by the member banks; one director in each class is chosen by the small member banks, one by the member banks of medium size, and one by the larger member banks. The chairman, by statute, is made the Federal Reserve agent. As Federal Reserve agent, he or she acts as a representative of the Board of Governors and has responsibility for obtaining new currency (Federal Reserve notes) and maintaining custody of unissued notes in the Federal Reserve vaults.

Although the nine members of the board of directors manage their Federal Reserve bank mostly subject to the approval of the Board of Governors, they do have considerable authority, as bank regulatory actions are administered and initiated in the regional banks. The president and vice-president, who serve five-year terms, are elected by the board of directors, subject to approval by the Board of Governors. Before 1935, the boards of directors' authority, both in the supervision of their Federal Reserve banks and in the policy decisions of the entire Federal Reserve System, was much broader.

The Federal Reserve banks are empowered to make loans to depository institutions, to provide check-clearing services, to act as a depository for reserves of all depository institutions, and to transfer these funds among the Federal Reserve banks. The Federal Reserve banks also act as **fiscal agents** for the U.S. Treasury by conducting the Treasury's sales of U.S. Treasury obligations. Federal Reserve banks supply research facilities for the member banks and publish a large number of reports and periodicals (over 3 million copies in 1979) for the public for little or no charge.

Each branch of the twelve regional Federal Reserve banks has either a five- or a seven-member board of directors. A majority of a branch board of directors is appointed by the regional Federal Reserve bank's board of directors, and the remainder, by the Board of Governors.

The Federal Advisory council (FAC) is composed of twelve members, each of whom represents one of the twelve Reserve banks. Before the 1930s, the FAC had considerable power, but it now has only advisory functions. It confers directly with the Board of Governors and makes recommendations on the system's operations. Even though the FAC has no decision-making authority, it is still very helpful in its advisory capacities. In Washington, D.C., politics, advisory groups often perform the useful function of reviewing topics that those in authority wish to delay (sometimes permanently) from their consideration. Whether or not the thrift institutions want to be relegated to this position—while their rival commercial banks can elect officials to the boards of directors of the Federal Reserve regional banks—is an interesting conjecture that may be brought forward in the new Thrift Institutions Advisory Council.

THE THRIFT INSTITUTIONS ADVISORY COUNCIL

The Monetary Control Act of 1980 brought thrift institutions under the Federal Reserve System's reserve requirements, opened the discount window to thrift institutions and allowed thrift institutions to buy Federal Reserve services—all for the first time. (Previously, only mutual savings banks had been allowed membership.) In response to this larger group subject to Federal Reserve policies, the Federal Reserve set up the Thrift Institutions Advisory Council (TIAC) in 1983, described in Exhibit 14-1. Its initial members were presidents and chief executive officers of savings and loan associations, a credit union, and two mutual savings banks.

Will the members of this group be satisfied to meet, discuss, and remain powerless in the Federal Reserve bureaucracy? Or will they want to elect their members of the boards of directors of the regional banks, just as their rival commercial banks have been able to do since 1914? Or, as unthinkable as this might now seem to many "in the system" (the Federal Reserve System), should all financial intermediaries be put on equal footing in regard to influencing the federal regulators? How could this be done? This is an excellent

EXHIBIT 14-1   Federal Reserve Press Release

FEDERAL RESERVE press release

For immediate release   March 15, 1983

The Federal Reserve Board today announced the appointment of seven new members of its Thrift Institutions Advisory Council and designated Harry W. Albright, President of the Dime Savings Bank, New York, as President of the Council for the current year. Thomas R. Bomar, President of AmeriFirst Federal Savings and Loan Association of Miami, Florida, has been designated Vice President of the Council.

The Council is an advisory group made up of ten representatives from nonbank depository thrift institutions. The panel was established by the Board in 1980 and includes seven savings and loan officials, two mutual savings bankers and one credit union representative. The Council meets at least four times each year with the Board of Governors to discuss developments relating to thrift institutions, the housing industry and mortgage finance, and certain regulatory issues.

Under the Monetary Control Act of 1980, thrift institutions, for the first time, became subject to Federal Reserve System reserve requirements; were required to provide reports on their deposits; and, had access to the discount window and other System services.

Will the thrifts settle for a role in this advisory committee inside the Federal Reserve System, or will they demand more equal treatment with banks?

discussion question as well as a question that may be skirted in the nation's capital for some time to come because of its sensitivity to so many powerful interest groups in the industries affected. Indeed, the consideration of touchy subjects such as this may well begin most fruitfully in an academic environment.

NONMONETARY FUNCTIONS

The nonmonetary powers of the Federal Reserve can be separated into three parts. First, the Federal Reserve is empowered to supervise and regulate the operation of member banks and all bank holding companies, whether or not the banks in the holding companies are members. Second, the Federal Reserve regulates the terms of credit of particular types of transactions throughout the economy, including the regulation of loans to depository institutions. This second group of powers can be referred to as *specific credit regulations.* Third is a group of miscellaneous *banking and currency services,* such as acting as fiscal agents for the U.S. Treasury, clearing checks, and inspecting, destroying, and printing new currency.

Bank Supervision and Regulation

Each of the twelve Federal Reserve banks supervises and examines the state member banks in its districts. They process branch and merger applications, review applications for membership or termination of membership of banks in the Federal Reserve System, and examine reports on the conditions of member banks. Bank examiners are sent out by the Reserve banks, but an examination usually "amounts to little more than making routine examinations and requiring the submission of condition and earnings reports." All bank holding companies are regulated by the Federal Reserve, which must pass on all mergers and acquisitions (see Chapter 7).

Specific Credit Regulations

The Federal Reserve has, at times, been given power to regulate the terms of consumer installment credit. From 1941 to 1947, in 1948, during the Korean conflict until 1952, and again beginning on March 14, 1980, the Board of Governors controlled the terms of consumer installment credit, and from 1950 to 1952 it exercised control over real estate credit. The Credct Control Act of December 23, 1969 (Section 205), provided that "whether the President determines that such action is necessary or appropriate for the general purpose of preventing or controlling inflation generated by the extension of credit in an excessive volume, the President may authorize the Board to regulate and control any or all extensions of credit."

The Federal Reserve Board also regulates the payment of interest on bank deposits. Since the Banking Acts of 1933 and 1935, explicit money interest payments have been prohibited on demand deposits of Federal Reserve member banks and nonmember banks. Legislation passed in 1980 set up a committee (the Depository Institutions Deregulation Committee) of government regulators to remove interest rate ceilings on NOW accounts and share drafts within six years (see Chapter 6).

The Securities Exchange Act of 1934 gave the Federal Reserve Board control over the margin requirements for loans to purchase stocks. The Reserve Board controls the margin requirements for most listed stocks and the more frequently traded over-the-counter stocks. The act was a consequence of the stock market declines in and after 1929. The purpose of the act was to restrict the use of loans for speculative purposes. Milton Friedman argued against this particular type of credit control and against its supervision by the Board of Governors:

> Because of their dramatic quality, movements in stock prices command more attention from the system and others than their role as a source rather than as a reflection of economic changes justifies. . . . I see no justification for singling out credit extended to purchase or hold securities for special attention. But if this is to be done it should be as part of a policy directed at regulation of security markets and by an agency charged with special responsibilities for such markets, not by the Federal Reserve System.[2]

The eligibility requirements that the Federal Reserve has imposed on collateral for loans it extends to depository institutions are another tool of specific credit policy. Depository institutions borrowing is discussed in Chapter 16.

Payments Mechanism Functions

The provision of currency and coin, check-clearing services, wire transfer of money, and automated clearinghouses for checks are some of the services the Federal Reserve renders to help maintain an efficient payments system in the United States.

Check clearing and the provision of currency and coin cost the Federal Reserve $460 million in 1979, when these services were provided at zero cost to member banks. Legislation passed in 1980 required the Federal Reserve to charge for these services by September 1981 and to offer them to all depository institutions on an equal basis, whether or not they are members.

Most of the paper currency in the United States consists of Federal Reserve notes issued in denominations of $1, $2, $5, $10, $50, and $100. The greenbanks, or U.S. notes, that the Treasury began printing after the Legal Tender Acts of 1862 are no longer issued by the Treasury, except for the $100 denomination notes.

The Federal Reserve has the primary responsibility for supervising and maintaining the quantity of currency and coin in circulation in the United States. When a purchase is made in a retail store, for example, the currency and coins are usually deposited in a depository institution. The depository institution, through its correspondent or directly, deposits most of the currency and coin at the regional Federal Reserve bank or its branch.

Expert handlers at the Federal Reserve check the currency for counterfeited, mutilated, and worn-out currency. In 1982 the Federal Reserve announced the purchase of improved currency quality sensors (automatic machines) to be installed in the high-speed currency sorters at 35 Federal Reserve banks and branches and to check for damaged and worn-out currency. In 1983, after two years of study and $1 million in development costs, new fitness sensors were designed, tested, and approved for use. The new sensors distinguish soiled and damaged currency from currency suitable for circulation. They can also detect and reject bills with transparent tape and missing corners.

The life of a dollar bill was, on the average, approximately three years in 1941 and five years in 1976. The actual printing of new paper money and the minting of coins at the Bureau of Engraving and Printing (BEP) and the Bureau of the Mint are under the jurisdiction of the U.S. Treasury. There has been a demand for higher-quality currency (which is not limp and dirty) because of the use of automated teller machines (ATMs) that jam unless they are stocked with undamaged currency. Also, in the early 1980s, the Bureau of Engraving and Printing reached the limits of its capacity to print low-denomination bills. This resulted in fewer bills being turned in to the Federal Reserve where they might be taken out of circulation. In addition the Federal Reserve could not set its fitness standards in the sorting process at the maximum quality level. By 1983, the BEP's capacity had increased, and new fitness sensors and higher standards were scheduled for implementation at the Federal Reserve. This should lead to an improved quality of the notes in circulation (approximately 9 billion in 1983).

Our discussion will now turn to the **electronic transfer of funds (EFT)** and the **automated clearinghouse (ACH)**, a system using EFT to clear payments. The Federal Reserve plays a major role in and is the largest supplier of these services for the electronic transfer of funds.

The automated clearinghouse (ACH) is a payments system that clears funds without creating paper checks, by using computers and electronic impulses.[3] In April 1968, the San Francisco and Los Angeles Clearing House Associations made recommendations for paperless entries among banks. Then in 1970, a group of ten California banks began a pilot program for the interbank paperless exchange of funds. Also in 1970, a group of ten California banks began a pilot program for the interbank paperless exchange of funds. Also in 1970 the American Bankers Association, the largest trade association for commercial banks in the United States, formed the Monetary and Payments System (MAPS) Committee to improve the payments system. MAPS suggested an electronic payments system. In 1971 the Federal Reserve Bank of

Atlanta, working with the Georgia Institute of Technology, studied paperless funds transfer. Several banks in Atlanta formed the Committee on Paperless Entry (COPE), which agreed to begin a Federal Reserve–managed ACH. This ACH became the second ACH in the country, beginning operation in 1973.

In 1971 the Federal Reserve Board also stated that it favored an electronic funds transfer system, and in 1972 the Federal Reserve began operating ACH systems for the San Francisco, Los Angeles, and Atlanta clearinghouses. The National Automated Clearing House Association (NACHA) was formed in 1974 to establish rules and regulations for ACHs, and by 1975, thirteen ACHs were in operation. The federal government began processing social security checks through the ACHs in 1975, and in 1983 the Federal Reserve and the NACHA began a pilot program to handle corporate trade payments (CTPs) through ACHs. The CTPs worked well and in 1984 were open to all users.

By 1986 there were 31 ACHs operating in the United States, serving over 16,000 financial institutions and 34,000 corporations. In 1986 most ACHs used the Fedwire facilities, a wire transfer facility owned and operated by the Federal Reserve. The ACHs processed 48.1 million electronic payments per month, of which 23.2 million were commercial transfers and 24.9 million were government transfers of funds. The use of ACHs reduces the cost of transferring funds below that of using paper checks. ACHs also eliminate bank float, the double counting of funds between the time of the credit to an account at the bank where the funds are deposited and the deduction from the account at the bank at which the funds are drawn.

The Fedwire is operated by the Federal Reserve system. The 12 Federal Reserve banks and their 25 branches, as well as many depository institutions, use the Fedwire. It began operations in 1918 and in 1986 was the largest of the wholesale electronic funds transfer systems in operation in the United States.[4] On an average day in 1984, there were 166,410 transfers, with an average size of $2.2 million. The Federal Reserve modernized its Fedwire in 1983 when its contract with American Telephone and Telegraph ended. The Federal Reserve thus no longer relies on a central switch at Culpepper, Virginia, and its new communication system is more efficient. In addition, the Depository Institutions and Monetary Control Act of 1980 required the Federal Reserve to charge for its services, including the use of its Fedwire, and in 1985 it received $65.2 billion for these services, as shown in Table 14-3.

There also are other national wire systems, such as CashWire, which began operations in 1982. In addition, there are local wire systems, such as the Clearing House Electronic Settlement System (CHESS), which operates in the Chicago Federal Reserve district. The Clearing House Interbank Payments System (CHIPS), operated by the New York City Clearing House Association, is used to clear international transactions for 1,000 member banks. CHIPS is controlled by the 12 largest New York City commercial banks. SWIFT (Society for Worldwide Interbank Transactions) is a Belgian communication network with 800 members.

On an average day in 1984, all of the domestic wire systems together trans-

TABLE 14-3   1985 Income Statement for Services of the Federal Reserve System (in millions of dollars)

Income Statement for Priced Services
Federal Reserve System
For the year ending December 31, 1985
(in millions)

	Total	Commercial Check Collection	Wire Transfer and Net Settlement	Commercial ACH	Definitive Safekeeping and Noncash Collection	Book-Entry Securities	Cash Services
Income from services	$613.8	$464.5	$65.2	$23.2	$21.1	$24.3	$15.6
Operating expenses, net of subsidies	476.7	356.7	52.6	18.8	19.2	14.2	15.3
Income from operations	137.1	107.8	12.7	4.4	1.9	10.1	0.3
Imputed costs	51.6	44.2	1.6	2.0	1.1	2.6	0.1
Income from operations after imputed costs	85.5	63.6	11.1	2.4	0.8	7.5	0.2
Other income and expenses, net	13.5	11.4	0.9	0.3	0.3	0.3	0.2
Income before income taxes	$99.0	$75.1	$12.0	$2.7	$1.1	$7.8	$0.4

Details may not add to totals because of rounding.
Source: Board of Governors of the Federal Reserve, press release, April 18, 1986, p. 11.

ferred $640 billion, an enormous operation that poses some risk of overdrafts. In an overdraft during the day—daylight overdrafts—one of the parties to the wire transactions extends credit to the other party until the overdraft can be covered with "good funds." The Board of Governors of the Federal Reserve System has established a policy for large-dollar transfer networks, which limits the size of the overdraft according to the individual bank's capital.

APPENDIX: HISTORY OF THE FEDERAL RESERVE SYSTEM FROM THE BANKING PANIC OF 1907 TO WORLD WAR II

The Panic of 1907

In the past during a banking panic, depositors often feared for the solvency of their commercial banks. The slightest rumor often prompted them to run to the bank and attempt to withdraw their money. The remedy devised by the private commercial banking system for such bank runs was a suspension of convertibility into cash. This device was used during the banking panics of 1893 and 1907. Checks could still be used to pay bills, but the banks temporarily refused to make payments in cash. Federal insurance of deposits, instituted in 1934, effectively reduced bank runs to a negligible number. However, before this solution to banking runs, two other solutions were suggested first: the formation of the National Currency Associations and the National Monetary Commission, which led to the organization of the Federal Reserve System. The primary purpose of the Federal Reserve was to lend money to banks that faced bank runs. Although the peculiar institutional framework of the Federal Reserve System can be traced back to the First and Second Banks of the United States and to the debates surrounding their formation, the impetus to form a central bank came from events such as the bank runs in 1907.

In March 1907, prices fell rapidly on the New York Stock Exchange, and in August, stock prices fell again. The Treasury transferred $28 million from its vaults to commercial banks. Otto Heinze and Company, a brokerage house, failed after gambling on copper stocks. A run started on the Mercantile National Bank, owned by members of the Heinze family. The Morse banking chain and then the Knickerbocker Trust Company, followed by the National Bank of America and other trust companies, were subject to runs by the depositors. The financial community and the federal government went to J. P. Morgan for assistance. Treasury Secretary George B. Cortelyou went to New York to confer with bankers and with Morgan.[5] The Treasury placed $42 million of interest-free deposits in banks controlled by Morgan's firm. Morgan decided which New York banks would receive loans to meet bank runs. Although the New York banks were criticized for not banding together more rapidly and extending loans to the banks that experienced bank runs, it is doubtful that this form of collusion would have prevented widespread banking panics. New York banks could not have increased the total amount of available reserves; they could only reallocate the existing reserves.

It was the rapid restriction of cash payments that allowed the banks to stay open and carry on their business. That is, they could sell their income-earning assets and recall their loans to raise needed reserves. The prompt restriction of payments was probably the single most important factor that prevented the recession of 1907 from becoming more than a mild contraction.[6]

The Aldrich–Vreeland Act

The banking panic of 1907 and the subsequent restriction of payments in cash by commercial banks led to renewed outcries for some type of banking reform. The government responded by passing the Aldrich–Vreeland Act on May 30, 1908. This act provided for the organization of the National Currency Associations, to be composed of ten or more national banks, which would pool their reserves in case of a banking emergency. The National Currency Associations would be empowered to issue to their member banks emergency currency up to 75 percent of the value of private credit instruments and up to 90 percent of the value of certain state and local government bonds. The secretary of the Treasury also could authorize national banks to issue the same kind of currency against credit instruments deposited with the Treasury.

The Aldrich–Vreeland Act also stipulated that a National Monetary Commission be appointed to investigate the banking system. The commission was composed of nine senators and nine representatives. Its chairman was Senator Nelson B. Aldrich, and its vice-chairman was Congressman Edward B. Vreeland. The commission held hearings and employed a staff of economists and financial experts that wrote 23 volumes and made important contributions to monetary analysis. One of the commission's recommendations, which became known as the Aldrich plan, was the establishment of a national reserve association. Aldrich published his *Suggested Plan for Monetary Legislation*, which he had presented to Congress in 1912. The plan called for a weak central bank but failed to pass in Congress. A stronger type of central bank was established when President Woodrow Wilson signed the Federal Reserve Act on December 23, 1913.

The remedies set forth in the Aldrich–Vreeland Act were tested once during the banking panic of 1914 before that act was superseded by the formation of the Federal Reserve System. (The Federal Reserve, authorized in December 1913, was not yet in operation; it began operations in November 1914.) At the outbreak of World War I, Europeans attempted to unload securities on the New York Stock Exchange. The New York Stock Exchange thus closed on April 30, 1914, in an attempt to prevent a sharp decline, but an "outlaw" market on the Wall Street sidewalk began operating when the New York Stock Exchange opened for restricted trading. Country banks started to withdraw their balances from their New York correspondents, and depositors began runs on banks. The emergency currency allowed by the Aldrich–Vreeland Act provisions was immediately circulated and amounted to as much as one quarter of the total amount of currency that the public held before the outbreak of the war. The remedy proved successful. The banks did not have to restrict payments, and a banking panic was prevented. The provision of the Aldrich–Vreeland Act and the 1907 remedy of suspending cash payments turned out to be far superior to the actions taken by the Federal Reserve in the banking panics between 1929 and 1933.

History of the Federal Reserve System to 1929

Before the establishment of the Federal Reserve, the United States was on a gold standard. The quantity of the monetary base in circulation was determined primarily by the balance of payments, the profitability and availability of gold mining, and alternative uses for gold. The Federal Reserve was not established, therefore, with the primary responsibility of controlling the money supply. Instead, it was created mainly to stop banking panics. The cause of banking panics was seen as the difficulty of converting one form of money, demand deposits, into another form of money, currency and coin. Thus, the Federal Reserve, as noted in the subtitle to the act by which it was established, was called upon "To furnish an elastic currency," and it was to be the "lender of last resort."

Those primary functions that were crucial to the Federal Reserve's formation became irrelevant immediately after it was founded.[7] As soon as the Federal Reserve Act was passed and before the system began operations, World War I began; the gold standard countries abandoned the gold standard; and the flow of gold into the United States increased to pay for exports to the Allies. The gold standard regulations that had served as a major determinant of the money supply no longer effectively controlled it. Therefore, the responsibility for controlling the money supply fell upon the Federal Reserve and the Treasury, even though the Treasury resumed gold purchases and sales at $20.67 per ounce after the war.

When the United States entered the war on April 2, 1917, an important power center inside the Federal Reserve was the governors' conference. It was composed of the twelve presidents of the Federal Reserve banks. (They were called "governors" until the 1935 reorganization.) The Federal Reserve bank governors wanted to play an indirect role in financing the war. They chose to make loans to Federal Reserve member banks that presented government securities as collateral. Thus the Federal Reserve's first major action consisted of financing the government's World War I expenditures with money that was lent to the member banks for buying securities sold by the Treasury.

Under the provisions of the Federal Reserve Act, the Federal Reserve Board in Washington, D.C., was composed of seven members. Five of these were appointed; the other two were the Comptroller of the Currency and the secretary of the Treasury, who were ex-officio members of the Board. The Banking

Act of 1935 changed the name of the Federal Reserve Board to the Board of Governors of the Federal Reserve System and shifted to it much of the power of the presidents of the regional Reserve banks. The act also stipulated that the secretary of the Treasury and the Comptroller of the Currency were to be removed from the Board of Governors. Seven secretaries of the Treasury and six Comptrollers of the Currency served on the Federal Reserve Board between 1913 and 1936, which gave the Treasury and the supervisory agency of the national banking system important voices in the Federal Reserve System. The chairman and vice-chairman of the Federal Reserve Board were designated governor and vice-governor before 1935. The seven chairmen who served before 1936 and the other appointed members of the Federal Reserve Board, during their tenure, formed another block of power that sought to control the actions of the Federal Reserve System.

Under this system of control, the Federal Reserve's power was diffused, which made it difficult to hold any individual responsible for the Federal Reserve's actions and made the actions themselves dependent on a widespread power struggle within the system. The Federal Reserve not only was free from accountability to the electorate, which did not elect its officials, but also was not clearly under the direction of the executive or legislative representatives of the public. The twelve bank presidents frequently disagreed, prevented necessary continuity in Federal Reserve policy, and often pursued different open market and member bank borrowing policies in their separate Federal Reserve districts.

The monetary base grew rapidly from 1914 through World War I and continued to grow in the postwar period. The Federal Reserve reacted with policies to reduce member bank borrowings. Governor Benjamin Strong of the New York Federal Reserve Bank was chairman and the dominant influence in the governors' conference. He recommended higher discount rates and more restrictive eligibility requirements for member bank borrowing. Other Reserve bank governors opposed an increase in the discount rate and recommended instead an increase in the coupon rate paid by the Treasury on government bonds. At first, the Treasury wanted to refund its debt without raising the interest rates it paid. Meanwhile, Governor Strong changed his position somewhat, indicating that the time to increase the discount rate had passed and that, if it should be increased, a crisis would result.

There was a failure to understand that the effect of changes in the discount rate on the level of the monetary base depended on the level of other rates of interest. The discount rate at the Federal Reserve Bank in New York had been raised to 3.5 percent in December 1917 and to 4 percent in April 1918. It was then kept at that level until November 1919, with the other Reserve banks following along. These low rates were below the other market rates of interest and encouraged increased member bank borrowing, which caused the money supply to expand. That is, the member banks could make a substantial profit by borrowing from the Federal Reserve and using the loans to purchase short-term assets at the prevailing market rates.

And then the pendulum swung too far the other way. The discount was first raised to 4.75 percent at the end of 1919; then in 1920, the rate was raised to 7 percent by the New York Bank and three other banks and to 6 percent by the rest of the regional Reserve banks. This large increase in the discount rate produced a sudden turnaround in the profitability of member bank borrowing. The rate of increase in the money supply immediately declined, then monetary growth turned negative, in a sustained decline matched only once since the Civil War, in the 1929–1933 period. The peak of the economic expansion is dated by the National Bureau of Economic Research as January 1920. A mild recession followed which grew more severe in its later phases. The recession after the middle of 1920 has been described as one of the "most rapid declines on record."[8] By June 1921, wholesale prices had fallen to 56 percent of their level in May 1920. Although the recession was relatively brief, with the trough in July 1921, it was one of the worst in the country's history.

In its first peacetime monetary policy, the Federal Reserve precipitated a much more severe contraction than might otherwise have occurred. There were 63 bank failures in 1919, 155 in 1920, and 560 in 1921. There was, however, no widespread evidence of bank runs. An inflow of gold in 1920 offset the effects of the decrease in member bank borrowing, causing the monetary base to fall less rapidly.

A centralized open market committee was first tentatively organized in 1922 and then reorganized in 1923 as the Open Market Investment Committee of the Federal Reserve System. It was composed of five members, appointed by the Federal Reserve Board. Regional Reserve banks still conducted small amounts of their own open market purchases and sales.

Between October 1921 and May 1922, regional Federal Reserve banks purchased approximately $400 million of government securities as investments that would bring earnings to their banks. These Federal Reserve banks were acting as profit maximizers.

The discount rate was kept low enough to allow member banks to borrow with commercial paper as collateral, so that Federal Reserve credit could support the needs of trade. It was thought that the Federal Reserve System should supplement member bank borrowing with open market activities that were intended to stabilize and control the market but not to dominate it.[9]

There is no indication that in the 1920s any official of the Federal Reserve System, except Governor Strong of the New York bank, saw price stability as a proper target of the Federal Reserve policy. Rather, an article in the July 1926 *Federal Reserve Bulletin* showed that short-run interest rate stability was considered to be an important target: "Under present conditions . . . the currency is elastic and both expands and contracts in response to seasonal demands while money rates fluctuate over a much narrower range."[10] Governor Strong attempted to carry out countercyclical policy, and the Federal Reserve System took credit for ending business downturns in 1923–1924 and 1926–1927. Only a minority of the Federal Reserve officials favored a countercyclical objective for open market policy.

The Federal Reserve System and the
1930s Depressions

The Federal Reserve System had been concerned throughout the 1920s with the increasing amount of sales volume in the stock market. After 1928, the Federal Reserve attempted to keep interest rates low enough to stimulate the economy but high enough to reduce the amount of money invested in the stock market. At first, the Federal Reserve Board urged the Federal Reserve banks to use their influence to prevent the member banks from borrowing money that would be used to speculate in the stock market. Then in August 1929, the Federal Reserve Board began to raise the discount rate and to pursue a restrictive policy to control the stock market boom.

The death of Governor Strong in 1928 led to a vacuum of power in the system as well as the absence of a strong voice for countercyclical actions. Some of the officials of the Federal Reserve System asked that the Open Market Investment Committee be abolished and that the control of open market operations be returned to the Federal Reserve governors. As the economy fell into a severe depression, the Federal Reserve officials failed to take significant countercyclical actions or to lend sufficient funds to banks in trouble, a primary purpose of the lender of last resort.

Following the huge decline in stock prices in October 1929, the Federal Reserve banks lowered their discount rates. The New York Bank made some open market purchases, but the Board felt that a more liberal discount policy was preferable to additional open market purchases and refused to allow the open market purchases requested by the president of the New York Federal Reserve Bank. The Board did allow $155 million more in open market purchases, plus an additional $100 million of purchases that had been previously authorized at the end of 1929, but no further securities purchases were made before March 1933.

The Open Market Investment Committee was in the process of being reorganized in the early part of 1930. Approval for a policy required a majority of the Federal Reserve Board and of the 108 directors of the twelve Federal Reserve banks, with the right reserved by each Federal Reserve bank to refuse to participate in the actions. The twelve Federal Reserve Board governors were now equal with the members of the Federal Reserve Board in their influence on Federal Reserve policy. As the House Banking and Currency Committee commented in 1935, "It would be difficult to conceive of any arrangement better calculated than this for diffusing responsibility and creating an elaborate system of obstructions."[11]

Between October 1930 and July 1931, almost 1,400 commercial banks, holding approximately $1 billion in deposits, failed. The money stock declined by 6 percent, and deposits of commercial banks fell by 8 percent. While this occurred, the Federal Reserve, which was originally organized to be the lender of last resort, reduced the quantity of bills discounted for member banks and maintained the same volume of Federal Reserve credit outstanding, which was one half the amount outstanding at the end of 1928.

The economy began to recover in 1931, but the recovery was blunted by additional bank failures. After Great Britian went off the gold standard in 1931, the major concern of the Federal Reserve was not the renewed rash of bank failures but, rather, the threat of a reduction in the amount of gold held in the United States. The discount rate was raised from 1.5 percent on October 8, to 2.5 percent the next day, and to 3.5 percent the following week. Between August 1931 and January 1932, an additional 1,860 commercial banks, with $1,449 million in deposits, failed.

In September 1932, Governor George Harrison of the Federal Reserve Bank of New York advocated open market purchases to help alleviate the depression. A majority of the governors opposed this action. Governor George Norris of the Philadelphia Bank stated this majority view in a memorandum:

> We have always believed that the proper function of the System was well expressed in a phrase used in The Tenth Annual Report of the Federal Reserve Board (1923)—"The Federal Reserve supplies the needed additions to credit in times of business expansion and takes up the slack in times of business recession." We have therefore, necessarily found ourselves out of harmony with the policy recently followed by supplying unneeded credit in a time of business recession, which is the exact antithesis of the rule above stated.[12]

The minutes of the November 15, 1932, Open Market Policy Conference stated:

> All the Members of the Conference were of the opinion that there is no occasion to buy more securities at the present time. The question for the decision of the Conference, therefore, was whether the System should now sell some of its present holdings or leave the account stationary.[13]

A period of open market purchases by the Federal Reserve in 1932 ended on August 10. It was now too late. From July 1929 to March 1933, the supply of money had fallen by approximately one third, and the depression hit a deep trough in the first quarter of 1933.

President Franklin Roosevelt announced at midnight on March 6, 1933, that all banks would be forbidden to open until March 9. He later extended this federally imposed **banking holiday** to the middle of March, after which many states further extended the holiday. Unlike the earlier banking panics, in which the banks remained open and transacted their business, the imposed banking holiday completely closed the banks. This action prevented bank managers from taking steps to increase their reserves to meet the demands for withdrawal. The number of commercial banks, which had peaked in 1921 at 31,076, fell to 22,242 in 1931 and then to 14,771 by the end of 1933, where it remained (reaching 15,072 in December 1985).

The convertibility of the dollar into gold was suspended from 1933 until 1934, when a new official price of $35 an ounce was established. This was an official devaluation of the U.S. currency relative to gold.

At the end of 1934 President Roosevelt appointed Marriner S. Eccles, a banker from Utah who was working for the Treasury, to the position of chairman of the Federal Reserve system. Eccles and members of his staff proposed a reorganization of the Federal Reserve System, concentrating the decision-making power within the Board of Governors in Washington. A number of laws were passed. The Banking Act of 1935 was the major piece of legislation that changed the organization of the Federal Reserve. Under this law, ex-officio members of the Federal Reserve Board were eliminated; the Open Market Committee was organized to include twelve members, seven of whom were the Board of Governors; regional Federal Reserve banks were prohibited from participating in open market activities without the permission of the Federal Open Market Committee; and the term of office of the members of the Board of Governors was lengthened. Unfortunately, the first major action of the newly organized Federal Reserve was to double the reserve requirements in 1936 and 1937, thereby restricting monetary growth. This action was a major determinant of the second severe depression of the 1930s.

During World War II, the Federal Reserve again financed the federal government by the equivalent of printing money. This time the major institutional mechanism for printing money was not member-bank discounting as in World War I, but rather open market purchases of government securities.

STUDY QUESTIONS

1. Describe the functions, composition, and level of management of the following groups in the Federal Reserve System:

   a. Managers of member banks
   b. Board of Governors
   c. Federal Advisory Committee
   d. FOMC
   e. Presidents of the regional Federal Reserve banks
   f. Boards of directors of the regional and branch Reserve banks

2. Does the U.S. Congress or the twelve-member FOMC have legal and direct control of the U.S. money supply? Explain the meaning of the assertion "Congress appropriates money."

3. Who formulates monetary policy directives? Who receives monetary policy directives? What kind of information do monetary policy directives contain?

4. Describe the nonmonetary functions of the Federal Reserve. How and when has the Federal Reserve supervised the allocation of credit and the terms for buying common stock?

5. Why would a bank's management want the bank to be a member of the Federal Reserve System? What are the costs and the benefits? Did these costs or benefits change substantially after 1980? (Review the reserve requirements in Chapter 8.)

6. What are federal funds, the federal funds market, and the funds rate?

7. Now (since 1981) that all depository institutions can use the Federal Reserve discount window, are authorized to buy services from the Federal Reserve, and (except the very small depository institutions) are covered by Federal Reserve requirements, should they all be treated equally in their representation in the Federal Reserve? Should the present system continue, in which only member commercial banks can elect members of the board of directors of the Federal Reserve's regional banks? How would such equality be achieved? Describe the necessary institutional changes.

8. Should regulated depository intermediaries have any managerial authority inside the Federal Reserve System, or should the regulated be separated from the regulators? Explain your answer.

9. How did the Federal Reserve System serve in its function as a lender of the last resort in the 1930s?

10. Read again the excerpts of the Federal Reserve minutes from the early 1930s, and describe the rationale for the arguments made.

GLOSSARY

ACH. Automated clearinghouse. A payments system that clears funds without creating paper checks, by using computers and electronic impulses.

Banking holiday. The action taken by President Franklin D. Roosevelt on March 6, 1933, that forbade banks in the United States to open until March 13 of that year. The terminal date was later extended to the middle of March, after which many states extended it even further.

EFT. Electronic transfer of funds.

Federal Reserve bank. The bank in each of the designated twelve districts of the United States, formally set up along the lines of a private corporation but functioning as a central bank branch and as part of the Federal Reserve System, largely under the control of the Board of Governors.

Fiscal agents. In the Federal Reserve System, the individuals who officially handle the functions of the U.S. Treasury. The Federal Reserve System acts as the agent for the Treasury in the sale of U.S. government securities.

Monetary base. Currency and coin outside depository institutions plus the cash reserves of depository institutions. These cash reserves consist of vault cash (cash on the premises of depository institutions) plus deposits at the Federal Reserve banks or deposits at other depository institutions or regulatory agencies authorized to pass them through—dollar for dollar—to the regional Federal Reserve banks or their branches.

Open market operations. The purchase and sale of securities. In the case of Federal Reserve open market operations, transactions are carried out by the New York Federal Reserve Bank.

NOTES

1. The Federal Banking Agency Audit Act of 1978 (Public Law 95-320) allows the General Accounting Office (GAO) to review and audit the activities of the Federal Reserve, except those relating to "deliberations, decisions, and actions on monetary policy matters, including discount window operations, reserves of member banks, securities credit, interest on deposits, and open market operations." In a report to Henry S. Reuss, former chairman of the Banking Committee of the House of Representatives ("Response to the Honorable Henry S. Reuss on Questions Bearing on the Feasibility of Closing the Federal Reserve Banks," Comptroller General, U.S. General Accounting Office, May 21, 1981), the GAO estimated the following: in October 1980, the value of the Federal Reserve System's land, machinery, and buildings was $853.9 million.

2. Milton Friedman, *A Program for Monetary Stability* (New York: Fordham University Press, 1960), p. 27.

3. Pamela S. Frisbee, "The ACH: An Elusive Dream," in "The ACH in a New Light," *Economic Review*, Federal Reserve Bank of Atlanta, March 1986, pp. 4–8. See also Bernell K. Stone, "Electronic Payments Basics," in ibid., pp. 9–18.

4. See David L. Mengle, "Daylight Overdrafts and Payments System Risks," *Economic Review*, May–June 1985, pp. 14–27.

5. See *The American Heritage Dictionary of Business and Industry* by Alex Groner and the editors of *American Heritage* and *Business Week*, with an introduction by Paul Samuelson (New York: American Heritage, 1972), pp. 210–213.

6. See Milton Friedman and Anna Schwartz, *A Monetary History of the United States, 1867–1960* (Princeton, N.J.: Princeton University Press, 1963), p. 163.

7. See Friedman and Schwartz, "Early Years of the Federal Reserve System, 1914–1921," in *A Monetary History*, pp. 189–239; and *Federal Reserve Structure and the Development of Monetary Policy: 1915–1925*, staff report of the Subcommittee on Domestic Finance, Committee on Banking and Currency, House of Representatives, 92nd Cong., 1st sess., December 1971 (Washington, D.C.: U.S. Government Printing Office, stock number 5270-1304), Chap. 2, pp. 23–29.

8. Friedman and Schwartz, *A Monetary History*, p. 231.

9. *Federal Reserve Structure*, p. 71.

10. *Federal Reserve Bulletin*, July 1926, p. 471, reprinted in *Federal Reserve Structure*, p. 91.

11. *Federal Reserve Structure*, p. 125.

12. Ibid., p. 128.

13. Ibid., p. 131.

CHAPTER 15

THE TREASURY, THE FEDERAL RESERVE, AND THE MONETARY BASE

CHAPTER PREVIEW

Introduction. The organization of the material and its importance are presented.

The Federal Reserve. Its assets and liabilities and the sources and uses of depository institutions' reserves are described.

The Government Budget Constraint or Monetary Base Identity. First, the U.S. Treasury financing transactions (for the deficit) are shown; then these are combined with transactions of the Federal Reserve to obtain the monetary base identity (or government budget constraint). Each of the components of the monetary base identity is discussed. Five practice problems with answers are presented.

INTRODUCTION

The last chapter discussed the structure of the Federal Reserve and its non-monetary functions. This chapter and Chapters 16 and 17 examine the monetary functions of the Federal Reserve. The term *monetary* refers to money, and monetary functions include the Federal Reserve's management of the nation's money supply. This chapter is concerned with the monetary base. Remember from the last chapter that the monetary base is created by the government. It is composed of currency and coin outside depository institutions plus the reserves of the depository institutions.

The monetary base is only part of the money supply; it is not the complete money supply. For example, in September 1986, M-1 stood at $693.5 billion, and the monetary base was only 33 percent of that amount, or $231.6 billion. Who is making all that money, and what effect does the Federal Reserve have on the control of the money supply? You will not find out in this chapter; that fascinating enquiry is left to Chapters 16 and 17. Once you have mastered these chapters, you will understand the supply of money and will be able to turn to the next three parts of the book, which describe the effects of changes in the money supply on the economy.

In describing the monetary base and how it is related to the Federal Reserve's balance statement and to other government transactions in general, there is an annoying collection of accounting details that must be considered. It therefore is important to keep the plan of this chapter firmly in mind so that you will not be drowned in accounting details and fail to arrive at your destination. The plan of this chapter is as follows:

1. The assets and liabilities of the Federal Reserve are described first. These assets and liabilities contain many of the elements of the monetary base. Knowing them is the first step in understanding how the monetary base is changed by the Federal Reserve.
2. The Federal Reserve publishes in its monthly *Bulletin* a different way to look at its assets and liabilities, called the *Sources and Uses of Reserves* statement. When the uses are subtracted from the sources on this statement, the reserves supplied to the banking system, a major part of the monetary base, falls out as a residual. The monetary base is an important variable in the analysis of how the money supply is determined.
3. A more meaningful arrangement of the transactions of the entire federal government and their relationship with the monetary base can be used. It adds to the sources-and-uses-of-reserves statement and allows the relationships between changes in the monetary base and other government transactions to be precisely related. To develop this view, the transactions of the U.S. Treasury must be taken into account.

As a result of this journey through the house of accounting concepts, you will be able to answer complicated questions about the relationship of government transactions that seem hopelessly complicated, simply by plugging in values in a simple identity. Second, and much more important, you will find it much easier to organize and understand the analysis of financing the federal deficit. The effects of federal government deficits on the economy critically depend on how these federal deficits are financed. They can be financed, for example, by issuing more monetary base. This is one of the most important subjects of macroeconomics and has come to the forefront in recent years during the Reagan administration and in much theoretical work.

First we shall discuss the meaning of the federal government deficit. Federal government expenditures can, in general, be financed by borrowing (selling bonds to the public), issuing new federally created money (increases in the monetary base), or levying taxes. The federal deficit is the cash value of the federal government's expenditures for goods, services, and transfer payments (such as unemployment payments by the federal government) minus the federal government's income, mostly from taxes. The federal deficit therefore is essentially the government's expenditures minus taxes, and is financed (paid for) by either borrowing or creating new money.

THE FEDERAL RESERVE

Assets and Liabilities

Table 15-1 presents a generalized T-account classification of the Federal Reserve's assets and liabilities, consolidated to include all twelve district Federal Reserve banks. Table 15-2 presents a specific itemized T-account of these assets and liabilities for September 1986. This record is a starting point for gaining insight into the Federal Reserve's transactions that change the

TABLE 15-1   Generalized Accounting Record of the Federal Reserve's Assets and Liabilities

This T-account shows the categories of assets and liabilities held by the Federal Reserve. It should be thought of in a completely different light from a private bank's balance sheet. The Federal Reserve is an arm of the government.

Assets	Liabilities and Capital Accounts

1. Cash assets
  a. Coin and currency
  b. Gold certificates
  c. Special drawing rights certificates
2. Loans to depository institutions
3. Uncollected cash items
4. Securities held
5. Miscellaneous assets
	6. Federal Reserve notes outstanding
	7. Deposits from depository institutions, international organizations, foreign central banks, and the U.S. Treasury
	8. Deferred availability cash items
	9. Other liabilities and capital accounts

The basic accounting identity holds: assets = liabilities + equity (or capital accounts).

T A B L E 1 5 - 2   The Federal Reserve's Assets and Liabilities,* September 1986† (in billions)

Now consider the actual amounts of each category of Federal Reserve assets and liabilities. Again, turn to the huge liability, Federal Reserve notes outstanding, amounting to $184.2 billion. Cash items in process of collection stood at nearly $9.1 billion. The depository institutions owe the Federal Reserve this money. However, the Federal Reserve has already credited the depository institutions' reserve accounts with $8.3 billion, the deferred availability cash items liability. Remember from Chapter 8 that the difference, $0.8 billion, is Federal Reserve float. Coins are a relatively small item, only $500 million, although those counting pieces are expensive to maintain and transport. They are made at the Treasury and are shipped to the Federal Reserve, as are all those Federal Reserve notes. The notes listed as a liability are those in circulation. The coins in circulation are not an asset or a liability of the Federal Reserve. The $500 million in coins in its vaults are an asset.

Assets		Liabilities and Capital Accounts	
Gold certificates (and special drawing rights)	$16.1	Federal Reserve notes outstanding	$184.2
Coin	.5	Deposits from depository institutions	36.8
Loans to depository institutions	.9	U.S. Treasury account	7.5
U.S. and agency securities held‡	100.6	Foreign and other accounts	1.0
Cash items in process of collection	9.1	Deferred availability cash items	8.3
Other assets	17.0	Other liabilities and capital accounts	6.4
Total	$244.2	Total	$244.2

* Consolidated for all twelve regional Federal Reserve banks.
† End-of-month estimates, slight inaccuracy because of rounding.
‡ Bankers' acceptances in relatively small amounts and repurchase agreements are included.
Source: Federal Reserve Bulletin, December 1986, p. A10.

monetary base. A brief description of each of the classes of assets and liabilities follows. First the assets, as numbered in Table 15-1, are identified.

1a. *Coin and currency.* The metal coin and currency are held by the Federal Reserve banks in their vaults in order to supply depository institutions, as part of the Federal Reserve's central bank function of maintaining the payments system, described in the last chapter.

1b and c. *Gold certificates and special drawing rights certificates* (SDR certificates) arise in transactions with the U.S. Treasury. The gold certificates are claims against the Treasury's gold. The SDR certificates are claims against the Treasury's SDRs, an international money issued by the International Monetary Fund.

2. *Loans to depository institutions* are also called *discounting* and are said to be made through the discount window at each Federal Reserve bank.

3, 8. *Uncollected cash items,* an asset, minus the liability, *deferred availability cash items,* equals Federal Reserve float. This is described in Chapter 8, along with estimates of float for a number of years.

4. The *securities held* by the Federal Reserve amounted to $200.6 billion. They comprise its portfolio of U.S. government and federal agency obligations, from which it earned most of its current "earnings." The word *earnings* is enclosed in quotation marks because these interest payments are from the U.S. Treasury and government agencies to the Federal Reserve. A consolidated balance sheet of the government, in which the Federal Reserve is defined as part of the government, would net them out at zero. The transfers would be internal ones. Most of these funds that are not used for expenses are returned to the U.S. Treasury as "interest on Federal Reserve notes."

5. The *miscellaneous assets* include the Federal Reserve's real estate, buildings, and equipment.

The liabilities, as numbered in Table 15-1, are described next.

6. The *Federal Reserve notes,* amounting to $184.2 billion, are the bulk of the currency and coin in circulation. Examine a U.S. dollar bill, which is a Federal Reserve note. The name, number of the Federal Reserve district, and the letter of the alphabet corresponding to that number identify the regional Federal Reserve bank that originally issued it. Technically, it is a liability of that Federal Reserve bank, although an attempt to return it would produce only a blank stare.

7. *Deposits* from depository institutions amounted to $36.8 billion and were confined mostly to reserves. International organizations, foreign central banks, the U.S. Treasury, and government-sponsored agencies, accounts also hold deposits at the Federal Reserve.

9. *Other liabilities and capital accounts* include the accumulated funds paid in to the regional Federal Reserve bank by member banks in the district for their stock. (The total paid in amounted to $1.8 billion.) Capital accounts also include the "profits" of the Federal Reserve, which are to be paid (back) to the U.S. Treasury, and accrued dividends for the 6 percent return on member bank stock.

Notice that Table 15-1 embodies the accounting identity that equates the total value of assets, something of value, with the total value of liabilities plus capital (or equity), the claims against the assets. It is a statement reflecting double-entry bookkeeping, the rule requiring everything to be entered at least twice.

Sources and Uses of Reserves

By rearranging the assets and liabilities in Table 15-1 and adding a few items from the Treasury, the accounting balance sheet for sources and uses of reserves shown in Table 15-3 is obtained (and estimates are shown in Table

TABLE 15-3   Sources and Uses of Private Depository Institutions'
Reserves

There are three changes from Table 15-1. Federal Reserve float is consolidated into one item. The currency created as a liability of the U.S. Treasury is added as a *source* of funds. The *use* of funds includes all the currency in circulation and cash held by the U.S. Treasury. This item does not include the Treasury's deposit accounts. The result is a listing of all the sources and uses for cash in the Federal Reserve, the U.S. Treasury, and in circulation (in private hands). The table is arranged so that the reserves (their cash) of depository institutions is the last item (8).

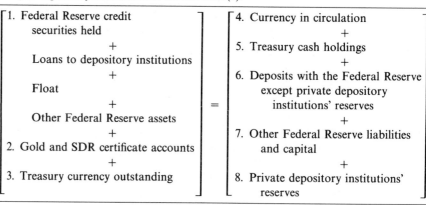

15-4). It is similar to the T-account in Table 15-1 except for these three changes:

1. Federal Reserve float has been consolidated into one item.
2. The currency created by the Treasury, "Treasury currency outstanding," is added as a source of funds. There was $17.4 billion of this currency.
3. The use of funds includes all the currency in circulation ($200.7 billion) and cash held by the Treasury ($.4 billion).

The changes bring into the picture all the currency and coin created by the U.S. Treasury and the Federal Reserve. The accounting record is arranged in Table 15-3 so that all the factors that supply funds that could be used for reserves are separated from all the factors that use these funds. The residual is the reserves of depository institutions.

Following convention, the assets of the Federal Reserve, except gold and the SDR certificate accounts, are brought under a variable called "Federal Reserve credit."

The sources and uses statement of private depository reserves is a useful classification for determining the effect of government transactions on reserves. For example, an open market operation in which the trading desk at the New York Federal Reserve bought U.S. securities would increase "Federal Reserve credit," item 1 in Table 15-3. One of the other items must change to preserve the identity that defines a use for every source of reserves. This identity is in the spirit of the saying "Everyone (a source) must be somewhere (a use)." Other things in the identity being the same, reserves of private institutions would increase.

The other items that are not likely to be changed by the open market purchase alone and therefore can be assumed to be constant are item 2, "Gold and SDR certificate accounts"; item 3, "Treasury currency outstanding"; item 2, "Treasury cash holdings"; and item 4, "other Federal Reserve liabilities and capital."

The other things that might change are as follows: The bond seller (to the Federal Reserve) may wish some cash. In that case, the Federal Reserve will increase its note issue, and so item 1, "currency in circulation," will increase. If the bond seller is a foreign central bank, the proceeds may be deposited at the Federal Reserve, which will increase item 3.

T A B L E 1 5 - 4   Estimates of the Sources and Uses of Private Depository Institutions' Reserves, December 1986 (in billions)

This table presents estimates, as given in the monthly *Federal Reserve Bulletin* (for December 1986), for the general categories shown in Table 15-3. This format for arraying these items is frequently used in reporting Federal Reserve activities, sometimes appearing weekly in the newspapers in connection with the announcement by the Federal Reserve of new money supply estimates. The trouble is that most readers of those statements probably do not know how it all fits together with government operations and what effect the changes in the items shown have on the monetary base and the money supply.

Supplying Reserve funds	
1. Federal Reserve credit*	
(4) Securities held	$200.6
(2) Loans to depository institutions	.9
(3–8) Federal Reserve float	.8
(5) Miscellaneous assets	17.0
2. (1b, 1c) Gold and SDR accounts	16.1
3. Treasury currency outstanding	17.4
Total	$252.8
Absorbing Reserve funds:	
1. Currency in circulation	$200.7
2. Treasury cash holdings	.5
3. (7) Deposits with Federal Reserve other than reserves	7.9
4. (9) Other Federal Reserve liabilities and capital	6.4
Total	$216.0
5. (7) Reserve accounts	36.8

* Consolidated for all twelve regional Federal Reserve banks.
Note: Numbers in parentheses refer to items in Table 15-1.
Source: Federal Reserve Bulletin, December 1986, p. A10.

THE GOVERNMENT BUDGET CONSTRAINT OR MONETARY BASE IDENTITY

U.S. Treasury Financing Transactions

A final useful identity is called the **government budget constraint** or **monetary base identity.**[1] This relationship will tie together the transactions of the government that affect not only the reserves of depository institutions but also the rest of the monetary base: currency and coin outside depository institutions.

An easy way to understand the Treasury's transactions is to ask how the Treasury finances the government deficit. The deficit is the difference between the expenditures for goods and services that the federal government buys, plus transfer payments and the taxes it collects. Notice that the question does not ask how deficits are financed by the federal government as a whole. That second question can be answered after the Federal Reserve is brought into the picture and the monetary base identity, in all its glory, shines forth.

Table 15-5 shows the different ways the Treasury and U.S. federal government agencies finance their deficits. They can sell bonds, item 2. The Treasury

TABLE 15-5   U.S. Treasury Financing of Its Deficit

The table shows that the U.S. Treasury can obtain funds to finance the federal deficit by borrowing (selling bonds, item 2) from its deposits (at the Federal Reserve, item 3, or private banks, item 5), from its cash holdings (item 4), or by increasing and using new cash (item 6). The Treasury directly puts into circulation only a small amount of cash and prints the rest for the Federal Reserve. This description of the financing of the federal deficit is incomplete without bringing in the Federal Reserve, which is done next.

Deficits (expenditures minus taxes)	equals	Sources of funds
1. [The deficit, *DEF*]	=	2. Bonds sold by Treasury (Treasury borrowing)*
		—
		3. Change in Treasury deposits at the Federal Reserve
		—
		4. Change in Treasury cash holdings
		—
		5. Change in Treasury deposits at private banks, ΔUS
		+
		6. Change in Treasury cash outstanding

* Sales of U.S. agency securities are included.

TABLE 15-6 The Monetary Base or Government Budget Constraint Identity*

In this table the Federal Reserve and the Treasury transactions are consolidated. The change in the monetary base on the left side of the table (item 1) is shown to be equal to the sum of all the different ways the monetary base can be changed on the right side of the table (items 2 through 7). For example, if the federal deficit increases and all the other items on the right side of the table are zero (meaning that there are no changes), the change in the monetary base will be the same amount as the change in the deficit.

$$
\begin{bmatrix}
\text{1. Change in the monetary base, } \Delta B \\
\quad \text{a. Change in reserves on deposit} \\
\qquad \text{at the Federal Reserve} \\
\qquad + \\
\quad \text{b. Change in currency} \\
\quad \text{(1) Held as reserves at depository} \\
\qquad \text{institutions (vault cash)} \\
\quad \text{(2) Held by the nonbank public}
\end{bmatrix}
=
\begin{bmatrix}
\text{2. The deficit } (DEF) \\
\quad + \\
\text{3. Purchase minus sale of bonds† by} \\
\quad \text{the Federal Reserve and the U.S.} \\
\quad \text{Treasury, } \Delta BOND \\
\text{4. Change in loans through the} \\
\quad \text{discount window, } \Delta DISC \\
\text{5. Change in Federal Reserve float,} \\
\quad \Delta FLOA \\
\quad + \\
\text{6. Change in government gold} \\
\quad \text{stock, } \Delta G \\
\quad + \\
\text{7. Change in Treasury accounts in} \\
\quad \text{private depository institutions,} \\
\quad \Delta US
\end{bmatrix}
$$

* All changes refer to dollar values of the changes.
† Recall, from Chapter 3, that *bonds* is a general term used for all debt instruments in this analysis.

can use the funds it has on deposit at the Federal Reserve, item 3; it can use its own cash holdings, item 4; or it can use its deposits at commercial banks, item 5. Finally, the Treasury can sometimes obtain funds by creating more of its own currency, item 6, though this alternative is no longer an important source of funds.

The monetary base identity shown in Table 15-6 is then obtained by (1) putting the items in Table 15-4 in the form of changes, (2) substituting into Table 15-4 the Treasury identity in Table 15-5, and (3) consolidating the variables. What comes out is a statement about the consolidated transactions of the Federal Reserve and the U.S. Treasury.[2] The government budget constraint or monetary base identity can also be viewed as the equality between the change in the monetary base and the different ways that it can be changed.

This second view will become clear if the symbols shown in Table 15-6 are written in quotation form:

$$\Delta B = DEF + \Delta BOND + \Delta FLOA + \Delta G + \Delta US + \Delta DISC \qquad (1)$$

The use of this identity in understanding the relationships between government transactions and the monetary base is illuminated by a closer examination of the individual variables.

The Federal Deficit

The **federal deficit** (*DEF*) is the cash value of the government's expenditures minus income, including goods, services, and transfer payments (mostly taxes) but excluding transactions in gold. It is item 2 in Table 15-6. This is a cash deficit as opposed to an accrual deficit. (An **accrual deficit** records taxes and expenditures at the time they become due rather than at the time the actual exchange of cash is made.)

If all the other components of the change in the monetary base on the right side of identity (1) are equal to zero, a deficit will increase the monetary base, and a surplus (a negative deficit) will decrease the monetary base. If, however, the deficit equals the value of government bond *sales* (the negative of bond purchases) to the public ($DEF = -\Delta BOND$), and the other components of the change in the monetary base equal zero, the change in the monetary base will be zero.

A deficit of this type, when it is accompanied by an equal amount of bond sales, was used as a policy variable by John Maynard Keynes in his famous book, *The General Theory of Employment, Interest, and Money*.[3] In Keynes's analysis, which became the foundation of much of macroeconomics, a **borrowed budgetary deficit** or **loan expenditure**, as he called it, was a major policy tool with which the government affected total real income. One of the most prominent controversies in the postwar period has been about the relative effects on nominal and real income of a borrowed budgetary deficit versus a change in the money supply. Identity (1) includes important government variables in this controversy, as it ties together the government's fiscal and monetary policy actions. **Pure fiscal policy** actions can be identified with the level of a borrowed federal deficit. This is a deficit that is "financed" by the equivalent of borrowing from the public, leaving the monetary base unchanged.[4] **Pure monetary policy** actions can be identified with a change in the monetary base (or a more broadly defined concept of money) when the deficit is zero.

In statistical tests of the effects of monetary and fiscal policy, neither the deficit nor the change in the monetary base is usually found to be equal to zero. An attempt is then made to isolate the separate effects of monetary and fiscal variables to be explained (such as real or nominal income).

Bond Transactions

The variable $\Delta BOND$ is the consolidated value of the purchases minus the sales of bonds by the Federal Reserve and the rest of the government to the public. This is item 3 in Table 15-6. If all the other variables on the right side of identity (1) are equal to zero, a purchase of bonds will increase the monetary base, and a sale of bonds will decrease the monetary base.

Federal Reserve Loans to Depository Institutions

Federal Reserve loans to depository institutions, or **discounts and advances**, $\Delta DISC$ in identity (1), is the net increase in these loans. When the Federal Reserve increases the volume of its loans to depository institutions, and other components of the change in the monetary base are equal to zero, the monetary base increases.

Float

An increase in item 5 in Table 15-6, "Federal Reserve float," $\Delta FLOA$, increases the monetary base (see Chapter 8).

TAX AND LOAN ACCOUNTS

Until 1978, substantial amounts of federal government funds were placed on deposit in commercial banks at a zero rate of interest return. Most of these funds were in **tax and loan accounts**, which are Treasury accounts authorized to receive corporate income taxes, excise taxes, unemployment insurance taxes, and payroll withholding taxes.[5] The commercial bank receiving these funds gives the depositor a depository receipt, which is used when his or her next tax form is sent to the Internal Revenue Service, as evidence that the tax was paid. Because the commercial bank could buy income-earning assets with these funds, they were specially profitable before 1978.

The profitability of tax and loan accounts to private banks was reduced by a 1977 law, which took effect in November 1978. It required each tax and loan private bank depository to select one of two options. It could either pay interest to the Treasury on its tax and loan balance (the **note option**) or immediately—by the next day—remit to the Treasury any such fund received (the **remittance option**). Under the note option, the bank pays an interest equal to 25 fewer basis points than the average federal funds rate for the week. Thus, if the federal funds rate is 12 percent, the bank will pay the Treasury 11.75 percent. Funds held under the remittance option are subject to regular reserve requirements, but funds credited to the note option are free from reserve requirements.

During December 1983, the Treasury had $23.9 billion in tax and loan accounts and $7.5 billion in its accounts at the Federal Reserve banks. From November 1978, when the banks started paying interest on their tax and loan accounts, until August 1979, the Treasury balances averaged $5.9 billion in the tax and loan accounts and $3.8 billion at the Federal Reserve. During this period, the Treasury received $540 million in interest payments from the private banks on these tax and loan balances and $3 million in late charges for funds that were not sent by the next day under the remittance option.

It is frequently argued that government deposits of tax proceeds in private bank accounts (tax and loan accounts) promote monetary stability because they do not change the monetary base. In identity (1), the tax payment by the taxpayer is a **surplus** or **negative deficit**, which is equal to an offsetting change in government deposits at commercial banks.

$$DEF + \Delta US = 0 \qquad (2)$$

The monetary base is constant.

The deposit of tax proceeds into tax and loan accounts, however, does change the money supply, though by less than if the taxes were deposited in the Treasury's account at the Federal Reserve. Government deposits at private banks are not part of the private money supply, defined as M-1, so that the money supply declines with the transfer of funds from private to government accounts, though by not as much as if the monetary base changed. Of course, the Federal Reserve could rapidly offset changes in the monetary base through open market operations.

Government Deposits at Private Depositories

The change in government deposits at commercial banks, ΔUS, is part of the monetary base identity. This is because a change in these deposits, when the other components of the right-hand side of identity (1) equal zero, changes the monetary base. The Treasury may withdraw funds from its deposits at commercial banks and deposit them at its account at the Federal Reserve, thereby reducing the size of the monetary base.

The Treasury uses its accounts at the Federal Reserve banks for making payments, by shifting the money stored in deposits at commercial banks to the Federal Reserve accounts. Commercial banks are usually given advance warning if the Treasury expects to make a withdrawal. The Federal Reserve System, acting as the agent for the Treasury, announces a **call date** and the percentage of funds that the Treasury expects to withdraw.

Gold

Item 6 in Table 15-6 is the change in the stock of gold, ΔG, held by the federal government and measured by the cash value of transactions in gold. For example, when the Treasury buys $100 in gold, the monetary base will rise by $100 if all the other components of ΔB in equation (1) equal zero.

Only the value of the dollars actually exchanged for gold is used to compute ΔG. A change in the value of the Treasury's gold stock, arising from the way it is valued (capital gains and losses), has no effect on the monetary base. For example, in 1934, the official U.S. price of gold was raised from the price of a year earlier, which was $20.67 an ounce, to $35.00 an ounce. This action by iteself had no effect on the monetary base. In August 1971, the U.S. Treasury ceased an unlimited commitment to buy and sell gold from foreigners; that is, the " gold window" was closed. Since 1971, the Treasury has occasionally sold some of its gold at market prices.

Expanding and Contracting the Monetary Base

Any combination of changes in the variables on the right side of identity (1) that add up to a positive number will increase the monetary base. The government can then be said to be expanding the monetary base, or **running the**

TABLE 15-7   T-Accounts Reflecting Balance Sheet Entries from $100 Purchase of Gold by the U.S. Treasury

The bookkeeping entries of a Treasury gold transaction with the private sector have been found to be as fascinating as any other story about those shiny ingots of precious metals, which are buried in vaults and believed to mysteriously "back the money supply in circulation." Suppose Reginald Marsh sells $100 in gold to the Treasury. Marsh receives a $100 deposit, which is placed in his account at Southwest National Bank, which thereby also gains $100 in reserves, items 1 and 2 in the T-accounts in Table 15-7. The Treasury pays Marsh by a check against its account at the Federal Reserve (items 3, 4, and 5) and the Treasury increases its gold stock, item 6. Next, Southwestern National Bank clears Marsh's check at the Federal Reserve bank (items 7 and 8).

But this is not the end of the story. The Treasury replenishes its account at the Federal Reserve by giving the Federal Reserve a gold certificate, for which the Treasury receives $100 (items 9, 10, 11, and 12).

When the Treasury sells gold, the gold is frequently moved by armored car from the U.S. Assay Office in New York on the East River five blocks to the Federal Reserve Bank of New York on Liberty Street. The Federal Reserve vault is 50 feet below sea level and 76 feet below street level. Many foreign countries also store some of their gold in this vault at the New York Federal Reserve Bank. Each working day, gold bars are wheeled between the various countries' storage compartments, on instructions for international payments, rather than the countries' incurring expensive shipping and insurance charges from transporting gold between countries.

It is a weird and fascinating sight if one understands the implications. Men far underground, with steel covers over their shoes (to prevent injury if one of the bars drops), tote bars between compartments in the basement of the New York Federal Reserve Bank to settle a debt between Norway and Germany that arose from sardine imports into Germany. Many of the gold bars weight 400 troy ounces (12 troy ounces to a pound), or $33\frac{1}{3}$ pounds. They rose in price from $14,000 in 1971 (at $35 a troy ounce) to $334,000 in 1980 (at $835 per troy ounce), then back down to $168,000 in March 1983 (at $420 per troy ounce). Many of these bars are stamped with the insignia of the Soviet Union, which, along with South Africa, mines much of the world's gold.

U.S. Treasury		Federal Reserve		Southwest National Bank	
Period 1 $100 gold (6); −$100 deposit at FRB (5)		−$100 reserves (3); $100 reserves (8)	−$100 Treasury deposit (4); $100 deposit from Southwest National Bank (7)	$100 reserves (2)	$100 deposit to Marsh (1)
Period 2 $100 deposit at F.R. (9)	$100 gold certificate outstanding (10)	$100 gold certificate (11)	$100 Treasury deposit (12)		

printing press and putting the money in circulation. The name often given to these relationships is **financing**. If, for example, a deficit of $10 billion occurs in the same period in which $10 billion in bonds are sold to the public by the U.S. treasury, the deficit is said to be *financed by borrowing*. However, if many variables change in the period of the deficit, there will be no mileage to be gained in economic analysis by pretending that particular sources of funds are earmarked for the deficit and other sources are not.

STUDY QUESTIONS

1. What are the differences between the balance sheet of assets and liabilities of the Federal Reserve and the sources-and-uses-of-reserves statement?

2. What is the government budget constraint, and how is it related to the accounting records in Study Question 1?

3. What are pure fiscal and pure monetary policy, and how are they related to the monetary base?

4. Can the monetary base be changed in a period in which there is no government deficit?

5. How can you estimate the federal deficit if the two things you do not know are government expenditures and government taxes? (A complete answer is given in Auerbach's article, in note 1, but you can find the general solution yourself using identity (1).)

6. What strange things do people do with gold 76 feet below the ground in New York City?

7. Show, using T-accounts, the transactions involved in a $1 billion sale of gold by the U.S. Treasury to the public.

8. If $10.5 billion are withheld from payroll as withholding taxes and are paid to the U.S. Treasury, which holds it in accounts at commercial banks, how will the monetary base be changed, if at all?

9. If the federal government runs a deficit and adds all current tax proceeds to tax and loan accounts, will its expenditures be completely financed by bond sales equal in value to the size of the deficit and its tax proceeds? (*Hint:* Do Practice Problem 3 first.)

10. The Federal Reserve returns the interest it earns on government securities to the Treasury. This reduces the size of the federal deficit recorded by the government. Is this transfer of funds either fiscal or monetary policy, or is it neither? Would the transfer of the paid-in surplus from the member bank payments to the Federal Reserve (mentioned in the last chapter) be part of monetary or fiscal policy, or would it also be neither? The fact that such payments reduce the recorded federal deficit tells us what about the effect on the economy of the recorded deficit? (Do you think that such a transfer would stimulate private spending or even affect private spending in any way?) Why have some members of Congress praised the transfer of the paid-in surplus to the Treasury, declaring that the federal deficit would be reduced by this simple bookkeeping transaction? Would an authorization for the Federal Reserve to take money from its vaults and give it to the Treasury be equivalent in its effects on the economy and the deficit? Could the deficit thereby be reduced to zero? In your answer, distinguish cosmetic bookkeeping from meaningful economic changes that affect the economy.

Calculation Guide to use with the Practice Problems on the Monetary Base Identity (or Government Budget Constraint)

The seemingly complex sets of government transactions in the five problems can easily be analyzed for their direct effect on the monetary base by simply substituting the values into the variables of identity (1) at the top of the table, the monetary base identity. Much of the confusion and many of the mistakes that have arisen in discussions of the direct relationships of fiscal policy and other types of government transactions with the monetary base and the money supply can be eliminated by using this procedure.

$$\Delta B = DEF + \Delta BOND + \Delta DISC + \Delta FLOA + \Delta G + \Delta US$$

Change in the Monetary Base	Deficit	Bonds Purchased Minus Bonds Sold by Government	Change in Loans Through Discount Window	Change in Federal Reserve Float	Change in Government Gold Stock	Change in Treasury Accounts in Depository Institutions
1.						
2.						
3.						
4.						
5.						

FIVE PRACTICE PROBLEMS ON THE MECHANICAL RELATIONSHIPS BETWEEN THE COMPONENTS OF THE CHANGE IN THE MONETARY BASE

The following problems are designed to give you practice with the monetary base (or government budget constraint) identity. Use the accompanying table as a calculation guide for your answers. Fill in the appropriate boxes with the information given in each problem. Calculate the change in the monetary base as you finish posting the data for each problem. By the time you get to Problem 5, it will appear extremely simple, although trying to answer this problem without the identity would be very difficult. When you have completed the exercise, check your answers against those at the end of the chapter.

In each of the following problems, calculate the change in the monetary base, and show how your answer is derived:

1. The government incurs a deficit of $100 ($DEF = \$100$) in the same period in which $100 in bonds are sold ($\Delta BOND = -\$100$); the sum of the other components of the change in the monetary base is zero.

2. The government incurs a deficit of $100 ($DEF = \$100$). All other components of the change in the monetary base sum to zero.

3. The government incurs a deficit of $200 ($DEF = \$200$) in the same period in which all tax receipts of $100 are deposited in tax and loan accounts ($\Delta US = \$100$) and all other components of the change in the monetary base sum to zero.

4. The government purchases $10 in gold ($\Delta G = \$10$) in the same period in which Federal Reserve bank float increases by $20 ($\Delta FLOA = \$20$) and the government incurs a $30 surplus ($DEF = -\$30$).

5. The Federal Reserve buys $100 in bonds ($\Delta BOND = \$100$), and the Treasury makes a call on tax and loan accounts of $50 ($\Delta US = -\$50$). The Treasury sells $50 in bonds to the public ($\Delta BOND = -\$50$), and the government runs a $70 deficit ($DEF = \$70$).

ANSWERS TO PRACTICE PROBLEMS

1. The aggregate change in the monetary base is then zero. The deficit is a borrowed deficit, financed by bond sales.
2. The deficit is financed by "printing" money ($\Delta B = \$100$).
3. The monetary base must increase by $300 ($\Delta B = \$300$). The answer might not sound intuitively correct, even though it is consistent with the identity. This is the explanation: If the government's expenditures minus receipts (which form the deficit) equal $200 and the taxes (the receipts) are $100, then the expenditures will be $300. Because the full tax income was redeposited in Treasury accounts at private depositories, the $300 in

expenditures had to come from a new money issue (or its equivalent, such as a check against the Treasury deposits at the Federal Reserve).
4. The monetary base is constant.
5. The monetary base increases by $70.

GLOSSARY

Accrual deficit. A record of the deficit that shows expenditures and taxes when they become due instead of when the actual cash payments are made.

Borrowed budgetary deficit (or **loan expenditure**). Deficit financed by borrowing (selling bonds).

Call date. For tax and loan accounts, the date on which the Treasury will make a withdrawal.

Discounts and advances. Loans from the Federal Reserve to depository institutions.

Federal deficit. The expenditures on goods, services, and transfer payment to the private sector minus the receipts from the private sector (mostly tax receipts).

Financing. A method of obtaining funds for making a payment.

Government budget constraint. See **Monetary base identity.**

Monetary base identity (or **government budget constraint**). The accounting identity between the change in the monetary base and the sum of the different ways in which it is changed, classified by commonly used concepts such as the *deficit* and *government bond pur-*

chases.

Negative deficit. See **Surplus.**

Note option. One of two options for private depositories receiving government deposits in which interest is paid to the Treasury on the balance

Pure fiscal policy. A deficit (or surplus) financed by borrowing (or lending), leaving the monetary base constant.

Pure monetary policy. A change in the monetary base with no deficit or surplus.

Remittance option. One of two options for private depositories receiving government deposits, in which the funds are immediately remitted to the Treasury.

Running the printing press. An informal way of describing a government-implemented increase in the monetary base.

Surplus. The negative of a deficit for the federal government, when taxes exceed expenditures on goods, services, and transfer payments to the private sector.

Tax and loan accounts. U.S. Treasury accounts at private depositories used to receive tax revenues.

NOTES

1. The concept of the government budget constraint was developed by Carl Christ in "A Model of Monetary and Fiscal Policy Effects on the Money Stocks, Price Level and Real Output," *Journal of Money, Credit and*

Banking, November 1969, pp. 683–705; and by Robert Auerbach in "An Estimation Procedure for the Federal Cash Deficit Applied to the United States Interwar Period, 1920–1941," *Western Economic Journal*, December 1972, pp. 474–476. This derivation includes the variable for changes in Treasury deposits at private depositories.

2. A complete consolidation requires that the goods and services supplied by the Federal Reserve minus the service charges collected be added to the deficit. However, this is a minor correction and is noted only to emphasize that the Federal Reserve must be consolidated with the rest of the federal government in this analysis.

3. John Maynard Keynes, *The General Theory of Employment, Interest, and Money* (New York: Harcourt Brace, 1964), pp. 98, 128–129, footnote 1.

4. Usually pure fiscal policy is associated with a constant level of some broader monetary aggregate, such as M-1.

5. See the Federal Reserve Bank of Cleveland, "The Influence of Government Deposits on the Money Supply," *Economic Commentary*, June 28, 1971; and Richard W. Lang, "TTL Note Accounts and the Money Supply Process," *Review*, Federal Reserve Bank of St. Louis, vol. 61, October 1979, pp. 3–14.

CHAPTER 16

MONETARY POLICY TOOLS

CHAPTER PREVIEW

Introduction. The Federal Reserve has three major monetary tools.

The Desk in Action. The monetary base can be changed by billions of dollars in 30 minutes.

Discounts and Advances. Loans to depository institutions can also change the monetary base. The volume of these loans depends on the spread between the federal funds rate and the discount rate and the effect of nonprice rationing methods.

Reserve Requirements. This is an instrument of the Federal Reserve that can change the profits of depository institutions and the money supply, but not the monetary base.

The Treasury Draw. These are direct loans from the Federal Reserve to the Treasury, up to a limit of $5 billion.

Appendix: Management of the Monetary Base from 1862 to the Establishment of the Federal Reserve System. The Treasury had central banking responsibilities before the Federal Reserve was established. The Treasury's management of the monetary base was to a large extent a passive one because of the return to a gold standard in 1879.

INTRODUCTION

The three major tools of monetary policy (tools that can be used to affect the supply of money) are *open market operations, loans to depository institutions* (discounts and advances), and *reserve requirement changes.* The first two of these policy tools involve the purchase or sale of debt instruments, which causes the monetary base to increase or decrease, respectively. Open market operations consist of the purchase or sale of bonds to the public sector, whereas loans to depository institutions consist of granting and retiring loans. The third Federal Reserve policy tool, changes in member bank reserve requirements, affects the amount of money that depository institutions can create per dollar of reserves.

The following three sections will discuss these monetary tools, and the final section will describe direct loans by the Federal Reserve to the Treasury, called the Treasury draw.

THE DESK IN ACTION

The Federal Reserve system's open market manager, who manages open market operations at the New York Federal Reserve trading desk, often begins the day with early morning conferences with dealers in the New York money market. It is said that they do this to "get a feel for the market." They share information about the prices, yields, quantities, and qualities of debt instruments traded the day before, as well as the opinions of money market dealers.

The open market manager consults the FOMC instructions and may participate in a number of telephone conferences with the Board of Governors (members or staff) and occasionally with all the members of the FOMC in Washington, D.C., and the regional banks. The chairman of the Board of Governors and the FOMC may, in our hypothetical example, say, "O.K., that action seems proper this morning." The open market manager may then consult with the Treasury by phone to check on any transactions it may be making that would affect the monetary base. The manager then decides, "We'll go into the market at 10:30 (A.M.) and buy $3.5 billion."

The open market manager walks into the room on the eighth floor of the New York Federal Reserve Bank, where the trading desk is located. Approximately ten security traders are seated at several rows of desks against a backdrop of an array of yields and prices of debt instruments that covers two walls. Each trader has a telephone console on his or her desk that is connected with 3 or 4 of the 35 (the number in 1986, listed in Table 16-1) approved private dealers in the U.S. government securities market. They must be approved by the Federal Reserve. The private dealers are, in turn, brokers for large private customers, such as commercial banks, insurance companies, and large finance companies.

TABLE 16-1 Government Securities Primary Dealers and Brokers, 1986

The Federal Reserve designates a group of securities dealers and commercial banks as primary dealers. They are required to demonstrate their market-making capacity, creditworthiness, and other factors that indicate their fitness for a business relationship with the Federal Reserve. The Federal Reserve uses them exclusively in its purchases and sales of securities for monetary policy purposes.

Bank Dealers

Bank of America NT&SA
Bankers Trust Company
Chase Manhattan Government Securities, Inc.
Chemical Bank
Citibank, N.A.
Continental Illinois National Bank and Trust Company of Chicago
Crocker National Bank
First National Bank of Chicago
First Interstate Bank of California
Harris Trust and Savings Bank
Manufacturers Hanover Trust Company
Morgan Guaranty Trust Company of New York
Carroll McEntee & McGinley Incorporated
Irving Securities, Inc.

Registered Dealers

Bear, Stearns & Co., Inc.
Donaldson, Lufkin & Jenrette Securities Corporation
The First Boston Corporation
Goldman, Sachs & Co.
E. F. Hutton & Company, Inc.
Kidder, Peabody & Co., Incorporated
Morgan Stanley & Co., Incorporated
Paine Webber Jackson & Curtis, Incorporated
Prudential-Bache Securities, Inc.
Salomon Brothers, Inc.
Dean Witter Reynolds, Inc.
Greenwich Capital Markets, Inc.

Unregistered Dealers

Discount Corporation of New York
Drexel Burnham Lambert Government Securities, Inc.
Aubrey G. Lanston & Co., Inc.
Lehman Government Securities, Inc.
Merrill Lynch Government Securities, Inc.
Wm. E. Pollock Government Securities, Inc.
Refco Partners
Smith Barney Government Securities, Inc.
Kleinwort Benson Government Securities

TABLE 16-1 (continued)

Chapdelaine & Co., Inc.
Fundamental Brokers, Inc.
Garban Ltd.
Hilliard Farber and Company, Inc.
Liberty Brokerage Inc.
MKI Government Brokers, Inc.
RMJ Securities Corporation
Cantor Fitzgerald Securities Corp. (Telerate—available to the public)
Newcomb Securities Company, Inc. (Reuter— available to the public)

* Primary dealer status is determined solely by the Federal Reserve Bank of New York.
Source: U.S. General Accounting Office, *U.S. Treasury Securities, the Market's Structure, Risks, and Regulation,* Briefing Report to the Chairman, Subcommittee on Domestic Banking, Finance and Urban Affairs, House of Representatives, August 1986, pp. 21, 88, 89.

The open market manager's assistant tells the traders to notify the market. The traders push the buttons on their consoles, and via private lines, buzzers sound in the trading rooms of the dealers in the special government securities markets. The Federal Reserve trader announces, "We will be in the market shortly," and then hangs up. Sirens have sounded in the government securities markets: Billions of dollars of securities will be bought or sold in the next half-hour.

Then the second round commences ten minutes later, shortly after 10:40 A.M. The Federal Reserve traders tell the private dealers which securities the Federal Reserve will purchase. The phone calls are then terminated, and the private dealers may reconnoiter, perhaps by phone, with some of their customers. These customers may be domestic commercial banks and domestic insurance and finance companies.

Suppose, for example, that the buy list includes a particular maturity of U.S. Treasury notes and that a bank, First Bank of Kansas City, Missouri, wishes to sell $10 million of these notes. The dealer informs a Federal Reserve trader of the First Bank offer (the price and quantity) in one of several rounds of calls to the private dealers. Within 30 minutes from the time the initial calls were made, the open market manager calls for a last round, and the auction ends. The quantities and asking prices given by the dealers are recorded on separate pieces of paper. The open market manager and his or her assistants place the pieces of paper on a large board at the end of the room in order of the asking price (lowest first). He or she then selects for purchase $3.5 billion of the offers with the lowest asking prices to sell. The traders call the private dealers and notify them which offers to sell have been accepted. Three-and-one-half billion dollars in U.S. Treasury notes have been purchased by the open market desk, with delivery and payment on the same day. The monetary base is thus increased by $3.5 billion.

First Bank of Kansas City, Missouri, which offered, through its private dealer in the government securities market, to sell $10 million in U.S. Treasury notes, has an acceptable offer. The Kansas City Federal Reserve Bank wire room receives the acceptance through the Federal Reserve's special wire service. First Bank can take delivery of cash in an armored truck or, more likely, deposit funds in its account at the Federal Reserve for reinvestment in the money markets later in the same day. The securities sold by First Bank are already at the Federal Reserve of Kansas City, Missouri. The Federal Reserve provides vault and inventory services for the banks' securities.

The records of open market operations of the Federal Reserve through Wednesday, together with estimates of changes in the U.S. money supply, are accumulated and usually released to the press at a weekly press conference in New York City.[1]

The Federal Reserve conducts most of its open market operations (over 95 percent) in repurchase agreements, which were discussed in Chapter 12. The desk purchases securities from a dealer under a contract, which obligates the dealer to repurchase the securities at a specified price on or before a particular date. The interest dealers pay on the money they receive is determined by the same open market auctions. These contracts are called *repurchase agreements* or, simply, *repos*. They have the same effect on the monetary base as does an outright purchase of securities: They expand the monetary base. Repurchase agreements are not made by the Federal Reserve for more than fifteen days.

The Federal Reserve's open market operations can be said to be either dynamic or defensive. **Dynamic open market operations** are performed to affect bank reserves and thereby to affect the money supply and interest rates. **Defensive open market operations** are designed to offset disturbances to the level of bank reserves. These disturbances can arise from operations of the Treasury and government agencies, which affect bank reserves, as shown by the monetary base identity in the last chapter. They also arise from changes in the distribution of deposits in the banking system (which affects the amount of required reserves held by depository institutions) and from numerous other sources, discussed in the next chapter. The application of this classification to short-run Federal Reserve operations is somewhat blurred for individuals outside the Federal Reserve. This is because it is very difficult, if not frequently impossible, to determine whether the Federal Reserve is purposely moving to a new target or is offsetting a disturbance.

DISCOUNTS AND ADVANCES

The Federal Reserve Act of 1913 gave to each of the Federal Reserve banks the authority to make loans to private commercial banks that were members of the Federal Reserve System. The Depository Institutions Deregulation and Monetary Control Act of 1980 gave all depository institutions (credit unions, savings and loan associations, mutual savings banks, and all commercial banks) that have checkable accounts access to these loans on an equal basis. With the authorization in the same law for nationwide checkable accounts for all depository institutions, the number of eligible borrowers increased from slightly over 5,600 member banks in 1980 to over 35,952 depository institutions in 1986.

These loans are of two forms, *discounts* (sometimes called *rediscounts*) and *advances*, although they both are usually referred to as *discounting*. Certain types of commercial, agricultural, and industrial paper may be given to the Reserve banks by member banks in return for a loan equal to the value of the collateral minus a discount, that is, a discounted loan. A depository institution may also obtain a direct advance on which interest must be paid and against which eligible paper must be deposited with the Reserve bank. Virtually all

FIGURE 16-1   Short-Term Interest Rates, 1929–1982 (discount rate, effective date of change; all others, quarterly averages).

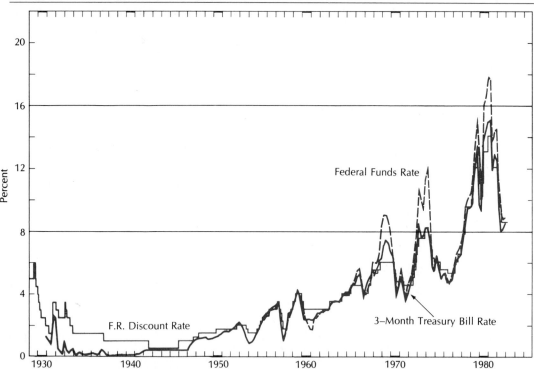

This historical record of the relationship of the discount rate to the Treasury bill rate and the federal funds rate shows periods when the spread (between market rates and the discount rate) was negative (1930s to the early 1940s) and periods when it was positive (during the peak interest periods in the 1970s and 1980s).

Source: Board of Governors of the Federal Reserve System, *Historical Chartbook, 1983,* p. 98.

FIGURE 16-2   Short-Term Monthly Interest Rates, 1966–1986

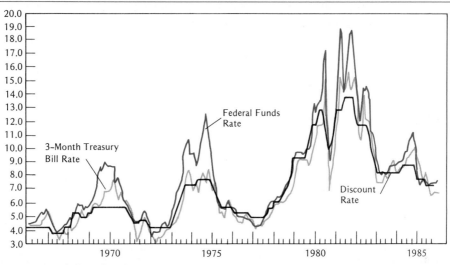

The twenty-year period ending in 1986 contains periods of sharply rising market interest rates in which the discount rate was substantially lower than the market rates. The low points in the market interest rate series also are below the discount rate. This pattern suggests that the discount rate is not changed to match completely the large changes in market interest rates. In addition—and this is counter to much media coverage and much folk knowledge of the discount rate—there is no evidence to suggest that discount rate changes consistently lead market rate changes. Generally, the changes in the Treasury bill rates reach a peak (a high point) or a trough (a low point) well before the discount rate changes. This evidence suggests that it is wrong to view the Federal Reserve as directly controlling market interest rates with discount rate changes—something like pulling a big lever at the Board of Governors to a desired interest rate, which then becomes the equilibrium rate in world markets for U.S. Treasury bills.

Source: Cambridge Planning and Analytics Inc., Boston.

borrowing is currently in the form of advances against which government securities are used as collateral.

The interest rate charged by the Reserve bank to the depository institution is called the *discount rate*. Each Federal Reserve bank's board of directors sets each Federal Reserve bank's discount rates at least once each month, subject to the approval of the Board of Governors. This has usually meant in the post–World War II period that the Board initiates a discount rate and the twelve regional Federal Reserve banks adopt it within two weeks. The discount rates from 1930 to 1986 are shown in Figures 16-1 and 16-2.

The officials at the Federal Reserve banks may deny a depository institution permission for a loan. The exact effect of nonprice rationing (including the threat of denial) on the volume of depository institution borrowing is difficult to determine. No precise policy of influencing banks is discernible, although the objectives of member bank borrowing privileges have frequently been studied, and the original Federal Reserve Act has been amended to redefine the objectives a number of times.[2]

The Federal Reserve was originally created "to furnish an elastic currency, to afford means of rediscounting commercial paper" as well as "to establish a more effective supervision of banking in the United States and for other purposes."[3] The instructions to furnish an **elastic currency**, if it refers to the entire money supply, are part of the commercial bills, or *real bills*, the doctrine of the "banking school." (See Chapter 7 for more details.) This doctrine asserts that an expansion of the money supply will not be inflationary if it is used to finance the needs of trade. Even open market operations were written into the Federal Reserve Acts as amended in 1933 and 1935, with the stipulation the "open market operations shall be governed with a view to accommodating commerce and business and with a regard to their bearing upon the general credit situation of the country."[4]

The major monetary tool of the Federal Reserve was originally *not* intended to be open market operations. The Federal Reserve was to be the "lender of the last resort" in the case of banking panics and to furnish loans to the member banks to support the needs of trade. The Federal Reserve Act, as amended (Section 13a, part 2), stipulates that "any Federal Reserve bank may discount notes, drafts, and bills of exchange arising out of actual commercial transactions; that is, notes, drafts, and bills of exchange issued or drawn for agricultural, industrial, or commercial purposes, or the proceeds of which have been used, or are to be used, for such purposes ... nothing in this Act contained shall be construed to prohibit such notes, overdrafts, and bills of exchange, secured by staple agricultural products, or other goods, wares, or merchandise from being eligible for such discounts."

Reserve banks were given permission to make loans to member banks that used U.S. government securities as collateral in order to finance World War I defense expenditures. The commercial banks bought securities from the Treasury and replenished their reserves by borrowing from the Federal Reserve. Lower preferential rates were established on member bank borrowings, for which government securities were used as collateral during World War I and World War II.

EXAMPLES OF DISCOUNT WINDOW TRANSACTIONS

Example 1   It is Wednesday afternoon at a regional bank, and the bank is required to have enough funds in its reserve account at its Federal Reserve Bank to meet its reserve requirement over the previous two weeks. The bank finds that it must borrow in order to make up its reserve deficiency, but the money center (that is, the major New York, Chicago, and California) banks have apparently been borrowing heavily in the federal funds market. As a result, the rate on fed funds on this particular Wednesday afternoon has soared far above its level earlier that day. As far as the funding officer of the regional bank is concerned, the market for funds at a price she considers acceptable has "dried up." She calls the Federal Reserve Bank for a discount regional loan.

Example 2 A West Coast regional bank, which generally avoids borrowing at the discount window, expects to receive a wire transfer of $300 million from a New York bank, but by late afternoon the money has not yet shown up. It turns out that the sending bank had due to an error accidentally sent only $3,000 instead of the $300 million. Although the New York bank is legally liable for the correct amount, it is closed by the time the error is discovered. In order to make up the deficiency in its reserve position, the West Coast bank calls the discount window for a loan.

Example 3 It is Wednesday reserve account settlement at another bank, and the funding officer notes that the spread between the discount rate and fed funds rate has widened slightly. Since his bank is buying fed funds to make up a reserve deficiency, he decides to borrow part of the reserve deficiency from the discount window in order to take advantage of the spread. Over the next few months, this repeats itself until the bank receives an "informational" call from the discount officer at the Federal Reserve Bank, inquiring as to the reason for the apparent pattern in discount window borrowing. Taking the hint, the bank refrains from continuing the practice on subsequent Wednesday settlements.

Example 4 A money center bank acts as a clearing agent for the government securities market. This means that the bank maintains book-entry securities accounts for market participants, and that it also maintains a reserve account and a book-entry securities account at its Federal Reserve Bank, so that

securities transactions can be cleared through this system. One day, an internal computer problem arises that allows the bank to accept securities but not to process them for delivery to dealers, brokers, and other market participants. The bank's reserve account is debited for the amount of these securities, but it is unable to pass them on and collect payment for them, resulting in a growing overdraft in the reserve account. As close of business approaches, it becomes increasingly clear that the problem will not be fixed in time to collect the required payments from the securities buyers. In order to avoid a negative reserve balance at the end of the day, the bank estimates its anticipated reserve account deficiency and goes to the Federal Reserve Bank discount window for a loan for that amount. The computer problem is fixed and the loan is repaid the following day.

Example 5 Due to mismanagement, a privately insured savings and loan association fails. Out of concern about the condition of other privately insured thrift institutions in the state, depositors begin to withdraw their deposits, leading to a run. Because they are not federally insured, some otherwise sound thrifts are not able to borrow from the Federal Home Loan Bank Board in order to meet the demands of the depositors. As a result, the regional Federal Reserve Bank is called upon to lend to these thrifts. After an extensive examination of the collateral the thrifts could offer, the Reserve Bank makes loans to them until they are able to get federal insurance and attract back enough deposits to pay back the discount window loans.

Source: David Mengle, "The Discount Window," *Economic Review*, Federal Reserve Bank of Richmond, May–June 1986, p. 3.

During the 1920s, officials of the Federal Reserve System were concerned about the allocation of bank loans, and the large flow of bank credit into the stock market. They thus attempted to prevent member banks from making loans for the purpose of speculating on stocks. Federal Reserve officials, however, did not wish to raise the discount rate because that would make it harder for banks to finance the "legitimate" needs of trade. On February 2, 1929, the Federal Reserve Board sent a letter to the Federal Reserve banks, which stated that

> The Federal Reserve Act does not, in the opinion of the Federal Reserve Board, contemplate the use of resources of the Federal Reserve Banks in the creation or extension of speculative credit. A member bank is not within its reasonable claims for discount facilities at its Federal Reserve bank when it borrows either for the purpose of making speculative loans or for the purpose of maintaining speculative loans.[5]

Individual Reserve banks managed their discount window in different ways. Member banks that were frequent borrowers or member banks that were considered to be in poor financial condition faced the possibility of being examined more frequently. Member banks were advised on the proper use of the discounting facilities. In 1928, just before the calamitous depressions of the 1930s, the Federal Reserve Board went so far as to state, "It is a generally recognized principle that Reserve bank credit should not be used for profits. . . ."[6] Member bank borrowing was not at a high level during the 1930s: In December 1939, member banks borrowed a daily average of $3 million.

In the post–World War II period, there has been extensive use of discount facilities. In 1945, the daily average December borrowing amounted to $334 million. Borrowing rose to nearly $3.5 billion in 1974, partly because of a loan of $1.75 billion to the troubled Franklin National Bank in New York, which failed. At the end of December 1982, borrowings of depository institutions were $700 million, as shown in the list of Federal Reserve assets in the last chapter.

Although most borrowing is for short periods—no more than a few days—under Regulation A, as amended in August 1976, a seasonal borrowing privilege for longer-term borrowing was liberalized. Banks suffering seasonal deposit drains borrow for as long as four weeks. Also, following the Depository Institutions Deregulation and Monetary Control Act of 1980, which opened the discount window to thrifts, there has been an extended credit facility for S&Ls.

Emergency loans were made in 1982 to depository institutions that were in trouble, as this 1983 report from the San Francisco Federal Bank indicates:

Credit Activity

The Bank continued to assist depository institutions in meeting their liquidity needs by providing funds through the discount window. In 1982, 105 Twelfth District institutions, including five thrift institutions, had occasion to borrow from the Federal Reserve. While most of these institutions borrowed for short-term adjustment purposes, several borrowed under seasonal lines of credit or to meet longer-term liquidity needs.

Each of the five offices of the District experienced a large increase in the amount of collateral pledged by institutions to secure potential borrowings at the discount window. At year-end the Reserve Bank held $18.5 billion in collateral accounts, an increase of $7.3 billion (65 percent) from the $11.2 billion level at year-end 1981.

Emergency loans were made in 1982 to seven institutions having serious financial difficulties. Working closely with other federal and state supervisory agencies, the District Credit Unit administered loans to enable these institutions to stay afloat pending mergers with stronger institutions or to regain financial health. By year-end, three of the institutions had merged with other institutions.

A major accomplishment of the Credit Unit during the year was the implementation of the Qualified Loan Review (QLR) program. The QLR program provides that qualifying institutions may pledge certain types of customer paper as collateral for advances at the discount window and for Treasury Tax and Loan deposits without the Reserve Banks' prior analysis and approval of the financial condition and credit-worthiness of the pledging institution's customers. To qualify for participation in the QLR program an institution must, in the judgement of its supervising agency and the Reserve Bank, be in sound financial condition and have a satisfactory internal loan review and examination program.[7]

The level of the federal discount rate, taken by itself, is a misleading determinant of the quantity of loans demanded from the Federal Reserve by banks. Rather, it is the *spread* between money market rates on other relatively risk-free, short-term debt instruments—primarily the federal funds rate—and the discount rate that should be used in predicting bank borrowing (see Figure 16-3). If the discount rate is lower than other short-term money market rates, banks will have an incentive to increase their profits by obtaining loans from the Reserve banks rather than from these more expensive sources. When the discount rate is below other short-term market rates of interest, banks receive a subsidy from the Federal Reserve in the form of a discount from market rates of interest. Of course there are nonpecuniary costs such as actually receiving, or the threat of receiving, a scolding at the discount window. The banks will include these costs in their decision making.

Therefore, the spread between the Federal Reserve discount rate and other short-term market rates of interest is not the only important variable for predicting the quantity of loans demanded by member banks. Some consideration must also be given to changes in the Federal Reserve's attitude or policy of discouraging "excessive borrowing" by member banks. A number of studies have attempted to estimate the member banks' demand for loans.

FIGURE 16-3   Reserve Adjustment Borrowing from the Federal Reserve and the Spread Between the Federal Funds Rate and the Discount Rate

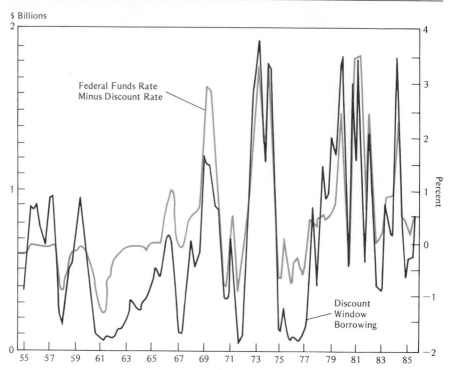

"If a bank could borrow from the Fed as much and as often as it desired at the discount rate, then the discount rate would serve as a cap to the federal funds rate. The fact that the federal funds rate is usually above the discount rate when nonborrowed reserves are less than required reserves is *prima facie* evidence that the discount rate does not measure the full cost of borrowing from the Fed. The full cost of borrowing from the Fed, or the effective discount rate, is the sum of the quoted discount rate plus the nonpecuniary costs resulting from discount window administration. Because the Fed tries to limit the amount and duration of borrowing by individual banks, by subjecting their lending and investment practices to 'surveillance,' and because banks wish to assure themselves access to the window in the future when they may face liquidity problems, the nonpecuniary costs of borrowing an additional dollar rise with the quantity and frequency of borrowing by an individual bank. These costs would rise even with the unchanged level of borrowing if the administration of the discount window were to get 'tougher.'

"To minimize its costs, an individual bank will manage its reserve position in such a way that the effective discount rate on an additional dollar borrowed from the Fed will be equal to the cost of acquiring reserves from alternative sources. At the margin, then, there is no subsidy involved in borrowing from the Fed when the effective rather than the quoted discount rate is compared with the cost of alternative sources of funds.* Because borrowing federal funds is a substitute for borrowing at the discount window, this cost can be measured by the federal funds rate, and the spread between the federal

Changes in the discount rate usually receive wide attention. The announcement may temporarily cause changes in economic variables, such as increased fluctuations in stock market prices. These **announcement effects** are sometimes interpreted as the major effect of discount rate changes. It is sometimes said for example, that an increase in the Federal Reserve discount rate is a signal that the Federal Reserve is raising market interest rates or that the Federal Reserve thinks rates will rise and is leading the way. Neither conclusion may be true; both usually are wrong. This is because the Federal Reserve discount rate is only one interest rate among many other interest rates on other assets throughout the domestic economy and worldwide financial markets. The Federal Reserve cannot directly raise market interest rates, but it can change the monetary base and thereby influence interest rates. A change in the Federal Reserve discount rate does not mean that all these other interest rates are thereby also changed. Very often, market interest rates may have risen earlier. The rise in the discount rate thus may merely reflect an effort by the Federal Reserve to bring the discount rate more in line with other market rates of interest (see Table 16-2).

Depository institution borrowing can significantly affect bank reserves and therefore the quantity of money. The change in bank reserves from this source is often very erratic, difficult to predict, and a major source of error, or *leakage*, in the relationship between open market policy and some desired level of bank reserves. Because of these problems, many economists have made suggestions for changing the Federal Reserve's policy on bank borrowing. Many economists think that bank borrowing should be a privilege at penalty rates and not a gift at less than market rates, allocated on a nonprice basis. The penalty rate could be some permanent high rate, such as a level equal to short-term market rates of interest plus a fixed amount. Milton Friedman suggested either a high penalty rate tied to a market rate or the complete elimination of borrowing and the imposition of a sufficiently high penalty or fine on any deficiency in reserves, to keep it from "becoming an individual form of discounting."[9] In July 1987 the Federal Reserve instituted a flexible discount rate on loans with maturities that exceed 30 days. The rate on these longer-term loans was made to vary with market rates, but had a lower limit of the basic discount rate plus one-half percentage point.

---

funds rate and the quoted discount rate measures the marginal nonpecuniary cost of borrowing from the Fed."

---

* However, there is a subsidy on average because the full nonpecuniary costs of borrowing are incurred only on the last dollar borrowed; on the intramarginal borrowing, the bank incurs below-market costs. For monetary policy purposes, of course, it is only the marginal cost that is relevant.

Source: The quotation is from Paul L. Kasriel, "The Discount Rate—Will It Float?" *Economic Perspectives*, May–June 1981, p. 21. The figure is from David Mengle, "The Discount Window," *Economic Review*, May–June 1986, p.5.

TABLE 16-2　Discount Rate Changes, October 1982–June 1986

After testing data from these discount changes Daniel L. Thornton concluded: "The evidence showed a statistically significant effect of a change in the discount rate on both the federal funds and Treasury bill rates immediately following the discount rate change. A series of tests provided evidence, consistent with the theory, that the direct effect of a discount rate change is nil. Consequently the impact of a discount rate change on market rates is due to an announcement effect, a policy effect or both. The rapidity with which market rates respond to the discount rate change suggests that the announcement effect is operative. Furthermore, some indirect tests of the policy effect produced results that are inconsistent with it, suggesting that discount rate changes have had no permanent effect on market interest rates."

Source: Daniel L. Thornton, "The Discount Rate and Market Interest Rates: Theory and Evidence," *Review*, Federal Reserve Bank of St. Louis, August–September 1986, pp. 14, 18.

Date Effective	Change	Classification	Reason
October 12, 1982	10% to 9.5%	T	Action taken to bring the discount rate into closer alignment with short-term market interest rates.
November 22, 1982	9.5% to 9%	P	Action taken against the background of continued progress toward greater price stability and indications of continued sluggishness in business activity and the relatively strong demand for liquidity.
December 14, 1982	9% to 8.5%	P	Action taken in light of current business conditions, strong competitive pressures on prices and further moderation of cost increases, a slowing of private credit demands, and present indications of some tapering off in growth of the broader monetary aggregates.
April 9, 1984	8.5% to 9%	T	Action taken to bring discount rate into closer alignment with short-term interest rates.
November 21, 1984	9% to 8.5%	P	Action taken in view of slow growth of M-1 and M-2 and the moderate pace of business expansion, relatively stable prices, and a continued strong dollar internationally.
December 24, 1984	8.5% to 8%	P	Essentially the same as before plus an attempt to bring the discount rate into more appropriate alignment with short-term market interest rates.
May 20, 1985	8% to 7.5%	P	Action taken in the light of relatively unchanged output in the industry sector, stemming from rising imports and a strong dollar. Rate reduction is consistent with the declining trend in market interest rates.
March 7, 1986	7.5% to 7%	P	Action taken in the context of similar action by other important industrial countries and for closer alignment with market interest rates. A further consideration was a sharp decline in oil prices.
Apirl 21, 1986	7% to 6.5%	T	Action taken to bring the discount rate into closer alignment with prevailing levels of market rates.

P = policy related
T = technical
Source: Federal Reserve Bulletin, paraphrased from statements in various issues, and *The Wall Street Journal*.

James Tobin suggested that discounting become the central monetary tool of the Federal Reserve.[10] Tobin advised that the Federal Reserve banks be allowed to pay interest at the discount rate on reserve balances and that prohibition against payment of interest on demand deposits be abandoned. By changing the discount rate, the Federal Reserve could change the quantity of borrowing and control the money supply.

Friedman also advocated the payment of interest on reserves and demand deposits, although he prefers open market operations rather than changes in the discount rate or reserve requirements as a method of controlling the money supply. Friedman contends that open market operations are a more precise method and that the effects on the money supply of changes in the discount rate or reserve requirements are difficult to predict.

RESERVE REQUIREMENTS

Reserve requirements changes do not change the monetary base. Rather, they change the amount of deposits that can be created per dollar of reserves and thereby change the profits that a depository institution can make per dollar of deposits. The lower the reserve requirement of sterile cash is, the more that can be invested in income-earning assets.

The Federal Reserve Act did *not* provide authority for changing reserve requirements on member bank deposits. Member banks were divided into three classifications, which corresponded to the classifications set up under the National Banking Act. Central reserve city banks were required to maintain 13 percent, reserve city banks 10 percent, and country banks 7 percent reserves as a percentage of their net demand deposits. All time deposits at all classes of banks were required to have 3 percent reserves. The power to change reserve requirements was granted to the Board of Governors during the 1930s as part of the general broadening of the discretionary powers that were granted. The Board of Governors and the banks blamed the failure of the Federal Reserve to stop the banking panics between 1929 and 1933 on limitations in its discretionary powers.

The Thomas amendment to the Agricultural Adjustment Act of 1933 gave the Federal Reserve Board the emergency power to change reserve requirements between the minimum percentages specified in 1917 and twice those percentages, provided it obtained the permission of the president. The Banking Act of 1935 extended the Board's power to change reserve requirements and eliminated the need to obtain permission from the president.

Changes in reserve requirements have been made infrequently and, in most cases, have been small. The first change in legal reserve requirements, which became effective on August 16, 1936, was, however, relatively large and produced a contractionary impact on the U.S. economy. Between August 16, 1936, and May 1, 1937, reserve requirements were doubled in three steps. This action was taken because the commercial banks had increased their excess reserves and the Federal Reserve wished to "soak up" these supposedly "idle reserves." Actually, the commercial banks had increased their excess reserves for a purpose that they considered justifiable, and these reserves were not idle in the sense of performing no function. The commercial banks had increased their reserves to ensure themselves against the possibility of renewed bank runs. They no longer relied on the "lender of last resort," the Federal Reserve, which had failed to lend to the commercial banking system the money it needed to stop the bank runs in the early 1930s. Commercial bankers had not yet learned that federal deposit insurance would eliminate almost all bank runs. The huge increase in reserve requirements forced commercial banks to increase further their total reserves so that excess reserves would be restored to a desired level. The first two increases in reserve requirements slowed the rate of increase in the money supply, and the third increment, on May 1, 1937, led to an absolute decline in the money supply. The U.S. economy, which was recovering from the disastrous depression of the early 1930s, suffered a new contraction.

In addition to changes in the reserve requirements, the Federal Reserve affects the amount of reserves that member banks are required to hold in another equally important manner. The Federal Reserve has at times changed the manner in which legal reserves and bank deposits are counted. In 1968, with the institution of lagged reserve requirements, it changed the periods over which reserves and deposits are averaged for reporting purposes.

During the 1960s and 1970s, the Federal Reserve lost members. The proportion of domestic deposits (in member banks) over which there were Federal Reserve reserve requirements fell from over 80 percent in the 1950s to 70.8 percent in 1978 (see Table 16-3). Banks left the Federal Reserve in order to benefit from the lower reserve requirements of the individual states. State requirements involved almost no sterile reserves. Instead, reserves could be held as deposits with correspondent banks (which yield a return in the form of services) and as investments in interest-paying financial assets, such as U.S. Treasury bills. Proposals to pay interest on reserves and/or make reserve

TABLE 16-3 Number of Member Banks and the Percentage of Domestic Deposits Covered by Federal Reserve Reserve Requirements, 1945–1978.

	Number of Member Banks	Percentage of Deposits
1945	6,884	86.3%
1950	6,873	85.7
1955	6,543 .	85.2
1960	6,174	84.0
1965	6,221	82.9
1970	5,767	80.1
1975	5,787	75.1
1976	5,758	73.8
1977	5,664	71.8
1978	5,593	70.8

requirements universal were introduced in Congress. On March 31, 1980, the Depository Institutions Deregulation and Monetary Control Act was signed into law, and universal reserve requirements were imposed. These reserve requirements were discussed in Chapter 8.

THE TREASURY DRAW

The Treasury is allowed to borrow up to $5 billion directly from the Federal Reserve. This authority is called the **Treasury draw**. It was authorized in 1942, and the authority has been renewed 21 times by Congress, from 1942 to 1979, indicating that Congress holds this authority on a short leash.

The Treasury was said to need this draw privilege for emergency periods when it finds itself short of cash, or if the Treasury is near its debt ceiling and its securities are difficult to sell without a big discount. (The debt ceiling cannot be broken by the draw.) Previously it took about three weeks' prior notice to prepare the necessary government securities to sell to the public to cover such shortages. Therefore, the Treasury wanted this draw as a safety valve, whereby it could temporarily obtain money directly from the Federal Reserve. The safety valve argument became less important in 1979, when the Treasury sold short-term **cash management notes**, maturing in a day or two, which can be produced rapidly.

Under the Treasury draw, the monetary base can be increased by as much as $5 billion. Such an increase can create a significant bubble in the money supply. The problem of offsetting such a bubble through open market operations is relatively minor; nevertheless, there is merit in reducing even small problems if the cost is small. A solution suggested by Professor William Poole and proposed by Congressman George Hansen (of the Subcommittee on Monetary Policy of the House Banking Committee) was signed into law in 1979. The law removes the bubble in monetary growth from the exercise of the Treasury draw. The Treasury was authorized to borrow securities from the Federal Reserve (in the manner of a short sale) and then sell these securities to the public. Under the proposal, the Treasury would sell these securities to the public and then use the money to cover its expenditures, so that there would be no change in the monetary base. The $5 billion limit has remained.

APPENDIX: MANAGEMENT OF THE MONETARY BASE FROM 1862 TO THE ESTABLISHMENT OF THE FEDERAL RESERVE SYSTEM

Fiat and Commodity Currency

The Legal Tender Acts of 1862 and 1863 authorized the Treasury to issue $450 million of United States notes to help finance the Civil War. This paper was fiat currency and was called **greenbacks**.

When the United States returned to the gold standard (which tied the supply of the monetary base to the quantity of gold sold to the Treasury) in 1879, the control of the money supply by the central government through the actions of the U.S. Treasury was substantially reduced. The balance of payments, which affected the inflows and outflows of gold from foreign transactions and the cost of gold mining relative to the official price of gold—$20.67 per ounce—influenced the supply of gold to the Treasury. The Treasury was obligated to buy or sell an ounce of gold at this price. There was also a great deal of public support for purchasing silver at a high enough price to make an effective standard of both gold and silver.

Political pressures such as those being voiced by the Greenback party (formed in 1875) and by the People or Populace party of the U.S.A. called for the government to purchase silver and to issue silver-backed money. The so-called crime of '73 was a temporary lack of authorization for the minting of the silver dollar, first coined in 1792. The heated denunciations of this alleged crime had their future echoes in the 1960s when, under the Lyndon Johnson administration, the silver was taken out of the quarter. The so-called crime had already occurred in 1853, when silver had once been taken out of the coins. (A further description of the gold standard is presented in Chapter 33.)

When the Treasury Ran Short

One of the most colorful events of the period of central banking before 1913, when the Federal Reserve was founded, was the attempt by the U.S. Treasury to negotiate loans from private bankers. The secretary of the Treasury was authorized in 1882 to suspend the issuance of gold certificates whenever the reserve of gold bullion or coin fell below $100 million.[11] (Gold certificates circulated as money beginning in 1863 and ending in 1934.) When President Grover Cleveland took office in 1893, the government's reserve exceeded that amount by less than 1 percent. In less than two months, it fell below $100 million and continued to drop. The Treasury attempted to replenish its supply with money it obtained by selling 5 percent bonds. In February 1895, the gold reserve was $41 million and falling at the rate of $2 million per day. Gold bullion was hoarded and carried abroad in anticipation of the rise in its price, as the Treasury attempted to replenish its reserves. Assistant Secretary of the Treasury William E. Curtis went to see John Pierpont Morgan, the affluent investment banker, and August Belmont, an agent for the Rothschilds, a leading European banking family. An agreement was worked out whereby a Morgan–Belmont syndicate would underwrite an issue of $50 million in 30-year bonds, with an option for another $50 million. Half the gold needed to pay for the bonds would come from foreign sources.

When the newspapers announced that an agreement had been drawn up to stop the gold drain, the outflow of gold temporarily subsided. But President Cleveland and Secretary of the Treasury John G. Carlisle considered the interest rate on the proposed loan to be too high. Morgan and Belmont went to

Washington to confer with the president but were met by Daniel Lamont, secretary of War, who told them that the president was against the sale of bonds and that he would not see the bankers. The following day they did meet with President Cleveland. The Morgan–Belmont syndicate was authorized to take $60 million in bonds. Morgan offered participation in the purchase to European financial institutions. The gold drain stopped during the summer, and the Treasury built up its reserves above the required amount.

The Treasury as a Central Bank

The Treasury had surpluses from the government budget for most of the period between the Civil War (1866) and World War I (1915). The surpluses tended to reduce the monetary base, as explained in the monetary base identity.

Laws permitting the deposit of Treasury funds in national banks were liberalized. The Treasury was permitted to change the size of the monetary base by transferring reserves into the private banking system from the Treasury vaults. The secretary of the Treasury in 1902, Leslie M. Shaw, officially ruled that funds could be transferred from the Treasury to private banks and then back again at the discretion of the secretary of the Treasury. He called in Treasury funds at private depositories during the summer and then released them in the autumn, to adjust the supply of money according to the seasonal needs of trade. Shaw also argued against the establishment of a central bank, as it would remove the supervision of monetary operations from the Treasury.

The most important determinant of the monetary base from 1897 to 1913 was the increase in the gold stock produced by the expanded production of gold in the world. The growth in the Treasury's monetary gold stock at an average annual rate of 3.8 percent was the largest source of change in the U.S. monetary base.[12] The second largest contributor to the growth in the U.S. monetary base was national bank notes, which grew at an average rate of 1.3 percent per year in this period. Treasury operations other than buying gold contributed to the monetary base at an average rate of only .3 percent per year for this period.

STUDY QUESTIONS

1. Trace the mechanics of an open market sale of securities by the Federal Reserve trading desk. How is the monetary base affected?
2. How do changes in the discount rate and reserve requirements affect bank profits?
3. Suppose that a less developed country has no viable capital markets—no bond market. How can a monetary policy be conducted?
4. Was Federal Reserve membership by a substantial number of commercial banks important to the conduct of monetary policy before 1981? Explain.

5. Does the Treasury draw refer to a card game in which the high card wins as a last resort in disputes between the Treasury and the Federal Reserve? Explain. How does the Treasury draw affect the monetary base?

6. Can the monetary base be controlled by open market policy alone? Explain.

7. Will the penalty discount tied to market rates improve the Federal Reserve's control of the monetary base? Explain.

8. Is the following statement true, false, or uncertain? "During a deep depression the Federal Reserve could not sell large quantities of bonds through the open market desk because there would not be enough buyers." Explain your answer.

9. Go back to Chapter 8 and review reserve requirements. Can the Federal Reserve change reserve requirements under the Monetary Control Act of 1980? What would be the effect on depository institutions' profits of a rise in reserve requirements on checking accounts? What would happen to their profits if the Federal Reserve paid interest on these increases in required reserves? Can the Federal Reserve pay interest on reserves?

10. How did the Treasury influence the monetary base before the establishment of the Federal Reserve? (From the appendix.)

GLOSSARY

Announcement effects. Temporary changes in economic variables, for example, increased fluctuations in stock prices, as a result of the announcement of some new information, such as an announcement by the Federal Reserve that it will change its discount rate.

Cash management notes. Short-term debt instruments of the U.S. Treasury that can be produced rapidly.

Defensive open market operations. Federal Reserve open market operations to offset disturbances to bank reserves so that money growth (and/or interest rates) is not affected by these disturbances.

Dynamic open market operations. Federal Reserve open market operations performed to affect bank reserves and thereby to affect the supply of money.

Elastic currency. A currency that grows with the "needs of trade." See Chapter 7 for an explanation of the needs of trade. In a more modern context than the Federal Reserve Act of 1913 in which it is used, the concept of an elastic currency means that the supply of currency will be changed with changes in the need for it, as evidenced by changes in nominal gross national product of a similar variable. It also is often meant to include an entire concept of money such as M-1, that is, an *elastic money supply.*

Greenbacks. Fiat money initially issued to help finance the Civil War in the United States.

Treasury draw. The authority

given to the U.S. Treasury to borrow a limited amount directly from the Federal Reserve. Follow- ing recent legislation, this loan now is in the form of securities rather than cash.

NOTES

1. For a further description, see Paul Meek, *Open-Market Operations*, Federal Reserve Bank of New York, June 1978.

2. See Clay J. Anderson, "Evolution of the Role and the Functioning of the Discount Mechanism," *Reappraisal of the Federal Reserve Discount Mechanism*, vol. 1, Federal Reserve Board of Governors, August 1971, pp. 133–163. For a review of views, see David Jones. "A Review of Academic Literature on the Discount Mechanism," *Reappraisal*, vol. 2, pp. 23–45.

3. This is from the preamble to the Federal Reserve Act.

4. Section 12-A, Part III, Federal Reserve Act, as amended.

5. Anderson, "Evolution . . . of the Discount Mechanism," pp. 146–147.

6. *Fifth Annual Report of the Federal Reserve Board*, 1928, p. 8.

7. Federal Reserve Bank of San Francisco, *1982 Annual Report*, January 26, 1983, pp. 25–26.

8. One important factor that is not discussed until Chapter 27 is the effect of lagged reserve requirements on the operation of the discount window and on monetary policy. Material on the discount window can be found in Jones, "A Review of Academic Literature"; and in Peter Keir, "Impact of Discount Policy Procedures on the Effectiveness of Reserve Targeting," *New Monetary Control Procedures*, Federal Reserve Staff Study, vol. 1, Board of Governors of the Federal Reserve System, February 1981, Study 7 (pages not numbered).

9. Milton Friedman, *A Program for Monetary Stability* (New York: Fordham University Press, 1959), pp. 44–45. In March 1980, Canada's central bank instituted a floating penalty discount rate one-quarter percentage point above the average yield on 91-day Canadian government Treasury bills.

10. James Tobin, "Toward Improving the Efficiency of the Monetary Mechanism," *Review of Economics and Statistics*, vol. 42, August 1960, pp. 276–279. The central bank of England uses changes in the discount rate as a major policy tool.

11. See *The American Heritage History of American Business and Industry* by Alex Groner and the editors of *American Heritage* and *Business Week*, with an introduction by Paul Samuelson (New York: American Heritage, 1972), pp. 194–197.

12. Philip Cagan, *Determinants and Effects of Changes in the Stock of Money, 1875–1960*, National Bureau of Economic Research (New York: Columbia University Press, 1965), Table F6, pp. 338–339.

CHAPTER 17

THE MONEY EXPANSION MULTIPLIERS

CHAPTER PREVIEW

Introduction. The money supply can be divided into two parts: money created by the banking system and the monetary base created by the central bank. This chapter is concerned with the relationship between these two parts of the money supply.

The Money Expansion Multipliers. This is a relationship between the money supply and the monetary base.

Can the Federal Reserve Control the Money Supply? Although many say yes, the issues involved, especially statistical problems, make the supporting evidence controversial.

INTRODUCTION

Suppose that there are no depository institutions and no deposit accounts. The entire money supply is currency and coin, printed and minted by the central government. You could then say that the entire money supply is made up of the monetary base.[1] Suppose, next, that depository institutions are added to the economy and that they have a substantial number of checking accounts that are included in the definition of money (M-1). Suddenly, the money supply is bigger than the monetary base.

How did it get bigger? The answer is that the depository institutions have created a large part of the money supply. The part that they have created will be called *bank money*. It follows that the money supply can be viewed as being composed of two parts:

1. The *monetary base* created by the government, composed of (a) currency and coin outside depository institutions and (b) reserves of the depository institutions.
2. *Bank money* created by the banking system.

Bank money is money created by the banking system in the manner described in Chapter 8. The central subject of this chapter can be described equivalently as the relationship between the monetary base and bank money or as the relationship between the monetary base and the money supply. If the Federal Reserve can control the monetary base and if the Federal Reserve can change the money base so that it can control bank money, then, equivalently, the Federal Reserve can be said to be controlling the money supply.

Important variables in the relationship between the monetary base and the money supply are illuminated in relationships called the **money expansion multipliers**. These multipliers are described first with special attention to two variables that determine the size of the multipliers: the *public's desire for currency and coin relative to deposits* and *depository institutions' desire for reserves relative to deposits*.

Components of M-1

There are many other ways of breaking apart a concept of the money supply, such as M-1, which are frequently referred to in newspaper accounts, in the Federal Reserve literature, and many other places. It is useful to have an easy reference to tie all these components together, such as that presented in Table 17-1. (The table is equivalent to many pages of difficult descriptions of each of these components and their relationships to one another.)

Different components of the money supply, defined as M-1, are also shown in Table 17-1. Currency in circulation, the monetary base, and depository institutions' reserves were explained in Chapter 15. Now we will discuss the determination of the larger aggregate, M-1. This concept of the money supply is the total currency, coin, and checkable deposits held by the public.

TABLE 17-1 The Components of M-1, August 1986 (in billions of dollars)

Currency Outside Depository Institutions	V. C.*				
$179.9	$21.4		Currency in Circulation		$201.3

Currency in Circulation	Reserves at Federal Reserve			
$201.3	$29.2		Monetary Base	$230.5

	V. C.	Reserves at Federal Reserve		
	$21.4	$29.2	Depository Institutions Reserves	$50.6

T.C. $7.3

Currency Outside Depository Institutions	V. C.	Reserves at Federal Reserve	Bank Money	
$179.9	$21.4	$29.2	$447.0	

T.C. $7.3   M-1 $684.8

Currency Outside Depository Institutions	V. C.	Reserves at Federal Reserve	Checkable Deposits
$179.9	$21.4	$29.2	$497.6

* V.C. is vault cash.
Note: Currency refers to currency and coin. The reserves shown may be held for other deposits as well as checking accounts.
Source: Board of Governors, Federal Reserve Bulletin (December 1986), pp. A4, 12, and 13, with slight adjustment for conformity. Data are not seasonally adjusted.

THE MONEY EXPANSION MULTIPLIERS

The money expansion multipliers (also called the monetary base multipliers) are derived from two identities.[2] The first identity states that the total money supply (M-1) is equal to the currency and coin outside depository institutions,

C, plus checkable deposits at depository institutions, D:

$$M\text{-}1 = C + D \tag{1}$$

The second identity defines the monetary base, B, as equal to the currency outside depository institutions, C, plus the reserves of the depository institutions, R:

$$B = C + R \tag{2}$$

If equation (1) is divided by equation (2) and the terms are rearranged, equation (3) will be the result:

$$M\text{-}1 = B\left(\frac{C + D}{C + R}\right) \tag{3}$$

Dividing the numerator and the denominator of the fraction by D, the final identity is

$$M\text{-}1 = B\left(\frac{C/D + 1}{C/D + R/D}\right) \tag{4}$$

The money supply is equal to the size of the monetary base multiplied by a ratio. The ratio in parentheses on the right side of equation (4) is sometimes called the money expansion multiplier. If R/D declines in value, the denominator, $C/D + R/D$, will become smaller, and the money expansion multiplier will become larger. If C/D declines in value, the numerator, $C/D + 1$, will decline by a smaller proportion than will the denominator, $C/D + R/D$. This is because the C/D ratio is added to 1 in the numerator and to a fraction, R/D, in the denominator. The same change added to a large number and a smaller number will increase the smaller number by a larger proportion.

Equation (4) classifies the determinants of the money supply into three groups. First are those government transactions, discussed in Chapter 16, that affect the size of the monetary base, B (see Figure 17-1).

Second are those factors that affect the **currency ratio**, C/D. The size of the currency ratio is determined primarily by the public. The public decides what proportion of its money it wishes to keep in the form of currency and coin. The greater the proportion of money the public wishes to keep in the form of currency and coin, the less will be available to the banking system as a reserve for expanding the supply of bank money.

FIGURE 17-1   The Determinants of M-1

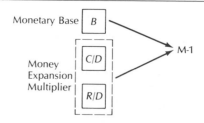

The third group of factors affecting the money supply is classified as the determinants of the **reserve ratio**, R/D. The managers of individual depository institutions determine the proportion of deposits they wish to keep in the form of reserves to meet reserve requirements and the liquidity needs of the bank. If the definition of money is M-1, time deposits at commercial banks will not be included in the money supply. Nevertheless, the bank managers will want to hold some reserves against the bank's time deposits. The government deposits in commercial banks are also not included in the money supply. Depository institutions may also want to hold reserves against government deposits. The proportion of checkable deposits maintained in the form of reserves by an individual depository institution therefore depends on the distribution of deposits among checkable deposits, time deposits, and government deposits.

The managers of each depository institution must assess their expected average deposits and the variations of that average in the forthcoming period so that there will be sufficient reserves to meet legal reserve requirements and withdrawals of funds by depositors.

The difference in the effect on the money supply resulting from a change in the currency ratio will be shown with two different values of the reserve ratio. Suppose that the monetary base is constant at \$100 billion. The currency ratio is assumed to be .2, and the reserve ratio is assumed to be .3. The total money supply is then determined from equation (4):

$$\$240b = \$100b\left(\frac{.2 + 1}{.2 + .3}\right) = \$100b(2.4) \tag{5}$$

The money expansion multiplier is equal to 2.4. Therefore, the money supply is equal to \$240 billion. Now if the currency ratio is increased to .3, the expression will become

$$\$216.67b = \$100b\left(\frac{.3 + 1}{.3 + .3}\right) = \$100b(2.1667) \tag{6}$$

The money expansion multiplier is equal to 2.1667, so that the total money supply is \$216.67 billion. The effect of increasing the currency ratio by .1 is a decrease in the money supply of \$23.33 billion.

If instead the currency ratio remains at .2 and the reserve ratio increases to .4, the money expansion multiplier will then equal 2, and the money supply will equal \$200 billion:

$$\$200b = \$100b\left(\frac{.2 + 1}{.2 + .4}\right) = \$100b(2) \tag{7}$$

which is a decline in the money supply of \$40 billion, compared with equation (5).

Now suppose both the currency and reserve ratios change together. Both increase by 0.1 from their values in equation (5):

$$\$185.71b = \$100b\left(\frac{.3 + 1}{.3 + .4}\right) = \$100b(1.8571) \tag{8}$$

The money supply is reduced by $54.29 billion, compared with the amount in equation (5). The sum of the changes in the money supply caused by the changes in C/D and R/D, taken separately in equations (6) and (7), is $63.33 billion. The $9 billion difference in equation (8), where both C/D and R/D

FIGURE 17-2 The Money Expansion Multiplier (with the monetary base adjusted for reserve requirement changes), 1959–1986

From 1960 to 1980 the value of the money expansion multiplier generally fell. Much of this decline can be attributed to the increase in the C/D ratio as the public chose to hold larger proportions of M-1 in the form of currency. The initial period of deregulation, from 1980 to 1983, contained a more erratic money expansion multiplier, and it did not continue its previous general decline in value. This was a period of new operating procedures by the Federal Reserve and abrupt changes in the C/D ratio, which will be explained in Chapter 27. From 1981 until 1986 there was a phaseout of the interest rate ceilings on consumer checking accounts. There was also a substantial rise in the value of the money expansion in 1985 and 1986. This was caused in large part by a switch from currency, the older demand deposits (which pay no pecuniary interest) that businesses could hold, and time deposits (which cannot be obtained on demand until maturity) into the new, interest-paying consumer deposits. From July 1985 to December 1986, M-1 grew by 22.1 percent, and the monetary base (adjusted for reserve requirements) grew at 10.8 percent. In most short periods—over a year—the money expansion multiplier did not change by a large proportion and had a predictable value for controlling the money supply. Between 1980 and 1986 the money expansion multiplier changed by roughly 11 percent from its low point in 1980, allowing M-1 to rise by roughly $71 billion from this change in the money expansion multiplier.

Source: Federal Reserve Bank of St. Louis, *U.S Financial Data,* October 14, 1983, p. 5; R. W. Hafer, Scott E. Hein, and Clemens J. M. Kool, "Forecasting the Money Multiplier: Implications for Money Stock Control and Economic Activity," *Review,* Federal Reserve Bank of St. Louis, October 1983, p. 27, updated.

change, reflects the interaction between the ratios. Interaction means that the effect on the money supply of a change in one of these ratios is not independent but depends on the size of the other ratio.[3] The values of the money expansion multiplier for M-1 from November 1959 to December 1986 are plotted on Figure 17-2.

Now the discussion turns to the components of M-1 contained in the multiplier, the two ratios shown in Figure 17-2. The third determinant of M-1, discussed in Chapter 15, is the monetary base and is controlled primarily by the Federal Reserve.

The Currency Ratio

The currency ratio is determined in the first instance by the public. The ratio is currency and coin outside depository institutions divided by checkable deposits.[4] The public's demand for currency relative to deposits may be viewed in a framework similar to the analysis of the choice among other kinds of assets.

The public may suddenly come to believe that a depository institution will be unable to exchange demand deposit claims for currency and coin. One of the best ways to spread this view is for a depository institution to refuse to exchange immediately a deposit claim for currency and coin. The depositor may respond to this refusal with some anxiety. News of one such refusal that reaches the ears of a few depositors will soon spread and cause a run on the depository institution. This happened during the 1930s and in earlier banking panics. Accordingly, bank runs cause an increase in the currency ratio.

A change in the interest paid on checkable deposits (with the same service charges or minimum balance requirements) changes the demand for currency and coin relative to checkable deposits. Some analysts claim that the changes in interest rates on deposits have a small effect on the currency ratio.[5] But changes in market interest rates have had a significant effect on the ratio of time deposits to demand deposits, especially in the periods in which there was at least a partially effective prohibition on interest payments on commercial bank demand deposits. A rise in interest rates with zero interest on demand deposits induced a shift to time deposits.

In general, the less developed and less urbanized an economy is, the greater the currency ratio will be. There is a long-term fall in the currency ratio as countries develop and as income and urbanization increase. The changes over the business cycle and seasonal changes in the currency ratio fluctuate around this long-term trend. There are many plausible explanations for this long-term trend, as many variables may affect the change in the currency ratio during periods of urbanization. An important part of the explanation lies in the development of banking systems and checking deposits or their equivalents, which offer a relatively inexpensive way to store and transfer money.

The long-run trend in the currency ratio in the United States from the 1880s to the 1930s was downward. The currency ratio rose from its trend during banking panics, with the largest rise coming with the bank runs in the early 1930s. The currency ratio also rose during World War I and World War II.

After World War II, the currency ratio again began to decline until 1960, when it reversed itself and began to rise.[6]

In 1986, the average currency holdings by the public amounted to approximately $729.80 for every man, woman, and child in the United States. It would have been difficult, however, to find many people who would admit to having this much currency and coin in their possession. The reasons for a high C/D were discussed in Chapter 2. To review, it seems likely that the high ratio of currency to income can be explained in part by the desire to negotiate transactions without the written records that come with the transfer of checking deposits. Also, because the U.S. dollar serves as an international currency, some of this cash, such as $100 bills, are probably held in large quantities outside the United States. They are a convenient form of wealth in places where there is a great deal of international trade, such as Hong Kong.

Although in 1985 and 1986 the value of the currency ratio was high, there was a switch from currency, the older demand deposits that businesses could hold, and time deposits into the new interest-paying consumer deposits. This was part of the adjustment to the phasing out, between 1981 and 1986, of interest rate ceilings on the payment of interest on consumer checking accounts. There was also a substantial rise in the value of the money expansion in 1985 and 1986, as shown in Figure 17-2, because of this shift of the monetary base into a form in which it could support consumer deposits. From July 1985 to December 1986, M-1 grew by 22.1 percent, and the monetary base (adjusted for reserve requirements) grew at 10.8 percent. Between 1980 and 1986 the money expansion multiplier changed by roughly 11 percent from its low point in 1980, allowing M-1 to rise by roughly $71 billion from this change in the money expansion multiplier.

The Reserve Ratio

The quantity of reserves that banks want to hold per dollar of demand deposits depends on a number of factors, which will be classified into three groups:

1. The level of reserve requirements
2. Liquidity needs
3. The distribution of deposits and deposit-type liabilities

The reserve ratio is the value of depository institutions' reserves (the sum of vault cash plus the deposits at the Federal Reserve) divided by checkable deposits adjusted. It is affected by changes in legal reserve requirements—which directly change the amount of vault cash and financial institutions' reserve accounts at the Federal Reserve—that banks must hold per dollar of adjusted deposits.

Liquidity needs is the name applied to the factors that explain the banks' desired level of excess reserves. Liquidity needs depend on the expected level and the uncertainty of the level of deposits minus withdrawals. They also depend on the cash requirements arising from the operations of the depository institutions that are not directly associated with the reserves held against deposits by the depository institution. These cash requirements include payrolls and other expenses.

The liquidity needs are also dependent on the composition of the bank's portfolios. The more highly liquid, nonmoney assets the bank holds in its portfolios, the less excessive reserves will be needed. Immediate access to the federal funds market allows an individual depository institution to hold less excess reserves at a given interest rate. For the banking system as a whole, however, an increased demand for federal funds can drive up the funds rate and force many depository institutions to borrow from the Federal Reserve.

What is the effect of interest rates on the R/D ratio? One approach to the answer can be divided into two parts. The first is the effect of interest rates on excess reserves, and the second is the effect of interest rates on shifts of funds between deposit accounts.

There is a hypothesis that holds that the higher are both the market rates and the opportunity cost of holding excess reserves, the more aggressively will the banks economize on their excess reserves, and the lower will the excess reserves become.[7] But this has been a rather empty argument since at least 1970, and it probably has not been of major importance since 1945 (see Figure 17-3). Interest rates simply cannot play much of a role in determining excess reserves because excess reserves are kept at an extremely low level through efficient cash management by depository institutions. All 5,413 member banks held an average of $924 in excess reserves in September 1979. Although that was especially small (.01 percent of reserves), the amount was not much larger in February 1980 (.4 of reserves, a relatively large amount). There is little value in developing a theory on how drinking habits affect the water level in a reservoir if the reservoir holds only a cup or two at any time.

Before 1945, the excess reserves of the member banks were sometimes substantial, but not primarily because of low interest rates. The huge rise in excess reserves in the 1930s was the commercial banks' reaction to the failure of the Federal Reserve to lend them money when the 1930–1933 bank runs occurred. Banks did not yet believe that federal deposit insurance would stop bank runs, and so they built up excess reserves for their own insurance. In 1936 and 1937, the Federal Reserve raised the reserve requirements to absorb these so-called idle reserves. The banks then rebuilt their excess reserves, as shown in Figure 17-3. Meanwhile, interest rates on three-month Treasury bills fell from a yield of 1.4 percent in 1931 to under 1 percent until 1949, averaging .4 percent from 1931 to 1940. It was not the high interest rates that made it profitable for the banks to devote their resources to economizing on cash balances.

There was a rise in excess reserves after 1980, as shown in Figure 17-3, which can be explained by technical factors and not by the hypothesis that higher nominal interest rates encourage depository institutions to carry less reserves. One technical factor was the phasing in of Federal Reserve requirements (after the passage of the Monetary Control Act in 1980) for the thousands of thrifts and nonmember commercial banks that were subject to these

FIGURE 17-3   Excess Reserves and Borrowings from the Federal Reserve, 1929–1986 (billions of dollars)

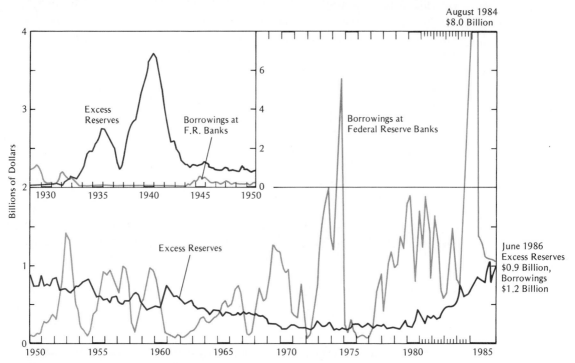

Before implementation of the Monetary Control Act of 1980, which opened the discount window to all depository institutions with checkable accounts on November 13, 1980, borrowings from the Federal Reserve were for member banks only. Notice that even when borrowings were relatively large, as they were in a number of periods since 1977, excess reserves did not increase until after 1980. This evidence is consistent with the view that borrowings are not primarily used for excess reserves (that is, they are not held by depository institutions); they are used by depository institutions to purchase investments and make loans. Therefore, the R/D ratio in equation (4) is not significantly affected by borrowings.

The rise in excess reserves in the 1980s was caused by a number of technical factors, one of the most important having to do with bookkeeping. "Before implementation of the Monetary Control Act of 1980 on November 13, 1980, reserves and borrowing related to member banks only. After this date reserves and borrowing are for all depository institutions."

Source: 1984 Historical Chart Book, Board of Governors of the Federal Reserve (updated from Federal Reserve *Bulletins*). The figure is from p. 3, and the quotation is from p. 31.

requirements for the first time. Their excess reserves were included for the first time with the member banks' excess reserves. Another technical factor was the Garn–St Germain Act of 1982, which exempted up to $2 million of reservable liabilities from reserve requirements in 1982. The exemption was raised in stages to $2.6 million in 1986, leaving small banks with little or no reserve requirements but with a need to carry some reserves for liquidity needs.

This evidence does not mean the R/D ratio is not affected by changes in interest rates. In the 1960s and 1970s, funds were shifted from zero interest-paying demand deposits to time deposits at commercial banks or to money market funds, which, in turn, purchased certificates of deposit from the banking system. Demand deposits at member banks would have reserve requirements as high as 16.25 percent if the member bank had more than $400 million in deposits, whereas in 1979, time deposits had reserve requirements from 1 to 8 percent in a complex maze of overlapping requirements. Changing market interest rates also led to shifts in deposits among depository institutions with different legal reserve requirements. All these changes related to interest rates and differing legal reserve requirements had significant effects on the money supply.[8]

After the implementation of the Monetary Control Act of 1980, with its relatively high 12 percent (initial) reserve requirement on checkable accounts, compared with the zero reserve requirements on savings accounts (when the phase-in is complete), the incentive to get deposits into savings account categories will be strong. The Garn–St Germain Act of 1982 has already allowed limited checking privileges on savings accounts. The higher the market rates are, the more profitable it will be for depository institutions to offer incentives to switch depositors into savings accounts. The main device to switch deposits will be widening the spread between savings account interest and checking account interest.

This analysis leads to a tantalizing suggestion. If different levels of required reserves cause instability in the R/D ratio, why not have uniform reserve requirements? To be uniform, given the many innovative ways of developing new monies that have no reserve requirements, why not have zero reserve requirements? This is a controversial idea. Opponents argue that without substantial reserve requirements, banks could lend out nearly all their deposits, which would be deposited at other banks and so on until the money supply ballooned up. This process of redepositing reserves is called **pyramiding**. Proponents argue that banks carry some excess reserves, small though they may be, and that the public has a desired R/D ratio. They hold that these two brakes on expansion are enough to prevent unlimited pyramiding. Would, however, the R/D become so unstable with no reserve requirements that the Federal Reserve would find it difficult, if not impossible, to offset undesirable fluctuations in the money supply?

It is interesting to note in Figure 17-3 that the level of borrowings at Federal Reserve banks is apparently not closely related to excess reserves. This means that when borrowings are high, there is no prolonged period of high excess reserves. The money borrowed from the Federal Reserve is used to support additional deposits, although at the moment of borrowing, it may appear that these borrowed funds are used to cover reserve requirements. Clearly, however, from the monetary base identity in Chapter 15, these borrowings are additions to the monetary base that enable deposits to be larger than otherwise, provided that the borrowed funds are not additions to excess reserves or to the public's holdings of currency and coin. The level of borrowing is related to the difference between market interest rates and the discount rate, but borrowings apparently primarily affect the monetary base, not the R/D ratio.

The long-term value of the reserve ratio from 1867 to 1960 roughly followed the currency ratio. The reserve ratio generally fell from 1867 to the early 1930s. The banking panics of the early 1930s caused banks to increase their reserve ratios to provide insurance against future bank runs. The reserve ratio was slightly smaller in value than was the currency ratio until World War II; then there was a rapid rise in the currency ratio and a fall in the reserve ratio. The currency ratio has remained higher than the reserve ratio.

The historical record of the reserve ratio also has had short-term fluctuations over the business cycle, which, if corrected for changes in reserve requirements, would "uniformly display inverse conformity to business cycles."[9] Excess reserves tend to decline during business expansions and expand during business contractions, though this historical finding has been less important in recent periods, when excess reserves have been very small.

CAN THE FEDERAL RESERVE CONTROL THE MONEY SUPPLY?

The Federal Reserve currently operates with short-term and long-term monetary targets that specify a target range of several percentage points for the rate of growth in a monetary aggregate such as M-1. For example, the target for M-1 may be an average rate of growth of 4 to 6 percent. Short-term targets are often for two months, whereas official long-term targets are currently one year. Can the Federal Reserve control the money supply within such a target range for two or three months, six months, or a year? In this section we will explore the answers to this question.

Suppose, first, that the central bank can precisely determine the size of the monetary base. This assumption alone is not trivial. Looking back at the monetary base identity (or the government budget constraint) in Chapter 15, the reader will recall that there are many ways of changing the monetary base. Many types of government transactions affect the monetary base other than those of the Federal Reserve open market desk. We will assume that all those factors that adversely affect the monetary base are offset by Federal Reserve open-market conditions and that these open-market operations are conducted in such a manner as to make the monetary base exactly what the Federal Reserve wants it to be. Does a particular size of the monetary base mean that bank money—the money created by the private banking system—will also be uniquely fixed at some level?

One way to consider this question is to ask whether or not undesirable changes in the money expansion multiplier in equation (4) can be offset by open market operations that change the monetary base. For example, assume that the money expansion multiplier suddenly rises, causing an undesirable increase in M-1 growth. Can this bulge be offset by open-market sales that pull down the monetary base?

This is a difficult problem in what is known as **control theory**. To understand the kind of short-term problems that can arise, consider the following example, using equation (4) as a guide. The monetary base is increased. Announcement of the increase sets into motion forces that cause the C/D and R/D ratios to rise considerably. This causes the money expansion multipliers to fall. The attempt to increase M-1 by increasing the monetary base can then result in a drop in M-1. If more monetary base is pumped into the system (through open-market operations) and the rise in the C/D and R/D ratios is short-lived, the money expansion multiplier may rise to its original value, and M-1 may rise significantly farther than desired. Whether or not this kind of reaction is likely to get the monetary policy off course for a considerable period is a matter for statistical tests.

A number of statistical problems can be explained in a simple way that makes the interpretation of such tests' results very difficult and perhaps, in many periods, impossible. Many of those statistical problems are caused by the fact that the Federal Reserve never has had the single target of controlling a particular definition of money for a sustained period of a year or more. From the middle 1950s, when an official policy of pegging interest rates at a fixed level was dropped, until 1970, the Federal Reserve has been primarily interested in stabilizing (which is a close cousin to pegging) interest rates over the short term.

Theoretically, there is always an interest rate that is consistent with a desired rate of money growth. Therefore, an open-market policy that achieved that interest rate would result in the desired rate of monetary growth. In other words, suppose the Federal Reserve's open-market manager knows that a federal funds rate target range of 7 to 9 percent is consistent with a desired rate of money growth of between 4 and 6 percent. This relationship is depicted for one instant in time and one price level in Figure 17-4. The Federal Reserve has frequently used a federal funds target range for this type along with its money supply target range. The open-market manager can then change the monetary base through open-market operations to achieve a federal funds rate in this target range and simultaneously achieve a rate of money growth in the money supply target range.

The Federal Reserve's policies of hitting a short-term federal funds target have, however, frequently been inconsistent with its money supply targets. It is evident from this experience that an attempt to select a federal funds target range consistent with a desired money growth range is a difficult, if not impossible, task. This issue is discussed further in Part VIII.

In 1970, with the appointment of Arthur Burns as chairman of the Federal Reserve Board, it was announced that more attention would be given to stabilizing the money supply. Nevertheless, this was certainly not the Federal Reserve's only objective. For much of the period from 1970 to 1979, the

FIGURE 17-4   The Money Supply Range Consistent with a Federal Funds Target Range of 7 to 9 Percent at One Point in Time

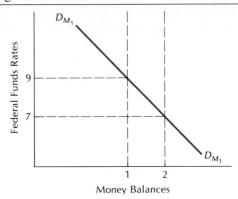

Theoretically, an interest rate band of from 7 to 9 percent for the federal funds rate would be equivalent to a money supply target between level 1 and level 2, if the money demand curve were as shown in the diagram. The trouble is, however, that on a short-term basis, it would be difficult to identify the demand schedule. Therefore, the interest rate consistent with a planned level of monetary growth is not known with any certainty, even for very wide ranges, over the short term.

Federal Reserve operated primarily to stabilize interest rates—the federal funds rate—over short periods of time. If the money supply moved far out of line, then corrective action might be taken. Then on October 6, 1979, Chairman Paul Volcker made a formal announcement that the Federal Reserve would concentrate on controlling the money supply.

Since 1979, the variability of the money supply has increased. Individuals such as Milton Friedman and Allan Meltzer, who had long advocated that the monetary aggregates should be targeted, held that it was a change in operations that was not accompanied by necessary changes in operating methods.

Using control techniques appropriate for interest rate targeting (including interest rate targets), the Federal Reserve attempted to control the money supply. It held that under these conditions, things got worse. The controversy that developed requires knowledge of targeting and operational procedures, which is presented in Chapter 27. This controversy is also covered there. For those who cannot wait, a substantial amount of material was produced by the Federal Reserve and academic economists and cited in note 10.

The statistical problem that arises in interpreting tests of the relationship between the monetary base and the money supply during those periods when the Federal Reserve was not trying to control the money supply most of the time is illuminated by the following example: Suppose that an investigator wanted to find out if a small ship could be confined to a predetermined course by manipulating the rudder. The only test periods available for collecting data were those in which there was no predetermined course and the rudder was used solely to keep the ship as stable as possible (so that if the ship drifted off course, the rudder might be turned to accommodate the drift) or periods in which the ship was under tow. Under those conditions, the relationship between the ship's rudder and the ship's course would shed little light on the effect of the rudder on the ship's course. The investigator would prefer to have a long period of data in which the rudder was intended to be a primary determinant of the ship's course, rather than periods in which the ship's course was a primary determinant of the direction of the rudder. Data collected from such a "passive rudder" period may be used in tests that appear to show a relationship between the rudder and the ship's direction, but it is doubtful that these results would throw much light on that relationship.

A number of experts, including Albert Burger, William Dewald, James Johannes, and Robert Rasche, have produced evidence that shows that the Federal Reserve can have fairly precise control over a two- or three-month average of common concepts of the money supply.[11] Dewald amazed his money and banking students by forecasting this relationship in his classes. He did so on a weekly basis with excellent results. Berger estimated the money expansion multiplier depicted in Figure 17-2 from prior data. The actual growth of the money supply was very close to the amount that Berger predicted. A study by Johannes and Rasche using modern time series methods supported the following conclusions:

> Our conclusion from the above analysis is that the money stock measured on any of several bases can be predicted with considerable accuracy over horizons of at least several months using simple time series models for the various multiplier components and given a knowledge of the path of the monetary base.[12]

Other studies, including one by Rasche, find that some of the procedures used by the Federal Reserve prevented precise monetary control.[13] One of the most interesting results regarding monetary control was that an attempt to control short-term movements too closely resulted in greater instability. Robert Rasche and Brian Motley performed tests on the stability of money from 1979 to 1982. This was a period in which the Federal Reserve announced that it would closely control M-1, but M-1 still became more variable. Motley and Rasche reported that

> . . . the relatively large errors in forecasting (money growth) suggest that the central bank's ability to "fine tune" the money stock in the short-run is very limited.
>
> The empirical findings in this article strongly suggest that both the Federal Reserve itself and the small army of "Fedwatchers" who keep tabs on its activities from the sidelines should focus their attention on longer run movements in money growth.[14]

A final problem arises with the way in which the money supply data are seasonally adjusted. This is the process of removing regular cycles that occur in the data within a year, in order to see the underlying direction of change. It is a necessary adjustment for many analyses. For example, a retail store manager would not proclaim that December (holiday) sales are great because they exceed August or November sales. Rather, he or she would want to correct for regular seasonal changes before making such comparisons.

The seasonal adjustment method used by many government agencies and by the Federal Reserve on its monetary data may grind up and significantly change underlying movements in the money supply, according to some observers.[15] Attempts to control a monetary aggregate such as M-1 that has been seasonally adjusted in this way may cause undesirable changes, and the underlying changes that are not part of the seasonal may be entirely missed.

STUDY QUESTIONS

1. In general terms, discuss some statistical problems associated with testing the relationships between a monetary aggregate and the monetary base.
2. Do you think the Federal Reserve can control the money supply? Separate weekly control from quarterly or six-monthly averages.
3. Discuss the reasons for the following conclusions: (1) If the central bank wants to control M-1, checkable deposits should have no reserve requirements. (2) If the Federal Reserve wants to control M-2, reserve requirements should be uniform over all M-2 components.
4. List the important determinants of the C/D and R/D ratios. How do increases in each of these ratios affect the money expansion multiplier and the monetary base?
5. How would a mail strike affect the supply of money?
6. How would a bank strike affect the supply of money?
7. If banks charged a higher parking fee for customers, how would the supply of money be affected?
8. If one dollar is shifted from a private demand deposit to a government demand deposit at a private bank, what will happen to the supply of money?
9. Why should the money supply data be seasonally adjusted?
10. The following is a list of six actions that a depository institution may take to change its reserve position. Explain how each action will affect the money supply (M-1 and M-2) and the monetary base.

    a. The management may *sell some of the depository institution's financial securities.* This can be done rapidly and at a small brokerage cost. The money markets allow low-cost rapid sales of relatively default-free securities such as U.S. Treasury bills, which banks hold as secondary reserves. Sometimes these securities and/or state and municipal securities must be pledged as collateral against state and municipal deposits. If this is the case, they cannot be sold to raise cash reserves.

b. The management may *call in some of its loans* from businesses or individuals. Many loans have call provisions or the equivalent. A business or personal loan is frequently made on a three-month (90-day) basis, with the exception by the borrower of the right to renew the agreement. If these loans are not renewed, the bank may lose the borrower's future business and incur unfavorable publicity. This is a costly way to increase reserves rapidly. Of course, a bank may allow loans to run off without actively seeking new borrowers.

c. The management may *borrow in the interbank federal funds market*, the loan market primarily among commercial banks. The management may also obtain funds from the other managed liabilities. The large minimum size of loans in the federal funds market, as well as other requirements, attract larger banks that frequently make short-maturity loans over as little time as 24 hours. Federal funds loans and repurchase agreements are the most common way to raise reserves very rapidly without borrowing directly from the Federal Reserve. The interbank market for borrowing is dominated by uncollateralized federal funds transactions. This market is a low-cost method of quickly allocating reserves among depository institutions to where they are most needed.

d. The management may *borrow funds from the Federal Reserve*. Some managers are reluctant to borrow from the Federal Reserve, preferring other loan sources. For the banking system as a whole, however, one conclusion is inescapable. If by the weekly settlement time (close of business on Wednesdays) there are not enough reserves in the banking system to meet reserve requirements, the depository institutions cannot increase their total reserves by borrowing from one another and thus must borrow at the Federal Reserve discount window.

e. The management may *obtain additional equity funds from present and new owners by selling additional stock in the depository institution*, or it may *sell debt instruments through the holding company that owns the depository institution*. These actions would require substantial time and be too costly to change reserves rapidly.

f. The management may try to *shift deposits from high-reserve categories to low-reserve categories*, thereby lowering the total reserve requirements. In general, this action takes considerable time. There are, however, techniques for slightly reducing recorded deposits in the current week.

GLOSSARY

Control theory. The study of the methods of controlling variables such as the money supply and the monetary base. The Federal Reserve, for example, can use these control procedures.

Currency ratio. The ratio of the amount of currency outside depository institutions to the amount of their checkable deposits.

Liquidity needs. A depository institution's need for cash for its daily operations.

Money expansion multiplier (or monetary base multiplier). The relationship between the monetary base and the stock of money. It is equal to the ratio of money divided by the monetary base (using a particular concept of money and the related money expansion multiplier).

Pyramiding. The process of redepositing funds in the banking system, resulting in an unstable level of deposits if the amount is not limited.

Reserve ratio. The ratio of the amount of reserves at depository institutions to the amount of their deposits.

NOTES

1. Some readers of the first edition had trouble understanding how the money supply could be viewed as being divided between the monetary base and bank money. This method of introducing that classification was suggested to me by Jack Rutner.

2. Milton Friedman and Anna Schwartz developed this identity in *A Monetary History of the United States, 1867–1960* (Princeton, N.J.: Princeton University Press, 1963), especially App. B, pp. 776–808. A formula similar to the one used by Friedman and Schwartz was used by J. E. Meade in "The Amount of Money in the Banking System," *Economic Journal*, March 1934, pp. 73–83, reprinted in *Readings in Monetary Theory* (Homewood, Ill.: Richard D. Irwin, 1951), pp. 54–62. Meade's formulation is less useful for analyzing the current U.S. money supply, as one of his proximate determinants is "the proportion of its note issue, which the Central Bank covers with gold."

3. A more complete formula for the expansion of M-1 is derived as follows: Let R (reserves) equal the sum of the reserves held against checkable deposits, D, time deposits, T, and government deposits, such as tax and loan accounts, G:

$$R = aD + bT + cG \tag{9}$$

where a, b, and c are constants. Again divide equation (1) by equation (2), substituting in the more detailed classification of reserves in equation (9). Then multiply by B and divide the numerator and denominator of the fraction by D. The following equation is obtained:

$$\text{M-1} = B\left[\frac{C/D + 1}{a + b(T/D) + c(G/D) + C/D}\right] \tag{10}$$

Both a payment of taxes to a tax and loan account and a shift of funds from a demand deposit to a time deposit at a commercial bank reduce M-1.

4. Some analysts, such as Phillip Cagan, use other ratios, such as currency and coin outside banks divided by the total money supply, M. This formulation is explained by the same analysis, as $M/C - 1 = D/C$. Much information on the currency and reserve ratios can be found in Phillip Cagan's classic work on the money supply, *Determinants and Effects of Changes in the Stock of Money, 1875–1960* (New York: Columbia University Press, 1965).

5. Cagan, *Determinants*, pp. 118–150.

6. The ratio of currency held by the public to adjusted demand deposits at commercial banks was .8 in January 1867. By October 1929, the currency ratio had fallen to .086. It then rose sharply during the banking panic of the early 1930s, reaching .225. The currency ratio then began to fall again, as it had during its secular decline from the 1880s to the 1930s. It rose slightly during the second recession of the 1930s, in 1937, but again fell, reaching a value of .137 in December 1938. It rose dramatically in World War II, as it had in World War I. In December 1944, it reached a value of .254. During the remainder of World War II and the postwar period, up to 1960, the currency ratio had a downward trend. In December 1960, the currency ratio was .159. After 1960, the trend of the currency ratio was upward, reaching .333 in January 1987.

7. Stated in this way, the logic of this hypothesis is not precisely correct. Banks will have an incentive to economize on excess reserves at any positive rates of market interest. However, because of the costs of buying and selling income-earning assets, they will be able to make more transactions when market interest rates are higher, to cover the added costs. It will pay to hire another portfolio manager, for example, at higher market rates of interest. This corrected logic was developed by James Tobin and William Baumol in a famous model of money demand, presented in Appendix C to Chapter 18.

8. For some views on the relationship of the money supply and interest rates, see S. Goldfeld, *Commercial Bank Behavior and Economic Activity* (Amsterdam: North Holland Press, 1966); S. Goldfeld and E. Kane, "The Determinants of Member Bank Borrowing," *Journal of Finance*, Vol. 21, September 1966, pp. 499–514; F. Modigliani, R. Rasche, and J. Cooper, "Central Bank Policy, the Money Supply and the Short-Term Rate of Interest," *Journal of Money, Credit and Banking*, Vol. 2, May 1970, pp. 166–218; R. Teigen, "Demand and Supply Functions for Money in the United States: Some Structural Estimates," *Econometrica*, Vol. 32, October 1964, pp. 476–509; and J. Tobin, "Commercial Banks As 'Creators' of Money," in D. Carson, ed., *Banking and Monetary Statistics* (Homewood, Ill.: Richard D. Irwin, 1966).

9. Cagan, *Determinants*, p. 221.

10. The *Journal of Money, Credit and Banking* published in November 1982 the results of a conference, "Current Issues in the Conduct of Monetary Policy," sponsored by the American Enterprise Institute for Public Policy

Research and held on February 4–5, 1982. Its 315 pages present the views of a number of economists. The Federal Reserve published a two-volume *New Monetary Control Procedures* in February 1981 with numerous members of its staff contributing studies.

11. Albert Burger, "Money Stock Control," Federal Reserve Bank of St. Louis, October 1972, pp. 10–18; and James M. Johannes and Robert H. Rasche, "Predicting the Money Multiplier," *Journal of Monetary Economics*, Vol. 5, 1979, pp. 301–325. Also see Michael J. Hamburger, "Behavior of the Money Stock: Is There a Puzzle?" *Journal of Monetary Economics*, Vol. 3, 1977, pp. 265–288; J. L. Pierce and T. D. Thomson, "Some Issues in Controlling the Stock of Money," *Controlling Monetary Aggregates II: The Implementation*, Federal Reserve Bank of Boston Conference Series No. 9, 1972, pp. 115–136; and William Dewald and William Gibson, "Sources of a Variation in Member Bank Reserves," *Review of Economics and Statistics*, May 1967, pp. 143–150. For a relatively easy-to-read analysis, see Neil G. Berkman and Richard W. Kopeke's excellent analysis in "The Money Stock: Out of Control or What?" *New England Economic Review*, Federal Reserve Bank of Boston, January–February 1979, pp. 5–19. Also see note 9.

For an early analysis of monetary control and financial intermediary deposits, long before the deregulation period of the 1980s, see David I. Fand, "Intermediary Claims and the Adequacy of Our Monetary Controls," in a book filled with classic statements that money and banking students can still profitably read, *Banking and Monetary Studies*, written in commemoration of the centennial of the National Banking System and edited by Deane Carson (Homewood, Ill.: Richard D. Irwin, 1963), pp. 234–253. Fand responded, in part, to the Heller Committee recommendations, a committee set up in March 1962 by President John Kennedy, which proposed introducing reserve requirements on savings and loan associations and mutual savings banks. Eighteen years later, reserve requirements were so extended.

12. Johannes and Rasche, "Predicting the Money Multiplier," pp. 323–324.

13. One study found that Federal Reserve policy had the effect of offsetting movements in the money expansion multiplier, even though the current money supply was not stabilized: Jack L. Rutner, "A Time Series Analysis of the Control of Money," *Monthly Review*, Federal Reserve Bank of Kansas City, January 1975, pp. 1–8. The Federal Reserve would, if this study is right, have followed a policy—not by design but perhaps because of the interest rate target it followed—of adjusting the monetary base to fit the money supply. If this adjustment usually happened over a short time period, say, two weeks, it could have been missed by most testing procedures, which would have revealed only the stability of the money expansion multiplier. The tests of Edgar L. Feige and Robert McGee in "Money Supply Control and Lagged Reserve Accounting," *Journal of Money, Credit and Banking*, November 1977, pp. 536–551, also

call these tests into question. Feige and McGee found that since 1968, bank reserves have lagged money growth, because of the system of lagged reserve requirements instituted by the Federal Reserve in 1968 and ended in 1984.

14. Brian Motley and Robert H. Rasche, "Predicting the Money Stock: A Comparison of Alternative Approaches," *Economic Review*, Federal Reserve Bank of San Francisco, spring 1986, p. 51.

15. The following article makes this point, but it should be consulted only if the reader is comfortable with intermediate statistics. See Robert Auerbach and Jack Rutner, "The Misspecification of a Non-Seasonal Cycle As a Seasonal by the X-11 Seasonal Adjustment Program," *Review of Economics and Statistics*, November 1978, pp. 601–603. Also see the report of the Advisory Commission on Monetary Statistics, called "Improving the Monetary Aggregates," Board of Governors of the Federal Reserve System, June 1976. The commission included G. L. Bach, Philip D. Cagan, Milton Friedman, Clifford G. Hildreth, Franco Modigliani, Arthur Okun, and, originally, Paul McCracken.

PART FIVE

MONETARY THEORY

CHAPTER 18

THE DEMAND FOR MONEY

CHAPTER PREVIEW

Introduction. The classical view of the demand for money in its modern form is central to the material in this chapter.

Fundamentals of Demand Curves. The concepts of the demand and supply of money and the price level are presented.

The Quantity Theory of Money Demand. The determinants of the demand for real money balances, an old subject of study, are examined.

The Velocity of Money. The velocity of money is an alternative way of looking at the demand for money. The changes in the velocity of money from 1895 to 1986 and the debate about the nature of velocity in the 1980s are discussed.

Appendix A: The Equation of Exchange. An alternative way of defining the velocity of money is described.

Appendix B: The Demand for Money by Business Firms. The demand for money by business firms requires a different analysis but may end up with similar variables.

Appendix C: The Transactions Demand for Nominal Money Balances. A model is derived that relates the demand for money to both the cost of selling bonds to obtain money balances and the interest forgone on bonds by holding money. A suggestion is made to update this model for the payment of interest on checking accounts.

INTRODUCTION

The study of theory begins in this chapter with the demand for money. The demand for money is not treated in nominal terms—a demand for nominal dollars—instead, it is treated in real terms, a demand for *real units of purchasing power*. These fundamental concepts are introduced at the beginning of the chapter, including the meaning of the *price index*, and the meaning of the real value of money.

The classical view of the demand for money, called the **quantity theory of money**, is "classical" because the study is so ancient in origin. We shall discuss this and the modern view, in this tradition, of the demand for money. Real income and a special way of looking at interest rates (which takes into account the costs and benefits of holding money) are described as determinants of the demand for real money balances. One famous property that is alleged for the demand for money, money illusion, is also explained. Next, the concept of the velocity of money is introduced and is shown to be an alternative, convenient way in which to speak about the demand for money. There are three appendices on interesting topics in the demand for money. We also will discuss one of the most important debates in regard to controlling the money supply of the United States, the income velocity of money in the 1980s.

FUNDAMENTALS OF DEMAND CURVES

The Demand and Supply of Money

Rather than referring to the demand and supply of a *flow* of funds per period of time, as was done for loanable funds in Chapter 4, it is customary to speak of the demand and supply of the *stock* of money at a given time, as depicted in Figure 18-1. The supply of money is assumed to be a vertical line (it is not discussed in this chapter). The demand for money at each nominal interest rate on bonds is shown along $D_M D_M$. The quantity of money demanded equals the quantity supplied at an interest rate of i_b. In equilibrium, i_b is the same interest rate that would be derived from the demand and supply of loanable funds analysis, discussed in the previous chapter.

An important difference between this analysis and that for loanable funds is that money balances are not stated in terms of the number of (nominal) dollars but, rather, in terms of the real value of money (its purchasing power). Thus, in this analysis it is assumed that purchasing power, not just dollar bills, is demanded. Because it is necessary to understand the concept of the real value of money, it is discussed next.

The Real Value of Money

The **real value** or **exchange price** of a unit of money, a dollar bill, is defined in the same manner as is the exchange price of any other unit of wealth: It is the value of the goods and/or services that must be exchanged to obtain a dollar bill in the market.

FIGURE 18-1   The Demand and Supply of Real Money Balances

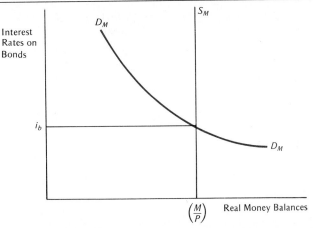

The demand for real money balances is drawn showing the *quantity of real money balances demanded* at each nominal interest rate on bonds (say, one-year Treasury bills). The supply of money is drawn here as a vertical line that shows that the quantity of real money balances supplied does not depend on nominal interest rates (a characteristic of the supply of money that need not be true). By assuming that the supply of money does not depend on interest rates and is at a given level, attention can be focused on the demand for real money balances.

Although the market price of money is a confusing concept to many students, the confusion usually disappears if money is compared with other commodities. Imagine that in a barter economy (no money) one dozen oranges are traded for one clock. The real (relative) price of oranges in terms of clocks can then be said to be one dozen oranges/one clock. The orange price of clocks is then one clock/one dozen oranges, or one twelfth clock per orange. All prices in the barter economy might be stated in terms of one commodity, say, peanuts. One could then derive the peanut price of each commodity. Peanuts are then the commodities used in the denominator of all relative prices, and peanuts are called the **numeraire** or the **deflator**.

In a money economy, the most convenient numeraire is money, and the price of each commodity can be stated in terms of money. If three dollars is the dollar price of a clock, the clock price of a dollar will then be one third of a clock. Because money is widely accepted in payment for many goods and services and because it is usually a common *unit of account*, its exchange price is not measured solely in terms of one commodity. That is, if one were asked if the exchange price of a dollar had declined, the following answer would be very incomplete: "It takes fewer clocks to buy a dollar." Therefore, some composite measurement that involves many goods and services that an indivdiual is likely to exchange for a dollar should be used.

A **price index** thus is formed, which is ideally a comparison between two periods of the average price per dollar for the purchase of a given group of goods and services. For example, if the average price is $1.00 in the first period and $1.15 in the second period, the *price level* is said to have increased by 15 percent. The *price level index* in period 2 is $1.15/$1.00 or, multiplying by 100 to make the first period equivalent to a base of 100, 115, a pure number with no units.

There is, in principle, an impossible problem in forming a price index. At any point in time, different market baskets of goods are consumed by different households, and therefore whenever there are changes in relative prices, a price index must fail to represent the change in the cost of buying a market basket for one or both of these different households. The same problem applies over time to a given household, because the market basket of goods purchased in 1970 will not be the same as that purchased in 1990, as relative prices change.

In the United States, price indexes—which are estimated by departments in the federal government—are frequently used to describe price level changes. The **producers price indexes** (of wholesale prices) and the **GNP deflator** (of all goods and services included in the gross national product) are regularly estimated. A number of price indexes result from extensive monthly surveys of the Bureau of Labor Statistics. Its **consumer price index (CPI)** is an index of prices based on a particular group of goods and services, called the **market basket**, which is supposed to include the types of things bought by most consumers. An index that is similar in its attempt to measure consumer prices is the **personal consumption expenditure deflator (PCE).** The PCE index measures the average prices of *all* consumer goods compared with those of a base period.

How to Make a Price Index

Price indexes are usually estimated from sample surveys using modern statistical procedures. The actual construction of a price index, together with some intuitive idea of what it means, can be illustrated best with a simple example.

Suppose that there are two goods in an economy, A and B. In Table 18-1, notice that good A was selling for $10 in the first period but then fell in price to $5 in the second period. The number of items sold fell from 15 to 7. The question is, What has happened to average prices?

It is not an easy question to answer. One cannot look at prices alone in computing such an average, the amount sold must also be taken into account. Imagine that the French berets with a bell on the top and with Tom Selleck's signature on the inside went from $10.95 to $75.95 after Selleck wore one on a television program. You would not want to say that the United States was having a rapid inflation, with prices going through the roof, if only 200 of the berets were sold, if in the same period, other goods, such as food, remained at constant prices per item. That is, it is intuitively natural to weight the price increase by the amount sold.

That example is easy to explain. But look at the A and B goods in Table 18-1. Different quantities are sold in each period. One could average the quan-

TABLE 18-1   Forming a Price Index for Two Goods

	Period 1	Period 2
Price A	$10	$ 5
Price B	6	20
Quantity of A sold	10	11
Quantity of B sold	15	7
Index using Period 1 weights*		

$$P_L = \frac{10(\$5) + 15(\$20)}{10(\$10) + 15(\$6)} = \frac{\$360}{\$190} = 1.84 \ (84\% \ \text{rise}) \tag{1}$$

Index using Period 2 weights†

$$P_A = \frac{11(\$5) + 7(\$20)}{11(\$10) + 7(\$6)} = \frac{\$195}{\$152} = 1.28 \ (28\% \ \text{rise}) \tag{2}$$

* This is called a Laspeyres index, a method used to calculate the CPI index.
† This is called a Paasche index, a method used to calculate the PCE index. Both indexes are usually multiplied by 100 so that $P_L = 184$ and $P_A = 128$, which is equivalent to making the base year outlay equal 100.

tities and use these averages to weight each price, but this can produce problems. For example, if 1 unit were sold in the first period and 1 million units in the second period, it would be misleading to give the price in each period a weight of .5 million. This is because the price in the period when only one was sold should have very little weight.

Another method is to use the weights in the first period. For A and B, they are 10 and 15, respectively. The weighted average of second-period prices is then

$$10(\$5) + 15(\$20) = \$350$$

and the weighted average for first-period prices is

$$10(\$10) + 15(\$6) = \$190$$

The proportional rise in (weighted) average prices is

$$\frac{\$350}{\$190} = 1.84$$

That proportion is multiplied by 100 to give 184 as the price index. This multiplication makes the index easier to use, because in the first period, the *base period*, the average is, by definition, 100. Thus, when the index rises to 184 in the second period, it can be said that average prices have risen by 84 percent from the base period.

Using base-period weights (the quantities of items sold in the initial period) to weight both periods in calculating a price index is called a *Laspeyres index*. Suppose that second-period weights are used. Try this to form such an index.

It is called a *Paasche index*. Then check your answer in equation (2) in Table 18-1.

The Laspeyres method of calculating an index tends to overstate the rate of inflation. That is, the calculation uses in the second period the same quantity of a good that has gone up in price, when relatively less is likely to be sold at the higher price. This weighting system thus gives too much weight to goods with rising prices and not enough weight to goods with falling prices.

But in the Paasche index, if the quantities sold in the second period are used as weights, the inflation will tend to be understated because the weights are biased in the other direction. That is, the lower quantities sold in the second period for goods that have risen in price are also used for the first period. This method of forming an index gives too little weight to goods with rising prices. Thus the calculations in Table 18-1 indicate a smaller rate of inflation, 28 percent. The "true" average is between the Laspeyres and the Paasche indexes.

The price level, P, is estimated by the value of the price index. In equations (1) and (2) of Chapter 8, $P = 184$ or 128 in the second period according to the method selected for its calculation. The **price level** is a measure of the amount of goods and services that can be exchanged for a dollar, on the average, compared with that in a base year. If P doubles (P would equal 200 in the second period), a dollar bill can, on the average, be exchanged for half as many units of goods and services. The **purchasing power of money** declines by half. The exchange price (or real value) of a dollar is given by $1/P$. The exchange price (or real value) of M units of money is M/P. Consequently, the nominal price of a dollar is $1. Its real price—like the real price of other goods and services—is its nominal price divided by the price level.

THE QUANTITY THEORY OF MONEY DEMAND

A Perspective from the Past

The study of the demand for money and the relationship of money to the price level are parts of monetary theory that have been discussed by scholars for a number of centuries. Depending on one's ingenuity in finding a connection between the ideas of ancient scholars and the central idea of this part of monetary theory, the beginnings of this discussion can be traced farther and farther back, even to Confucius. Skipping forward through the centuries, the subject is found in John Hale's *Discourse of the Common Weal of This Realm of England*, written sometime before his death in 1571, and in John Locke's *Some Consideration of the Consequences of Lowering the Interest and Raising the Value of Money*, written in 1692.[1]

It is probably difficult to find a well-known economist from Adam Smith (whose famous *An Inquiry into the Nature and Cause of the Wealth of Nations* was published in 1776) to the present time who has not devoted considerable space to analyzing the demand for money and the relationship of money to the price level. Many of these luminaries developed useful new analyses ("new" is a tenuous allegation in the presence of enterprising economic historians) or successfully reformulated hypotheses in a more useful way.

Throughout the history of this inquiry, there has been one frequently repeated assertion: The quantity of money is a primary determinant of the price level. Writing in his classic essay, "Of Money," David Hume (1711–1776) said, "Suppose four-fifths of all the money in Britain to be annihilated in one night. . . . Must not the price of all labour and commodities sink in proportion . . .?"[2] The rigid version of this central theme in the history of monetary theory (as in Hume's isolated assertion) is that of strict proportionality between the quantity of nominal money and the price level.[3]

The apparent absurdity of this unqualified rigid version of strict portionality between money and prices has been the focus of both derision and confusion. As a statement about the change from one equilibrium position to another in a mathematical model, it can, of course, be made to be true. But as an accurate description of individual behavior—at the microeconomic level—it is inaccurate. Individuals may indeed display offsetting behavior that allows the statement to be true for the economy as a whole under certain conditions. To go from the micro level, however, to an explanation of how the economy as a whole—the macro level—can achieve strict proportionality between a nominal money supply increase and a price level increase turns out to require some of the most brilliant academic acrobatics.[4] The conditions that are required for strict proportionality are unlikely to hold. Nevertheless, much insight can be gained into the demand for real money balances from knowing something about one of the most important underlying principles in this age-old subject. This principle, the absence of money illusion, is discussed later.

The Demand for Real Money Balances

The modern formulations of the demand for money in the quantity theory tradition make the demand for real money balances (M/P) depend on real income (Y/P), the nominal interest rates, summarized by the interest rates on bonds, i_B, and a variable determined by the public's tastes and preferences, Z. The next sections of this chapter will explain the first two variables, why they are important, and alternative formulations that may be more useful for some purposes. The variable Z will be explained later in the chapter. To tie these discussions together, the variables are put together here in a formula for the demand for real money balances.

The Effect of Real Income

The influence of the real income variable may be thought of in two ways. First, the greater the real income is, the more real purchases will be made, and so the more real money balances will be demanded. This motive for holding real balances was described by John Maynard Keynes as the **transactions demand for money**. It is included in a description of the Keynesian model in Chapter 23.

A second explanation of the effect of real income on the demand for real money balances treats money as one asset in a portfolio of assets. At higher levels of real income, an individual's wealth is likely to be greater. That is, the individual will have more assets, one of which will be real money balances. Real wealth itself is a more desirable variable, but because estimates of wealth are very rough, real income is used. Real wealth or real income indicates the scale of an individual's portfolio and is called a **scale variable**.

THE DEMAND FOR MONEY

The demand for real money balances, $(M/P)^D$, depends on

1. Real income Y/P (a national income aggregate).
2. Market (or nominal) interest rates on alternative assets, which will be summarized by the rate of interest on bonds, i_B.
3. Other variables determining the public's tastes and preferences for real money balances, Z.

In symbols, the equation is

$$\left(\frac{M}{P}\right)^D = f\left(\frac{Y}{P}, i_B, Z\right) \qquad (3)$$

The f before the parentheses means "depends on." It is a *functional notation* that means the following: The equation says that real money balances demanded *depend on* the three variables in the parentheses. It does not specify *how* they depend on these variables (that is, for example, the effect on money demand if real income rises by 10 percent). Rather, it is a general statement, and such a statement in the form of an equation is said to be in *functional form*.

The Costs of Holding Money

The cost of holding money can be viewed in two parts. First is the **opportunity cost**, the cost of not holding the next best alternative asset (or group of assets) such as a short-term bond, say, a three-month U.S. Treasury bill. If the interest rate on this Treasury bill is 8 percent per year, then that 8 percent will be an opportunity cost that the holders of money must bear. A $100 money balance would cost $8 per year to hold. Second are the explicit costs of holding money, such as charges on balances in bank accounts, insurance, and wallet and purse costs.

These statements are made clearer if they are put in a more precise form. Consider that individuals hold real money balances because of the services and money income that money produces.[5] A real money balance is a given amount of purchasing power. It provides both medium-of-exchange services to make payments and store-of-value services, described in Chapter 2.

At a given price level, individuals are viewed as increasing their money balances up to the point that additional services per dollar (the **marginal service yield**) equal the additional net costs per dollar. To illustrate this view, assume that

1. The bond rate of interest i_B is 10 percent.
2. The interest rate (from a NOW deposit) on money, R_m, minus any storage costs per dollar, C_M, is 4 percent.
3. The marginal service yield, i_M, is unknown.

This statement says that an individual will increase his or her money balances until

$$i_M = i_B + C_M - R_m \qquad (4)$$

To understand this equation, it can also be thought of as an equilibrium statement that says that the rate of return from holding more bonds is equal to the rate of return from holding more money. It is an equilibrium position because there will then be no incentive to shift into more bonds or more money. What is the rate of return from holding money? It is the nonpecuniary rate of return (the marginal service yield), i_M, minus the money cost per dollar, C_M, plus any interest on money, R_M. That rate of return on money is equal to the rate of return on bonds, i_B. In symbols, the equation says that in equilibrium, $i_M - C_M + R_M$ is equal to i_B.

Notice an important but sometimes confusing point about these interest rates: They are nominal interest rates. The demand for *real* money balances, shown in Figure 18-1, depends on *nominal* interest rates. That is, the expectation of a rise in the price level causes nominal interest rates to rise (see Chapter 4). A rise in nominal interest rates increases the cost of holding a given real money balance. Most other goods, such as a house, have income streams (such as rent from tenants) that rise in nominal value with a rise in the price level. The real rate of interest thus governs the demand for these goods. Therefore, the key to using nominal interest rates for the demand for real money balances is that money, unlike goods such as houses, has a nominal income stream that is not expected to change to offset the effects of expected price changes on its *real value*. These expected changes in the price level show up in nominal interest rates.

To further your understanding of equation (4), use the values given for each variable. Substitute these values in the equation. Then i_M is found to be 6 percent. Equation (4) is a condition for equilibrium-desired real money balances. If the individual values the services from real money balances at more than 6 percent, he or she will sell off some other assets and add real money balances. Simply stated, real money balances would offer a higher net rate of return than other assets would.

From this analysis, it appears that the rate of interest derived here, i_M, is the rate of interest that should be put into the demand-for-money equation, equation (3). This is because it takes into account the opportunity cost of holding money, i_B, and the direct costs, C_m, and returns, R_M. However, most modern macroeconomics analysis generally uses just the opportunity cost, the interest rate on bonds, i_B. Although that convention is generally followed, it is important to remember that because interest is now paid on many checking deposit accounts, the other variables in equation (4) will affect the demand for money.

To see how this would work, we will next explain the effect of the payment of interest on checking deposit accounts.

Absence of Money Illusion

An important property often alleged for equation (3)—the demand for real money balances—is worth learning if you do not want to be accused of having money illusion. Suppose that all money prices suddenly rise by 10 percent. This makes the real values of money and bonds fall; it also makes the value of money income fall. Suppose that each moneyholder simultaneously receives 10 percent more nominal money balances, 10 percent more money income, and 10 percent more "money" assets (assets such as time deposits and bonds) and that there is no expectation of price changes. This is a form of relabeling. It takes time to find out that all prices have risen by 10 percent and that, even though more units of dollars are needed to make the same real expenditures, there is just enough additional money and money income to buy as much as before and to save as much as before. In time, everyone will realize that his or her nominal income, his or her nominal money balance, and all nominal prices have risen proportionally.

A government decree that effectively changes the unit of account, including the units by which money income, nominal prices, and money balances are measured, could achieve the same result, except that the government decree would provide a more rapid announcement of the relabeling process.

To show what has happened in this example, let the Greek letter lambda, λ, be equal to 1.1, the compounding factor for a 10 percent increase in nominal money, nominal income, and the price level. Then equation (3) becomes

$$\left(\frac{\lambda M}{\lambda P}\right)^D = f\left(\frac{\lambda Y}{\lambda P}, i_B, Z\right) = \left(\frac{M}{P}\right)^D \tag{5}$$

THE EFFECT OF PAYING INTEREST ON CHECKING ACCOUNTS ON THE DEMAND FOR MONEY

With the authorization on January 1, 1981, for nationwide interest-paying checking accounts at all depository institutions, over 30 percent of M-1 was in the form of interest-paying money. To illustrate the effect of paying interest on money on the demand for money, refer to Figure 18-2. If market interest rates—using the nominal interest rate on bonds—rose from 8 to 10 percent, the quantity of real money balances demanded would decline along demand curve D_{M_1} from A to B. If in response, the depository institutions paid more interest on checking accounts, the demand for money would shift out to D_{M_2}, and the new equilibrium would be at point C. (The demand curve would shift because at every nominal interest rate on bonds, more interest is paid on money, so that more money is demanded.) The depository institution's raising interest payments on money would to some extent offset the effect of higher interest rates on the demand for money. In Figure 18-2, point C is above point A, and so there is a complete offset. If the payment of interest on money changes in tandem with changes in the market rates of interest, the

real money balances will be less sensitive to changes in the market interest rates than they would have been before the interest was paid.

Notice that the demand curves for money in Figure 18-2 become flatter (more elastic), even though the depository institutions have not changed the interest they pay on their interest-paying accounts in tandem with changes in the market rates. The depository institutions also do not appear to have significantly changed the interest they pay on deposits included in M-1 in this period. This reason alone indicates that there would be changes in the quantity demanded, as shown in Figure 18-2, from A to B. That change in quantity demanded is the same as it was before the payment of interest on money. Therefore, to make the demand for money more sensitive to interest changes, the elasticity of the demand for money must change

FIGURE 18-2   The Demand and Supply of Real Money Balances with an Increase in Demand*

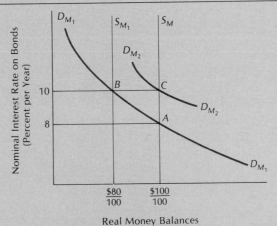

Remember from your introductory economics course that the following conventions hold: A movement along a demand or supply curve is stated as a change in quantity demanded or supplied. A shift in demand or supply curves is stated as a change in demand or supply. Those conventions are illustrated in this figure. A movement from A to B is a decrease in quantity demanded; a movement from B to C is an increase in demand.

* Real balances such as $100/100 are a specific form of M/P where M is the nominal balance and P is a price index.

as a result of paying interest on money. This means that individuals would have to treat the new M-1, with its NOW account component, differently than they treated the old M-1. They may treat NOW accounts differently than they do other forms of money. That is, they may treat a NOW account more like a bond and use it less frequently as a medium of exchange than they do other forms of money. Indeed, some observers have made this suggestion.

The evidence is not clear, however, because the test period from 1981 to 1986 is when the ceiling interest payments allowed on NOW accounts were phased out. In early 1983 there was a huge transfer of funds into the interest-paying checking accounts that had just been authorized, as described in Chapter 8. By March 1983, $300 billion had been transferred into these new accounts, and thus it is difficult to construct test results that rule out the effects of implementing these interest-paying checking accounts. In addition, market interest rates fell after the middle of 1982. But when the depository

institutions have had more experience with the ceiling-free environment and the problems of rising interest rates, they may well try to offset the rise in interest rates with a rise in the interest they pay on money. In the event of a rise in interest rates, the depository institutions probably will not suffer the large disintermediation (the withdrawal of funds) they did in the 1970s. They will be able to bid for funds with higher interest payments, and then the analysis in Figure 18-2 with the new equilibrium at point C would be relevant. Finally, the demand for M-1 would then be less sensitive to changes in market interest rates than it was in the 1970s.

Recent evidence that supports the view that the demand for M-1 has become more interest sensitive since 1981 is explained in easy-to-understand terms by Michael C. Keeley and Gary C. Zimmerman in "Interest Checking and M1," *Weekly Letter*, Federal Reserve Bank of San Francisco, November 21, 1986.

The property alleged for this equation is that under these conditions, individuals do not change their behavior; rather, they want the same real money balances $(M/P)^D$.

But if individuals do demand a different quantity of real money balances at the higher price level, they are said to suffer from **money illusion**. They do not base their behavior on real variables, none of which has changed. Instead, they base their behavior on nominal variables. But many economic analyses assume no money illusion.

MONEY ILLUSION IN THE CONSUMPTION OF PRUNES

Individuals do not base their demand for consumption on nominal values, regardless of the price level, unless they have a dread disease, *money illusion*. That condition is one

in which human behavior does not depend on real variables; it depends on *nominal values*. As will be shown, the disease could produce many problems—not only for eco-

TABLE 18-2   The Real and Nominal Value of Prunes and Their Consumption by
Individuals with and Without Money Illusion

	Period 1	Period 2	Change
Price of 5 lb of prunes	$10	$2.50	75 percent fall in price
The price level	100	25	75 percent fall in average prices
Real value of 5 lb of prunes	$10.00/100 = $.1	$2.50/25 = $.1	No change
Consumption by money illusion victim	5 lb	20 lb	$10 in prunes consumed in each period, causing medical complications
Consumption by individual without money illusion	5 lb	5 lb	No change in consumption

nomic analysis but also for the health of a money illusion victim. The example presented is also shown in Table 18-2.

To illustrate nominal and real values, think of $10 worth of prunes. Ten dollars is their nominal value. If that is all the consumption of prunes an individual undertakes in a period, the nominal consumption of prunes will equal $10.

Suppose that there is a fall in average prices so that the price level index falls from 100 in period 1 to 25 in period 2, a 75 percent drop. At the same time the individual's nominal income and money holdings also fall by 75 percent. Prune prices follow the price level down, also falling by 75

percent. In real terms, nothing has happened. Everything is relabeled at a lower price level, and nominal income and money holdings have fallen in tandem. With the individual's nominal income and money balances, the same amount of real goods and services that could be bought in the first period can be bought in the second period.

The money illusion victim looks at the price of prunes and says, "I still want $10 in prunes." Therefore, he or she consumes 20 pounds of prunes in period 2 rather than the 5 pounds of prunes consumed in period 1, as shown in Table 18-2. If a period is one week, need more be said about the effects of money illusion?

This property of equation (3) is a powerful insight, but not a fully tested proposition. It requires that the services from real money balances be independent of the nominal number of dollars in the real money balances. For example, the income from 100 one-dollar bills is assumed to be the same as that from 200 one-dollar bills if the price level doubles (and there is no expectation of a further price change). This assumption may not hold for commodity money, but it seems plausible for fiat money balances.

There are some costs and distribution effects arising from the adjustment process that could temporarily change equation (3). That is, it takes time to shop around and learn about prices. Some nominal prices are fixed by contracts that were made in the past, and so the property will not hold until the contracts are revised or the assets involved are revalued.

In addition, every monetary variable must change in proportion, including the exchange rates of the domestic currency with foreign currencies (adjusted for the change, if any, in the purchasing power of the foreign currencies).

THE VELOCITY OF MONEY

Income Velocity

A common and useful way to look at the relationship between money and income, with real or nominal variables, requires the introduction of a new concept, the **income velocity of money**, also referred to in this chapter simply as **velocity**. Velocity can be defined as the ratio of nominal income as computed in the national income accounts, Y, divided by the average stock of nominal money, M.

$$V = \frac{Y}{M} \tag{6}$$

The average stock of money, M, is measured in the same period as is nominal income, Y. Velocity is a number per unit of time. For example, during the third quarter of 1982, M-1 averaged \$458 billion, and GNP was \$3,088 billion. Thus, the M-1 velocity, using a GNP estimate for income, was \$3,088/\$458, or 6.7 per quarter of a year.

Equation (6) can be rearranged as

$$MV = Y \tag{7}$$

The meaning of this equation can be explained with an example. Twenty students are in a classroom. Each student is given 10 one-dollar bills. The students are allowed to sell hypothetical *final* goods and services to each other for one hour. Each student records the total money value of the final goods and services he or she has sold. Assume that the total sales of all students amount to \$600. Because there is a total of 200 dollar bills, each dollar bill must have changed hands an average of three times ($=600/200$). Nominal income is \$600, and the income velocity is 3/u.t., where u.t. (unit of time) is one hour.

The concept of velocity, can be stated in equivalent real terms as real income, Y/P, or simply y, divided by real money balances, M/P.

$$V = \frac{y}{M/P} \tag{8}$$

Equation (8) is identical to equation (6), except that both the income and money variables in equation (6) have been divided by P. The value of velocity has not changed. Rearranging equation (3),

$$MV = Py \tag{9}$$

This equation says that expenditures (money balances times their turnover) are equal to receipts (the "average" price times the quantity of goods and services in the national income accounts).

Dividing each side of equation (9) by P:

$$\left(\frac{M}{P}\right)V = y \tag{10}$$

At each level of real income, an increase in the demand for real balances is equivalent to a decline in velocity. One of these variables cannot go up without the other's falling if real income is constant. Therefore, the problem of finding the demand for money at each level of income can alternatively be defined as a problem of finding the value of velocity.

If there is a desired level of money balances at some income, there will be a desired velocity. Velocity, therefore, is also dependent on the interest rates discussed here. At higher bond interest rates, velocity rises, and with larger direct interest payments on money, velocity falls.

The concept of velocity is a useful way to organize the relationships between changes in money and changes in the price level and real income. It can be seen in equation (9) that if velocity can be predicted, then predictions of the relationship among the other variables, M, P, and y, will be simplified. Furthermore, this identity is a reminder that if a theory explains only the change in one of the variables, say a rise in the price level, it will be incomplete. That is, there must be offsetting changes in M, V, or y to preserve the equality of MV with Py.

INCOME VELOCITY, THE DEMAND FOR MONEY, AND MONEY SUPPLY GROWTH

An increase in velocity means that the ratio of real income to real money balances has increased. This can be interpreted as a decrease in the amount of real balances that people want to hold at a given level of real income. Thus, one can say that a *decrease* in velocity is another way to say an *increase* in the demand for money.

Temporarily, when the money supply expands rapidly, individuals find that they have larger-than-desired real money balances. Looking at equation (8), this is equivalent to a fall in velocity. Real income is, to a large extent, tied to past decisions about investment and consumption and usually does not show sharp changes from a general trend. Thus, fast money growth generally means that there will be a temporary fall in velocity. Equivalently, it means that there will be a temporary increase in the demand for real money balances.

The word *temporary* is used because the individuals with larger-than-desired real money balances do eventually try to lower them to desired levels. This behavior and its effects on the economy will be discussed in the next chapter.

Cambridge Cash Balance Equation and the Direction of Influence

Sometimes equation (9) is presented in a different form, called the **Cambridge cash balance equation**. In this form, a different variable is substituted for income velocity. The concept of income velocity is also a statement about the average cash balances that people demand as a proportion, K, of their income. Equation (10) may be rewritten as

$$\left(\frac{M}{P}\right) = Ky \tag{11}$$

where $K = 1/V$. This way of arranging the monetary identity stresses the view that the demand for real money balances, $(M/P)^D$, depends, in part, on the level of real income.

This chapter explains the effects of interest rates and real income on real money balances. The next chapter will discuss the effects of changes in the money supply on prices, interest rates, and real income. Thus, that discussion will incorporate the other direction of influence from M/P to y.

The existence of "bidirectional" influence of causation ($M/P \rightleftarrows y$) presents problems in statistical testing that were explained in the discussion of money and stock prices in Chapter 13.

Changes in the Velocity of Money

There have been a number of studies of the way in which income velocity changes over business cycles, **cyclical** changes, or over the long run, a trend. Velocity tends to rise during business expansions and fall during business contractions. This means that during business expansions, individuals hold less money per dollar of some measure of income—their demand for money per unit of real GNP declines. During business contractions, individuals hold more money per dollar of GNP.

Over a longer period of time, a different relationship has been observed. In tests of the long period from 1867 to the 1950s, real income and income velocity were found to move in opposite directions in the United States. That is, as income grew over this period, individuals tended to increase their demand for money per dollar of income. Therefore, an apparent contradiction arose. As income rose during business expansions, the demand for money declined, but as income rose over the long run, at lesat up to the 1950s, the demand for money increased.

One explanation for this contradiction is that the demand for money does not depend on the current period's income but, instead, depends on the average yearly income that individuals expect over a longer period of time.[6] Using this concept of **expected income**, a sudden rise in current income during a business cycle expansion will only slightly affect individuals' long-run expected income. Money demand that depends on expected income will not rise by as much as current income will. Income velocity will rise. Similarly, during a business contraction, expected income will not fall by as much as current income will. Money demand will not fall by as much as current income will. Therefore, velocity calculated on the basis of current falling income will fall. This explanation is consistent with the long-term fall in velocity from 1867 until the 1950s, as the trend in income (both current and expected) was upward.

Figure 18-3 shows that the long term decline in velocity of M-1 appears to have ended in 1948. What caused this long-term decline in velocity from at least the middle of the last century to the middle of this century? What caused the different behavior in velocity since approximately 1950?

The long-term decline in velocity from approximately 1850 to 1954 (except during World War II) was probably caused largely by growing confidence in the stability of the U.S. government, which issued the monetary base, and by familiarity with the use of checking accounts and the reductions in transactions costs that checking account money afforded. These long-term changes generated a willingness to hold an increasing proportion of income and wealth in the form of money. In addition, more of the transactions in the economy were conducted through the market, where money was used and less output was manufactured in the home. Initially, the home was an important factor in

FIGURE 18-3   Income Velocity of Money, 1910–1986

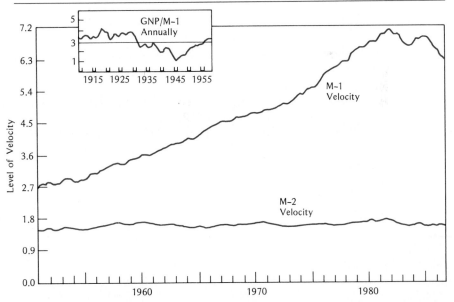

The velocity of M-1 fell until the late 1940s; then it rose until the early 1980s. (But if the decline in the velocity of M-1 during World War II is omitted, the velocity of M-1 fell until 1955.) The velocity of M-2 has been nearly constant since 1950.

Source: Cambridge Planning and Analytics Inc., Boston.

the production of goods and services for the household, from making clothes to processing food for storage. Modern technology and specialization not only removed the necessity for most household production but also made home production a relatively inefficient use of labor. A huge increase of women in the work force accompanied this change. And an increasing knowledge of and sophistication about the use of banking facilities accompanied the change in velocity.

One variable that captures part of this trend is the degree of urbanization—the size of the population in metropolitan areas relative to that in rural areas. The degree of urbanization is a good candidate for the symbol Z in equation (3), especially where the demand for real money balances is explained for developing economies.

Velocity in the 1950s and 1960s

Beginning in the 1950s, interest rates in the United States began to rise. Most of this rise can be attributed to rising rates of inflation, according to the cash balance explanation in Chapter 19. The interest rate ceiling on time deposits at commercial banks, a large component of old M-2, was raised to 5 percent in

FIGURE 18-4   The Rate of Change in the Velocity of M-1, 1951–1986

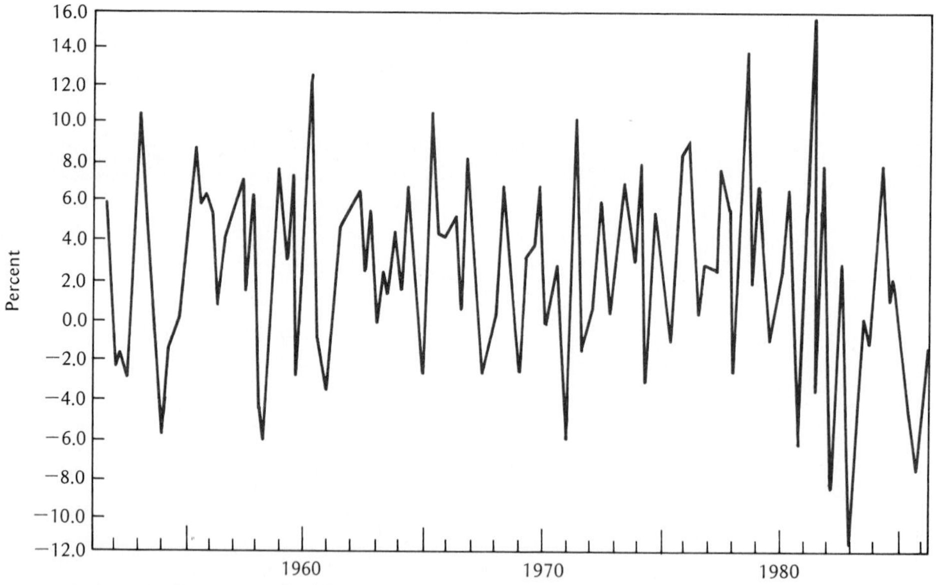

Although there was considerable variation, the average rate of growth in M-1 velocity up to the late 1970s was 3.2 percent. After 1979 the variation in the rate of growth was greater, and the average rate of growth was negative.

Source: Cambridge Planning and Analytics Inc., Boston.

the 1950s. The interest rate ceiling for demand deposits at commercial banks, a major component of M-1, was held constant at zero, except for the gifts and free services that banks provided as a legal way to evade partially the prohibition on interest payments.

It therefore became more and more costly to hold demand deposits. As interest rates rose, depositors had more incentives to economize on demand deposits, and so they switched more and more of their money to other assets. The quantity of M-1 they demanded continued to fall relative to income; that is, the velocity of M-1 rose, as shown in Figure 18-3. The rate of change in M-1 velocity averaged a little over 3 percent, as shown in Figure 18-4. But because in the 1960s competitive interest was paid on time deposits until the 1970s, there was no such incentive to economize, and the demand for time deposits remained roughly constant relative to income, so that the velocity of old M-2 also was roughly constant.

Velocity in the 1970s and 1980s

There is some evidence that the demand for and the income velocity of money changed after 1973 with the introduction of financial innovations.[7] These innovations lowered the transactions costs for financial asset purchases and sales, making it less costly to economize on cash balances. The innovations also took the form of new financial assets that offered less expensive ways to hedge against unexpected interest rate changes and changes in the price of stocks. (The new financial assets were described in Chapter 12.) The demand for these financial assets thus may have increased, and some of that increased demand may have come at the expense of money balances.

The changed character of the income velocity of money became quite apparent in the 1980s. As shown in Figure 18-4, M-1 velocity did not rise after 1980. It fell and then rose and then fell again, having a lower value in 1986 than in 1980. The reasons suggested for this are as follows:

1. The payment of interest on deposits was authorized under the Depository Institutions Deregulation and Monetary Control Act (sometimes referred to as the "Monetary Control Act"). These payments reduced the incentive to economize on cash balances, thus increasing the demand for money, as shown in Figure 18-2. The effect, according to this analysis, was that the income velocity of money fell to a new position during the adjustment period.

2. There were two recessions in this period, and the behavior of the income velocity of money is expected to change during a recession. John Tatom concluded his study of the behavior of the income velocity of money in 1982, as follows:

> It is not unusual, however, for velocity to decline in a recession. [See Table 18-3.] It is, in fact, quite typical. Short-term movements in velocity reflect diverse reactions of the economy to monetary policy actions. In a recession, all of these reactions generally contribute to a temporary decline in velocity. Given the length and severity of the recent recession,

TABLE 18-3   Growth Rates of Velocity in the Last Eight Recessions

Peak–Trough	Velocity Growth Rate*	Increase in the Unemployment Rate†
IV/1948–IV/1949	−2.8%	3.2%
II/1953– II/1954	−2.7	3.2
III/1957– II/1958	−3.2	3.2
II/1960– I/1961	−1.4	1.6
IV/1969–IV/1970	0.0	2.2
IV/1973– I/1975	1.5	3.5
I/1980–III/1980	−0.8	1.4
III/1981–IV/1982	−4.3	3.3

* Compounded annual rate of change in GNP/M-1, in which the old (pre-1980) measure of M-1 is used before 1959.

† Percentage-point change in the quarterly average of unemployment as a percentage of the civilian labor force.

Source: John A. Tatom, "Was the 1982 Velocity Decline Unusual?" *Review,* Federal Reserve Bank of St. Louis, August–September 1983, p. 7.

where the severity is measured by the unemployment rate or the gap between the nation's potential and actual real GNP, it is not surprising that velocity registered the largest decline in post–World War II recessions. . . .

Monetary growth tends to be most variable around a period of recession, especially when a sizable decline initially sets off the recession itself. Such a variation in money growth creates temporary movements in velocity; not only is the supply of money in flux, but real output is as well, as the demand for money adjusts to the money supply variation. Variations in real output and velocity are further enlarged temporarily by inventory adjustments.

In the recent recession, these processes were magnified by the degree and extent of monetary stringency during some periods prior to the recession. As a result, the normal cyclical movement of money demand was large, and swings in the inventory investment further distorted, temporarily, the movements of velocity. Other factors, including the temporary decline in inflation and movements in interest rates, federal expenditures and energy prices all worked in the same direction, reducing velocity in the recent recession. Thus, the extent of the decline in velocity in the recent recession was not unusual, nor did it represent an atypical shift with important, but unknown, implications for policy-making.[8]

3. The immediate effect of rapidly increasing the money supply is for the income velocity of money to fall. And the money supply grew rapidly after 1983. This is because individuals temporarily hold more money after a rapid

increase in the money supply and then adjust their money balances to a new desired level.

4. The rate of inflation was substantially reduced during the early 1980s, and nominal interest rates fell. This should indicate an increase in the quantity of money demanded, which would significantly lower the income velocity of money.

5. Between 1869 and 1954 the income velocity of M-1 fell at an average rate of 1.3 percent per year ater 1895, as shown in Figure 18-5A, although during World War II the income velocity of M-1 rose.[9] After World War II, interest rates and inflation began to accelerate. Combined with the prohibitions against paying pecuniary interest on deposits, the income velocity of M-1 rose at an average of a little over 3 percent per year from 1955 until 1981. Then the interest payment prohibition was lifted (phased out from 1981 to 1986). One hypothesis is that the income velocity of M-1 will drop to a lower level to reflect the phase-in of interest payment on 30 percent of the money supply. The income velocity of M-1 will then gradually return to its trend rate of growth of the period before 1954 if there are no long-term changes in interest rates. Velocity is strongly affected by interest rates, and so if the level of interest rates rises, the income velocity of M-1 will also rise, as shown in Figure 18-5B. But the income velocity of M-1 will not rise as much as it did between 1954 and 1980, when there was a prohibition on paying pecuniary interest on demand deposits. This is because 30 percent of M-1 was in the form of checking accounts on which interest can be paid. The rest of M-1 bears no pecuniary interest, and so it is in the holders' interest to economize on this part of their M-1 balances. Thus, rises in the market rate of interest will cause some switching out of M-1 into other assets, which will cause a rise in the income velocity of M-1, just as a decline in interest rates will cause a fall in the income velocity of M-1.

6. William Barnett holds that the monetary aggregates generally are not properly added together, that they are merely a *simple sum of the components.*[10] For example, M-1 simply adds NOW accounts to demand deposits and currency. Too much weight is usually given to interest-paying substitutes for the basic medium of exchange—as it was defined in 1972 to include only demand deposits and currency held by the public. Instead, Barnett uses a weighting scheme, called a *Divisia index,* to add together the components of monetary aggregates. It weights the components of a monetary aggregate by user cost, which includes the opportunity cost of using this component. The opportunity cost of using NOW accounts is the cost forgone on bond interest minus the direct payments made on NOW accounts. The monetary series formed using the Divisia index gives less weight to the monetary substitutes that grew so rapidly after 1972. Barnett's monetary series does not show any significant change in its relationship with GNP in the 1970s, as do the simple sum aggregates. The Divisia index of money also does not show as high a growth rate for 1985 and 1986 as do the simple sum aggregates. There is no decisive victor between these two indexes' ability to predict more accurately

FIGURE 18-5   The Commercial Paper Rate and the Level and Rate of
Change in M-1 Velocity, 1895–1985

A: The Rate of Change in M-1 Velocity

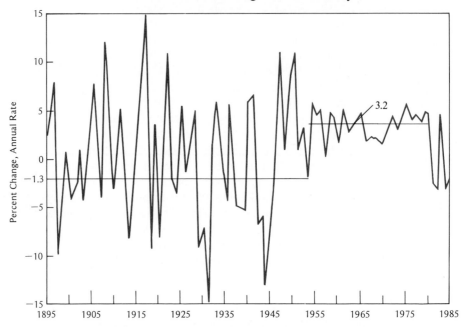

B: The Level of M-1 Velocity and the Commercial Paper Rate

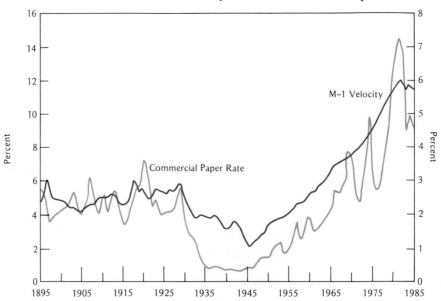

the GNP or other macroeconomic variables. But the Divisia index has a theoretical advantage of using microeconomic foundations on aggregations. It is not clear that the weights estimated are better than simple sum aggregation is, because a number of assumptions are required to pass from the micro foundations to the weights that are used. Further tests and more observations are needed. Barnett found that the money series that incorporates the broadest group of monetary components used by the Federal Reserve in publications of its monetary aggregates also does better in predicting GNP than do more narrowly defined aggregates. But from the standpoint of short-term open market operations, this is not very useful, as these aggregates are often not known until long after the open market operations are conducted.

Although all these theories are well argued, in 1986 one could not be sure of the values that the income velocity of M-1 would assume. Would it again begin to rise, or would it remain more nearly constant, as M-2 had done since 1950? Evidence about the income velocity of money was not persuasive in this period because there were no estimates in the U.S. data of the position of the demand for money vis-à-vis the payment of interest on deposits after the early 1930s, when pecuniary demand deposit interest payments were prohibited. How far out would the demand schedule in Figure 18-2 shift in response to interest payments?

The issues surrounding the income velocity of money in the 1980s led to a stimulating policy debate in the later 1980s, which will be discussed further in Part VII. Milton Friedman argued in 1986 (at the Western Economic Association meetings in San Francisco in July) that there should be no "fine tuning" of the money supply, especially in this period of increased uncertainty about the income velocity of money; that a monetary rule of constant money growth would lead to more economic stability. Others contended that the money

---

Between 1869 and 1954 the income velocity of M-1 fell at an average rate of 1.3 percent per year after 1895, as shown in part A, although during World War II it rose. Combined with the prohibitions against paying pecuniary interest on deposits and the rising interest rates, the income velocity of M-1 rose (at an average of 3.2 percent per year) from 1955 until 1980. Then the interest payment prohibition was phased out from 1981 to 1986. One hypothesis is that the income velocity of M-1 will drop to a lower level to reflect the phase-in of interest payments on 30 percent of the money supply. The income velocity of M-1 will then return to its rate of growth in the period before 1954 if there are no long-term interest rate changes. Velocity is strongly affected by interest rates, as shown in part B, and so if the level of interest rates changes to a new long-term level, the income velocity of M-1 will also change.

Source: The trend rate of growth of the income velocity in M-1 is calculated from Milton Friedman and Anna J. Schwartz, *A Monetary History of the United States 1867–1960* (Princeton, N.J.: Princeton University Press, 1963), p. 774. The plots, with the exception of a different trend rate of growth, are taken from William T. Gavin, "Monetarism and the M1 Target," *Economic Commentary*, Federal Reserve Bank of Cleveland, October 1, 1986, p. 2.

supply–GNP relationship had broken down and that the faster money growth had not ignited a new inflation by the beginning of 1987.

Among the many critics of the view of a stable demand for money was a group of economists generally associated with a classical free market viewpoint. Their so-called new school of monetary economics arose in the early 1980s, which questioned the notion of a unique concept of the demand for money such as M-1.[11] This group disagreed with the view that the demand for something like real M-1 was stable enough to enable the government to carry out monetary policy effectively. (A further note on their policy views is presented in Chapter 26.)

The reader might consider the proposal of one member of this group to control only currency in the conduct of monetary policy. What does that policy require? If the demand for M-1 is unstable, can the demand for currency be stable?

Friedman and Schwartz took a sharply different view. All their tests were conducted with M-2 before 1981.[12] Friedman used M-1 after 1981 because he held that the new M-1 concept corresponded more closely to the old M-2 concept than did the new M-2 concept.

APPENDIX A: THE EQUATION OF EXCHANGE

Up to this point, we have used the concept of income or wealth as a variable in explaining the demand for money. What about including a greater number of transactions than those that enter into an estimate of income? Why not include the sum of the value of all transactions?

Back in 1911, one of the most famous economists who has ever studied money and interest rates, Irving Fisher, developed the forerunner to equation (1).[13] Fisher's monetary identity is called the **equation of exchange**. Unlike equation (1), which defines income in national income accounting terms, the Fisher equation covers all transactions, including those transactions for intermediate goods and transactions involving financial assets. His equation of exchange is

$$MV_t = PT \tag{12}$$

where T is the total number of transactions, P is a price index for all transactions, and V_t is the transactions velocity of money.

This identity (12) was cast aside in favor of the income identity (1) in large part because of the availability of better data. Boris P. Pesek made a compelling case for bringing Fisher's equation back onto center stage.[14] Although it is not clear whether every transaction should be used in explaining the demand for money, a definition of transactions that includes those from the sale of financial assets seems appropriate. If income affects the demand for money, and individuals treat the income they derive from selling a stock or bond in the same way that they treat their wage income, then capital gains from the sale of financial assets should be included in the measure of their income (after adjusting for taxes). Pesek convincingly argued that many recent financial developments can best be understood by going back to Fisher and using the concept of velocity in equation (12). Find out for yourself. Stay home this weekend and read Boris Pesek's article.

The equation of exchange emphasizes the use of money in exchange. As more (or fewer) transactions are required, larger (or smaller) nominal money balances will be needed at each level of prices. Also, if workers are paid more frequently, they will hold smaller average nominal money balances at each price level because they will know that their money balances will be replenished more rapidly. This relationship between the average money holdings and the frequency of wage payments is subject to a number of other factors, some of which are contained in the famous model of the transactions demand for money, contained in Appendix C to this chapter.

APPENDIX B: THE DEMAND FOR MONEY BY BUSINESS FIRMS

Real money balances can be thought of as a **factor of production** in a business firm, the same as other inputs such as land, labor, and capital. It can be shown in price theory that each factor of production will be used up to the point that the additional output it produces per dollar of cost is equal to the additional output that could be produced by each of the other factors per dollar of their cost.

The **budget constraint** is the name given to the limitation placed on the amount of income available to a household in a given period. The budget constraint in a given period can be altered by a household if funds are borrowed against future income. The market for loans against future wage income is, however, imperfect. Households must borrow at a much higher rate than they can earn by lending. If one presumes that a budget constraint for a household will not be significantly shifted in a given period because of the difficulties associated with borrowing, the idea of a fixed budget constraint for households may be a roughly correct approximation. Then income can be usefully used to explain the real money demand. *But this is not the case for business firms.* The capital market will rapidly shift funds into firms that are expected to bring the greatest rate of return. Even if a firm has a small rate of profit in the current period, it may have a very large scale of operations because it is able to borrow in the capital market on the basis of expected increased profits in the future. The concept of a fixed budget constraint for a business firm operating in a fairly competitive capital market thus collapses. In this respect, business firms differ from households and require a different formula for the demand for real money balances. Perhaps a more important determinant is whether or not the business is relatively money intensive, such as a financial intermediary might be.

Nevertheless, the **scale of operations** may be a good explanation on the strictly mechanical grounds that a larger business needs more real money balances to operate. Business firms use real asset size and the total volume of transactions as scale variables in tests of the demand for real money balances.

But the results of tests of business demand for real money balances are not consistent.[15] Different results are obtained from **cross-section data** (estimates of different firms in the same time period) than from **time series data** (data from successive time periods). Tests have shown that

> differences in manufacturing industries' demands for cash can be explained by differences in firm sizes; ... What happens is that the velocity of cash (where velocity in sales divided by cash) at first declines and then rises, as firms increase in size. But the decline in velocity occurs only over a small fraction of the lower portion of the values the asset-size variable may take on.[16]

These results, which synthesize several investigators' findings, are interesting, but they tend to relate unsatisfactorily to theory and are therefore difficult to interpret. Test results in search of theoretical meaning may find many shoes that fit; unfortunately, they may walk off in several directions, thereby tearing apart the theory.

One of the most difficult aspects of interpreting the business demand for real money balances is having to take into account the output produced by real money balances. Real money balances are a factor of production that yields output for the business firm. The output produced by money in a business firm "is likely to be especially dependent on features of production and conditions affecting the smoothness and regularity of operations as well as those determining the size and scope of enterprises, the degree of vertical integration, and so forth."[17] That is, a business firm that has many unexpected payments and/or receipts may find it more profitable to carry larger quantities of real money balances than will a firm of similar size (with the same amount of transactions and the same size assets) that has a smoother, more predictable flow of receipts and payments.

The analysis of the demand for real money balances by business firms is further complicated by the necessity of distinguishing between *manufacturing firms* and *financial intermediaries*. The amount of reserves held by financial intermediaries depends to a large extent on the quantity of short-term liquid liabilities that they have issued to the public, and on the legal reserve requirements in the case of depository intermediaries. These financial intermediaries buy and sell assets in the money markets daily. The total volume of transactions is huge and is not related to their money balances in the same manner as is the volume of transactions of manufacturing firms.

Furthermore, new cash management techniques allow firms to economize on real money balances. These techniques include lock-box systems under which bill payments are collected in post office boxes throughout the country and local banks will immediately deposit the payments. This can be combined with zero-balance accounts: Bank accounts are reduced to zero each day, and the funds are transferred to a central account for immediate investment. The implementation of cash management techniques is probably very uneven among firms, thus making the aggregate business demand for money schedules difficult to estimate.

However, after lamenting the unsatisfactory state of estimates of the business demand for money, it can be said that the variables in the household demand for money—equation (3)—probably explain much of the relationship. This may be true, because variables such as the relative number of business firms that are cash intensive or the size distribution of business firms do not change enough to offer much explanation over and above the commonly used variables, such as income and interest rates.

APPENDIX C: THE TRANSACTIONS DEMAND FOR NOMINAL MONEY BALANCES

William Baumol and James Tobin made similar analyses of the demand for money, using an inventory approach.[18] These famous contributions combined the theories of the demand for money as a device for negotiating transactions with the analysis that views money as an asset dependent on interest rates. The Baumol–Tobin analysis, or a variant of it, has been applied to controlling business inventories of cash. It is similar to models for controlling the inventories of other commodities held by businesses.

The principles are illustrated in a model that makes a number of simplifying assumptions that do not change the underlying general principles. For convenience, all references are to nominal money, with the price level constant. Assume that Henry Boggs receives $400 each Thursday in the form of assets, say bonds, for his pay during the week. Boggs's expenditures are always at a constant rate, just enough to exhaust the value of his assets at the instant that he receives his next pay the following Thursday. Henry Boggs's asset balances over a five-week period are shown in Figure 18-6. Boggs cannot pay for goods and services with bonds; he must periodically sell some bonds to obtain the medium of exchange money. He wants to make as much interest return from the bonds as possible. How often should he sell bonds, and how much average money balance should he hold during the week? The problem is to find those values.

This decision depends in part on the cost of selling bonds. Every time Boggs sells bonds, there is a fixed cost of b dollars and a variable cost of $1/2K$ times the amount of bonds sold. Those costs are comparable to brokerage fees plus other transactions costs. Therefore, if T is the total value of the transactions balances received each Thursday, which for simplicity is assumed to be in the form of bonds, the total transactions cost, S, of periodically selling these bonds during the week will be

$$S = bN + \tfrac{1}{2}KT \tag{13}$$

FIGURE 18-6   Asset Balances with Thursday Paydays and a Constant
Rate of Expenditures That Exhausts the Weekly Pay

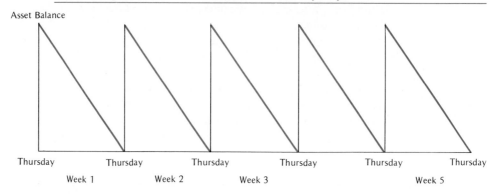

Asset Balance

Thursday   Thursday   Thursday   Thursday   Thursday   Thursday

Week 1   Week 2   Week 3   Week 5

where N is the number of transactions. A few changes in equation (13) will lead to the solution.

First, the average holdings of transaction balances, t, turns out to be equal to $T/2$. This is because T transaction balances are held at the beginning of the period and zero at the end. Adding T to zero and dividing by the number of observations, 2, gives the average, $T/2$. Using t allows the substitution of Kt for its mathematical equivalent, $\frac{1}{2}KT$, in equation (13).

Second, $N = t/c$, where c is average cash balances. This is so because total cash balances times the total number of transactions must equal total transaction balances, as every dollar of transaction balances received in the form of bonds is exchanged for a dollar of money during the period. By dividing the total of each of these two variables by 2, their averages are obtained. The resulting equality is $CN = t$, from which $N = t/c$ follows.[19]

Making these two substitutions into equation (13), the total transactions costs, S, becomes

$$S = b\left(\frac{t}{c}\right) + Kt \qquad (14)$$

The earnings from holding bonds are simply the interest rate, i, times the average bonds held, and average bond holdings are average transactions balances minus average cash holdings ($t - c$). The profit, R, from the bonds is the earnings minus the transactions costs:

$$R = it - ic - b\left(\frac{t}{c}\right) - Kt \qquad (15)$$

Profit is maximized with respect to changes in average money holdings when

$$\frac{dR}{dc} = \frac{bt}{c^2} - i = 0 \qquad (16)$$

so that the optimum average cash balance is

$$c = \sqrt{\frac{bt}{i}} \qquad (17)$$

The optimum average cash balance varies positively with the square root of the average transactions balance over the period and negatively with the square root of the interest rate.

The percentage change in average cash balances divided by the percentage change in income is called the *income elasticity of money*. It can be found from equation (17). The variable c is cash balances, and t is income. When t increases in value by a given percentage in that equation, c will rise by half that percentage. Plug in 10 percent for t and see whether c rises by 5 percent. (It can be precisely shown by putting the equation in the form of logarithms. The square root symbol (radical) makes the logarithm of c equal to one half the logarithm of t.) This income elasticity is smaller than that found from statistical tests on money data, which show the income elasticity nearer to 1. This difference may result because the model presented here does not capture all the costs, including inconvenience and decision-making time, for households. It is expensive, in terms of time and inconvenience, to sell small bonds continually to replenish cash balances. All that may be an academic curiosity with the advent of interest-paying checking accounts.

The elasticities of average cash balances with respect to average income and the interest rate (the ratio of the percentage change in average cash balances to each of these two variables) can be calculated from equation (17). Average cash balances are c, average income is t, and the interest rate is i in this equation. The elasticities are found to be $\frac{1}{2}$ and $-\frac{1}{2}$, respectively. This income elasticity is lower than that estimated from direct tests of income elasticity for the whole economy. This difference may result in part from the inability to capture all transactions costs, including inconvenience and decision-making time, for households.

If the model is amended for payment of direct interest on money (such as interest on NOW deposits), i can be defined as the difference between the bond rate and the direct rate of interest on money, and R is the extra profit gained by holding bonds. As that difference declines, desired cash balances increase, until $i = 0$ and $c = t$. At $i = 0$, the additional revenue from holding money is, by equation (15), then negative. It would be equal to the one-time cost of exchanging bonds for money $(b + \frac{1}{2}KT)$.

It is interesting (especially to students of price theory) that the variable for transactions costs, $\frac{1}{2}K$, drops out and does not determine optimum cash balances, c, whereas fixed transactions costs, b, are a determinant in equation (17). That is because $\frac{1}{2}K$ is a constant that cannot be changed by holding different cash balances, whereas the number of transactions, each requiring an expenditure of b, can be changed. The model has been extended to include conditions of uncertainty about receipts and withdrawals as well as the possibility of borrowing to cover cash shortages.[20]

STUDY QUESTIONS

1. Evaluate the following statement: The income velocity of money rises with a rise in market interest rates.
2. How do the equation of exchange and the Cambridge cash balance equation differ?
3. How does income velocity change over a business cycle?
4. How would an increase in service charges or a reduction in interest on NOW deposits affect income velocity?
5. How would a system of automatic transfer of money (with zero float) affect income velocity? Be careful. Income velocity is not a measure of the speed of payments; it is related to the proportion of income that individuals wish to hold as money. Would the loss of float cause households to hold more M-1 as a proportion of income? Would it affect business demand for real money balances? Explain.
6. How would the abolition of pennies affect the demand for U.S. money?
7. Should capital gains from bonds and stock sales affect the demand for money? Explain.
8. What does it mean to say that the demand for money is stable? Should that mean that quarterly changes in velocity are predictable? What difference does stability mean for monetary policy?
9. If real income is constant, the nominal supply of money increases, and a rise in bond interest rates causes income velocity to rise, what must happen to the price level? Use the monetary identities. Do these statements require that the change in money supply be the *cause* of a higher price level?

GLOSSARY

Budget constraint. The limitation of the amount of income available to a household in a given period, disregarding the availability of borrowing.

Cambridge cash balance equation. An accounting identity between the money stock and the proportion of income that is equal to the money stock. It can be stated in real or nominal terms.

Consumer price index (or CPI). The index of the market basket of goods bought by most consumers as estimated by the Department of Commerce. It is a widely used index in the United States.

Cross-section data. Data collected from the different values of a variable (such as consumer credit in each state) at one point in time. See **Time-series data.**

Cyclical. Denoting related movements in economic activity over a period greater than a year. A *business cycle* is a common type of cycle studied and identified by arbitrary standards such as those used by the National Bureau of Economic Research, a private research group.

Equation of exchange. An identity invented by Irving Fisher that defines velocity in terms of all transactions, not just the transactions included in national income accounting that define income, as in the income velocity of money.

Expected income. The income payment stream expected in the future.

Factor of production. One of the inputs in the production process, often classified as land, labor, capital, and entrepreneurship.

GNP deflator. A price index of all goods in the gross national product.

Income velocity of money or **velocity.** A ratio with aggregate income in an economy during a period divided by the average money supply in that period. GNP is frequently used in the numerator.

Marginal service yield of money. The change in the total services provided by money per dollar with an increase in money balances.

Market basket. In computing a price index, such as the consumer price index, the collection of goods surveyed and included in the index are called the market basket.

Money illusion. Economic behavior based on nominal rather than real variables.

Numeraire or **deflator.** A divisor used to bring variables into common units of purchasing power.

Opportunity cost. The value of a good or service in its next-best use (or some combination of optimum uses).

Personal consumption expenditure

deflator (or PCE). A price index of all U.S. consumer goods.

Price index. A measure of the weighted average price of a group of goods and services compared with a base period. If 100 is the base-period value of the index, as is customary, 110 will represent a 10 percent increase in the price level.

Price level. The average price of a group of goods and services in a period.

Producers price index. The wholesale price index.

Purchasing power of money. The amount of goods and services that can be exchanged (purchased) for a given quantity of money. See **Real value of money.**

Quantity theory of money. The classical study of the demand for money. Some claim that it also includes classical views of the relationship of money to prices.

Real value or exchange price of money. The amount of goods and services that can be exchanged (purchased) with a given quantity of money, in which the average value of money is determined with a price index that is used as a deflator. See **Numeraire.**

Scale of operations. The size of a business as measured by variables such as sales, work force, or the size of the capital stock. Notice that sales relate to output and that the other two variables are inputs.

Scale variables. Variables used to explain the size of something such as a business or an individual's assets (value of his or her wealth).

Time-series data. Data for the values that a variable takes over time (such as consumer credit in successive months). See **Cross-section data.**

Transactions demand for money. One of the determinants of the demand for money related to the level of income. The relationship can be stated in nominal or real terms.

NOTES

1. Edmund Whittaker, *Schools and Streams of Economic Thought* (Chicago: Rand McNally, 1960), pp. 37, 66. Hugo Hegeland traced "the quantity theory of money" (theories that emphasize the demand for money) back to the writings of Confucius (551–479 B.C.) in *The Quantity Theory of Money* (New York: Augustus M. Kelly, 1969).

2. Whittaker, *Schools and Streams of Economic Thought*, p. 78.

3. This subject is discussed by Milton Friedman, "The Money-Quantity Theory," *International Encyclopedia of the Social Sciences*, Vol. 10 (New York: Macmillan and the Free Press, 1968), pp. 432–447. For a description of what was called "the modern quantity theory" and famous studies, see Friedman, ed., *Studies in the Quantity Theory of Money* (Chicago: University of Chicago Press, 1956), with contributions by Friedman, Phillip Cagan, John Klein, Eugene Lerner, and Richard Selden.

4. See Don Patinkin, *Money, Interest, and Prices* (New York: Harper & Row, 1965). He elegantly develops conditions for strict proportionality on a macroeconomic level between nominal money balances and the price level at each level of real income. These conditions (roughly) include the requirements that the prices of all goods and services always vary in the same proportion with one another (as a composite good); that an excess demand for goods in one market be reduced by a decrease in excess supply in other markets, so that equilibrium can be attained in all markets; that the distribution of wealth be unchanged; that the size and age profile of the population be constant with given tastes; that the money supply be fiat government issue; and that there be no expectation of changing prices. In general, the literature on this subject is too difficult for beginners. But the curious reader may examine the nonmathematical parts of these few articles to obtain some flavor of the subject. The historical development of these conditions was reviewed by Kenneth Arrow and F. H. Hahn in *General Competitive Analysis* (San Francisco: Holden-Day, 1971), Chap. 1. An excellent but advanced discussion of this subject is found in Douglas Fisher, *Monetary Theory and the Demand for Money* (New York: Halsted Press, 1978), Chap. 3. On the same level of difficulty, an alternative to the Patinkin model that enlarges the model to better describe real capital goods is found in Karl Brunner and Allan Meltzer, "Money, Debt, and Economic Activity," *Journal of Political Economy*, September–October 1972, pp. 951–977.

5. See Benjamin Klein, "Competitive Interest Payments on Bank Deposits and the Long Run Demand for Money," *American Economic Review*, December 1974, pp. 931–949; and David Laidler, *The Demand for Money, Theories and Evidence* (New York: Dun-Donnelly, 1977), especially "The Role of Interest Rates," pp. 122–130.

6. See Milton Friedman, *A Theory of the Consumption Function* (Princeton, N.J.: Princeton University Press, 1957), where *expected income* is called *permanent income*. See also Friedman, "The Demand for Money: Some Theoretical and Empirical Results," *Journal of Political Economy*, August 1959, reprinted in *The Optimum Quantity of Money and Other Essays* (Chicago: Aldine, 1969), Chap. 6, pp. 111–139. Friedman could not explain all of the demand for money with permanent income.

    Friedman has been criticized for not giving greater weight to the effect of interest rates on the demand for money, though some of the interest rate effect is captured by the single variable, permanent income. A classic and early study that shows that interest rates have a major effect on the demand for money is by Henry A. Latane, "Cash Balances and the Interest Rate—A Pragmatic Approach," *Review of Economics and Statistics*, Vol. 36, November 1954, pp. 456–460. Also see Stephen M. Goldfeld, "The Demand for Money Revisited," *Brookings Papers on Economic Activity*, Vol. 3, 1973, pp. 577–638; Karl Brunner and Allan H. Meltzer, "Predicting Velocity. Implications for Theory and Policy," *Journal of Finance*, Vol. 18, May 1963, pp. 319–354; Gregory Chow, "On the Short-Run and Long-Run Demand for Money," *Journal of Political Economy*, Vol. 74, April 1966, pp. 111–131; and David Laidler, "The Rate of Interest and the Demand for Money—Some Empirical Evidence," *Journal of Political Economy*, Vol. 74, December 1976, pp. 545–555.

7. See Ross Milbourne for a description of this analysis and a bibliography of recent articles, "Financial Innovation and the Demand for Liquid Assets," *Journal of Money, Credit and Banking*, November 1986, pp. 506–511. Also see Vance Roley for evidence of a change in the income velocity of money in 1973, "The Demand for M1 by Households: An Evaluation of Its Stability," *Economic Review*, Federal Reserve Bank of Kansas City, April 1985, pp. 17–27. Diane F. Siegel also reviewed this subject in "The Relationship of Money and Income: The Breakdowns in the 70s and 80s," Federal Reserve Bank of Chicago, July–August 1986, pp. 3–15. For an argument between Milton Friedman and Anna Schwartz and their critics on the stability of the demand for money, see Milton Friedman and Anna J. Schwartz, *Monetary Trends in the United States and the United Kingdom, Their Relation to Income, Prices, and Interest Rates, 1867–1975* (Chicago: University of Chicago Press, 1982); and Thomas Mayer, "An American View," Charles A. E. Goodhart, "A British View," and Robert E. Hall, "A Neo-Chicagoan View," all in Friedman and Schwartz, "Monetary Trends," *Journal of Economic Literature*, December 1982, pp. 1528–1556.

8. John A. Tatom, "Was 1982 Velocity Decline Unusual?" *Review*, Federal Reserve Bank of St. Louis, August–September 1983, p. 15.

9. This is an average compound interest for the 85 years from 1869 to 1954 when the income velocity of M-1 fell from 4.57 to 1.49. The data are taken from Milton Friedman and Anna J. Schwartz, *A Monetary History of the United States 1867–1960* (Princeton, N.J.: Princeton University Press, 1963), p. 774. Robert Weintraub calculated the average rate of rise in velocity between 1956 and 1981 to be 3.31 percent. See Robert Weintraub, "What Type of Monetary Rule," *Cato Journal*, spring 1983, p. 179.

10. William A. Barnett, "The User Cost of Money," *Economic Letters*, Vol. 1, 1978, pp. 145–149; "Economic Monetary Aggregates: An Application of Aggregation and Index Number Theory," *Journal of Econometrics*, September 1980, pp. 11–48; and "The Microeconomic Theory of Monetary Aggregation," in William Barnett and Kenneth Singleton, eds., *New Approaches to Monetary Economics* (New York: Cambridge University Press, 1987).

11. Eugene Fama, "Fiduciary Currency and Commodity Standards," unpublished paper, University of Chicago, January 1982, from a citation in Hall, "A Neo-Chicagoan View," p. 1556.

12. The old definition of M-2 provides a more consistent series before and after the 1930s because interest was paid on at least part of this aggregate. The aggregate M-1 (which is part of M-2) was changed in the 1930s by the prohibition of interest on commercial bank demand deposits. The new M-2 (since 1982) includes money market funds and may be an entirely different animal from the old M-2. Tests will reveal which aggregate is best to use, but the arguments presented in Chapter 2 suggest that M-1—the basic medium-of-exchange aggregate—should be a central part of any definition of money.

13. Irving Fisher, *The Purchasing Power of Money, Its Determination and Relation to Credit, Interest, and Crisis* (New York: Augustus M. Kelley, 1963).

14. Boris P. Pesek, "Monetary Theory in the Post-Robertson 'Alice in Wonderland' Era," *Journal of Economic Literature*, Vol. 14, September 1976, pp. 856–881. Also, for a discussion of these identities with a slightly different view, see Friedman, "Money-Quantity Theory," p. 436.

15. A summary of these studies up to the late 1960s is found in a book by William J. Frazier, Jr., *The Demand for Money* (New York: World, 1967). More sophisticated works include Thomas Saving, "Transactions Costs and the Firm's Demand for Money," *American Economic Review*, June 1971, pp. 407–420; and Stanley Fischer, "Money and the Production Function," *Journal of Economic Inquiry*, December 1974, pp. 517–533.

16. Frazier, *The Demand for Money*, pp. 214–215.

17. Friedman, *Studies in the Quantity Theory*, p. 12.

18. William J. Baumol, "The Transactions Demand for Cash: An Inventory Theoretic Approach," *Quarterly Journal of Economics*, November 1952,

pp. 545–556; and James Tobin, "The Interest-Elasticity of Transactions Demand for Cash," *Review of Economics and Statistics*, August 1956, pp. 241–247. The excellent synthesis presented by Harry Johnson, including most of his symbols, is used here. See Johnson, "Notes on the Transactions Demand for Cash," in *Essays in Monetary Economics* (Cambridge, Mass.: Harvard University Press, 1967), Chap. 5, pp. 179–191.

19. It can be shown that under these conditions individuals will maximize their profit if they sell off their assets in equally spaced sales of equal amounts. Assume that only one transaction in the middle of the period is to be made. A proportion, X, of assets must initially be sold, leaving $1 - X$ assets for a proportion, X, of the time period. The earnings on the bonds held will be $X(1 - X)iT$. These earnings are maximized when $X = \frac{1}{2}$, as can be seen by taking the first derivative of revenue with respect to X. It follows that an individual should sell half his or her assets and use this money for half the period. Thus, if two sales of bonds are to be made, revenue will be maximized by equally spaced sales of equal value. Similarly, each subperiod can be analyzed in the same way, to show that further sales should be of equal size at equal time intervals.

It can also be shown that if the individual is paid in money instead of bonds, the optimum average cash balance will vary inversely with the rate of interest and directly with average transactions balance, but the relationship is more complex. (See Johnson, "Notes," pp. 184–187.)

20. Merton Miller and D. Orr extended the model for conditions of uncertainty in "A Model of the Demand for Money by Firms," *Quarterly Journal of Economics*, August 1966, pp. 413–435. They criticize the Baumol model for its derivative elasticities (p. 426).

CHAPTER 19

MONEY AND INFLATION, A CASH BALANCE APPROACH

CHAPTER PREVIEW

Introduction. An inflation is a sustained rise in the price level.

The Cost of Inflation. The costs are somewhat different for expected and unexpected inflations.

The Explanation of Income and Interest Rate Changes During an Inflation Caused by an Increase in Money Supply Growth. Three effects on interest rates are discussed.

Evidence: The Money–Price Relationship. Rough but persuasive evidence is presented.

Evidence: The Monetary Deceleration–Recession Relationship. A significant decline in money growth from its trend will be likely to lead to a decline in spending and even a recession.

Some Problems in Finding a Short-Run Relationship. Some difficult problems arise in attempting to verify the cash balance explanations.

Appendix A: The Price Expectations Effect. Important additional evidence and problems in finding the real rate of interest are presented.

Appendix B: The Effects of Income Tax Rates and Inflationary Expectations on the Nominal Rate of Interest. The Irving Fisher equation is amended to include the effects of income tax laws on the nominal rate of interest.

INTRODUCTION

An **inflation** is a sustained rise in the price level. It could be a period of a quarter of a year, a year, or five years. When does it end? That is a very arbitrary decision.

A **hyperinflation** is defined as an inflation in which the price level rises by 50 percent or more per month. It is said to end in the month that the rise in the price level drops below 50 percent per month and stays below 50 percent for at least a year.[1]

When does the run-of-the-mill inflation end? A similar arbitrary definition would do: say, in the month that is followed by one year of no more than 2 percent (average) inflation. Two percent inflation is probably indistinguishable from no inflation, given the errors in the price indexes.

Those theories of inflation that emphasize the supply and the demand for money as central relationships in the explanation of inflation are called the *cash balance analyses of inflation.* They rely on a predictable demand for real money balances. Another way of making this point is to say that they rely on a predictable value for income velocity, which was described in the previous chapter. When combined with other relationships that determine real output and the rates of return on assets, a theory of inflation is developed.

First we shall discuss the costs of inflation, but not the costs of stopping inflation, a subject that is covered in Chapters 21 and 26. Then we shall consider the cash balance explanation of inflation.

The cash balance explanation of inflation can be understood more easily if it is dissected into two parts. One part is the effect of money growth on prices and real income, and the other is the effect of money growth on interest rates. The effect of money growth on interest rates is further divided into three parts: (1) the liquidity effect, (2) the income effect, and (3) the price expectations, or Fisher effect. All these will be covered in a general section, in which the evidence for the effects of money growth on prices, output, and price expectations is given additional attention. When the cash balance explanation of inflation is understood, the discussion of the effects of price controls presented in Chapter 21 will provide a useful and timely counterpoint.

For simplicity, real output is considered constant in the explanation of inflation in this chapter, but that limitation is removed in the discussion in Chapter 24.

The appendices provide information about how individuals form expectations about inflation and how income tax rates affect the difference between the real and nominal rates of interest.

THE COST OF INFLATION

If an inflation is *not* expected, many individuals throughout the society will have made no arrangements for the higher rate of price increases. Those living on incomes rising by less than the rate of inflation will suffer a decline in the real purchasing power of their incomes. Those groups will include older people who do not receive adjustments for inflation in their retirement income, workers under fixed wage contracts, and unemployed individuals without benefits that increase with inflation. Also lenders who charged an interest rate that does not cover the inflation rate plus the real rate of interest will be hurt, as will money holders who do not receive an inflation-adjusted interest rate on their money. The list can go on and on; there is also a list of those who benefit. All this is frequently summarized in one sentence: There will be a transfer of wealth in the society from those on fixed incomes to those on variable incomes, nominal incomes that rise faster than does the rate of inflation.

The benefits and costs are not only a redistribution of wealth that makes the society in total no less wealthy. The sudden change of expected real income streams because of unexpected inflation also causes many distortions and produces much uncertainty about the future.

CONTRACTING FOR INFLATION

How does one contract for an expected inflation? The answer is that contracts have prices built into them for the future delivery of goods and services that take into account the expected rise in the price level. Home builders tell home buyers that the house they will build and have ready for occupancy next year will sell for a price that the home builder estimates will take into account the expected cost of inflation. Laborers attempt to get jobs that will pay an amount that rises with the rate of inflation. If a formal contract for labor is involved, these estimates will be reflected in that contract. Such provisions in a contract are called **escalator** or **cost-of-living clauses**.

If no formal contract is involved, some employers may indicate that their pay scale will keep up with the cost of inflation as reflected in the prices of their products, and these employers will attract workers. Employers who fail to keep their pay scales in line will be giving their workers a decrease in real pay, and these employers will tend to lose workers. Sellers of merchandise to be delivered in the future will build into the price of that merchandise the expected price level at the time of delivery. If prices are expected to rise by 15 percent, their prices may be increased by 15 percent.

In some countries such as Brazil, that have rapid rates of inflation, wages are adjusted periodically, such as twice a year, throughout the economy, by government edict.

Although the foregoing description for perfectly expected inflation indicates that only money is not indexed to inflation, that need not be the case. The rate of interest on money can go up with the rate of inflation if interest is paid on money. Once the ceiling interest rates no longer effectively block the payment of market interest rates on checking accounts, those accounts can pay interest that keeps up with inflation. However, currency does not bear interest, and that component of the money supply is not indexed for inflation.

Government bonds can be indexed for inflation by making their payment stream dependent on a price index or a market interest rate. So can private bonds. That provision has been adopted on some mortgage bonds, called variable-rate mortgages, and some private corporate bonds, called floating-rate notes or floaters. For example, in March 1983, Manufacturers Hanover Bank and Citibank in New York City issued floaters, such as a nine-year note with a rate of interest floating at 75 basis points (three quarters of a percentage point) above the three-month Treasury bill rate and a three-year note at 50 basis points (half a percentage point) above the three-month Treasury bill rate. Savings and loan associations and other thrifts that had large inflows of funds into the new money market deposit accounts, described in Chapter 8, bought many of these floaters.

What is the cost of a perfectly expected inflation—an inflation in which everyone has sufficient time to make contracts with inflation adjustments built into them on everything except the return for holding money? Everything except the return on money is indexed to the price level.

A major cost of a perfectly expected inflation is the real cost of economizing on cash balances. If the rate of return on money does not rise with the rate of inflation, holders of money will suffer a loss in purchasing power. No interest is paid for holding currency. The rate of return on demand deposits is zero (although the ceiling on other accounts has been lifted). There is, therefore, even in a perfectly expected inflation, a strong incentive to get rid of cash balances. A significant part of the society's resources is involved in getting rid of cash balances, of passing the hot potato to someone else. Business firms produce all manner of cash management schemes. Indeed, much of the frenzied level of activity in the capital markets—the bond markets and the equity markets—consists of passing the hot potato or, more precisely, the money that is being burned up by inflation.

There is, of course, no perfectly expected inflation or perfectly unexpected inflation. The inflationary environment in the United States since World War II has produced some long-term expectations of inflation throughout the economy. Most inflations are a combination of redistribution of wealth from those on fixed incomes to those on variable incomes and the expenditure of significant amounts of real resources to economize on cash balances.

The cost of economizing on cash balances is extremely high during hyperinflations. Employees must leave work every hour or so with the wages they have accumulated and run to the store with shopping bags of money before prices shoot upward even farther. It is interesting that these extremely rapid inflations are not accompanied by an abandonment of the use of money and a substantial return to barter, or to a substitute money system, unless they are accompanied by a system of price and wage controls that eliminates the monetary services provided by the money.

The costs of inflation just mentioned are probably smaller than a third category of costs, which cannot easily be measured. Inflation is an *unsteady state* because societies are incapable of fully adjusting to it. It might well be true that in some conceptual sense, a 7 percent rate of inflation, for example, could be a long-term equilibrium inflation rate to which the society could fully adjust. All contracts would be indexed to the 7 percent inflation; all government expenditures and government taxes would be indexed to the 7 percent inflation; the exchange rate of the currency (which determines the purchasing power of the domestic money supply for imports) would be depreciated to take into account exactly the internal 7 percent inflation; there might be a system of paying 7 percent on individuals' currency and coin balances; and there would be no expectation that anything would ever be done to reduce this rate of inflation. But these kinds of adjustments do not seem likely to occur; certainly they are unlikely in the near future in the United States.

As the inflation rate accelerates, there are all manner of dislocations, all manner of uncertainties, together with the government's reactions brought about by pressures from the public for quick solutions such as wage and price controls (discussed in Chapter 21) that may further impair the operation of the economy. Under these conditions, employers are unlikely to make ambitious plans for new investment, including the hiring and training of new workers. Employment suffers, unemployment rises, and there is general instability, all of which have severe negative effects on the welfare of the population.

THE EXPLANATION OF INCOME AND INTEREST RATE CHANGES DURING AN INFLATION CAUSED BY AN INCREASE IN MONEY SUPPLY GROWTH

Initial Conditions

Suppose that initially the nominal money supply, M, and the price level, P, are constant. The initial position where the demand and supply of real money balances are in agreement is at point B in Figure 19-1. All these "pictures" of important economic variables are in the initial position before inflation begins.

We can now explain the mechanics of the cash balance explanation of inflation. The initial and underlying stimulus in this explanation is the nominal money supply, which will be assumed to increase continually at an annual rate of 7 percent after the initial period.

Liquidity Effect

The money supply schedule moves to $(M/P)_2$ in Figure 19-1, in the first period of time. The supply of real money balances increases while the demand is constant. In response to an increase in the supply of money, interest rates fall. The fall in the real rate of interest caused by this increase in the supply of real money balances is called the **liquidity effect**. In Figure 19-1, the interest rates move from r to r_1. The intersection of the demand and supply for real money balances moves from B down to C as M/P grows larger.

FIGURE 19-1   Liquidity, Income, and Price Expectations Effects
Following an Increase in the Rate of Money Growth

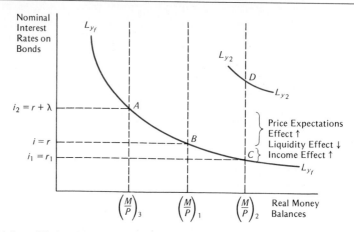

The initial equilibrium is at point *B*. As the money supply is increased, interest rates fall
(both the real and the nominal interest rates). This decline in interest rates due to an
excess supply of real money balances is called the *liquidity effect*. Individuals' desire for
real money balances does not change as rapidly as does the increase in the real money
supply, so they begin spending (running down) their new real money balances. At first,
income increases, raising nominal and real interest rates—a change in the interest rates
called the *income effect*. The level of interest rates moves toward a new equilibrium at
point *D*. Prices start to rise, lowering real money balances toward their initial position,
reducing spending, and eliminating the income effect. As inflation becomes expected,
nominal interest rates rise above real interest rates, incorporating the expectation of
inflation. This is called the *price expectations effect*. The final equilibrium is at point *A*.

The Income Effect

There is a lag in the public's adjustment to the new lower rate of interest.
Individuals initially find that they are holding higher real money balances
than they want, higher real money balances than they have been holding. They
thus attempt to maintain their former desired real cash balances by spending
more and trying to reduce their real money balances.

Just as everybody has to be somewhere, every dollar in circulation also has
to be somewhere, and dollars become hot potatoes as the public attempts to
get rid of them. The result is a rise in real income, created by the new demand
for goods and services, and a much slower and more delayed rise in prices.
The rise in real income causes the whole demand for real money balances
curve in Figure 19-1 to shift out to the right, through point *D*. The resulting
rise in interest rates is called the **income effect**.

The real money supply $(M/P)_2$ begins to shrink. A rise in prices shrinks real
purchasing power. In terms of the symbol M/P, it gets smaller as the denomi-

FIGURE 19-2 Time Paths of the Variables in the Cash Balance Explanation of Inflation with Constant Real Income

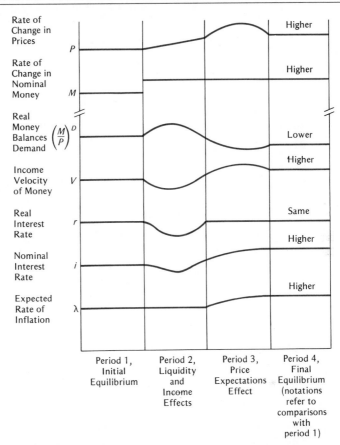

This figure shows the paths of the variables in the cash balance explanation of inflation with the simplifying assumption that real income is constant. The figure is conveniently divided into four periods, although in an actual episode, the periods are not of equal length, and the effects shown along the bottom of the figure may occur simultaneously. The final positions are as follows:

Prices rise, as this is a story of inflation. Rising prices mean higher nominal income (with constant real income, Y/P, where P is prices and Y is nominal income). At higher interest rates, individuals keep spending their money to run down their cash balances until M/P is lower. Lower real money balances at constant real income mean higher velocity. Real interest rates are assumed to be unchanged, although Chapter 24 gives some reasons for a change in real interest rates. Nominal interest rates are higher, reflecting inflationary expectations. And finally, the expected rate of inflation is higher. These final positions are straightforward, but the interesting adjustments are not so obvious. The most interesting is the rise in the price level at a rate that is faster than that of the money growth, as individuals reduce their real money balances when nominal interest rates rise.

nator P gets larger. Real money balances start to move back to their original position $(M/P)_1$ in Figure 19-1.

In period 2, shown in Figure 19-2, real money balances rise and fall, and the real rate of interest falls and then rises until it returns to approximately where it was before. The income effect tends to push up interest rates, offsetting the liquidity effect.

HOW LONG DO THE INCOME AND LIQUIDITY EFFECTS LAST?

It was thought that the liquidity effect would last for a long time. William Gibson concluded, from tests of the period 1947 to 1966, that the liquidity effect lasted for about three months following a change in old M-1 and for about five months following a change in old M-2.[2] In the 1970s, however, it appeared that the financial markets in the United States became more sophisticated and reacted more rapidly. The liquidity effect may now be washed out quite rapidly in a day or two. That is, the mere announcement of fast nominal money growth may send interest rates up rather than down.

On the other hand, the income effect may take a great deal longer to show up. The increase in spending generated by issuing new nominal money does create new demand, which has most of its impact on real income in three to nine months. Some economists believe that the initial income effect is offset by later declines in real income associated with the problems caused by inflation. (This is discussed in Chapter 27 under "Dilemmas in Choosing Ultimate Targets.")

The Price Expectations Effect

The cash balance explanation of inflation brings the expectation of inflation into the analysis, by using the simple equation that Irving Fisher first published in 1896.[3] It was explained in Chapter 4 as

$$i_B = r_B + \lambda \tag{1}$$

where i_B is the nominal rate of interest on bonds, r_B is the real rate of interest on bonds that would prevail if there were no inflation, and λ (the Greek letter lambda) is the expected rate of inflation. Equation (1) rests on the belief that lenders would not lend out their real money balances at the real rate of interest (the interest rate with zero inflation expected) if they knew there was going to be inflation and that they would be paid back smaller real money balances, money that had less purchasing power. Lenders would want to be compensated for the expected rate of inflation. Borrowers would agree to pay this extra premium on their interest rate because they would have uses for the real money balances, such as buying real estate, that are expected to appreciate at least as fast as the rate of inflation. (The effect of income taxes on the nominal rate of interest is discussed in Appendix B.)

When individuals begin to expect inflation, λ begins to rise in value, as shown in period 3 of Figure 19-2, a period containing the **price expectations effect**, or **Fisher effect**. The price expectations effect is nothing more than a rise in the nominal rate of interest because of the expectation of inflation.

In Figure 19-1 the quantity of real money demanded (a movement along the original demand curve) declines to $(M/P)_3$. Individuals attempt to economize on their cash balances because the opportunity cost of holding money is higher. The cost of holding money is high because individuals now expect inflation. The full rise in the price level takes less time than the three to nine months that it takes for the impact of increased money growth on real income to be felt. The major impact on the price level occurred, on the average, about two years after the initial increase in the money growth with the rates of inflation experienced in the United States since World War II. The lag would be shorter with more rapid inflations or with more contracts with prices tied to the consumer price index (escalator clauses). This long adjustment period for the price level means that the real balances that people desire at the interest rate of i_2 in Figure 19-1 are not achieved until after the long adjustment period. Period 4 in Figure 19-2 gives the values of the various variables in the final equilibrium levels. Some variables, such as interest rates, reach that position far in advance of the final equilibrium rate of rise in the price level.

The real money balances demanded are lower than they are initially in period 4 in Figure 19-2, which leads to an interesting conclusion about the adjustment process: Prices rise during the adjustment process not only because the nominal money supply has been increased and individuals initially try to restore their desired real money balances by spending the new nominal money, but also because individuals try to economize on their real money balances.

Inflation has thus made real money balances more expensive to hold. (Notice that this assumes that there is no fully compensating increase in the direct interest paid on nominal money.) Individuals do not want to hold as much in real money balances as they did before, as this causes prices to rise faster than the nominal money supply increases during the adjustment period.

EVIDENCE: THE MONEY–PRICE RELATIONSHIP

There is no convincing evidence of a short-term relationship between money and prices except during very rapid inflation, such as hyperinflation. Many factors influence prices in the short term, everything from bad weather in Iowa to an increase in oil prices. However, there is rough evidence of a long-term relationship between money and prices.

The rough evidence is that inflation is associated with rapid money growth. The average growth rates of prices and M-1 of the previous year since World War II are plotted in Figure 19-3. The rate of change in M-1 two years pre-

FIGURE 19-3   Growth Rates of Prices and Money, 1952–1987

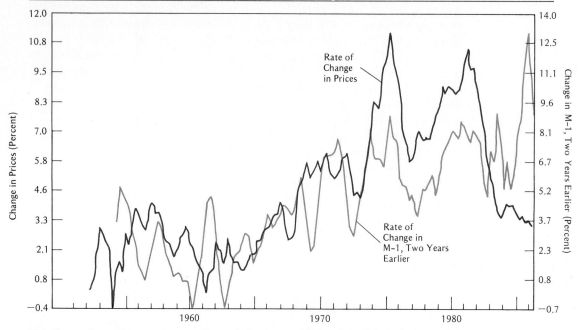

This figure shows the average growth rates of prices and M-1 of the previous year. For example, above the 1986 number, in the horizontal scale, M-1 is shown to have grown between 8.1 and 9.6 percent, two years previously, and the current rate of growth of prices (the GNP deflator) is a little under 3.3 percent. The rate of change in M-1 two years previously roughly tracks prices. But there are enough exceptions to make the lag between money and prices variable and the relationship imprecise. The two variables are twelve-month moving averages.

Source: Cambridge Planning and Analytics, Inc., Boston.

viously roughly tracks prices. The lag between the change in the rate of growth in the money supply and the rate of change in prices has been about one and one-half to two and one-half years. There are enough exceptions to make the lag between money and prices variable and the relationship imprecise. Between 1915 and 1935, the relationship was concurrent and the fit as close as it was after World War II. From 1935 to 1946, a period of depression and then wartime price controls, the relationship is not discernible.

A closer fit is found between the rate of growth in the money supply one year earlier and a measure of total spending, the rate of change in the GNP. The rate of change in the money supply one year earlier tracks the rate of change in the GNP rather closely over the long period from 1946 to 1986, as shown in Figure 19-4. This evidence supports the hypothesis that rate of change in nominal spending is strongly related over the long term to the rate of change in the money supply. The total spending induced by prior money growth can be broken apart into rates of changes in prices and real output. The effects on prices have a longer lag than do the effects on real output, and

FIGURE 19-4   Growth Rates of Money and GNP

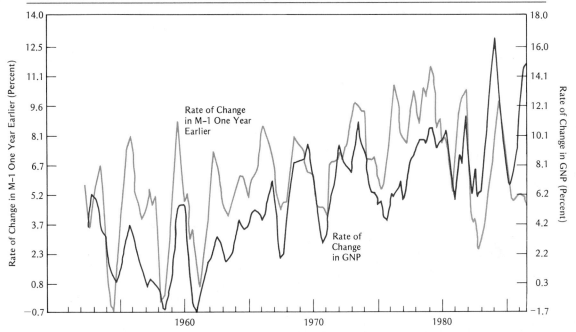

The rate of change in money one year earlier tracks the rate of change in GNP rather closely over the long period from 1952 to 1987. This evidence supports the hypothesis that the rate of change in nominal spending is strongly related over the long term to the rate of change in the money supply. The two variables are twelve-month moving averages.

Source: Cambridge Planning and Analytics, Inc., Boston.

the average effect on spending is shown by the relationship in Figure 19-4. In some periods, spending affects prices more than output does, and in other periods, output is affected more. Thus the relationship in Figure 19-4 is more precise than is the relationship in Figure 19-3.

The cash balance view of inflation is that money growth that is more rapid than the long-term growth of output cannot be offset by continuous adjustments in velocity or by short-term adjustments in output. That is, the purchasing power of each unit of money will fall.

EVIDENCE: THE MONETARY DECELERATION–RECESSION RELATIONSHIP

Sustained changes in the rate of growth in the nominal money supply are associated with changes in output in the same direction three to nine months later, according to the view of proponents of the cash balance approach. That

FIGURE 19-5   Money Supply Growth Relative to Its Trend, 1952–1986

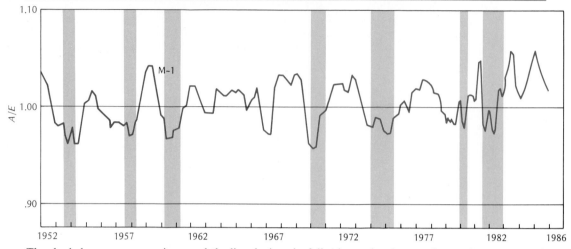

The shaded areas are recessions, and the line depicts the following ratio: the actual rate of money growth divided by its prior trend rate of growth. This ratio is sometimes called the *A/E* ratio. If the money supply is significantly pulled down from its previous trend rate of growth, there will be a drop in purchasing power in the public's hands. Spending declines, and output is affected. There is a downturn in economic activity that is sometimes severe enough to be labeled a recession. But the downturns that occurred in 1967 and 1979 were not severe enough to be classified as recessions.

Source: Bryon Higgins, "Monetary Growth and Business Cycles," Part II, "The Relationship Between Monetary Decelerations and Recessions," *Economic Review*, Federal Reserve Bank of Kansas City, April 1979, p. 18. Updated.

is, a significant decline in money growth that was sustained for at least three months would be expected to reduce the rate of growth in output three to nine months later. Sharper contractions than those generally experienced between 1940 and 1982 may affect output with a shorter lag.

The evidence of an association between sharp declines in money growth (monetary deceleration) and recessions between 1952 and 1979 was tested by Bryon Higgins, William Poole, Dallas Batten, and R. W. Hafer.[4] Poole found

"The evidence presented here suggests that sizable and sustained reductions in short-run money growth below its trend rate portend declines in the growth of real GNP. Of the 14 recessions in the four countries examined, only one—the fourth quarter 1974–third quarter 1975 recession in the United Kingdom—was not preceded by a substantial decline in short-run money growth. Moreover, in only one instance—the third quarter 1975–fourth quarter 1976 period in West Germany—did short-run money growth fall substantially below trend without a recession following. In that instance, however, West German real GNP growth fell about 10 percent to zero, a result consistent with the theoretical discussion."

Source: Dallas S. Batten and R. W. Hafer, "Short-Run Money Growth Fluctuations and Real Economic Activity: Some Implications for Monetary Targeting," *Review*, Federal Reserve Bank of St. Louis, May 1982, pp. 18–19. The quotation is from p. 20.

FIGURE 19-6 Gross National Product, GNP, and Growth and Deviations of Short-Term Money Growth from Its Trend in (A) the United States, (B) the United Kingdom, (C) West Germany, and (D) Italy, 1973–1981

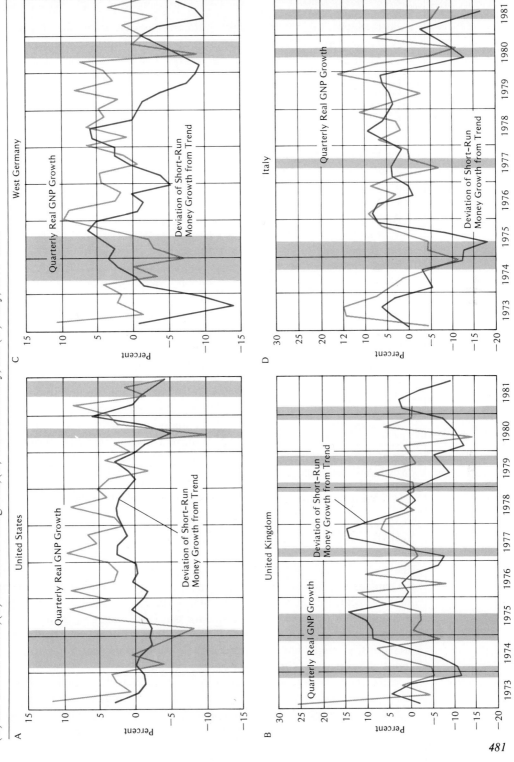

481

a close relationship between peaks in the business cycle and significant monetary decelerations. The basic evidence presented by Higgins is shown in Figure 19-5. The shaded areas are recession periods. The A/E ratio is simply the ratio of actual money growth to money growth that would have occurred if the established trend had continued. In other words, the lines in Figure 19-5 for real money and nominal money show how abrupt the changes were. If the ratio was 1, there were no changes from the trend. Higher or lower ratios signify upward or downward deviations, respectively. Statistical tests have revealed that although there is not a precise relationship, the likelihood of recession increases with the degree of monetary deceleration. In Figure 19-6, Batten and Hafer present the same kind of evidence for four countries, including the 1980 and 1981 recessions in the United States.

A sustained increase in the rate of money growth has been held to increase output and employment in the near term. Therefore, the effect of decelerations could be partially offset and even reversed by a 180-degree turn toward rapid monetary growth. The effects of faster monetary growth on unemployment are analyzed in Chapter 20. Erratic monetary policy can produce uncertainty, which will increase the real rate of interest.

The analytical meaning of the effect of declines in nominal money growth from its trend follows from the cash balance explanation of inflation. According to this theory, the trend rate of money growth is a primary determinant of the long-run price level that people expect. If the money supply growth rate is significantly decreased below this rate, then real money balances, M/P (where P is the long-run price level), will decline. That is, this decline in wealth will cause individuals to curtail their spending.

The short-term price level depends on many other factors that could change and offset this effect on real money balances. Thus, the deviation of the growth in nominal money from its long-term trend must be sharp enough to swamp any of these short-term effects.

SOME PROBLEMS IN FINDING A SHORT-RUN RELATIONSHIP

The cash balance explanation is complicated by several problems that make the explanation difficult to verify for short-term changes in the money supply. First, the central bank in the United States, the Federal Reserve, has frequently attempted to *accommodate* or *finance* the GNP. That is, it increased the money supply as the GNP rose. This was done to avoid any contradictory pressure that might have occurred if there were insufficient funds to buy the goods and services at their higher prices.

Whether or not accommodation is a correct policy, it is a policy in which a rise in prices *causes* the GNP to rise, which, in turn, *causes* the nominal money supply to be increased. This policy makes it difficult to test just how much of the rise in prices is caused by a rise in the money supply in the short run—less than about two years. Simple tests that do not take into account the feedback from prices to money in the short run are faulty. You may think that your garden grows better with more fertilizer, but in reality you may be putting more fertilizer down when your garden is growing faster anyway. Likewise, some tests that conclude that there are extremely strong relations between money and prices in the short run are biased, and so the conclusions are unwarranted.[5]

A FURTHER EXPLANATION

Review equation (1) in the last chapter. Rearrange its terms to see that the price level is equal to money per unit of output times velocity:

$$P = \frac{M}{y} V \qquad (2)$$

Assume that over the previous two years real income, y, velocity, V, and the nominal money supply, M, have produced an average price level of 9 percent. Suddenly money growth falls to 2 percent. Individuals will consider the real purchasing power of their money balances, its real value, to be suddenly growing at a slower rate. They thus will cut back on the rate of growth of their spending, and the economy will be slowed down, possibly into a recession.

The money supply is assumed to be the primary variable in determining the long-run growth in the money supply, according to the following view: The real income variable, y, and velocity, V, in equation (2) will fluctuate widely over the business cycle, but their long-run variation will be small. The belief in a stable long-run velocity may also be stated as a belief in the long-run stability of the demand for money. This view is controversial, with many observers believing that such forces as financial innovation (which they contend reduces or eliminates the distinctive properties of money) make the demand for money unstable over the long run.

APPENDIX A: THE PRICE EXPECTATIONS EFFECT

A few additional words about the price expectations, or Fisher effect, are in order, as this is an essential part of the cash balance explanation of inflation. Suppose that inflation is expected to last for one year, after which the price level is expected to remain constant. This price expectation would have its greatest effect on interest rates during the forthcoming year, but not on the interest rates that are expected to prevail in future years. A one-year bond would tend to fall in price, so that its nominal interest rate exceeds the real rate of return by the expectation of inflation. A bond with a longer maturity, say 30 years, would have a much smaller change in price. All expectations of price level changes for the next 30 years enter into the public's valuation of the

FIGURE 19-7   The Rate of Change in Prices and the Federal Funds Rate

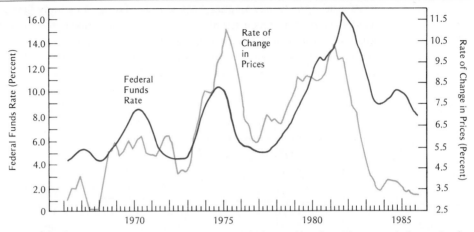

There has been a fairly close relationship between the rate of change in prices (the rate of change in the GNP deflator) and short-term interest rates (the federal funds rate). Twelve-month moving averages were used.

Source: Cambridge Planning and Analytics, Inc., Boston.

30-year bond. This result can be applied to the term structure of interest rate analysis in Chapter 11.

Numerous monetary studies have directly tested the price expectations effect and have provided substantial evidence of its existence.[6] Countries, such as Brazil, that have had rates of inflation as high as 5 percent per month have also had very high nominal rates of interest (also as high as 5 percent per month), which are explained most plausibly by the existence of a large price expectations effect.

Examination of evidence for the United States in Figure 19-7 shows the close relationship between the federal funds rate and the rate of change in the consumer price index. That relationship indicates that in spite of the Federal Reserve's frequent attempts to control the federal funds rate, the underlying inflationary expectations and arbitrage between markets have kept the funds rate fairly closely associated with the rate of change in the price level.

Various methods are used to explain how price expectations are formed. Many studies have employed some form of a weighted average of past price levels or past price level changes. More recent periods are given larger weights, which decay toward zero as more distant prior periods are included.[7] More recent methods of estimating price expectations were developed in a theory called *rational expectations*, discussed in Chapter 20, which takes into account a wide range of variables in estimating price expectations.

Inflation began accelerating during World War II, and yet *low* interest rates persisted into the 1950s. Why was the government so successful in its interest rate policy, which was directed at keeping interest rates low during this period? One answer is simply that after the horrendous depressions of the 1930s, no one expected a long, robust expansion and rising inflation. The inflation thus appeared as a short-term deviation from normal. Views of recession, theories of stagnant levels of investment, and assumptions of price stability were tightly held. By the middle 1970s, these long-term views of the economy had probably turned around 180 degrees.

During most of the post–World War II period (since 1945) in the United States, prices have been rising. A full adjustment to a prolonged period of *constant* or *falling* prices after the 1970s would take six to nine years, according to one study.[8] People became accustomed to rising prices in the post–World War II period and so they regarded some inflation as a normal state of affairs. Generally rising interest rates reflect expectations of generally rising rates of inflation, which are usually correct expectations.

Then came the very sharp slowdown in the money supply during 1980, the first half of the last year of the Carter administration. A recession followed, and both long and short interest rates fell, as shown in Figure 19-8. This

FIGURE 19-8   Interest Rates for U.S. Treasury Debt Instruments with Maturities of Three Months, One Year, and a Composite Long Maturity, 1980–1986

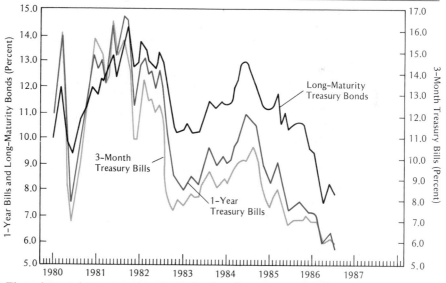

These data on interest rates support the view that expectations of inflation were rapidly revised in the face of a strong negative shock to the system in 1980 and 1982. Both long and short interest rates fell by large amounts. When more rapid money growth was implemented by the Federal Reserve in 1985 and 1986, these revised expectations, following two recessions, were evidently strong enough to cause interest rates to continue to be revised downward in 1985 and 1986.

Source: Cambridge Planning and Analytics, Inc., Boston.

evidence supports the view that expectations of inflation were rapidly revised in the face of a strong negative shock to the system. The same phenomenon was repeated following the sharp slowdown in the money growth during the first one and one-half years of the Reagan administration, 1981 and the first half of 1982. There followed a relatively severe recession in 1982 in which over 10 percent of the labor force was officially unemployed. Expectations of inflation were rapidly revised downward, and the revision was great enough to cause nominal interest rates to fall. When the money supply grew more rapidly in 1985 and 1986, these revised expectations, following the two recessions, were evidently strong enough to cause interest rates to continue to be revised downward in 1985 and 1986.

If price level changes are large, as in rapid inflations, the price expectations effect would explain virtually all of the nominal interest rate changes.[9] Extremely rapid inflations did occur in the United States during the Revolutionary War and in the Confederacy during the Civil War. Smaller changes in the price level, such as those experienced in the post–World War II period in the United States, have a smaller, though sometimes dominating influence on nominal interest rates.

Estimates of interest rate variation in the post–World War II period after the early 1950s have indicated that something like 50 percent of the variation in nominal rates of interest was accounted for by changes in expectations of inflation, not changes in the real rate of interest. The words *something like* are used because these types of estimates are imprecise. They suffer from the problems of trends and periodicities in the data, discussed in Chapter 13, and the difficult task of isolating movements in the interest rates that are caused by the price expectations effect. Remember that the income effect and the price expectations effect change interest rates in the same direction. They cannot be untangled easily.

Estimating the Real Rates of Interest

In 1982, some individuals began to demand that the Federal Reserve stop concentrating on trying to keep the money supply within a specific range, a subject discussed in Part VIII. One alternative that was suggested was a target range of real interest rates. It is important, therefore, to look at some work that has been done on esimating real interest rates. This work is also important to ecomonic analysis because real investment depends on real rates of interest.

The way to estimate real rates of interest that has been used most frequently is to utilize equation (1), Fisher's relationship between real and nominal rates of interest. Nominal rates of interest are the observed market rates of interest. From these rates, simply deduct the expected rate of inflation, λ, in equation (1). The residual is an estimate of the real rate of interest. How accurate is it?

The evidence of the price expectations effect is difficult to pin down precisely. This imprecision is illustrated by a number of studies that attempted to estimate real rates of interest by simply subtracting some average rate of change in the price level from previous periods from the market rates of interest. The deduction is based on the idea that the public generally expects the rate of inflation that has occurred in recent years to continue. It is interesting to look at one of these attempts to estimate price expectations, in this case by the research department at the Federal Reserve Bank of St. Louis.

A series of reports published by the Federal Reserve Bank of St. Louis showed the market interest rate on high-grade corporate bonds and an adjusted series. The adjusted series is the bond yield less the average annual rate of change in consumer prices over three previous years. It can be considered as a series of predictions of price level changes, based on current and prior information. These series are depicted in Figure 19-9 from 1964 to October 1972.

FIGURE 19-9   Interest Rates on Highest-Grade Seasoned Corporate Bonds and an Adjusted Yield, Based on Past Rates of Inflation, 1964–1972

The adjusted rate curve is sometimes interpreted as an estimate of real rates of interest. It is derived by subtracting the average of the current and prior two years' inflation rates from the market yield estimate shown (for corporate bonds). The deduction does not take into account other factors such as income tax rates (discussed in Appendix B).

* Market yield less average annual rate of change in consumer prices over three previous years.
Latest data plotted: market yield, October; adjusted yield, October estimated.
Source: Federal Reserve Bank of St. Louis.

TABLE 19-1   Attempt to Estimate the Real Rate of Interest by
Subtracting Past Inflation Rates from the Nominal Rate of Interest

A	B	C	Column B
		Arithmetic Average of	
	Corporate	Current and Previous	Column B
	Aaa Bond Rate	Two Years' Inflation Rate	Minus C
Year	(percent)	(percent)	(percent)
1973	7.4	5.2	2.2
1974	8.6	8.1	0.5
1975	8.8	9.3	−0.5
1976	8.4	8.0	−0.4
1977	8.0	6.2	1.8
1978	8.1*	7.2	0.9

* October 1978.

The adjusted rate curve was viewed as a very rough estimate of the long-run *real* rates of interest, that is, the rates that would prevail if there were no inflation. The real rate (ignoring premiums for risk and adjustments for taxes), as determined by this method, dropped from 2.2 percent in 1973 and continued down to *negative* numbers in 1975 and 1976, as shown in Table 19-1. It stood at approximately 1 percent in 1978. The long-run actual real rate is probably nearer the trend rate of growth of output, approximately 3 percent; it is doubtful that it was negative for a year, so that the average return on real investment was a future stream of losses.

This method for predicting interest rates may have produced unrealistic results largely because of U.S. oil imports. The huge dollar payments for oil in this period caused a return inflow of dollars that was largely invested in U.S. Treasury bills. Treasury bills offered a most attractive place for oil exporters to invest huge amounts of dollars, at least until they became more familiar with the alternatives. The demand for Treasury bills pushed up their price and lowered their yield. Thus, the nominal rate of interest probably did not exceed the real rate of interest by the expected rate of inflation.

Another series of estimates of real interest rates was developed by Stephen G. Cecchetti, as shown in Figure 19-10. These estimates are based on the information contained in current market interest rates, in which the rate of inflation is assumed to be fully incorporated. This information is combined with past rates of inflation and real growth in output in a statistical procedure.

The results confirm other estimates that show high real rates of interest occurring after 1980. Because higher real rates of interest are associated in economic analysis with lower real rates of investment, this finding is of considerable importance. That is, the higher real rates of interest could be caused by increased uncertainty about the future health of the economy, especially after periods of rapidly changing monetary policy—indeed, which changed rapidly enough to be a major cause of two recessions. A higher real rate of return is therefore required to entice investors to invest. Another explanation of high interest rates has to do with the exploding federal budget deficit in the

FIGURE 19-10   Estimates of the Real Rates of Interest on U.S. Treasury Securities with Three Months to Maturity, 1952–1986

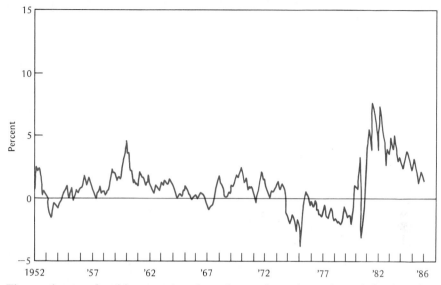

These estimates of real interest rates show them to have risen substantially after 1980. Because higher real rates of interest are associated in economic analysis with lower real rates of investment, this finding is of major importance.

Source: Stephen G. Cecchetti, "High Real Interest Rates: Can They Be Explained?" *Economic Review*, Federal Reserve Bank of Kansas City, September–October 1986, p. 34.

1980s. The resulting increase in bonds that the U.S. government had to sell to finance its deficits could have affected interest rates. The analysis of this alleged cause of high real interest rates is given in Chapter 25.

When considering real interest rates, it is useful to separate the yield as an investment before and after taxes are deducted. The investor looks at the after-tax interest rate. The lower tax rates enacted in 1981 increased the profitability of real investment and the demand funds for real investment, thereby temporarily increasing the real interest rate.

APPENDIX B: THE EFFECTS OF INCOME TAX RATES AND INFLATIONARY EXPECTATIONS ON THE NOMINAL RATE OF INTEREST

Consider a risk-free bond that, for simplicity, is assumed to pay $1,500 per year for every future year. (Such a bond is called a *perpetuity*.) The bond costs $10,000, and so the yield or interest rate is 15 percent, other things being the same. But other things rarely remain the same for the careful lender or borrower. For example, an inflation rate expected to be 25 percent per year would reduce the real value of the income stream by 25 percent a year. This effect can be stated generally in the following way: Unity plus the *nominal* rate of interest on bonds, i_B, is the compounding factor by which the investment in the bond increases each year. This compounding factor—for readers who are not familiar with compound interest—was reviewed in Chapter 10. This compounding factor is simply $(1 + i_B)$. It equals the compounding factor for the real rate of interest (the interest rate with no inflationary expectations) multiplied by a compounding factor for inflation. If the inflation is expected to increase at a rate of λ (the Greek letter lambda) per year, the compounding factor for inflation will be $1 + \lambda$. Thus,

$$(1 + i_B) = (1 + r_B)(1 + \lambda) \tag{3}$$

Multiplying the right side out and subtracting unity from each side of equation (3), the following expression of the nominal interest rate on bonds is obtained:

$$i_B = r_B + \lambda + r_B \lambda \tag{4}$$

The term $r_B \lambda$ is sometimes ignored on the grounds that it is small. Then the nominal rate of interest on bonds is simply stated as the real rate on bonds plus the expected rate of inflation, as was done in equation (1).

This is an equilibrium relationship to which market adjustments will lead if lenders and borrowers share these expectations of inflation, other things being the same. Lenders wish to cover themselves for the decline in the value of future interest payments and return of principal. Borrowers are willing to pay because the nominal return on the investments for which they wish to use funds is also expected to rise by the rate of inflation.

Again, some important factors are not the same. This story is far from complete because the borrowers (the bond sellers) can deduct the interest payments from their income, thereby reducing their taxes. That is, the government pays part of the interest. The borrowers would be willing to pay a higher interest rate because of this subsidy. The lenders must pay tax on interest income (except for tax-exempt issues such as municipals), and so they need a higher rate of return to cover the real rate of interest plus the expected rate of inflation.

These tax considerations can be taken into account by looking at the effective real after-tax cost of funds, $r_{B, \text{AT}}$. If there were no expectation of inflation, it could be obtained by deducting the tax rate on income, K, from the nominal rate of interest, or simply

$$i_B(1 - K) = r_{B, \text{AT}} \qquad \text{for } \lambda = 0 \tag{5}$$

with no expectation of inflation. Therefore, if inflation is expected at a rate of λ, equation (3), using the tax rate adjustment in equation (5), will become

$$1 + i_B(1 - K) = (1 + r_{B, \text{AT}})(1 + \lambda) \tag{6}$$

Solving for the effective real after-tax costs of funds, $r_{B, AT}$,

$$r_{B, AT} = \frac{1 + i_B(1 - K)}{1 + \lambda} - 1 \tag{7}$$

Now rearrange the furniture. Multiply out the right-hand side of the equation, collect terms, drop the term $\lambda r_{B, AT}$ on the grounds that it is small enough to ignore, and then divide each side by $(1 - K)$. The result is

$$i_B = \frac{r_{B, AT} + \lambda}{1 - K} \tag{8}$$

Try an example. Suppose that the inflation rate is expected to be 12 percent, the rate of taxation on income averages 20 percent, and the underlying after-tax real rate of interest is 3 percent. What is the equilibrium nominal rate of interest?

$$i_B = \frac{.03 + .12}{1 - .2} = .1875 = 18.75\% \tag{9}$$

Notice from equation (1) that without considering the tax rate, the nominal rate would be 15 percent. The computations in equation (9) indicate that a 20 percent tax rate increases the nominal interest rate to 18.75 percent.[10]

STUDY QUESTIONS

1. What is inflation?
2. Describe the cash balance explanation of inflation.
3. What is the evidence of the relationship between money growth and the price level, and on what grounds can it be questioned?
4. What is the evidence of the relationship between interest rates and the rate of change of prices, and on what grounds can it be questioned?
5. In what ways would the senario regarding the cash balance explanation of inflation be changed if it were assumed that real income was growing at a long-run trend rate of growth of 3 percent?
6. How could bad weather in Iowa change the price level? Could it be predicted? How long would it affect prices?
7. What is the Gibson paradox? How is it related to the price expectations effect? (See note 6.)
8. According to the cash balance explanation of inflation, prices can rise at a more rapid rate than can the rate of growth of the money supply. Can you explain this phenomenon?
9. Suppose that an inflation subsides, price expectation changes cause nominal interest rates to fall, and the demand for real money balances increases. In response, the Federal Reserve increases the money supply so

that the level of spending will not decline. Some Federal Reserve officials gave this line of reasoning for the large increase in the money supply in the last half of 1982. (See Michael W. Keran, "Velocity and Monetary Policy in 1982," *FRB Weekly Letter*, Federal Reserve Bank of San Francisco, Research Department, March 18, 1983, p. 3.) Keran cautioned, "How long this rapid M1 growth rate should continue is a matter of judgment. In principle, however, M1 growth should not exceed the increased desire to hold M1 as a result of the decline in inflation expectations" (p. 3). What would happen to interest rates and prices if the Federal Reserve were wrong and provided too much money, and how long would it take for this to occur? What actually happened? What kind of monetary policy does this line of reasoning call for during a period of rising interest rates? What are the dangers and benefits of this type of response?

10.   What has been the association between nominal GNP and M-1 in the volatile period of money growth from 1980 to 1984? Why did this occur? Would you expect it to continue?

11.   Why did the trend in M-1 velocity end in 1980?

GLOSSARY

Cost-of-living (CLC or escalator) clauses. Provisions of contracts, debt instruments, or government payment programs (such as social security retirement payments) that tie payments to a price index (the rate of change of the consumer price index, for example) to prevent changes in the real value of the payments stream. Limits may be placed on the variability of the payments.

Escalator clauses. See **Cost-of-living clauses.**

Gibson paradox. The apparent paradox between high price levels and high nominal interest rates that was found by A. H. Gibson and cited by John Maynard Keynes. (See note 6.)

Hyperinflation. An inflation in which the price level rises by 50 percent or more per month. It is said to end in the month that the rise in the price level drops below 50 percent per month and stays below 50 percent for at least a year. This definition was devised by Phillip Cagan in his famous "The Monetary Dynamics of Hyperinflation," in Milton Friedman, ed., *Studies in the Quantity Theory of Money* (Chicago: University of Chicago Press, 1956), p. 25.

Income effect. The change in real and nominal interest rates in the same direction as the change in real income, in the cash balance explanation of inflation.

Inflation. A sustained rise in the price level.

Liquidity effect. A fall in real and nominal interest rates from an excess supply of real balances or a rise in interest rates from an excess demand for real balances.

Price expectations effect or **Fisher**

effect. A rise in the nominal interest rate caused by an expectation of more rapid inflation or a decline in the nominal interest rate caused by the expectation of a more rapid deflation. It is a relationship between the rate of change in the price level and the nominal interest rate.

NOTES

1. Phillip Cagan, "The Monetary Dynamics of Hyperinflation" in Milton Friedman, ed., *Studies in the Quantity Theory of Money* (Chicago: University of Chicago Press, 1956), p. 25.

2. William Gibson, "Interest Rates and Monetary Policy," *Journal of Political Economy*, May–June 1970, pp. 431–455.

3. Irving Fisher, *Appreciation and Interest*, published by the American Economic Association in 1896 (Vol. 11, No. 4) and repeated in his later books, *The Rate of Interest* and *The Theory of Interest*. The relationship alleged by Fisher is probably slighlty altered by tax laws. Borrowers (bond sellers) can usually deduct interest expense. Lenders (bond buyers) usually have interest income added to their taxable income. Therefore, borrowers may be willing to accept a slightly higher interest rate for a given expected rate of inflation, as their payments are reduced by tax reductions. Lenders will need a slightly larger interest payment so that their after-tax income will cover the rate of expected inflation and the real rate of interest. Thus the nominal rate may exceed the real rate by slightly more than the expectation of inflation, in equilibrium.

4. Bryon Higgins, "Monetary Growth and Business Cycles," Part II, "The Relationship Between Monetary Decelerations and Recessions," *Economic Review*, Federal Reserve Bank of Kansas City, April 1979. Higgins used a procedure developed by William Poole, "The Relationship of Monetary Decelerations to Business Cycle Peaks: Another Look at the Evidence," *Journal of Finance*, Vol. 30, June 1975. The old M-1 was used in Higgins's tests. Except for 1959 and 1979, in the period tested, the differences between it and M-1 are insignificant. M-1 growth was larger than M-1 growth in 1959 by 2.2 percent and smaller in 1979 by 4 percent.

5. See Robert D. Auerbach and Jack L. Rutner, "Money and Income, Is There a Simple Relationship?" *Monthly Review of the Federal Reserve Bank of Kansas City*, May 1975, pp. 13–19; and Robert D. Auerbach and Jack L. Rutner, "A Causality Test of Canadian Money and Income: A Comment on Barth and Bennett," *Canadian Journal of Economics*, August 1978, pp. 583–594. Although money income, rather than prices, is used in these two articles, the statistical problems are applicable. The price indexes are probably no better, perhaps even worse, indicators of short-run price changes than money income is (which is affected by price changes and changes in real income), at least in periods when prices rise

rapidly. The second article is too complicated for most students, who should read only the conclusion. The subject is also covered in Robert Auerbach, "A Convergence of Views" in *The Federal Reserve Authorities and Their Public Responsibility* (Rochester, N.Y.: University of Rochester, 1980).

6. There is substantial evidence that indicates that the price expectations effect does exist. Where can an important piece of this evidence be found? It is almost in the work of the famous economist John Maynard Keynes, who did not use the price expectations effect in his analysis. See John Maynard Keynes, *A Treatise on Money*, Vol. 2 (New York: Harcourt Brace, 1930), p. 198. Also see John Maynard Keynes, *The General Theory of Employment, Interest, and Money* (New York: Harcourt, Brace, 1935; reprinted 1964), pp. 141–144. Keynes was puzzled by the observation that nominal interest rates almost always rose during inflations and fell during deflations. Increases in the money supply, his analysis indicated, should shift the supply of money to the right (in Figure 19-1) during the expanding part of the business cycle, when inflation would occur. This should lead to a reduction in interest rates (the liquidity effect). The evidence showing a positive correspondence between interest rates and the rate of change in the price level appeared to contradict this analysis. A. H. Gibson observed a high and positive correlation between the interest rate on British consols and the level of prices. Labeling this puzzle the **Gibson paradox**, Keynes wrote, "For the extraordinary thing is that the 'Gibson paradox'—as we may fairly call it—is one of the most completely established facts within the whole field of quantitative economics, though theoretical economists have mostly ignored it. It is very unlikely indeed that it can be fortuitous, and it ought, therefore, to be susceptible of some explanation of the general character" (ibid).

A confusing point that is sometimes overlooked is that Keynes and Gibson were talking about the relationship of interest rates to the *level* of prices. The price expectations effect (which Irving Fisher invented) is a relationship between the *rate of change* in prices and interest rates. In their 1982 book, Friedman and Schwartz reported the following: "Our results strongly support the doubts expressed by Frederick Macaulay more than forty years ago about the universality of the 'Gibson paradox'—a positive correlation between interest rates and prices levels. . . ." See Milton Friedman and Anna J. Schwartz, *Monetary Trends in the United States and the United Kingdom, Their Relation to Income, Prices, and Interest Rates, 1867–1975* (Chicago: University of Chicago Press, 1982), p. 11, and a further elaboration on pp. 585–587. They found that such a relationship does not hold true for most of the period they studied (mid-1870s to mid-1970s) except in a "much-muted form" between World War I and World War II. They interpreted their evidence as supporting the price expectations effect for much of the period studied, especially after 1960, when the relationship was especially strong. It is important to add that Keynes did not accept the explanation of this phenomenon developed by Irving Fisher, presented earlier.

Other studies of the price expectations effect are by David Meiselman, "Bond Yields and the Price Level: The Gibson Paradox Regained," in Deane Carson, ed., *Banking and Monetary Studies* (Homewood, Ill.: Richard D. Irwin, 1963), pp. 112–133; Milton Friedman, "Factors Affecting the Level of Interest Rates"; Gibson, "Interest Rates"; and William Yohe and Denis Karnosky, "Interest Rates and Price Level Changes, 1952–1969," *Federal Reserve Bank of St. Louis Review*, December 1969, pp. 18–38. Colin D. Campbell analyzed the adjustment of price expectations during the rapid postwar inflation in Brazil and compared it with the inflationary episodes in South Korea in "The Velocity of Money and the Rate of Inflation: Recent Experiences in South Korea and Brazil," pp. 339–386, in *Varieties of Monetary Experience*, in which the editor, David Meiselman, also collected empirical studies by John Deaver (pp. 7–68), Adolfo Diz (pp. 69–162), Michael Keran (pp. 163–248), George Macesich (pp. 249–296), and Morris Perlman (pp. 297–338) on inflationary episodes in other countries (Chicago: University of Chicago Press, 1970).

7. Yohe and Karnosky, in "Interest Rates," surveyed the weighting patterns used by others and explained their own tests, which used different weighted averages of prior price data. William Gibson used survey data rather than past prices to estimate price anticipations in "Interest Rates and Inflationary Expectations: New Evidence," *American Economic Review*, December 1972, pp. 854–865. Gibson concluded, "The results lend support to the hypothesis that the real rate of interest is not affected by price expectations over a six-month period and that interest rates fully adjust to expectations within six months."

8. Irving Fisher concluded from his research that it took approximately 20 years for changes in the rate of inflation to have their full effect on long-term interest rates, whereas Milton Friedman and Anna Schwartz came to a different conclusion in their 1982 book: "Our estimate of the period of price change entering into the formation of price anticipations is some six to nine years, distinctly shorter than the period estimated by Fisher and others. . . ." (*Monetary Trends*, p. 12).

In explaining Fisher's conclusions, one could say that it takes a long time to change entrenched beliefs based on many years of consistent experience. People have to die, or at least radically change their opinions as a result of some very persuasive new experiences. In explaining Friedman and Schwartz's more recent findings from tests on a century of data (from the mid-1870s to the mid-1970s), one could say that individuals remember best what happened most recently. Still, six to nine years is not very long—not in a class with the expression, "as old as yesterday's newspaper." One type of learning behavior seems plausible. In the environment of the 1970s and 1980s, with fast-changing interest rates and inflation, individuals may learn to be more flexible in their beliefs. Unfortunately, that could lead to more, not less, variation in these variables, as it is the lags in reaction time that slow economic processes. For example, consider a lag in the time it has taken for the money supply growth to affect the price level in the United States since World War II.

9. Cagan, "The Monetary Dynamics of Hyperinflation," pp. 25–117. The effect of changes in price anticipations swamps the effects of changes in real income and real rates of interest on the demand for money in Cagan's study. See also Andrew Abel, Rudiger Dornbusch, John Huizinga, and Alan Marcus, "Money Demand During Hyperinflation," *Journal of Monetary Economics*, January 1979, pp. 97–104.

10. For a detailed analysis of this subject, see Michael R. Darby, "The Financial and Tax Effects of Monetary Policy on Interest Rates," *Economic Inquiry*, June 1975, pp. 266–276; and Martin Feldstein, "Inflation, Income Taxes, and the Rate of Interest: A Theoretical Analysis," *American Economic Review*, December 1976, pp. 809–820.

CHAPTER 20

THE PHILLIPS CURVE AND PRICE EXPECTATIONS

CHAPTER PREVIEW

Introduction. A number of explanations of inflation in the post–World War II period revolved around the Phillips curve. More recently, expectations of inflation and the theories of rational expectations were added.

In Search of an Explanation. Explanations of inflation after World War II were divided into cost-push and demand-pull varieties. The more recent wedge theories of inflation are a form of cost-push explanations, as are wage-push theories of inflation.

The Expectations-Augmented Phillips Curve. Expectations of inflation were added to the analysis.

Rational Expectations. New formulations of expectations in which individuals take into account all available information were developed into a new theory of inflation and its effect on employment and output.

INTRODUCTION

A number of theories of inflation that are still generating new speculation began as attempts to explain the test results of A. W. Phillips. His test results were published in 1958, and **Phillips curve** analysis, named after the curve he estimated, was applied broadly to the offshoots of his famous work. This chapter will discuss the development and current nature of the Phillips curve analysis.

An important development in this theory occurred in the late 1960s, when inflationary expectations were introduced into the analysis. Some economists branched off into a new type of analysis that made adjustments to inflationary expectations a centerpiece of their macroeconomic analysis. This group's theories are called **rational expectations**. These developments will be described, with special attention to the expectations-augmented Phillips curve.

IN SEARCH OF AN EXPLANATION

The association between rising prices or wages and lower rates of unemployment received much attention in the press and among economists after World War II, even before 1958, when Phillips published his findings. Explanations of inflation based on money supply growth were in doubt, overshadowed by the impact of early Keynesian analysis of the determinants of employment and real output. The observations that full employment was accompanied by inflation were sometimes attributed to the actions of large unions or large businesses, as it was believed that these organizations were largely free from economic constraints.

Wage Push

Early in the post–World War II period, Sumner H. Slichter took the position that creeping inflation was an inevitable result of **wage push** by trade unions. The unions won increasingly higher wage settlements which exceeded the rate of increase in the productivity of labor.[1] When the rate of wage increases exceeds the rate of increase in the productivity of labor, Slichter held, the employer is forced by higher costs to raise the prices of the goods he or she sells. The employer must (1) pay laborers more money wages and (2) attempt to substitute capital for labor, a substitution that was not economical before the wage increase. Both actions drive up costs.

It is important to point out a possible contradiction in this explanation. Employers who can freely raise product prices when wages rise may well have been able to do so previously. Then why do they wait to increase their profits? It thus is difficult to use this explanation for either sustained inflations of two years or more or for periods of price stability, such as occurred in the United States from 1960 to 1964.

According to the wage-push explanation, wages rise; sellers mark up their prices; workers demand more goods and services; and the **wage-price spiral** begins. Albert Rees pointed out that the wage-price spiral hypothesis, which is based on only the direct effects of an increase in the wages of unionized employees, unrelated to demand-and-supply conditions, is not applicable to rapid inflations. "Unions tend to lose ground in relative wages, or at least not to gain new ground, during very rapid inflations when the rigidities introduced by collective agreements act as a brake on the upward pull of demand on wages."[2] (This observation is consistent with our later assumptions in explaining the Phillips curve, using *expectations* of price level changes.) The wage-price spiral can be financed by a government policy of increasing the money supply to avoid unemployment at the higher wage rate levels.

Cost Push and Demand Pull

The wage-push and wage-price spiral analysis of inflation was replaced in some analyses by the broader **cost-push inflation** explanation. A cost-push inflation begins with an increase in nominal wage rates and/or nominal material prices unrelated to past conditions of demand or supply.

Many of the analyses of the Phillips curve phenomenon use a second type of explanation, called **demand-pull inflation**. A demand-pull inflation is caused by an increase in spending, so that the demand for goods and services exceeds the supply; that is, there is excess demand for goods and services.

Wedge Theories of Inflation

A special form of cost-push inflation is thought to result when the government applies a tax that forms a wedge between an employer's costs and either the wages paid or the prices received for goods and services sold. The existence of this type of cost-push explanation of inflation was suggested by some economists who carefully spelled out the necessary conditions and by many others who regard it as a commonsense explanation.

It is a controversial idea with a number of problems that makes it inapplicable to most inflationary episodes. But it is useful for the reader to navigate this theory and the criticisms of it to avoid reaching incorrect conclusions based on this type of cost-push reasoning.

Higher wage taxes, such as social security taxes, have been held to reduce equilibrium employment and to cause a higher price level. This view appears, at first glance, to contradict the notion that higher taxes reduce spending and inflation. Conventional models have, however, been used to explain these results.

Here is how the theory works: An increase in the minimum wage or social security taxes makes it more expensive to employ the same number of workers. Employment drops as employers reduce the number of workers in order to reach a profit-maximizing level of workers after the tax is imposed.

But with fewer people working, output falls. Refer back to the monetary identities in Chapter 18. The price level is equal to money per unit of output times velocity. If the money supply is constant, there will be less output, no change in velocity, and an excess demand for goods and services. (That is, the same amount of money is spent on fewer goods and services.) Prices rise.

The term *wedge problem* is most appropriately used for social security taxes, as they form a wedge between take-home wages and the cost of the worker to the employer. The analysis of social security taxes is, however, similar to that used for the minimum wage. In addition, even a sales tax could form a wedge between the price paid by the consumer and the price obtained by the seller. So even a sales tax could be said to cause higher prices. These explanations will be called **wedge theories of inflation**.[3]

One problem with these wedge theories is that they usually explain a one-time rise in prices, not a sustained rise in prices. Only with constantly rising taxes and minimum wages can one explain a constantly rising price level with these theories. Furthermore, if social security taxes and sales taxes are raised, one should not neglect the macroeconomic effects that would tend to lower prices, offsetting the price change described by the wedge theories. Imagine, for example, that the minimum wage or social security tax were raised to such a high level that half the work force was thrown out of work. The economy would take a nosedive, and spending would fall. Prices would fall (or rise at a slower rate). The rise in unemployment would put downward pressure on wages, though if they were sticky, as is usually assumed, money wages would not fall by much. All this is merely the stuff of conventional (Keynesian) economics, which says that an increase in government taxes reduces the aggregate demand for goods and services. But it cannot be neglected because it may swamp the opposite effects, emphasized by the wedge theories.

Some of the analyses of the wedge problem include a permissive monetary policy. That is, if the sales taxes, social security taxes, or minimum wages create unemployment, the monetary authority is supposed to step in with a more rapid monetary policy that restores full employment. In this case, the increase in the money supply fuels inflation, as is consistent with cash balance explanations of inflation. But again, these theories still acccount for only a one-time increase in the money supply, not for a sustained increase.

Two technical details also tend to make these wedge theories apply only to short-lived inflations. First, with prices rising, the causal elements of these explanations would soon be washed out. Inflation would soon wash away the *real* value of a social security tax, an increase in minimum wage, or other *nominal* wedges. The wedge theories are self-liquidating in this respect. The real value of these wedges would decline and, if the wedge theories are to be believed, would then be a factor in reducing the rate of inflation. As in the case of an airplane with a motor fixed to slow down as altitude increases, the wedge theories may never get prices very far off the ground. An additional problem with the wedge theories as they are applied to social security payroll taxes is posed in Study Question 7 at the end of this chapter.

One related form of the wedge theories of inflation is the **markup inflation** theory. This is a wedge between cost and selling price, a wedge of profits. Under this theory, sellers have sufficient latitude that they can maintain their selling prices at a fixed proportion above their costs. This markup of costs can be maintained despite the pressures of temporary insufficient demand. An increase in costs is transferred to an increase in prices. A decline in demand does not cause prices to fall; the markup over costs is maintained.

Another problem with the markup hypotheses is the belief that firms generally have unused monopoly power to boost prices when costs rise, regardless of demand conditions. If firms have this kind of power, why do they wait for a rise in costs to raise prices; why not increase profits earlier? One answer to this question is that some large firms incur governmental wrath and adverse public opinion when they raise prices unless they have something like a cost increase to blame it on. This may be the case for specific episodes, but it may be difficult to find any sustained relationship between some measure of monopoly power and inflation.

The Phillips Curve

An article by A. W. Phillips appearing in the November 1958 issue of the British economics journal *Economica* had an important impact on the analysis of inflation.[4] In this article, "The Relation Between Unemployment and the Rate of Change of Money Wage Rates in the United Kingdom, 1861–1957," Phillips fitted a curve to observations of the percentage of unemployment and the percentage rate of change in money wage rates per year in Great Britain. The general appearance of this curve—a limp noodle—is shown in Figure 20-1. Separate curves were fitted to observations for different subperiods from 1861 to 1957.

The relationship interpreted from these curves and other evidence was that at low levels of unemployment, money wage rates increased more rapidly than they did at high levels of unemployment, with several exceptions. Phillips concluded that

> The statistical evidence . . . seems in general to support the hypothesis . . . that the rate of change of money wage rates can be explained by the level of unemployment and the rate of change of unemployment, except in or immediately after those years in which there is a sufficiently rapid rise in import prices to offset the tendency for increasing productivity to reduce the costs of living.[5]

Phillips explained his findings in the following way: When the demand for labor is relatively high compared with the supply, and there is little unemployment, employers bid up wage rates quite rapidly. Workers thus will be in a stronger position to ask for wage increases during a period of rising business activity, when there is relatively full employment. However, "workers are reluctant to offer their services at less than the prevailing rates when the demand

FIGURE 20-1   A Phillips Curve*

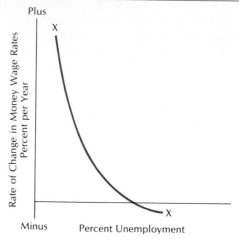

The Phillips curve is a relationship between the rate of change in money wage rates or the price level and the rate of unemployment. It has a negative slope, which means that higher rates of inflation are associated with lower levels of employment.

* A curve of the type fitted by A. W. Phillips to data from the United Kingdom, 1861–1957.

for labor is low and unemployment is high so that wage rates fall only very slowly."[6]

Cost-of-living adjustments in wage rates were held to have little or no effect on the average rate of change in the money wage rates "except at times when retail prices are forced up by a very rapid raise in import prices (or, on rare occasions in the United Kingdom, in the prices of home-produced agricultural products)."[7]

Because the value of imports was estimated to be one fifth of national income. Phillips explained that the relationship depicted in Figure 20-1 would not apply in years in which import prices rose rapidly, such as war periods.

Much of the subsequent Phillips curve analysis substituted the rate of change in the price level for the rate of change in money wage rates.

The Record

Albert Rees and Mary T. Hamilton made a number of tests of the Phillips curve relationship on United States data from 1900 to 1957 and reached the following conclusion:

we regard the construction of a plausible Phillips Curve from annual data for a long period as a tour de force somewhat comparable to writing the Lord's Prayer on the head of a pin, rather than as a guide to policy. This is because it is highly probable that the relationship is changed during the period, because the data are of poor quality for much of the early part of the period, and because of the large changes in some of the variables that take place during the course of a calendar year and are blurred in the annual data. If we were making policy recommendations we would prefer to test them on an analysis of monthly or quarterly data for the post War period.[8]

In addition, Guy Routh noted only one year after Phillips's work appeared that the data Phillips used were faulty; he asserted that Phillips had exaggerated the relationship for U.K. data.[9]

However valid these doubts were, a great many tests were run, using all kinds of data on periods before 1970 that appeared to support some form of the Phillips phenomenon. Edward Foster, in a survey of the literature on the costs of inflation, contended that "there has been overwhelming empirical evidence of the association of low unemployment with high inflation, and vice versa; the evidence covers wide spans of time and a varied collection of economies."[10]

And then came the 1970s. High rates of unemployment coexisted with high rates of inflation. Had the Phillips curve shifted? Some said it had. Others applied the new name *stagflation* to these episodes, illuminating in some of their views a new phenomenon in economics. (Paul Samuelson used the term **stagflation** to describe periods of slow real growth combined with inflation.) Still others said that continued and accelerating inflation caused such disruptions in the economy that inflation produced more unemployment, not less.[11]

In 1980 and 1981, inflation and high unemployment existed in tandem. In 1982 and 1983, as inflation dramatically dropped, the unemployment rate surged to over 10 percent of the labor force and then fell two percentage points at the end of 1983. The simple Phillips curve could not explain these diverse episodes.

The original Phillips curve literature presented a *trade-off* between the rate of inflation and unemployment. That is, policymakers would need higher rates of inflation in order to lower unemployment. There was considerable support for the existence of this trade-off in the short run, at least up to the middle 1970s, but much more controversy about the existence of such a long-run relationship. Indeed, some economists believed that long-run full employment could not be maintained as long as there was a high rate of inflation.

Nominal and Real Wages

One problem that sometimes creeps into an analysis of the relationship between the wages of labor and inflation is the confusion between nominal wages and real wages. The **real wage of labor**, W/P (nominal or money wages, W, divided by the price level), can rise even if W is falling. When it is alleged that an excess demand for labor raises the wages of laborers, careful attention must be given to what is meant by wages. If the excess demand for labor is alleged to cause *nominal* wages to rise, regardless of the change in the price level, the analysis needs to explain why *real* wages are not an important determinant of the quantity of labor demanded and supplied, why workers but not employers ignore the purchasing power of money wages.

This confusion arose in the Phillips curve analysis. It is, for example, possible to have a 10 percent inflation (P is rising by 10 percent) with different rates of change in real wages, W/P. Compare two alternative changes in real wages under this inflation rate. Suppose that nominal wages are rising by 5 percent, so that W/P is falling by 5 percent. Then assume that nominal wages are rising by 15 percent so that W/P is rising by 5 percent. Can both these changes in real wages be associated with the same level of unemployment and the same inflation rate on a single Phillips curve? It seems doubtful.

The next development in the Phillips curve analysis, the incorporation of inflationary expectations, remedied this problem. Careful attention was given to the difference between nominal and real wages.

THE EXPECTATIONS-AUGMENTED PHILLIPS CURVE

Edmund Phelps and Milton Friedman both developed explanations of the Phillips curve that depended on expectations of price changes by workers and employers.[12] Those analyses are sometimes called the **expectations-augmented Phillips curve analyses**.

There are two basic assumptions in these explanations of the Phillips curve. First, although employers and workers adjust their expectations of inflation equally rapidly, they receive different signals. From the point of view of the worker, what matters is the general price level, the real buying power of his or her wage. From the point of view of the employer, who decides whether or not to hire workers, what matters is the price of the products he or she sells (and the prices of inputs). These are the prices on which profit depends. The employer is able to react more rapidly to a new rate of inflation because he or she has fewer prices to consider, only the increased price of the relatively few goods and services with which the firm is associated.

The second assumption is related to the equilibrium level of employment. The long-run free market equilibrium level of employment (where the long-run demand and supply curves for labor intersect) is never attained. Imperfections exist in the labor market, such as labor monopolies and minimum wage laws. Disturbances, such as unexpected changes in the demands and supplies for labor and search, as well as moving costs, also prevent long-run equilibrium from being attained. All these constrain the long-run unemployment rate to some higher rate of unemployment, called the **natural rate of unemployment**. The second basic assumption is, therefore, that the natural rate of unemployment is stable and predictable, although not necessarily constant. That is, it can change with changes in any of its underlying determinants, which include the productivity of labor and competition in the labor market.

Whether or not the natural rate of unemployment is stable and predictable is, therefore, a controversial question.

The short-run Phillips curve based on these two assumptions can be explained by example. Suppose that the natural rate of unemployment is 4 percent and the steady state of inflation is 3 percent. This is depicted in Figure 20-2, in which the natural rate of unemployment is ON and the 3 percent rate of inflation is equal to OD. The long-run Phillips curve is NN', a line that is perpendicular to the horizontal axis at N.

Now suppose that the inflation increases to a rate of 7 percent per year. Workers still expect a 3 percent inflation, and so the increased rate of inflation does not lead them to seek higher nominal wages right away. As a result, the real wage, W/P, falls. Employers perceive the increase in the actual prices for the goods and services they sell and the decline in real wages they pay. It is then profitable for the employers to increase the quantity of labor demanded, thereby reducing the employment rate to 2 percent ($=OF$).

As workers begin to expect and adjust to the new rate of inflation, they obtain higher nominal wages. The real wage rises, the quantity of labor

FIGURE 20-2   The Expectations-Augmented Phillips Curve*

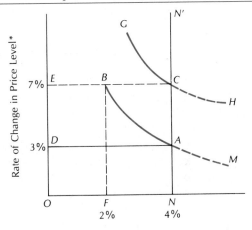

Rate of Unemployment

The expectations-augmented Phillips curve is BAM, and the natural rate of unemployment curve, NN', touches the horizontal axis at N. If the inflation rate unexpectedly rises, it will cause a decline in the unemployment rate. Thus, an unexpected rise in inflation from 3 percent to 7 percent causes a movement from A to B along the expectations-augmented Phillips curve. The dashed segment, AM, is for an unexpected decline in the inflation rate below 3 percent. The unemployment rate would rise. Curve GCH is another short-run Phillips curve that would result if the unexpected rate of inflation became 7 percent.

* This axis may be scaled for $(\dot{P} - \dot{P}^e)$ so that Friedman's depiction of the short-run Phillips curve is a function such as BAM, which does not shift with different rates of change in the actual price level, only with changes in the differences between the actual and unexpected rates of change in the price level.

demanded declines, and the natural rate of unemployment is restored. There is a movement from B to C in Figure 20-2. In equation (1), the unemployment rate then equals the natural rate, and $\dot{P}_t$ equals $\dot{P}_t^e$.

If the government wishes to keep the rate of the unemployment below the natural rate, it must increase the money supply at an even more rapid rate. This will cause prices to continue to rise at a more rapid rate than is anticipated. The need for prices to rise faster and faster to maintain a rate of unemployment below the natural rate has led to one name for this explanation of the relationship between unemployment and inflation: the **accelerationist hypothesis**.[13] There is a major, 180-degree difference between this explanation of the Phillips curve and much of the long line of analytical explanations that followed the publication of A. W. Phillips's work in 1958. The former Phillips curve analysis makes the rate of change in prices depend on the level of unemployment (and other variables). But the expectations-augmented Phillips curve analysis makes unemployment a function of changes in the rate of change in prices (and price expectations).

AN ALTERNATIVE WAY TO EXPLAIN THE EXPECTATIONS-AUGMENTED PHILLIPS CURVE

An alternative explanation uses an equation and some hypothetical numbers. The curve AB in Figure 20-2 is a short-run Phillips curve derived from this analysis. The equation for the Phillips curve is then[14]

$$K(N - U_t) = \dot{P}_t - \dot{P}_t^e$$

or

$$U_t = N - \frac{\dot{P}_t - \dot{P}_t^e}{K} \qquad (1)$$

where N is the natural rate of unemployment; $\dot{P}_t$ and $\dot{P}_t^e$ are the actual and expected (by workers) rates of change of the price-level changes, respectively; U_t is the unemployment rate; and K is a constant. The greater is the positive difference between the actual rate of change in prices and the rate of change expected by workers, the smaller the unemployment rate will be.

Suppose that the expected rate of inflation is 3 percent, $\dot{P}_t^e = 3$ percent. If the actual rate also equals 3 percent, $\dot{P}_t = 3$ percent, the difference between the actual and the expected

rate will be zero, $\dot{P}_t - \dot{P}_t^e = 0$. Then from equation (1), the natural rate will equal the actual rate of unemployment.

Now suppose that the actual rate of inflations jumps unexpectedly to 7 percent, $\dot{P}_t = 7$ percent. Assume further that K is found, through testing, to be equal to 2. Equation (1) then takes the following values:

$$U = .04 - \frac{.07 - .03}{2} = .02 \qquad (2)$$

The unemployment rate falls to 2 percent. This shows that as inflation unexpectedly rises, unemployment rates fall.

Equation (1) can be used to check your understanding of the mechanics of the expectations-augmented Phillips curve. What if inflation suddenly falls to 1 percent? Can you calculate what would happen to unemployment and explain why? The numerical answer is given at the end of the chapter.

Which direction of causation is correct? Additional statistical tests with new methodologies for dealing with the problems of data in time series appear to have promise for solving this puzzle. It is likely that there is a two-way causality. Price changes affect unemployment, and vice versa. Meanwhile, if the reader wishes to delve into some simple models that hypothesize different directions of causation for the Phillips curve, see note 15.

RATIONAL EXPECTATIONS

Economists have long been interested in people's expectations of changes in economic variables.[16] Early work on the term structure of interest rates, cited in Chapter 11, revolved around people's expectations in regard to what interest rates would be in future years. The price expectations effect, described in the nineteenth century by Irving Fisher (and discussed in the last chapter), is another example from the field of monetary theory. There are numerous examples from many fields, including the famous cobweb model found in nearly every price theory book. The cobweb model is used to show how the price of an agricultural product approaches (or diverges from) equilibrium. Farmers are modeled as adjusting their output (the supply of an agricultural product) to expected prices.

A key question in analyzing expectations is, How should they be estimated? Before the theories of rational expectations were developed, the most common method of estimating expectations of a variable such as the price level was to take a weighted average of past price levels. That method is still used. Individuals generally base their expectations of future price levels on past price levels, with more weight given to more recent price levels. In a path-breaking article, John Muth questioned this formulation and suggested that more information than the past history of a variable is taken into account in predicting the future course of a variable.[17] (See Study Question 11.) Indeed, economic theories also are used to predict future values of variables, and they take into account many factors besides the variables' past history. (The predictions of these theories can be made known to the public through the widespread communication network in the developed countries. The business publications are like vacuum cleaners in their search for predictions of what course variables will take.) John Muth stated his hypothesis as follows:

> I would like to suggest that expectations, since they are informed predictions of future events, are essentially the same as the predictions of the relevant economic theory. At the risk of confusing this purely descriptive hypothesis with a pronouncement as to what firms ought to do, we call such expectations "rational."[18]

Muth's rational expectations hypothesis is stated in terms of a probability, the probability of a given future value for a variable, given all available information. (This formulation conforms to the idea of a stock price in an efficient market, described in Chapter 13.) A second important characteristic of Muth's rational expectations hypothesis is that people include in the information on which they base their forecasts any systematic (predictable) errors in past predictions. If, for example, they have been consistently overshooting their prediction of inflation, they will lower their forecasted values for future inflation. Only random (unpredictable) errors in the forecast will be left if people remove such systematic errors. Therefore, people's average forecasts are, except for random deviations, equal to the value that a variable actually takes.

The next important question in studying expectations after estimating what they are is, What difference do they make? The rational expectations theorists have developed an extensive and sophisticated literature on this subject. One important basic hypothesis is closely related to the hypothesis of Friedman and Phelps described in the last section. The central variable in this hypothesis is the price level. To illustrate this hypothesis, consider what will happen if people fully expect the growth in the money supply to be rapid and to result in a more rapid inflation. This faster money growth, in turn, may be part of a policy by the government to stimulate employment.

Suppose that the workers adjusted their expectations of inflation without any hesitation. Then, using the Friedman–Phelps analysis, there would be no real effects; wages and prices would be set up simultaneously by the new expectations, so that the real wage, W/P, would be constant and the unemployment rate would remain at the natural rate. The rational expectations hypothesis holds that this rapid adjustment may well be the case some of the time.

Several impediments are thought to prevent a rapid adjustment even if the price level change is to be expected. One is the existence of contracts—labor contracts and contracts for the purchase of goods in the future. These contracts will slow down price adjustments even if new expectations of price level changes are formed. In addition, there is the cost of information in different markets, which is held to be high enough to prevent the simultaneous and rapid change of prices by participants in all markets. According to these assumptions, even prices that are expected to change in some markets may respond slowly, thus causing changes in unemployment and other real variables. Therefore, a key to the explanation of what happens under the rational expectations hypothesis is to discover what causes expectations of price level changes and to separate these price level changes into those that are free to change and those that are not.

A primary contribution and the emphasis of the rational expectations theorists have been on the formation of expectations of price level changes. Rather than base expectations of the rate of inflation on past rates of price level changes alone, every other common macroeconomic variable that can be found to affect significantly these expectations is used.

The most important variable for explaining inflationary expectations in the rational expectations theory is the rate of change in the money supply. Changes in the money supply that are not part of the trend in money supply growth and are not predictable on the basis of current general information are classified as *unexpected* changes in the money supply. Unexpected changes in the money supply cause changes in unemployment, output, and other real variables. The same type of explanation as is used for the expectations-augmented Phillips curve is used here.

The rational expectations hypothesis is in the tradition of classical economics with its emphasis on markets being cleared and correct information being discounted into market prices. Over time, it is held, errors in expectations will average zero. However, some economists in this tradition do not agree with a major part of rational expectations theories. Milton Friedman and Anna Schwartz, in their 1982 book, questioned the belief that correct information will be discounted into prices if one averages enough periods of information into the prices. The problem is, they contended, that in any given period—often a number of years—the prices will not reflect market-clearing correct information. That is, prices may be such that real variables *are* affected for long periods, which could cause prolonged business cycles, which Friedman and Schwartz illustrated in an example. They referred to a period from 1880 to 1896 when individuals in the United States incorrectly thought that the country would go off the gold standard:

> Given a sufficiently long sequence of observations, of course, it could be maintained that all such events will ultimately average out, that in the century of experience our data cover, for example, there are enough independent episodes so that it is appropriate to test rationality of expectations by their average accuracy. But that is cold comfort, since few studies cover so long a period. . . .[19]

In 1981 a symposium on rational expectations was held at New York University, and the papers and some comments were published in 1983.[20] Frank Hahn criticized the rational expectations literature and the models of one of its main developers, Robert Lucas, for adopting a market-clearing model consistent with Walrasian equilibrium, an economywide equilibrium in which every market in the economy is in equilibrium:

> The arguments that are offered in support of the view that we can treat the world as if it were in continuous Walrasian equilibrium are so appallingly bad and so much at variance with the Lucasian resolve to pursue serious and rigorous economics that they are barely worthy of consideration. One is told that not only will all Pareto-improving [moving toward the optimum allocation of resources] possibilities be exploited by markets but also they will be exploited the instant they arise. . . . There is even the more disreputable argument that some three or four log-linear econometric equations not immediately at variance with microeconomics of a single agent and economy-wide equilibrium " work."[21]

Allan Meltzer explained that the rational expectations literature bypasses issues concerning the expectations of most importance to Keynes.[22] That is, the rational expectations literature generally assumes expectations of economic events to be held with certainty and to be widely shared. But Keynes's discussion of long-term expectations stressed that there could be sudden changes in expectations as well as persistent expectations based on habit and convention. Thus expectations could be persistently mistaken, and individuals would have little idea of what other people's expectations were.

There are also some other disputed areas in the literature of rational expectations. No completely reliable way has been found to separate expected changes from unexpected changes in the money supply. This is because the statistical tests used to estimate expected changes in the money supply have such a large residual (the unexpected part) that little weight can be put on the expected part. In other words, if the money supply is estimated to grow in the future by 10 percent, subject to a huge error (the unexpected part of money growth), people may put little weight on the estimate of future growth. As an estimate of the effects of money supply growth, one may be forced to fall back on the rough evidence presented in Chapter 19, and there is an average two-year lag between money growth and price level changes and an average three- to nine-month lag between money growth and output changes. These crude approximations bypass the sophisticated rational expectations concepts of expected and unexpected money growth.[23]

The rational expectations theorists have attacked Keynesian models in which the relationships have not been derived on classical economics grounds in which individuals are viewed as trying to optimize their welfare. Again, this is similar to the point earlier about the rough evidence lags for monetary policy described in Chapter 19. The "best" explanation therefore may be judged on which works the best, which leads to policies that have the most desirable effects.

In the meantime, many economists have been drawn to the rational expectations theorists' results that show that much of the monetary and fiscal policy does get discounted into prices and has little effect on real variables such as employment. Test results that support these rational expectations conclusions are presented in Chapter 25.

STUDY QUESTIONS

1. What is a Phillips curve? What does it show, and how did Phillips explain it?
2. If increases in the quantity of money or wedges are important causes of inflation, what effect do they have on the Phillips curve explanation of inflation?
3. What is stagflation? Is it consistent with a Phillips curve explanation of inflation? Explain.
4. Is it important to Friedman's explanation of the Phillips curve that the natural rate of unemployment be predictable and stable? Is it important

to this explanation that the direction of causation be from price changes to unemployment?

5. If the government adopted a policy, as it does in some countries, whereby wage increases were announced and allowed on specific dates for all workers in the economy, how would this policy affect the level of unemployment, according to the theories of inflation presented in this chapter?

6. According to the accelerationist hypothesis, a government policy, such as those found in the Employment Act of 1946 and the Humphrey–Hawkins Act of 1978, that sought to maintain full employment in the United States at a level that might be less than the natural rate of unemployment would lead to accelerating inflation. Explain why this is so.

7. Assume that those who pay their social security taxes—all covered workers—believe that this is an insurance payment for which they receive full value in the form of pensions and insurance. How would this affect the wedge explanation of inflation that results from an increase in the social security payroll tax? Is this assumption reasonable?

8. According to the rational expectations theories, would monetary policy become more potent if data on the money supply were kept secret? Explain.

9. According to the rational expectations theories, what will happen if a money supply change is perfectly expected and individuals are able to adjust their contracts to that expectation? How will your answer change if the effect of such a money supply change on prices is uncertain? Will expectations be corrected over time, leading to a "correct" setting of prices? What is meant by "a 'correct' setting of prices"? (*Hint:* Review the controversy arising from the Friedman–Schwartz 1982 criticism of the rational expectations theories.)

10. Suppose that imports rise in price (imports are goods purchased from other countries). The price level suddenly rises because of this rise in import prices (as it did in 1974, 1979, and 1980, following increases in the price of oil). Actual inflation is greater than expected inflation. What will happen to the unemployment rate, according to the expectations-augmented Phillips curve? What is wrong with this result? (*Hint:* When more is paid for imports to foreigners, purchasing power in the country drops. It is like an eternal tax on domestic income, and recession can result. Unemployment rises.) Can you explain why these so-called external shocks have a different effect on unemployment than does an internal cause of inflation, such as increases in the money supply? Does the natural rate of unemployment shift from these external shocks? (*Hint:* Can the adjustment to the new rate of inflation occur at a higher rate of unemployment?)

11. Expectations are estimated by rational expectations theorists from all available information, which means that the expectations conform to the values predicted by economic theories. An alternative, commonly used method uses the past history of a variable for which expectations are

being estimated. For example, this latter method of estimating the rate of change in the price level that people expect in the future uses the rates of change in the price level in the past, with more weight given to more recent rates of change in the price level. This is called the *extrapolative method*, an extrapolation of past trends. When will this method yield as good or better results than an economic model will? To help with your answer, two examples are presented. First, consider the efficient markets hypothesis covered in Chapter 13—in which there is an instantaneous adjustment in prices to all new information. That hypothesis makes the current price of a stock the best prediction of what it will be in the next period of time (plus the interest cost of holding the stock). No other information is needed. The second example occurred during a question-and-answer period at an American Finance Association meeting when an individual was describing the rational expectations hypothesis. Asked what he thought the Federal Reserve would do next, he said that he would extrapolate from its past behavior.

ANSWER TO PRACTICE PROBLEM

Unemployment rises above the natural rate of unemployment to 5 percent.

GLOSSARY

Accelerationist hypothesis. A hypothesis stating that the rate of change in the price level must continually accelerate so as to maintain an unemployment rate below the natural rate of unemployment.

Cost-push inflation. Inflation that results from an autonomous change (a change in a variable not explained by changes in prior economic variables) in one or more types of costs of inputs in businesses.

Demand-pull inflation. An inflation caused by an excess demand for goods and services.

Expectation-augmented Phillips curve. A Phillips curve that relates the difference between actual and expected rates of changes in the price level to the rate of unemployment.

Markup inflation. An inflation that results from the ability of sellers to maintain their markup over costs combined with an autonomous rise (see **Cost-push inflation**) in costs, despite conditions of demand.

Natural rate of unemployment. The rate of unemployment that would prevail if the rate of inflation (or deflation) were perfectly expected and wages were perfectly adjusted to that rate.

Phillips curve. A schedule relating different levels of inflation (or deflation) of the price level or wage rates to levels of unemployment. Newer versions use the difference between actual and expected prices.

Rational expectations. A group of theories based on the premise that economic actors take into account all available evidence for such decisions as setting prices and wages and adjusting their money balances.

Real wage of labor. The nominal wage, *W*, divided by the price level, *P*, which equals *W/P*.

Stagflation. A condition in an economy of slow real growth combined with inflation.

Wage-price spiral. A theory of inflation based on an initial autonomous rise in wage rates (see **Wage-push inflation**), the resulting increased demand for goods and services by workers (see **Demand-pull inflation**), and the ability of sellers to mark up their selling prices (see **Markup inflation**).

Wage-push inflation. An inflation caused by an autonomous increase (see **Cost-push inflation**) in wage rates.

Wedge theories of inflation. Theories of inflation based on a decline in output caused by a wedge (the *wedge problem*) between take-home pay and the cost of labor to employers (from a social security tax, for example) or a wedge between costs and retail prices from industry or taxes. See **Markup inflation**.

NOTES

1. The rate of increase in productivity of labor can be defined as the rate of increase in the average output per worker, holding constant the contributions of other inputs. Because the contributions of other inputs are usually not taken into account, the resulting statistics are imprecise.

2. Albert Rees, *The Economics of Trade Unions* (Chicago: University of Chicago Press, 1962), p. 102.

3. See, for an example of a wedge hypothesis, Frank Breckling and Kathleen Classen Utgoff, "Taxes and Inflation," *Policies for Employment, Prices, and Exchange Rates*, a supplement to the *Journal of Monetary Economics*, Vol. 11 (Amsterdam: North-Holland, 1979), pp. 223–246.

4. A. W. Phillips, "The Relation Between Unemployment and the Rate of Money Wage Rates in the United Kingdom, 1861–1957," *Economica*, November 1958, pp. 283–299. Reprinted in M. G. Mueller, ed., *Readings in Macroeconomics* (New York: Holt, Rinehart and Winston, 1966), pp. 245–256 (these pages cited).

5. Ibid., p. 255.

6. Ibid., p. 245.

7. Ibid., p. 246.

8. Albert Rees and Mary T. Hamilton, "The Wage-Price Productivity Complex," *Journal of Political Economy*, February 1967, p. 70.

9. Guy Routh, "The Relation Between Unemployment and the Rate of Change of Money Wage Rates: A Comment," *Economica*, November 1959, pp. 299–315.

10. Edward Foster, "Costs and Benefits of Inflation," Federal Reserve Bank of Minneapolis, March 1972, p. 12.

11. Milton Friedman, "Nobel Lecture: Inflation and Unemployment," *Journal of Political Economy*, June 1977, pp. 451–472. Paul Samuelson used the term *stagflation* to describe the periods of slow real growth combined with inflation.

12. Milton Friedman, "The Role of Monetary Policy," *American Economic Review*, March 1968, pp. 1–17; Edmund S. Phelps, "Money Wage Dynamics and Labor Market Equilibrium, in *Microeconomic Foundations of Employment and Inflation Theory* (New York: W. W. Norton, 1970), pp. 124–166. The explanation here follows Friedman, but the Phelps version is similar.

13. There are some tests that contradict the accelerationist hypothesis; see Foster, "Costs and Benefits of Inflation," p. 16. Thomas Sargent, in "A Note on the 'Accelerationist' Controversy," indicated why tests of the accelerationist hypothesis may be false because of the way that expected prices are formulated in the models; see *Journal of Money, Credit and Banking*, August 1971, pp. 721–724.

14. For a further description of this presentation, see Robert D. Auerbach and Ronald Moses, "The Phillips Curve and All That: A Comment," *Scottish Journal of Political Economy*, November 1974, pp. 299–301.

15. See Auerbach and Moses, "The Phillips Curve and All That"; and James Tobin, *Inflation: Its Causes, Consequences and Control* (New York: New York University Press, 1968). Tobin's article was reviewed by Harry Johnson in *Macroeconomics and Monetary Theory* (Chicago: Aldine, 1972); see especially pp. 162–163. Other models are found in R. G. Lipsey, "The Relation Between Unemployment and the Rate of Change of Money Wage Rates in the United Kingdom, 1862–1957: A Further Analysis," *Economica*, February 1960, pp. 1–31; Edmund Phelps, "Phillips Curves, Expectations of Inflation and Optimal Unemployment over Time," *Economica*, August 1967, pp. 254–281; and Warren Smith, "On Some Current Issues in Monetary Economics: An Interpretation," *Journal of Economic Literature*, September 1970, pp. 767–782.

16. A highly readable review of the theories of rational expectations with an extensive bibliography was written by Steven M. Shefrin, *Rational Expectations* (Cambridge, England: Cambridge University Press, 1983). Some important articles on this topic are by John F. Muth, "Rational Expectations and the Theory of Price Movements," *Econometrica*, July 1961. A sampling of the literatures should include Thomas J. Sargent and Neil Wallace, "Rational Expectations and the Theory of Economic Policy," *Studies in Monetary Policy 2*, Federal Reserve Bank of Minneapolis, 1975, also in *Journal of Monetary Economics*, Vol. 2, April 1976; David Laidler, "Expectations of the Phillips Trade Off: A Commentary," *Scottish Journal of Political Economy*, February 1976; Robert J. Barro, "Rational Expectations and the Role of Monetary Policy," *Journal of Monetary Economics*, Vol. 2, January 1976; and R. E. Lucas, Jr., "Expectations and the Neutrality of Money," *Journal of Economic Theory*, April 1972.

17. Muth, "Rational Expectations," pp. 315–335.

18. Ibid., p. 316.

19. Milton Friedman and Anna J. Schwartz, *Monetary Trends in the United States and the United Kingdom, Their Relation to Income, Prices, and Interest Rates, 1867–1975* (Chicago: University of Chicago Press, 1982), pp. 556–557.

20. Roman Frydman and Edmund S. Phelps, eds., *Individual Forecasting and Aggregate Outcomes, "Rational Expectations" Examined* (Cambridge, England: Cambridge University Press, 1983).

21. Frank F. Hahn, "Comment," *Individual Forecasting and Aggregate Outcomes, "Rational Expectations" Examined*, p. 224.

22. Allan Meltzer, in a forthcoming book that interprets some of John Maynard Keynes's theories. Meltzer's interpretation is discussed in the appendix to Chapter 25.

23. On these points see Robert Auerbach, "A Convergence of Views," in *The Federal Reserve Authorities and Their Public Responsibility* (Rochester, N.Y.: Center for Research in Government Policy and Business, Graduate School of Management, University of Rochester, 1980), pp. 5–33.

CHAPTER 21

WAGE AND PRICE CONTROLS

CHAPTER PREVIEW

Introduction. Inflation imposes costly distortions and is costly to stop.

Arguments in Favor of Wage and Price Controls. The free market system produces undesirable results and/or the high cost of tight money as a method of stopping inflation are two common arguments for wage and price controls.

Theory and Evidence. What has the record been, and what can be expected from wage and price controls?

INTRODUCTION

Inflation is a costly phenomenon, not only because of the distortions it imposes, elaborated on in Chapter 19, but also because there are significant costs of stopping it. These costs of stopping inflation are a major reason that some analysts support wage and price controls. This and another reason are discussed in the next section. We then will describe the kind of inflation that will result if wage and price controls are imposed on an inflationary economy. The last part of the chapter considers the theory and evidence of the effects of wage and price controls.

ARGUMENTS IN FAVOR OF WAGE AND PRICE CONTROLS

Some countries have formal wage controls or, as they are sometimes called, an **incomes policy**. Some economists argue that an incomes policy in the United States also is necessary.[1] The late Abba Lerner suggested a government-imposed plan to remedy what he called sellers' inflation.[2] In a sellers' inflation, the sellers join together with labor, agreeing to give raises if they can pass the costs along in the form of higher prices for the goods and services they sell. (For an explanation and evaluation of a similar cost-push type of inflation, see the *wedge theories* of inflation in the last chapter.) Henry Wallich and Sidney Weintraub advocated a special wage insurance plan to reward workers who received wage increases below a given percentage amount. Such a plan was also reportedly advocated by Gary Hart, a United States Senator who sought the Democratic nomination in the 1984 presidential primary. It is discussed later in this chapter. In addition, John Kenneth Galbraith has been a consistent proponent of an incomes policy in the United States.

The arguments for wage and price controls generally present one or both of the following reasons: First, the free market system does not lead to desirable results. It does not allocate resources properly, and/or it distributes the goods and services produced in an undesirable way. Some of the arguments along these lines hold that consumer sovereignty does not work. (That is, consumers cannot effectively affect market decisions by "voting" with their dollars.) The central government would better serve these functions with direct allocations and price setting.

Second, the kind of tight money needed to halt most inflation is too costly a policy, as it produces serious recessions. For example, the 1981–1982 recession during the Reagan administration was due in large part to a change from a generally loose money policy (with rates of growth in the money supply at over 8 percent for much of the previous Carter administration years) to a slower rate of growth of the money supply, down to slightly more than 2 percent from February 1982 to August 1983. (Then the slowdown in money supply growth was sharply reversed.) Inflation dramatically slowed down, but a costly recession ensued, with the unemployment rate exceeding 10 percent of the labor force.

Proponents of wage and price controls hold that this type of cost of bringing an inflation under control would be reduced by a firm government announcement that prices will be prevented from rising as rapidly (or at all), by some type of government-imposed control system, such as wage and price ceiling regulations. In this way, the *expectations* of inflation could be sharply changed without a long, costly adjustment. When inflation is halted, many who hold this view would wish to return to a free market system.

Repressed Inflation: What Is It?

Defining a repressed (or suppressed) inflation is something like describing the illness of a patient who has a high fever, with the constraint that the patient's temperature must be taken with a thermometer fixed at normal. **Repressed** or **suppressed inflation** occurs when the conditions for a rising price level exist, but a rise in the price of a significant number of commodities and services is made illegal by wage and price controls. Repressed inflation is associated with widespread effective maximum wage and price ceilings and an underlying inflationary equilibrium. **Inflationary equilibrium** is defined as the rate of change in prices that would have occurred over a year or two if the price controls had not been adopted.

Suppose that wage and price controls are imposed on every good and service in an economy with no foreign trade. Suppose also that these wage and price regulations are perfectly effective. There are no **black markets** (illegal markets in which price controls are ignored) and no substitutes for the legal currency and coin. What if, under these conditions, the nominal quantity of money is increased at a rate that is higher than the rate of growth of national income minus the rate of change in the long-run (secular) velocity of money?

Hold on to your hats. The winds of inflation are blowing; however, a gust of price increases is illegal. There would be an increase in demand for goods and services. As long as, at the controlled prices, real output cannot grow as fast as does the increase in demand, inventories will be depleted below their desired levels. Under these conditions, shortages of goods and services will be the result. Long lines of shoppers waiting for a chance to make a purchase are a sign that price controls are working.

A method for *rationing* goods and services, other than the one that existed under the unconstrained price system, would have to be instituted. Entrepreneurs might give their favorite customers and friends priority in the selection of goods and services. The government might institute formal rationing methods, as was done in the United States during World War II. In a rationing system, persons might be issued books of coupons that entitled them to purchase limited quantities of goods and services. This example may be unrealistic, however, if the underlying pressures of increased demand cause consumers and sellers to resort to black markets and other methods for evading the price regulations. That is, instead of paying the regulated price, consumers may be forced to pay an illegal premium "under the table" to obtain goods and services.

Various methods for evading the price regulations will be instituted. Quality and quantity of changes, which are often difficult to detect, will be used to alter the prices of goods and services. Consumers will substitute commodities and services that are not regulated for those commodities and services that are regulated. Sellers thus will have an incentive to produce nonregulated commodities and services instead of regulated commodities and services.

Biased Price Indexes

The price indexes published by the government during a period of repressed inflation may be seriously inaccurate. (Review the discussion of price indexes in Chapter 18.) First, the quality and quantity changes in the commodities that are sold may not be taken into account in the government survey of prices. (The shrinking size of candy bars is a favorite example.) This omission will cause the recorded price index to understate the actual rise in prices. Also, government price indexes will be little affected by the price of goods and services sold in the black markets.

The price indexes may significantly underestimate the price rise if the prices of uncontrolled goods rise rapidly. The quantity of uncontrolled goods sold during the regulated periods is likely to be greater than the quantity sold during the base period of the price index—before price controls—because of the switching from controlled goods when there are shortages. If the method of calculating the U.S. consumer price index is used, the *quantities* of goods sold in the *base* period will be used as weights for prices in the subsequent periods. If the base period is before the price regulations were anticipated, unregulated commodities with rising prices and quantities purchased in the current period will receive relatively small weight in the calculation of the price index. This downward bias in price indexes during repressed inflation may be severe.

Output

The rationalization for wage and price controls in the United States often has the following general line of argument: Spending is expected to rise rapidly. Entrepreneurs can expand their output, raise their prices, or do both to meet increased demands. Therefore, if wage and price increases are made illegal, output will rise rapidly.

The sudden disruption of the price mechanism and the adoption of alternative methods for rationing goods and services impose numerous costs of buying and selling inputs on the production process and lead to the misallocation of resources. In labor markets in which employers need additional laborers, they are presented from raising wages. In markets for controlled goods and services, in which there are excess supplies, many employers are reluctant to reduce prices for fear the new price regulations may force them to maintain lower prices permanently.

Even the expectation of wage and price controls causes wage and price distortions. For example, employers may raise prices to achieve a higher base price for the anticipated price control period.

Therefore, instead of promoting a more rapid rate of growth of real output, price controls can reduce the rate of growth in real output below the level that would have occured without price controls.

THEORY AND EVIDENCE

Some Evidence

There is, unfortunately, insufficient evidence regarding the effect of wage and price controls in reducing the rate of mild inflations. This lack of reliable information is partly caused by the lack of precise data on price movements during the control period. Also, as in the 1971–1972 price control period in the United States, the contribution of controls is on the borderline of being too small to identify.

There is some evidence regarding the effect of controls during wartime periods.[3] In the United States, the price level rose during the Civil War, World War I, and World War II. The peaks in price level rises came at the end of the Civil War, a year and a half after World War I, and three years after World War II. If the periods immediately following these three wars are included in each of the wartime episodes of inflation, it will be found that prices rose by approximately the same percentage in the three wartime periods.

Direct controls were not used during the Civil War. There were some direct controls during World War I, and extensive price regulations were used during World War II. These differences in controls are consistent with the following conclusions: During World War II and, to a lesser extent, during World War I, price controls prevented markets from reaching their underlying equilibrium until after the wars, when these controls were abolished. In addition, the published price indexes during the World War I and World War II periods of regulation underestimated the actual rise in prices. These effects delayed the rise in the published price level index until after the period of controls. Apparently, the controls did not change the underlying inflationary equilibrium. These conclusions also explain why government officials may be reluctant to remove price regulations: They may justifiably fear an upward surge in the published price indexes.

Temporary and Permanent Price Controls

In an excellent study of open and repressed inflations in the United Kingdom and Spain, Juan J. Toribio, in a somewhat inaccessible essay, discovered some interesting and important results.[4] He also developed a useful explanation for the demand of money during repressed inflations. He noted that the literature on repressed inflation arrives at two apparently contradictory conclusions. One is that repressed inflation produces a greater demand for money. This conclusion supports the view that price regulations can not only reduce the rate of inflation, as reflected in the published price indexes, but can also temporarily reduce spending by the public. On the other hand, the literature on repressed inflation often warns that excessive regulation may lead to a **flight from cash**, a complete collapse of the monetary system, and the adoption of a barter system or an alternative form of money. Toribio resolved this apparent contradiction by looking at the services that money is expected to produce and how these services are affected by the expected duration, effectiveness, and extent of controls.

The more extensive the price controls are, the longer they will be expected to be effective and pervasive; the more efficient is a government-imposed rationing system in equating the quantities of goods and services demanded and supplied according to underlying equilibrium prices, the smaller will be the demand for real money balances. As the prices of more and more goods are regulated by the government, and more goods or services other than money are bartered in trade for the controlled goods and services, the monetary services per dollar of money decline. Legal money loses more and more of its *medium-of-exchange* services. These conditions cause a decline in the demand for real money balances or, equivalently, a rise in the desired velocity of money. Therefore, the implementation of extensive, effective price controls and rationing that are expected to be *permanent* reduces the demand for real money balances, causing an *increase* in spending. The upward pressure on prices, the inducement to form more extensive black markets, and the rewards for finding legal ways to evade price regulations are intensified.

Permanent, effective controls and permanent rationing are therefore extremely difficult forms of government regulation to impose on a free society. There must be extensive policing facilities, and indeed, the central authority may prefer to allow widespread violations of the price control and rationing regulations. In many sectors, these regulations may impose huge costs that could be significantly reduced by a price system flourishing in black markets. Insofar as black markets do arise, thereby reducing the effectiveness of the price controls, the demand for real money balances will be increased. The services from money will be greater than they would otherwise have been, because money may be used as a medium of exchange in the black markets. The timing of the availability of particular goods in the black market may be difficult to predict, because many of the common forms of advertising are not available to black marketeers. This will increase the value of monetary services provided by money as a reserve for unexpected opportunities to purchase goods. There is likely to be an increased demand for currency and coins relative to checking accounts, so as to avoid written records of the transactions. The currency ratio discussed in Chapter 17 is likely to rise with an increase in black market activity. This increase in the currency ratio will tend to reduce the money expansion multiplier and the money supply, and therefore the rate of inflation.

The effects on the demand for money of the imposition of a **control system** (formal price regulation and rationing) that is expected to be temporary may be significantly different. Again, it is true that the more extensive and effective are the price controls, the greater will be the reduction in the services provided by money. This reduces the demand for real money balances. The longer the control system is expected to remain in force, the greater will be the reduction in demand for real money balances.

However, the conditions that are expected to prevail at the time that price controls are lifted also affect the demand for real money balances during the control period. If more goods are expected to become available after the temporary control system is lifted, the demand for real money balances will increase during the control period. Toribio found that this latter effect dominated the repressed inflations he studied in the United Kingdom and Spain.

Interest Rates

One additional important effect, which Toribio found in the repressed inflations in the United Kingdom, is relevant to other advanced countries with well-developed financial markets. Because bonds were not one of the controlled commodities, the demand for bonds increased during the controlled periods. (A *maximum* bond interest rate control would be a *minimum* price on bonds.) The price of bonds rose until the interest rates were relatively low.[5] This may partly explain periods of abnormally low nominal interest rates during price control periods. In 1972, a period of price controls in the United States, short-term interest rates were low compared with their subsequent level after a rapid rise in 1973, when most wage and price controls were abandoned. Short-term prime commercial paper rates were 4.69 percent in 1972 and 8.15 percent in 1973. This rise in interest rates may be explained by (1) a sharp upward revision in the expectation of inflation, (2) a premium for increased uncertainty associated with the explosion of prices as wage and price controls ended, and (3) a reduction in this *Toribio effect*.

Price Expectations

The belief that the institution of wage and price ceilings will cause the public to revise downward its expectation of inflation needs to be clarified. Suppose that the average rate of increase of the nominal money supply has been 7 percent per year. Suppose also that the consumer price index is rising at an average annual rate of 3 to 4 percent per year. Because any reduction in the rate of growth in the nominal money supply would take two to three years to affect significantly the equilibrium rate of inflation, the government wants to end inflation by an alternative means, that is, wage and price controls. This is one of the reasons given for the price regulations begun in August of 1971 by the Nixon administration and effectively ended in 1973.[6]

Short-run price anticipations can be temporarily changed if the public believes the price freeze will be effective. In other words, if the public believes that the rate of inflation will be reduced, short-term nominal rates of interest are likely to fall, and the quantity of real money balances demanded will increase. The expectation that the inflation will be reduced will temporarily reduce public spending below the level that would have occurred without the controls.

If the nominal money supply is still being increased at 7 percent per year, the public will soon find that it has more nominal money balances than it desires, even at the lower nominal rates of interest. Individuals will attempt to reduce their money balances. The temporary effect of controls, inducing the public to increase the quantity of real money balances demanded and to reduce spending temporarily, will be rapidly dissipated. Spending will then increase. The new powerful forces from increased spending will cause the regulatory apparatus to give way in more and more sectors in which legal and illegal methods are found to evade the regulations. Individuals will reduce the quantity of money they hold as they again come to expect higher rates of inflation. The reduction in the quantity of real money balances demanded on top of the continual increase in the nominal money supply of 7 percent per year will cause an even greater upward pressure on prices.

When, for example, a 60-day price and wage freeze was instituted in June 1973, short-term interest rates rose. This episode is consistent with the hypothesis that the public had lost faith in wage and price controls and revised upward their expectations of inflation.

Government officials "produced" forecasts that severely underestimated the price increases for the beginning of 1973. The public lost some confidence in the government's ability not only to control inflation but also to foresee it in the immediate future. But these government officials were not solely, and perhaps not even primarily, at fault. The public, the press, and many people in government demanded actions that would *immediately* halt inflation. It thus was in an atmosphere of pressure for instant solutions to inflation that the price controls were instituted in August 1971. Once an inflationary equilibrium is built up and sustained for several years or more, there is no known way to instantaneously eliminate its effects.

Mild Inflation

Whether or not the price controls in the United States from August 1971 to December 1972 reduced the rate of inflation by 1 percent or 2 percent is a matter for research that may demand more accuracy in the price indexes than can be expected. As in the inflations during the three war periods, there is some presumption that the underlying equilibrium rate of inflation was not significantly affected if the immediate postcontrol period in 1973 is included (see Figure 21-1). The popular cry during early 1973 that meat retailers and producers were to blame because meat prices caused the price explosion only

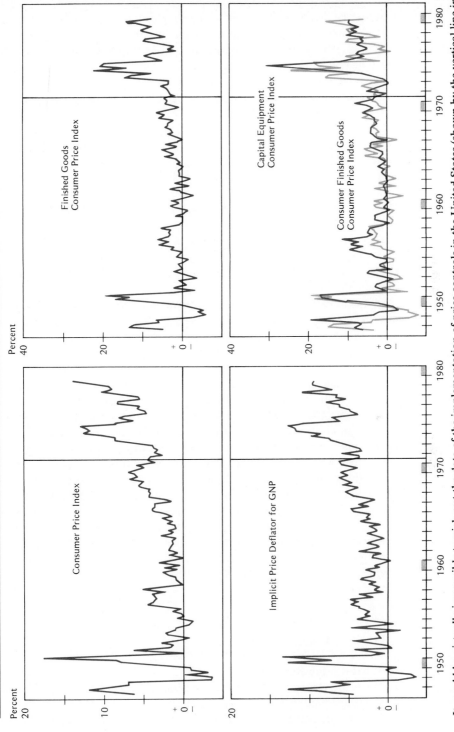

FIGURE 21-1   Rates of Change of the Price Level for Four Categories of Components with the Institution of Price Controls in 1971 (vertical line) (changes at annual rates, seasonally adjusted, quarterly), 1947–1980

It would be virtually impossible to pick out the date of the implementation of price controls in the United States (shown by the vertical line in 1971), from the record of price indexes alone. The controls self-destructed in 1973 under strong inflationary pressures, and prices surged into the double digits.

Source: Board of Governors of the Federal Reserve System, *Historical Chart Book*, 1979, p. 37.

temporarily diverted the public's attention from the underlying, much more general inflation and the changes in the world supply of food. Nevertheless, meat boycotts and other expedient responses were part of an atmosphere in which instant solutions were demanded.

The reinstitution of price controls in 1973 produced food shortages and was not effective in reducing expectations of inflation in 1973. The extent of the severe shortages produced by the episode of total price controls that began in August 1971 was not fully realized until the end of 1973, when the shortages were dramatically intensified by an Arab imbargo of oil shipments to the United States.

In November 1978, President Jimmy Carter announced a new program of quasicompulsory price controls. The Council on Wage and Price Stability, COWPS, was given the job of running the program. Firms that did not abide by the price standards were not eligible to sell products to the government. The legality of this form of compulsion was questionable. Could the lowest bidder be denied a sale because his or her firm had not abided by the price regulations? It is impossible to discern the contribution of COWPS to reducing the rate of inflation.

An ingenious form of wage insurance was proposed by President Carter and sent to the Congress, where it died. The idea for this insurance came from the late Arthur Okun, former chairman of the Council of Economic Advisers, who in turn took the idea from Henry Wallich of the Federal Reserve Board and Professor Sidney Weintraub. If employees settled for a wage increase of 7 percent or less and the actual rate of inflation in the following year was greater than 7 percent, they would be eligible for a tax refund for the difference, up to a 10 percent rate of inflation. Although the plan was ingenious, it was difficult to conceive of an administrative and regulatory apparatus with the rules and regulations necessary to make sure that the insurance was fairly provided. The inducements to evade such regulations are enormous. For example, employers could informally agree to pay the employees and themselves more in a future year so that they could get their subsidy immediately. Some unions said that they would disregard the 7 percent ceiling on wages whether or not the insurance was provided. Assuming that the plan could effectively be implemented, a key question is whether or not such an insurance plan would reduce the cost of bringing inflation under control.[7] The costs of implementing the plan, some of which are presented in note 7, must be weighed against the costs of other methods of reducing inflation.

STUDY QUESTIONS

1. What is repressed inflation?
2. What are the costs of inflation, and how do they differ when the inflation is expected and when it is unexpected?
3. Why are price indexes biased during a period of price controls?

4. What are the different effects on the demand for real money balances of temporary and permanent price controls?

5. What conditions are most favorable for implementing wage and price controls?

6. What methods can be used to bring inflation under control, and what kinds of costs arise with each method?

7. Stopping an inflation with slower money growth is an expensive process that many countries have experienced. The United States suffered severe recessions in the early 1980s that caused millions of workers to lose their jobs as the central bank slowed down the money supply to disinflationary (reducing the rate of inflation) levels. Some observers said that the process could have been less costly if price controls were implemented and the money supply were not slowed as rapidly. Assess this alternative. Consider the special problems that would occur if the public were told (or perceived) that the control system was temporary.

GLOSSARY

Black markets. Markets in which goods and services are purchased at prices that exceed the ceiling prices of the price control system. The word *market* may be misleading, as there may be no formal organization of buyers and sellers; rather, there is negotiated trading by transactors operating in secrecy or with word-of-mouth information systems.

Control system. Formal price regulations and rationing.

Flight from cash. A sharp decline in the demand for the currently used money supply and the adoption of a barter system or a different form of money.

Incomes policy. A system of government wage controls.

Inflationary equilibrium. The economic conditions that allow a constant rate of change of the price level over several years or more.

Repressed or **suppressed inflation.** An episode in which an underlying inflationary equilibrium is prevented by price controls from being registered in recorded prices. It may be partly—or even substantially—reflected in *black market* prices.

NOTES

1. *On Incomes Policy: Papers and Proceedings from a Conference in Honour of Erik Lundberg* (Stockholm: Studieforbundat Narungsliv och Samhalle, Industrial Council for Social and Economic Studies, 1969). Many distinguished American economists participated, including Paul Samuelson, Walter Heller, James Dusenberry, James Tobin, and Fritz Machlup. Gunnar Myrdal and Nicholas Kaldor were among the European partici-

pants. For a negative viewpoint on price controls and a survey, see Robert L. Schuettinger and Eamonn F. Butler, *Forty Centuries of Wage and Price Controls—How Not to Fight Inflation*, with a foreword by David Meiselman (Washington, D.C.: Heritage Foundation, Caroline House, 1979).

2. Abba P. Lerner, *Economics of Employment* (New York: McGraw-Hill, 1954).

3. See Milton Friedman, "Price, Income, and Monetary Changes in Three Wartime Periods," in *The Optimum Quantity of Money* (Chicago: Aldine, 1969), Chap. 8. Paul Evans investigated general price controls during World War II. He found that if the Federal Reserve had adopted a tight monetary policy during World War II in place of general price controls, "employment and output would have been at least 11.7 and 7.1 percent higher than they were." "The Effects of General Price Controls in the United States During World War II," *Journal of Political Economy*, 1982, p. 965.

4. Juan J. Toribio, "On the Monetary Effects of Repressed Inflation," Ph.D. diss., University of Chicago, June 1970.

5. The responsiveness (or elasticity) of the demand for money with respect to bond interest rates increases during the control periods, according to Toribio: "In the extreme case, if all goods other than money and securities are rationed, it is conceivable that a liquidity trap might appear in the money market, as Keynesian theory pretended. Notice, however, that such a liquidity trap would be due to the special circumstances of price control and rationing, and it would not necessarily appear in a free market economy" (p. 123). See Chapter 23 for a description of the liquidity trap.

6. See Roger Miller and Rayburn Williams, *The New Economics of Richard Nixon: Freezes, Floats, and Fiscal Policy* (San Francisco: Canfield Press, 1972). Also see Edgar L. Feige and Douglas K. Pearce, "Inflation and Incomes Policy: An Application of Time Series Models," in Karl Brunner and Allan Meltzer, eds., *The Economics of Price and Wage Controls* (Amsterdam: North Holland, 1976), pp. 273–302.

7. The costs of the insurance plan, in addition to those arising from a new nationwide administrative bureaucracy, are incurred from the resultant misallocation of labor and capital. The plan would provide a subsidy for industries in which wage increases were low because of low productivity, overabundant labor sources, or declining demand for the product being manufactured. Insofar as the plan is effective in holding down wages in an inflationary environment, it would induce a shift out of capital (away from machinery and automation) to labor (as inputs in the productive process). This shift would be reversed when inflation subsided, so that its welfare benefits from higher employment would be transient.

PART SIX

KEYNESIAN EXPENDITURE THEORY

CHAPTER 22

AGGREGATE DEMAND AND SUPPLY

CHAPTER PREVIEW

Introduction.   What is Keynesian expenditure theory?

The Supply of Goods and Services.   The labor market and the production function are described.

Classical and Keynesian Positions on Unemployment.   Say's law and the cause of short-run unemployment equilibrium are explained.

The Demand for Goods and Services.   The consumption function and the components of aggregate demand are described.

Equilibrium.   Equilibrium in the Keynesian cross diagram is derived.

Government to the Rescue.   The government expenditure and tax multipliers and the size of the deficit necessary to close the unemployment gap are described.

The Lessons of Keynesian Expenditure Theory.   The use of fiscal policy is developed.

Appendix A: Money Illusion of Workers, a Standard Interpretation.   Sticky wages are part of a standard interpretation, though the nature of *The General Theory* makes other interpretations (presented at the end of the next chapter) likely candidates for what Keynes meant.

Appendix B: An Algebraic Derivation of the Government Expenditure Multiplier.   This alternative derivation of the multiplier uses the device of summing a geometric series.

Appendix C: The Effects of Permanent and Short-Run Changes in Fiscal Policy.   Some recent evidence on fiscal policy is presented.

INTRODUCTION

The previous two parts of the book analyzed the demand and supply of money for their effects on other variables and even for their effects back on themselves. In this part of the book, the central variable is *expenditures*, the determinants and effects of expenditures. A general expenditure model explaining short-run unemployment and some proposed remedies is presented. Interest rates and the important role played by investments will be introduced in Chapter 23, in which money is given a prominent role in the determination of interest rates. Chapter 24, the last chapter in this part, explains inflationary equilibrium, building on the analysis of the demand for money and the relationship between money and inflation developed in the last part of the book, this time bringing in the effects of the rate of change in real income.

The material covered in this part of the book is called Keynesian expenditure theory because it was first introduced and developed by John Maynard Keynes as a general body of theories that explained short-run unemployment, a condition that Keynes thought was more common than was full employment of the labor force.

Much of macroeconomic analysis has been dominated by the ideas of John Maynard Keynes since at least 1936, when he published *The General Theory of Employment, Interest, and Money*. Keynes drew attention in *The General Theory* (as it is usually called) to the determinants of the aggregate demand for goods and services necessary to achieve full employment. That is, he analyzed those conditions that keep the economy from achieving full employment equilibrium. The timing for this publication could not have been better. The United States and a number of other countries were in deep depressions. Nearly 25 percent of the labor force was out of work in the United States, and obviously, policies for full employment were needed. Keynes's analysis can be viewed as justifying the need for the federal government to carry out those policies through increased deficit spending.[1]

This chapter uses several simplifications to make the main points of the analysis easier to understand. There are two concepts of income. **National income**, the income earned from producing the current year's output, is referred to simply as *income*. **Disposable income** is income after income taxes. In addition, all variables except nominal wages are in real terms. The precise way to indicate this is to divide a variable such as nominal consumption, C, by the price level, P, to obtain C/P, real consumption. Only the symbol C is used in this chapter, but that symbol along with the other symbols for investment, I, government expenditures, G, and so on all are to be understood as being divided by the price level.

THE SUPPLY OF GOODS AND SERVICES

In this section the aggregate supply of goods and services is discussed. The schedule is simplified to show how much output will be supplied by the entire economy at each level of real income. Attention is drawn to the level of real income that is large enough to require the full employment of labor to produce the output. To find this level of output the discussion turns first to the demand and supply of labor in the labor market and then to the relationship between the quantity of labor employed and the level of output.

The Full Employment Level of Income

The concept of full employment is determined from the demand and supply schedules in what is called the *labor market*. The labor market consists of those workers supplying labor and those employers demanding labor. With injustice to all nuances (changes necessary to make the analysis more precise), it is presented in aggregate form in Figure 22-1. On the horizontal axis is the quantity of labor, measured in units of millions of ("average") workers per week. On the vertical axis is the real wage, W/P, where W is the nominal wage and P is the price level. If W were $500 per week and P were $200, the real wage would be $500/$200 per week, or $2.50 per week.

The demand and supply schedules for labor are drawn for a "normal" economy growing at near-capacity levels. At the equilibrium real wage of $(W/P)_F$, the hypothetical number of 110 million workers per week will be the quantity of labor supplied and demanded. That equilibrium level is defined as the *full employment level.*

FIGURE 22-1   The Demand and Supply of Labor*

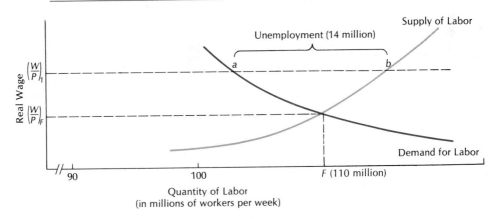

This figure shows the demand and supply schedules of labor for a "normally" growing economy near capacity output. Equilibrium at (the hypothetical) 110 million workers per week and a real wage of $(W/P)_F$ defines the full employment level. If the real wage rises to $(W/P)_1$, there will be an excess supply of labor *ab*. This excess supply of labor is also the amount of unemployment.

* The numbers are hypothetical.

The Production Function

To describe the relation between the quantity of labor employed and the real output in a society, an aggregate *production function* is frequently used. A production function shows the relationship between the quantities of inputs going into the productive process and the quantity of output.

For example, for a cake, the production function is given by the recipe—a complete recipe that also contains the input of labor and equipment, such as an oven—to make a given number of cakes. The aggregate production function for the entire economy is made into a simple recipe by assuming only two classes of inputs, also called *factors of production*:

1. Labor, humans who supply services.
2. Capital, the stock of all other resources, such as equipment, and the resources obtained from the land.

A further simplification in the Keynesian analysis in this and the next two chapters is the assumption that the stock of capital is constant.

The rationale for this assumption is that in a short period of time, say less than a year, capital will not change enough to affect significantly the results of the analysis. With the capital stock constant, only the quantity of labor can be changed to produce different quantities of output. The relationship between the different quantities of output and labor is shown by the production func-

FIGURE 22-2   Aggregate Production Function (in millions of base-year dollars per week)

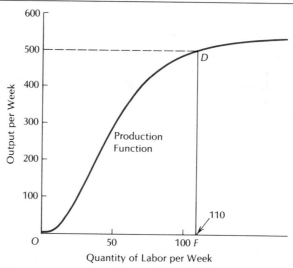

The full employment quantity of labor is *OF*. With that quantity of labor and the existing stock of wealth, an output of $500 million per week could be produced. (The output is in real units so that if the price level doubles, the nominal dollar amount of output will also double.)

tion drawn in Figure 22-2. The full employment equilibrium output of Figure 22-1 is 110 million workers per week. That amount of employment is consistent with $500 million in output per week. (Output is measured in real units per week, so that if the price level doubled, the same output would be measured by twice as many dollars.)

CLASSICAL AND KEYNESIAN POSITIONS ON UNEMPLOYMENT

Classical Equilibrium

The classical position—that is, the conventional analysis before the work of John Maynard Keynes—was that the economy would settle down to an equilibrium position, as shown for the labor market. Prices in the markets for goods and services and for labor would adjust so that the quantities supplied and demanded in each market would approach equality, the equilibrium position. The classical position that Keynes attacked is most vivid in Say's law.

Say's Law

Jean Baptiste Say (1767–1832) was first a businessman and then after 1819 taught economics. He presented the following perplexing statement:

> It is worthwhile to remark that a product is no sooner created, than it, from that instant, affords a market for other products to the full extent of its own value.[2]

Say meant that when new goods are produced, those that produce them are paid. That is, the workers and owners of other factors of production receive pay from the producers. They can immediately buy other goods. The producer has the unsold output that can be exchanged for other goods and services. The supply of goods thus appears to create a demand for other goods. This notion is sometimes abbreviated in something you might call a rough translation for **Say's law**: *Supply creates its own demand.*

Say also said that *there cannot be general overproduction.* A society cannot make too much of everything. Consumers are never completely satisfied with the available goods and services. A society can have overproduction or a glut of some goods or services, but not all goods and services.

The Criticism by Keynes

Something is fundamentally wrong. What if the workers and the owners of production do not spend all their income? In that case, their demand for goods will be less than the value of the output they produce. If this is not offset by other consumers' spending, that is, if this is an economywide phenomenon, more will be produced than is demanded. This was Keynes's point. In a *money economy*, in which people are paid in money, they may choose to save their earnings in the form of pieces of paper called financial assets. If it is a *barter economy*, which is an economy with no money, they will not be able to do this. They can only try to stockpile goods, which will create a demand for goods. The attempt to store beer, blankets, gold coins, and bicycles in the basement—because of the fear of a coming depression—will itself nourish the demand for goods. But storing pieces of paper called financial assets does reduce the demand for goods and services, causing an excess, or surplus, supply of goods and services, as shown in Figure 22-3. Keynes agreed with Say that this was not a condition of a *general oversupply of goods and services*. Rather, it was a condition of *insufficient demand for goods and services*.

To illustrate Keynes's use of it, Say's law can be put into better form for an economy that uses money or bonds. It is the assertion that *there will not be an excess demand for money and/or bonds that causes an excess supply of goods and services*. Keynes said in effect, "Say, it isn't so." In a money economy, there can be a general excess demand for money and bonds, especially if people become frightened about the economy's future health. This is because the threat of a recession can choke consumption expenditure. The types of assets that people can hold—instead of buying the physical output that is produced in the economy—include many financial assets other than money. Those financial assets were discussed in Chapters 3 and 12.

What is the important point of the discussion about Keynes's criticism? Keynes did not believe that recessions—especially the massive depressions in the 1930s when *The General Theory* was published—were caused by producing too many goods and services. They were, instead, caused by an insufficient demand for goods and services.

FIGURE 22-3   Demand and Supply of All Goods and Services

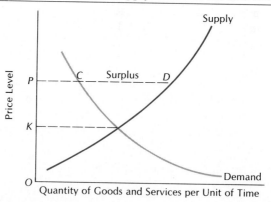

This is a diagram of the demand and supply of all the goods and services in the economy (measured in some form of a standardized unit, each containing the same proportion of every good or service). Notice that at a price level of *OP*, there is an excess supply of *CD* (called a surplus).

The "classical solution" was simply a decline in the price level and nominal wages as insufficient demand arose. Equilibrium would be restored at a price level of *OK* in Figure 22-3. At the lower level of prices, nominal wages would also have to be lower in order to preserve the full employment real wage of $(W/P)_F$ in Figure 22-1.

Keynes objected to this line of analysis. Although he devoted considerable space in *The General Theory* to explaining why equilibrium would not be achieved even if nominal wages fell, an important point for Keynesian analysis was that nominal wages would not fall in the short run.

Sticky Wages

One of Keynes's most important contributions was to show that full employment would not be a common condition because nominal wages are slow to fall. This characteristic of nominal wages is called **sticky wages**. Nominal wages can rise rapidly but fall only slowly. Like a ratchet on a jack that is used to raise a car and keep it in position, this behavior of nominal wages is also called a **ratchet effect**.

What causes this effect? Employees get angry and morale drops if the employer says, "I must lower your wages." The employer might even add, "Such a reduction is caused by poor business conditions, but it will allow me to retain all of you. Jane and Sylvester, don't fret as I lower your wages from $8.00 per hour to $6.00 per hour. Because the price level is falling, your real wage is constant. Why are you screaming?" Indeed, it may be better for the employees' morale—of those that are still retained—to lay off workers than to lower nominal wages.

In addition to the morale problem, there is the legal impediment to rapid wage changes from contracts that fix many prices and nominal wages. Union wage contracts and contracts are common for many goods and investment projects that fix prices and nominal wages. (Some of these contracts have *escalator clauses*—also called *cost-of-living clauses* or *COLAs*—that increase the contracted prices and nominal wages when the price level rises. But many contracts have no such provision.) Thus, contracts often prevent particular nominal wage rates and prices from changing.

WHAT DID KEYNES REALLY WRITE?

Keynes did not emphasize sticky wages in *The General Theory*. To see why sticky wages are part of the standard interpretation, read Appendix A. The interpretations of what Keynes said are more than historical curiosities. They are part of the discussion leading to new theories from which ideas for full employment policies have been and will be derived.

THE DEMAND FOR GOODS AND SERVICES

Desired and Actual Expenditures

The remedy that Keynes proposed for unemployment as it has been developed in the mainstream of what is called *Keynesian economics* is understood best by beginning with the basic determinants of the expenditures for goods and services.

There are two types of expenditure variables: *desired* and *actual*. For example, an individual may desire to spend $300 per week on consumption. Actual consumption may be something else, say, $400. Desired consumption is then less than actual consumption.

The desired values of variables are marked with a superscript D, as for desired consumption, C^D. The actual values of variables have no superscript, as in actual consumption expenditures, C.

The Components

The components of aggregate demand for goods and services are

C^D = desired real private consumption

I^D = desired private investment

G^D = desired real government expenditures

The variable G^D may take the form of (1) desired government consumption or (2) desired government investment expenditures. (See Figure 22-4 for the historical record.)

Examples of actual expenditures for each type of expenditure are

1. *Government consumption*: government expenditures for electricity for the lights on top of the Washington monument and for the food eaten by military personnel on duty.
2. *Government investment*: government expenditures for the construction of the Rayburn House Office Building (for some members of the House of Representatives).

Consumption and Saving

The amount that individuals spend on consumption goods and services, called *private consumption*, depends to a large extent on their income after taxes. Income, Y, after taxes, T, is called *disposable income*.

It is easy to show that when aggregate disposable income rises, so too do aggregate personal consumption expenditures. After all, personal consumption expenditures are a major part of what is counted to obtain the concept of income. As shown in Table 22-1, personal consumption expenditures in the

FIGURE 22-4   The Components of Aggregate Expenditures in the United States, 1951–1987 (current dollars)

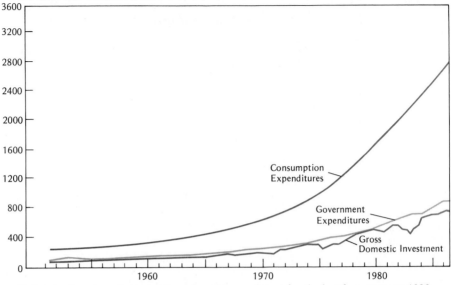

Estimates based on the trend in each series are shown for the last four years to 1990.

Source: Cambridge Planning and Analytics, Inc., Boston.

United States as a percent of disposable income fell until the 1980s. Then the percentage rose. The fact that aggregate personal consumption expenditures rise with aggregate disposable income does not provide much evidence that personal consumption expenditures depend on disposable income because little *dependence* is involved; they both are nearly the same thing.

TABLE 22-1   Personal Consumption Expenditures in the United States As a Proportion of Disposable Income, Selected Years, 1933–1987 (in billions of dollars)

This table shows that the ratios of personal consumption expenditures to disposable income in selected years from 1933 to 1987 ranged from .89 to .95 except during the deep depression of the 1930s, when the ratio was 1.

(1) Year	(2) Personal Consumption Expenditures	(3) Disposable Income	(4) Ratio of Column 1 to Column 2
1933	$ 45.8	$ 45.6	1.00
1940	71.0	75.3	.94
1950	192.0	206.6	.93
1960	324.9	352.0	.92
1970	621.7	695.3	.89
1987	3,046.6	3,216.0	.95

The relationship of private consumption expenditures to disposable income is derived from an examination of what consumers do when their disposable income changes.

When a consumer receives income, he or she can either spend it or save it. For the individual, disposable income, Y_{DI}, is related to its two broad uses, consumption, C, and saving, S. For example, if Herbert Brown receives $100 and consumes $100, none will be saved. But a decision to consume $90 is a decision to save $10.

Disposable income saved can be invested to produce new output, or it can be kept in money or in some other asset. Investment goods (the capital stock) have an income stream in the future. Thus, investment increases the capital stock and provides income for the future consumption of goods and services. Money holdings can also be transformed into goods and services in the future. Thus, the decision to save is a decision about how much to consume now or in the future. That decision depends on Herbert Brown's preference and on the return from saving. If there is a relatively high reward for saving, in the form of a high real rate of interest, the consumer may be encouraged to save more. Herbert Brown could also consume more than his income, by borrowing funds or running down his wealth. This is called *dissaving*.

Consumption and Disposable Income

As disposable income rises, the individual has more funds for consumption expenditures. Suppose, as Keynes did, that Herbert Brown—the typical, average consumer—maintains his consumption expenditures so that they are related to his disposable income in the following way (see Table 22-2): Even at a zero level of disposable income, Brown consumes something each week. His consumption at a zero level of disposable income is $75 per week, and according to this theory, that amount will be a constant level of consumption that will be added to the proportion of any additional income used for consumption. Any additional disposable income received will be divided between consumption and saving in the following proportions: 90 percent will be spent on consumption and 10 percent will be saved.

Keynes assumed that individuals would continue to consume a constant proportion of any additions in income. This proportion is called the **marginal propensity to consume**, defined as the change in consumption, ΔC (where Δ, the Greek capital letter delta, is the symbol for change) divided by the change in disposable income, ΔY_{DI}.

$$\text{marginal propensity to consume} = \frac{\Delta C}{\Delta Y_{DI}} = b \tag{1}$$

where b is the letter generally used to signify the marginal propensity to consume. Using these concepts regarding consumption, the determinants of desired consumption can be derived.

Figure 22-5 shows Herbert Brown's consumption behavior. At the origin, O,

TABLE 22-2 The Consumption Schedule with Respect to Disposable Income per Week

This table shows that with a constant add-on (the zero-level consumption) and a constant marginal propensity to consume, total desired consumption rises and average desired consumption falls.

(1) Disposable Income	(2) Desired Consumption at Zero Disposable Income That Is a Constant Addition at All Levels of Disposable Income	(3) Marginal Propensity of .6 Times Income	(4) Total Desired Consumption (column 2 plus column 3)	(5) Average Propensity to Consume (column 4 divided by column 1)
$ 0	$75	$ 0	$ 75	ND*
100	75	60	135	1.35
200	75	120	195	.975
300	75	180	255	.85
400	75	240	315	.7875

* Not defined.

FIGURE 22-5 The Consumption Schedule That Plots Values in Table 22-2

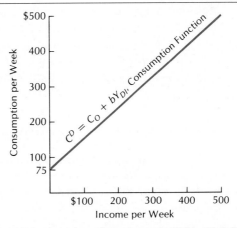

This consumption schedule plots the values shown in Table 22-2. It is linear (a straight line), sloped up at an angle determined by the marginal propensity to consume. Because the marginal propensity to consume is constant, so is the slope. The intercept is at $75. The line for the consumption equation is drawn for the condition of zero taxes, so that disposable income equals income. If taxes are imposed, the consumption line will shift down.

disposable income is zero. Look up the vertical axis to $75 and notice that that is where the straight line showing Herbert Brown's level of desired consumption intersects the vertical axis. Seventy-five dollars is called the *intercept* of that line.

Suppose that Herbert Brown's disposable income jumps from zero to $100 per week. He will still spend $75 on consumption plus an additional amount that depends on his marginal propensity to consume, b. The example assumes that b is .6. Therefore, $Y_{DI} = \$100$, and that change in disposable income from zero, times the marginal propensity to consume, is

$$bY_{DI} = .6(\$100) \tag{2}$$

Herbert Brown's total consumption is $75 plus $60, or $135, when his disposable income is $100.

Is there an easier way to write out this simple computation than with this large flock of words? Yes, there is. It all can be stated in symbols

$$C^D = C_0 + bY_{DI} \tag{3}$$

where C_0 is the constant add-on to consumption even at a zero level of disposable income. This equation is called the *Keynesian consumption equation*.

Examine how easy equation (3) makes the example. The value of b is .6 and C_0 equals $75, so that when Y_{DI} is $100,

$$C^D = C_0 + bY_{DI} = \$75 + .6(\$100) = \$135 \tag{4}$$

The picture of this equation is shown in Figure 22-5, drawn from the numbers shown in Table 22-2.

Recall that disposable income, Y_{DI}, is equal to income, Y, minus taxes, T. The consumption equation in Figure 22-5 is drawn for the case in which taxes are zero. This makes disposable income, Y_{DI}, equal to income, Y. If taxes are increased, there will be less disposable income and less consumption at each level of income, and the line for the consumption equation will shift down. The size of this shift is shown later in the chapter.

Desired Investment and Desired Government Expenditures

Investment expenditures do depend on interest rates, as discussed previously. In Figure 22-6, desired investment is considered to be a constant $25 million per week. In Figure 22-7, desired government expenditures are also assumed to be a constant, at $75 million per week.

The Aggregate Demand Schedule

The desired expenditures on consumption and investment by the private sector plus the desired government expenditures are added up at each level of income to obtain the aggregate demand schedule, shown in Figure 22-8.

FIGURE 22-6   Investment Expenditures Are Assumed to Be Constant

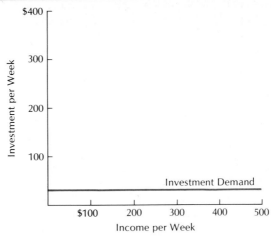

Investment demand is, for simplicity, assumed constant at $25 million per week.

Notice the intercepts. First $C_0 = \$75$ is the intercept of the consumption function, which is equal to $75 million in consumption per week. The intercept of the investment equation is $25 million higher in investment per week. The investment plus consumption lines are parallel because that difference, $25 million in investment per week, is the same at every level of income. Following the same procedure, notice that the intercept of the aggregate demand sched-

FIGURE 22-7   Government Expenditures Are Assumed to Be Constant

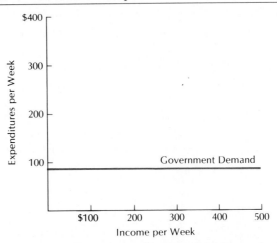

Desired government expenditures are, for simplicity, assumed constant at $75 million per week.

FIGURE 22-8 Aggregate Demand Schedule (millions of dollars per week)

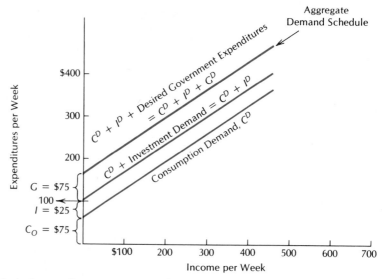

The desired expenditures on consumption and investment by the private sector plus the desired government expenditures are added up at each level of income to obtain the aggregate demand schedule.

ule is $75 million higher per week and, again, parallel to the consumption schedule. Thus, the intercept of the aggregate demand schedule is at $75 million per week.

If you understand these steps, you will understand the derivation of this aggregate demand schedule. Test yourself before you proceed.

PRACTICE PROBLEM: TEST ON THE DERIVATION OF THE AGGREGATE DEMAND SCHEDULE

Draw an aggregate demand schedule based on the following values:

$C_0 = \$100$ million per week, marginal propensity to consume $= .5$
$I^D = \$100$ million per week
$G^D = \$150$ per week
$T = 0$

Answer: To check the correctness of your derivation, see if $700 million in income is consistent with $700 million in aggregate demand (the same point on the aggregate demand schedule).

EQUILIBRIUM

The Keynesian Cross Diagram

In equilibrium, desired expenditures ($C^D + I^D + G^D$) equal income. A line used to locate that equilibrium statement is drawn in Figure 22-9. It is a 45° line, meaning that the angle it forms with the horizontal axis is 45°. The 45° line depicts the possible points of equilibrium, as it is an accounting identity between expenditures and receipts (income), the two sides of every transaction:

$$C + I + G = Y \tag{5}$$

The 45° line is copied in Figure 22-10 and so is the aggregate demand schedule from Figure 22-8. Equilibrium is defined where the two lines intersect, at point A. At that point, desired expenditures, actual expenditures, and income all are equal.

$$C^D + I^D + G^D = Y \tag{6}$$

Equation (6) is not an accounting identity; it is the value at which income will settle, based on people's behavior. In Figure 22-10, equilibrium is at $437.5 million per week. This diagram with the crossing lines is sometimes called the **Keynesian cross diagram** because the 45° line crosses the curve showing the aggregate demand for goods and services, as shown in Figure 22-10.

Consider the income level of $600 billion per week in Figure 22-10. Could that be an equilibrium level of income? Less than $600 billion per week in goods and services is demanded at that level of income.

FIGURE 22-9   45° Equilibrium Line

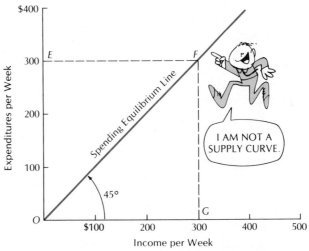

The 45° equilibrium line is equidistant from each axis. For example, $EF = GF$. It identifies possible equilibrium positions.

FIGURE 22-10   Aggregate Demand (in millions of dollars per week)

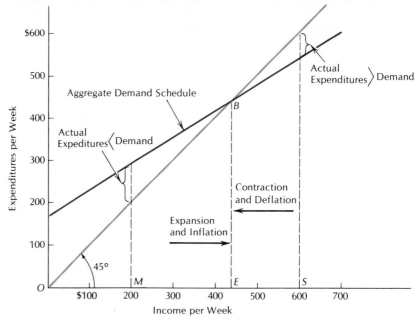

The Keynesian cross diagram shows that equilibrium is *OE*. Larger incomes, such as *OS*, result in economic contraction because actual expenditures exceed the demand for goods and services. This results in a reduction in spending. Smaller incomes, such as *OM*, result in economic expansion because the demand for goods and services exceeds actual expenditures.

Consumers and business managers correct this problem by reducing their spending. What happens when businesses and consumers reduce their purchases of goods and services? Sellers in wholesale and retail markets get caught with bigger inventories than they expected. To the shoe store owner with few customers and shoe boxes piled to the ceiling in the storeroom, the situation is described as, "I'm lousy with shoes and business stinks."

Economists call the buildup in inventories *involuntary investment*. Employers of firms that produce these goods find their orders dwindling, and workers are laid off all down the line.

The shoe store owner has two immediate courses of action: to lower prices and/or to lay off employees. This means "special sale prices" and more unemployment. The owner also reduces shoe orders from manufacturers; but this takes time to affect production, especially if previous orders cannot be canceled.

This situation is reflected throughout the economy by economic contraction and deflation (or less rapid price increases). Income declines toward $437.5 million per week in Figure 22-10.

Alternatively, suppose that income is less than $437.5 million per week, say at $200 million per week. At that level of income, aggregate demand is seen to be above the 45° line, which is the actual level of income. Consumers and businesses react by spending more on goods and services.

To the shoe store owner, it means lower-than-desired stocks of shoes. "They can't get enough of my shoes. It's glorious." The shoe store owner may react immediately by trying to hire more employees and/or raising prices. He or she may also place orders for more shoes.

The effects of economywide actions of this type cause an economic expansion and an upward push on prices. Expenditures will move back toward $437.5 million per week, *OE* in Figure 22-10.

Thus, $437.5 million per week is the equilibrium level of income.

GOVERNMENT TO THE RESCUE

The Unemployment Gap

Suppose that full employment is defined in the labor market depicted in Figure 22-1 as 102 million workers employed each week. From the production function in Figure 22-2, it follows that the full employment output would be $500 million per week in output (measured in the real terms of dollars for the base year of the price index). Suppose also that the equilibrium income is given in the Keynesian cross diagram, Figure 22-10. The aggregate demand schedule from Figure 22-10 is redrawn in Figure 22-11 (labeled Aggregate Demand Schedule I) along with the full employment line from the labor market/production function diagrams.

Point *A* is a point of **unemployment equilibrium**. This is an equilibrium real income at which there is substantial unemployment. There is a gap of $62.5 million per week between the income needed to achieve the equilibrium demand for full employment goods and service production and the equilibrium level of expenditures. That is the unemployment gap. To close that gap, the government can run a deficit and count on the effects of what is called the government expenditure multiplier. To see how this is done, we will describe two types of Keynesian expenditure multipliers.

The Government Expenditure Multiplier

The **government expenditure multiplier** is a relationship between changes in government expenditures (with taxes, *T*, constant) and income. To understand the government expenditure multiplier, we will follow, step by step, a series of expenditures resulting from a change in government expenditures, to see the effect on income. We will also explain this in a mathematical form.

FIGURE 22-11 A Government Deficit, *AB*, Causes the Aggregate
Demand Schedule to Shift to a Position Consistent with Full Employment

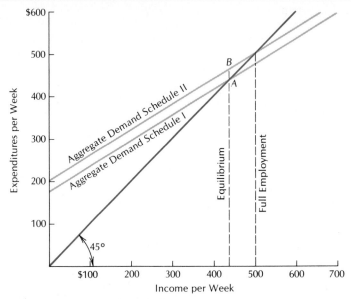

This figure shows that a $25 million deficit per week causes the aggregate demand
schedule to shift from I to II. The $25 million-per-week deficit is equal to *AB*, Equi-
librium income changes from $437.5 million per week to $500 million per week. The
explanation requires the evaluation of the government expenditure multiplier. Because
the marginal propensity to consume is .6, that multiplier equals $1/(1 - .6)$, or 2.5. A
deficit of $25 million per week times 2.5 equals $62.5 million more income per week,
just enough to increase expenditures to the full employment level.

An Explanation Using a Series

How would a $10.00 additional expenditure by the government in the form of
a bonus for beautiful rose production to White House gardener, Alfred Seed,
affect income? Assume that taxes are constant (so that income does not
increase taxes) and that the marginal propensity to consume, *b*, is also constant at .9. That last assumption means that

$$b = \frac{\Delta \text{ consumption}}{\Delta \text{ disposable income}} = .9 \qquad (7)$$

Alfred Seed uses nine of the ten dollars to buy a $9.00 shirt from Thomas
Look, a street vendor, and Seed saves $1.00. Follow the cumulation effect on
income in Table 22-3.

Thomas Look immediately buys lunch from Luigi Jones, the pizza man.
Luigi Jones spends 90 percent of that income, or $8.10, for flowers for his wife
from Edgar Pollen, the flower man. Pollen pays Roscoe Clear $7.29 to wash

TABLE 22-3   The Multiplier Process Using a $10.00 Government Expenditure

This table shows how income cumulates from a $10.00 government expenditure with taxes constant and the marginal propensity to consume equal to .9. It is continued on Table 22-4. These numbers are rounded to two decimal points. For complete numbers to step 9, see the answers at the end of the chapter.

| | (1) | (2) | (3) |
| | | | Cumulative Effect on Income (cumulating |
Step	Income	Expenditure	column 1)
1	White House gardener, Alfred Seed, receives $10.00 bonus for beautiful roses.	$9.00 shirt purchase from Thomas Look	$10.00
2	Thomas Look receives $9.00 in income.	$8.10 purchase of pizza from Luigi Jones	19.00
3	Luigi Jones receives $8.10.	$7.29 expenditure for flowers for his wife from Edgar Pollen	27.10
4	Edgar Pollen receives $7.29.	Roscoe Clear given $6.56 to wash windows	34.39
5	Roscoe Clear receives $6.56 in income.	$5.90 purchase at Jensen's bookstore	40.95

TABLE 22-4   The Multiplier Process Continuation of Table 22-3*

This table is a continuation of Table 22-3. Fill in the boxes, using your imagination for the consumption examples, and check your arithmetic to see if $65.13 (with no rounding at previous steps) or $59.21 (with rounding to two decimal points at each previous step) is the cumulated income at step 10. Also see Appendix B.

Step	Income	Expenditure	Cumulation Effect on Income (cumulate column 1 in Table 22-3 and in this table)
6	Cecil Jensen receives $5.90		
7			
8			
9			
10			

*This is a self-help test with answers at the end of the chapter. Fill in the boxes.

the windows of his flower shop. Clear buys a book on space travel from Jensen's bookstore for 90 percent of $7.29, which is $6.56.

Notice that the cumulative income in Table 22-3 from the original $10.00 government expenditure is $40.95 after the book purchase. Continue the calculations in Table 22-4 to ensure that you understand the multiplier process. The explanation of the algebraic derivation of the government expenditure multiplier will greatly simplify this problem.

An Algebraic Derivation of the Government Multipliers

Substitute the consumption equation (4) into the equilibrium equation (6) to obtain

$$C^D + b(Y - T) + I^D + G^D = Y \tag{8}$$

Solve for Y:

$$\frac{C^D - bT + I^D + G^D}{1 - b} = Y \tag{9}$$

To find the *government expenditure multiplier*, assume that the only variable that changes on the left side of the equation is G^D, desired government expenditures. The change in that variable is denoted by the Greek letter delta, ΔG^D, as is the resultant change in income, ΔY:

$$\Delta G^D \left(\frac{1}{1 - b} \right) = \Delta Y \tag{10}$$

The multiplier is in parentheses, $1/(1 - b)$. To find the *government tax multiplier*, assume that the only variable that changes is taxes, T. The change in that variable is denoted as

$$\Delta T \left(\frac{-b}{1 - b} \right) = \Delta Y \tag{11}$$

The government tax multiplier in parentheses is $-b/(1 - b)$.

For a more intuitive approach to this algebraic derivation, see Appendix B.

Closing the Unemployment Gap

The unemployment gap is $62.5 million per week. The government expenditure multiplier, $1/(1 - b)$ when the marginal propensity to consume is .6, is $1/(1 - .6)$, which equals 2.5. The right deficit to close this gap is a deficit that, when multiplied by 2.5 (the multiplier), will cause equilibrium expenditures to increase by $62.5 million per week. That is, $62.5 million per week divided by 2.5, which equals $25 million per week, is the correct size for a government deficit. Such a deficit shifts the aggregate demand curve from I to II in Figure 22-11.

So simple is the story, it is a wonder that nations are not always at full employment. But this is only half the story; the picture changes radically in Part VII, which considers the problems of inflation and financing.

The Real Deficit

The introduction to this chapter described an important form for most variables in the chapter: They are considered to be real variables unless otherwise specified. This assumption allowed the symbols for the various variables, such as consumption, investment, and government expenditures, to be simplified. The Keynesian analysis described here is in real terms; it uses variables that are corrected for the rate of inflation. The full employment level of output is a real variable. To get there, real expenditures must be the appropriate size.

The deficit in this analysis is also the real deficit. The real deficit must be large enough to produce full employment demand for goods and services. If the price level doubles, the same real stimulus from a deficit will require a nominal deficit of twice the size, other things being the same. (The real deficit from 1946 to 1986 is plotted in Figure 22-12, and the ratio of the deficit to GNP is shown in Figure 22-13.)

FIGURE 22-12   The Real U.S. Government Deficit, 1951–1987

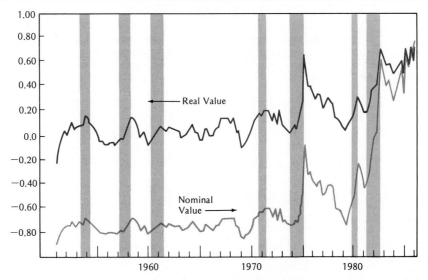

Estimates based on the trend in the series are shown for the last four years to 1990. The shaded areas are recessions. Although the real deficit rose sharply during and immediately following the 1974–1975 recession, it fell until 1980. Then it began to rise until 1986. Immediately following the stock market crash of October 1987, steps were taken to reduce the deficit.

FIGURE 22-13   The Ratio of the U.S. Government's Deficit to GNP, 1951–1986

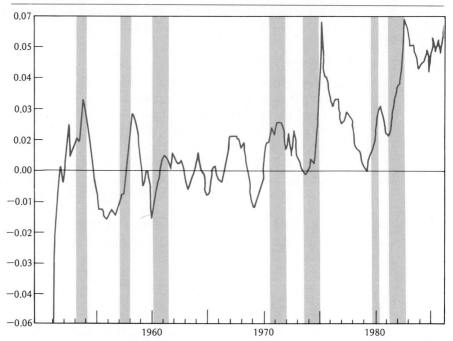

Estimates based on the trend in the series are shown for the last four years to 1990. The shaded areas are recessions. The deficit reached to almost 7 percent of GNP at the end of the 1974–1975 recession and in 1983. The ratio continued to take a high value by historical standards in the three years after 1983.

The real deficit is harder to predict than the nominal deficit is because the future price levels must be predicted as well. They depend on such variables as the previous rates of change in the money supply. That means that a policy plan of deficits just large enough to counteract the future conditions of insufficient demand would be very difficult to achieve. In addition to that, the real size of the gap between the **unemployment equilibrium** and full employment will change as the price level changes.

THE LESSONS OF KEYNESIAN EXPENDITURE THEORY

Keynesian theory elevates fiscal policy to a tool for achieving and maintaining full employment equilibrium. It has become the foundation of a vast number of policy actions of many countries and much additional analysis that builds on the basic notions it presents. Its descriptions of the reasons for unemployment equilibrium, especially a ratchet effect on wages, are widely used in macroeconomic analysis. If an economy is at an unemployment equilibrium and wages and prices will only rise, what policy should be adopted? That subject, discussed in Chapter 27, is called the stagflation dilemma.

Financing and Inflation Considerations, Vital Missing Links

After mastering the Keynesian expenditure theory, you will not be pleased to find out that it is only half of the story. The other half of the analysis concerns the effects of financing the deficit or, more broadly, financing the government's expenditures. Without this second part of the story, the expenditure theory is suspended in midair. It is an incomplete analysis to say that a borrowed deficit has a particular effect on aggregate demand given by the government expenditure multiplier, without also considering the effects of borrowing, which will be examined in Chapter 25.

An Important Missing Variable

The Keynesian analysis in this chapter bypasses an important variable that is central to Keynesian analysis, the real rate of interest. In the next two chapters, that variable will be brought into the analysis. In this chapter, investment demand was tied down and gagged, by holding it constant at a given level. Allowing interest rates into the analysis cuts loose these restrictions, and investment is shown to play a key role in the analysis.

APPENDIX A: MONEY ILLUSION OF WORKERS, A STANDARD INTERPRETATION

Keynes did not make a big point of sticky money wages. Rather, he devoted much more space in *The General Theory* to why full employment could not be achieved even if money wages fell. That statement might be made by observers who have read some of the alternative interpretations of Keynes's analysis in *The General Theory* or have themselves read *The General Theory*.

Keynesian economics grew from the work of Keynes as interpreted in the early post–World War era by economists who analyzed what Keynes meant. It is their work from which most of the Keynesian analysis has been developed. And it is their work on which much fiscal policy has been based. They have tried to make their work faithful to the spirit of Keynes's intriguing analysis. For example, John Hicks developed the model described in the next chapter. This is a Keynesian model, but the reader would have a terrible time trying to glean it from *The General Theory*.

The General Theory is a very imprecise book, with a multitude of statements that can be interpreted in many different ways. A Nobel laureate in economics, Paul Samuelson, summed it up in this way:

> Herein lies the secret of *The General Theory*. It is a badly written book, poorly organized; any layman who, beguiled by the author's previous reputation, bought the book was cheated of his five shillings. It is not well suited for classroom use. It is arrogant, bad-tempered, polemical, and not overly generous in its acknowledgments. It abounds in mares' nests or confusions; in it, the Keynesian system stands out indistinctly, as if the author were hardly aware of its existence. . . . An awkward definition suddenly gives way to an unforgettable cadenza. When finally mastered, its analysis is found to be obvious and at the same time new. In short, it is a work of genius.[3]

Nonetheless, Keynes put forth new ideas and new ways of looking at the economy that were extremely fruitful, if not precisely worked out in detail. Such analysis is always difficult because the details, the nuances, can often invalidate the general ideas. It was Hicks's genius that put these important ideas in the form of a precise model that could be tested and would become the most popular model in economics, selling Keynesian economics to many students for many decades.

The process of putting Keynes's analysis into usable form is still going on, with new interpretations still being made, as described at the end of the next chapter.

However, it is the body of Keynesian work that has been incorporated into "standard presentations" that is important to present analysis. Much of that work grew out of the early interpretations of Keynes by famous economists such as Abba Lerner and James Tobin. For example, in an important source book published two years after Keynes's death, they emphasized sticky wages as the main point of Keynesian analysis.

In a summary article that Keynes read and approved, Lerner said: "It is time for economists who wish to give statesmen practical advice to realize that money wages are sticky—that workers will, in fact, refuse to reduce money wages."[4] James Tobin said: "Clearly one of Keynes' basic assumptions— Leontief calls it *the* fundamental assumption—is that money illusion occurs in the labor supply function."[5] That is, workers had money illusion because they would not take a lower money wage, regardless of the change in real wage. (Review Chapter 18 for a further discussion of money illusion.)

APPENDIX B: AN ALGEBRAIC DERIVATION OF THE GOVERNMENT EXPENDITURE MULTIPLIER

If you looked at the answers to the missing numbers of Table 22-4 or if you did them by hand or on a calculator, you would now be ready to proclaim, "There must be a better way!" There is.

Suppose that the increase in government expenditures is $1, holding taxes constant and again letting the marginal propensity to consume, b, equal .9. The value of income in step 1 is the value of the increase in government expenditures, $1. The individual receiving the dollars spends b times that amount, or $b$$1. The individual receiving $b$$1 spends b times that amount, or $bb$$1 = $b^2$$1. It goes on and on that way. The sum, S, of all those expenditures is

$$S = \$1 + b\$1 + b^2\$1 + b^3\$1 + \cdots + b^N\$1 \tag{12}$$

where ... means "and so on" and N is a very large number.

Now, a trick to simplify this series of values, called a *geometric series*, is employed. First, take out the $1 in each term by writing the equation in this equivalent way:

$$S = \$1(1 + b + b^2 + b^3 + \cdots + b^N) \tag{13}$$

Take out the dollar sign for convenience in the notation so that equation (13) becomes

$$S = 1 + b + b^2 + b^3 + \cdots + b^N \tag{14}$$

Multiply each side of equation (14) by b, a perfectly legal algebraic operation, to obtain

$$bS = b + b^2 + b^3 + b^4 + \cdots + b^{N+1} \tag{15}$$

The last term, b^{N+1}, is obtained from multiplying b times b^N.

Subtract equation (14) from equation (15). What is left?

$$S - bS = b^{N+1} \tag{16}$$

Here, b is a fraction, such as 9/10, that when it is multiplied by itself many times, gets smaller. Because N is a very large number, b^{N+1} is approximately zero and may be dropped. Then the $S - bS$ in equation (16) can be simplified to $S(1 - b)$.

Divide each side of equation (16) by $1 - b$ to obtain

$$S = \frac{1}{1 - b} = \text{the government expenditure multiplier} \tag{17}$$

The expression $1/1 - b$ is the expenditure multiplier for an increase in government expenditures of $1, holding taxes constant.

For any change in government expenditures, ΔG, the multiplier is

$$\Delta G\left(\frac{1}{1 - b}\right) = \Delta Y \tag{18}$$

where ΔG is the change in government expenditures and ΔY is the change in income.

For example, if $b = .9$, the multiplier $1/(1 - b)$ will be, using decimals,

$$\frac{1}{1 - .9} = \frac{1}{.1} = 10 \tag{19}$$

or, using fractions,

$$\frac{1}{1 - 9/10} = \frac{1}{1/10} = 10 \qquad (20)$$

If $G = \$10$, as in the foregoing example,

$$\$10 \frac{1}{1 - .9} = \$10(10) = \$100 \qquad (21)$$

where $100 is the change in income. Notice that the cumulative income in the tenth step in Table 22-4 is $65.13. If you continue through step 8 in Table 22-4, the cumulative total will be very close to $100 (actually $99.98).

APPENDIX C:
THE EFFECTS OF PERMANENT
AND SHORT-RUN CHANGES
IN FISCAL POLICY

What have been the effects of fiscal policy on output, income, and employment? Some evidence and conclusions are presented in this section.

The tax cut of 1964 did appear to stimulate the economy. However, Professors Franco Modigliani and Charles Steindal[6] found that the *one-time* tax rebate and the reduction in withholding in the second quarter of 1975 were largely saved. In other words, unlike the 1964 tax cut, the 1975 tax cut did not significantly stimulate aggregate demand.

The conclusion from empirical tests is that *permanent changes* in tax revenues or the level of spending have more effect than do *temporary changes*, such as the tax cut of 1964.

This evidence is important to government tax and expenditure changes that are caused by business cycle fluctuations. Taxes on income depend on the level of income. Taxes rise during expansions and fall during contractions. Government expenditures on unemployment benefits and other income supplements tend to rise when income falls and to fall when income rises. According to the analysis in this chapter, these changes in taxes and government expenditures will tend to offset the effect of either a decline or a rise in income on the aggregate demand for goods and services. Such automatic changes in government taxes and expenditures are called **automatic fiscal stabilizers**. They are part of the tax policy that needs no congressional approval and therefore can rapidly be put into place.

How effective are they? Because they are temporary, the type of evidence just provided supports the contention that they are not too effective.

J. Ernest Tanner reviewed his and other evidence and stated

> The automatic fiscal stabilizers which have been part of the system in the post–World War II period appear to have significantly less effect than

commonly thought. Any change in the deficit which occurs as a result of the normal fluctuations in the economy is widely expected and would be offset by changes in savings. As a result, the higher tax rates at cycle peaks do not curb consumption demands nor do the lower tax rates during cycle downturns stimulate consumption demands. Consumption remains more or less constant over the cycle with savings rates climbing in periods of recessions but falling during expansions.

Discretionary fiscal policies may not be any better as stabilizing tools. Because the consumer takes into account known public action in making his consumption decisions, discretionary fiscal actions such as those in 1968 and 1975 would be expected to affect only savings rates, leaving consumption largely unaffected. As a result, neither discretionary fiscal actions nor the automatic stabilizers should be expected to serve our needs for a policy tool contributing to short-run economic stability.

The empirical evaluation and testing of this theory is not inconsistent with the hypothesis. Unexpected deficits—largely unexpected government spending changes—lead to increases in aggregate demands. . . . The evidence for unexpected deficits appears to conform exactly to the Keynesian theory.[7]

Conclusions such as Tanner's follow from the expected income hypothesis discussed in Chapter 18 and from the rational expectations hypothesis presented in Chapter 20. If consumers take into account many factors in estimating their expected income, an income change in one time period will not dramatically change their expected income, thereby causing their consumption expenditure to change only slightly. The appearance of a bigger or smaller deficit will not have a large effect on consumption. However, a sustained deficit may have such an effect.

STUDY QUESTIONS

1. Assume the following model:

   $$C = C_0 + b(Y - T)$$
   $$I = \$50 \text{ million per week}$$
   $$C_0 = \$10 \text{ million per week}$$
   $$b = .8$$
   $$T = 0$$
   $$G = 0$$

   Full employment is $900 million per week.
   What is the size of the increase in government expenditures or tax reductions needed to achieve full employment?

2. What is Say's law?
3. Why would Keynes say about Say's law, "Say, it isn't so"?
4. Draw a diagram of the labor market.

5. What is full employment?
6. What is a production function?
7. What is full employment income? Define and describe it. In the hypothetical example in this chapter, it is $500 million per week. What is the actual approximate estimate for the current year?
8. Why is the analysis in this chapter short-term analysis?
9. What is unemployment equilibrium?
10. If wages changed rapidly in times of widespread unemployment, what would happen?
11. Describe a condition for maintaining the unemployment equilibrium that Keynes noted.
12. During a period of unemployment equilibrium, how could full employment be restored without government intervention?
13. What is the connection between unemployment equilibrium and insufficient demand?

ANSWERS FOR TABLE 22-4*

Step	Income	Cumulative Income
1	$10	$10
2	9	19
3	8.10	27.1
4	7.29	34.39
5	6.561	40.951
6	5.9049	46.8559
7	5.31441	52.17031
8	4.782969	56.953279
9	4.3046721	61.2579511
10	3.87420489	65.13215599

* See Appendix B.

GLOSSARY

Automatic fiscal stabilizers. Automatic changes (induced by extreme changes) in government expenditures and taxes that tend to offset business cycle changes on aggregate demand for goods and services.

Disposable income. After-tax income.

Dissaving. The negative of saving, in which saving is defined as income minus consumption. Dissaving results in the running down, spending, of wealth.

Government expenditure multiplier. The ratio of the cumulative consumption expenditures induced by a government deficit relative to the size of the deficit. It is equal to $1/(1-b)$, where b is the marginal propensity to consume.

Keynesian cross diagram. A diagram showing the aggregate desired expenditure schedule and a 45° line showing equilibrium between desired expenditures and income at each level of income.

Marginal propensity to consume. The change in consumption associated with a change in income.

National income. The value of the current year's output for the entire economy.

Ratchet effect. A condition in which nominal wages can rise but tend not to fall.

Say's law. In one general form, it asserts that all markets clear so that there is no excess supply of goods and services. In the restricted form that Keynes attacked, it says that there can be no excess supply of goods and services. This can be true for a barter economy but not for an economy in which individuals can hold financial assets such as bonds and money.

Sticky wages. Nominal wages that tend to stick at their level even in the presence of declines in the demand for labor.

Unemployment equilibrium. The state in which income has settled down to a level that is consistent with significant unemployment of the labor force as determined by an excess supply of labor on the demand and supply schedules for labor (drawn for "normal" trend growth in the economy).

NOTES

1. John Maynard Keynes (1883–1946) was born more than 100 years ago. His father, John Neville Keynes, was an economist at Cambridge University, and his mother, who had been active in politics, became the mayor of Cambridge. His parents survived him when he died in 1946.

   Keynes won a scholarship to King's College at Cambridge in mathematics and classics and in 1906 passed a test for the Civil Service with his worst mark in a test in economics. "The examiners presumably knew less than I did," he remarked. He served in the India office but was persuaded by Alfred Marshall, a famous economist, to come back to Cambridge. He eventually became bursar of King's College, managing the college's finances and greatly increasing its resources through wise investments.

   He was active in many government posts, including that of a director of the Bank of England. He ran an investment company, organized the Camargo Ballet, and managed the construction and finances of the Arts Theatre at Cambridge. He married Lydia Lopokova, a star of the Russian Imperial Ballet. After his serious heart attack in 1937, she was "a tireless nurse and vigilant guardian against the pressures of the outside world." In 1942, he was knighted Lord Keynes of Tilton.

   Keynes's writings in economics are voluminous in number and subject matter, innovative and scholarly, and written in a highly readable style. As Paul Samuelson points out, Keynes's most famous book was "written badly, poorly organized," yet it was to change the course of macroeconomics and to serve as a guide for fiscal policy in many countries because of its important policy prescriptions and brilliant analysis. It is *The General Theory of Employment, Interest, and Money* (New York: Harcourt Brace, 1964; first published in 1936), usually referred to as *The General Theory*. It was the second to last of Keynes's seventeen books.

The timing of Keynes's *The General Theory* could not have been better. Many of the world's leaders and many economists were eager to find solutions to mass unemployment. Although they listened to Keynes in the 1930s, it was not until late in the 1940s that his ideas began to take root in the economics profession. They are still taking root in government policies in a form that is sometimes generations behind in the development of these theories. In the United States, great economists, such as Abba Lerner, Alvin Hansen, and Paul Samuelson, explained Keynes's new ideas in the 1940s and 1950s and convinced most economists that they were correct.

The two quotations are from "Obituary: *The Times* (London), April 22, 1946, Lord Keynes," in *The New Economics: Keynes's Influence on Theory and Public Policy* (New York: Knopf, 1948), pp. xviii–xix.

2. Jean-Baptiste Say, "Of the Demand or Market for Products," reprinted from the first American edition of Say's *A Treatise on Political Economy, or the Production, Distribution, and Consumption of Wealth*, Chap. 15 (reprinted in 1880 by Claxton, Rensen & Haffelfinger in Philadelphia); Charles W. Needy, ed. *Classics of Economics*, (Oak Park, Ill., Moore, 1980), p. 58.

3. Paul A. Samuelson, "The General Theory," in *The New Economics*, pp. 148–149.

4. Abba Lerner, "The General Theory (1)," in *The New Economics*, p. 116.

5. James Tobin, "Money Wage Rates and Employment," in *The New Economics*, p. 580.

6. Charles Steindal, "Is a Tax Rebate an Effective Tool for Stabilization Policy?" *Brookings Papers on Economic Activity*, 1977, p. 182.

7. J. Ernest Tanner, "Fiscal Policy: An Ineffective Stabilizer?" *Economic Review*, Federal Reserve Bank of Atlanta, August 1982, p. 50.

CHAPTER 23

THE *IS–LM* MODEL

CHAPTER PREVIEW

Introduction. The reader is introduced to Hicksian macroeconomic equilibrium.

The Consumption and Saving Functions. Real interest rates are added to the consumption equation developed in the last chapter.

Determinants of Net Investment. Net investment is the change in nonfinancial wealth. Its determinants include the real rate of interest.

Equilibrium in the Goods and Services Sector. The *IS* locus is derived.

Equilibrium in the Money Market. The *LM* locus is derived.

Deriving the Full Employment Level of Real Income. The same development in the last chapter is reviewed.

Full Employment Equilibrium and Price Level Changes with Flexible Prices. Overall equilibrium in the goods and services sector and the money market, as determined by the *IS* and *LM* loci, forms the real rate of interest at the full employment level of real income.

Aggregate Demand and Supply Schedules. Demand and supply schedules are developed.

Unemployment Equilibrium. Specific conditions that prevent full employment from being achieved are described.

Driving Away in the IS–LM *Model.* It is a useful model with some major defects, such as its theory (or lack of theory) of the price level.

Appendix A: Promising Frontiers of Research from the Keynesian Model. The work of Robert Clower and others on the nature of unemployment disequilibrium opens up important areas of research on the cost of information, a subject joined by those in the tradition of conventional price theory, such as George Stigler, and the rational expectations theorists.

Appendix B: Another Interpretation of What Keynes Meant. Allan H. Meltzer interpreted Keynes's main point as the need to stabilize investment at a level that will produce maximum employment.

Appendix C: The Accelerator. A condition that makes income (or sales) a determinant of real investment is described.

INTRODUCTION

This chapter puts into place additional building blocks to explain the effect of real interest rates and other important variables left out of the simple explanation of equilibrium in the Keynesian model in Figure 22-10 in the last chapter.[1]

For this purpose, we will use a model first developed by John Hicks in 1937.[2] Hicks attempted to portray some of the central ideas of Keynes's analysis in *The General Theory*. The set of equations Hicks developed became the most popular model in the macroeconomic literature. It is also referred to as the *Hicksian solution to macroeconomic equilibrium*, but the *IS–LM* analysis (investment, savings–liquidity, money) will do.

Following the usual classification, the model will be separated into three sectors:

1. The goods and services sector
2. The money market sector
3. The production and labor sector

The goods and service sector contains the consumption and savings functions. The term *money market* is used differently from the way in which it was used in Chapter 12, where it was used to describe markets for short-term liquid debt instruments. The money market sector in this model has an equation that is geared to explain the real money demand in the entire nonbank, private part of the economy. The production and labor sector contains the demand and supply of labor schedules and a curve relating the number of workers employed to the output produced by the economy, the production function. The next sections will describe the relationships in these sectors.

In understanding this chapter, the reader should keep the following points in mind:

1. Real variables such as real income are noted either by Y/P (nominal income over the price level) or by a lowercase letter, y. Lowercase letters are

often used in economics to signify real variables. The symbol for real disposable income is y_D.

2. It is assumed that people expect the price level to remain constant. That does not mean that the price level is constant, only that there is no expectation of inflation or deflation. The reason for this assumption is found by going back and looking at the Fisher equation in Chapter 19. This assumption makes the real and nominal interest rates equal. In the next chapter, the assumption is dropped so that the reader can see what happens when the two concepts of interest rates differ because of the expectation of inflation.

3. The *policy* variables, real government expenditures, G, and real taxes, T, are *not* labeled with a D for "desired," so as to separate them sharply from the *behavioral* variables, such as desired real investment, $(I/P)^D$, and desired real consumption, $(C/P)^D$, of the private sector.

4. The *IS* and *LM* curves each are called a *locus* (plural, *loci*) (a set of points whose location is determined by stated conditions) because the name *locus* helps emphasize that they are different from the underlying behavioral relations. Any of the lines plotted may be called *curves* (because that is the proper mathematical name) or *schedules* (because they plot sets of values for two variables). It is not wrong to call them *IS* and *LM* functions if they are thought of as functions (dependent on) of all the underlying variables that determine them (what economists call a *reduced form*). In a description that repeatedly refers to them, they can also be labeled as simply *IS* and *LM*.

Why all the technical problems? Because you, oh once-happy reader, are about to enter into an economic model that ties together many important macroeconomic variables. It must be put in good order because in a model, all the pieces fit together (even if some of them have to be bent slightly to get them in place). You will behold the beauty of consistency that laypersons often say they cherish but will not tolerate because of its complexity. When you finish and can say, "I've got it. It all fits together," you will be profoundly happy at being able to jump through a flaming hoop into Hicksian macroeconomic equilibrium.

THE CONSUMPTION AND SAVING FUNCTIONS

At least one more variable should be added to the consumption function in the last chapter to explain real consumption. That is the real interest rate. At higher real interest rates, there will be a greater incentive to save rather than to consume at each level of disposable income. The consumption function becomes

$$\left(\frac{C}{P}\right)^D c_0 + b_1 y_D - b_2 r \tag{1}$$

where b_1 and b_2 are the marginal propensities to consume with respect to changes in real disposable income, y_D, and real interest rates, r, respectively. As real income rises, desired real consumption rises. And as the real interest rate rises, desired real consumption falls.

Equation (1) can be rewritten as an explanation of desired real saving. Because real saving, S/P, is equal to the value of income that is not consumed, the decision to consume more of one's income is a decision to save less. Thus, an alternative way to write equation (1) is in terms of desired real saving:

$$\left(\frac{S}{P}\right)^D = s_0 + s_1 y_D + s_2 r \tag{2}$$

where both s_1 and s_2 are positive. More real saving will be desired if either real disposable income or real interest rates rise.

Two real saving curves are plotted in Figure 23-1 with taxes constant so that they can easily be drawn against real income. The saving curves are *upward* sloping with respect to the interest rate, on the assumption that individuals will save more if they are more highly rewarded with higher interest rates.[3] As real income rises, there is more private real savings at each interest rate, which is reflected by a shift in the savings function to the right in Figure 23-1. Savings curve $S_{(y_1)}$ is drawn for a higher level of real income—income level 2—than saving curve $S_{(y_2)}$ is, which is drawn for income level 1. There is one such saving curve for each level of real disposable income. This array of saving curves is called the **map of saving functions**. If there is an increased desire to save at every level of real income, the entire map of saving curves will shift to the right. This is shown in Figure 23-1 by a shift to the new saving functions, which are marked with a prime, $S'_{(y_1)}$ and $S'_{(y_1)}$.

FIGURE 23-1   Real Saving Functions

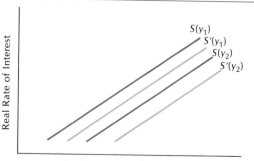

The saving functions $S(y_1)$ and $S(y_2)$ are positively sloped to show that more income is saved at higher real rates of interest. There is one such saving function for each level of real income. If there is an increased desire to save (to consume more) at every level of real income, the saving functions will shift to the right, such as to $S'(y_1)$ and $S'(y_2)$.

DETERMINANTS OF NET INVESTMENT

Net investment is equal to the change in the economy's *stock of nonfinancial wealth* or, as it is sometimes called, its *capital stock.*

This leads to an interesting general view of the determinants of net investment. Net investment demand is the demand for additional wealth (or capital stock). That demand for additional wealth depends on

1. The rate of return from investing—that is, adding to the capital stock—compared with
2. The rate of return on alternative uses of the funds.

To explain these statements, we will use an example using Christopher Brent, the owner of Trees and Lawns Company.

Brent wants to build a new factory, a rat extermination firm, that is completely independent of his present operation. (The reason for the assumption of independence is that it makes it easier to estimate the costs and benefits. They do not depend on other parts of his operation that may change because of the investment.) Suppose that Brent calculates that he can earn $90,000 a year from the new investment after all further costs of operation, as far in the future as he can see. This is the *expected return.*

This estimate takes into account the possibility of bad years. The actual average optimum return is $125,000 a year, but the lower figure results from making an adjustment for the risk that the earnings will be less than optimum.

AN EXPLANATION OF THE RELATIONSHIP BETWEEN NET INVESTMENT AND THE GROWTH OF NONFINANCIAL WEALTH

The value of nonfinancial wealth falls because of **depreciation**. Depreciation occurs because wealth

1. Is used up.
2. Is worn out.
3. Becomes **obsolescent** or **obsolete** (a *capital loss*) or appreciates (a *capital gain*)—negative depreciation.

As inventories of goods manufactured in previous periods are consumed, (1) they are used up. As capital equipment wears out and becomes less productive, (2) it is worn out. Even if physical wealth is maintained

intact (say, an automobile on blocks that is never used), it may become less valuable (a better automobile—in the eyes of investors—may be built). This is called (3) *obsolescence,* and it shows up as a capital loss. Or an item of nonfinancial wealth may appreciate. For example, a work of art by an old master or an antique item may gain in value through the years. This appreciation is *negative depreciation*—an awkward name for a simple capital gain.

Investment used to maintain the capital stock—to restore the depreciated nonfinancial capital stock—is called **replacement**

FIGURE 23-2   Investment and Nonfinancial Wealth

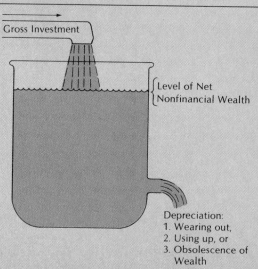

Gross Investment

Level of Net
Nonfinancial Wealth

Depreciation:
1. Wearing out,
2. Using up, or
3. Obsolescence of
   Wealth

Gross investment increases nonfinancial wealth, and depreciation reduces it; the difference, the net increase in nonfinancial wealth, is equal to net investment.

investment. If the depreciation is covered by replacement investment, any additional investment will add to the stock of nonfinancial capital stock. This addition per year is called *net investment*, and it is the concept used to derive the investment schedule in Keynesian analysis. Finally, **gross investment** is the term used for the sum of net investment plus replacement investment. A simple picture, Figure 23-2, clarifies all these terms. Gross investment is shown as adding to the level (fluid in a vessel) of wealth. Part of the value of wealth declines (leaks out of the vessel) in each period. This is called *depreciation* (or capital consumption).

Net real investment is equal to the change in real nonfinancial wealth.

The explicit cost is assumed to be a one-time payment of $1 million to build the new factory. This makes the *rate of return* on the investment equal to

$$\text{rate of return on this investment} = \frac{\text{return per year}}{\text{explicit cost}} = \frac{\$90,000}{\$1,000,000}$$

$$= .09 \text{ or } 9\% \text{ per year} \qquad (3)$$

The *alternative* or *opportunity cost per dollar* invested is the value of the funds in their next-best use. That next-best use may well be a government bond.

If a $1 million government bond has an interest payment of 10 percent a year, Brent can make a greater return by buying such a bond by than investing in rat extermination. The 10 percent interest represents the alternative cost of funds that can be used for investment. That critical interest rate is compared with the rate of return on investment to determine whether it is profitable to invest. (The adjustment to put the bond rate into a real after-tax rate—as is necessary in this comparison—was discussed in Chapter 19. Happily, that detail can be ignored here because nominal and real interest rates are assumed to be equal.)

If Christopher Brent buys a $1 million government bond at an interest rate of 10 percent, he will receive

$$.10/\text{years}(\$1,000,000) = \$100,000/\text{year} \tag{4}$$

Why should he chase rats?

This example brings out the critical variables that determine net investment. Stated compactly, the demand for net investment depends on the difference in the following variables (after adjusting each variable so that they represent comparable risk levels): the real rate of return from investment minus the real rate of return on government bonds.

The rate of return on this investment is a real rate of return. It is not affected by inflation. If prices rise throughout the economy, Brent can raise the cost of his rat extermination services. This preserves the 9 percent return. For example, suppose that there is a 50 percent rise in the price level. The $90,000-a-year return is reduced in half in real terms. If Brent's prices keep up with the inflation, he will raise them so that he takes in $180,000. *The important point is that the real rate of interest is a determinant of investment.* The rate of interest on bonds should also be stated in real terms, which has been conveniently done by assuming that no inflation is expected.

Suppose that the real rate of return on many investments is higher than is the interest rate on bonds. Investors borrow money by selling bonds. This is the essential process of transferring savings to investors. In some cases, the consumer who saves part of his or her income also invests it by buying consumer durables: television sets, toasters, automobiles, home computers, and so on. Most of the savings from consumers—who are the ultimate wealth owners—must be transferred to investors. One vital process by which this transfer is made, which was explained in Part II, is through *intermediation.*

As the transfer is made and more investment takes place, investment goods rise in price. This is caused by an increased demand for all the inputs needed to make the investment goods. They therefore must be pulled out of the production of consumption goods (or other investment goods) and services. In addition, without technological improvements, the capital stock becomes less productive per unit of capital, as it becomes larger. That is because all the other inputs in the productive process do not grow as rapidly in the short run as does the capital stock. (This is called *diminishing returns to the capital stock.* The added cost per unit of capital stock for producing it are summarized as *diminishing returns to the production of capital.*)

The Investment Function

From an equilibrium position, net investment will be undertaken only if someone has an idea for investment that is expected to bring a real rate of return that is higher than the going equilibrium real interest rate. At lower real interest rates, there will be more such ideas than at higher real interest rates. How many ideas for investment will bring more than a 20 percent equilibrium real rate of return (after deducting part of the expected incomes to cover the risk that the investment may return less and deducting taxes)?

As the capital stock grows larger in the short run, more and more of these profitable ideas are exploited. So the observation that more ideas for net investments will be forthcoming at higher rather than lower interest rates needs to be refined a bit. Although this hypothesis may be true for a given size of the capital stock, the larger that stock becomes, the fewer will be the opportunities for profitable investment at any interest rate, in the short run.

In symbols, the investment function takes the following form: The desired real investment, $(I/P)^D$, is assumed to depend on the real rate of interest,

$$\left(\frac{I}{P}\right)^D = g_0 - g_1 r \tag{5}$$

where g_0 and g_1 are constants. At lower real rates of interest, there is assumed to be a greater real investment demand. The constant g_0 is the intercept of this linear equation. The investment schedule is drawn in Figure 23-3 and is a picture of equation (5).

The investment function is a *short-run* function that shows the quantity of real investment demanded at each real rate of interest, assuming that the quantity of wealth is fixed. If the quantity of wealth were to change, the invest-

FIGURE 23-3   The Investment Schedule for a Size of the Capital Stock

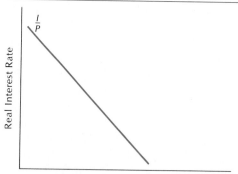

Real Interest Rate

$\frac{I}{P}$

Real Investment per Unit of Time

The investment demand schedule depicts the hypothesis that for a given size capital stock, more profitable investment opportunities are available at a lower real rate of interest.

ment demand (which is a demand for additional capital) would also change at each real rate of interest. How can the quantity of wealth be constant if there is positive net investment that adds to the quantity of wealth? As an exact description of reality, the assumption must be wrong. However, in the short run—and this model pertains only to the short run—the flow of investment is assumed to alter insignificantly the stock of capital.

Investment and Income

What about income? Will the net investment function shift around with different levels of income? Will not an increase in income cause an increase in net investment? The answer is an emphatic "Maybe so," with emphasis on the *maybe*. If income is expected to increase and this is expected to raise the *real rate of return from investment* above the real rate of interest on bonds, net investment can increase.

Suppose, for example, that Brent's rat extermination business is expected to bring in (after adjustment for risk) $130,000 a year rather than $90,000 (in the example) because of increased sales. With a slightly larger investment of $1.1 million to accommodate the increased sales, the real rate of return would be

$$\text{real rate of return} = \frac{\$130,000}{\$1,100,000} = .118 \text{ or } 11.8\% \tag{6}$$

That rate of return is considerably higher than the 10 percent return on the bond. It is "All systems go" for the new investment.

Suppose, however, that an increased investment of $1.7 million is needed to accommodate the expected increased sales. The real rate of return is

$$\text{real rate of return} = \frac{\$130,000}{\$1,700,000} = .076 \text{ or } 7.6\% \tag{7}$$

That is considerably lower than the 10 percent interest on bonds assumed to be available. It is a signal to "Shut down all systems" and let the increased income remain an interesting datum for some economist's charts.

Remember that expected income changes change the real rate of interest. Saying that net investment is dependent on the difference between the real rate of return on investment and the (real) interest rate on bonds *plus* the level of income or sales can be overkill. To find out how income can be brought in as a determinant of investment, see Appendix C to this chapter.

It is impossible to estimate as neat an investment schedule from actual data as that shown in Figure 23-3. One reason is that there is a time lag between a decision to invest (say, to build a new factory) and the investment expenditures themselves. That is, the investment expenditures may be spread over two or three years. Therefore, the investment schedule in Figure 23-3 expresses the idea of the relationship between real interest rates and net investment, but it is not a good depiction of when the net investment takes place. By that time, real interest rates may have changed dramatically.

EQUILIBRIUM IN THE GOODS AND SERVICES SECTOR

The equilibrium equation is taken from the last chapter. It shows that aggregate demand for goods and services (desired private-sector real expenditures on consumption and investment and government expenditures) equals actual real income, y:

$$\left(\frac{C}{P}\right)^D + \left(\frac{I}{P}\right)^D + \frac{G}{P} = y \tag{8}$$

Because the saving = investment identity of Chapter 4 is used to identify equilibrium, equation (8) will be changed into that form. Also, the concept of real disposable income used in the consumption function will be substituted into the equation. Real disposable income, y_D, equals $y - T/P$. This definition can be rearranged as y equals $y_D + T/P$. Substitute this expression into equation (8) and rearrange the terms.

$$y_D + \frac{T}{P} - \left(\frac{C}{P}\right)^D = \left(\frac{I}{P}\right)^D + \frac{G}{P} \tag{9}$$

The left-hand side is real desired saving (real income minus real consumption); the right-hand side is desired real private investment, $(I/P)^D$, plus real government expenditures, G/P. Real government expenditures are assumed to be investment expenditures. (If some government expenditures are on consumption, G can be broken into two parts, one for consumption expenditures and one for investment expenditures.)

Now subtract real taxes from each side of the equation to obtain the following:

$$\left(\frac{S}{P}\right)^D = \left(\frac{I}{P}\right)^D + \frac{G - T}{P} \tag{10}$$

The left-hand side of the equation is desired real private saving, or what is left from real disposable income after real consumption. On the right side is private real investment expenditures plus real government investment expenditures minus real taxes, the *leakage*, as it is sometimes called, to the government from (before-tax) private saving. This is a neat form of the saving = investment identity, as it isolates the real deficit, $(G - T)/P$, a major policy variable.

Both the saving and the investment functions are drawn together in Figure 23-4. Suppose that investment is given by the function labeled I/P. Income is at level 1, so that saving function $S(y_1)$ is the appropriate saving function. Where these two functions intersect, saving equals investment. The real interest rate, r, is determined at the intersection of these saving and investment schedules at a specified level of income. The equilibrium statement, equation (10), showing desired real saving equal to desired real investment, is satisfied. If the government adds to investment by running a real deficit, $(G - T)/P > 0$, then the investment curve will move out as shown.

FIGURE 23-4   Saving and Investment

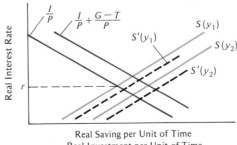

The saving functions and the investment demand functions are drawn together in this figure. The investment function shifts to the right from a real government deficit, $(G - T)/P$, made up of investment expenditures. These investment and saving functions determine an equilibrium rate of interest for the goods and services sector. For example, if I/P is the investment demand function and $S(y_1)$ is the saving function for a given level (y_1) of income, then the rate of real interest consistent with saving and investment in the real goods and services sector will be r.

Deriving the Equilibrium Locus

The next step is to derive a curve that will show all the possible equilibrium sets of real income and real interest rates that would be consistent with equilibrium in the goods and services sector.

It is easiest to understand how it is drawn by referring to Figure 23-5, which shows the saving, investment, and government deficit functions from Figure 23-4. For simplicity, begin by assuming $G = T$, so that the government is out of the picture. The deficit is zero.

There is again an entire map of saving curves for every level of real income. Notice that real investment equals real saving at interest rate r_2 when real income is at level 1 in Figure 23-5A. These equilibria values of interest rates and income are duplicated in Figure 23-5B, in which the vertical axis is scaled for real interest rates and the horizontal axis is scaled for real incomes. Similarly, at income level 2 and interest rate r_1 in Figure 23-5A, real savings and real investment are also in equilibrium. This set of values for real interest rates and real income identifies two points, A and B, in Figure 23-5B. Points A and B in Figure 23-5B are two points on the IS locus. *The IS locus is the locus of all the values of real income and real interest rates that are consistent with equilibrium in the expenditure sector.* Additional equilibria values can be found by drawing in savings curves for other levels of income in Figure 23-5A, but two points are sufficient to approximate the IS locus here.

If real government expenditures, G/P, are added, the investment plus government curve in Figure 23-5A will shift to the right. Then the IS locus in Figure 23-5B will also shift to the right to $I'S'$. The line QQ' in Figure 23-5B

FIGURE 23-5   The *IS* Function

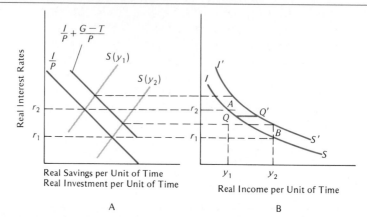

A   B

This figure shows the derivation of the *IS* locus of equilibria values for the goods and services sector. Figure 23-4 is redrawn as Figure 23-5A. At real income level 1 and no government deficit, the equilibrium real rate of interest is r_2. That set of values is consistent with point *A* on the *IS* locus in Figure 23-5B. If real income increases to the level of 2, the consistent point on the *IS* locus for that income level and equilibrium real interest rate, r_1, will be *B*. If the investment function shifts out because of government deficit expenditures on investment, the equilibria locus will shift to *I'S'* in Figure 23-5B.

equals the change in real government expenditures multiplied by the simple multiplier $1/(1 - b)$.

Recall from the last chapter that *b* is the marginal propensity to consume. The line *QQ'* measures the total change in real income resulting from the real government deficit. The last chapter showed that this total change is equal to the real deficit multiplied by the government expenditure multiplier.

EQUILIBRIUM IN THE MONEY MARKET

The demand for real money balances, $(M/P)^D$, conforms, in regard to the influence of the variables, to the general analysis developed in Chapter 18,

$$\left(\frac{M}{P}\right)^D = hy_D - lr \tag{11}$$

in which real money demand is positively related to real income and negatively related to the real interest rate. The symbols *h* and *l* are positive constants.

The demand for money is explained in Chapter 18 in a slightly different way from its development in the Keynesian literature. The Keynesian literature traditionally gives three motives for holding money. The **transactions motive** relates real income to the demand for real money balances. At higher levels of real income, people demand more real balances because they have more transactions to undertake. That motive conforms to the discussion in Chapter 18.

The **precautionary motive** relates the demand for money to the need to maintain a liquid money reserve for emergencies. This reserve is thought to be drawn down when interest rates (on other assets) rise. At higher rates of interest on *bonds* (with other things the same, such as the interest on checking accounts), it is more costly to hold real money balances for emergencies.

The **speculative motive** or **demand** for holding money has been reformulated. In the early Keynesian literature, the speculative demand was held to be related to the price that was expected on bonds that were close substitutes for money. When the price of bonds was high (that is, when bond interest rates were low), individuals would increase the quantity of real money balances that they demanded. They would do this because they wanted to wait for lower bond prices, so they could earn a higher rate of return on bond purchases.

The speculative demand for money was improperly stated in the early Keynesian literature. Even if bond prices were high and interest rates were low, it might still pay individuals to exchange their money for short-term bonds if they could earn a higher return.

The negative relationship between the interest rates on bonds and the demand for real money balances is an important property of the Keynesian analysis that was given other foundations. Such a relationship was developed for the transactions demand for money in Appendix C to Chapter 18. Another approach depends on the additional returns of bearing the risk of not being liquid.[4] Holding money ensures liquidity. However, as interest rates on bonds rise, there is a temptation to reduce real money balances and switch to much less liquid, more profitable financial assets.

All three motives for holding money—the transactions demand, the precautionary demand, and the speculative demand—are consistent with the relationship described by equation (11).

The supply of nominal money balances, M_s, depends on A_0, the monetary base, and w, the money expansion multiplier from Chapter 17.

$$M_s = wA_0 \tag{12}$$

It is assumed here for simplicity that the money supply can be controlled by the government, that is, that w is constant and A_0 is given by government policy.

Equilibrium in the money market occurs when real money demand equals the real money supply,

$$\left(\frac{M}{P}\right)^D = \frac{M_s}{P} \tag{13}$$

FIGURE 23-6   The LM Function

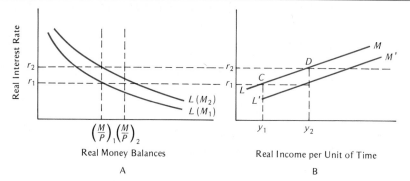

A

B

If real income is at level 1, the demand for money function will be $L(M_1)$ in Figure 23-6A. The real interest rate, r_1, is consistent with this set of equilibria values and is translated onto the LM locus, identifying point C of that locus in Figure 23-6B. At a real income level of 2, the demand for money function is $L(M_2)$. The real interest rate consistent with that set of equilibria values for real income and the demand for money is r_2. That set of equilibria values forms point D on the LM locus of Figure 23-6B. If the demand for money functions were to shift out (individuals want to hold more real balances at every level of real income), the LM locus in Figure 23-6B would shift out to $L'M'$.

where $P = P_0$, a given price level. The price level has not yet been explained in this analysis, but it can be changed to different levels to see what happens to the variables that are determined in the analysis.

The demand for money functions, shown in Figure 23-6A, are sometimes called the **liquidity preference functions**. Figure 23-6A is taken from Chapter 18. $L(M_1)$ is the demand for money functions at income level 1. The demand for money at a higher real income level, income level 2, is shown as function $L(M_2)$. The supply of real money balances is $(M/P)_1$. When real income is at level 1, the money market equilibrium real interest rate is r_1. These equilibria values for real income and the real interest rate are plotted in Figure 23-6B. The vertical axis of Figure 23-6B is scaled for the real interest rates, and the horizontal axis is scaled for real income. When real income is at level 1 and the money market equilibrium real rate of interest is r_1, the money market equilibrium is plotted at point C in Figure 23-6B. When real income is at level 2, the money market equilibrium real rate of interest given in Figure 23-6A is r_2. This money market equilibrium is plotted in Figure 23-6B as point D. The curve described by the line through points C and D is the LM locus. *The LM is the locus of all the equilibria values of real incomes and real interest rates that are consistent with equilibrium in the money market sector.*

Notice that if the supply of real money increases to $(M/P)_2$ in Figure 23-6A, equilibrium in the money market sector at each level of income will be at a lower interest rate. The LM locus in Figure 23-6B shifts to the right to $L'M'$.

DERIVING THE FULL EMPLOYMENT LEVEL OF REAL INCOME

We will define full employment in terms of the demand for labor and the long-run supply of labor, as we did in the last chapter.

Figure 23-7B shows the long-run demand and supply of labor: curves *DD* and *SS*, respectively. At point *B* the demand and supply of labor intersect at labor market equilibria values for the real wage, W/P, and the number of workers employed, *N*. This is **full employment equilibrium** in the labor sector. Reading off the production function (explained in the last chapter) in Figure 23-7A, this full employment level of workers is found to be consistent with real income level Oy_f.

The discussion of the different sectors of the *IS–LM* model ends here. The next sections will describe the relationship between the sectors when all the parts of the model are consistent with one another in general equilibrium. The relationship of the price level to output and some famous conditions that prevent full employment equilibrium from being achieved will also be discussed.

FIGURE 23-7   The Production Function and the Labor Market

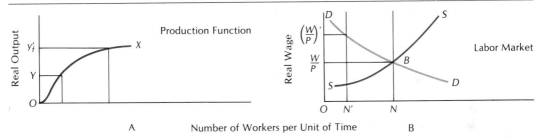

The production function shows the change in output associated with a change in the number of workers employed. The demand and supply of labor determine the number of workers employed. (These diagrams were explained in the last chapter.)

FULL EMPLOYMENT EQUILIBRIUM AND PRICE LEVEL CHANGES WITH FLEXIBLE PRICES

The *IS* and the *LM* loci are drawn together in Figure 23-8. They intersect at point *A*, where a unique set of a real interest rate and real income satisfies all the relationships embedded in the *IS* and *LM* loci. The real income is *Oy*, which is less than the full employment income of Oy_f, depicted by a vertical line.

If prices and nominal wages are assumed to be **elastic** or flexible (and the nominal money supply is constant), the real income level *Oy*, determined by

FIGURE 23-8   General Equilibrium

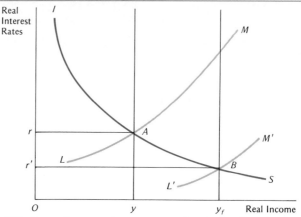

The *IS* and *LM* loci are shown to intersect at point *A*, a point of unemployment. As prices fall, the real money supply becomes larger, moving the *LM* locus to *L′M′*. Equilibrium is achieved at full employment. In the process, the real rate of interest falls from *r* to *r′*.

the intersection of *IS* and *LM* at point *A*, will be consistent with an *excess supply of labor*. In Figure 23-7B, this level of real income corresponds to *ON′* workers employed at a wage of *(W/P)′*. Suppose that some workers would be willing to take a lower money wage to obtain a job. Wages would fall, and more workers would be employed. Because of the depressed demand conditions caused by the unemployment, prices would fall also.

As output increases with the higher level of employment, the price level falls. If *P* falls, then the supply of real money balances, *M/P*, will rise. The real supply of money increases from $(M/P)_1$ to $(M/P)_2$, as shown in Figure 23-6A. This shifts the *LM* locus to the right until full employment is reached. The final equilibrium is shown in Figure 23-8 at point *B*, the full employment level. The interest rate has declined to *r′*. *Equilibrium in the simple* IS–LM *analysis with flexible prices is at the full employment level.*

Suppose that the economy is in equilibrium so that the *IS* and *LM* loci intersect at point *B* in Figure 23-9. This is the full employment level of output. Now assume that the government runs a deficit by increasing real investment. The deficit is financed by borrowing (selling bonds). Therefore, there is no charge in the money supply, and the *LM* locus does not shift. The *IS* locus shifts out to *I′S′*, and the new equilibrium appears to be at point *C* in Figure 23-9. This is an unattainable point of equilibrium, as it exceeds the full employment level of output. There is an *excess demand for goods and services*, which drives up the price level. As prices increase, the real money supply, *M/P*, declines. This shifts the *LM* locus to the left to *L′M′*, and the final equilibrium is at point *D*. The effect of the government deficit at full employment income has been to raise the price level and the real interest rate.

FIGURE 23-9   Changes in Full Employment Equilibrium

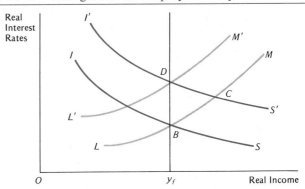

From a position of full employment equilibrium, *B*, the government runs a deficit pushing out the *IS* locus to *I'S'*. The intersection with the *LM* locus at point *C* is one in which expenditures exceed full employment output, driving up prices of the available goods and services. As the price level rises, real money balances, M/P, decline, causing the *LM* locus to shift to the left to *L'M'*. Real interest rates rise so that the new full employment equilibrium is established at point *D*.

Thus the model will produce the following type of price level changes if prices are perfectly flexible: At unemployment levels of output, prices fall, and at full employment, any additional spending causes prices to rise. The unemployment level of output is called the *Keynesian position*. The full employment position is called the *classical position*, which was described in the last chapter.

Keynes forcefully and eloquently described the conditions that prevent the achievement of full employment equilibrium. The view that nominal wages are "sticky" or "rigid downward" is an important contribution of Keynesian analysis, and it is one explanation of short-run unemployment.

AGGREGATE DEMAND AND SUPPLY SCHEDULES

If prices are not perfectly flexible—in particular, if the nominal wage is constant—the model may be used to produce a more conventional-looking relationship between output and the price level. Conventional-looking demand and supply of output schedules at each price level are produced.

First, the aggregate demand curve can easily be found. All the variables in the *IS* locus are real variables that *do not* change in value with changes in the price level. The *LM* locus, however, *does* change with changes in the price level, *P*, and a *constant nominal money supply, M*. As *P* increases, M/P declines, and the *LM* moves from *LM* to *L'M'* in Figure 23-9. (Ignore the full employment level, as prices are fixed and the equilibrium can be at any level of

FIGURE 23-10   Aggregate Demand and Supply Schedules

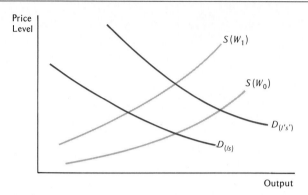

These aggregate demand and supply curves are derived from the *IS–LM* model. The aggregate demand curve is derived by changing the price level. At each different price level, the *LM* takes a different position, defining an aggregate demand curve from the series of equilibria points with the *IS* locus. The aggregate supply curve is derived by changing the price level and then plotting the different labor market equilibria as the quantity of labor employed changes with different wages, W/P. (The supply of labor is assumed to adjust to each level of quantity demanded.) If the nominal wage increases, the aggregate supply curve will shift from $S(W_0)$ to $S(W_1)$. If *IS* is shifted out to $I'S'$, as in Figure 23-9, the aggregate demand curve will shift from $D_{(IS)}$ to $D_{(I'S')}$.

real income.) Therefore, there is a different *LM* locus for each price level as *LM* shifts along the *IS* locus. These different price levels and real incomes at each intersection of *IS* and *LM* trace out the aggregate demand schedule, $D_{(IS)}$, in Figure 23-10. The equality between real income and real output in equilibrium allows the horizontal axis to be scaled with either variable. If the *IS* locus shifted to $I'S'$ in Figure 23-9, the aggregate demand curve would shift to $D_{(I'S')}$ in Figure 23-10.

The aggregate supply curve is derived by assuming that a given nominal (money) wage, W_0, is constant. Then as the price level, P, changes, a different real wage is attained in Figure 23-7B. Each real wage is associated with the employment of a specific number of workers on the demand for labor function. (The supply curve of labor, *SS*, is ignored in this derivation. It is replaced with a horizontal supply-of-labor curve for the real wage associated with the price level being used.) Corresponding to each given amount of labor employed, the production function in Figure 23-7A gives a particular level of real output. Thus each price level is associated with a level of real output to form the aggregate supply schedule, $S_{(W_0)}$ in Figure 23-10. If the nominal wage is increased to W_1, the aggregate supply curve will shift to $S_{(W_1)}$ in Figure 23-10. These more conventional demand and supply schedules can be used to illustrate the relationship between a given price level and the equilibrium level of output.

UNEMPLOYMENT EQUILIBRIUM

Keynes proposed a number of ways in which the economy can remain at an unemployment equilibrium. One condition that would lead to unemployment equilibrium is the workers' refusal to take a lower money wage in the short run. Money wages are then said to be *rigid downward* in the short run. This is the *ratchet effect* described in the last chapter.

Suppose that the economy is at point A in Figure 23-8, where the level of real income is less than the full employment level. Despite widespread unemployment, workers are unwilling to take a smaller money wage even if the price level, P, falls so that the real wage, W/P, that they were offered actually increases. Employers may also be unwilling to pay a smaller nominal wage, not only because some workers may have union contracts, but also because lower nominal wages tend to reduce worker morale and productivity. In the short run, a worker who finds his or her nominal wage reduced by 5 percent may not rejoice at receiving a 5 percent real wage increase after he or she learns that the price level has decreased by 10 percent. The worker has *money illusion* if nominal rather than real wages guide his or her behavior. It may take a considerable period of time (and substantial unemployment) for workers to adjust their expectations to deflation so that they would embrace lower money wages in line with this new lower level of prices. (Can you imagine wage negotiations in which the workers plead for a dollar less per hour because that would be a substantial increase in real wages?) The economy remains at point A in Figure 23-8 at unemployment equilibrium until the workers' wages are "adjusted."

In terms of the aggregate demand and supply schedules in Figure 23-10, this point may be made in a simple way: If the workers insist on a money wage, the resulting aggregate supply schedule can be derived, say $S(W_1)$. There is some lower money wage, say W_0, that will shift the aggregate supply curve to the right to full employment income. This is supply curve W_0 in Figure 23-10. The resulting price level is lower than before. If prices and wages are rigid downward, it cannot be attained. The government must step in with deficit spending that shifts the IS locus and the aggregate demand curve in Figure 23-10 to the right to $D_{(I'S')}$. Full employment is reached at a higher price level.

An interesting condition for unemployment equilibrium that Keynes posed is the liquidity trap, although it is not applicable to most of the post–World War II period in the United States.[5] The **liquidity trap** is that portion of a demand-for-money function that is horizontal or, using price theory language, **perfectly elastic** at a sufficiently low positive rate of interest. Such demand-for-money functions are shown in Figure 23-11A. The demand-for-money function $L(1)$ becomes horizontal at a rate of interest r_0. At this rate of interest, individuals are assumed to be willing to hold an infinite quantity of real money balances. All the other demand-for-money functions also contain a liquidity trap, so that the equilibrium LM locus, described by LM in Figure 23-11B, is horizontal up to a real income that is greater than full employment

FIGURE 23-11 *IS–LM* with a Liquidity Trap

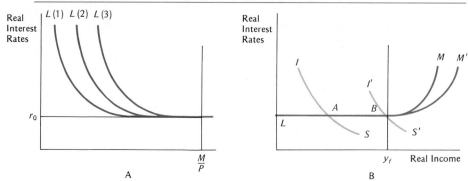

If the demand for money becomes flat (perfectly elastic), the *LM* locus will have an associated flat section. This is called a *liquidity trap.*

income. The *IS* and the *LM* intersect at point *A*, which is a level of real income below the full employment level. Even if prices are flexible, the unemployment equilibrium will not be altered under these conditions. The price level may fall, increasing the real quantity of money balances and shifting the *LM* locus to *LM'*. This shift does not affect the unemployment equilibrium.

With a liquidity trap, an increase in the money supply is an impotent policy tool for increasing spending. Only deficit spending will increase real income by moving the *IS* locus to the right.[6] This is an important point that may be

FIGURE 23-12 Changes in the Effects of Deficit Spending with *LM* Loci of Different Slopes

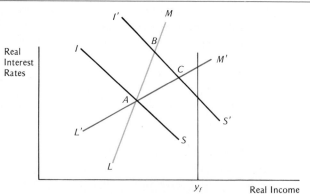

Suppose that a deficit causes the *IS* to shift to *I'S'*. Real income increases by a greater amount with a more horizontal (more elastic) *LM* locus such as *L'M'* than with a more vertical (more inelastic) money market locus, such as *LM*. Thus, fiscal policy is more effective with a more horizontal *LM* locus. Similarly, the reader can show that the more vertical the *IS* locus is, the more ineffective the monetary policy will be.

generalized: As the demand for real money balances curve becomes more horizontal, it takes larger and larger increases in the real money supply to produce the same increase in real income.

In the opposite case, in which the demand for money is more vertical (more inelastic, thus making the money demand less responsive to interest rate changes), it takes larger and larger real deficits to produce the same increase in real income. This can be seen in Figure 23-12, where LM is steeper than L'M'. (LM is steeper because of the more inelastic money demand curves from which it is derived.) Suppose that a deficit causes a shift from IS to I'S'. The equilibrium of the money and expenditures sectors will move from A to B along the steeper function LM. If L'M' is the money market equilibrium curve, more real income will be produced as the equilibrium moves from A to C.

DRIVING AWAY IN THE *IS–LM* MODEL

The ability to demonstrate easily the relationships of many macroeconomic variables has made the simple *IS–LM* model useful. But it is of doubtful use in predicting the price level.

The derivation of the price level was not the primary objective in the early development of Keynesian analysis. Rather, the analysis focused on levels of output, employment, and the real rate of interest. The price level or the money wage rate was often taken as fixed. In many tests of the *IS–LM* model, the production function is not included, and the price level is determined outside the model. Attention is turned to the interest rates and real incomes associated with the *IS* and *LM* loci. In its simple form, the model's theory of the price level is weak. No one is likely to accept its result that prices will not rise in the short run if output is less than the full employment level—at least no one who is familiar with recent history.[7] It is a time-honored tradition for economists to complain about the *IS–LM* model, much as you would yell at an old car that has a defective engine and bad tires, and then get in and drive it away.

APPENDIX A:
PROMISING FRONTIERS OF RESEARCH
FROM THE KEYNESIAN MODEL

Robert Clower tied together the conditions put forth for unemployment equilibrium, including wage rigidity and the liquidity trap.[8] Rather than viewing these conditions as unrelated special conditions, Clower believes that Keynes's view of the way in which the market works was very different from conventional price theory analysis. Clower said that Keynes thought that market information was very imperfect. In conventional price theory (*classical* in the sense that it goes back to Leon Walras, 1834–1910, and *neoclassical* because it includes the work of Alfred Marshall, 1842–1924), the wrong view of the market is assumed, according to Clower. In conventional price theory, workers and employers look at the prevailing market prices and then make their plans to sell or buy their goods or labor services at these prices. (In a formal model of their actions, any demand for goods and services in excess of supplies formed in this way Clower called **notional excess demands**.)

But actual effective demand and supply of goods and services may be quite different in a market in which buyers and sellers of goods and services find that they cannot buy or sell all they had planned at market prices. This is because the producer may cut back on his or her demand for labor. Suddenly the worker is confronted with an unexpected decline in current income. The amount of labor services that he or she planned to sell is curtailed. There is a chain reaction throughout the economy, with workers and producers basing their actions on disequilibrium prices that will not clear the market. There is no head auctioneer in the market who says, "Look, these are the correct prices to clear the market. Now base your demands for goods and services and the amounts you will supply on these market-clearing prices." Instead, the shoe store owner says, "Where are the customers? I'm going to have to put my employees on half days or lay some off." No one has the correct information about prices that would clear the markets for goods and services and labor.

Trades do not occur at equilibrium prices, as many analyses contend. Instead, production plans by firms and workers are formulated from current imperfect market information. Any disturbance in the system—say, an unexpected shortfall in the production of some good because of a rise in the prices of the imported inputs needed to make the good—pushes market prices farther from equilibrium, where demands and supplies are equal (or excess demands or supplies are zero). Inventories pile up.

The same type of reaction occurs in the bond markets in which any decline in interest rates appears at first as abnormal, causing people to think that the "normal rate" will be restored. Axel Leijonhufud suggested that the Keynesian liquidity trap can exist if Keynes's description is interpreted in the following way: The participants in the market are unable to forecast the equilibrium rate (the so-called normal rate) accurately so that their

> estimate—the "normal rate"—will often diverge from the justified or natural rate. In particular, the market may be slow to adjust to changes in the natural rate—changes which may be induced by any of a large number of "real factors." For "to diagnose the position precisely at every stage . . . may sometimes be . . . beyond the wits of man."[9]

The *natural rate* is the long-run equilibrium rate of interest.

There has been controversy over whether these interpretations of Keynes are correct. These doctrinal debates (who meant what) cause economists interested in the history of ideas to have protracted arguments spanning decades.

The issue for analysis is whether these views are useful in understanding the economy. Clower's explanation makes interesting analysis of the nature of disequilibrium. It fits with the work of many economists, including those identified in the classical tradition, who emphasize the cost of information.[10] Economists who developed rational expectations theories (described in Chapter 20) used the cost of information (along with contracts) to describe why the economy does not quickly reach new equilibrium prices. This is a useful avenue of inquiry and is important to economic policy. Would the provision of better information substantially reduce the time it takes to achieve full employment?

The new developments in the futures markets described in Chapter 12 allow some of the uncertainty ascribed disequilibrium prices (following a shock to the economic system) to be reduced. This can be done with financial assets such as financial asset futures, including stock index futures, which allow producers to hedge against general changes in economic activity.

APPENDIX B:
ANOTHER INTERPRETATION OF WHAT KEYNES MEANT

Allan H. Meltzer touched off a new debate on what Keynes meant.[11] Meltzer stated that "Keynes identified full employment—the level of employment at which the economy produces the maximum output that available capital and technology permit." The resulting policy interpretation is thus not based on a liquidity trap or sticky wages. "Keynes believed that the way to raise the economy's average output was to raise the average level of investment and reduce risk premiums in interest rates by reducing the amplitude of cyclical fluctuations in investment."[12] Thus, Meltzer contends that Keynes primarily focused on the need to increase the capital stock to raise the level of real income.

Critics disagree, and excerpts from *The General Theory*, letters of Keynes, and a cable from an individual who quoted Keynes were marshalled in this debate.[13] One thing appears certain. If this explanation by Meltzer had been made and accepted decades ago, the literature in macroeconomics and many countries' fiscal policies would have been different. That is, instead of running deficits, they would have tried to increase and stabilize real investment.

On the likely success of the policy that he interprets Keynes as advocating, Meltzer concluded that

> Where governments have controlled the rate of investment, they have often yielded to pressures to preserve declining industries or to invest where the expected return is low or negative. . . . Time may deal more kindly with Keynes' perception that the object of economic policy should be to reduce risk to the minimum inherent in nature and trading arrangements. . . . Perhaps those assignments are, at last, of major interest for economists.[14]

Early in the post–World War II period, some who had interpreted Keynes to mean that investment would stagnate because of lack of profitable investment opportunities may have suggested policies for managing investment. The rise of the computer and the nuclear age soon put to rest the notion of the stagnation of investment opportunities. In addition, this was not a valid reason for assuming that full employment equilibrium could not be reached. If prices were flexible, consumption goods could fall in price until full employment was reached, even if investment came to a halt. The adjustment period could be shortened by expansionary fiscal policy that moved the *IS* locus to the full employment level, given the simplified assumptions of this model.

APPENDIX C: THE ACCELERATOR

The *accelerator* is the name given to the relationship that can occur between the rate of change in income (or sales) and the level of gross investment. Remember that gross investment is composed of replacement investment (to cover the depreciation of the capital stock) plus net investment (which is equal to a change in the capital stock).

A central condition that helps produce the acceleration principle is a fixed ratio of nonfinancial wealth—also called *capital stock*—to sales (or income). We will begin our discussion by showing that this condition is similar to assuming a constant real rate of interest.

If a company's after-tax profit per dollar of sales is constant, then a constant ratio of sales to capital stock will maintain a constant ratio of profit to capital stock. That ratio, if maintained, was described in the example in the last chapter (with Christopher Brent) as the *real rate of return*. If it is the equilibrium real rate of return, it may be approximately maintained on average over time.

As sales rise, say from $1 million per year to $1.4 million per year, the capital stock must rise along with it at the same rate if the ratio of sales to capital stock is to remain constant. That rate of increase in sales is $1.4 million divided by $1 million, or 40 percent. Therefore, the capital stock must also rise by 40 percent.

At the level of capital stock that was needed to produce $1 million in sales, the only investment that was needed was that required to replace worn-out capital—the replacement investment. To get to a 40 percent higher level of capital stock, a much higher level of investment is required. That is, not only the replacement investment, but also a higher level of net investment, is required. To get an idea of the increase in investment needed, recall that net investment is equal to the change in nonfinancial wealth. Therefore, gross investment (replacement investment plus net investment) must grow. Now, if you have the patience for a few numbers, Table 23-1 contains a worked-out numerical example.

TABLE 23-1   An Example of the Accelerator

The sales shown in column 2 require capital stock of half that size to produce them in each period. So column 4 is half the size of column 2. Net investment, column 5, is the change in the desired capital stock in column 4. Replacement investment, column 6, is 20 percent of the capital stock in the previous period. Add replacement investment to net investment to obtain total gross investment in column 7.

The Result of the Accelerator: As the rate of sales rises in column 3, gross investment rises to a higher level. As the rate of increase in sales declines or turns negative, the level of gross investment falls.

(1)	(2)	(3) Rate of Change of Sales from Period 1 Through Period 4	(4) Desired Capital Stock (50% of sales)	(5) Net Investment	(6) Replacement Investment (20% of capital stock per year)	(7) Gross Investment (columns 5 and 6)
Period	Sales (millions)	(%)	(thousands)	(thousands)	(thousands)	(thousands)
1	$1	0%	$500	$ 0	$100	$100
2	1.2	20	600	100	100	200
3	1.4	33	700	100	120	220
4	1.5	71	750	50	140	190
5	1.5	0	750	0	150	150
6	1.2	−20	600	0	0	0

An Example of the Accelerator

The sales shown in column 2 of Table 23-1 require a capital stock of half that size to produce them in each period. So column 4 is half the size of column 2. Net investment, column 5, is the change in the desired capital stock in column 4. Replacement investment, column 6, is 20 percent of the capital stock in the previous period. Add replacement investment to net investment to obtain total gross investment in column 7.

The Results of the Accelerator

As the rate of increase of sales rises in column 3, gross investment rises to a higher level. As the rate of increase of sales declines or turns negative, the level of gross investment falls.

This finding, known as the *accelerator effect*, shows that the level of investment can be related to the rate of change of sales (or income). This means that as sales rise rapidly, the level of investment can be whipped upward to a multiple of its original level. As the rate of sales increases declines, the level of investment can take a nosedive. This can be an important reason for business cycles.

Changes in the rate of growth of sales whip around the level of investment. The change in the level of investment changes the total income by a multiple amount, according to the value of the expenditure multiplier.

The main point is that the level of gross investment expenditure is volatile in the face of changes in the rate of change in sales (or income) if the ratio of sales to capital stock is nearly constant. That condition is equivalent to a constant real rate of interest.

Although the assumption of a constant real rate of interest is not realistic in the short run—the kind of period in which business cycles occur—the principle could still work: Changes in real rates of interest would amplify (make larger) or reduce business cycle fluctuations, depending on which way real interest rates move.

STUDY QUESTIONS

1. Describe the following functions: the real consumption function, the real investment function, the real savings function, the demand for real money balances, the production function, and the demand for labor.

2. What is a liquidity trap? What implications does it have for monetary policy?

3. Trace through the effects of an increase in the nominal money supply on real interest rates and output, using the *IS–LM* model.

4. Using the *IS–LM* analysis, show the difference in the effects on real income and real interest rates of a government deficit financed either by borrowing or by money creation.

5. If gross investment minus expenditures for the maintenance or replacement of the capital stock equals net investment, what will happen if the capital stock is not maintained? Are the two concepts of investment then equal? (*Hint:* The difference between the two concepts of investment is equal to depreciation, whether or not the capital stock is maintained.) Explain.

6. What are some of the problems with the *IS–LM* analysis? Why is it a short-run model?

7. Explain why the simple government expenditures multiplier used for a government deficit does not result in its full increased expenditure flow in an *IS–LM* analysis unless there is a liquidity trap. What additional expenditure will result from a government deficit if the *LM* is perfectly vertical? What do these conditions say about monetary and fiscal policy?

8. How are aggregate demand and supply schedules relating the price level and output derived in the *IS–LM* analysis? Draw these schedules and use them to explain that full employment equilibrium may not be automatically achieved if workers are unwilling to lower their money wages. What must the government then do to achieve full employment in the *IS–LM* model?

GLOSSARY

Depreciation. A fall in the value of nonfinancial wealth.

Elasticity. The ratio of the percentage changes in two variables, such as the percentage change in real interest rates divided by the percentage change in real income (along an *IS* or *LM* locus).

Full employment equilibrium. An equilibrium level of real income consistent with full employment.

Gross investment. Investment expenditures for maintaining and replacing the capital stock *plus net investment* to increase the capital stock.

Liquidity preference function. Demand-for-money function.

Liquidity trap. A demand function for real money balances that is flat (perfectly elastic). If the *LM* locus is also flat all the way up to full employment, the liquidity trap means that individuals want to hold an infinite amount of money at the liquidity trap real rate of interest. See **Perfectly elastic.**

Map of saving functions. An array of saving functions, each showing the amount of saving that individuals want to undertake at different rates of real interest. Each function is drawn for a different level of real income.

Net investment. Investment that adds to the real stock of capital. It consists of goods that are produced during a period and continue to yield services (income) in future periods.

Notional excess demands. Robert Clower's name for the excess demands that are faced by market participants in markets in which each market participant draws up plans so that expenditures of each participant are financed by its individual income. Such a market is conceptually different from one in which an auctioneer records bids and offers and provides market-clearing prices, as does a specialist on a stock exchange.

Obsolescent or **Obsolete.** A fall in the price of a good because it is outdated or outmoded. This fall in valuation can occur even if there is no change in the physical form of the good; that is, it is not worn out in any way. Thus, an automobile that is up on blocks and is never used may fall in value just because it is an older model.

Perfectly elastic. An elasticity of infinity occurring in a liquidity trap when the demand for real money balances is parallel to the horizontal (real money balance) axis. As the demand-for-money curve approaches this flat position, the ratio of the percentage change in interest rates divided by the percentage change in real money balances demanded approaches infinity, as the denominator of the ratio approaches zero.

Precautionary motive. A (Keynesian) motive for holding money as a reserve for emergencies.

Replacement investment. Investment used to maintain the capital stock— to restore the depreciated nonfinancial capital stock.

Speculative motive or **demand.** Originally, a (Keynesian) motive for holding money incorrectly based on individuals' presumed desire to buy bonds only when their price was low. This meant that people held more money at lower interest rates. It has been reformulated on the basis of transactions costs from buying and selling bonds and on the riskiness of interest-paying assets other than money to yield the same negative relationship between interest rates and the demand for real money balances.

Transaction motive. A (Keynesian) motive relating real income to the demand for real money balances.

NOTES

1. Recall that the last chapter made consumption and saving dependent on levels of disposable income.

2. John Hicks, "Mr. Keynes and the 'Classics': A Suggested Interpretation," *Econometrica*, Vol. 5, 1937, pp. 147–159. A presentation of this model, together with some problems of including the labor sector, is found in Robert D. Auerbach, "A Demand-Pull Theory of Deflation and Inflation," *The Manchester School*, June 1976, pp. 99–111. These problems are summarized in note 7.

3. It is possible that people will save *less* at higher real rates of interest. See Martin Bailey, "Saving and the Rate of Interest," *Journal of Political Economy*, Vol. 65, 1957, summarized in his *National Income and the Price Level: A Study in Macroeconomic Theory* (New York: McGraw-Hill, 1971), pp. 102–118.

4. James Tobin wrote the classic article on this, "Liquidity Preference As a Behaviour Toward Risk," *Review of Economic Studies*, February 1958, pp. 65–86.

5. There has been some confusion between nominal and real interest rates in analyzing the alleged liquidity trap in the 1930 depressions. The central problem with interest rates was not that the nominal interest rate was too low; rather, it was that the real interest rate was too high. A real interest rate series is shown in Chapter 19. Real interest rates were high because of the expectations for the economy that were both dismal and uncertain. This prevented real investment and would have done so whether or not there was a liquidity trap. (I am thankful to Jack Rutner for discussion of this point.) For arguments against the concept of a Keynesian liquidity trap, see Karl Brunner and Allan Meltzer, "Liquidity Traps for Money, Bank Credit, and Interest Rates," *Journal of Political Economy*, January–February 1968, pp. 1–37. This article also contains a bibliography of articles dealing with the liquidity trap. An argument against the concept of a liquidity trap is also made by Don Patinkin, *Money: Interest, and Prices: An Integration of Monetary and Value Theory* (New York: Harper & Row, 1965), p. 225. A few studies found a liquidity trap during the depressions of the 1930s, when interest rates sank to less than 1 percent, though this finding is not generally accepted.

Keynes himself, in his 1936 book, *The General Theory,* said of the liquidity trap, "But whilst this limiting case might become practically important in the future, I know of no example of it hitherto." A liquidity trap can be created by government actions that peg the interest rate at a fixed level, as was done in the United States after World War II until 1951. A liquidity trap may also be produced under a system of government price controls, according to Toribio's hypothesis, discussed in Chapter 21.

6. A. C. Pigou held that consumption depends on real money balances, M/P. As prices fall, even though a liquidity trap exists, real consumption will increase and the *IS* will shift to full employment. This effect has been called the "Pigou effect," or more correctly, as Gottfried Haberler also described it, the "Haberler–Pigou effect." Later formulations put all wealth in the consumption function, including bonds and money. Bonds and money issued by the government (outside money) exhibit positive wealth effects when the price level falls. Bonds and money created by the private sector (inside money) have no net wealth effects. The lenders' net worth declines, and the borrowers' net worth increases from a decline in the price level. The inside-outside money distinction was invented by John G. Gurley and Edward S. Shaw in *Money in a Theory of Finance* (Washington, D.C.: Brookings Institution, 1960). The hypothesis was amended by Boris P. Pesek and Thomas R. Saving; see their *Money, Wealth, and Economic Theory* (New York: Macmillan, 1967). They held that the net worth of banks would rise when they created inside money, thus increasing wealth. Don Patinkin replied that the net worth of the banking system does not come from the production of deposits alone, but also from the monopoly right to produce deposits; see "Money and Wealth: A Review Article," *Journal of Economic Literature,* Vol. 7, 1969, pp. 1140–1160.

7. See Auerbach, "A Demand-Pull Theory of Deflation." That analysis shows that the *IS–LM* model with a production function/labor sector has too many relationships; that is, in the jargon of the models, it is *overdetermined.* The labor market/production function sector is shown to give a locus of equilibrium levels of real output and real interest rates so that only one of the other markets is needed to describe equilibrium values. It also shows that an increase in demand for goods and services can increase supply more than demand, causing prices to *fall* in this model.

8. Robert W. Clower, "The Keynesian Counter-Revolution: A Theoretical Appraisal," in F. H. Hahn and F. Brechling, eds., *The Theory of Interest Rates,* International Economic Association Series (New York: Macmillan, 1965), pp. 103–125; reprinted in Robert W. Clower, ed., *Monetary Theory, Selected Readings* (Baltimore: Penguin Books, 1969), pp. 270–297. Walras's law holds that if all but one market is cleared, the remaining market will be cleared. In a system of simultaneous equations

representing the excess demand for all goods and services in the economy (called a Walrasian system), if all but one of the equations contain values that make their excess demands equal zero, so too will the excess demand of the one remaining equation equal zero. If the labor market has an excess supply of labor, then some other market (or markets) will not be cleared—will still have excess demands. Because Keynes was talking about unemployment equilibrium, Clower's description was as follows: "We may say that Keynesian economics is price theory without Walras's law, and price theory with Walras's law is just a special case of Keynesian economics" (p. 295 in *Monetary Theory*). This sweeping statement is based on Clower's view of the disequilibrium process. Without an auctioneer to present prices that clear markets, the signals received by market participants may not be market-clearing prices.

9.   Axel Leijonhufud, *On Keynesian Economics and the Economics of Keynes: A Study in Monetary Theory* (New York: Oxford University Press, 1968), p. 377. The quotes within the quote are from Keynes, *A Treatise on Money*, Vol. 1 (New York: Macmillan, 1930), p. 255.

10. David E. W. Laidler presented a good discussion of the topic, "Information, Money and the Macro-economics of Inflation," in Laidler's *Essays on Money and Inflation* (Chicago: University of Chicago Press, 1975), pp. 1–18. Also see Leijonhufud, *On Keynesian Economics and the Economics of Keynes*; and George Stigler, "The Economics of Information," *Journal of Political Economy*, June 1961, pp. 213–225.

11. Allan H. Meltzer, "Keynes's *General Theory*: A Different Perspective," *Journal of Economic Literature*, March 1981, pp. 34–64.

12. Ibid., p. 61.

13. Don Patinkin, Paul Davidson, Sidney Weintraub, James R. Crotty, and a reply from Allan H. Meltzer, "On Meltzer's Interpretation of Keynes," *Journal of Economic Literature*, March 1983, pp. 47–78.

14. Meltzer, "Keynes's *General Theory*," p. 63.

CHAPTER 24

INFLATIONARY EQUILIBRIUM

CHAPTER PREVIEW

Introduction. Suppose that the price level settles into a steady state of 7 percent growth per year?

Nominal and Real Interest Rates. The Fisher equation from Chapter 19 reappears.

The IS *Locus.* It is invariant (does not change) with changes in the expected or actual rates of inflation in this model.

The LM *Locus.* It depends on the nominal rate of interest.

Equilibrium Positions. With the vertical axis scaled for nominal rates of inflation, the *IS* must be shifted so that it is consistent with the real rates of interest associated with each higher nominal rate of interest on the vertical axis. Then equilibrium values for the variables are determined for a steady state of inflation.

Interest on Money. The payment of interest on money can reduce the rate of inflation during the adjustment to higher nominal interest rates in an inflationary episode.

Changes in the Real Rate of Interest. Wealth effects from inflation can reduce the real rate of interest, and uncertainty can increase it. Tax rate changes alter the difference between the nominal and real rates of interest.

INTRODUCTION

Suppose that the price level settles into a steady state of 7 percent growth per year. How will all the macroeconomic variables in the *IS–LM* model delineated in the last chapter be related under this condition of an inflationary equilibrium? Those relationships compared with equilibrium relationships with zero inflation are described in this chapter. The analysis ties in with the discussion in Chapter 18, even borrowing a monetary identity to clarify part of the discussion.

The Fisher equation from Chapters 4 and 19 is used at first in this chapter to develop the analysis of inflationary equilibrium. Tax rates are brought into the Fisher equation, using the same equation developed in Appendix B of Chapter 19. That discussion uses the after-tax real rate of interest on bonds. In equilibrium, it is equal to the real rate of interest used in this chapter and does not present a new variable for this analysis.

NOMINAL AND REAL INTEREST RATES

The first building block was developed in Chapters 4 and 19. It is the Fisher equation, which relates nominal to real interest rates under a hypothesis that will hold in equilibrium if tax considerations discussed in Appendix B of Chapter 19 are ignored:

$$i_B = r_B + \lambda \tag{1}$$

where i_B is the nominal rate of interest on bonds, r_B is the real rate of interest on bonds, and λ is the expected rate of inflation, say 7 percent.[1]

Real desired investment depends on the real rate of interest.[1] Thus, real desired investment is not changed by changes in the nominal rate of interest caused by the expectation of more rapid inflation. (See Chapter 23 for a review of this point.)

In the same way that expected inflation increases the expected price of shoes and nominal profits from an investment in a shoe factory, it also increases the expected cost of the factory. The real rate of return relating the expected future *real* income to the present *real* cost of the shoe factory will not change.[2]

THE *IS* LOCUS

This consideration leads to an important property of the *IS* locus with increased rates of inflation. Because all the variables are real variables and only the real rate of interest is used, the *IS* locus will not shift because of changes in the expected or actual rate of inflation.

One more example will further illuminate this point. Consider real consumption, C/P. If the prices of food and clothing and other consumption goods begin to rise at a more rapid rate, this will normally cause the average nominal price of all consumption goods to rise at a similar rate. The symbol C will have a value that is rising at a more rapid rate. If these price increases are part of a general inflation, the price level, P, will normally also rise at the same rate. Therefore, C/P will not be affected.

If real disposable income and real interest rates, the determinants of desired real consumption examined in the last chapter, are unchanged, desired real consumption will also be unchanged. Thus, with both the consumption and investment functions constant, the *IS* locus will not shift with changes in the rate of inflation.

THE *LM* LOCUS

The *LM* locus is built from the demand and supply for real money balances. As indicated in Chapter 18, the demand for real money balances depends on *nominal* rates of interest. An increase in expected inflation raises the nominal rate of interest in equation (1), making it more expensive to hold real money balances. Thus there is an incentive to reduce real money balances.

In Figure 24-1B, the expectation of inflation at a rate of λ (say, 7 percent) encourages individuals to reduce their real cash balances from M/P_2 to M/P_1, where the lenders are just being fully compensated by the higher rate of interest, i'_B. The nominal rate of interest has risen from its level with no inflation,

FIGURE 24-1   The Money Market and Full Employment Equilibria During Inflation

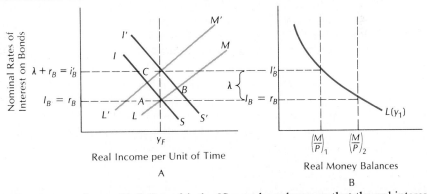

With an expected rate of inflation of λ, the *IS* must be redrawn so that the real interest rate corresponds to the associated higher nominal interest rate on the vertical axis. The *LM* is derived from the liquidity preference functions and the supply of real money balances, as it was in the last chapter. It depends on nominal rate of interest. As the *IS* is shifted to *I'S'*, a shift equal to λ, the curves intersect at point *B*, requiring a rise in the price level so that full employment equilibrium can be restored at point *C*, as the *LM* locus shifts to *L'M'*.

where $i_B = r_B$, to its equilibrium position under an expected inflation at a rate of $\lambda + r_B$, which equals i'_B.

At income level 1, for which the demand-for-money (or liquidity preference) curve is drawn, equilibrium is at a higher nominal interest rate. This is also the case for other demand-for-money curves that can be drawn for other real incomes. (Recall that there is a family of such curves, scaled by real income.) Every level of real income will be associated with a higher nominal interest rate as a possible value for the new inflationary equilibrium. Equilibrium is designated here at the full employment level of real income.

EQUILIBRIUM POSITIONS

In Figure 24-1A, equilibrium is depicted in terms of real income and the nominal rate of interest on bonds. This differs from the last chapter, which used the real rate of interest.

With price stability, equilibrium is at point A in Figure 24-1A. Because no inflation is expected, the nominal and real rates of interest are equal. In equation (1), $\lambda = 0$.

After equilibrium is reached for a steady state of inflation at a rate of, say, 7 percent, the nominal rate of interest exceeds the real rate by λ (which is a difference of 7 percent). Because the IS locus is based on the real, not the nominal, rate of interest, it must be redrawn for the corresponding nominal rate of interest on the vertical axis, given by equation (1). The IS locus is thus moved upward in Figure 24-1A by an amount equal to λ. This causes an intersection of LM and $I'S'$ at B where expenditures exceed full employment output. As seen in Chapter 19, the attempt to economize on real money balances causes more spending and inflation. The expectation of inflation, by itself—apart from the increase in the rate of nominal money growth—causes inflation in the adjustment to a new equilibrium. As prices rise and real money balances are reduced, LM shifts back to $L'M'$ and a new equilibrium at C.

To maintain real balances at $(M/P)_1$ with prices rising at a rate of λ per year (say, 7 percent), the nominal money supply must also increase. That is, the nominal money supply must grow at a rate that exceeds the growth rate of full employment output by the percentage rate of λ (7 percent).

This point is illustrated by using a monetary identity from Chapter 18, after translating each variable into a rate of change per unit of time (the same symbol with a dot over it):

$$\dot{M} + \dot{V} = \dot{P} + \dot{y} \tag{2}$$

where $\dot{M}$ is the rate of change of the nominal money supply, $\dot{V}$ is the rate of change of income velocity, $\dot{P}$ is the rate of change of the price level, and $\dot{y}$ is the rate of change of real income. All these variables are in the form of percentages per year. At a nominal interest rate of i'_B, there is some equilibrium level of income velocity. Therefore, $\dot{V} = 0$ in equilibrium. If $\dot{y}$ is 4 percent and $\dot{M}$ is 11 percent, $\dot{P}$ must be 7 percent in equilibrium.

INTEREST ON MONEY

Would things change if interest were paid on money? Assume first an extreme case. The interest on money varies with the interest on bonds. It varies by just enough so that the difference between the two interest rates eliminates the incentive to switch into bonds when bond interest rates rise. Meanwhile, the nominal interest rate on bonds corresponds to the equilibrium position in equation (1). Under these conditions, the expectation of inflation does not cause a decrease in the quantity of real money balances demanded. The *LM* locus would have to be changed from *LM* to *L'M'* in Figure 24-1—just as is true for the *IS* locus—when it is plotted against nominal interest rates. This is because only a change in real interest rates, not nominal interest rates, would affect the demand for real balances in this special case. In fact, the interest rate axis could be scaled in real interest rates, and the analysis could be carried out in the same manner as in the last chapter. That is, the equilibrium positions would change from *A* to *C*, without going to *B*. In other words, the mere expectation of inflation would *not* fuel inflation during the adjustment process. Only the actual change in the nominal money supply would generate inflation.

Put differently, if individuals were not prompted by the expectation of inflation to switch out of real money balances, the expectation of inflation by itself would not cause inflation. An increase in the rate of growth of the money supply would continue to cause increased inflation. The real balances that people hold would be "indexed" against inflation by an interest return tied to the expected inflation. This could be done if the government paid interest on bank reserves and currency.[3] Of course, this extreme case would not be applicable for a number of reasons, such as the inability to pay interest on currency and coin inexpensively. As interest rate ceilings on checkable deposits were raised and became ineffective constraints, finally being removed in 1986 (pursuant to 1980 legislation), more competitive interest was paid on money. These more competitive interest payments will reduce the inflationary effects of the expectation of inflation that occur during the adjustment to a new inflationary equilibrium. The association (or correlation) between the growth rate of the nominal money supply and the rate of inflation should be greater. This will make monetary policy easier to gauge, and it could even make the inflation rate less variable.

CHANGES IN THE REAL RATE OF INTEREST

Up to this point, the real rate of interest, r_B, has been assumed to be unaffected by a change to a new inflationary equilibrium. But this may not be true if real consumption depends on real money balances (see note 6 in Chapter 23). If this were the case, real consumption would decline as the rate of inflation increased. This would occur because real money balances would be

FIGURE 24-2   Full Employment Equilibria During Inflation with a
Change in the Real Rate of Interest

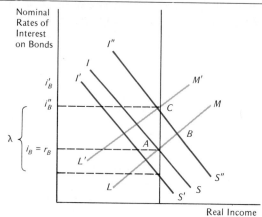

Real rates of interest may fall because of wealth effects or rise because of uncertainty
during an inflationary episode. In the figure, *IS* has shifted down to *I'S'* because of
wealth effects, and then as inflationary expectations set in, it shifted up to *I"S"*.

smaller; people would feel less wealthy, so they would cut down their real
consumption.[4] This is a short-term **wealth effect**.

The *IS* in Figure 24-2 would shift to a new equilibrium position from a
curve drawn for a lower real rate of interest. The *I'S'* is drawn on the basis of
this new lower real rate of interest. It must be redrawn in terms of the nominal
rate of interest corresponding to this lower real rate of interest. The *I"S"* is
higher than *I'S'* by the expected rate of inflation. The intersections of the *IS*
and *LM* would go from *A* to *B* to *C* in Figure 24-2. The result of the fall in the
real interest rate is that the nominal rate does not rise to i'_B, as in Figure 24-1,
but only to i''_B in Figure 24-2.

The important point is that nominal interest rates in an inflationary equilibrium may not rise above the zero inflation nominal rate by the full expected
rate of inflation, even though equation (1) may be true. The reason is that the
real rate of interest may decline with the expectation of inflation.

Tax rates were brought into the Fisher equation in Appendix B of Chapter
19. Equation (1) becomes

$$i_B = \frac{r + \lambda}{1 - K} \tag{3}$$

where *r* is the real interest rate and *K* is the average income tax rate. Subtract
the real rate of interest from both sides of the equation to see the difference
between the real and nominal rates of interest. The difference is greater than it
was before tax rates were introduced and becomes larger with a higher tax
rate. Recall from Chapter 19 that the deductibility of interest payments from

taxable income for those making interest payments and the inclusion in taxable income of interest payments for those receiving them causes this effect.

A fuller analysis of the effects of tax rates is necessary to understand the changes in the real rate of interest from these effects in the short run. Some of these considerations will be discussed in the next chapter in some timely and important analyses that bring in fiscal policy, including taxes. For this stage of analysis, simply be aware that income tax rates affect the difference between nominal and real rates of interest so that the difference is greater than the expected rate of inflation.

The real rate of interest may *rise* if the new rate of inflation produces uncertainty regarding its continuation and its effects. A risk premium is added to the real rate of interest. This rise in the real rate will push nominal interest rates up from the zero inflation level by even more than the full expected rate of inflation.

True, uncertainty is not part of a pure, steady-state equilibrium inflation rate in which everyone sleeps soundly without a thought that the steady-state rate of inflation will ever change. Most of this world's rather more messy inflations may at most provide five or ten years of a fairly steady rate of inflation, which is not long enough to eradicate uncertainty about their continuation.

STUDY QUESTIONS

1. Use the *IS–LM* model developed in this chapter to show the change from a 10-percent inflationary equilibrium to a 5 percent inflationary equilibrium.

2. What happens to real and nominal interest rates as a result of an increase in inflationary expectations in the *IS–LM* analysis?

3. Suppose that both the inflation rate and the level of uncertainty about the economy increase. Could nominal interest rates fall? If this could happen, show it on the *IS–LM* diagram.

4. Under what conditions will the expectations of increased rates of inflation fail to raise the rate of inflation above the rate of growth of the money supply, given that it is an inflation caused by rapid money growth?

5. Bringing in the effect of income tax rates on the difference between real and nominal rates of interest developed in Appendix B of Chapter 19, explain how this difference can change during an inflation caused by a reduction in tax rates. Show this change on the *IS–LM* diagram.

6. Show on the *IS–LM* diagram the effect of temporary price controls during an inflationary episode. Review Chapter 21 for this purpose.

7. What will be the effect on the rate of inflation during an inflationary episode if the expectation of inflation causes a decline in investment caused by uncertainty about the future? Explain using the *IS–LM* model.

8. From an inflationary equilibrium, what effect would an announcement by

the government that everyone believed that money growth would be reduced to a lower rate have on interest rates? Explain using the *IS–LM* model.

9. It has been alleged that the removal of ceiling rate limitations on checking accounts caused interest rates to rise. One reason given for this contention is that higher interest rates cost depository institutions more, so they had to charge more on their loans. Assess this argument. How would the *IS–LM* change if this argument were true? Is this likely? (*Hint*: Bond markets have never been controlled, and secondary bond markets, as discussed in Chapter 13, are very competitive.)

GLOSSARY

Wealth effect. A change in consumption from a change in wealth. It can be produced by putting real money balances in the consumption function so that a change in real money balances changes consumption. This is a wealth effect limited to real money balances, and it is called a *real balance effect*. See note 6 in Chapter 23.

NOTES

1. The real rate of interest is the internal rate of return developed in Chapter 10. With a constant capital stock, it is equal to what Keynes called "the marginal efficiency of capital." The marginal efficiency of capital is the increase in output per microscopic increase in capital.

2. This requires, along with some other things, that the purchase of the shoe factory does not include the purchase of nominal assets such as accounts due or payable or bonds owned or issued, which, together, have a positive or negative net worth. If this assumption is not true, then the purchase of the shoe factory will be affected by the expectation of inflation in the same way as a borrower or a lender will.

3. This indexing requires that the depository institutions receiving interest on their reserves be part of an industry that expands to perfectly competitive equilibrium and pays perfectly competitive interest on the deposits. In other words, the interest payments on reserves do not partly increase monopoly profits in an industry with limited entry.

4. It is assumed that those deriving the benefits from issuing new money, such as the government, do not increase their consumption.

PART SEVEN

APPLICATIONS OF THEORY

CHAPTER 25

THE EFFECTS OF MONETARY AND FISCAL POLICY

CHAPTER PREVIEW

Introduction. All three methods of financing government expenditures impose costs.

The Effects of Financing Expenditures Through Money Creation. This is a short review of the effects of money creation covered in Part V.

The Effects of Borrowing to Finance the Deficit. Alternative theories of the effects on real interest rates, real investment, and real saving are discussed.

The Effects of Financing Through Taxation. A theory is presented that such financing is equivalent in its effects on consumption and real interest rates to financing through borrowing.

Can Deficits Be Continually Financed By Borrowing? Public concern and an interesting debate among economists in the face of unprecedented peacetime budget deficits has raised the issue of whether it is possible to keep running borrowed government deficits without resorting to financing them with money creation.

Appendix: Supply-Side Economics—The Effects of Neglecting Financing Transactions. An example of the failure to specify financing transactions for government expenditures is presented.

INTRODUCTION

The expenditure theory developed in Part Six was half of the picture of the effects of government expenditures. The other half concerns the method of financing these expenditures.

Borrowing and printing money are two ways of financing government deficits—expenditure on goods and services that are in excess of taxes. A third way, taxation, to finance government expenditures is also discussed. All three methods of financing expenditures impose significant costs on the private sector. It is a mistake to emphasize the cost of one type of financing and forget the costs of the other types. Government expenditures are not free of cost, regardless of whether or not they are worth the cost.

When someone says that government deficits are bad and therefore that the better course is to increase taxes, the following question should be asked: Are taxes better, or worse, or the same as printing money or borrowing in their effects on the welfare of the population? Looking at the effects of financing on the real saving, real investment, and real rate of interest is an important part of assessing the total effect on government expenditures.

IT DID NOT COST A DIME; IT COST MUCH MORE

There have been instances in which the federal government has helped entities outside the federal government with federal government guarantees of the entity's loans, such as it did with part of the debt of New York City. Is that a costless form of federal help if no defaults occur so that the federal government is not called upon to pay even a dime on the loans? No, it is a very expensive form of aid.

To see this, imagine that *your* debts were guaranteed by the federal government. How much in income-earning assets could you acquire at the lowest (risk-free) interest rate? If the guarantee was large, say, on $500 million of debt, you could acquire $500 million in assets. Suppose that you bought corporate bonds that yielded 2 percent more than your borrowing rate. You would earn the difference, subject to the risk that the 2 percent premium entails. The ability to garner part of the nation's output and wealth from these government guarantees of debt is a cost imposed on the remainder of the population, a cost that is substantial.

THE EFFECTS OF FINANCING EXPENDITURES THROUGH MONEY CREATION

The first method of financing expenditures—a change in the monetary base accompanying a deficit—combines monetary and fiscal effects. In this case, the deficit is said to be financed by new money issue or, equivalently, by the printing press. The deficit has the *multiplier effect* described in Chapter 22.

FIGURE 25-1 The Effect of the Deficit on Aggregate Demand When It Is Financed by Borrowing and Money Creation

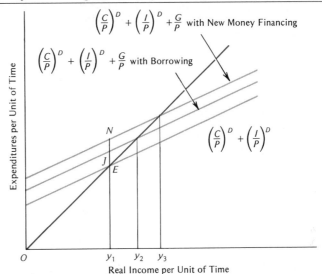

The real deficit is equal to *NE*. With new money, financing the full effect of the deficit and the expenditure multiplier causes real income to rise to y_3. With borrowing, the effect of the real deficit is reduced because of *crowding out*.

This can be seen in Figure 25-1, the Keynesian cross diagram. Private demand for goods and services is labeled $(C/P)^D + (I/P)^D$ for desired real private consumption plus desired real private investment. For simplicity, there are initially no government expenditures. Now the government spends G/P, which is equal to a real deficit of *NE* in Figure 25-1. Government expenditures equal the real deficit because real taxes are assumed to be zero, again for simplicity. The government expenditure multiplier then causes real income to rise from y_1 to y_3.

This is the complete analysis as far as the simple expenditure model goes. It simply reveals a rise in real income. In the next period of time, say, the following year, real income would revert to its initial level if there were no additional real deficit.

However, the results of faster money growth have been shown to be *split* between real income changes (in six to nine months) and price increases (having their full impact in approximately two years in the U.S. post–World War II period). Therefore, the money used to finance the deficit has its own effect.

If the extra money growth to finance the deficit is a one-time injection, then output will temporarily rise, the price level will permanently rise to a new level, and the effect of the deficit financing by money creation will end. However, there may be a series of deficits that keep the money supply growing at a faster rate of growth for a number of years. This will keep prices rising at a faster rate of growth unless real income rises rapidly or people are willing to hold the extra money (velocity falls).

To see the effects of changes in these variables, look back at the monetary identity in Chapter 18, repeated here,

$$\frac{M}{P} V = y \tag{1}$$

where M is nominal money balances, P is the price level, V is the income velocity of money, and y is real income.

Notice that if M grows rapidly to finance the deficit, people will hold more money at a given price level (V falls); more goods and services will be produced (y rises); prices (P) will rise; or all three variables will change to values consistent with equation (1). Velocity has generally risen, not fallen, in recent decades in the United States, as rising interest rates have caused people to reduce the quantity of money they demanded. Faster money growth over this period has been associated with more rapid rates of inflation.[1]

If this observation is correct, so that faster money growth caused by the financing of deficits increased the rate of inflation, the following conclusion about financing through the use of the printing press (money creation) will be valid. Such financing imposes an *inflationary tax* on all forms of financial wealth holdings, including money balances, that do not pay an interest rate that fully offsets the rate of rise in the price level. Put simply, if inflation is humming along at 10 percent per year and you own $100 in currency and coins or a demand deposit at a commercial bank that pays no interest, you will be paying an inflationary tax of $10 per year (10 percent of $100). Furthermore, the purchasing power of your money holdings will fall by 10 percent a year as the inflation proceeds at a 10 percent rate. Unless your money balances paid a 10 percent interest, such a method of financing taxes would be equivalent to paying an explicit income tax.

THE EFFECTS OF BORROWING TO FINANCE THE DEFICIT

Effects on Interest Rates

Suppose that the deficit is composed of consumption expenditures by the government and is financed by selling bonds to the private sector. Another way of describing this financing is to say that it increases the **national debt**. Thus, our discussion of borrowing will also consider the effects of changes in the national debt.

To analyze the effects of the deficit, we must look at private investment. The real private investment curve, I_0/P, is plotted in Figure 25-2A. As explained in the preceding part of the book, there is more real investment at lower real interest rates. So the real investment curve is negatively sloped (downward sloping).

FIGURE 25-2   Saving and Investment

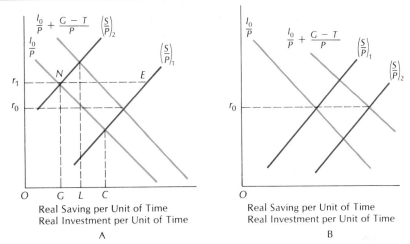

Real Saving per Unit of Time
Real Investment per Unit of Time

A

Real Saving per Unit of Time
Real Investment per Unit of Time

B

Crowding out is shown in Figure 25-2A. Government bonds are sold to finance the deficit. The bonds are considered items of net wealth. Because they are wealthier, individuals consume more and save less (at the constant full employment level of real income). The saving function shifts from (1) to (2). Private investment declines by GC, a decline called *crowding out*. The real investment by the government may take the form of a real deficit, $(G - T)/P$, where G/P is government spending and T/P is taxes. This increases real investment by GL.

An alternative hypothesis showing that bond financing is *neutral* on real interest rates is shown in Figure 25-2B. Bonds sold to finance the deficit are perceived to create a future tax liability (to pay the interest and return of principal on the bonds). This causes individuals to save more at every level of real interest rates, shifting the saving function from $(S/P)_1$ to $(S/P)_2$. The effect on real interest rates, if any, depends on the value of the government's deficit expenditures to the society. If government expenditures are as valuable as private expenditures are, the investment curve will shift out, as shown in Figure 25-2B, exactly maintaining the real rate of interest. If the society puts a smaller value on these government expenditures, total investment will not be given by the curve $I_0/P + (G - T)/P$ in Figure 25-2B. Rather, it will be something less, crossing the saving function, $(S/P)_2$, at a lower real interest rate.

Initially, the real interest rate is r_0. If nothing happens to that real interest rate, then aggregate demand will increase by NE in Figure 25-1. The multiplier effect will cause real income to rise to y_3. If the real interest rates in Figure 25-2A rise to, say, r_1, there will be less real private investment.

That reduction in real private investment due to a rise in real interest rates is called **crowding out**. If real interest rates do rise and real investment falls, the decline in real private investment will reduce the effect of the deficit on aggregate demand. Instead of the aggregate demand's shifting up by NE in Figure 25-1, it may shift up only by JE (NJ is the decline in real private investment caused by crowding out). Then real income will rise to only y_2.

Two explanations of why the real interest rate will rise are presented next. The first concerns an adjustment in the bond market (a general term for financial assets markets for debt instruments), in which the government is selling bonds to finance the deficit. The second explanation brings in the effects on saving behavior.

After you have mastered those explanations, we will turn to an alternative hypothesis that a borrowed deficit has no effect on aggregate demand. And once you understand this, we can discuss the controversy.

Bond Market Effects

Real interest rates may rise, at least temporarily, as the government sells bonds to finance the deficit. (To simplify the analysis, we will use the simplest type of bond—that is, simplest in terms of computing its interest rate.)

SIMPLIFYING BONDS

Economists frequently use the simplification explained in Chapter 10 of transforming bonds into *perpetuities* (or *consols*). These are bonds that have no maturity; they pay a continuous, fixed return each year, forever. The British government issues consols, and in the United States, private corporations issue *preferred stock*, which has the same property. Preferred stock may pay, for example, $70 a year forever. At a price of $1,000, the interest rate, r_1, on this income stream is found from the relation in Chapter 10, $PV = R/r$:

$$r_1(\$1,000) = \$70 \text{ per year} \qquad (2)$$

$$r_1 = \frac{\$70 \text{ per year}}{\$1,000} = 7\% \text{ per year} \qquad (3)$$

Now suppose that the government enters the bond market to finance its deficits. The supply of bonds increases. In Figure 25-3, the supply curve of bonds shifts out, and the price of bonds falls from P_2 to P_1. Suppose that this causes the price of the bond in equation (3) to fall to $900 in the market. Then

$$r_2 = \frac{\$70 \text{ per year}}{\$900} = 7.78\% \text{ per year} \qquad (4)$$

The yearly interest rate rises from 7 percent to 7.78 percent. (The same effect is true for bonds with a stated maturity, although the computation is more difficult. As their price falls, the interest rate on the fixed stream of income that those bonds provide rises.) The huge increases in the supply of government bonds, of the type generated in the United States since 1975, may have driven up real interest rates slightly. See Table 25-1 for a tabulation of the huge increase in funds raised by the U.S. government from 1975 to 1981.

The financial markets are very competitive. A small rise in interest rates on

TABLE 25-1 Funds Raised by Government Borrowing and Federal Deficits from 1965 to 1981

This table shows the amount of funds raised by the U.S. government (debt instruments sold) from 1965 to 1981. Total funds raised by all nonfinancial sectors are shown for comparison. The deficits and the funds raised by the U.S. government are associated.

Calendar Year	Deficits	Funds Raised by Nonfinancial Sectors (billions of 1972 dollars)		Percentage of U.S. Government
		Total	U.S. Government	
1965	+0.7	$ 96.4	$ 1.7	1.8%
1966	2.3	88.9	3.0	3.4
1967	16.7	103.3	11.3	10.9
1968	7.3	119.8	12.7	10.6
1969	+9.7	104.0	−1.5	(1.4)
1970	13.6	104.2	14.1	13.5
1971	22.9	148.4	27.1	18.3
1972	16.8	166.3	14.3	8.6
1973	5.3	184.3	7.5	4.1
1974	10.0	163.1	10.5	6.4
1975	55.2	160.7	68.4	42.6
1976	40.2	199.0	52.3	26.3
1977	33.2	238.5	41.2	17.3
1978	19.5	264.1	36.7	13.9
1979	9.1	242.1	23.8	9.8
1980	34.5	201.3	44.9	22.3
1981	32.0	206.5	45.3	21.9

+ In deficit column denotes surplus.
− Under U.S. government and parentheses in the last column show a reduction in the national debt (equivalent to government lending during the period).

Source: Stephen O. Morrell, "Cyclical and Secular Components of the Federal Budget: Implications from Credit Market Activity," *Economic Review*, Federal Reserve Bank of Atlanta, August 1982, pp. 22–23.

government bonds will attract a huge amount of funds away from alternative uses of funds. The effect is temporary with a single deficit. The funds raised are returned to the private sector in deficit expenditures, eventually replacing the funds borrowed from the private sector.

With a series of deficits and government credit demands, as in the 1975–1981 period, the real interest rate may have been affected throughout the period. Estimates of real interest rates show that they were generally higher from 1976 to 1982 (with the exception of 1978), compared with the 1965–1975 period. There are, however, other factors (such as uncertainty) affecting real interest rates; so the evidence is very weak.

FIGURE 25-3 The Demand and Supply of Bonds with an Increase in Government Bonds Supplied

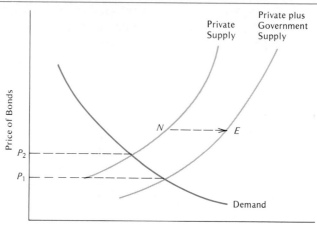

Quantity of Bonds per Unit of Time

Government borrowing (the sale of bonds by the government) to finance a deficit shifts the supply of bonds by NE, causing the price of bonds to drop from P_2 to P_1 if the supply of private-sector bonds is constant. This is equivalent to a rise in real interest rates. But the rise is temporary, as the supply curve will shift back.

Effects on Saving

The Case for Decreased Saving

Figures 25-2A and B show real investment and real saving schedules. Each saving schedule reflects the view that consumers will save more if the reward for saving is higher. That is, they will save more at higher real rates of interest. The saving schedule is positively sloped (upward sloping).

Equilibrium is initially at a real interest rate of r_0 in Figures 25-2A and B. If individuals regard the new government bonds they hold as additions to their real wealth, they will feel wealthier, even though their real income has not changed, and they will consume more (save less) at every real rate of interest. The saving function shifts from (1) to (2) in Figure 25-2A, and the real interest rate rises from r_0 to r_1. Real private investment declines by GC, a decline called crowding out.

The real government deficit, $(G - T)/P$, where G/P is real government spending and T/P is real taxes, may be viewed as adding to the private expenditures, shifting the investment curve out to $I_0/P + (G - T)/P$. This restores some of the real private investment that is crowded out.

A Note on Outside Bonds and the Real Rate of Interest

When a private entity (such as a corporation or an individual) sells a bond, no net wealth is created. Review this point in the discussion of financial wealth in Chapter 3. Nonetheless, the individual (or corporation) who owns the bond feels wealthier, and the individual (or corporation) who owes the payment stream on the bond feels poorer (other things being the same). These are **inside bonds**. When the government sells a bond to the private sector, the government presumably feels no poorer, but the bondholder feels wealthier. So the argument is made that the government bond is an item of *net wealth*.[2] It is called an **outside bond**. (The views of those who think it is not an item of net wealth are presented next.)

The Debt Neutrality Hypothesis: The Case for Increased Saving

Some economists believe that government bonds do not add to the wealth of consumers because every time the government issues a bond, it creates a liability for the payment of tax to make the payments on the bond.[3]

If taxpayers fully take into account these future tax payments, the total wealth effect on bondholders and other taxpayers will be zero. The bonds will have a *neutral* effect; hence, the name **neutrality hypothesis**.

Because of the new liability for future taxes to pay the interest on these bonds, taxpayers will save more out of their incomes. The saving schedule will move to $S(y_2)$ in Figure 25-2B.

Victor A. Canto and Donald Rapp presented this view in an example:

> Suppose the government reduces the current tax bill of every taxpayer by one dollar and finances this tax reduction by issuing bonds which bear the market rate of interest. A lump-sum tax equal to one dollar plus interest will be levied on each taxpayer next year in order to retire the current bond issue. Will taxpayers feel wealthier today as a result of this transaction? Will they therefore increase their consumption and lower private capital accumulation?
>
> If people behave rationally, the argument goes, the answer to these questions must be "no." People will save the dollar they currently receive so as to be able to meet their increased future tax liabilities. Current saving will increase by the amount of the government debt issue.[4]

Back in the Keynesian cross diagram, Figure 25-1, the government shoots a blank. The deficit considered alone pushes the aggregate demand out by NE. The additional government expenditures from the deficit have a multiplier effect. However, the tax liability from the bonds that must be sold caused real private saving to increase by NE (and real consumption falls by NE). The two effects are offsetting, and the aggregate demand curve never changes. The borrowed deficit leaves real income at y_1. Real interest rates do not change at all in the extreme case of perfect neutrality.

In terms of the real saving and real investment diagram in Figure 25-2B, the bond sales cause a future tax liability that induces people to save more. The saving function shifts from (1) to (2). The deficit causes an addition to the real private investment function so that the real rate of interest is maintained.

If the government is wasteful and its investments are not valued as highly as private investments are, real rates of interest may fall. The future real income for society's stock of wealth will then decline, creating a lower rate of return, and that is equivalent to a lower real rate of interest. That effect depends on the efficiency of government expenditures, not on the bond financing.

Robert Barro worked out the assumptions for the neutrality effect—including the effect of current taxes on future generations, the heirs of the present generation.[5]

This hypothesis regarding the results from a bond sale by the government to the public, taken alone, may leave you incredulous. Can it be true that the tax liability from the sale of bonds will be accurately taken into account, causing an increase in real saving and a reduction in real consumption in the current period? This will happen even if the tax liability is expected to fall on great-grandchildren, yet unborn. In our following explanation, however, we show that the great economist David Ricardo thought that the tax liability would not be *fully* taken into account. He wrote 160 years ago, and his views may still be correct.

One should not dismiss the idea as foolish. A great deal of wealth in the United States has been set aside by individuals for their heirs. This can be called **bequest wealth** or **assets**, which was estimated to have been $3 trillion in 1974, or 72 percent of total wealth in the United States.[6]

It may seem that the reason for these bequest assets is to make sure that the heirs can pay their future taxes. Indeed, this wealth is often deliberately planned as a tax shelter for heirs. Wealth is transferred to children who are in a lower income bracket, and it is kept in trust (often by a commercial bank) until the children are old enough to be given the income.

But one inconsistency in this reasoning is that many people may leave zero or *negative bequests*. An example of a negative bequest is a pile of bills left by the deceased that the heirs must pay, such as a mortgage on a house and loans cosigned by the heirs. Negative and zero bequests contradict the notion that future tax liabilities that fall on heirs are completely taken into account.

There are other explanations for so-called bequest wealth. It could be a reserve for emergencies because of the inability to hedge future possibilities for great losses. Or this reserve could be provided for one's heirs quite independently from the size of the national debt (the present value of future tax liabilities). What is needed for stronger proof of the neutrality effect is more direct evidence. Some tests have shown that deficits are not closely related to changes in real interest rates. That finding alone is not strong evidence of the neutrality hypothesis, although it is consistent with that hypothesis.

When a Borrowed Deficit Has a Large Effect

There are conditions in which a borrowed deficit may have a large effect on the aggregate demand for goods and services. To illuminate this point, consider an example of a private company, Zebra Rentals, that runs a deficit. Zebra Rentals invests $100 million to build a new factory and borrows $100 million by selling bonds. These are inside bonds, because although the holders of the bonds have an asset that makes them feel wealthier, the owners of Zebra

Rentals have a liability that reduces the net worth of their company. If the investment is very profitable, the owners of Zebra Rentals will feel wealthier even after taking account of their new debts, and Zebra Rentals will provide more real income for the economy.

The example illustrates a central point about government deficits. If the government's deficit expenditure is efficient, it can produce a valuable real income stream. This is most apparent during a period of high unemployment, as existed in the 1930s, when investors were very pessimistic. If under these conditions, the government starts spending more than it takes in in taxes (it runs a deficit), it may brighten investors' expectations that the demand for goods and services will pick up again. *The entire private investment curve will shift to the right.* This shift in the investment curve is called **crowding in**. This reaction will have stimulative effects even if the bonds used to finance it are viewed as a future tax liability. The benefits of the government deficit may be well worth the cost.

A NOTE ON SOME TEST RESULTS

In a few words, test results generally show that borrowed deficits have only a small effect on aggregate demand. You need read no further unless you wish to get a flavor of the immense amount of testing to which modern economists have subjected hypotheses in this area of analysis. Gerald P. Dwyer, Jr., summed up a huge amount of test results on the effects of government borrowing (that increases the government's debt):

Tests of the proportion that increased government debt increases households' consumption uniformly indicate that such an effect is not significant. Using time-series data for the United States, Levis Kochin, J. Ernest Tanner, John J. Seater, J. Walter Elliot, William H. Buiter, and James Tobin and Martin J. Feldstein found evidence consistent with the hypothesis that government debt does not affect consumption expenditure in the economy. Some of these studies have also tested the hypothesis that deficits are accompanied by compensating changes in saving. The test results, which are subject to problems of interpretation, suggest some although perhaps not complete compensating changes.

In some of these same studies, however, there are tests of hypotheses derived from the proposition that increased government debt does increase households' consumption. These hypotheses are not rejected. Hence, the results in these studies are consistent with both propositions—that government debt does affect consumption and that it does not. The resolution of this question must await more powerful tests.

Because Social Security is part of the federal government's unfunded debt, tests of the hypothesis that anticipated future Social Security payments affect consumption are also relevant. Using time-series data for the United States, Martin Feldstein finds a substantial effect, but Dean R. Leimer and Selig D. Lesnoy find that this result does not survive correction of an error in Feldstein's calculations. Feldstein has replied with evidence in favor of an effect, but Leimer and Lesnoy show that the evidence is not robust to small changes in the tests. Using other data, Michael

R. Darby finds that Feldstein's initial esti- mated effect of Social Security wealth is implausibly large as well. As a result, the hypothesis of no effect of Social Security debt seems to be quite consistent with the available data.[7]

Asghar Zardkoodi, Randall G. Holcombe, and John D. Jackson examined data from 1929 to 1976 to find the effect of deficits on saving. They found evidence of crowding out.[8] The evidence they cited includes the observation that the budget deficit as a per- centage of GNP increased substantially after 1974. But the personal savings rate in the United States showed a substantial *decline* after 1975.

However, if the economy is more robust and real private investment is sub- stantial, some government spending programs may not be efficient. The gov- ernment may invest in less productive ventures than the private sector may. What are the results when the government runs a borrowed deficit when there is no crowding in and no equally productive (with the private sector) govern- ment expenditures? That is a controversial question. You may want to wade through some of the test results to get a flavor of the controversy.

We should emphasize that just because government expenditures, financed by borrowing, may not increase aggregate demand does not mean that they are not desirable. Expenditures on defense and social programs may be highly desirable. They may, however, have little stimulative effect on aggregate demand.

Conclusions from Recent Evidence

Borrowed deficits have been found to have much less effect on real income than was thought a decade ago. Large models generally give much less weight to borrowed deficits than to deficits financed by money creation. It also appears from the evidence that borrowed deficits of the size run in the United States from the 1950s to the 1980s do not have much effect on real interest rates. However, as noted, small changes in real interest rates can greatly affect real investment. But the effects on real rates of interest of larger borrowed deficits—especially a *series* of larger deficits—is controversial.

THE EFFECTS OF FINANCING THROUGH TAXATION

The Equivalence Theorem

The third method of financing expenditures is taxes. Many people prefer this method of financing to borrowing or printing money. Borrowing or printing money, they say, is bad because these alternatives cause higher interest rates and inflation, respectively.

The question asked in modern macroeconomic theory is, Are the effects on saving and real interest rates significantly different from tax increases compared with borrowing? Those that support the neutrality hypothesis say no. They hold that a tax increase is *equivalent* to borrowing in its effect on real interest rates and saving. This form of the neutrality hypothesis is called the **equivalence theorem**. As shown, under the neutrality hypothesis, more is saved to offset future tax liabilities from government bond financing. Real consumption declines by the same amount as it would with a tax on disposable income.

A Note on David Ricardo, the Equivalence Theorem, and the Burden of the National Debt

David Ricardo (1772–1823) remains one of the most respected economists in the history of economics. He was born in London, worked for his father at the London Stock Exchange, and, after reading Adam Smith's *Wealth of Nations*, took an interest in economics.

Although he became an important contributor to classical economic thought, his labor theory of value became the foundation for Karl Marx's theory of surplus value. Ricardo's abstract models are the basis for a great amount of later work on the distribution of wealth. He also gestated analyses of the effect of changes in the money supply that are part of the historical development of monetary theory called the *quantity theory of money*.

In the early 1800s, Ricardo analyzed the effect of the national debt.[9] Although Ricardo developed the idea of the equivalence theorem, Randall G. Holcombe explained that Ricardo did not believe the equivalence theorem to be true and that the theoretical debate "seems to remain much as Ricardo left it in 1821."[10] (See Table 25-2.)

The debate about borrowing versus taxation is also a debate about changes in the size of the national debt (the outstanding debt of the government). Borrowing increases the national debt. The debate can be described as asking the question of whether or not an increase in the national debt is a burden on future generations. (The debt from 1789 to 1981 as a percentage of GNP is shown in Figure 25-4.)

Holcombe summarized the history of the debt burden controversy as follows:

> The generally accepted answer at that time was explained by Abba Lerner in 1948. Lerner said the national debt was really not a burden because the debt was, for the most part, owned by Americans, and therefore we owe it to ourselves. This, of course, is the same argument made more than two centuries before by Jean François Melon. Given the history of the debate, it is surprising that Lerner's argument generally went unchallenged through most of the 1950s.
>
> The first serious questioning of Lerner's theory was done by James M. Buchanan in 1958. Buchanan argued that the present sellers and purchasers of the public debt voluntarily argree to the transaction, and so are not bearing the burden of the debt. However, future taxpayers who face

higher taxes as a result of the debt are being made worse off. The government, because of its ability to force future taxpayers to pay higher taxes, pushes the debt burden into the future. Once again, we note the similarity between Buchanan's argument and that made by Adam Smith. In 1776, Smith said that deficit finance would gradually enfeeble a nation because the government has the power to burden future taxpayers. This certainly appears to be a case of intellectual history repeating itself, but the story is not finished yet. . . . Surprisingly, the state of the theoretical debate seems to remain much as Ricardo left it in 1821.[11]

Even if the subject is still controversial, there is one inescapable change from views of this issue a decade ago. As stated, borrowed deficits are now thought to have much less—and probably very little—effect on aggregate demand or aggregate supply than was formerly believed.

TABLE 25-2 Expenditures of a Hypothetical Individual with or Without Equivalence

The first column shows how the individual spends his or her income of $30,000 under the current state of affairs. The individual's income can be divided into three general categories: consumption, saving, and taxes. The debate over the Ricardian equivalence theorem then asks the hypothetical question: What if government spending does not change, but the government lowers taxes and borrows the money to make up for the forgone taxes? The second column shows the answer if the equivalence theorem is true. The person's taxes go down by $1,000, and saving increases by $1,000 to offset the lower present taxes and higher future taxes triggered by the deficit spending. Consumption remains unchanged. The hypothetical example illustrates the equivalence theorem in action.

The third column shows the result that Ricardo thought would be more likely if debt finance were used instead of taxation. The individual's income remains unchanged, and taxes are lowered as they were in the second column, but in the third column the individual does not save all the reduction in taxes. Saving goes up by only $200 in this example, and consumption rises by $800. In this case, financing by taxes and financing by debt are not equivalent because debt finance causes consumption to rise. Individuals do not save for their future higher taxes but, instead, use the money from lower taxes primarily for consumption.

	Original Position	Taxes Lowered by $1,000 and Borrowed by Government	
		Equivalence	*Partial Adjustment*
Consumption	$20,000	$20,000	$20,800
Saving	2,000	3,000	2,200
Taxes	8,000	7,000	7,000
Total Income	$30,000	$30,000	$30,000

Source: Randall G. Holcombe, "Deficits, Savings, and Capital Formation," *Economic Review,* Federal Reserve Bank of Atlanta, August 1982, pp. 39–41. Caption is adapted from 39–41.

FIGURE 25-4 Public Debt as a Percentage of GNP, 1790–1985

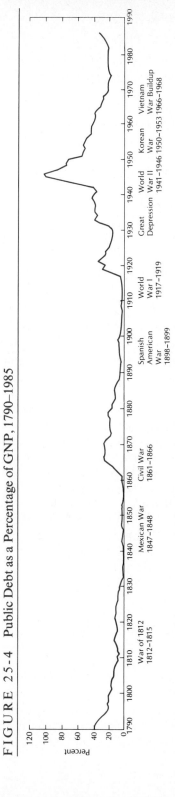

Wartime financing increased the ratio of government debt to gross national product.

Source: James R. Barth and Stephen O. Morrell, "A Primer on Budget Deficits," *Economic Review*, Federal Reserve Bank of Atlanta, August 1982, pp. 12–13, updated.

CAN DEFICITS BE CONTINUALLY FINANCED BY BORROWING?

U.S. government outlays and the federal deficit, which increased after the mid-1970s, have continued at historically high peacetime levels, as shown in Figure 25-5. There is some concern that these growing budget totals may injure the economy, leading to an interesting debate about whether large deficits (net of interest payments on the debt) will destabilize the economy.[12] The debate is over whether or not the economy can reach a stable equilibrium if the government continues to finance its spending through borrowing rather than money creation. How rapidly can the government's debt grow before it will have to resort to printing money? To understand part of the problem, consider the interest payments on the government debt. The interest payments grew from $19.3 billion (or 10 percent of general outlays) in 1970 to $178.9 billion (or nearly 19 percent of federal outlays) in 1985. Can the government continue to spend more than it collects and finance the deficit by borrowing, that is, continue to run up the national debt?

To answer this question, suppose that the government is spending more than it collects in taxes plus the "revenue" it collects from inflation. (The inflation tax is a tax on money held by the public when inflation lowers the value of the money that the government has printed and used to buy goods and services from the public.) Michael Darby argued that there can be a stable debt-to-income ratio (he used the ratio of debt to net national product) if the output (that is, real income for the economy) grows more rapidly than does the after-tax real interest rate. If the interest rate, net of taxes that the government collects, is lower than the growth rate of real income, the government can borrow enough to make the interest payments. This borrowing will not increase the ratio of government debt to output. Darby maintains that this is the case because the after-tax real interest rate generally is less than the rate of growth of output.

Suppose, alternatively, that the after-tax interest rate is higher than the growth rate of output. Then if the government borrows to make interest payments on its debt, the interest payments will rise faster than real private income will. If the government keeps running deficits net of interest payments on the debt that it is financing by borrowing, it must continue to pay more interest. If the increase in the interest payment is greater than is the increase in output, the ratio of government debt to income will grow without limit. This situation occurs when the after-tax interest rate that the government must pay on its debt is greater than the rate of growth of output. Preston Miller and Thomas Sargent hold that this will be the case sooner or later if the government continues to run a deficit that it will have to finance by increasing the monetary base. They pointed out that the current monetary and fiscal policies can cause a change in the difference between the real growth rate and the real interest rate. Miller and Sargent also claimed that the estimates of this difference that Darby used do not take this into account, especially the probability

FIGURE 25-5 U.S. Government Outlays, Deficit, Revenues, and Debt Financing as a Percentage of GNP, 1960–1985

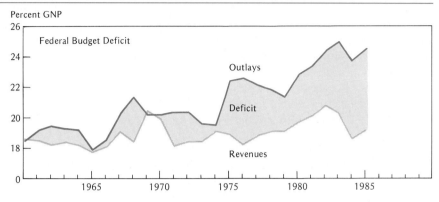

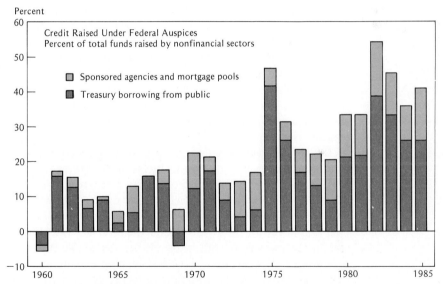

U.S. government outlays and the federal deficit, which increased after the mid-1970s, have continued at historically high peacetime levels. The stock market crash of October 19, 1987, was attributed in part to concern that these growing budget totals might injure the economy. Interest payments on the debt grew from 10 percent of outlays in 1970 to nearly 19 percent in 1985.

Source: Federal Reserve Bank of Cleveland, *Economic Trends*, December 1985, p. 14.

of a higher interest rate that will be partly determined by a rising ratio of government bonds to the monetary base. Miller and Sargent pointed out that since 1980 the real interest rate has risen relative to the real growth rate of output in the face of historically unprecedented peacetime government deficits. Clearly, the answer to this debate has not been resolved.

Printing money to finance a deficit furthermore imposes an inflationary tax on cash balances that reduces the real value of workers' money holdings. This may reduce their incentive to work—if they keep their savings partly in this form—as does a tax directly on their wages. Borrowing to finance deficits may, at least temporarily, raise real interest rates, reducing investment, as does a direct tax on the returns from investment. Concentrating only on the supply-side effects of one form of financing, that is, taxation, is as incomplete as is concentrating on the effects of only one form of financing in analyzing the effects on aggregate demand. An example of such a concentration and some of the problems of that type of analysis follows in the appendix.

APPENDIX: SUPPLY-SIDE ECONOMICS— THE EFFECTS OF NEGLECTING FINANCING TRANSACTIONS

One view of supply-side economics allows a good way to summarize the errors in analyzing the financing of government expenditures.

Supply-side economics is the term used to cover the study of ways to increase the supply of goods and services. Suggestions range from eliminating frictions (such as lack of information about job openings) in the labor market and providing training to improve the labor force to ways of increasing real investment. These suggestions for the labor market would increase the number and the hours of the people employed, and they would also increase their productivity (their output per hour of work).

One of the ideas popularized by Ronald Reagan in his successful campaign for the presidency in 1980 and in the first year of his administration (1981) concerned the supply-side effects of tax rates. It was held that lower tax rates would rapidly increase the incentive to work and invest. Economists have long believed that a wedge between labor costs and take-home wages or between the rate of return on investing and the after-tax rate of return was related to the incentive to work and invest.[13] (See the wedge theories in Chapter 20.) It was, however, generally believed that changes in tax rates (over the entire economy) would take a long time to have a substantial impact on employment and real investment. The reasons for the long time lag include the costs of adjustment (workers do not immediately run out and bargain for more work because of a moderate change in income tax rates). Real investment requires considerable planning plus the assurance that the tax rate change is a long-term one. These kinds of long-term adjustments are found in the average two-year lag for the effects of money supply changes on the price level in the post–World War II period in the United States.

The supply-siders of the Reagan era did more than spur useful additional research into the effects of changes in tax rates. They popularized a view of what they claimed was a rapid response to tax rate reductions. That response would keep the government deficit from rising because of a tax rate reduction.

As will be seen, that result requires an instant response and does not apply to nominal tax revenues.

The supply-siders who came to prominence during the Reagan administration were widely viewed as incorporating their tax rate hypothesis in a diagram called the *Laffer curve*. It was reportedly first drawn in 1974 in a Washington, D.C., restaurant by Arthur Laffer, an economist. Arthur Laffer and his curve became famous. The curve appeared in the media, was incorporated into some introductory economics books in the early 1980s, and was heralded as an insightful summary of the effects of tax rate changes on total tax revenues.

The Laffer curve, shown in Figure 25-6, is explained as follows: At a tax rate of 100 percent, no income will be produced, and total tax revenues will be zero. Likewise, at a tax rate of zero, total tax revenues will be zero as well. Between these two tax rates is a range of tax revenues with a maximum at *OR* below point *M* on the Laffer curve. The supply-siders claim that tax rates were so high in 1980 that they were above point *M* on the Laffer curve (Figure 25-6). A rise in tax rates above *M* would reduce tax revenues. Income would decline under the burden of higher tax rates, and tax revenues would decline. Therefore, tax rates should be lowered. Tax revenues would then increase, and the nominal deficit would be smaller.

Assume that from a position of a balanced budget, tax rates—but not government expenditures—are reduced. If the average tax rate is 20 percent, nominal income must instantly rise by five times the nominal deficit expendi-

FIGURE 25-6   The Laffer Curve

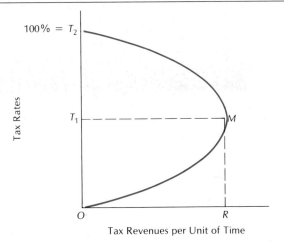

Tax Revenues per Unit of Time

The Laffer curve shows that at a tax rate of zero, no tax revenues will be collected. At a tax rate of T_2, 100 percent of all income will be taxed so that there is no incentive to produce income in the private sector. Income will fall to zero, and no tax revenue will be collected. At a tax rate of T_1, the maximum amount of tax revenue will be collected.

ture to keep the tax revenues from decreasing. For example, if the deficit expenditure is $100 billion, nominal income must instantly rise by at least $500 billion so that the tax revenues of 20 percent of $500 billion will raise enough revenues to cover the nominal deficit.

Certain types of tax responses are quite rapid. Individuals in high income brackets respond to large tax rate reductions by coming out of their tax shelters because they find it more profitable to switch into taxable assets. There was some evidence of this in the middle 1960s. They could switch, for example, from tax-free municipal bonds to taxable corporate bonds that pay a higher rate of interest. But even this effect is not immediate.

It must be immediate, or the Laffer curve is misspecified. The Laffer curve cannot be viewed correctly as a relationship showing the effects of one variable—tax rate changes—on revenue, holding other variables constant. The monetary base identity (or government budget constraint) developed in Chapter 15 shows that if the deficit changes at all, other variables in the identity must change simultaneously. Once the financing transactions come into play, their effects on real and nominal income must be taken into account. As the analysis and evidence in this chapter indicate, those financing transactions are a major area of study in modern macroeconomics, and recent evidence shows that borrowed deficits have little impact on real income. The Laffer curve leaves all that out and is, therefore, badly misspecified.

In addition, the level of employment and real investment, which lower tax rates stimulate, are real variables associated with *real* income. Tax revenue depends on *nominal* income. Nominal tax revenues can rise with inflation if the tax rates rise, fall (within a given range), or stay constant. The shape of the Laffer curve is, therefore, not specified unless the determinants of nominal income are specified. Nominal income is equal to real income times the price level. To discover the connection between a reduction in income tax rates and nominal tax revenues, one must analyze how real income and the price level are affected. The Laffer curve did not provide a theory of the price level. Therefore, there was no bridge between tax rate cuts and nominal tax revenues. *The nominal Laffer curve never existed.* At best it can be said to be a relationship between income tax rate reductions and real tax revenues; but even here it can be faulted on the basis of the problems discussed previously.

To understand how price level changes might affect nominal tax revenues, consider a large nominal deficit that results from a reduction in income tax rates. Suppose that money creation is used to finance the deficit. After the adjustment period between the increase in the money supply and its effect on the price level, a higher price level would mean higher nominal income and higher nominal tax revenues.

A rapid rise in the money supply can cause a rise in nominal tax revenues as prices and nominal income rise, even if tax rates remain constant. That is, the rise in inflation and nominal income will put individuals into higher tax rate brackets under the progressive income tax schedule used in the United States.

But the supply-siders of the Reagan era sidestepped the advent of much larger deficits following the 1981 tax rate reduction, saying that their ideas would have worked with a gold standard, described in Part Nine.

STUDY QUESTIONS

1. Trace through the effect of a government expenditure, using the Keynesian cross diagram, with each of the following types of financing for government expenditures: (a) borrowing, (b) money creation, and (c) tax increases.
2. What is the neutrality hypothesis?
3. What is the equivalence theorem?
4. What is the evidence regarding the effect of a borrowed deficit?
5. What is crowding in?
6. What is crowding out?
7. What did David Ricardo think about the equivalence theorem?
8. What are inside and outside bonds?
9. How is saving affected by a borrowed deficit? State your assumptions carefully, and give alternative views.
10. How is the real rate of interest affected by the deficit financed by new money issue?
11. Can small changes in real interest rates have much effect on real investment? Explain.
12. Do tax revenues depend directly on real or nominal income? Will a policy to induce hours of work increase tax revenues? Explain. (What if nominal income declines?)
13. What is the burden of the national debt? What connection do these considerations have for the effects of a borrowed deficit?

GLOSSARY

Bequest wealth or assets. Wealth held for heirs.

Crowding in. An increase in real private investment induced by government expenditure that raises expectations of improved economic conditions.

Crowding out. A decline in the quantity of real private investment, caused by a rise in real rates of interest that results from govern-ment bond sales to the public.

Equivalence theorem. A theorem that states that government bond sales are equivalent to current taxes in their effect on real saving caused by the complete discounting of all future tax liabilities from the payments on the bonds into the present value of the population's net wealth valuations.

Inside bonds. Bonds issued by and

held by individuals or private corporations in the domestic economy.

National debt. The value of the federal government's outstanding debt.

Neutrality hypothesis. The view that government bond sales (or purchases) to the public have no effect on real rates of interest.

Outside bonds. Bonds issued by entities outside the private sector, such as the government and foreign bond issuers.

NOTES

1. However, the income velocity of money (M-1) dropped by 4.8 percent in 1982. The phasing out of effective ceiling rates on deposits will tend to reduce velocity.

2. If government bonds are considered outside bonds, what will happen to the real rate of interest as a result of a purchase of these bonds from the public? This is part of a protracted but stimulating discussion in the academic literature. The discussion began with an article by the late Lloyd A. Metzler, "Wealth, Saving, and the Rate of Interest," *Journal of Political Economy*, April 1951, pp. 93–116. Robert A. Mundell extended Metzler's work in "The Public Debt, Corporate Income Tax, and the Rate of Interest," *Journal of Political Economy*, December 1960, pp. 622–626. These two articles were followed by a number of papers, including that by John Wood, "Metzler on Classical Interest Theory," *American Economic Review*, March 1980, pp. 135–148. Wood holds that Metzler's results improperly rely on bond trading at disequilibrium prices. Wood's bibliography (pp. 147–148) is a good reading list for this subject.

3. The liability is a claim from bondholders against future taxpayers.

4. "The 'Crowding Out' Controversy: Arguments and Evidence," *Economic Review*, Federal Reserve Bank of Atlanta, August 1982, pp. 34–35.

5. Robert J. Barro, "Are Government Bonds Net Wealth?" *Journal of Political Economy*, November–December 1974, pp. 1095–1117.

6. Lawrence J. Kotlikoff and Lawrence H. Summers, "The Role of Intergenerational Transfers in Aggregate Capital Accumulation," *Journal of Political Economy*, August 1981, p. 730.

7. Quotation is from Gerald P. Dwyer, Jr., "Is Inflation a Consequence of Government Debt?" *Economic Review*, Federal Reserve Bank of Atlanta, August 1982, pp. 22–30. Parts of Dwyer's footnotes 15 and 17 follow: Levis A. Kochin, "Are Future Taxes Anticipated by Consumers?" *Journal of Money, Credit and Banking*, Vol. 6, August 1974, pp. 385–394; J. Ernest Tanner, "Fiscal Policy and Consumer Behavior," *Review of Economics and Statistics*, Vol. 61, May 1979, pp. 317–321, and "Empirical Evidence on the Short-Run Real Balance Effect in Canada," *Journal of Money, Credit and Banking*, Vol. 2, November 1970, pp. 473–485; John J. Seater, "Are Future Taxes Discounted?" unpublished paper, September

1980; J. Walter Elliot, "Wealth and Wealth Proxies in a Permanent Income Model," *Quarterly Journal of Economics*, Vol. 95, November 1980, pp. 509–535; William H. Buiter and James Tobin, "Debt Neutrality: A Brief Review of Doctrine and Evidence," in George M. von Furstenberg, ed., *Social Security Versus Private Saving* (Cambridge, Mass.: Ballinger, 1979); and Martin J. Feldstein, "Government Deficits and Aggregate Demand," *Journal of Monetary Economics*, Vol. 9, January 1982, pp. 1–20. There are three studies based on international data, but the results are conflicting and of little value because of poor data. See Martin J. Feldstein, "International Differences in Social Security and Saving," *Journal of Public Economics*, Vol. 14, October 1980, pp. 225–244, and "Social Security and Private Savings," in Martin J. Feldstein and Robert P. Inman, eds., *The Economics of Public Services* (London: Macmillan, 1977); and Robert J. Barro and Glenn M. MacDonald, "Social Security and Consumer Spending in an International Cross Section," *Journal of Public Economics*, Vol. 11, June 1979, pp. 275–589.

8. Randall G. Holcombe, "Deficits, Savings, and Capital Formation," *Economic Review*, Federal Reserve Bank of Atlanta, August 1982, p. 42. Bruno Sakak, then my student, ran a number of tests on quarterly estimates for recent periods up to 1984 of the real and nominal deficit, and real and nominal interest rates that uniformly showed no correlation.

9. David Ricardo, *The Principles of Political Economy* (London: J. M. Dent, 1912; originally published in 1821).

10. Holcombe, "Deficits, Savings, and Capital Formation," p. 41.

11. Ibid., pp. 39–41. References are made to the following: John Maynard Keynes, *The General Theory of Employment, Interest, and Money* (New York: Harcourt Brace, 1936); Abba P. Lerner, "The Burden of the National Debt," in *Income, Employment, and Public Policy* (New York: W. W. Norton, 1948); James M. Buchanan, *Public Principles of Public Debt* (Homewood, Ill.: Richard D. Irwin, 1958); and Robert J. Barro, "Are Government Bonds Net Wealth?" *Journal of Political Economy*, Vol. 82, November–December 1974, pp. 1095–1117. See, for example, James M. Buchanan, "Barro on the Ricardian Equivalence Theorem," *Journal of Political Economy*, Vol. 84, April 1976, pp. 337–342; and Martin Feldstein, "Perceived Wealth in Bonds and in Social Security," *Journal of Political Economy*, Vol. 84, April 1976, pp. 331–336.

12. This debate is discussed in the Federal Reserve Bank of Minneapolis, *Quarterly Review*, Winter 1985. See especially Thomas J. Sargent, "Some Unpleasant Monetarist Arithmetic," pp. 15–31; Michael R. Darby, "Some Pleasant Monetarist Arithmetic," pp. 32–37; and Preston J. Miller and Thomas J. Sargent, "A Reply to Darby," pp. 38–43.

13. For views of this issue, see *The Supply-Side Effects of Economic Policy*, Proceedings of the 1980 Economic Policy Conference, cosponsored by the Center for the Study of American Business and the Federal Reserve Bank of St. Louis, May 1981, p. 83.

CHAPTER 26

KEYNESIANS VERSUS MONETARISTS

CHAPTER PREVIEW

Introduction. The general views of the monetarists and the antimonetarists are described.

Big Models Versus Little Models. Monetarists generally prefer smaller models.

Interest Rates and Monetary Aggregates. Monetarists emphasize target ranges for the monetary aggregates; many nonmonetarists emphasize control of interest rates.

Who's Who and the Truth. In 1979, views on monetary policy were widely shared.

Attacks in 1982 and 1983 on Monetarism and Keynesianism. The perception of monetarism changed in the 1982 recession. Keynesian policies were also criticized.

The 1980–1986 Evidence Appears to Contradict Monetarists' Theory. A number of changes in macroeconomic variables in the 1980s seemed to contradict monetarist analysis. Some explanations for the changes in velocity (presented in Chapter 18) are consistent with monetarist analysis, but even the monetarists generally failed to use these explanations to predict the phenomena.

Appendix: Some Theoretical Positions Illustrated by IS–LM Loci. The *IS–LM* analysis of Chapter 23 can be used to illustrate some monetarist and Keynesian theoretical positions.

INTRODUCTION

The field of money and banking is sometimes characterized as having two views, the monetarist and the nonmonetarist, or Keynesian. It certainly makes good press and convenient cataloging to be able to group experts and their views into two neat camps. But are there really two such camps? The answer is that there are many camps, some of which are labeled as monetarist, but it is difficult to explain how they differ. Even the leading economists in the United States have tried and failed to persuade one another how they precisely differ.

There is a group labeled monetarists who generally hold the following views:

1. Sustained nominal money growth that is more rapid than the long-run growth of output cannot be offset by continuous adjustments in velocity or short-run adjustments in output. The purchasing power of each unit of money will fall. The adjustment process was slow with the moderate rates of inflation in the United States between 1946 and 1978. That is, it took two to three years for money growth to have a full impact on the price level. With more rapid inflation, the adjustment is more rapid.

2. A sustained change in nominal money growth affects real output in the same direction, three to nine months later, but these effects are largely offset by real output changes over a longer run. For this reason, attempts to reduce short-run unemployment with fast money growth will have moderate short-run success at the expense of increased rates of long-run inflation. A return to price stability will require a much more severe period of monetary restraint and higher unemployment than would occur under the monetary rule.

3. It is difficult to predict the length of the lag between the implementation and the effects of monetary policy. Also, given our present knowledge, there is no way to forecast accurately the state of the economy two to three years in advance. Therefore, attempts to offset future price level movements with present changes in the money supply are likely to produce increased variability in the price level. This "fine tuning" is undesirable. A monetary rule, with the money supply growing at a rate geared to the long-run growth of output (say around 2 percent for M-1), would produce more long-run stability in the price level (and real output) than would occur under a policy of "fine tuning" (offsetting even minor disturbances) or a more stable counter-cyclical policy (offsetting only expected sustained and significant disturbances).

   There is the implication here that monetarists believe the private sector is essentially stable.[1] That is, it will not have long swings in the rate of inflation with a monetary rule in force.

4. Fast money growth first reduces nominal interest rates (the *liquidity effect*)—although the length of that effect has at times been negligible—and then raises nominal interest rates (the *price expectations effect*). (See Chapter 19.)

5. Fast money growth causes high nominal interest rates, via the Fisher effect reviewed in Chapter 19. This view is gaining wider acceptance and is no longer (after the 1977–1980 experience of rapid money growth and high nominal interest rates) a distinguishing factor. Nonmonetarists, however, give much more weight to movements in the real rate of interest than do monetarists.

Karl Brunner coined the term *monetarist*. Allan Meltzer and Karl Brunner founded the Shadow Open Market Committee, a private group that gives its view on open market operations and is also labeled monetarist. The late Robert Weintraub was influential and effective in promoting monetarist views in Congress. He had major responsibility in both the House and Senate Banking Committees for developing a joint resolution (House Concurrent Resolution 133) and part of a law (Federal Reserve Reform Act of 1977) that set up reporting requirements for the Federal Reserve. This law directed that long-run money growth be geared to the long-run growth of output. (This subject is discussed in Part VIII.) Milton Friedman, a Nobel Prize winner, is the dean of the monetarists, author of a large collection of books and articles, many written with Anna Schwartz, also a renowned monetarist. Friedman taught at the University of Chicago (1941–1977), where he led (and still leads) a school of thought known as the Chicago School. It is identified with monetarism and conservative political beliefs.

Monetarists may blame Keynes's theories for encouraging countries to inflate by running deficits financed by new money issue in order to carry out the basic policy message of *The General Theory*, "demand management," with fiscal policies. Nevertheless, there is no easy way to separate monetarists from others on the basis of a theoretical model. Indeed, monetarists sometimes use the Keynesian *IS–LM* device to make their points, and they certainly draw on many of the valuable contributions made by Keynes. Still, the division is frequently made, as the title of this chapter suggests, between the monetarists and the Keynesians. Those are the more familiar labels. A more accurate classification is *monetarist* and *nonmonetarist*, as many nonmonetarists do not consider themselves to be Keynesians.

TWO POINTS OF POLITICAL CLARIFICATION

Two points of clarification about the monetarists' political views were suggested to me.

1. The advocacy of conservative beliefs is not a necessary component of monetarist ideas, such as the monetarist view that money supply growth should be fairly con- stant. A government that does not have conservative beliefs, such as a socialist or communist government, can adopt such a monetary policy. (For example, China has indicated that it has adopted a monetary policy that could be described as consistent with the "monetarists' rule" for steady mon-

etary growth.) It would be interesting to discover how these governments would handle the implication that the private sector is essentially stable, or the view of James Tobin, a critic of monetarism, that monetarism reveals a preference for minimizing the public sector. It is likely that no such implications are acknowledged.

These considerations lead to an interesting question for further consideration after the reader has read the descriptions of monetarism and the critics' arguments against monetarism. Does monetarism imply a particular political viewpoint? In particular, does it imply a libertarian viewpoint?

2. *Libertarian* rather than *conservative* is the name preferred by many Chicago School proponents for their political beliefs. This is because in the 1800s, the label conservative was given to those who advocated the maintenance or increase of central government control of the economy, and the liberal label was attached to those who wanted free markets and more individual and less government control of economic decision making. The labels were switched in the current century, with the name conservative applied to those who want greater emphasis on free markets, the price system, and individual decision making. Another reason that many proponents of the Chicago School do not want to be called conservatives is that the label conservative has been applied to what may be called *social conservatives*. Social conservatives want more government intervention in areas where libertarians would argue for nonintervention by the government. For example, one area is the banning of books that teach what social conservatives consider to be immoral.

Describing the nonmonetarist views is a much more difficult task. One cannot point to the University of Chicago as the center of the monetarist school of thought and then try to define the rest of the world as nonmonetarist. Friedman is now in California at the Hoover Institution, and other well-known monetarists are in many other places. Meanwhile, back at the University of Chicago and other places, a new school of monetary economics has developed.[2] Defining all other views would lead to some rather vacuous generalities. Instead, our attention will be confined here to some *antimonetarist* views.

1. Countercyclical monetary policy is rational and essential. In the case of major changes in the economy, it would increase the stability of both the price level and real income to change monetary policy to offset business cycle fluctuations, rather than slavishly to follow a rule. Franco Modigliani has been an especially strong supporter of this view.[3] Nobel laureate Paul Samuelson summarized this view as follows:

> It is not fine tuning that I am after. Minor short term movements will not bulk large in my welfare indicator, and I dare say that much of such Brownian movements [random changes] are irreducible. But often, I believe, the prudent man or prudent committee can look ahead six months to a year and with some confidence predict that the economy will be in other than an average or "ergodic" state [the

average over time of a series tends to equal, via the mean square rule of law of large numbers, a fixed expected value]. Unless this assertion of mine can be demolished, the case for a fixed growth rate for M, or for confining M to narrow channels around such a rate, melts away.[4]

2. Monetarists overemphasize the long-run alleviation of inflation with slow rates of money growth, while failing to take adequately into account the extremely high costs of the resulting recession. Keynesians (as in the Keynesian *IS–LM* model) place more emphasis on the short run. Keynes's famous statement that we all are dead in the long run emphasized this point. James Tobin, a leading theoretician who has made many contributions to monetary theory and who is one of the most critical antimonetarists, stated this view of monetarist preferences:

   > Distinctive monetarist policy recommendations stem less from theoretical or even empirical findings than from distinctive value judgments. The preferences revealed consistently in those recommendations are for minimizing the public sector and for paying a high cost to stabilizing prices.[5]

3. Velocity is a "catchall" for everything that happens in the economy outside changes in the money supply. It cannot be relied on to remain stable or to return to a trend.
4. There is a two-way causation between MV and Py in the monetary identities. Joan Robinson, a renowned British economist, claimed that monetarists emphasize $MV \rightarrow Py$ when it is the other way around. Money is a passive variable and not a discretionary policy tool.
5. The monetarist view is an oversimplification of a complex economy with many structural problems and money market frictions that influence the price level and output and are largely unrelated to changes in the money supply. The wedge theories and the markup theory of inflation discussed in Chapter 20 are two examples of a broad array of views of this type, extending all the way to a disavowal of all conventional macroeconomic analysis.

These are general differences of opinion that do not universally apply to every monetarist or antimonetarist. From a more rigorous standpoint—differences in theoretical analysis—there is no consensus on the precise distinctions between monetarists and nonmonetarists. Two excellent published debates in 1974, with a number of leading experts participating, failed to find distinguishing theoretical differences that participants would agree were the differences that divided them.[6]

BIG MODELS VERSUS LITTLE MODELS

Monetarists prefer to use smaller models, whereas many nonmonetarists use very large models. This choice can be explained by the methods that monetarists employ. They often begin with large aggregates and then analyze their effects on smaller sectors. Some nonmonetarists who use larger models prefer to begin with small sectors and combine their effects to predict aggregate changes. Perhaps a more basic explanation for this difference in approach is the following: Some monetarists may believe that the effect of the money supply on the price level is, in the large models, crowded into insignificance by being included with a long "laundry list" of other variables that influence prices. Because the influence of a variable in a model depends partly on what is left for it to explain after the effects of other variables are accounted for, there is the possibility of arbitrarily reducing the influence of a variable. The large modelers would reply that of course, money is not the only or even the most important influence on the price level in each and every inflationary episode. It is essential also to have all the other variables that influence prices in the model.

INTEREST RATES AND MONETARY AGGREGATES

Monetarists emphasize target ranges for the control of the monetary aggregates. Many nonmonetarists regard control of interest rates by open market operations as a more desirable objective. Once it is realized that changes in monetary aggregates affect interest rates and that a monetary policy that targets interest rates may produce a desired money supply growth (as noted in Chapter 17), much of this argument is seen to depend less on differences in theory than on application.

It is true, however, that nonmonetarists often put less emphasis on money as a distinct financial asset separate from credit (loan instruments). By influencing interest rates, they contend that a broader spectrum of financial assets can be affected by monetary policy. However, the analytical distinctions in these two positions are hazy. Because the interest rates of a number of assets are included in many monetarist models, any doctrinal emphasis on money relative to other assets may be lost. In other words, both use theoretical models that are often nearly identical in their treatment of the yields on different assets.

Perhaps a more important distinction is that monetarists believe that monetary aggregates are distinct and unique variables that can be controlled by central bank policies. Some nonmonetarists believe that such control is largely futile and that the money supply is a passive variable that adjusts along with a much broader range of financial assets. Any attempt by the central bank to interfere, by not allowing the money supply to grow or contract along with these other assets or along with the business cycle, will cause intolerable distortions or the invention of substitutes for the conventional money supply. One aspect of this view, with respect to advice given to the U.S. Congress, is that it seems to surface mostly when money growth is slow.

In line with these preferences, monetarists call monetary policy "tight" or "loose," depending on the rate of growth of the nominal money supply. A rapid rate of change in the nominal money supply is "loose." But when non-monetarists use those terms, they often are referring to high or low nominal interest rates, respectively.

WHO'S WHO AND THE TRUTH

The distinction between the views of the monetarists and the Keynesians or all nonmonetarists is much less clear than was the case for the Hatfields and the McCoys. It is often difficult to tell from the labels which way the monetarists and the nonmonetarists are shooting. For example, in the first part of 1979, many economists labeled as monetarists thought the money supply was growing too slowly, that it might cause a recession, which characteristically results in fast money growth by the Federal Reserve. Conversely, many economists labeled as nonmonetarists and some monetarists thought the money supply was growing too rapidly. They looked at all the near-money substitutes and brisk credit expansion. These positions were opposite to the ones expected from these two groups. Paul Samuelson said it reminded him of a concert pianist whose hands crossed on the keyboard.

An example of the difficulty in knowing which school of thought was on which side occurred before the Banking Committee of the U.S. House of Representatives in 1979. The monetary policy hearings before that committee had two witnesses from different camps, Professors Karl Brunner and Lester Thurow. There was anticipation of a heated debate on how fast the money supply should grow. In reply to Chairman Henry Reuss, Professor Brunner agreed that a gradual slowing down of the rate of growth in the money supply would be desirable. "That indeed goes in the direction toward which I and my friends are looking. . . ."[7] Later in the hearing Chairman Reuss asked Professor Thurow if he was in agreement:

> Turning to a more cosmic subject, it is indeed fortunate for this Committee that we have an eminent monetarist and an eminent non-monetarist ranged side by side here. This Committee always grasps pathetically at whatever chance there may be to reconcile the apparently inharmonious testimony of witnesses.
>
> . . . would you sail for your policy of attacking the commanding heights of price increases by direct methods such as you have described? The forms would include fiscal policy among them, and also you would make a proprietary bow towards the monetarists by saying "alright, Dr. Friedman, Dr. Brunner and the business community and the banking community, as far as that goes we will sail for a Federal Reserve statement backed by the Administration of M-1 targeted growth for 1979 of 6 percent as the Federal Reserve suggests."
>
> Good fellow that you are, would you go for that?[8]

Professor Thurow answered that he favored a number of structural reforms and that "talking about M-2, that you have to have some modest, slow deceleration in the rate of growth of M-2 or the money base or whatever you want to look at."[9]

Even James Tobin, who in the past had sharply disagreed with monetarists' positions, supported the Federal Reserve's October 6, 1979, announcement of slower money growth: "The Volcker recession of 1980–82 is a terribly expensive way to restrain the American appetite for imported oil. But with more efficient energy prices not yet in place, the Federal Reserve Chairman, Paul A. Volcker, had little choice."[10]

Despite all the controversy between monetarists and nonmonetarists, as shown in the 1974 debates, there was a broad consensus on monetary policy in the last quarter of 1979. Was this a pinpoint in time of accidental agreement or a sign of a convergence of views on the vital issues of monetary policy?

Apparently each of the various views will not be validated or contradicted by the logic of an economic model. A model can always be constructed to support a position. The models are necessary in setting up experiments that must then meet the test of repeated episodes in the economy. It is these test results that will eventually tell the tale. The facts will not speak for themselves; they will be used to estimate parts of economic models. Perhaps it will take more extreme economic changes than occurred in the 1946–1984 period in the United States to produce persuasive evidence and a convergence of views.

Such was the case in 1979 and 1980 and in the 1930s. The 1979–early 1980 experience of inflation's reaching 20 percent with 20 percent interest rates for several months seemed to bring forth a consensus in favor of a monetarist prescription. Looking from the other camp, the depressions of the 1930s turned Keynes, who had been more monetarist, into a Keynesian. He downplayed the effects of changes in the money supply. For less extreme variations, the jury has not delivered a consensus.

ATTACKS IN 1982 AND 1983 ON MONETARISM AND KEYNESIANISM

The agreement in 1979 on the course of money supply growth appeared as a point in time of accidental agreement in 1982 and 1983. Not only members of the press and representatives of the public in the nation's capital but also many economists attacked monetarism. Some of these economists suggested targets for monetary policy other than the monetary aggregates. This is discussed in the next chapter. There was a divergence of opinion about the correct course for monetary policy. Monetarists had favored a gradual, smooth reduction in monetary growth rates (using three- or six-month averages) to levels of growth consistent with lower rates of inflation or even price stability.

When the money supply grew rapidly in the last half of 1982 and the first five months of 1983 (12.1 percent from August 1982 to May 1983), monetarists indicated their desire for more moderate growth to prevent expectations of more rapid inflation, and thus to allow interest rates to continue falling, and to prevent a new inflation two years later. They also feared that a rapid braking of the monetary growth would cause a new recession. Many monetarists advocated a continuation of faster money growth to reduce more rapidly the high level of unemployment.

In May 1983, Preston Martin, the vice-chairman of the Federal Reserve Board, told Congress that monetary policy would *accommodate* the recovery but that the Federal Reserve would watch for any signs of renewed inflation. Apparently, he planned to lean against the prevailing wind, which at that time was high unemployment.

Nonmonetarists pointed to the severe drop in income velocity in 1982 (4.8 percent for M-1) and said that with millions unemployed, the nation could not afford to take a chance that velocity might remain low. Now was the time for discretionary anticyclical monetary policy. Faster money growth was in order.

Monetarists rejoined that the nation should not pay for the same ground twice, as General Patton had once said. Rapid money growth could rekindle a new round of inflation that would require yet another contraction to stop it. Monetarists thought the low velocity in 1982 could be explained and that velocity would again grow at its previous average rate. (See Chapter 18.) Fast money growth from the middle of 1982 to the middle of 1983 was a product of Federal Reserve policy, they held. It was associated with a rapid increase in the monetary base, a variable the Federal Reserve could control. The monetary base grew at 10.5 percent from the third quarter of 1982 to the second quarter of 1983. They also held that fast money growth would cause nominal interest rates to rise. If nominal interest rates were pushed up by new fears of inflation induced by fast money growth, so too would increased uncertainty push up—or keep from falling—real interest rates. Another recession would be needed two or three years down the road to bring the inflation under control.

The division of opinion was especially severe in 1982 and 1983, when the following three events made many people—including many members of the U.S. Congress and the media—look with disgust on monetarism.

1. Ronald Reagan had campaigned in 1980 and had taken office in 1981 espousing a particular type of supply-side economics—the Laffer curve type of analysis described in the last chapter—and monetarism—a gradual slowdown in monetary policy to disinflationary levels. Reagan stated that tax cuts would be beneficial for the country in restoring the incentive to work and invest. Many economists agreed with this contention. But there was widespread disagreement with the additional claim that tax rate cuts would *reduce* deficits. This led to the prediction that the 1981 tax cut would be primarily responsible for balancing the budget by 1984.

The associated forecast for no recession, even though the money supply would be dramatically slowed and inflation brought down, was even more questionable. It was directly contrary to the evidence from monetary theory regarding the output effect of declines from trends in monetary growth presented in Chapter 19. A large tax bill was passed in 1981. Beryl Sprinkel, a well-known monetarist, was appointed undersecretary for monetary affairs at the U.S. Treasury. Two other undersecretaries were generally known as supply-siders. With the claims that were issued, it appeared that supply-side Laffer curve analysis had won the day, despite the monetarists' opposite views on recession.

A deep recession ensued. Unemployment rates that had hit 7.5 percent during the preceding Carter administration (May 1980) rose to over 10 percent of the civilian work force in September 1982, reaching 10.8 percent in December 1982. The Federal Reserve had slammed the brakes on money growth, holding the growth in M-1 for the six months ending in the week of August 10, 1982, to 1.8 percent and for the three months before August 19, 1982, to only .4 percent (all at annual percentage rates). This slow money growth made the recession worse than it would have been with more stable money growth. It also helped reduce inflationary expectations, causing interest rates to drop sharply. By August 20, 1982, the three-month Treasury bill rate had fallen to 7 percent from nearly 13 percent in June 1982 and 14 percent in February 1982.

The episode was associated with a rash of inaccurate analyses in the media. The dramatic fall in interest rates was held to be the result of a current rumor in financial markets that the Federal Reserve would ease money growth. The theories were buttressed with the observation that the Federal Reserve had lowered its discount rate in August and that this had been a fundamental factor in causing interest rates to decline. They did not take into account that the Federal Reserve was catching up with the decline in rates, which had fallen below the discount rate a month before. The buyers of financial instruments—in a worldwide market—did not change the amount they were willing to pay for these securities because the Federal Reserve had decided to bring its lending rate in line with interest rates. That Federal Reserve action, the announcement by major banks of lower prime rates, and an announcement by Henry Kaufman did have powerful *announcement effects* on the stock markets.

Henry Kaufman, the chief economist at Salomon Brothers, was widely quoted in the media. He had forcefully stated his forecast for higher interest rates on the basis of fiscal policy. On July 19, 1982, he stated

> In any event, *U.S. Treasury* cash needs, for which there is a greater certainty for the next six months starting July 1, are likely to total between $90 billion and $95 billion net. This compares with $58 billion during the same period last year when the economy was in recession. . . .
>
> While the Treasury will surely be financed, the market is not capable of accommodating these needs without higher interest rates and without increasing financial vulnerability of some credit demanders in the private sector. . . . Both short- and long-term interest rates will rise further in the second half of 1982, with long-term interest rates reaching their 1981 highs, while short-term rates will probably fall shy of their previous peaks.[11]

(The effects of financing covered in the last chapter should be consulted. Also, the apparent neglect of the decline in inflationary expectations causing the difference between real rates and nominal rates, described in Chapter 19, is important to understanding this improper interpretation and forecast of this episode.)

Henry Kaufman announced that his predictions of higher interest rates had been wrong and abruptly changed his prediction to lower interest rates on the basis that the economy was weaker than he had anticipated. He criticized the slow-growth monetary policies. During the week of August 16–20, 1982, the stock market surged with record volume and rising prices. The announcement that even Henry Kaufman, who had predicted that interest rates would rise, was now convinced of lower interest rates helped trigger a reaction. But to say that the decline in interest rates was a result of that announcement, the decline in the prime rate, the Federal Reserve's lower discount rate, and the rumor of faster money growth was myopic.

Beginning in August 1982, the money supply grew rapidly. Many individuals took this rapid growth as the reason for the decline in interest rates, although once it began, interest rates stopped falling.

This episode appeared to be the last straw in the toleration of monetarist policies by many people who identified the Reagan administration's policies as monetarist. They had combined the supply-side rhetoric of the administration, which had claimed balanced budgets and no recession, with its intention to reduce monetary growth. The result was seen to be opposite to these claims. The stock market surge and the decline in interest rates were perceived to be due to more rapid money growth and a welcomed departure from monetarism. (The monetarist policies were sometimes given credit for a decline in the rate of inflation.)

2. On October 6, 1979, the Federal Reserve announced that it would change its policies to a more monetarist approach, targeting the monetary aggregates more accurately. Both the money supply and interest rates became more variable. It was widely viewed as a failed experiment.

Monetarists, such as Milton Friedman, believed that the Federal Reserve, despite its announcement, had not changed its methods of monetary control to fit the new objectives:

> The Federal Reserve System, not forces outside its control, is responsible for the yo-yo pattern of monetary growth. It has ample power to produce a more stable pattern of monetary growth. The change in "method" on October 6, 1979 was highly desirable and long overdue. However, it was not accompanied by the changes in detailed procedures and regulations that were required to make that "method" effective.[12]

Those changes in procedures are discussed in Part Eight. As an explanation of the perceived failure of the "monetary experiment," it left many people unimpressed. Details of the Federal Reserve's operating procedures are, to say the least, of little interest to politicians and members of the press. For five years, an effort by a staff economist in Congress to get the Federal Reserve to change from lagged to contemporaneous reserve accounting was endorsed only by Henry Reuss, former chairman of the House Banking Committee. Other members of the Congress who were consulted were mostly still back at the stage of asking, "What do reserve requirements have to do with the money supply?" and "Who cares?"

Several reactions in the press indicate some of the views of this monetarist period. Jude Wanniski, a supply-sider, wrote on October 13, 1982, a *Washington Post* editorial entitled "Monetarism Died Last Week, and the Markets Are Celebrating." As did Congressman Jack Kemp, a leading supply-sider in the Congress, Wanniski blamed the state of the economy on a failed monetarist experiment, and both suggested a return to the gold standard (described in Part Nine).

Wanniski heralded the Federal Reserve's deemphasis of M-1 late in 1982 as the death of monetarism. He asserted

> This does not mean that inflation will soon rear its ugly head. If it did mean that, we would not expect to see declining interest rates and life again in the long-term bond markets. The end of monetarism simply means the end of an experiment with a central-bank quantity target. . . .
>
> The supply siders observe that since the Fed began targeting the money supply three years ago the price of gold—the most monetary of commodities and thus the most sensitive—has swung wildly between $298 and $840, and interest rates have swung widely as well.[13]

Thus, the supply-siders let it be known that the price of gold must be stabilized, an action that would follow the adoption of the gold standard. In the U.S. Congress, the Republican gold standard proponents and supply-sider Kemp were joined by many Democrats in their attack on the Federal Reserve for following monetarist policies. We will discuss shortly several alternatives suggested by some Democrats.

On August 3, 1982, Senator Robert C. Byrd, then the minority leader for the Democrats in the Senate, was joined by many colleagues in a proposal to set monetary policy targets for real interest rates as well as targets for the money supply because the monetarist experiment had failed. The subject of setting real interest rate targets is discussed in the next chapter. Here Byrd's reference to the failed experiment is cited:

> Mr. President, I rise to introduce the Balanced Monetary Policy Act of 1982, legislation which is designed to bring down interest rates and thus to move our Nation out of a tragic and ever-widening recession.
>
> Bold action by Congress is imperative, because the administration has embraced two economic experiments which together have brought our Nation to the brink of depression.
>
> One of these, the "supply side" economic theory, which holds that tax cuts for the wealthy will bring prosperity to all, is now widely recognized as a failure.

The other administration economic policy is less well known, but no less of a disaster. I refer to the administration's support of tight money and high interest rates.

The Federal Reserve Board, in October of 1979, undertook a dramatic and far-reaching policy change. It embraced the monetarist economic theory that reducing the growth of the money supply is the only way to stop inflation. It therefore abandoned any attempt to control interest rates. The assumption was that if the growth of the money supply was sufficiently slowed down, and if interest rates were allowed to float freely, inflation would be halted and in time interest rates would come down on their own. Stripped of all the technical jargon, monetarists believe the only way to stop inflation is to start a recession.

Mr. Reagan, as a candidate for President, wholeheartedly embraced this monetarist dogma. As President, he has repeatedly affirmed his support for the Federal Reserve's tight-money, high-interest rate policy.

Some of us, I must say, had severe doubts about the monetarist theory from the start. On October 19, 1979, only days after the Board adopted this new policy, I said on the Senate floor:

Ultimately, to control inflation we must produce more, not less. Attempting to control inflation or protect the dollar by throwing legions of people out of work and shutting down shifts in our factories and mines is a hopeless policy. . . . The Congress will be watching closely to ensure that the recession of 1974 and 1975 will not be repeated. . . . We will watch with concern the impact of this policy on small businesses which depend on credit markets for financing. We will watch its impact on the construction industry. . . .

Mr. President, we have now seen the results of this experiment with monetarism.

Mr. President, too many innocent lives have already been sacrificed on the "alter of monetarism," too many men, women and children are suffering because of the theories of economic idealogues who do not have to pay the price of their mistakes.[14]

The timing of this speech to bring down interest rates by directing the Federal Reserve to do it without tight money was not good. Following the tight money policies of the Federal Reserve in the first half of 1982, nominal interest rates fell by nearly half in July and August, as noted previously for the Treasury bill rate. In this period, the members of the Congress who had been loudly arguing for faster growth to bring down market interest rates found their arguments demolished by these dramatic economic events. Without missing a step—and unnoticed by much of the public, which is not trained to distinguish nominal from real interest rates—they abruptly changed to real interest rates. Not even Senator Byrd had completely made the change, for his statement shot back and forth between nominal and real interest rates in a muddled manner. For example, he said that high interest rates significantly increase the interest on the national debt. Those are nominal rates that can be perfectly consistent with high or low real interest rates. (Review this point in Chapter 19.)

In the following statement by Senator Byrd, quoting Lester Thurow, the appropriate concept of the interest rate is the real rate of interest, the rate of return on investing:

> Today, high interest rates are "public enemy number one." More than any other single factor, they have caused this present, tragic recession.
>
> The economist Lester Thurow summed up the problem succinctly in a recent *Newsweek* article: "Capitalism, a system where individuals invest today to get more back tomorrow, simply doesn't work with high interest rates and the stagnant business conditions they create."[15]

But Senator Byrd followed this statement by reverting back to nominal (market) interest rates associated with usury ceilings.

> The truth of this proposition is everywhere around us. The administration may choose to hide its head, ostrich-like, in the warm sands of economic dogma, but the rest of us must face the facts. We cannot tolerate these sky-high killer interest rates—rates that until recently would have been considered usurious. Congress must act to bring down these killer interest rates before they bring down our economy and the strength and security of our Nation.[16]

Senator Byrd's bill would also have kept real interest rates from becoming negative:

> The Federal Reserve Board would be required to keep real interest rates positive; that is, interest rates would have to stay above the level of inflation.

This speech thus had elements of ardent outcries against high interest rates and a call for legal restrictions against low interest rates, without carefully separating the nominal and real concepts. Caught with a decline in nominal interest, the critics of monetary policy in the Congress had to keep the campaign going even if the new concept of real interest rates did not technically fit the polemics of the campaign.

In March 1982, Hobart Rowan, a staff writer for the influential *Washington Post*, attacked Milton Friedman and the "monetarist mania created by Friedman and his followers" for making a career of "dumping on the Federal Reserve Board" (although Rowan did allow that Friedman had won the "Nobel award"). The attack, based on data presented by Federal Reserve Chairman Paul Volcker, is especially interesting because Friedman later claimed that Chairman Volcker had the wrong numbers. Rowan said of Friedman,

> Even when confronted with evidence that he may have overstated the case—or God forbid, may actually be wrong—he won't admit it. Federal

Reserve Chairman Paul Volcker, for example, testified before the Senate Banking Committee that there is no "obvious link" between the growth of monetary aggregates and "our current economic problems." If there were, Volcker asks, how come countries whose economic performance we tend to admire—like Japan, Switzerland, and West Germany—have so much wider swings in their rates of monetary growth?

Volcker supplied committee Chairman Jake Garn (R., Utah) with figures for the narrowly defined money supply last year that showed a range between minus and plus 138 points for Japan, 60 points for West Germany, 56 points for Switzerland, and 29.5 points for the United States. The only better record among industrial powers—if stability is some kind of virtue—was Italy (which incidentally had one of the highest inflation rates!).[17]

After an unsuccessful period of trying to obtain these numbers from the Federal Reserve, Friedman was finally given data up to 1979 that showed Volcker's data to be misleading. The Federal Reserve said that more recent data would be costly to obtain, and Friedman decided not to ask the Fed to spend funds to give him comparable data for accurate comparisons between these countries. Instead, he obtained cooperation from the Bank of Japan that supplied comparable data. The results appeared in an article Friedman published in August 1983.[18] He wrote that comparisons had been made with monthly averages for U.S. data against data based on single-date estimates for six foreign countries. This selection of data made the conclusions subject to error, as single-date estimates generally vary more widely than do monthly averages. But this is a statistical property that does not necessarily mean that the U.S. money supply series is more stable.

3. The phaseout of ceiling rates on deposits, described in Chapter 8, produced a hodgepodge of new deposit instruments and regulations. The Federal Reserve said that the rapid increase in the money supply beginning in the last half of 1982 and ending in the middle of 1983 was a result of shifting funds into these new instruments and not a result of their monetary policy. This subject will be discussed in the next chapter.

The result of these forces was a decline in support for what was perceived to be monetarism. There were instead new calls for credit controls to control inflation. This view is captured especially well in the law proposed by Alan Cranston, a Democrat and a U.S. senator. He made the following statement on the floor of the U.S. Senate on May 13, 1982:

Senate Speech on Proposed Low Interest Rate Act

S.2526. A bill to reduce interest rates, control inflation, and insure the availability of credit for productive purposes, and promote economic recovery by extending the Credit Control Act, and for other purposes; to the Committee on Banking, Housing, and Urban Affairs.

Mr. Cranston. Mr. President, I am introducing legislation today to renew the President's authority to act to lower interest rates through the policies and powers of the Federal Reserve Board.

The Low Interest Rate Act which I am introducing on behalf of myself and Senators Riegle, Burdick, Baucus, Ford, and Moynihan, will extend permanently the Credit Control Act of 1969 which is due to expire on June 30, and would strengthen the authority of the President to authorize the Federal Reserve Board to act to lower interest rates and to prescribe limitations on credit for unproductive corporate takeovers and for other generally nonproductive purposes. . . .

One effect of the bill could be to free up more than $70 billion in credit tied up in financing the corporate takeover game which adds nothing to increased productivity.

This credit could be used productively by agriculture, housing, the automotive industry, and other interest rate sensitive sectors of the economy now in a state of depression.

The Credit Control Act, which was enacted in 1969, empowers the President to "authorize the Federal Reserve Board to regulate and control any or all extensions of credit" when he determines that such action is necessary for the purpose of preventing or controlling inflation.

The Low Interest Rate Act would extend the use of Presidential power over credit "to reduce high levels of unemployment in any sector of the economy, or to prevent or control inflation or recession."

The bill permits the Federal Reserve, when authorized to do so by the President, to apply monetary restrictions selectively rather than relying solely on across-the-board tight money which strangles the entire economy. . . .

The Low Interest Rate Act gives the President the authority to tell the Federal Reserve Research to ease up selectively on those sectors of the economy which have been flattened out by high interest rates while at the same time keeping up the pressure against highrolling corporate takeover artists who find it cheaper and easier to merge than to build new assets. . . .

The increasing use of credit for nonproductive purposes is a leading cause of high interest rates. And it is clear that unless rates go down this year there will be widespread failures of major businesses, greater numbers of farm mortgage foreclosures and lengthening unemployment lines. . . .

Interest rates must come down. But the blunderbuss approach of tight money, causing as it does massive business failures and high unemployment, is far, far too costly. There are better ways of bringing down interest rates, all of which must be used if we are to succeed in saving ourselves from an economic disaster.

These include reducing the deficit and enacting a budget which will continue to reduce deficits in future years with a definite downward trend; judicious expansion of the money supply; a planned, phase lowering of interest rates, and limitations on the use of credit for expensive and unproductive corporate takeovers and similar unproductive activities. . . .

I ask unanimous consent that the text of the bill be printed in the *Record* at the conclusion of my remarks.

There being no objection, the bill was ordered to be printed in the *Record*, as follows;

Be it enacted by the Senate and House of Representatives of the United States of America in Congress assembled. That this Act may be cited as the " Low Interest Rate Act of 1982." . . .

Sec. 3. (a) Section 205(a) of the Credit Control Act (12 U.S.C. 1904(a)) is amended to read as follows:

"(a) Whenever the President determines that such action is necessary or appropriate to reduce high levels of unemployment in any sector of the economy, or to prevent or control inflation or recession, the President may authorize the Board to regulate and control any or all extensions of credit. . . .

"(7) prescribe limitations with respect to credit for nonproductive purposes, including corporate takeovers, and otherwise ensure the availability of credit for productive and necessary purposes." . . .[19]

The proposed Low Interest Rate Act is an authority for credit rationing, according to the uses that the central authority deems worthy or productive. If fully implemented, it would require a huge bureaucracy inside the Federal Reserve to monitor credit for millions of people and businesses. Free credit markets would be serverely curtailed. A central tenet of free enterprise, the ability to borrow to open freely a business or to buy one in existence, would be significantly curtailed.

Keynesian policy was also suffering from a loss of confidence because of the large deficit in 1982 and the simultaneous rise in unemployment. The Democratic party supported a return to balanced budgets, long the domain of Republican rhetoric. Many individuals turned from macroeconomic policy suggestions such as Keynesian deficits to stimulate the economy to intervention of the type proposed by Senator Cranston. Calls for expedient solutions are to be expected in a deep recession with millions of people out of work and intense political pressures for solutions. However, the truth or falseness of the principal ideas of macroeconomics—the monetary and macroeconomic theories presented in Parts Five, Six, and Seven—was not affected by this rhetoric.

Those theories will be supported or contradicted by the type of evidence presented in the last chapter. Careful testing by economists of the historical record will throw additional light on the analyses. However, the attitudes reported in this section did have important effects on the nation's policies, and they did bring monetarism and Keynesianism into many individuals' vocabularies as somewhat contemptible beliefs.

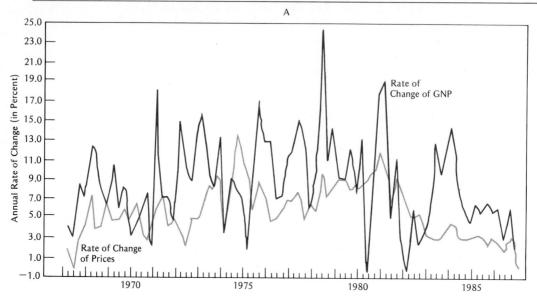

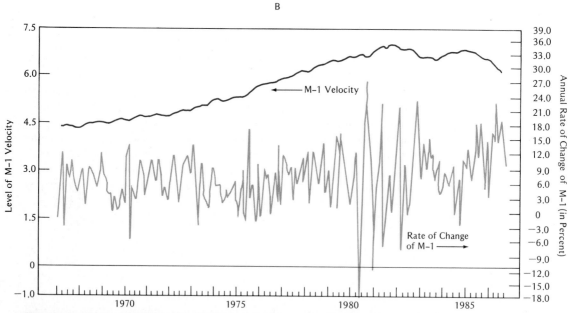

Changes in these variables in the 1980s appeared to contradict monetarist analysis. (1) The roughly 3 percent trend rate of growth in velocity ended after 1980. (2) The money supply spurted, with some twelve-month average growth rates of over 10 percent, whereas the rate of inflation (the rate of change of the GNP deflator) declined. There were some plausible explanations for the changes in velocity (presented in Chapter 18), and the rate of change of GNP was actually more closely associated with prior money

THE 1980–1986 EVIDENCE APPEARS TO CONTRADICT THE MONETARISTS' THEORY

A number of changes in macroeconomic variables in the 1980s, as shown in Figures 26-1 and 26-2, seemed to contradict monetarist analysis:

1. The roughly 3 percent rate of growth in velocity ended after 1980.
2. The money supply spurted, with some twelve-month average growth rates of over 10 percent, whereas the rate of change in prices (the rate of change in the GNP deflator) declined.

Some explanations for the changes in velocity (presented in Chapter 18) are consistent with monetarist analysis, but even the monetarists generally failed to use them. The rate of change in GNP was actually more closely associated with prior money growth in the 1980s than it had been in earlier periods.

The 1983 decline in velocity seemed to contradict the monetarists' analysis. The growth in M-1 velocity had fallen or become negative in each of the recessions shown in Figure 26-1—1970, 1974–1975, 1980, and 1982–1983, as well as in the downturn in 1967. In 1986 money growth surged to twelve-month average rates of over 12 percent, and the economy did not fall into a recession. The unemployment rate ended the year by slightly falling to 6.7 percent. How could the large drop in velocity in 1986 be explained?

These seemingly contradictory changes in macroeconomic variables were seen by many to be a repudiation of monetarism. Many observers believed that the Federal Reserve was correct in implementing fast money growth in the 1983–1986 period to offset the decline in velocity. Milton Friedman stated that the unexpected decline in velocity supported his view that short-run changes in velocity cannot be predicted and that an attempt to do so would create more instability over the longer run than if the rate of growth of the money supply were constant. Nevertheless, the monetarists did not predict the slowdown in velocity, and furthermore, they, including Friedman, made incorrect predictions about the rapid increases in inflation in the 1983–1986 period. Accordingly, many observers saw the apparently contradictory evidence as a clear refutation of monetarist analysis. Frank Morris, president of the Federal Reserve Bank of Boston, wrote:

> The M1/nominal GNP relationship has become even more unpredictable than I anticipated three years ago. In the autumn of 1983, promi-

---

growth in the 1980s than it had been in earlier periods. Nevertheless, the slowdown in velocity caught the monetarists making incorrect predictions about rapid increases in inflation in the 1983–1986 period. Many others saw the evidence as a clear contradiction of monetarist analysis. Twelve-month moving averages are used.

Source: Cambridge Planning and Analytics, Inc., Boston.

FIGURE 26-2   M-1 Velocity and Recessions, M-1 Lagging One Year

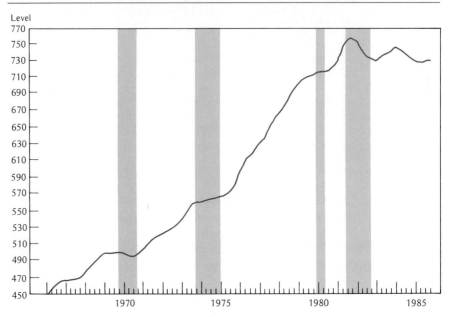

The ratio of current GNP to M-1 one year before is plotted as velocity. The 1983 decline in velocity seemed to contradict the monetarists' analysis. The growth in M-1 velocity (computed in this manner to reflect the major impact of money on GNP) had declined or become negative in each of the recessions shown, 1970, 1974–1975, 1980, and 1982–1983, as well as in the downturn in 1967. Money growth surged in 1986 to twelve-month average rates of over 12 percent, and the economy did not fall into a recession. The unemployment rate ended the year slightly reduced at 6.7 percent. How could the large drop in velocity in 1986 be explained? Some said it was a repudiation of monetarism and that the Federal Reserve was correct in implementing fast money growth to offset the decline in velocity. Milton Friedman said that the unexpected decline in velocity supported his view that short-run changes in velocity cannot be predicted and that an attempt to do so would create more instability over the longer run than if the rate of growth of the money supply were constant.

Source: Cambridge Planning and Analytics, Inc., Boston.

nent monetarist economists forecast that the economy would move into recession in the first half of 1984 and that inflation would accelerate sharply in the second half.[20]

The 1980 experience had apparently torn Morris between the discipline of a rule for controlling money growth, as advocated by the monetarists, and the need to disregard the rule. This view was probably shared by Federal Reserve officials and was expressed by Morris in the list of things he learned from the 1980 experience:

To Sum Up

Asked the question "What have we learned since October 1979?" I would list the following:

1. A targeting procedure for monetary policy has great disciplining values which we should not discard.
2. There is no variable that the Federal Reserve can target which has a highly predictable relationship to the nominal GNP.
3. It is not feasible for monetary policy to focus solely on the price level, since there is no other policy tool available with which to deal with an unexpected weakness in the economy—à la 1982—or unexpected strength.
4. If one accepts the first three propositions, then it follows that the optimum monetary policy regime is one of rules tempered by discretion.
5. I would choose a total liquid assets rule for two reasons: (1) unlike all of the other aggregates its meaning has not been changed by the events of the past 10 years; and (2) if we can no longer measure transaction balances, controlling liquidity is the next best choice.[21]

Morris noted that total liquid assets had "a disastrous year in 1982, when its velocity was 6.5 percent below trend."[22] So in general, not only had Morris regarded the monetarist analysis as grossly wrong; the episode also had played a major role in depleting theoretical support for the conduct of any predictable monetary policy.

The evidence of three years, 1983–1986, is useful but too short to be the basis for strong generalizations. But the reader will soon have more observations on which to base his or her judgment of the analysis presented in Chapter 18 to explain velocity in this period.

APPENDIX: SOME THEORETICAL POSITIONS ILLUSTRATED BY *IS–LM* LOCI

Some of the theoretical differences alleged by participants in the 1974 debates can be illustrated with the *IS–LM* analysis. Although there was no general agreement that these demonstrations identified the "true" differences, they do give much of the flavor of each position.

Friedman believes that the long-run real rate of real interest is fairly stable and is tied to the long-run growth in real output. An extreme version of this position is depicted in Figure 26-3A. This *IS* is horizontal, indicating that a constant real rate of interest clears the expenditure sector at any level of real income. It is also obtained from the so-called open economy case. Suppose that there is perfectly free mobility of investment funds across countries, as

FIGURE 26-3   Three Configurations of *IS* and *LM* in the Keynesian Versus Monetarist Debate

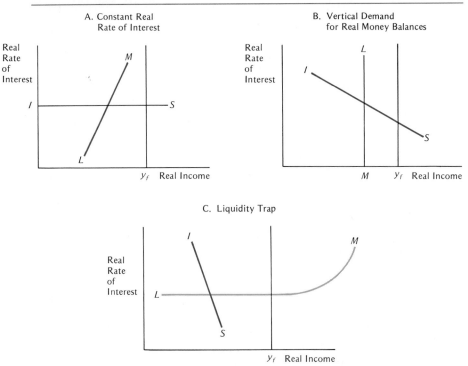

between the United States and Western Europe. There is then a given real rate of interest determined by an area of trade that is larger than the domestic economy. If changes in the *IS* and *LM* loci are not sufficiently powerful to change the world's real interest rates, the interest rate will be fixed, as in the extreme Friedman case. Fiscal policy is impotent; only monetary policy changes real income. Only shifts in the *LM* locus, from changes such as different nominal monetary growth rates or different price levels, can change real income.

Sometimes the monetarist position is alleged to be represented by a vertical (or nearly vertical) *LM* locus, caused by the real money demand's being unresponsive to interest rate changes (meaning that it is vertical). It is a limiting case (see Figure 26-1B). As explained in Chapter 25, this makes monetary policy more potent and fiscal policy less potent. With a perfectly vertical *LM* locus, fiscal deficits raise only the real rate of interest and have no effect on real income.

The limiting case of the Keynesian position is given by the liquidity trap in Figure 26-1C. Here monetary expansion is impotent. Individuals merely hold all additions to the money supply, but there is no new spending. Only fiscal policy will restore full employment, by shifting the *IS* locus.

STUDY QUESTIONS

1. State how monetarists and nonmonetarists differ in their views of (a) nominal and real interest rate changes, (b) big and little models, and (c) countercyclical monetary policy.

2. If there are no fundamental disagreements on the logic of economic analysis, why should there be disagreements between monetarists and nonmonetarists?

3. Describe the monetary policies that would be advocated by monetarists and nonmonetarists during the next twelve months.

4. Demonstrate Keynesian and monetarist views using the *IS–LM* framework.

5. What events transpired during the first years of the Reagan administration that caused monetarism to be viewed as a poor guide for policy? Assess these events.

6. What events in the economy, if any, would cause either monetarism or Keynesian policies to be viewed more favorably? When is a resort to credit controls and wage and price controls likely to occur?

7. Are there benefits or harm in classifying theory under such titles as monetarism and Keynesianism? Would it be better to organize the discussion into monetary theory and expenditure theory, combining the work from many schools of thought?

8. Explain how efficient and free international capital markets can make monetary policy more and fiscal policy less potent. (*Hint:* Review the Friedman and Keynesian extreme versions in the *IS–LM* demonstration in the appendix to this chapter.)

NOTES

1. Karl Brunner and Allan H. Meltzer, two monetarists, state that "the stability of the private sector" is "one of the principal monetarists conjectures," in Jerome L. Stein, ed., *Monetarism* (Amsterdam: North-Holland, 1976), p. 99.

2. The new school of monetary economics is described by Robert Hall, "Monetary Trends in the United States and the United Kingdom: A Review from the Perspective of New Developments in Monetary Economics," *Journal of Economic Literature*, December 1982, p. 1555: "The new school of monetary economics has two cases against the constant growth rule. First, the macroeconomic performance of the policy, while much better than the actual policy of the past century, could be quite a bit better. Second, and more fundamental, the money stock itself is a creature of inefficient regulation. Standard microeconomic principles dictate the deregulation of transactions and intermediation for exactly the same reason they call for free-market policies in other markets like

air travel. But the school is far from united on where to turn for a better monetary policy. Fama (1982) has proposed the application of the money growth rule to currency alone. Black (1981) advocates Irving Fisher's (1920) variable gold standard. Hall (1982) suggests a variable commodity standard not based on gold. Bilson (1981) favors a fiduciary money paying, in effect, market interest rates. All of these proposals share a basic microeconomic goal—full deregulation of transactions services and intermediation. None of them would rely on the concept of a money stock or its stability relative to total income. Whether their macro-economic performance would equal that of a simple money growth rule is still a matter of controversy."

The works cited by Hall are the following: Fischer Black, "Banking and Interest Rates in a World Without Money: The Effects of Uncontrolled Banking," *Journal of Bank Research*, Vol. 1, Autumn 1970, pp. 8–28, and "A Gold Standard with Double Feedback and Near Zero Reserves," unpublished paper, Massachusetts Institute of Technology, December 1981; John F. O. Bilson, "A Proposal for Monetary Reform," working paper in economics, No. E-80-7, Domestic Studies Program, Hoover Institution, Stanford University, March 1981; Eugene Fama, "Banking in the Theory of Finance," *Journal of Monetary Economics*, Vol. 6, January 1980, pp. 39–57, and "Fiduciary Currency and Commodity Standards," unpublished paper, University of Chicago, January 1982; Irving Fisher, *Stabilizing the Dollar* (New York: Macmillan, 1920); and Robert E. Hall, "Explorations in the Gold Standard and Related Policies for Stabilizing the Dollar," in Robert E. Hall, ed., *Inflation* (Chicago: University of Chicago Press, 1982).

The idea of commodity standards is described in Part Nine. There is a fundamental problem with these ideas that must be reconciled by fairly clear evidence before they become viable alternatives. Unless they provide the functions now available from present money supplies, their adoption may cause official money to lose its important medium-of-exchange functions. Private money supplies will arise, and one monetary unit will no longer be accepted across areas such as the United States. This method of making payment could be costly. The system could be closer to pre–Civil War peacetime conditions in the United States with a hodgepodge money supply issued by many different private issuers. The optimum size for an area having one currency, an optimum currency area, is discussed in Part Nine. This consideration does not preclude improvements in present arrangements. For example, it would be beneficial to allow the payment of interest on required reserves at depository institutions so as to remove the incentive to invent close substitutes for money.

3. There is an excellent 48-page booklet on this point and much of the monetarist–nonmonetarist controversy. It contains Franco Modigliani's presidential address to the American Economic Association in 1976

(*American Economic Review*, March 1977), "The Monetarist Controversy, or Should We Forsake Stabilization Policies?" as well as a debate between Modigliani and Milton Friedman. See "The Monetarist Controversy: A Seminar Discussion" with Michael Keran, moderator, in *Economic Review, Supplement*, Federal Reserve Bank of San Francisco, Spring 1977.

4. Paul Samuelson, "Reflections on Recent Federal Reserve Policy," in a Symposium on "The Variability of Monetary Policy" in the *Journal of Money, Credit and Banking*, February 1970, pp. 33–34.

5. James Tobin, "Is Friedman a Monetarist: A Reply," in *Monetarism*, p. 336.

6. The books are *Milton Friedman's Monetary Framework, a Debate with His Critics* (Chicago: University of Chicago Press, 1974) and *Monetarism*. *Monetary Framework* includes Friedman's "A Theoretical Framework for Monetary Analysis" and comments by Karl Brunner, Allan H. Meltzer, James Tobin, Paul Davidson, and Don Patinkin. All the comments were submitted. *Monetarism* contains the proceedings of a 1974 conference held at Brown University. The editor, Jerome Stein, in a brilliant attempt to find a theoretical division, presented "Inside the Monetarist Black Box." Other participants whose comments are found in *Monetarism* were Modigliani, Tobin, Friedman, Albert Ando, Anna Schwartz, L. R. Klein, Robert Gordon, Michael Darby, Rudiger Dornbush, Robert Rasche, Thomas Mayer, Brunner, Meltzer, Carl Christ, Jurg Niehans, Robert Solow, John Scadding, Willem Buiter, Phillip Cagan, Stanley Fischer, and William Bomberger.

7. *Hearings on the Conduct of Monetary Policy*, Committee on Banking, Finance and Urban Affairs, U.S. House of Representatives, 96th Cong., 1st sess., February 21–22, 1979, p. 127. See Robert Auerbach, "A Convergence of Views" in *The Federal Reserve Authorities and Their Public Responsibility* (Rochester, N.Y.: University of Rochester, 1980), pp. 5–33.

8. *Hearings*, pp. 146–147.

9. Ibid., p. 147.

10. James Tobin, *The New York Times*, 1979.

11. Henry Kaufman, "Caution at the Start of Renewed Economic Growth: An Unusual Investment Posture," *Bondweek*, July 19, 1982, p. 7.

12. Milton Friedman, "The Federal Reserve and Monetary Instability," *The Wall Street Journal*, February 1, 1982, editorial page.

13. Jude Wanniski, "Monetarism Died Last Week, and the Markets Are Celebrating," *The Washington Post*, October 13, 1982, p. A23. *The Washington Post*, the most influential paper in the nation's capital, read by members of Congress and the executive, branch, was a good source for articles attacking monetarism and advocating faster money growth. Although this article appears as an editorial, articles appearing on news pages, such as the article by Hobart Rowan, subsequently quoted, often conveyed these opinions.

14. Senator Robert C. Byrd (for himself, Mr. Cranston, Mr. Inouye, Mr. Ford, Mr. Baucus, Mr. Bentsen, Mr. Biden, Mr. Boren, Mr. Bumpers, Mr. Burdick, Mr. Cannon, Mr. DeConcini, Mr. Dixon, Mr. Dodd, Mr. Eagleton, Mr. Huddleston, Mr. Jackson, Mr. Johnston, Mr. Kennedy, Mr. Levin, Mr. Matsunaga, Mr. Melcher, Mr. Metzenbaum, Mr. Mitchell, Mr. Moynihan, Mr. Pell, Mr. Pryor, Mr. Randolph, Mr. Riegle, Mr. Sarbanes, and Mr. Sasser) where all listed are U.S. senators, *Congressional Record, Senate*, August 3, 1982, pp. S.9699–9700.

15. Ibid., p. S.9699.

16. Ibid., pp. S.9699–9700.

17. Hobart Rowan, "It Is Time to Relegate Monetarism to a Museum," *The Washington Post*, March 28, 1982, p. G5; article begins on the first page of the Business and Finance section.

18. Milton Friedman, "Monetary Variability in the United States and Japan," *Journal of Money, Credit and Banking*, August 1983, pp. 339–343.

19. Senator Alan Cranston (for himself and Senators Riegle, Burdick, Baucus, Ford, and Moynihan), *Congressional Record, Senate*, May 13, 1982, p. S.5270-1.

20. Frank E. Morris, "Rules plus Discretion in Monetary Policy—An Appraisal of Our Experience Since October 1979," *New England Review*, Federal Reserve Bank of Boston, September–October 1985, p. 6. Morris cited Milton Friedman's forecasts of the likelihood of a slowdown in the first half of 1984 and the strong possibility of a 9 percent inflation rate by the end of 1984. On September 1, 1983, Friedman wrote an article, which appeared on the editorial page of *The Wall Street Journal*, entitled "Why a Surge of Inflation Is Likely Next Year": "In short, excessive monetary growth over the past year means that we are facing the near-certainty of an overheated economy for the next few quarters at least, which will almost certainly mean a subsequent acceleration of inflation, probably in middle or late 1984." But instead of an increase in the rate of inflation, there was a decrease in 1984, 1985, and 1986 despite continued rapid money growth, as shown in Figure 26-1. By September 1986 the rate of change in a twelve-month moving average of the GNP deflator was 2.61 percent, and the rate of change in a twelve-month moving average of the consumer price index was 1.76 percent.

21. Frank E. Morris, "Rules plus Discretion," p. 8.

22. Ibid., p. 7.

MONETARY POLICY

TARGETS AND INSTRUMENTS

The Change in Operating Procedures in October 1982: Targeting Borrowed Reserves. In October 1982, the short-run target objectives for M-1 were suspended. The new operating procedure targeted borrowed reserves, a procedure that called for controlling interest rates in order to induce depository institutions to borrow the desired amount from the Federal Reserve.

Appendix: Coordination of Monetary and Fiscal Policies. Monetarists and Keynesians generally want opposite monetary policies in response to change in fiscal policy.

INTRODUCTION

In this chapter, we will first discuss the selection of the objectives of monetary policy—the **ultimate targets**—of the Federal Reserve. The ultimate targets include price level stability and full employment. They are not the lofty objectives of the "great debate" among philosophers, but their achievement does help put the food on the table so the loftier debate may proceed. From this subject, a step backward is taken to the **intermediate targets**, which are changed with the intention of achieving—or approaching—the ultimate targets. The intermediate targets are set for different concepts of the money supply.

Our discussion will then take yet another step backward, to the **operating instruments**, the variables that the Federal Reserve's open market desk can affect directly in its day-to-day operations. These instruments include the monetary base or that part of the monetary base that is not borrowed from the Federal Reserve—the nonborrowed base.

The federal funds rate is treated as an intermediate target in Chapter 31. There the issue of guiding open market operations by the levels of the federal funds rate, the levels of some monetary aggregate, or a combination of both, as is currently the practice, is discussed. However, open market operations affect the price and yield on securities by changing their demand and supply, thus directly affecting interest rates. Therefore, under some operating procedures, it may be natural to call the federal funds rate an operating instrument. Another classification of the federal funds rate might be as a *signal* of underlying demand and supplies of reserves.

This chapter begins with a discussion of the ultimate and intermediate targets and then describes operating instruments. This allows an interesting discussion of the issues surrounding the need for new operating procedures at the Federal Reserve, especially following the October 1979 announcement by the Federal Reserve that it would concentrate more on controlling the money supply. A major problem in setting targets that arises during an economic phenomenon called stagflation is explained next. The record of the Federal Reserve's one-year targets since 1975, the end of its 1979 experiment with monetary aggregates, and the operating procedure begun in 1982 are discussed. As an introduction to those sections, the reader would benefit from rereading the end of the last chapter. The appendix contains some interesting issues in coordinating monetary and fiscal policy.

THE ULTIMATE AND INTERMEDIATE TARGETS

The official ultimate targets for economic policy were stated in the Employment Act of 1946 (Public Law 79–304):

> The Congress declares that it is the continuing policy and responsibility of the Federal Government to use all practicable means consistent with its needs and obligations and other essential considerations of national policy, with the assistance and cooperation of industry, agriculture, labor, and State and local governments, to coordinate and utilize all its plans, functions, and resources for the purpose of creating and maintaining, in a manner calculated to foster and promote free competitive enterprise and the general welfare, conditions under which there will be afforded useful employment opportunities, including self-employment, for those able, willing, and seeking to work, and to promote *maximum employment, production,* and *purchasing power.*

Presumably, the Federal Reserve is guided to some extent by those ultimate targets. In its statement of purposes to the public, the Federal Reserve asserted:

> From the outset (of the establishment of the Federal Reserve), it was recognized that the original purposes of the System were in fact aspects of broader U.S. economic and financial objectives. Over the years, economic stability and growth, a high level of employment, stability in the purchasing power of the dollar, and reasonable balance in transactions with foreign countries have come to be recognized as primary objectives of governmental economic policy.
>
> Such objectives have been articulated in many acts of Congress, including particularly the Employment Act of 1946.[1]

Thus in this 1974 statement the Federal Reserve statement added balance-of-payments considerations to the triumvirate of objectives actually "articulated" in the 1946 act (employment, purchasing power, and production).

The international objective can be inconsistent with the objectives of the Employment Act of 1946.[2] If the Federal Reserve does follow those *four* objectives, then both higher real interest rates to improve the international balance of payments and lower real rates to promote investment can be consistent with its ultimate targets.

It is difficult to determine what a poorly specified ultimate target means. The ultimate target of "reasonable balance with foreign countries" has much less precision than do the three objectives of the Employment Act. Even these three objectives are not too clear, because there is no specification of whether they are long-run or short-run objectives.

To fathom what "reasonable balance with foreign countries" might mean to the Federal Reserve, it is sometimes necessary to see what it has done to implement this balance.[3] Presumably, when the Federal Reserve intervenes by buying U.S. dollars and selling foreign currencies, it is implementing this foreign objective. At a July 29, 1977, oversight hearing on monetary policy, Chairman Henry Reuss of the U.S. House of Representatives Banking Committee said the following to Chairman Arthur Burns of the Federal Reserve (p. 97, Hearings Before the Committee on Banking, Finance and Urban Affairs, House of Representatives, *Conduct of Monetary Policy*):

> If the dollar depreciates, we have to pay more for essential imports, and that is going to add to our price levels. Furthermore, although our soybeans become cheaper to foreigners, we may need them at home, but some foreigner can grab them because of the lower international price, and that may hurt. . . .
>
> On the other side of the coin . . . the prevention of overvalued competitive currencies like the mark and the yen hurts the other two goals of national policy, namely maximum production and maximum employment, because if the dollar is overvalued vis-à-vis other currencies, then we export less and people lose jobs at home in the export industries. We import more and people lose jobs at home in import-competitive industries.
>
> So, my way out of that dilemma has always been to go with Adam Smith and say, "Let the market—supply and demand—determine the price of the dollar, and keep our hands off it, absent disorderly markets."

Chairman Reuss then asked Chairman Burns when the Federal Reserve actually does intervene. Chairman Burns replied (p. 98):

> The Federal Reserve has a certain responsibility for the position of the dollar in the exchange markets. Our broad policy is, as you know, to intervene only in the event of disorderly markets. But I must say to you in all honesty that no two of us may agree as to the precise definition of a disorderly market or the precise way to recognize one when it exists. And I must say that when I see the dollar, which is intrinsically strong, depreciating against currencies of countries whose economy is demonstrably weak, I sometimes ask myself the question whether the market is an orderly market.

Thus it appears that the fourth ultimate target of the Federal Reserve is the preservation of the international value of the U.S. dollar at a level that is judged to be "correct." "Incorrect" levels are most likely to arise when the international value of the U.S. dollar falls rapidly. This definition is similar to the analogy drawn by Chairman William Proxmire of the Senate Banking Committee in response to Federal Reserve replies. He said it was like nailing a custard pie to the wall.

Keeping in mind those ultimate targets, consider also the 1975 directions of the U.S. Congress to the Federal Reserve in House Concurrent Resolution 133 (H. Con. 133) to

(1) pursue policies in the first half of 1975 so as to encourage lower long-term interest rates and expansion in the monetary and credit aggregates appropriate to facilitating prompt economic recovery, and

(2) maintain long-run growth of the monetary and credit aggregates commensurate with the economy's long-run potential and increase production, so as to promote effectively the goals of maximum employment, stable prices, and moderate long-term interest rates.

The second part was changed from resolution form, which conveys the will of the Congress, to law in the Federal Reserve Reform Act of 1977 (Public Law 95–188).

Additional, more specific ultimate targets were given in the Full Employment and Balanced Growth Act of 1978, known as the "Humphrey–Hawkins Act" (Public Law 95–523), which directed the Federal Reserve to testify before the banking committees of both the House and Senate twice a year (in February and July). Since the Federal Reserve began reporting to Congress in 1985, the chairman of the Board of Governors has always testified at these oversight hearings. The Federal Reserve, as required under the law, gives the following information at these hearings:

1. The Federal Reserve presents specific forecasts of many selected macroeconomic variables (but not interest rates) that it expects during the coming year. For example, in the July 18, 1986, statement Chairman Paul Volcker (*Monetary Policy Objectives for 1986, Midyear Review of the Federal Reserve Board*) made the following forecasts for 1987 (p. 4):

1987 Economic Projections, Percentage of Change, Fourth Quarter 1986 to Fourth Quarter 1987

	Range	Central Tendency
Nominal GNP	5.0 to 8.25	6 to 7.5
Real GNP	2 to 4.25	3 to 3.5
GNP deflator	1.5 to 4.25	3 to 4
Fourth quarter 1987 civilian unemployment rate	6.5 to 7	"around" 6.5

2. Target ranges for its monetary policy in 1987 were forecast as follows (p. 2):

Rates of Growth in Monetary and
Debt Aggregates for 1987, Percentage
of Change from Fourth Quarter 1986
to Fourth Quarter 1987

	Range
M1	(3 to 8)*
M2	6 to 9
M3	6 to 9
Debt	8 to 11

* "Indicative of likely range if more stable velocity behavior shows signs of re-emerging."

The Humphrey–Hawkins law also reaffirmed the objectives of policy in the Employment Act of 1946 and even called for specific targets in the next several years after its passage. It directed that policy be aimed at achieving 4 percent unemployment and 3 percent inflation by 1983 and zero inflation by 1988. (The inflation rate was lowered dramatically by 1986—with consumer prices rising by only 1.9 percent in 1986—but unemployment was near 7 percent, ending 1986 at 6.7 percent.)

After the chairman of the Federal Reserve reports in February and July to each of the banking committees, these committees submit reports to the Senate and the House. The report in the House of Representatives is delivered to the Speaker of the House. The object of these reports is to encourage the committee members to take a discerning and enthusiastic interest in the Federal Reserve's record and intentions for monetary policy, including the way that monetary policy will affect the economy. This objective has generally failed, according to some of the staff members of the banking committees who helped write and win support for the reporting requirements for these hearings and assisted with them in the 1970s and early 1980s, shortly after the reporting procedure was first introduced. For example, the hearings have drifted onto other topics than the monetary aggregates. The members often solicit and emphasize at the hearings the views of the chairman of the Federal Reserve on budget policy and any disagreements he may have with the administration. These latter topics make better press than do the arcane monetary targets and are better understood by most committee members. But they are not the responsibility of the Federal Reserve.

Often the report submitted by the banking committees contains the views of dissenting members. The majority party on the committee may write the report, and the minority party may write its own dissenting report. Individual members may add their own views.

In its 1984 book *Purposes & Functions*, the Federal Reserve again stated its objectives:

> Over the years, stability and growth of the economy, a high level of employment, stability in the purchasing power of the dollar, and reasonable balance in transactions with foreign countries have come to be recognized as primary objectives of governmental economic policy. Such objectives have been articulated by the Congress in the Employment Act of 1946, and more recently in the Full Employment and Balanced Growth Act of 1946. . . .
>
> The Federal Reserve contributes to the attainment of the nation's economic and financial goals through its ability to influence money and credit in the economy. As the nation's central bank, it attempts to ensure that growth in the money and credit over the long run is sufficient to encourage growth in the economy in line with its potential and with reasonable price stability. In the short run the Federal Reserve seeks to adapt its policies to combat deflationary or inflationary pressures as they may arise. And as lender of last resort, it has the responsibility for utilizing the policy instruments available to it in an attempt to forestall national liquidity crises and financial panics.[4]

This statement of policy objectives uses time dimensions for policy objectives: long term and short term. The Congress's formal acts, cited in the statement, do not recognize the lag between policy implementation and its effects. For example, if the monetary policy is aimed at correcting short-term problems of deflation and inflation, the policy may produce worse problems in the long term. If there is a rather long lag, say an average of one to two years, for the full impact of a monetary change on the price level, the attempt to provide price stability will require long-term forecasts and planning. Thus it is more reasonable to attempt to influence output when the lags are much shorter, such as three to nine months. Even here the proponents of the rational expectations hypothesis, discussed in Chapter 20, would claim that only unexpected changes in monetary policy would significantly affect unemployment. The positioning of objectives in the preceding policy statement is the opposite of what one would expect from theoretical considerations. But given the type of oversight hearings and media coverage with which the Federal Reserve was confronted in the 1980s, this contradiction in timing patterns will be of little concern except to academic analyses of money and banking.

The ultimate targets of price stability and full employment cannot be achieved directly. Rather, the Federal Reserve can try to influence these variables by using its monetary tools, that is, open market operations, the level of discounting, and reserve requirement changes (rarely used), discussed in Chapter 16. The variables that the Federal Reserve can directly control through its monetary tools, such as open market operations, are its operating instruments.

OPERATING INSTRUMENTS

The Federal Reserve must go one step backward and determine the best operating instrument to change those intermediate targets. Open market operations directly affect the monetary base, and all or part of the monetary base may be viewed as the operating instrument. The desired level of those variables is the immediate target of the Federal Reserve's open market desk.

The operating instrument may be thought of as the entire monetary base. However, the open market trading desk does not control borrowing at the discount windows of the twelve regional Reserve banks. Therefore, the desk can be said to have the **nonborrowed base**, NB, as its operating instrument. That is, the monetary base, B, minus borrowings, BOR:

$$NB = B - BOR \tag{1}$$

Subtracting currency outside depository institutions from the monetary base gives reserves of depository institutions, R. The open market trading desk uses the value of **nonborrowed reserves**, NR, as an immediate target,

$$NR = R - BOR \tag{2}$$

where R is total reserves. Nonborrowed reserves are only one step away from **free reserves**, FR, which also have served as an immediate target. Subtracting required reserves from total reserves gives **excess reserves**, ER. Free reserves are excess reserves minus borrowings:

$$FR = ER - BOR \tag{3}$$

For each bank, a higher level of free reserves is sometimes viewed as indicating a greater potential for expanding loans and investments. For the economy as a whole, it can be a misleading variable as an indicator of a "tight" or "loose" money supply policy. This can be seen from the following example: Suppose that there is heavy borrowing so that BOR in equation (3) rises. According to the monetary base identity and the money expansion multipliers in Chapters 15 and 17, the money supply will expand. In recent decades, with efficient case management the depository institutions normally carry small excess reserves. The free reserve variable, FR, in equation (3) will fall, even turning negative. Negative free reserves are then sometimes incorrectly alleged to signify "tight money" when in fact the monetary aggregates are growing rapidly.

In practice, the Federal Reserve has targeted on a **total reserve path** covering the four weeks after the short-run targets are set at its FOMC meetings. This is converted into a **nonborrowed reserve path** by subtracting out an assumption about borrowing from the discount window. Each week's nonborrowed reserve target is updated on Friday on the basis of the most recent data. The immediate target in this procedure is nonborrowed reserves, and the objective is to hit the short-run intermediate targets. The development of those intermediate targets is discussed in Chapter 30.

OPERATING PROCEDURES AND MONEY CONTROL PROBLEMS, 1979–1982

On October 6, 1979, the newly appointed chairman of the Federal Reserve Board, Paul Volcker, announced steps to slow inflation and bring monetary growth under control. The discount rate was increased, and reserve requirements were imposed on increases in the "managed liabilities" of some banks.[5] More important, Mr. Volcker announced a revolution in monetary policy: The Federal Reserve would shift its emphasis from controlling the federal funds rate to controlling the monetary aggregates.

After October 1979, the money supply growth rates and nominal interest rates became more variable than in any period in the post–World War II period. The sharp decline in M-1 (it fell at a rate of 5.2 percent for three months) during the first part of 1980, for example, was the sharpest three-month decline in the entire period from 1947 to 1980. The sharp decline in the money supply in 1980 contributed to a deepening of the recession that year, as did the very slow growth in M-1 in 1982 contribute to the recession in 1982. Part of the explanation for the more variable monetary growth rates and interest rates is that the Federal Reserve had faulty operating procedures. That contention is developed here. However, it may not be the underlying reason for the large variations in the money supply. A case will be in Chapter 29 that the Federal Reserve was driven by political considerations to produce this money growth. Even if the tools were faulty, the Federal Reserve could have changed its open market operations sufficiently to get back on track, although an argument could be made that lagged reserve requirements and other operating procedures would have made the adjustment more difficult.

In announcing that it would change its emphasis to a monetary aggregates policy, the Federal Reserve failed to take sufficient steps to enable it to carry out that policy. The federal funds rate range was broadened to a range of 11.5 to 15.5 percent initially (see Figure 27-1). The New York desk, which carries out open market operations, reported that

> Previously, the desk had managed non-borrowed reserves as necessary to achieve the Committee's (Federal Open Market Committee) Federal funds rate objectives. The Committee's dissatisfaction with the excessive growth of money in the second and third quarters provided much of the impetus for adapting a new approach.
>
> From the total reserve path, the non-borrowed reserve path is derived by subtracting the level of member bank borrowings from the Federal Reserve indicated by the Committee at its meeting. Typically, the Committee has chosen levels close to the recently prevailing average though the level chosen on October 6 was shaded higher to impose some additional initial restraint. Ideally, the assumed initial borrowing level should be such that the resultant mix of borrowed and non-borrowed reserves

FIGURE 27-1   FOMC Ranges for the Federal Funds Rate, January 1979–1980

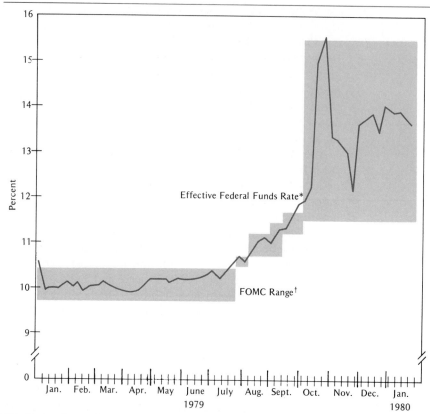

This figure shows that when the Federal Reserve announced a change in its targeting procedures in October 1979, it widened the federal funds target range.

* Weekly averages of effective daily rates.

† At each meeting during 1979, the FOMC established a range in the federal funds rate. These ranges are indicated for the first full week during which they were in effect.

Source: Richard W. Lang, "The FOMC in 1979: Introducing Reserve Targeting," *Review,* Federal Reserve Bank of St. Louis, March 1980, p. 11.

would tend to encourage bank behavior consistent with the emergence of desired required reserves, and hence of desired monetary growth. In practice, there seems to be significant short-term variations in the willingness or desire of banks to turn to the discount window. This adds to the difficulty of choosing an appropriate level . . . , and may necessitate adjustments in a path in response to changes in bank attitudes toward the discount rate.[6]

Essentially, the desk sought to control nonborrowed reserves in its daily operating procedures.

An "assumption" would be made about borrowings. Because in any week required reserves were fixed by the level of deposits two weeks earlier, under the system of lagged reserve requirements initiated by the Federal Reserve in September of 1968 (and ended in 1984), control of nonborrowed reserves meant that the desk was trying to influence only excess reserves. Insofar as borrowings varied, the Fed's target could also have been described as free reserves, which are excess reserves minus borrowings.

This was an operating procedure that did not provide close short-run control of the money supply because assumptions about borrowed reserves must turn out to be wrong if the Federal Reserve attempts to change nonborrowed reserves. Nonborrowed reserves and borrowings were not independent under these procedures. Banks hold, as an aggregate, trivial amounts of excess reserves. Thus under a system of lagged reserve requirements, in which current required reserves are fixed, any resulting decrease in reserves from contractionary open market operations necessarily drives the banks to the discount window. There was some confusion in understanding this reaction to contractionary open market operations, as each bank separately can borrow in the federal funds markets. All banks together, however, cannot increase the total reserves available to the banking system. If nonborrowed reserves are increased, excess reserves will rise briefly, after which loans and investments will increase. This causes deposit growth, which, again, cannot affect reserve requirements for two weeks. The federal funds rate then falls, and borrowings are reduced. Under this system, it is the discount manager, not the open market desk, who runs much of the short-run monetary policy.

Discount window operations are difficult to predict. Consider, for example, the instruction booklet, *Everything You Always Wanted to Know About Borrowing at the Discount Window* (*but Did Not Ask*), published by the Federal Reserve Bank of Kansas City in January 1978. On page 8, under "What Questions Will the Reserve Bank Ask?" the first sentence is "We generally ask no questions of the member bank when a loan is requested." Down the page it says that "In addition if a bank's borrowing becomes less clearly appropriate, we will also make an informational contact during the term of the loan after weekly analysis of the bank's loans, investments, and deposits or when the bank requests renewal." The key words here for researchers attempting to model the determinants of borrowing are the ambiguous "less clearly appropriate." A better monetary aggregates–targeting procedure would tie the discount rate to a market rate, add a penalty, and thereby replace the ambiguous effect of "moral suasion" with price rationing.

The Credit Restraint Program

A credit restraint program implemented in March 1980 caused stricter terms to be placed on credit card credit, which reduced the incentive to use credit cards. Because credit cards are a substitute for currency and coin, the credit restraint program further and dramatically increased the currency to deposit ratio from what could be predicted from its own past history, thereby causing a temporary decline in the money expansion multiplier. The currency-to-deposit ratio is plotted in Figure 27-2.

Under an aggregates target procedure in which the entire monetary base was being controlled, these shifts in the currency-to-deposit ratio would be

FIGURE 27-2   M-1 Multiplier and Ratio of Currency to Total Checkable Deposits, 1979–1982

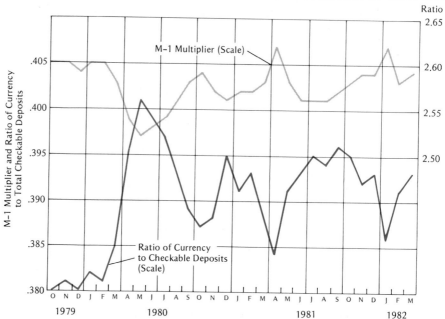

"Once credit controls were removed, the Weintraub hypothesis suggests, the multiplier would come back within its historical ranges.* Thus real money balances could be expected to return to more historical levels as well. This is what happened; actual real balances rose to about $226 billion in III/1980. . . . If the money multiplier declines, banks have to reduce the amount of deposits they create for a given amount of source base (or bank reserves). According to Weintraub's hypothesis, M-1 balances declined because monetary authorities did not anticipate the *increased* demand for currency and offset it by increasing the base. Therefore, the observed decline in real money balances was due not to a reduction in the *demand* for real balances, but to this unanticipated change in the supply of money caused by an increased demand for currency as a result of the credit controls."

*Robert Weintraub, *The Impact of the Federal Reserve System's Monetary Policies in the Nation's Economy*, Second Report, Staff Report of the Subcommittee on Domestic Monetary Policy, House Committee on Banking, Finance, and Urban Affairs, 96th Cong., 2nd sess. (Washington, D.C.: U.S. Government Printing Office, 1980), p. 17.
Source: Scott E. Hein, "Short-Run Money Growth Volatility: Evidence of Misbehaving Money Demand," *Review*, Federal Reserve Bank of St. Louis, June–July 1982, p. 33; the caption is from pp. 32–33.

offset rapidly by open market operations. There would be no need to allow the money supply to decline at record rates for three months, as it did until May 1980. The Federal Reserve statements at the time that nonborrowed reserves were growing rapidly in this period were irrelevant. Over a three-month period, it would have been possible to increase reserves sufficiently to offset the currency-to-deposit ratio and to put M-1 back on target. The adherence to a nonborrowed target during this episode was consistent with political objectives discussed in Chapter 29.

Suggested Improvements in Operating Procedures

It was suggested that the Federal Reserve not only return to synchronous reserve requirements, as it did (except for a two-day lag every two weeks) in February 1984, but also that it adopt a penalty rate at the discount window (see Exhibit 27-1). This would give the Federal Reserve better control over the monetary base, which has determined a substantial part of the growth path of the monetary aggregates (see the discussion of the money expansion multiplier in Chapter 17). In addition, the payment of interest on reserves would reduce the incentive to invent substitutes for reservable deposits. These substitutes make more difficult the control of the medium of exchange.

Another improvement in operating procedures was proposed by Milton Friedman partly in response to what he and some other observers considered churning at the Federal Reserve open market desk. **Churning** is the unecessary buying and selling of securities that run up transactions costs (brokers' fees, in the case of a private broker).

Churning

Total sales and purchases at the New York trading desk were approximately $800 billion in 1980, whereas the net change in the Federal Reserve's portfolio was $4.5 billion. Thus there was an incredible amount of transactions for a relatively small net change in the Federal Reserve's portfolio, indicating that the Federal Reserve had objectives other than gradually and smoothly changing the monetary base and that it was reacting to many disturbances. Are all these transactions necessary to achieve its objectives, or is this an example of churning? This is an interesting question that attracted the attention of a few—not many—people. Fernand J. St Germain, chairman of the Committee on Banking, Finance, and Urban Affairs of the U.S. House of Representatives, inquired about this subject in June 1981 (see Exhibit 27-2; the $1,634 trillion figure from the *Federal Reserve Bulletin* includes transactions for foreign central banks). Milton Friedman, in an article published in 1982, stated

> In the year 1980, the Federal Reserve made gross open market purchases of securities of something over $800 billion, and gross transactions, including sales of maturities being rolled over, of more than double that

EXHIBIT 27-1

FEDERAL RESERVE press release

For immediate release
October 5, 1982

The Federal Reserve Board today announced final approval of a change — from lagged to contemporaneous reserve requirements (CRR) — in the way depository institutions maintain reserves.

The change will become effective February 2, 1984. At that time, medium sized and larger depository institutions will begin posting reserves on transaction accounts with a two-day rather than the current two-week accounting delay. (Transaction accounts include checking, NOW, automatic transfer and share draft accounts.) Reserve requirements on nontransaction liabilities will be met on a lagged basis, as described below.

The Board acted after consideration of comment received on proposals published in November 1981 and after extensive staff study during the past several years. The Board decided in principle on June 28, 1982 to adopt contemporaneous reserve requirements on transaction deposits, but left open for later decision the questions of an effective date and whether reserve periods for different sets of institutions should be placed on a staggered basis, with half the institutions settling every other week. The Board has decided against staggering settlement periods.

It is expected that contemporaneous reserve requirements will improve the implementation of monetary policy to a degree by strengthening the linkage between reserves held by depository institutions and the money supply. The Board noted that sizable slippages will remain between reserves and money, as short-run flows are inherently volatile.

Under the present lagged reserve system, depository institutions must post their required reserves in any given week based on their deposit levels two weeks earlier.

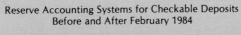

Reserve Accounting Systems for Checkable Deposits
Before and After February 1984

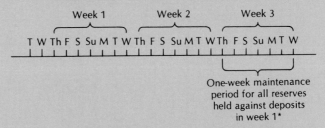

Lagged Reserve Accounting System 1968–1984

Week 1   Week 2   Week 3

T W Th F S Su M T W Th F S Su M T W Th F S Su M T W

One-week maintenance
period for all reserves
held against deposits
in week 1*

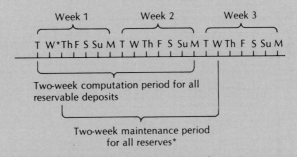

Contemporaneous Accounting System: Since February 1984

Week 1   Week 2   Week 3

T W*Th F S Su M T W Th F S Su M T W Th F S Su M

Two-week computation period for all
reservable deposits

Two-week maintenance period
for all reserves*

*February 2, 1984.

Under the reserve accounting system in effect from 1968 to 1984, the average required reserves of the current week depended on the average checkable deposits (also called transactions accounts) two weeks before. Under the contemporaneous reserve accounting system used since February 2, 1984, the average required reserves of the two weeks ending on Wednesday have depended on the average deposits held during the two-week period ending two days before, on Monday. (The current so-called contemporaneous accounting system thus still has a two-day lag.) The current two-week accounting period ends on Monday, and the required reserves do not need to be held until Wednesday.*

* One complicating factor is that the required reserves under the lagged reserve requirement system include the average reserves on deposit with the Federal Reserve in the current week ending Wednesday plus vault cash held at the bank two weeks before. Under the current system, required reserves include all reserves except vault cash held in the two-week period ending on Monday plus average vault cash held for the two weeks ending Wednesday. (This exhibit was simplified from the diagram published by the Federal Reserve.)

amount. The net change in the portfolio was $4.5 billion. The open market desk therefore made $184 worth of purchases gross and roughly twice that amount of transactions (purchases plus sales) in order to add one dollar to its portfolio. Why all this churning? It accounts for some-

EXHIBIT 27-2

U.S. HOUSE OF REPRESENTATIVES

COMMITTEE ON BANKING, FINANCE AND URBAN AFFAIRS

NINETY-SEVENTH CONGRESS
2129 RAYBURN HOUSE OFFICE BUILDING
WASHINGTON, D.C. 20515

Mr. Anthony M. Solomon, President
The Federal Reserve Bank of New York
33 Liberty Street
New York, New York 10045

Dear Mr. Solomon:

Federal open market transactions records (Federal Reserve Bulletin, April 1981, page A10) indicate that the Federal Reserve conducted $1.634 trillion in sales and purchases of repurchase agreements (including matched securities) in 1980 through its New York open market desk with governmental securities dealers. (The 34 dealers operating on this market on April 2, 1981 are attached.) These transactions constituted 99 percent of total purchases and sales at the open market desk. In a year in which the Federal Reserve was ostensibly on an aggregates target and when M1-B changed by $25 billion (December to December), the huge amount of repurchase agreement transactions poses some questions.

First, to help answer these questions would you provide me a summary for May and November, 1980, of:

a. Interest rates, amounts and maturities on repurchase agreements and matched sales submitted during the auctions at the desk, indicating which were accepted and which were not;

b. The Federal funds rate in effect at the time; and

c. The average repurchase agreement rates in effect during that time.

Second, would you describe the rationale for the Federal Reserve's 1980 open market desk policy and any changes that are being carried out in 1981?

Third, I assume that you closely monitor the transactions costs to the Federal Reserve and the gross profits to the government securities dealers which result directly from these operations. Would you give me your estimate of the gross profits made by the government dealers from these repurchase agreement transactions during 1980?

I would appreciate your answer as soon as possible so that my staff can study the material prior to receiving the Federal Reserve's July 20 report.

Sincerely,

Fernand J. St Germain
Chairman

thing like one-quarter to one-half of all the transactions of U.S. government securities dealers other than the Fed itself. It generates millions of dollars of fees for the dealers involved.[7]

Is this immense amount of buying and selling short-term repurchase agreements necessary to achieve the objectives the Federal Reserve has announced:

namely, the monetary objectives of targeted money growth and targeted interest rate changes? Both targets are stated as ranges between which no action is taken.[8] Obviously, the Federal Reserve thought that its activities in the financial markets were necessary. Here are some reasons the Federal Reserve gives for its immense number of purchases and sales: It frequently wants to offset changes in the federal funds rate and intervenes when the federal funds rate is near the end of the target range. (After October 1979, it said that it would intervene only if the federal funds rate appeared to remain persistently outside the target range.) Also, insofar as the federal funds rate is thought to be an indicator of depository institution reserve changes, the Federal Reserve may go into the market in response to federal funds rate changes even when the federal funds rate is not outside its target range. This was especially true before 1979 but may still be true to the same extent. In 1977, the Federal Reserve reported

> One objective of current operating procedure is to insulate the monetary aggregates to the extent feasible from the effects of supply-related disturbances by limiting associated movements in the funds rate. These supply shocks include movements in noncontrolled factors affecting nonborrowed reserved—such as float or Treasury deposits at the Reserve Banks—and changes in the amount of excess reserves that banks wish to hold. If open market operations have the effect of stabilizing the Federal funds rate, they will at the same time substantially moderate—although not necessarily eliminate—the effects of supply-related disturbances "on the monetary aggregates."[9]

Insofar as the federal funds rate maintains some sort of relationship with other rates, as would be expected in competitive markets, and insofar as the markets are efficient, this operating procedure is a prescription for nearly unlimited intervention, with little success in causing interest rate changes to be far from a random walk. (See Chapter 13 on efficient markets.) Insofar as the funds rate is temporarily controlled, there are very large profits to be made by those who understand the temporary effects of the Federal Reserve's intervention.

In 1982, Milton Friedman, then an adviser to President Reagan, advocated a return to synchronous reserve requirements and an end to churning.[10] He suggested that the Federal Reserve set targets for the monetary base over the next three or six months. Assume, for example, that a $10 billion increase is targeted for the monetary base over the next six months. The Federal Reserve would go into the market only once a week, say each Monday morning. It would buy one twenty-sixth of $10 billion, or $384.62 million in securities, plus the amount needed to replace maturing securities. If the single monetary aggregate designated for targeting veered off course, the base target could be adjusted at the end of the three- or six-month period. A penalty rate would be put in place at the discount window to reduce substantially the amount of borrowing. Changes in borrowing at the discount window can alter the monetary base, moving it off the targeted rate of growth.

Such a plan would end the fine-tuning of the money supply. Short-run variance in the money supply may increase, but this conclusion is controversial, as fine-tuning at the open market desk may introduce disturbances. Long-run money growth, it is argued, would be perceived as being more reliably within the projected target ranges.

It would leave to the market the day-to-day and seasonable adjustments that the market is well qualified to handle—and could do more effectively if it knew precisely what the Federal Reserve intended to do, then in the present state of uncertainty with the weekly guessing game about the Fed intentions that follows each Friday's release of the figures on the money supply.[11]

Data Problems

Another operating problem concerns supplying data to the Federal Reserve. This would not be so important if a system such as that proposed by Friedman were adopted. But it is important if the Federal Reserve attempts to fine-tune weekly changes in the money supply.

The Federal Reserve cannot continuously receive accurate estimates of the size of the money supply. Up to 1980, the approximately 5,600 member commercial banks reported on the size of their deposit liabilities each Wednesday. The deposit liabilities in the approximately 8,800 nonmember commercial banks and the thrifts were predicted on the basis of other variables, including previous reports, called **benchmark data**. Benchmark data reports on the nonmember commercial banks were sent to the Federal Reserve by the Federal Deposit Insurance Corporation in June and December. (The weekly changes in the checkable deposit liabilities of the thrifts were very small and unimportant at that time.) Sometimes the corrections in the money after these benchmark estimates were received were substantial. Thus, the FOMC and the open market trading desk did not have correct data for guiding money growth.

Perhaps the most important part of the Depository Institutions Deregulation and Monetary Control Act of 1980 was the provision that authorized the collection of more accurate and timely information on the deposit liabilities of *all* the depository intermediaries. This information is more important for monetary control than uniform reserve requirements, reduction in float, or other changes that some economists and the Federal Reserve believe will also improve monetary control. The open market desk can take offsetting action when the money supply is off course if it has correct, up-to-date information on the money supply.

Even with correct information from all depository intermediaries, which is reported once a week, there is still a control problem. Suppose that all data on deposits are collected as of the opening of business on Wednesday. That weekly observation point can give distorted estimates. For example, in Figure 27-3, average nominal growth is increasing, whereas average growth at the weekly observation points is falling.

FIGURE 27-3   Rising Average Nominal Money Growth with a Falling
Average Estimate from Wednesday Observation Points

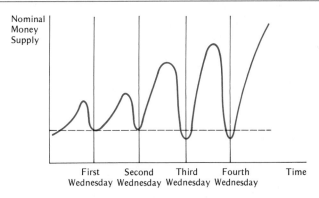

The figure shows that periodic observations, on Wednesday of each week when the
Federal Reserve receives its weekly reports from the banking and thrift industries, can
be misleading. The dated observations are falling, whereas the average value of the
money supply is rising.

The Federal Reserve has obtained samples of deposit size from a survey of
the large banks at observation times other than on Wednesdays, but this information is incomplete. Experts at the open market trading desk can also use
the federal funds rate change as a signal of changes in the banks' reserve positions.[12] This is tricky because it requires separating changes in the federal
funds rate caused by changes in the demand and supply of reserves from those
caused by changes from other sources. One other source is a general rise in
short-term rates because of the expectation of increased rates of inflation.[13]

The example in Figure 27-3 pertains to short-run control but not to periods
of several months or more when the average estimates catch up to the actual
average daily growth. Even this short-run disturbance is unnecessary with
modern technology. In an age when market participants in the stock and bond
markets can stay in instant contact through relatively low-cost computer terminals, why should information on the nation's money supply be in the mode
of a former age? Deposit and reserve information could be typed into a computer console once a day and transmitted through a phone line by simply
calling a local Federal Reserve computer terminal. This information from all
depository intermediaries would greatly facilitate short-run monetary control.
Although many depository institutions have this information readily available,
others would incur significant costs in collecting it. Therefore, consideration
should be given to alleviating those hardships when they are not the result
of a deficient bookkeeping system, possibly by reducing deposit insurance
premiums.

DILEMMAS IN CHOOSING ULTIMATE TARGETS

The selection of different ultimate targets is not easy, as some ultimate targets are sometimes inconsistent with one another.[14] In addition, the specification of what is meant and whether the target should be achieved in the long or the short run are often not made clear.

An example of an inconsistency arises with an ultimate target of a stable foreign exchange value for the U.S. dollar, which may, at times, call for a short-run policy of high interest rates. High enough real interest rates can cause an increase in demand for U.S. dollars as foreign investors demand more U.S. financial assets. They are attracted by the higher *real* rate of return. However, policies aimed at driving up real interest rates can reduce real private investment and cause higher unemployment, which is inconsistent with targets of domestic prosperity.

An example of mixing short-run and long-run ultimate targets can arise with an attempt to reduce unemployment rapidly by fast money growth. This can be viewed as an attempt to use the objectives of the Employment Act of 1946 as immediate, short-run "ultimate" targets. The results can be higher inflation and more unemployment in later periods.

This policy problem, which could be called the "stagflation dilemma," is shown in Figure 27-4. (See Chapters 18 and 19 for a more detailed description of the underlying analysis.) Starting from an initial period with a constant money supply, the monetary policy changes to a constant positive rate of inflation growth for the money supply.

Unemployment declines at first and then increases as uncertainties about future inflation and government policies to control it also increase. Threats of government wage and price controls and credit allocation schemes can discourage business owners from expanding their payrolls and investing in the future. Nominal interest rates rise, registering expectations of increased rates of inflation. If money growth is accelerated even more (as shown by the dashed line on the money supply trend), unemployment will fall at first and then rise. (See the expectations-augmented Phillips curve in Chapter 20.) The economy is in a state of stagflation—high unemployment plus inflation.

Attempts to stop the inflation raise the unemployment level, and attempts to reduce unemployment are increasingly ineffective as they kick off increased inflationary expectations and uncertainties. The attempt to reduce the unemployment with accelerated money growth causes high nominal interest rates (the dashed line on nominal interest rates) and more unemployment when the money supply is again brought back on trend (the dashed line on the unemployment path). The timing of these events is not portrayed accurately in Figure 27-4; only the general relationships are shown. The stagflation period could last for several years or more. Although the price level is shown as a trend line, long periods of money growth in different directions can cause greater variations in the price level, increasing uncertainties and impairing the

FIGURE 27-4   A Period of Stagflation

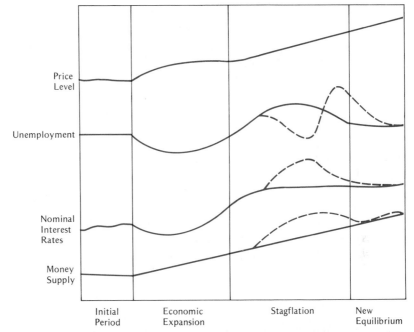

Initial Period	Economic Expansion	Stagflation	New Equilibrium

Starting from an initial position of a constant money supply, monetary growth is accelerated to reduce unemployment. Unemployment declines at first and then increases as uncertainties about future inflation increase. Rising nominal interest rates indicate expectations of increased rates of inflation. If money growth is accelerated even more because of the attempt to stop rising unemployment (as shown by the dashed line on the money supply trend), unemployment will fall and then rise as new fears of inflation are registered in increasing nominal rates of interest. The attempt to bring money growth back in at the trend growth rate also raises unemployment. The timing of these events is not accurately portrayed in the figure, only their general relationships. The stagflation period could last for several years or more.

stable environment needed to induce maximum investment and hiring of the unemployed.

The ineffectiveness of sustaining lower unemployment rates through faster money growth is supported by the relationship shown in Figure 27-5. Three-year moving averages of the rate of money growth and the unemployment rate show no close long-term relationship. If anything, the rate of unemployment appears to be positively correlated with the faster money growth after 1975 (higher rates of unemployment are associated with higher rates of money growth) and negatively correlated before 1975 (higher rates of unemployment are associated with lower rates of money growth). The use of three-year moving averages obscures the shorter relationships between money growth rates and unemployment rates. The intention of this evidence is to show that

FIGURE 27-5   Three-Year Average Money Growth and Unemployment Rates, 1954–1986

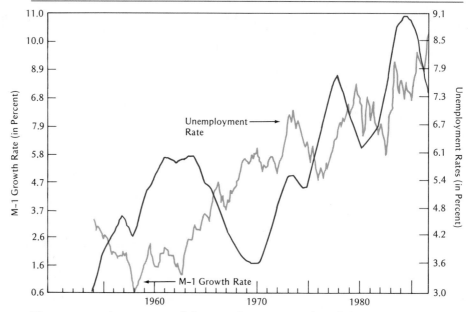

Three-year moving averages of the rate of money growth and the unemployment rate show no close long-term relationship. If anything, the rate of unemployment appears to be positively correlated with the faster money growth after 1975 (higher rates of unemployment are associated with higher rates of money growth) and negatively correlated before 1975 (higher rates of unemployment are associated with lower rates of money growth). By using three-year averages, this figure obscures the shorter relationships between money growth rates and unemployment rates.

Source: Cambridge Planning and Analytics, Inc., Boston.

although money growth may have short-term effects on output and unemployments, it is not apparent in the long term. If the evidence of a positive relationship after 1975 between fast money growth and unemployment rates persists, it will support the view that high rates of money growth cause inflation, which disrupts the economy and causes higher rates of unemployment.

So what is a policymaker to do? Suppose a member of the U.S. House of Representatives is running for reelection in his or her congressional district. It is best for that person to look for other work rather than to give the following type of speech before the families of the unemployed or those employed without tenure or other guarantees: "I could urge the Federal Reserve to run a more stimulative monetary policy which would, at least temporarily, put most of the unemployed back to work. Trouble is, this policy will cause more inflation in two or three years, which will require more unemployment in order to subdue it. All I can say to help you understand the basis of the present situation is that the market has cleared without those of you who are unemployed."

One way that a long-range policy might be sold to the public is to explain the long-term (two to three years later) targets *and* to support programs to help the unemployed in the short term. These programs would provide sufficient income insurance for the potentially unemployed as well as for the actually unemployed. Long-term strategies for economic policy may not be implemented in a free society if the short-term adjustments are too painful.

TWELVE-MONTH MONETARY TARGET RANGES

Beginning in 1975, the Federal Reserve began to present twelve-month target ranges for monetary growth to the banking committees of the House and Senate of the U.S. Congress, under House Concurrent Resolution 133. At first this was done quarterly, as shown in Table 27-1. Then under the Humphrey–Hawkins law, the Federal Reserve began reporting twice a year (in February and July) (see Table 27-2).

From March 1975 to the third quarter of 1979, the old medium-of-exchange concept of money, M-1, missed the fifteen target ranges 47 percent of the time (see Table 27-1). From March 1975 to the fourth quarter of 1979, the old M-2 and M-3 missed their separate sixteen target ranges 31 percent and 44 percent of the time, respectively. In the 1980–1986 period, shown in Figure 27-3, the money supply, especially M-1 growth, overshot most of the target ranges.

The record is bad, as it injured the credibility of Federal Reserve's announcements. The consequences are substantial. When the central bank of the Federal Republic of Germany announces from Bonn that the rate of growth of its money supply will be reduced, the adjustment process is rapid. Inflation soon slows. But after this record, when the U.S. Federal Reserve makes an announcement, confusion abounds.

Financial experts who specialize in reading between the lines of Federal Reserve announcements and who keep close track of monetary policies often opt for some variety of the "unintended reversal." That is, they interpret an announcement by the Federal Reserve of slow money growth as indicating a short period of very slow growth that will raise money growth far above its previous level. But the interpretations are not always that simple.

For comparison, examine the monetary targets of nine countries, as shown in Table 27-3. Japan and Switzerland had a target point. Japan came very close to its target in the two years shown. Canada was within, and West Germany nearly within, their target ranges in the two years shown. Japan had little inflation (ranging from 2.9 percent in the first quarter of 1981 to 2.1 percent in the first quarter of 1986). Real output in Japan grew vigorously except for the first quarter of 1986, when it fell. Inflation in West Germany fell from 5 percent in 1982 to 2.5 percent in 1986. The rate of growth of output in

TABLE 27-1   Federal Reserve System One-Year Target Ranges and Actual Growth Rates for Monetary Aggregates Under Old Definitions for Money, 1975–1979*

From 1975 to 1979, the Federal Reserve reported quarterly, presenting one-year targets at each of these hearings. It missed the M-1 target 47 percent of the time, the M-2 target 31 percent, and the M-3 target 44 percent.

Period	M-1		M-2		M-3	
	Target	Actual	Target	Actual	Target	Actual
Mar., 1975–76	5.0–7.5%	5.3%	8.5–10.5%	9.7%	10.0–12.0%	12.2%
Q2, 1975–76	5.0–7.5	5.3	8.5–10.5	9.6	10.0–12.0	12.1
Q3, 1975–76	5.0–7.5	4.6	7.5–10.5	9.3	9.0–12.0	11.5
Q4, 1975–76	4.5–7.5	5.8	7.5–10.5	10.9	9.0–12.0	12.7
Q1, 1976–77	4.5–7.0	6.5	7.5–10.0	11.0	9.0–12.0	12.9
Q2, 1976–77	4.5–7.0	6.8	7.5– 9.5	10.8	9.0–11.0	12.5
Q3, 1976–77	4.5–6.5	8.0	7.5–10.0	11.1	9.0–11.5	12.7
Q4, 1976–77	4.5–6.5	7.9	7.0–10.0	9.8	8.5–11.5	11.7
Q1, 1977–78	4.5–6.5	7.7	7.0– 9.5	8.8	8.5–11.0	10.5
Q2, 1977–78	4.0–6.5	8.2	7.0– 9.5	8.6	8.5–11.0	10.0
Q3, 1977–78	4.0–6.5	8.0	6.5– 9.0	8.5	8.0–10.5	9.5
Q4, 1977–78	4.0–6.5	7.2	6.5– 9.0	8.7	7.5–10.0	9.5
Q1, 1978–79	4.0–6.5	5.1	6.5– 9.0	7.6	7.5–10.0	8.7
Q2, 1978–79	4.0–6.5	4.8	6.5– 9.0	7.7	7.5–10.0	8.6
Q3, 1978–79	2.0–6.0	5.3	6.5– 9.0	8.2	7.5–10.0	8.7
Q4, 1978–79	1.5–4.5†	5.5	5.0– 8.0	8.3	6.0– 9.0	8.1

* Old definitions for money: M-1, private commercial bank demand deposits plus currency; M-2, M-1 plus commercial bank time and savings deposits other than large negotiable CDs; M-3, M-2 plus deposits at mutual savings banks, savings and loan associations, and credit unions.
† The M-1 range initially announced for this period, 1.5 percent to 4.5 percent, was based on the assumption about the rate at which the public would shift balances from bank checking accounts to new interest-earning transactions accounts. The Federal Reserve estimated that use of new account forms would dampen M-1 growth by three percentage points over the year. During the year, the Federal Reserve noted the use of these accounts as alternatives to M-1 deposits was more moderate than initially anticipated and accordingly adjusted the growth range for M-1 upward. As of October 1979, the Federal Reserve's adjusted range for M-1 was 3.0 percent to 6.0 percent.
Source: Conduct of Monetary Policy, Hearing Before the Committee on Banking, Finance, and Urban Affairs, House of Representatives, February 14, 1980, pp. 185–186. Prepared by F. Jean Wells and Roger S. White, Congressional Research Service. Actual growth data are based on seasonally adjusted money supply series of the Board of Governors of the Federal Reserve System as revised in January 1980. Target ranges are those announced before the House and Senate Banking Committees beginning in May 1975 according to procedures developed under H. Con. Res. 133 of the 94th Congress and later under P.L. 95–188. Beginning in 1979, target ranges were announced in accordance with provisions of P.L. 95–523.

TABLE 27-2 Federal Reserve One-Year Target Ranges and Actual
Growth Rates for Monetary Aggregates, 1980–1987

Targets for 1980 through 1986 for three concepts of money are shown. The numbers in
parentheses are adjusted for shifts of funds from savings accounts into NOW accounts
on the questionable grounds that such funds were all still treated like savings accounts.
The yearly growth rates partly mask the *most* variable growth (for periods of five or six
months) in the money supply since the data have been collected—back to World
War II.

The target ranges for M-1 in 1983 were changed three times, and those for M-2 were
changed twice. The changes involved not only new set of numbers but also different
time periods within 1983. The 1984 target range for M-2 was changed twice, as of May
1984.

The record for hitting monetary targets (the Federal Reserve first announced for the
year) is not good for the period 1980–1983 either, as only one of the twelve targets
originally announced for the three aggregates was hit (the M-1 target for 1981).

In 1983 the Federal Reserve introduced a semitarget (called "a monitoring range")
for domestic nonfinancial sector debt. This credit aggregate grew at 10.5 percent in
1983 (in the top half of its 8.5- to 11-percent range). In 1984 the target range was set at
8 to 11 percent and the debt grew at 11.5 percent. In 1984 the debt target range was 8
to 11 percent, and debt grew at 14.3 percent. Debt continued to be targeted at 8 to 11
percent through the tentative target ranges for 1987. It grew at 14 percent in 1985.

(1) Year	(2) Monetary Aggregate	(3) Target Range	(4) Actual	(5) Target Range Miss
1980	M-1	4.5–7% (4–6.5%)*	7.5% (6.75%)	.5 (.25)
	M-2	6–9	9.0	0
	M-3	6.5–9.5	9.6	.1
1981	M-1	6–8.5 (3.5–6)	5.1 (2.5)	−.9 (−1)
	M-2	6–9	9.3	.3
	M-3	6.5–9.5	12.4	2.9
1982	M-1	2.5–5.5	8.8	3.3
	M-2	6–9	9.1	.1
	M-3	6.5–9.5	10.0	.5
1983 (Targets announced on July 20, 1982):				
	M-1	2.5–5.5	10.4	4.9
	M-2	6–9	12.2	3.2
	M-3	6.5–9	10.0	1
1983 (New targets announced on Feb. 19, 1983 to apply to the remainder of 1983):				
	M-1	4–8	7.8	0
	M-2	7–10	7.7	0
1983 (New target for M1 growth announced in June 1983 for the remainder of 1983):				
	M-1	5–9	7.3	0
1984 (Targets announced July 1983):				
	M-1	4–8	5.2	0
	M-2	6.5–9.5	7.7	0
	M-3	6–9	10.5	1.5

TABLE 27-2 (*Continued*)

(1) Year	(2) Monetary Aggregate	(3) Target Range	(4) Actual	(5) Target Range Miss
1984 (New targets announced February 1984):				
	M-2	6–9	7.7	0
1985 (Targets announced February 12, 1985):				
	M-1	4–7	11.9	4.9
	M-2	6–9	8.6	0
	M-3	6–9.5	8.0	0
1985 (Targets announced July 9, 1985, for the last three quarters of 1985):				
	M-1	3–8	12.4	4.4
1986 (Targets announced July 18, 1986):				
	M-1	3–8	12.7^P	4.7^P
	M-2	6–9	7.7^P	0
	M-3	6–9		
1987 (Targets announced July 18, 1986):				
	M-1	3–8		
	M-2	5.5–8.5		
	M-3	8–11		

P: preliminary.
* These are data for different definitions of money adopted in these years.
Source: For the period up to 1983, the Board of Governors of the Federal Reserve System, Monetary Policy Objectives, 1981–1983. M-1 was called M-1B in 1980 and 1981. (The definitions of the aggregates were changed slightly on February 11, 1983, and these changed estimates were not used.) 1984 targets are found in "Monetary Report to the Congress," *Federal Reserve Bulletin*, February 1984, p. 69. The Federal Reserve changed its estimates of the monetary aggregates in February 1984 but continued to put the old "wrong" numbers in the *Federal Reserve Bulletin* as late as March 1984, creating confusion about its own record in a period in which uncertainty about its intentions needed no catalyst.

The data for 1985 and 1986 are taken from *Monetary Policy Objectives for 1986, Midyear Review of the Federal Reserve Board*, July 18, 1986, p. 9; and "Monetary Policy Report to the Congress," *Bulletin*, April 1985, pp. 187–199; R. W. Hafer, "The FOMC in 1985: Reacting to Declining M1 Velocity," *Review*, Federal Reserve Bank of St. Louis, February 1986, pp. 5–21.

West Germany was not as vigorous as that in Japan, and it declined in 1985. Part of the Reagan administration plan in 1985 and 1986, fostered by Secretary of the Treasury James Baker, apparently was to persuade West Germany and Japan to increase the rate of growth of their money supplies. The objective was to reduce the exchange value of the U.S. dollar, which was rising in the early 1980s. Was the fast money growth in the United States in 1985 and 1986 desirable, and did (or should they have) Japan and West Germany change their more stable monetary policy to comply with these pressures? The reader will have more observations over time with which to judge the effects.

TABLE 27-3 Targeted Monetary Aggregates in Nine Countries

Definitions:

Canada (M-1): Currency plus demand deposits less private-sector float.

France (M-2): Currency plus demand, savings, and time deposits.

Germany (Central Bank Money): Currency plus minimum required reserves on domestic bank liabilities using the reserve ratio existing in January 1974.

Italy (Private Sector Credit): Bank and special credit institution loans plus bonds issued by local authorities, public and private companies (net of loans consolidating debt of local authorities) less state-sector borrowing requirement.

Japan (M-2 + CDs): Currency plus demand, savings, and time deposits plus certificates of deposit.

Netherlands (M-2): Currency plus demand, short-term time, liquid savings, and foreign-currency-denominated deposits plus claims on government.

Switzerland (Monetary Base): Currency plus clearing accounts of commercial banks at the Swiss National Bank.

United Kingdom (Sterling M-3): Currency plus private-sector sterling demand and time deposits.

United States (M-1): Currency plus demand deposits and other checkable deposits plus travelers' checks.

		Annual Rates		
Country	Target Period	Target	Current†	Past‡
Canada	Three months centered on 9/1980 to present*	4–8%	4.5%	7.3%
France	1/1985–1/1986	4–6	6.0	8.3
Germany	IV/1984–IV/1985	3–5	4.5	4.6
Italy	12/1984–12/1985	12	8.5	17.5
Japan	III/1984–III/1985	8	8.2	8.4
Netherlands	12/1981–present*	6.5	8.4	5.7
Switzerland	12/1984–12/1985	3	−0.4	4.2
United Kingdom	2/1985–4/1986	5–9	15.1	12.3
United States	II/1985–IV/1985	3–8	13.2	5.2

* Canada and the Netherlands did not officially report a target for 1985 but unofficially continued their 1982 targets.

† Growth rates from the beginning of the current target period through the latest period for which data are available are as follows:

Canada (1/86)	Italy (11/85)	Switzerland (12/85)
France (9/85)	Japan (III/85)	United Kingdom (1/86)
Germany (IV/85)	Netherlands (9/85)	United States (IV/85)

‡ Growth rates for the year preceding the above target period, except for Canada (II/1979–3 months centered on 9/1980), Japan (II/1984–II/1985), the Netherlands (12/1980–12/1981), the United Kingdom (2/1984–4/1985), and the United States (IV/1983–IV/1984).

Source: International Economic Conditions, Federal Reserve Bank of St. Louis, (April 1986), p. 7.

ALTERNATIVE TARGETS

There are many other targets that the Federal Reserve could use, other than targeting some concept of the money supply. During the 1930s, an early member of the Chicago School (Henry C. Simons, who is quoted in Chapter 29) suggested that the price level be targeted. Later evidence in the 1950s determined that direct targeting of the price level would be a very poor operating procedure for the Federal Reserve's open market desk. This is because there was an average two-year lag between the implementation of an open market change in the monetary base over a three- or six-month period and a change in the price level. The feedback as to whether the change in the monetary base was too little or too much thus would be too long delayed to be of any help in correcting current policies. This does not mean that stabilization of the price level is not an excellent ultimate target, but one should be careful not to mix ultimate targets with intermediate targets or operating instruments.

M-4 IS COMING IN NICELY

Tables 27-1 and 27-2 hardly do justice to the confusion in interpreting the targets. The Federal Reserve actually has five commonly cited M's, which can be represented in seasonally adjusted form or seasonally unadjusted form. When Chairman Burns appeared before the House Banking Committee with a huge matrix of innumerable concepts of the monetary aggregates, eyes glazed over. No member of Congress was eager to take him on with a statement such as "You are not on target." "I beg your pardon," Burns might say as he puffed on his pipe, "the seasonally unadjusted M-4 is coming in nicely."

The next chairman, William Miller, invented a new aggregate in 1978, M-1+, that mixed the medium-of-exchange definition with savings accounts at commercial banks. It withered away and soon disappeared from Federal Reserve records. In an attempt to bring the M-1 concept up to date, as the basic medium of exchange, NOW accounts were brought in, and M-1B was the name used for the new aggregate. Having learned that new symbol, the public was soon told that the Federal Reserve did not want to count all NOW accounts during the adjustment period; it would target M-1B adjusted. By now, money and banking students were writhing in pain. The Federal Reserve had also brought in M-1A, which was promptly dropped when it changed the name of M-1B to M-1. Then, on February 11, 1983, it redefined M-1 slightly, just enough to change all the tables. Underneath all this complexity, the simple record in Tables 27-1 and 27-2 conveys an essential message.

What about looking at everything? An official of a Federal Reserve bank once told Milton Friedman that, unlike Friedman, who concentrated on one thing, money, the Federal Reserve looked at everything. Friedman replied (approximately), "After you do that, what changes do you prescribe for the money supply?" The point is that the Federal Reserve does not control everything; it works directly with the monetary base. However, it need not conduct open market operations according to the level of some monetary aggregate, such as the nonborrowed reserves of the monetary base. Instead, it could and does also use an interest rate target. Changes in the federal funds rate are registered rapidly enough after open market operations to make that variable a viable candidate for an operating instrument (or intermediate target), as it now is used along with the nonborrowed monetary base. The choice between money supply aggregates and the interest or the use of both for intermediate targets is discussed in Chapter 31.

Benjamin Friedman made a forceful case for using a credit aggregate along with monetary aggregates. His arguments and the rejoinder by Allan Meltzer are useful and interesting differences of view.[15] Benjamin Friedman may have been the main individual who convinced the Federal Reserve in 1983 to begin formally publishing material on a credit aggregate target. There is little doubt that credit (borrowed funds) is related to gross national product, as the Federal Reserve indicated in its 1983 monetary report to the U.S. Congress, shown in Table 27-4. As an ultimate target, it is almost as good as nominal GNP, real output, or the price level, although they would be preferable.

The real issue is whether it can be used as an intermediate target or an operating instrument. Suppose that an expansionary open market purchase is made. How soon will the manager of the open market desk know whether he or she overshot or undershot the target? That is not an important issue if monetary policy is conducted as Milton Friedman suggested, that is, correcting for overshooting or undershooting every six months. In that case, nominal GNP might be better. But Benjamin Friedman did not subscribe to that approach, indicating that some credit aggregates are available monthly. "Indeed, the Federal Reserve currently maintains, on an unpublished basis, a monthly credit file."[16] Therefore, the manager might get some kind of feedback at the end of the month.

However, the credit aggregates in the flow-of-funds accounts are not in the best of company. The flow-of-funds accounts kept by the Federal Reserve have a number of fundamental problems.[17] For example, to make them conform to national income accounts, assets are carried at book value instead of at market value. (Book value is the present net worth of a firm.) There is a problem of double-counting when the newly issued debt of one firm is lent to another firm that then issues new debt. Just how good the monthly data are has yet to be fully determined.

There is also the danger with multiple targets, such as a monetary and credit aggregate, that no clear decision rule between them is available, so that there is only political expendiency. To a large extent, this has been true with the array of monetary aggregates, as noted. The credit aggregates may merely get dropped into an array of targets. Like the missionaries who believed that

T A B L E 2 7 - 4   Behavior of Domestic Nonfinancial Sector Debt, 1960–1982*

"The specific measure of aggregate credit used by the FOMC in establishing a range of growth is the total debt of domestic nonfinancial sectors, as derived from the Board's flow-of-funds accounts. This measure includes borrowing by private domestic non-financial sectors and by the federal and state and local governments, in U.S. markets and from abroad; it excludes borrowing by foreign entities in the United States."

Year	Change in Debt	Change in Ratio of Debt to GNP	Year	Change in Debt	Change in Ratio of Debt to GNP
1960	5.2%	3.1%	1972	10.9	−1.4
1961	5.7	−1.6	1973	11.3	−0.2
1962	6.7	0.9	1974	9.3	2.1
1963	6.9	0.3			
1964	7.2	1.2	1975	8.9	−1.0
			1976	10.7	1.3
1965	7.2	−3.0	1977	12.3	0.1
1966	6.9	−1.1	1978	12.9	−1.6
1967	6.8	0.5	1979	12.3	2.4
1968	8.4	−0.9			
1969	7.1	0.3	1980	9.9	0.4
			1981	10.1	0.4
1970	6.9	1.9	1982	9.1	5.7
1971	9.3	−0.3	Average	8.7	0.4

* Changes in percent, fourth quarter to fourth quarter.
Source: Federal Reserve Board of Governors, *Monetary Report to Congress, Pursuant to the Full Employment and Balanced Growth Act of 1978*, February 16, 1983, pp. 35–36. Caption is taken from this source.

they had won many converts when their deity was accepted, Benjamin Friedman may have been dismayed to find that they have ten other deities, some seasonally adjusted, some not, and one in the White House. Giving them more targets may not constrain their control procedures to some more desirable outcome; it may set them free.

As noted in the last chapter, real interest rates were suggested in 1982 as a target for monetary policy. The reader should carefully review the estimation processes for real interest rates, including the effects of inflationary expectations and income taxes, surveyed in Chapter 19. Two conclusions can be drawn from that analysis. First, there are at present no exact ways to estimate real interest rates. The real interest rate or real rate of return will differ among individuals according to the rate at which they discount the future. (See Chapter 10 for a definition of the rate of discount.) Second, a given real rate of interest can be consistent with any rate of inflation. Real interest rates rise when there is a great deal of uncertainty in the economy, when it takes a high real rate of return to get investors to invest in the future. If the money supply is accelerated when real interest rates rise, the monetary acceleration can cause a further increase in uncertainty. The result is not hard to guess.

Other interesting and popular targets among many individuals are commodity standards, such as the gold standard, which are covered in Part IX.

THE CHANGE IN OPERATING PROCEDURES IN OCTOBER 1982: TARGETING BORROWED RESERVES

At an FOMC meeting in October 1982 the short-term target objectives for M-1 were suspended.[18] The event that initiated this change was the maturing of a large volume of all-savers certificates (time deposits with tax-free income that, in 1981, depository institutions were temporarily allowed to offer). It was feared that M-1 would be enlarged by a shift of funds from these certificates into checking accounts. Commercial banks and thrifts were also introducing money market–type accounts at the time, and it was feared that this would also influence M-1 in an unpredictable way. The change was made more permanent, perhaps because the fast money growth between 1983 and 1986 did not produce inflation in those years and the Federal Reserve saw no reason for directly controlling the monetary aggregates until it could better predict velocity. Controlling the money supply is an issue different from the effects of money growth on prices and output. The new operating procedure will be shown to be primarily a system to smooth interest rates.

Chairman Paul Volcker in his testimony to the Congress in 1983 denied the existence of monthly data for the credit aggregate that the Federal Reserve had halfway adopted.[19] It did "not have the status of a 'target,'" but the Federal Open Market Committee "does intend to monitor developments with respect to credit closely for what assistance it can provide in judging appropriate responses to developments in other aggregates." Simultaneously, he announced that less emphasis would be put on M-1 "because of institutional distortions and the apparent shift in the behavior of velocity." His statements indicated that the 1979 announcement of a concentration on monetary aggregates was an experiment that, at least for the near future, had ended.

> In addition, the Committee set forth for the first time its expectations with respect to growth of total domestic nonfinancial debt, and felt that a range of $8\frac{1}{2}$ to $11\frac{1}{2}$ percent would be appropriate. Data for such a broad credit aggregate are not yet available monthly, nor are the tools available to influence closely total flows of credit. While the credit range during this experimental period does not have the status of a "target," the Committee does intend to monitor developments with respect to credit closely for what assistance it can provide in judging appropriate responses to developments in the other aggregates. The range would encompass growth of credit roughly in line with nominal GNP in

accordance with the past trends; the upper part of the range would allow for growth a bit faster than nominal GNP in recognition of some analysis suggesting a moderate increase in the ratio of debt to GNP may develop.

Premium on Judgment

I appreciate the complexity—for the Federal Reserve and for those observing our operations—of weighing performance with respect to a number of monetary and credit targets, of taking account of institutional change, and of assessing the possibility of shifts in relationships established earlier in the postwar period—a possibility that can only be known with certainty long after the event. But we also can sense something of the dangers of proceeding as if the world in those respects had not changed.

I neither bewail nor applaud the circumstances that have put a greater premium on judgment and less "automaticity" in our operations; it is simply a fact of life. In making such judgments, the basic point remains that, over time, the growth of money and credit will need to be reduced to encourage a return to reasonable price stability. The targets set out are consistent with that intent.

I understand—indeed to a degree, I share—the longing of some to encompass the objectives for monetary policy in a simple fixed operating rule. The trouble is, right now, in the world in which we live, I know of no such simple rule that will also reliably bring the results we want.[20]

Because the Federal Reserve had gone over the upper limit of its target range for M-1 in 1982 and in May 1983 was on a path of growth above the M-1 target range for 1983, Volcker's statement carried an additional message other than that the 1979 experiment with concentration on monetary aggregates was over. Chairman Volcker's statement clearly implied that the monetary targets that are set for aggregates such as M-1, after taking into account many other factors, including the important ultimate targets of price stability and full employment, were no longer a constraint. They could be violated as a matter of policy at any time. There thus was a question as to whether or not this type of policy would keep real interest rates high because of continued uncertainty that required the financial community to hang on every weekly announcement of money supply growth, every offhand and formal comment by a Federal Reserve official, to see what the Federal Reserve policy currently comprised.

The new deemphasis of M-1 required a new operating procedure because the previous operating procedure—of targeting nonborrowed reserves—gave too much weight to controlling M-1. Although the FOMC continued to issue short-run targets for M-1 in its directive to the open market desk at the New York Federal Reserve Bank, the open market manager was not directed to target nonborrowed reserves. Rather, the new short-run target was borrowed reserves.

The FOMC tells the open market manager to target borrowed reserves by directing the following for the attainment of various levels of reserve restraint: "more restraint" (implying a higher level of borrowing from the Federal Reserve), "less restraint" (implying a lower level of borrowing), or "unchanged restraint" (implying the same level of borrowing).

The open market manager carries out the directive in the following way: Estimates are made of the two expected total reserves that will be available during the two-week accounting period (under the present system of contemporaneous reserve accounting). The open market desk then supplies reserves up to the level of the estimated total reserves minus the targeted level of borrowing. Suppose that the targeted borrowing is increased. By lowering the amount of reserves fed into the banking system through open market operations, a shortage of reserves will develop. The depository institutions that are short of reserves will be forced to borrow from those that have more reserves in the federal funds market. The federal funds rate will rise. Recall from Chapter 16 that the amount of funds borrowed by depository institutions depends on the difference between the federal funds rate and the loan rate posted by the Federal Reserve, called the *discount rate*. A sufficiently high federal funds rate will drive the banks to the discount window—rapidly if there are insufficient reserves to support deposits. Banks cannot increase the total reserves in the banking system by borrowing from one another.

The depository institutions will attempt to sell off assets and reduce deposits as the price of reserves—the federal funds rate—rises. The quantity of checking accounts in the banking system will change, and thus the quantity of money will change as part of this operating procedure.

The main part of the operating procedure is not control of the money supply, but a method for controlling interest rates in order to lead depository institutions to borrow the desired amount from the Federal Reserve. It is an operating procedure similar to that employed by the Federal Reserve before the October 1979 announcement in which it switched to nonborrowed reserves for its short-term operating target. (Before that announcement the Federal Reserve emphasized the federal funds rate as a target.) The new procedure has much wider bands for the acceptable federal funds rate than in the earlier period in which the federal funds rate itself was the target.

The new system can be one in which short-term interest rates are stabilized. Suppose that the FOMC wants the same level of borrowed reserves; this would be called "unchanged restraint." Under the new system, changes in the demand for reserves for depository institutions will have little effect on the federal funds rate because these demands are met by open market procedures to keep the federal funds rate just where it is so that the spread between the federal funds rate and the discount rate does not change. The new system could thus be described as one in which stability in interest rates is preferred to stability in the monetary aggregates.

Such an operating procedure is not assisted by the contemporaneous reserve accounting that was adopted in 1984. That is, contemporaneous reserve makes it more difficult to estimate the reserves of the depository institutions than under lagged reserve accounting. The new accounting system has increased the Federal Reserve's ability to control the money supply if the monetary base or nonborrowed reserves are used, as was the case between 1979 and 1982.

One difficulty with stabilizing interest rates is that the short-term stability of interest rates is traded for their longer-term stability. This is because interest rates are basically determined on world markets, and attempts to hold interest rates at levels not consistent with world interest rates cannot be maintained. Accordingly, there will be periods of large shifts from what had appeared to be, in the short term, a stable level of controlled interest rates.

APPENDIX: COORDINATION OF MONETARY AND FISCAL POLICIES

Alan Blinder wrote an interesting paper on the coordination of monetary and fiscal policy, and William Poole and James Tobin provided discussion papers.[21] Blinder used the government budget constraint (or monetary base identity) together with rational expectations theory to show that if people think that a deficit will be financed by money creation or the issuance of new government bonds, it will affect their behavior.

Discussion of the effects of financing, using the monetary base identity, produces useful analysis; but whether the label "coordination" or "noncoordination" is appropriate for intended relationships of monetary and fiscal policies depends on one's analysis. The following reply to Blinder from William Poole refers to the hypothesis that in the long run, changes in the money supply affect only prices, not real variables—the **neutrality of money**.

> Even if the coordination issue disappears in the long run due to the neutrality of money, there is still a short-run coordination issue that needs discussion. For there to be a coordination issue, the policy ineffectiveness proposition in the rational expectations macro literature must fail. More conventionally, it must also be assumed that countercyclical stabilization policy is feasible in spite of policy lags and the inaccuracies of economic forecasts. If stabilization policy is not feasible, Blinder has no paper.[22]

The uninitiated may find discussions about the coordination of fiscal and monetary policy to be quite harmonious. Everyone is for coordinated, as opposed to uncoordinated, policy. Yet monetarists and Keynesians may mean exactly the opposite when they discuss this topic.

Monetarists want the Federal Reserve to stay on its money target paths. They believe that actions of the Treasury that affect monetary growth—expenditures, tax collections, buying and selling securities—should be offset by the Federal Reserve's open market operations. Other actions, such as a borrowed deficit, that do not affect the money supply should be ignored.

FIGURE 27-6   Coordinating Fiscal and Monetary Policy: Opposite
Views of Monetarists and Keynesians

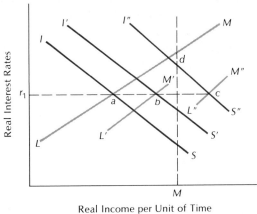

Keynesians believe that a deliberate expansionary policy of deficit spending
should not be hamstrung by tight (read high interest rates) monetary policy.

For those who have read Chapter 23, this is a demonstration of these points
in terms of the *IS–LM* framework in Figure 27-6. For simplicity, it is a static
analysis—a series of snapshots in time. Assume that a deficit financed by borrowing (selling bonds) moves *IS* to *I'S'*. Monetarists advise no change in the
money supply (if the money supply is on its long-run target). Some Keynesians
might suggest an increase in the money supply sufficient to move the *LM*
locus to *L'M'*. This monetary change keeps real interest rates at r_1 and allows
the full multiplier effect of a change in real income equal to *ab* (the government expenditure multiplier times the deficit).

Suppose that the deficit shifts *IS* to *I"S"*. The full multiplier effect, *ac*, can be
achieved only if the *LM* is shifted to *L"M"* by an increase in the money
supply. This is an unattainable position. The demand for goods and services
will exceed the supply, and inflation must result, so that the *LM* locus will
shift up to a full employment equilibrium position at point *d*. Thus, even under
the restrictive assumption that inflation will not occur until the full employment level is reached, a monetary policy that complements fiscal policy can be
inflationary. However, if the *LM* locus is nearly vertical, a government policy
to expand demand by running a deficit will fail without a complementary
monetary expansion.

STUDY QUESTIONS

1. Identify the common ultimate targets, intermediate targets, and operating
    instruments of monetary policy. Explain with several examples of how
    they can be inconsistent.

2. What has been the Federal Reserve's record since 1975 for hitting its target ranges for monetary growth? What have been the effects of this record?

3. What improvements in estimates of the money supply resulted from 1980 legislation? What improvements are still needed? What difference does this information make for monetary control under a system that targets borrowed reserves?

4. Under what conditions are nonborrowed reserves a better operating instrument than the monetary base is?

5. In Chapter 2, money was said to be an important variable for specific study, in part because it is a *policy variable*, a variable that can be changed by government policy. Under what conditions will money fail to be a policy variable and instead become a passive variable in another government policy? Describe such a policy and explain why money loses its importance in terms of the criteria used in Chapter 2.

6. How would one try to forecast Federal Reserve policy if the announced objectives were thought to be misleading, inconsistent, or unattainable nearly half the time? What variables and what other things would be useful in making such a forecast?

7. What is Milton Friedman's suggestion for stopping churning at the Federal Reserve open market desk? Would it work?

8. What improvements could be made in the Federal Reserve's procedures for controlling the money supply? Could the Federal Reserve have had a better record of achieving its target with the control procedures that it had at the time? Explain.

9. What are the benefits and harmful effects, if any, of combining a credit aggregate target with a monetary aggregate target in the conduct of monetary policy?

10. Assess the use of free reserves as an intermediate target for monetary policy.

11. Explain and assess the desirability of multiple intermediate targets for monetary policy. Then assess the following statement by Lawrence K. Roos, the former president of the Federal Reserve Bank of St. Louis: "The decision last fall by the Fed to abandon M-1 (currency and demand deposits) as a target and instead to focus on M-2, M-3, credit and Gross National Product signaled a retreat from its decision of October 1979 to concentrate on monetary aggregate targeting. It represented a return to the kind of intuitive fine-tuning that produced the double-digit inflation of the 1970s." (Quoted from "We'd Better Pay Attention to M-1," *The Wall Street Journal*, April 7, 1983, p. 28.)

The St. Louis Federal Reserve has been noted for its monetarist positions, with which Mr. Roos, as in the foregoing statement, apparently agreed. What would you have advised the Federal Reserve to do in the face of a recession with over 10 percent unemployment at the end of

1982? Should it have stuck to its monetary targets? Answer your question on the basis of the welfare of the population determined by the then current and expected future levels of unemployment and inflation.

GLOSSARY

Benchmark data. Source data from which future estimates or interpolations can be made. For example, if data are collected only twice a year from sources, those twice-a-year entries are called benchmark data. The series may be estimated from other sources between those dates or simply interpolated on the basis of past trends from the benchmark data.

Churning. The unnecessary buying and selling of securities that run up transactions costs.

Excess reserves. Total reserves minus required reserves.

Free reserves. Excess reserves minus depository institutions' borrowings from the Federal Reserve.

Intermediate targets. Targets in the chain of causation between the operating instruments and the ultimate targets of policy.

Neutrality of money. The hypothesis that in the long run, changes in the money supply do not affect real variables.

Nonborrowed base. The monetary base minus depository institutions' borrowings from the Federal Reserve.

Nonborrowed reserve path. The sequence of the desired target levels of total nonborrowed reserves planned by the Federal Reserve over time.

Nonborrowed reserves. Total reserves minus borrowings.

Operating instruments. The immediate and proximate variables changed by policy, such as the federal funds rate and nonborrowed reserves in the Federal Reserve's open market operations.

Total reserve path. The sequence of desired target levels of total reserves over time planned by the Federal Reserve for all depository institutions.

Ultimate targets. The targets that a policy is ultimately intended to achieve, such as price stability and full employment.

NOTES

1. Board of Governors of the Federal Reserve, *The Federal Reserve System, Purposes and Functions*, September 1974, p. 1.

2. The emergence of balance-of-payment problems did not appear in the president's Council of Economic Advisors' report until 1960. (Both the annual reports and the CEA were authorized by the Employment Act of 1946.) See Reuben E. Slesinger, *National Economic Policy: The Presidential Papers* (New York: D. Van Nostrand, 1968) for a review of the act and all the CEA reports to 1967.

3. One can study past actions of intervention or read the following elaboration in *The Federal Reserve System, Purposes and Functions* without gaining a precise idea of what the Board of Governors and the FOMC have in mind. Are they turning to foreign exchange intervention and a policy of high interest rates and away from emphasis on the monetary targets and domestic considerations? Such a question often arises in monetary policy oversight hearings. Here is some more custard pie from the Federal Reserve ready for nailing to the wall:

- "The Board of Governors and the FOMC take account of the U.S. balance of payments, movements in exchange rates, and other international economic and financial developments in making U.S. monetary policy.
- "The Federal Reserve Bank of New York handles the mechanics of official reserve transactions with foreign central banks, and in some cases these transactions call for Federal Reserve open market operations to offset undesired effects on domestic monetary conditions.
- "Transactions may be undertaken by the Federal Reserve in the foreign exchange markets, and these transactions, as well as similar transactions by foreign central banks, may be facilitated by currency 'swap' operations.
- "The Board of Governors takes various actions of a regulatory or supervisory nature that affect the international transactions and foreign operations of U.S. banks and the U.S. activities of foreign banks.

"In forming the judgments about prospective economic developments that underlie monetary policy decisions, Federal Reserve policymakers regularly take into account the relationships that link the domestic economy to the rest of the world—for example, the forces that affect foreign demand for U.S. goods and services, the determinants of supply and demand in this country for the U.S. products that compete with imports, the factors influencing international flows of funds, and the effects of international flows of funds on domestic financial markets. These relationships are viewed from two related perspectives. First, developments in the rest of the world may have significant implications for the domestic economic objectives of the United States and for the use of monetary policy in attaining these objectives. Second, economic developments in this country have important influences on the net balance of goods and services transactions and the net flow of long-term and liquid capital between the United States and foreign countries, which in turn affect the international value of the dollar and the international reserve position of the United States" [pp. 91–92].

There is nothing inherently wrong with imprecise targets from the standpoint of a governmental unit that desires to ensure a broad scope for future actions. For the analyst, however, it is useful to know what, if any, limits are put on future actions. How precise are the targets for future actions?

4. Board of Governors, Federal Reserve System, *Purposes & Functions* (Washington, D.C.: U.S. Government Printing Office, 1984), p. 1.

5. The managed liabilities are discussed in Chapter 8.

6. "Monetary Policy and Open Market Operations in 1979," *Quarterly Review*, Federal Reserve Bank of New York, Vol. 5, Summer 1980, pp. 60–61.

7. Milton Friedman, "Monetary Policy," *Journal of Money, Credit and Banking*, January 1982, p. 113. Friedman later revised his estimates of gross transactions to $800 billion. "A Reply by Milton Friedman," *Journal of Money, Credit and Banking*, August 1982, pp. 404–406.

8. In October 1979 the Federal Reserve announced that it would change its operating procedures so as to emphasize control of the money supply. It then widened the permissible band—before intervention—on the federal funds rate.

9. "Analysis of the Impact of Lagged Reserve Accounting," a report prepared by the staff of the Board of Governors of the Federal Reserve System, October 6, 1977, p. 15.

10. Friedman, "Monetary Policy," p. 117.

11. Ibid.

12. An excellent book that describes some of these points on monetary control is unfortunately out of print but may be found in the library: Albert E. Burger, *The Money Supply Process* (Belmont, Calif.: Wadsworth, 1971).

13. At first glance, it may appear that an overnight federal funds rate could not be affected by an expectation of increased rates of inflation. After all, how much inflation could occur in one day from an increase of even 10 percent in the expected rate of inflation over the entire year? The answer is that if one-year rates rose by 10 percent and arbitrage brought the one-day rates in line, they too would rise by a percentage that, on an annual basis with 365 compounding periods, would be 9.53 percent. At this rate, $261.10 interest would be paid on a $1 million loan for one day. (See Chapter 10 for the formulas used for these calculations.)

14. There is a sophisticated literature on this issue of assigning particular variables to influence particular other variables. In the context of a mathematical model, it can be shown that one independent variable (the policy variable) can be assigned to change only one other independent variable. Some of the important works on this assignment problem, which the beginner might scan only to obtain the flavor, are J. Tinbergen, *Economic Policy: Principles and Design* (Amsterdam: North-Holland, 1956); Henri Theil, *Economic Forecasts and Policy* (Amsterdam: North-Holland, 1961); and Franklin Fisher, "On the Independent Use of Two

or More Sets of Policy Variables," *Journal of Political Economy*, February 1967, pp. 77–85.

15. Benjamin M. Friedman, "Using a Credit Aggregate Target to Implement Monetary Policy in the Financial Environment of the Future," and Allan H. Meltzer, "Discussion," *Monetary Policy Issues in the 1980s*, a symposium sponsored by the Federal Reserve Bank of Kansas City, at Jackson Hole, Wyoming, August 9–10, 1982, pp. 19–247 and 249–255, respectively.

16. Benjamin Friedman, "Using a Credit Aggregate Target," pp. 239–240. Chairman Volcker said that the Federal Reserves semitarget credit aggregate is not available monthly, as quoted later.

17. The flow of funds and its problems are covered in Robert Auerbach, *Financial Markets and Institutions* (New York: Macmillan, 1983), pp. 52–70.

18. See R. Alton Gilbert, "Operating Procedures for Conducting Monetary Policy," *Review*, Federal Reserve Bank of St. Louis, February 1985, pp. 13–21.

19. Paul A. Volcker, "Testimony of Paul A. Volcker, Chairman, Federal Reserve Board," in *Monetary Policy Objectives for 1983, Summary Report of the Federal Reserve Board*, February 16, 1983, pp. 12–20.

20. Ibid., p. 20.

21. Alan S. Blinder, "Issues in the Coordination of Monetary and Fiscal Policy," William Poole, "Discussion," and James Tobin, "Discussion," in *Monetary Policy*, pp. 3–34, 35–40, and 41–46, respectively.

22. William Poole, "Discussion," p. 36.

CHAPTER 28

SELECTED POLICIES AND THE RECORD SINCE 1942

CHAPTER PREVIEW

Introduction. The events of the period after World War II are important background for understanding who controls monetary policy, the discussion in the next chapter.

The Bond Price Support Period. Interest rate pegging can make the money supply a passive variable.

The Character of the Post–World War II Period. From the Treasury–Federal Reserve Accord in 1951 to 1986, the Federal Reserve ran the monetary policy. Important trends in deficits and inflation are described. The period after the Volcker announcement of a change in Federal Reserve Policy in 1979 is given special attention.

Debt Management: Operation Twist and Bills Only. The losing bout of the U.S. government with the term structure of interest rates is presented.

INTRODUCTION

This chapter is an important prologue to the discussion in the next chapter of who makes monetary policy. First, it is necessary to understand the nature of the post–World War II period. Interest rate pegging was a policy of the government until the early 1950s. That and then the period up to 1987 are described. The chapter ends with a discussion of debt management and a losing bout the U.S. government had with the term structure of interest rates.

THE BOND PRICE SUPPORT PERIOD

In April 1942, the Federal Open Market Committee announced a plan to keep the interest rate on short-term Treasury obligations pegged at three eighths of 1 percent per year by buying or selling these securities at that rate. The interest rate was pegged at that low rate to reduce the cost of debt finance for World War II. Extensive amounts of other securities with longer maturities were purchased, though their interest rates were not pegged quite as rigidly.[1]

The nominal money supply will become a passive variable if it is regulated in order to hold interest rates constant in the short run. Figure 28-1 shows this

FIGURE 28-1   Pegging Interest Rates at i_p

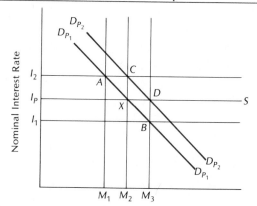

Nominal Money Supply Demanded

The figure shows how the central bank pegs the interest rate at i_p. It relies on the liquidity effect and then disregards the price expectations effect (discussed in Chapter 19). If interest rates rise so that the initial equilibrium point is A with a nominal money supply of M_1, the nominal money supply must be increased to M_2 so that the new equilibrium point is X. If interest rates fall so that the equilibrium point is B with an initial nominal money supply of M_3, the nominal money supply must be contracted to M_2. If the demand for nominal money balances moves out, say because the price level rises, so that the equilibrium point moves from X to C, the nominal money supply must be expanded to move the equilibrium point down to D.

with the interest peg set at a nominal bond interest rate of i_p. Suppose that bond prices fall, so that interest rates rise to i_2 (point A on the demand for nominal money balances $D_{P_1}D_{P_1}$) and initially the nominal money supply is M_1. The Federal Reserve's open market desk must buy bonds until their price rises and interest rates fall to i_p (at point X). The nominal money supply must be increased from M_1 to M_2, whether or not that money growth is desired. Similarly, if bond prices rise and the interest falls to i_1, at point B on $D_{P_1}D_{P_1}$, and initially the money supply is M_3, the Federal Reserve will be forced to sell bonds. The money supply contracts from M_3 to M_2, moving the interest rate from i_1 to i_p at point X.

Any change in the price level, say an increase from P_1 to P_2, that shifts the demand for nominal money balances to $D_{P_2}D_{P_2}$ would cause a change in nominal interest rates. Such a change could occur during an economic expansion, raising interest rates to i_2 at point C on the nominal money demand function in Figure 28-1. The Federal Reserve would then be forced to buy bonds and expand the money supply to M_3 to achieve a new equilibrium at D on the demand-for-money schedule. The money expansion, if expected to continue, would, after a short lag, raise nominal interest rates even more (via the Fisher effect described in Chapter 19). This, in turn, would require an open market purchase of bonds, which would expand the money supply even further. **Interest rate pegging**, therefore, can require the government to change the money supply in the wrong direction, so that it induces greater inflation or deflation. That is, it follows a **procyclical policy**.

The interest rate support program also meant that short-term Treasury bills had a relatively constant price and were a close substitute for money. The commercial banks reduced their excess reserves and purchased these price-supported Treasury bills. The ratio of bank deposits to bank reserves rose from nearly 4 to 1 in November of 1941 to more than 6 to 1 in January of 1946.

THE CHARACTER OF THE POST–WORLD WAR II PERIOD

There were dire predictions that the post–World War II period would produce widespread unemployment, as the 16,353,000 members of the U.S. armed forces joined the civilian labor force. In addition, many prognosticators thought that World War II had created increased demand for goods and services that brought an end to the depressions of the 1930s and that the end of hostilities would see a reduction in the demand for goods and services, as well as a deep depression.

The innovative work of John Maynard Keynes during the 1930s focused the attention of the economics profession on the availability of the central government's fiscal tools for achieving and maintaining prosperity. By injecting increased spending into the private sector through deficit spending, the central government could stimulate increased economic activity and prevent or alleviate a depression. Monetary policy was overshadowed by the new Keynesian theories. Alvin Hansen, a well-known proponent of Keynesian economics, wrote in 1948,

> Keynesian theory pushed still farther off the center stage the already dying "MV" type of monetary analysis. Followers of the MV analysis could never see why the "circular flow," once a certain money supply had been created, should not continue on indefinitely. So the fiction had to be invented that there was a villain in the piece. The villain was the monetary authority who maliciously at periodic intervals interfered to curtail the volume of money.[2]

Many governments throughout the world ran deficits and financed them in large part by printing new money. The allegation by monetarists that the depressions of the 1930s had been severely intensified by improper monetary policy and that the quantity of money was the primary determinant of the long-run price level was not widely debated until the late 1950s, when economists began to produce a large quantity of test results from newly estimated money data. Most of the period between World War II and 1970 in the United States and many other countries was one of rapid economic growth and almost continuous moderate rates of inflation, accompanied by large deficits and increased nominal money supplies. But there were exceptions, such as the period from 1961 to 1965, when inflation was negligible in the United States.

The much-touted predictions that the American economy would collapse without war were found to be completely off course. The peace in 1945 brought one of the most prolonged periods of economic growth in the history of the country, rivaling the post–Civil War period. There were recessions in the post–World War II period, but they were minor by almost any measure compared with the depressions of the 1930s.

One of the most notable differences between the recessions in the post–World War II period and those of earlier periods was that prices rose rather than fell in most of the postwar recessions. Prices fell in the 1948–1949 recession, were fairly constant in the 1953–1954 recession, and rose during all the other recessions: 1957–1958, 1960–1961, 1970–1971, 1973–1975, 1980, and 1981–1982. Although the first half of 1979 was not classified as a recession, real growth in that period was negative, and prices, as measured by the consumer price index, rose by 14 percent.

At the end of World War II, the commercial banks held large quantities of government bonds. The policy of pegging the interest rates on these bonds was continued. Under this policy, the Federal Reserve could do little to reduce inflation or to carry on any kind of an independent monetary policy. The federal budget was in surplus in the early postwar period, and so the Treasury did not have to finance government expenditures through borrowing. The federal government's cash surplus was $6.6 billion in 1947, $8.9 billion in 1948, and $1 billion in 1949. Then, in 1950, it had a deficit of $2.2 billion.[3] The deficit had to be financed either by borrowing (that is, selling bonds to the public) or by printing money. The deficit could be financed by printing money if the Federal Reserve bought the securities sold to the public by the Treasury. Partly because of the concern over the desirability of pegging interest rates on the new securities issued by the Treasury, the Federal Reserve became more interested in exercising an active discretionary role in determining the country's money supply. It had moved cautiously in this direction ever since 1946, with the events of the 1949 recession dramatically illustrating the deleterious effects of a passive monetary policy. When bond prices rose during the 1949 recession, the Federal Reserve sold bonds to maintain the interest rates at the pegged levels. Thus, the Federal Reserve was required to reduce the money supply during the middle of a recession.

On June 28, 1949, the Federal Open Market Committee announced that "it will be the policy of the Committee to direct purchases, sales, and exchanges of Government Securities by the Federal Reserve Banks with primary regard to the general business and credit situation."[4] A study by the Congressional Joint Economic Committee in 1950 asserted that the Federal Reserve should conduct monetary policy for the purpose of achieving full employment, price stability, and other objectives of the Employment Act. The officials of the Treasury wished to continue the support of long-term government bonds at 2.5 percent interest. This policy conflicted with the objectives supported by the Federal Reserve officials.

In June 1950, the Korean War began, accompanied by increased government spending and borrowing and a sharp increase in the rate of inflation.[5] The Federal Reserve was now acutely aware of the dangers of rapidly increasing the money supply during an inflation to keep low the interest rates on government bonds.

The Treasury–Federal Reserve Accord and the Return of Discretionary Monetary Policy

There was a struggle between the Treasury and the Federal Reserve, with the Treasury arguing for a passive monetary policy and continued support of bond interest rate pegging and the Federal Reserve arguing for greater discretionary power over the money supply. On March 3, 1951, the two sides reached an agreement, called the Treasury–Federal Reserve Accord.

William McChesney Martin, Jr., an official of the U.S. Treasury, was sent by President Harry Truman to negotiate the Treasury–Federal Reserve Accord. Although the more rigorously maintained peg had already been lifted before the accord, there was still intervention to control the interest rate. It was not Truman's wish to end this intervention but, rather, to give the interest rate greater freedom to rise somewhat before intervening. Not until Truman left office and was succeeded by Dwight D. Eisenhower in 1953 was the policy of intervening to keep the interest rate permanently below a given level dropped. Intervention to control interest rates between target ranges set by the Federal Reserve at different levels in different periods has remained.

From the Accord to 1986

William McChesney Martin, Jr., was appointed chairman of the Federal Reserve Board in April 1951 and served longer than any previous chairman, until January 1970. Chairman Martin played a dominant role in directing the monetary policies of the Federal Reserve in this post-accord period. In January 1970, Chairman Martin was succeeded by Arthur Burns. In March 1978, Chairman Burns was succeeded by G. William Miller, and in August 1979 Paul Volcker became chairman, and President Jimmy Carter made Miller the secretary of the Treasury. Chairman Volcker indicated at a press conference on November 19, 1980, his intention to remain as chairman (his term expired in 1983) in the Reagan administration, which he did.

There were eight recessions from the end of World War II until 1983: 1948–1949, 1953–1954, 1957–1958, 1960–1961, 1970–1971, 1973–1975, 1980, and 1981–1982. There was also a significant downturn in the 1966–1967 period. The 1966–1967 downturn did not quite reach the proportions necessary for the National Bureau of Economic Research to stamp the period "diseased," but nonetheless it has been labeled a "credit crunch." The rate of real GNP growth declined from 6.5 percent in 1966 to 2.6 percent in 1967; the rate of increase for industrial production declined from 9.8 percent to 2.1 percent; corporate profits had a negative growth rate equal to −6.6 percent in 1967. The 1967 episode was similar to the other declines, which were marked by a slowing or slightly negative rate of growth for real GNP, except that the unemployment rate was low, only 3.8 percent in 1967.

In all the post–World War II recessions since the late 1950s, the unemployment rate rose above 6 percent. In 1958 (6.8 percent), 1961 (6.7 percent), and December 1970 (6.2 percent), the unemployment rate was between 6 and 7 percent. The unemployment rate rose all the way to 9 percent in 1975. After the 1975 record, the post–World War II unemployment rate fell to just under 6 percent in 1978, hovered at that level in 1979, and then rose to 7.5 percent in the 1980 recession and above 10 percent in the 1982 recession.

Insofar as the Federal Reserve was primarily following a nominal interest rate target, and that seems to have been the case until October 1979, it could be argued that it may have helped deepen or precipitate some of these recessions. This conclusion can be drawn directly from that presented previously for interest rate pegging, which shows that such monetary policy can lead to procyclical movements in the money supply. Money supply growth would be slowed during a downturn as nominal interest rates fell below the target range. This explanation requires that the Federal Reserve change its target rates more slowly than the change in market interest rates. There were other, often more important, factors, such as oil price increases in 1973, that caused and deepened recessions.

In 1979 there was extremely rapid growth in the money supply. The three-month rate of change in M-1 ranged from over 9 percent to nearly 12 percent during April, May, June, July, and August 1979. With inflation soaring and a belief by participants in the financial markets that the Federal Reserve could not control the money supply, there was a sigh of relief on July 25, 1979, when Paul Volcker was named to succeed G. William Miller as head of the Federal Reserve Board after Miller had been named to replace Michael Blumenthal as secretary of the Treasury on July 19. The stock market rallied in anticipation of a Federal Reserve that would be better able to control the country's money supply and combat inflation. There was great uncertainty in the economy, not only from the rampant inflation and seemingly uncontrollable money supply growth, but also from national and world events.

On August 1, Chrysler reported large operating losses and asked for federal aid to avoid bankruptcy. On August 15, Andrew Young resigned as ambassador to the United Nations. The following day, the Federal Reserve announced an increase in the discount rate to a record 10.5 percent. And on September 12, the major banks raised their advertised prime rate to 13 percent. On October 5, 1979, the Dow-Jones Industrial Average closed at 898, the high for the year. The low occurred after the Volcker announcement on October 6, with Dow-Jones hitting 707 on November 7.

Just 60 days after Paul Volcker became chairman of the Federal Reserve Board, the Federal Reserve announced changes in policy. The new policy was described as more concentration on the monetary aggregates and less on the federal funds rate. In practice this meant that the target band for the federal funds rate was widened.

The Volcker announcement of major policy changes produced great uncertainty. As indicated in the last chapter, much of the time the Federal Reserve had missed its target for M-1, the medium-of-exchange definition of money, since it began reporting to the Congress on its long-range targets, and so this record lost its credibility. There was extreme uncertainty as to the effect of Volcker's announcement as well as the rather general prediction among economists and others that a sudden braking of the money supply as might occur (though it need not have if a gradual deceleration were implemented) would produce a recession in 1980.

Nominal interest rates rose rapidly, incorporating a premium for high uncertainty about Volcker's policy and world events. On October 12 the major banks raised their prime to 15 percent. A momentous shock occurred on November 4 when the U.S. embassy in Tehran was invaded and 52 hostages were seized. The Big Three automakers announced further layoffs, and gold rose in price, passing for the first time on December 26 the $500-per-ounce level. Then on December 30 Soviet troops invaded Afghanistan.

Nearly everyone had underestimated the effect of uncertainty on interest rates that would be produced by the new monetary policy, and no one foresaw the November 4 and December 30 shocks that dramatically increased uncertainty about the future. The uncertainty premium raised both short-term and long-term rates. The rise in long-term rates could not be explained in terms of inflationary expectations, given that the public thought that the new monetary policy would at least not significantly raise the long-run rate of growth of the money supply.

No serious analyst would have suggested that the lag between the deceleration in the rate of monetary growth and the price level would be as short as three months, given the average two-year lag that had been seen in the United States since 1947. Nevertheless, the new monetary policy was perceived by some to be inadequate to control inflation when the annual rate of inflation soared to 18.2 percent, as measured by the CPI, in January, February, and March 1980. (Part of this rise was caused by rising imported oil prices. See Chapter 7.) Along with this rise in the rate of inflation, interest rates rose, with the federal funds rate hitting 17.61 percent in April 1980.

It required unusual perseverence and courage on the part of Paul Volcker and the members of the Federal Open Market committee to follow any intended policy in such a period of extreme economic changes and dramatic international news. The reduction in monetary growth, on the average, from 1980 to 1982 and the sharp reduction in inflation over this period were acclaimed to be a great accomplishment. The political aspects of this period are important to monetary policy and are described in the next chapter.

The nominal deficit was persistently large by historical standards after 1975, but that is partly a reflection of the higher nominal values (due to inflation). It is more meaningful to compare the deficits with GNP, as in Figure 28-2, or to compute the real deficit, as was shown in Chapter 22. The deficit as a fraction of GNP has been generally larger by historical standards that go back to 1790 (except for wartime periods) since the 1930s, although the general trend increased after 1965. The Reagan administration signed a new tax law in 1981 that significantly lowered tax rates.

When the fiscal 1982 budget deficit looked as if it would go over $100 billion (which it did, as noted in Chapter 22), and future deficits looked large, the Reagan administration switched policies and supported a large tax increase bill that was signed into law in 1982. This was a procyclical fiscal policy that was followed by sharply faster money growth in the last half of 1982 and the first half of 1983 as unemployment rose to over 10 percent. Unemployment fell to near 7 percent in June 1984, but it failed to fall much farther for at least two more years. It stood at 6–7 percent at the end of 1986.

Because the budget process of the U.S. Congress failed to slow the growth of expenditures and because large deficits persisted after 1980, Congress tried to discipline itself by passing the Gramm–Rudman–Hollings law, known formally as the Balanced Budget and Emergency Deficit Control Act of 1985. Targets for deficits were set, as shown in Table 28-1. The law would automatically reduce the budget if it were expected to exceed the legislated targets, but the mechanism was severely weakened by a Supreme Court decision in 1986 that prevented executive branch agencies (that were to make estimates of the forthcoming deficit) from legally limiting the congressional budget decisions. In May 1987 an embarrassed Reagan administration announced that its most

FIGURE 28-2 Federal Government Surplus or Deficit As a Percentage of GNP, 1790–1986

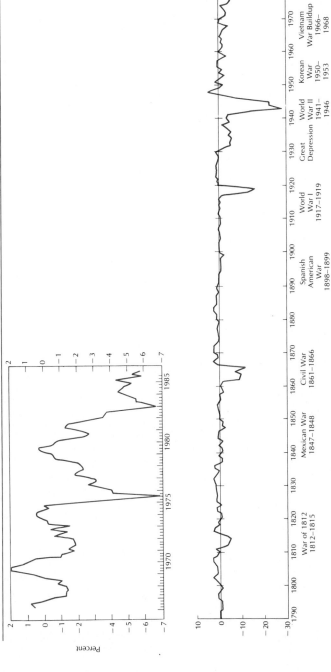

The deficits (shown as negative values) as a fraction of GNP were large during most war periods (War of 1812, Civil War, World War I, and World War II). They were not as large during the Korean War or the Vietnam War as they were in the peacetime period after 1975 and into the 1980s. In 1975 and 1983 they reached nearly 7 percent of GNP.

Source: James Barth and Stephen O. Morrell, "A Primer on Budget Deficits," *Economic Review*, Federal Reserve Bank of Atlanta, August 1982, pp. 10–11. Updated from Cambridge Planning and Analytics, Inc., Boston.

T A B L E 2 8 - 1   Targets for the Deficit in the Gramm–Rudman–Hollings Law (known formally as the Balanced Budget and Emergency Deficit Control Act of 1985)

The GRH law directed that deficits be reduced to meet certain targets so that the budget would be balanced by 1991. The targets applied to both the administration's submitted budget and the budget passed by Congress.

Fiscal Year	Deficit Target
1986	$171.0
1987	144.0
1988	108.0
1989	72.0
1990	36.0
1991	0.0

recent projections showed the proposed budget would produce a deficit that was substantially over the Gramm–Rudman targets that it supported.

The progressive income tax that produced rising marginal tax rates because of inflation in the 1970s and early 1980s was dramatically changed in 1986. The new law had only a few tax rate categories. It eliminated the capital gains tax and many tax shelters, but it kept the deduction for interest mortgages on owner-occupied residences. The highest marginal tax rates before 1981 were as high as 70 percent, until the 1981 tax law reduced them to 50 percent, and the 1986 law reduced them to 33 percent of taxable income. The 1986 tax law applicable to individual income was phased in from 1987 to 1988. It was esti-mated that three quarters of all taxpayers would pay a 15 percent income tax rate, which applied to a single person with a taxable income (after allowable deductions) of up to $17,850, and a couple, of up to $29,750. A 28 percent tax rate would apply above those levels. Couples whose income exceeded $71,900 and single individuals whose income exceeded $43,150 would pay a 5 percent surcharge, making the effective tax rate on this income equal to 33 percent. The surcharge would not apply to income over a certain cutoff ($149,250 for married couples); that is, there would be no surcharge, making the marginal rate above that amount equal to 28 percent. This reduction in tax rates for the highest incomes was a regressive tax feature in the 1986 law. Generally, the 1986 tax law tried to achieve the objective of taxing all activities at the same rate so that the rate of return, and not more favorable tax treatment, would guide the allocation of resources in the U.S. economy.

There were unexpected changes in important macroeconomic variables in the 1980s (see Figures 28-3 and 28-4). The variability of M-1 growth increased in the 1980s after October 1979, when the Federal Reserve announced that it would pay closer attention to the growth rate of M-1 and after 1982, when the Federal Reserve changed its operating procedures to concentrate on rate targets, as explained in the last chapter. There also were periods of slow growth in M-1 in the early 1980s, such as in the first half of 1980, when the money growth rate reached −5.4 percent. From 1983 to the beginning of 1987, the growth rates were very high by historical standards. After the recession of 1982, the rate of change in the consumer price index fell to very low levels and remained low despite the fast money growth in 1985 and 1986. In 1986, wholesale prices fell overall by 2.5 percent, helped by a collapse in wholesale oil prices, which caused wholesale energy costs to drop by 39.1 percent. The preliminary unofficial estimate of the rate of rise in the consumer price index for 1986 was 1.9 percent.

There was increased variability in short-term interest rates from 1980 to 1982. The three-month Treasury bill rate then fell in 1982, and after rising slightly to the middle of 1984, it fell to nearly 5 percent, the lowest it had been since 1977.

DEBT MANAGEMENT: OPERATION TWIST AND BILLS ONLY

The term *debt management* has several meanings. One refers to the methods by which the Treasury replaces maturing federal debt with new issues. This view of debt management is concerned with the mechanics of reissue and the

FIGURE 28-3   The Rate of Change of Money and Prices, 1980–1986

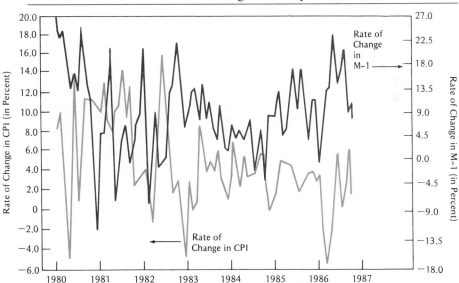

The variability of M-1 growth increased in the 1980s, and despite the fast money growth in 1985 and 1986, the rate of change in the consumer price index fell. The preliminary unofficial estimate of the rate of rise in the consumer price index for 1986 was 1.9 percent.

Source: Cambridge Planning and Analytics, Inc., Boston.

FIGURE 28-4   Rate of Change in M-1 and the Three-Month Treasury
Bill Rate, 1980–1986

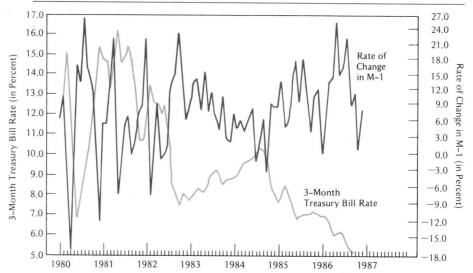

From 1980 to 1982, short-term interest rates were quite variable. The three-month
Treasury bill rate then fell in 1982, and after rising slightly to the middle of 1984, it fell
to nearly 5 percent, the lowest it had been since 1977. M-1 growth was rapid in 1985
and 1986.

Source: Cambridge Planning and Analytics, Inc., Boston.

methods of auctioning new issues. Another meaning of debt management concerns the management of the composition of government debt with respect to
its maturity.

A widely held view is that the maturity composition of the government debt
is an important determinant of the total level of spending. This view holds that
the shorter the average maturity of the government debt is, the more inflationary will be its effect.[6] This view is based on the concept of capital risk, the risk
that a debt instrument may fall unexpectedly in value (an unexpected rise in
interest rates). That is, a three-month U.S. Treasury bill has less such risk than
does a twenty-year U.S. government bond. If it is necessary to change the debt
instruments into money and interest rates suddenly rise, one could wait until
the maturity of the three-month bill, but the wait for twenty years for the bond
would be too long. A capital loss would be taken on the sale. But a checking
account or a unit of currency has no such risk. The hypothesis holds that the
shorter the maturity of debt instruments is, the more they are like money.
Changing twenty-year bonds into overnight loans or even into money will
make the population feel more liquid (with financial wealth that is less subject
to capital risk) and therefore wealthier, according to this view. Spending will
rise as a result.

In 1953 the Federal Reserve adopted a *bills-only* policy to improve the operations of the bond market.[7] Recall that bills have a maturity of one year or less. In the 1970s and at least up to 1984, open market operations were carried out with repurchase agreements. Repurchase agreements (discussed in Chapter 16) involve the sale of securities—Treasury bills are used by the Federal Reserve—with a contract to repurchase the securities that allows an interest return to the lender and temporary holder of the securities. The repurchase agreements often have a maturity no longer than several days. The continual buying and selling of these short-term debt instruments may help some of the market participants who profit from the immense amount traded that is generated by this policy.

An argument for the U.S. Treasury's carrying out a policy of issuing short-term debt instruments is sometimes advanced. This policy is not named bills-only; rather, it is referred to as a policy of *shortening the maturity of the* (U.S. Treasury) *debt*. (It is sometimes also referred to as *shortening the maturity of the national debt*. But both names can be incorrect if the Federal Reserve offsets the Treasury's actions by buying up the short-term debt or selling from its inventory of long-term debt in sufficient quantities to keep the average maturity of the debt in private hands from declining.) The argument is that when long-term rates are high, the issuance of short-term debt instruments saves the Treasury from paying interest costs. This aspect of the argument for short-term debt instruments has been shown to be misleading. The Treasury may not save significant interest costs by shortening the average maturity of its debt when its short-term debt bears a smaller rate of interest. Phillip Cagan explained this point:

> It follows that the Treasury cannot, given a desired level of liquidity, reduce its total interest cost by retiring bonds and issuing Treasury bills, which have a lower interest rate attributable to their liquidity. The increase in liquidity from the exchange requires a further issue of bonds to withdraw money, and the interest cost remains almost the same.[8]

In other words, the government cannot replace $500 of long-term bonds on which it pays 8 percent with $500 of short-term bills on which it pays 3 percent (saving $25 per year), if it does not want to affect the level of spending, provided that it is true that short-term securities are more inflationary. Additional long-term bonds would have to be issued to offset the increased inflationary effect of the short-term bills. There may be no reduction in the Treasury's interest cost. This argument should be added to the more fundamental view, that the net social cost of the Treasury's actions should not be measured solely by the interest cost on the debt. The other effects of the Treasury actions on the economy should also be considered.

One form of debt management consists of a policy to change the term structure of interest rates, discussed in Chapter 11. The Council of Economic Advisers suggested in 1965 that short-term interest rates be raised to reduce the unfavorable balance of payments and that long-term rates be lowered to stimulate investments.[9] Aside from the logic or desirability of this action, the question arose of whether debt management could achieve a significant effect on the term structure. The policy became known as **operation twist**.

Such a twist of the term structure is attempted by the following open market operations: The government buys long-term bonds to drive down long-term rates and sells short-term bills to drive up short-term rates. The private arbitrager who wants a profit can take the reverse actions—borrow long (sell long-term bonds) and lend short (buy short-term bonds). This is operation "straighten what the government has twisted." It is unlikely that when the government climbed into the ring with the demand and supply curves of the capital market—reaching worldwide—it did more than throw a few punches and then run for the corner to announce a victory. Such was the conclusion of several tests.[10]

STUDY QUESTIONS

1. What was the Treasury–Federal Reserve Accord? What policy did it terminate?
2. How does interest rate pegging work?
3. Did the U.S. economy have periodic recessions after World War II? If so, did Federal Reserve policy help alleviate them? (Interested readers will want to read Franco Modigliani and Milton Friedman's discussion and statements, cited in Chapter 26.)
4. What important change in policy did the Federal Reserve announce in 1979? Has it made a difference in monetary policy since then?
5. Is it true that when short-term rates are lower than long-term rates, the Treasury can save financing costs by adopting a bills-only policy? Explain.
6. What was operation twist, and how was it supposed to work?
7. Describe the monetary, interest rate, and inflation conditions of the period from Volcker's 1979 announcement to 1987. How did these conditions affect real interest rates? Were there other phenomena in this period that affected real interest rates? Would faster money growth in 1983 have lowered real interest rates?

GLOSSARY

Interest rate pegging. A government policy of buying and selling securities to maintain a given interest rate.

Operation twist. A U.S. government policy in the mid-1960s to twist the term structure of interest rates so that short-term rates would rise and long-term rates would fall.

Procyclical policy. A government policy of changing the money supply or its budget (taxes and expenditures) so that it induces greater inflation or deflation.

NOTES

1. For a description of this policy, see Milton Friedman and Anna Schwartz, *A Monetary History of the United States, 1857–1960* (Princeton, N.J.: Princeton University Press, 1963), pp. 561–567.

2. Alvin Hansen, "Keynes on Economic Policy," in Seymour Harris, ed., *The New Economics: Keynes' Influence on Theory and Public Policy* (New York: Knopf, 1948), p. 201.

3. See Daniel S. Ahearn, *Federal Reserve Policy Reappraised: 1951–1959* (New York: Columbia University Press, 1963) for a discussion of this period.

4. *Federal Reserve Bulletin*, July 1949, p. 776, reprinted in Ahearn, *Federal Reserve Policy*, p. 19.

5. Hostilities in Korea broke out on June 25, 1950. President Truman ordered U.S. assistance to the Republic of Korea on June 27. A cease-fire and armistice talks began in July 1951, and prisoner repatriation did not end until September 6, 1953.

6. Warren Smith, "Debt Management in the United States," *Study of Employment, Growth and Price Levels*, Joint Economic Committee, 86th Cong., 2d sess. (Washington, D.C.: U.S. Government Printing Office, 1960), pp. 1–15, reprinted in Harold Wolf and R. Conrad Deenges, eds., *Readings in Money and Banking* (New York: Appleton–Century–Crofts, 1968), pp. 385–403.

7. A debt management policy could be carried out with only two types of instruments: money and consols. By varying the amount of these two instruments, any liquidity composition of these government liabilities could be maintained. The problems of refinancing the debt would be abrogated.

8. Phillip Cagan, "A Partial Reconciliation Between Two Views of Debt Management," *Journal of Political Economy*, December 1966, p. 627. In 1979, the short-term interest rates were significantly higher than were the long-term rates. When this occurs, even the superficial argument for lowering costs by shortening the maturity of the debt instruments sold has no basis.

9. *The Annual Report of the Council of Economic Advisers*, January 21, 1965, Gardner Ackley, chairman, Otto Eckstein, and Arthur Okun. See especially p. 69.

10. Myron Ross discussed some points in the controversy in "'Operation Twist': A Mistaken Policy?" *Journal of Political Economy*, April 1966, pp. 195–199. Franco Modigliani and Richard Sutch were unable to find a relationship between the composition of the federal debt and the term structure of interest rates: "Innovations in Interest Rate Policy," *American Economic Review*, May 1966, pp. 178–197.

CHAPTER 29

WHO MAKES MONETARY POLICY?

CHAPTER PREVIEW

Introduction. The Federal Reserve has been referred to as an independent entity—something like a small foreign country—which issues policy directives but cannot be reached except by establishing arm's-length diplomatic relations. It is useful to learn that all this may be a false perception.

Political Independence or Dependence? This section discusses political independence and dependence, the latter as found in monetary policy and the politicization of research, and how the president influences the Federal Reserve.

Rules Versus Authority in Monetary Policy. The discussion in Chapter 26, this time with the advantage of the material presented on the Weintraub hypothesis, is continued.

INTRODUCTION

Considerable, though not conclusive, evidence supports the hypothesis that from 1951 to 1987, the president of the United States determined the course of U.S. monetary policy. Anyone who is not familiar with the peculiar institutional framework of the Federal Reserve would find nothing startling about that hypothesis. However, since the formation of the Federal Reserve, it has been regarded by many as an independent central bank, making monetary policy independent of political pressures or even of the desires of the president of the United States. The Federal Reserve has been referred to as an independent entity—something like a small foreign country—which issues policy directives but cannot be reached except by establishing arm's-length diplomatic relations. It is useful to learn that all this may be a false perception.

A subject that falls naturally into place, after reviewing the evidence of the preceding hypothesis, is whether the government should have some type of monetary rule or should practice discretionary monetary policy. This is a continuation of the discussion in Chapter 26, this time with the benefit of some evidence about political realities.

POLITICAL INDEPENDENCE OR DEPENDENCE?*

Born Under the Banner of Independence from Politics

The framers of the Federal Reserve Act (1913), which originated the Federal Reserve System, attempted to create a central bank that was independent from politics. Initially, the Federal Reserve was controlled mainly by two power groups, the Governors' Conference (composed of the twelve presidents of the regional Reserve banks) and the seven-member Federal Reserve Board in Washington, D.C. Five members of the Board were appointed by the president; the other two, the Comptroller of the Currency and the secretary of the Treasury, were ex-officio members of the Board. At the time, there was no understanding or desire for the Federal Reserve to engage in active open-market operations to control the money supply. Instead, it was to "furnish an elastic currency" and be the "lender of last resort."

During the early 1930s, however, power groups within the Federal Reserve were unable to agree to lend money to the many failing banks. The Federal Reserve did not become lender of the last resort, and approximately one third of the commercial banks closed.

In 1935, the Federal Reserve was reorganized to concentrate more power

---

* Parts of this section are adapted from Robert D. Auerbach, "Politics and the Federal Reserve," *Contemporary Policy Issues*, Fall 1985, pp. 43–58. By permission of Eldon J. Dvorak, Editor.

with the Board of Governors in Washington, D.C. All seven Board members are appointed by the president and approved by the Senate. The two ex-officio members were dropped from the Board. This reorganization made the Federal Reserve much more vulnerable to the political appointment process, but the belief in political independence has been strongly maintained and proclaimed to this day.

Waving the Banner of Independence from Politics

Each new Federal Reserve chairman traditionally reaffirms the System's political independence. For example, during the oversight hearings of the House Banking Committee on April 10, 1978, Congressman Charles E. Grassley (who later became a senator) discussed this subject with G. William Miller, chairman of the Federal Reserve:

Mr. Grassley: Mr. Miller, I have a general question or two dealing with the independence of the Fed. I think the independence of the Federal Reserve System is very closely connected with the maintenance of a sound monetary policy in this country, so you understand then what direction I am coming from when I ask these questions.

Previous Fed chairmen and previous administrations usually met to discuss general matters, at breakfast, or other meetings, particularly with the secretary of Treasury of those administrations.

My first question to you is: What kind, how often and in what environment do you have discussions with administration officials; and are these discussions any compromise of the principles of independence of the Fed?

Mr. Miller: I will answer in reverse order. I think there is no compromise of the independence of the Fed in carrying on discussions with other officials in the Government who are interested in economic policy. There is none because we continue to use these discussions only as a basis for considering matters of mutual interest and policies of mutual concern.

I do meet with the secretary of the Treasury once a week if we are both in town. Our staffs tend to meet once a week. These meetings may not involve me; they may just involve some of our staff working on technical aspects or coordination of our activities. We act as fiscal agent for the Treasury and do a lot of other things with the Treasury.

I usually meet periodically with the chairman of the Council of Economic Advisers. And I also meet occasionally with the officials in other agencies of the government who are dealing with economic issues.

As you probably know, on occasion the president asks for a number of us to come in and sit down with him and discuss economic matters; that may, I think, be a continuing procedure.

Mr. Grassley: From that standpoint, I would detect that your relationship with the administration doesn't depart too much from what we have been told have been the patterns of previous administrations and previous chairmen.

Mr. Miller: I know of no difference. I have really picked up the agenda that was established by Dr. Burns.

Mr. Grassley: Are you taking any new and/or different actions to insure the independence of the Fed as it might be within your power to so do?

Mr. Miller: I don't know of any action that is necessary. Our commitment to independence is absolute. I think there is no one in the Federal Reserve who is not fully committed to the concept of independence. I detect, in the arrangements that have been made since I succeeded Dr. Burns, no evidence of efforts to subvert that independence. I do not think our discussions entangle us or require us to become silent supporters of something in which we don't believe. So I haven't found any forces at work that seem to require a new initiative as far as independence.

Mr. Grassley: This final question would probably give you an opportunity to sum up what you have previously said. But is the independence of the Fed in any danger from either political pressure from this administration or from the Congress?

Mr. Miller: I don't detect it at this time. The president has stated over and over again that he believes in the independence of the Fed. He has stated that, at the time that I was nominated and at the time I was sworn in. There was a slight slip when I was sworn in giving us constitutional blessing, but I know it is only the Congress that has created the Fed, not the Constitution—although perhaps that is an amendment we should look into (Laughter). [pp. 142–143]

One year and four months later, President Jimmy Carter replaced the then secretary of the Treasury with G. William Miller, ostensibly because the former secretary was a little too independent.

A *Wall Street Journal* article in 1984 by David Meiselman on the relationship between Federal Reserve monetary policies and election years brought a reply from David R. Eastburn, former president of the Federal Reserve Bank of Philadelphia. Eastburn wrote a letter that was published under the headline, "The Fed Steers Clear of Politics":

As a former president of the Federal Reserve Bank of Philadelphia, I'm tired of reading that the Fed will bring interest rates down because of the coming elections, as intimated by David I. Meiselman. . . .

In two decades of observing and participating in meetings of the Fed's primary policymaking body, the Federal Open Market Committee, I've never once heard anyone even suggest slanting a decision to facilitate anyone's election.

As November comes close, Fed officials undoubtedly will follow their usual seasonal pattern: lying low. They will try not to call unnecessary attention to the Fed, will avoid public speeches where possible, and may postpone certain kinds of actions—like changes in the discount rate— that have a larger public impact than their importance warrants. This behavior should be interpreted for what it is: steering clear of politics, not engaging in them.[1]

In response to my (Robert Auerbach's) statement published in *The Wall Street Journal*[2] that the Federal Reserve was politically influenced in its monetary policy, Federal Reserve Board member Henry Wallich called the charges "mistaken" and "entirely wrong." Vice-Chairman Preston Martin asserted that it is too perilous for the Board to play favorites: "You risk bringing down the wrath of Congress and losing your independence."

A Hypothesis

This chapter suggests the following two-part hypothesis:

1. The Federal Reserve System is not independent of politics. It is a powerful political entity that influences and is influenced by state and federal elected officials.
2. One way that it preserves its political power is to carry out the monetary policy desired by the president of the United States. This part of the hypothesis is called the Weintraub hypothesis.[3]

What is meant by "independence from politics"? Like all large bureaucracies, the Federal Reserve has many "internal" political forces, which include the political process of electing regional bank presidents (subject to the approval of the Board of Governors).[4] The Federal Reserve was not designed to be independent of these "internal" political forces, as some individuals hold it to be. Rather, it is supposed to be independent of the political process on a state and national level by which legislative and executive elected officials influence Federal Reserve operations and policies and, in turn, are influenced in their decision making by Federal Reserve lobbying. The first part of the hypothesis holds this belief in independence to be wrong. Instead, it holds that the Federal Reserve is a powerful political force. The second part of the hypothesis is that the Fed's efforts to preserve its political strength prevent it from carrying out a monetary policy that deviates significantly from that desired by the U.S. president.

We will present several types of evidence. One is the frequency with which Federal Reserve policy matches that desired by the administration. Of course, both the administration and Federal Reserve may want the same policy in response to the same external events (e.g., a recession). However, if there are sharp turns in administration policies—perhaps because of a change in administrations—extra weight will be given to the continued synchronization of the Fed's policy under essentially the same Federal Reserve officials. Another kind of evidence is the minutes of the Federal Open Market Committee (FOMC).[5] We will also present excerpts from minutes of the twelve regional Federal Reserve Banks' boards of directors' meetings.[6] Other evidence, though compelling, is more difficult to detail precisely, so we will not present it. This includes the activities of the Federal Reserve's congressional liaison contingent and of the chairmen, who lobby and negotiate with Congress. It also includes the regular weekly meetings of the Federal Reserve's top personnel with Treasury officials.

Some Evidence of Political Dependence: The Historical Record of Monetary Policy

The evidence begins with a short summary of the work of the late Robert E. Weintraub, which has been updated and, as it pertains to the Nixon administration, expanded. Weintraub served part time from 1962 to 1965 and full time from 1972 to 1983 as a staff member for both political parties in Congress. His government service included the House Banking Committee, where he became staff director of the Subcommittee on Domestic Monetary Policy; the Senate Banking Committee; the Joint Economic Committee; and, briefly, the Treasury, after a distinguished academic career. He was an influential staff member, an astute political observer, and a gifted economist, who wrote important articles until he died in 1983.

Weintraub held that the Federal Reserve does not independently control U.S. monetary policy. Instead, he said, the Fed's monetary policy conforms to that desired by the president. To support that view Weintraub presented the following evidence: The Federal Reserve shifted course in 1953, 1961, 1969, 1971, 1974, and 1977—all years in which the presidency changed. (Except for the change from Kennedy to Johnson, those were the only years of a presidency change between 1953 and 1977.)

President Harry Truman (1945–1953) wanted the Federal Reserve to peg interest rates at a slightly higher rate, according to Weintraub.[7] President Dwight D. Eisenhower (1953–1961) wanted slow money growth, and during those years, the basic money supply grew by 1.73 percent—the slowest rate of any administration since World War II. President John F. Kennedy (1961–1963) wanted to stimulate the economy with slightly faster money growth, but not with rapid growth that would injure the balance of payments. From January 1961 to November 1963, the basic money supply grew at an annual rate of 2.31 percent. President Lyndon B. Johnson (1963–1969) wanted to promote economic growth, and so the Federal Reserve provided faster money growth during his presidency. The basic money supply grew at an annual rate of nearly 5 percent, a rapid rate by historical standards.[8] These different rates of money growth under Truman, Eisenhower, Kennedy, and Johnson occurred under the same Federal Reserve Board chairman, William McChesney Martin.

President Richard M. Nixon (1969–1974) appointed Arthur Burns as chairman. Nixon wanted wage and price controls. The paraphrased minutes of the FOMC meeting on August 15, 1972, show that Burns informed the members that he had been for "a wage and price policy long before the administration had decided to adopt one." The coincidence of views does not necessarily support the Weintraub hypothesis. However, some weak support is provided by the enthusiasm with which Burns championed wage and price controls in the secret FOMC meetings, as reported in the minutes. At the October 17, 1972, meeting—shortly before the election and after he had urged fast money growth—Burns told the FOMC that he "predicted the program (wage and price controls) to remain relatively effective." Stronger support for the Weintraub hypothesis was found in Burns's advocacy of faster money growth before the 1972 election. (Burns's comments were made in the secrecy of the FOMC meetings, the minutes of which were not made public until 1977.) Burns's staff presented him with the "strictly confidential" forecasts of money growth, as shown in Exhibit 29-1.

The forecasts called for a 10.5 percent growth in the basic money supply (M-1) in the third quarter of 1972 and 7.5 percent in the fourth quarter. Despite these forecasts of very high growth, Burns argued for fast money growth. His assertions, followed by part of the counterargument from Governor J. L. Robertson (Federal Open Market Committee, August 15, 1972, 805 and 810, September 1972, 928), included the following:

> In conclusion, Chairman Burns reiterated that the remaining margins of unutilized resources were great enough to permit rapid expansion in real output and still leave extensive unemployment of labor and of machinery and equipment. At the same time, the blue book projections of even more liberal money growth suggested a rate of increase in M1 that was no greater than the rate of growth in real output. *At this stage of the expansion, he saw no need to be afraid of prosperity and to adopt a restrictive monetary policy.* (Emphasis added.)

> Mr. Robertson commented that the Committee was confronted with a vigorously expanding economy and a price performance that was still too strong for comfort. . . . *In that kind of environment, acceleration in monetary expansion significantly beyond the moderate growth the Committee had intended was a cause for real concern.* (Emphasis added.)

At the FOMC meeting of September 19, 1972, shortly before the election, Burns argued for preventing the federal funds rate from rising—which, in Federal Reserve *modus operandi*, is a policy for faster money growth.

> Chairman Burns said he wanted to make it clear that he would much prefer not to see the funds rate ride to five and three-eighths percent in the coming period. He would be willing to tolerate a five and three-eighths percent rate if required by circumstances, and he had proposed

EXHIBIT 29-1

935   ATTACHMENT B

September 22, 1972

STRICTLY CONFIDENTIAL (FR)

Points for FOMC Guidance to Manager In Implementation of Directive	SPECIFICATIONS (As agreed, 9/19/72)
1. Guiding rate of growth in aggregate reserves expressed as a range rather than a point target.	9-1/2 to 13-1/2% seas. adj. annual rate in RPD's in Sept.-Oct. 1/
2. Range of toleration for fluctuations in Federal funds rate--enough to allow significant changes in reserve supply, but not so much as to disturb markets.	4-3/4 to 5-3/8%
3. Federal funds rate to be moved in an orderly way within the range of tolerance (rather than to be allowed to bounce around unchecked between the upper and lower limit of the range).	

4. Guiding expectations for monetray aggregates (M_1, M_2, and bank credit), to be given some allowance by the Manager as he supplies reserves between meetings.		Sept.	3rd Q. (SAAR)	4th Q.
	M_1:	11	10-1/2	7-1/2
	M_2:	11	10	7-1/2
	Proxy:	9	10-1/2	11

5. If it appears the Committee's various objectives and constraints are not going to be met satisfactorily in any period between meetings, the Manager is promptly to notify the Chairman, who will then promptly decide whether the situation calls for special Committee action to give supplementary instructions.

1/ Modified from range of 11-1/2 to 15-1/2 per cent initially approved at 9/19/72 meeting, in order to allow for nonimplementation of changes in Regulations D and J.

specifications under which the Manager would have the authority to move to that level. *But he definitely did not want to press eagerly toward higher funds rates, regardless of other circumstances.* (Emphasis added.)

In the secrecy of the FOMC meetings, and despite his public image at the time as an inflation fighter, Burns argued for and received fast money growth before the 1972 Nixon election. Burns's actions were strong support for the Weintraub hypothesis. The growth rate in the money supply during 1972 was the fastest for any entire year since World War II. For the whole Nixon presidency, the growth rate of the money supply was more than 6 percent.

When Gerald Ford assumed the presidency (August 1974 to 1976), the Federal Reserve provided money growth at an average annual rate of 4.7 percent—in line with the president's desire for slower money growth. However, in 1977, Jimmy Carter assumed the presidency (1977–1981) and again wanted faster money growth. The Federal Reserve, under Burns's chairmanship, dramatically increased the growth rate of the money supply. This apparent audition for Burns to retain his chairmanship was consistent with the Weintraub hypothesis. However, the effort was not successful; in March 1978, Carter appointed G. William Miller, who continued to give Carter exactly what he wanted—very fast money growth, by historical standards. And by October 1978, money growth had reached an annual rate of 8.5 percent.

In a speech on November 1, 1978, Carter indicated a change in his priorities from stimulating the economy to fighting inflation. Indeed, the fast money growth had pushed the inflation rate up into double digits. Almost immediately, the basic money supply was dramatically slowed. Then, in August 1979—after the Federal Reserve had again increased the growth rate of the money supply, in an attempt to stabilize interest rates—Carter appointed Paul Volcker as Federal Reserve Board chairman.

The Federal Reserve fought inflation by allowing the money supply to decline at an annual rate of 6.3 percent for five months in early 1980. There was deep concern within the administration, and near panic among some congressional Democrats who were seeking reelection, when the unemployment rate rose to more than 7 percent in May 1980. Should the Federal Reserve change course in response to political pressures, or would it maintain the stance promised by Volcker in his testimony during the summer of 1980? In the "Midyear Monetary Policy Report to Congress," Volcker told the House Banking Committee, ". . . the FOMC is prepared to contemplate that M1 measures may fall significantly short of the midpoint of the specified ranges for the year."[9] On July 24, 1980, Volcker told the Budget Committee of the U.S. Senate that the Federal Reserve would not reinflate the money supply. But some House Banking Committee members and staffers suspected that the short-run political pressures of an administration that faced a recession in an election year again would prevail, rather than the Federal Reserve's stated longer-run objectives. Evidence of this change in the direction of the monetary policy surfaced in two ways at that time. First, at the July 1980 oversight hearings, Volcker appeared to put a slight smokescreen over the Federal Reserve's intended future monetary policy when he would not state numerical target variables for 1981. He was pressed at the oversight hearings by Congressman John Cavanaugh, who said that because of Volcker's failure to comply with the Humphrey–Hawkins law, "In my mind, Mr. Chairman, you violated the law."[10] Second, the monetary base, which had grown at 6.2 percent in the second quarter of 1980, was now growing even more rapidly. Third-quarter growth of the monetary base turned out to be 9.7 percent.[11] In fact, the money supply was already increasing at a rapid rate. For the five months before the November 1980 election, the money supply increased at an annual rate of 16.2 percent—a record for the period since World War II.

The Federal Reserve received no clear instructions from the Reagan administration, and the money supply began to accelerate at the end of 1980. Beryl Sprinkel, the newly appointed under secretary for Monetary Affairs of the Reagan administration, announced publicly in the spring of 1981 that the Federal Reserve should slow the growth in the money supply. The Fed did so, and the money supply growth rate fell below the lower end of its target range. Secretary of the Treasury Donald Regan, fearing that the recovery projected by the administration would not materialize, called for faster money growth near the end of 1981—fast enough, in fact, to bring the Federal Reserve back into its target range for all of 1981. This meant extremely rapid money growth for the last few months of 1981, which caused concern among some officials inside the Reagan administration. Nevertheless, the Federal Reserve apparently followed the treasury secretary's advice, and the money supply growth remained rapid until February 1982, when Volcker met with Reagan. The president wanted slower growth, and so the Federal Reserve produced much slower growth until the end of August 1982. By that time, there was a large recession, and the unemployment rate had risen to more than 10 percent. Administration officials began to call for faster money growth. The Federal Reserve followed through with fast money growth from mid-1982 to mid-1983.

The administration's message for fast money growth was very clear. On November 21, 1982, on the television program *Meet the Press*, Martin Feldstein, chairman of the Council of Economic Advisers (CEA), said:

> It is true that M1, one of the measures of the money supply, has been going up very rapidly for the past couple of months, but that is not at all surprising when one thinks about the decline in interest rates that have occurred.

> I think looking at the broadest measures of the money supply and looking more generally at what is happening in financial and credit markets gives one no reason to be concerned about the Fed's expanding too quickly.

Treasury Secretary Regan reportedly stated that the Federal Reserve should accommodate its money supply to "an expanding economic base," and that would generate more federal revenues and reduce looming budget deficits. "Then as the economy strengthens, money growth should be phased back slowly."[12]

The Federal Reserve then said it had given up its close control of the basic money supply, because such control was no longer meaningful, as discussed in

Chapter 27. Again, there were strong signals from the administration that faster money growth would cause inflation at a bad time—when Reagan would be seeking reelection in 1984. Feldstein expressed "serious concern" over the "rapid recent growth of M1."[13]

The Federal Reserve produced a generally declining rate of growth of the money supply in the last part of 1983, which was the desired policy of the Reagan administration. Then in February 1984, the Federal Reserve widened the target ranges of M-1 to 4 to 8 percent.

The growth rate of the money supply in 1984—an election year—was not according to the pattern generally observed in election years. Meiselman called the pattern "the political monetary cycle" that he had observed before and after national elections in 1960, 1964, 1968, 1972, and 1980.[14] Monetary growth began to fall a year and a half before the election, started to rise two to three quarters before the election, and fell again after the election. The presumed intentions of this pattern were to stimulate the economy during the election year—without having an inflationary episode from the previous money growth (so that the incumbent would win the election)—and then to take corrective action to prevent an inflationary response from the election-year stimulus. This pattern was not followed by the Ford administration when Burns was Federal Reserve chairman, nor was it followed in 1984 under the Volcker chairmanship. In both cases, the historical record indicates that neither administration wanted fast money growth. For this reason, the failure to follow the historical pattern of the political monetary cycle, or the failure to find persuasive evidence that such a pattern exists, does not necessarily contradict the Weintraub hypothesis. More relevant are the wishes of the president during election periods. In this respect, the exceptions to the pattern cited by Meiselman do support the Weintraub hypothesis.

By 1987, with the resignation of some Board members and the end of Volcker's term as chairman in August 1987, President Reagan had the opportunity to appoint all the seven members of the Board of Governors. It was clear that the Reagan administration had obtained control over the Board of Governors and the FOMC by this direct appointment process. Although Reagan appeared preoccupied with a number of issues (including the Iranian arms scandal that erupted at the end of 1986), it appeared that the monetary policies of the secretary of the Treasury became the dominant view in the Reagan administration. They apparently called for and were successful in obtaining fast money growth. This may not have been the view of Paul Volcker, who received immense praise for governing the Federal Reserve between 1980 and 1987 when the inflation rate dropped from double digits to a low level in 1986. But the problems that Volcker confronted—in what may have been a desire for less rapid money growth—in contrast with the administration's policies, surfaced in 1986. In 1986 it was reported that the Reagan appointees had outvoted Chairman Volcker to win a lowering of the discount rate:

A dramatic demonstration of the clout of the two newcomers—Manuel Johnson and Wayne Angell—came this week with the disclosure that on Feb. 24 they and two other Reagan appointees outvoted Mr. Volcker, 4 to 3, to cut the discount rate.

. . . Mr. Volcker finds himself increasingly isolated on a board that he once dominated.[15]

But not all the administration appointees were in favor of the fast money growth of 1985 and 1986, as indicated by the comments of the chairman of the Council of Economic Advisers, Beryl Sprinkel: "Thus money growth so far in 1985 implies the need for a slowdown in money growth."[16] But Sprinkel chose not to press his views. It appeared that the faster money growth was the administration's preferred policy and was being carried out by its appointees on the Board of Governors. Sprinkel delivered a speech in an open meeting of the Western Economic Association (July 2, 1986, San Francisco) that noted the problems of uncertainty that can be caused by government economic policies. In the ensuing question-and-answer period, Sprinkel was asked to describe the country's current monetary policy, but he declined to do so. *The Wall Street Journal* criticized Sprinkel when he was rumored to be a candidate for chairman of the Board of Governors at the next time of appointment, August 1987:

Mr. Sprinkel is a personable fellow, but in his Treasury and White House posts he's not built the perception of someone able to defend the Fed's integrity against political sallies. And, of course, he made his name as a doctrinaire monetarist; with the monetary aggregates rising as inflation fell over the past four years, a monetary policy guided solely by aggregates easily could have converted vigorous recovery to a dismal slump. The economics profession and Wall Street have abandoned their fascination with the various Ms, but we have been given no reason to doubt that Mr. Sprinkel still believes.[17]

These comments contradict the hypothesis that the Federal Reserve is political and would continue to keep its monetary policy in line with the administration's requests.

The unsigned editorials of *The Wall Street Journal* on monetary and fiscal policy favored the supply-side policies advocated by Arthur Laffer and Congressman Jack Kemp. These policies include the strict discipline of the gold standard and, in the absence of a return to the gold standard, faster growth and little discipline (at least, no discipline of the type proposed by the monetarists), so that the supply-side tax cuts would work. Some of the Reagan appointees to the Federal Reserve were characterized as supply-siders rather than monetarists, as they favored and helped implement fast growth in 1985 and 1986.

Therefore, if the hypothesis in this chapter is correct, the theoretical beliefs of the chairman of the Federal Reserve should not be as important as are the wishes of the president in the formulation and conduct of monetary policy.

How Does the President Influence the Federal Reserve?

The influence of the president of the United States over the Federal Reserve Board of Governors and the Federal Open Market Committee stems not only from the president's ability to name the chairman of the Federal Reserve Board and at least two other members of the Board during each presidential term but also because there have been close contacts between the administration and the Federal Reserve Board. Former top members of the Federal Reserve staff have served in the Treasury and on the Council of Economic Advisers, and several Reserve Board governors and Reserve Bank presidents were formerly in policymaking positions in the executive branch.

The president's real influence is his or her power. The president can turn the rest of the federal bureaucracy against a recalcitrant member of the executive branch (which includes the Board of Governors). The president also has strong powers of persuasion, including a justified appeal to one's patriotism to join with the policies of the person duly elected by the entire voting public. For example, when Chairman William Martin raised the discount rate in 1965, President Johnson called Martin to his ranch in Texas. The discount rate was soon lowered.

One does not get to such a high political office in a democracy without developing skills in persuasion, in which President Johnson was especially proficient. Against the background of the importance of this great office, it is doubtful that many individuals in the executive branch can answer a phone call from the president or a request in a personal audience with, "I don't care what you say, I have my own monetary policy."

We should emphasize again that evidence of the validity of the Weintraub hypothesis should not necessarily be taken as evil; rather, it merely holds that the often stated "independence" of the Federal Reserve from politics is incorrect.

RULES VERSUS AUTHORITY IN MONETARY POLICY

The Weintraub hypothesis and the record it illuminates lead naturally into a subject that was discussed in Chapter 26, "Monetarists Versus Keynesians." Only a few subjects have been as hotly debated in monetary economics as has the effectiveness of discretionary monetary policy versus a rule such as directing the monetary authority to attempt to increase the money supply defined as M-1 within a range of from 2.5 to 3.5 percent per year. The proposals of Henry C. Simons in the middle 1930s have had an important influence in the development of a monetary rule. He concluded,

> A monetary rule of maintaining the constancy of some price index, preferably an index of prices of competitively produced commodities,

appears to afford the only promising escape from present monetary chaos and uncertainties. A rule for money, however, definitely merits consideration as a perhaps preferable solution in the more distant future.[18]

Henry Simons's proposal directed attention to a particular target variable, the price level, that he thought should be stabilized.

In 1947, Milton Friedman suggested a number of proposals that illustrate a view that policies should be more automatic and less dependent on the views of individuals currently responsible for policy decisions.[19] These views included a 100 percent reserve proposal for commercial banks to reduce pro-cyclical fluctuations in bank money, a progressive tax system relying only on direct income taxes, and a federal fiscal budget based on a predetermined level of expenditures. Taxes would be held at a level that would produce a balanced budget over an entire cyclical episode. That is, the budget would have a deficit when taxes were low, during downturns, and an offsetting surplus when taxes were high, during expansions. This concept is similar to more recent sugges-tions that the budget be balanced at the estimated full employment level of output. Friedman also advocated a permanent limit on government expendi-tures.

Friedman recommended interest payments on required reserves at com-mercial banks and the policy that if 100 percent reserves could not be imple-mented, reserve requirements be permanently set at one arbitrary level.[20] He also suggested that the money supply be increased at a continuous rate approximately equal to the long-run growth in real output minus the long-run secular change in velocity.[21] A rate of growth in the money supply of slightly over 4 percent per year in old M-2 should produce an average rate of growth in the price level that would be approximately zero.

These rules were advocated because of the difficulty in predicting future levels of economic activity at the time when monetary policy would have its impact and because of the difficulty in estimating the duration of lags, given the current state of economic knowledge. The advocates of these rules claimed that many unpredictable events affect economic activity and the price level and that only the long-run trend in these variables could be predicted with reasonable accuracy. They claimed that *fine-tuning* the economy with fiscal and monetary policy in an attempt to eliminate the short-run fluctuations in these variables would probably introduce increased stability.[22] The policy variables themselves would introduce additional oscillations that might not offset other disturbances; they even might add unpredictable variations in the ultimate target variables.

A monetary policy of slightly over 4 percent growth in the money supply was not held to be a cure for all cyclical movements in the price level and other variables affected by money; rather, it was held to be the best way to reduce fluctuations and to stabilize prices around some long-run, approx-imately constant trend. These rules, especially the 4 percent monetary rule, were attacked by those who believed that discretionary policy could produce better results. Paul Samuelson's eloquent rebuttal is given in Chapter 26.

There have been numerous simulation tests of the outcome that would have occurred had a given discretionary policy or monetary rule been followed. The results of these tests are as persuasive as is the credibilty of the underlying model and the assumptions used to simulate actual conditions. Given the problems in developing precise adjustment models that will accurately predict short-run fluctuations, the results of these simulations can be regarded as only roughly suggestive.

The issue is not a choice between two distinct options, a given rule or a given discretionary policy. Rather, discretionary policies can be rules of a sort in which decisions are based on prior and present values of economic variables. But the monetary rules are not specified and, within a small range, are not the primary concern of those advocating a rule. Proponents of a rule would agree that a price level that was fairly steady at approximately a 3 percent trend instead of an average change of zero—because of the adoption of a slightly higher monetary growth rate rule—would be preferable to a more erratic and variable result that might be obtained from discretionary policy. But this statement begs the question. Those in favor of a discretionary policy believe that such a result can be more closely approximated if the monetary authority is given more leeway. If the economy were in a prolonged recession, for example, they would want the Federal Reserve to be free to accelerate monetary growth.

STUDY QUESTIONS

1. Who determines monetary policy, and what is the evidence for this position?
2. Looking back at the 1985–7 period, for which evidence was not fully available to support or contradict the Weintraub hypothesis, can more be said, now that more time has elapsed and perhaps more information is available?
3. Reread the sections in Chapter 26 on a monetary rule versus discretionary policy, combine it with the material in Chapters 27, 28, and this chapter, and come to your own decision on this controversy. Support your decision.
4. Have the party (Democrat or Republican) affiliations of the presidents of the United States since 1945 been good indicators of the type of monetary policy they pursued (rapid or slow money growth)?
5. Who determined monetary policy after the October 19, 1987, stock market crash?
6. Consider the following possibilities for the instability of the money supply during the 1979–1983 period:
   a. The Weintraub hypothesis plus unstable policy advice from the administration.

    b. Poor money supply control procedures (described in Chapter 27).

    c. The impossibility of control as stated by President Frank Morris of the Federal Reserve Bank of Boston (in the study questions in Chapter 26).

    Assess the validity of each.

7. David R. Eastburn, former president of the Federal Reserve Bank of Philadelphia, disputed the view that the FOMC responds to political pressures. ("The Fed Steers Clear of Politics," *The Wall Street Journal*, January 30, 1984, p. 27.) Eastburn claimed that FOMC members would have no motive to be politically motivated. He said that the party-loyalty theory will not hold because they come from many parties. He asserted that there was no silent conspiracy, nor was there "reason for a member to influence interest rates for a personal gain." He explained: "In two decades of observing and participating in meetings of the Fed's primary policymaking body, the Federal Reserve Open Market Committee, I've never once heard anyone even suggest slanting a decision to facilitate anyone's election."

    Assess these statements in the light of the Weintraub hypothesis. Assuming the observations made by Eastburn are correct, under what conditions could the Weintraub hypothesis be true?

NOTES

1. David Meiselman, "The Political Monetary Cycle," *The Wall Street Journal*, January 10, 1984, editorial page; and David R. Eastburn, "The Fed Steers Clear of Politics," *The Wall Street Journal*, January 10, 1984, p. 27.

2. Laurie McGinley, "Traditional Target, the Fed Is Bracing for Political Criticism As Campaign Goes On," *The Wall Street Journal*, February 1, 1984, p. 1.

3. This part of the hypothesis, called the *Weintraub hypothesis*, was first described by Robert E. Weintraub in "Congressional Supervision of Monetary Policy," *Journal of Monetary Economics*, Center for Research in government Policy and Business, Graduate School of Management, University of Rochester, April 1978, pp. 341–362. New important evidence consistent with the hypothesis is presented by Thomas Havrilesky, "Monetary Policy Signaling from The Administrations to the Federal Reserve," *Journal of Money, Credit and Banking* (forthcoming, February 1988). No attempt has been made to apply the hypothesis before the 1951 Treasury–Federal Reserve Accord, though it would be interesting. One problem in applying the hypothesis to earlier periods is that it is not clear that the presidents wanted the Federal Reserve to carry out any particular policies other than acting as the lender of the last resort, as specified in the Federal Reserve Act of 1913. Monetary policy was not a concern in the early history of the Federal Reserve. A tentative open

market committee was not even formed until 1922, and officials in the Federal Reserve in the 1920s, except for Governor Benjamin Strong of the New York Federal Reserve Bank, did not even see price stability as a proper target of Federal Reserve policy.

There were numerous disputes between the Treasury and the Federal Reserve up to the time of the accord. Two congressional investigations by subcommittees under Senator Paul Douglas (1949–1950) and Congressman Wright Patman (1951–1952) produced extensive evidence on the inconsistent policies of the Treasury and the Federal Reserve and provided support for the accord. Friedman and Schwartz provided a detailed description of disputes between the Treasury and Federal Reserve both before 1935, when the ex-officio members of the administration sat on the Board, and after 1935 up to the accord. The application of the hypothesis is clearer after the accord, when the authority to control the money supply was given solely to the Federal Reserve and the objectives of monetary policy were formally stated (in the Employment Act of 1946) and known by the presidents. See Milton Friedman and Anna Schwartz, *A Monetary History of the United States, 1867–1960* (Princeton, N.J.: Princeton University Press, 1963).

4. "Internal" is in quotation marks because although the selection of the presidents of the Reserve Banks is internal to the Federal Reserve System, it involves private commercial member banks and the two-way influence between bankers and the Federal Reserve, a subject not discussed in this chapter.

5. So far as is publicly known, the Federal Reserve stopped taking minutes of the Federal Open Market Committee meetings in 1976, but before that time they were recorded and kept secret until they were delivered to the Congress and made public five years later.

6. After a protracted dispute, the minutes for three years in the early 1970s were delivered to the Banking Committee of the House of Representatives. After I read them, I helped Chairman Henry Reuss incorporate them in a speech he delivered in the House.

7. The intentions of President Truman, who sent William McChesney Martin to carry out the understanding (and then appointed him chairman of the Federal Reserve) are controversial. Weintraub, in a number of personal conversations on this point, contended that, based on first-hand sources, he believed Truman did not want to remove the interest rate peg target; he wanted a higher peg. Other observers believe Truman wanted the practice ended. The more rigorously maintained peg had already been dropped by the time of the accord. However, in support of Weintraub's interpretation (and in support of the Weintraub hypothesis if that interpretation is correct), it was not until September 24, 1953, that Chairman Martin was able to announce that "we have arrived at the point where we hoped we did not have to ever again directly support Treasury securities. (Friedman and Schwartz, *A Monetary History*, pp.

625–626, note 22.) Interest rates continued to serve as a Federal Reserve target variable.

8. An incident in which Martin raised the discount rate against the wishes of President Johnson has been cited as contradicting the Weintraub hypothesis. Weintraub did not think that the brief interval before a meeting with the president at his ranch in Texas—which resulted in a lowering of the discount rate—was a significant departure from his hypothesis.

9. *Conduct of the Monetary Policy*, Hearing Before the Committee on Banking, Finance and Urban Affairs, House of Representatives, July 1980, p. 23. Volcker did hold that M-1 had begun to grow again. "As the *Report* illustrates, M-1 growth has clearly resumed and the broader aggregate M-2 is now at or above the mid point of its range" (p. 23).

10. *Conduct of Monetary Policy*, July 1980, p. 102. Volcker finally did submit numerical targets, by letter, to Chairman Reuss. The Full Employment and Balance Growth Act of 1978, P.L. 95-523, is known as the Humphrey–Hawkins Act.

11. The change in the rate of growth in the monetary base was even more pronounced than the data indicate, as the growth of the money supply in the second quarter was slowed by the imposition of the Credit Restraint Program of 1980. As we indicated in Chapter 27, this action increased the ratio of currency to deposits over what it would have been without the program.

    Volcker later argued, in response to a question submitted by Congressman George Hansen, that the Federal Reserve could not control the monetary base in 1980 because of borrowing at the discount window. See *Conduct of Monetary Policy*, February 1981, p. 168. After Hansen pointed out that "the monetary base, adjusted for reserve requirements, increased from May to November [1980] by about 10 or 11 percent . . . then turned flat, . . ." Volcker responded, "Under the present institutional arrangements, with banks able to borrow from the Federal Reserve, we cannot have assured control over the monetary base. . . ." Volcker's answer does not appear meaningful for 1980, with five months of record negative growth followed by five months of record positive growth. The Federal Reserve can ration loans through the discount window and raise the discount rate if it so desires.

12. John M. Berry, "Reagan Says Fed Policy Should Serve Recovery," *The Washington Post*, January 13, 1983, p. C1.

13. Caroline Atkinson, "Money Growth Is Too Rapid, Feldstein Says," *The Washington Post*, June 6, 1983, p. C1.

14. David A. Meiselman, "The Political Monetary Cycle."

15. Paul Blustein, "Tense Fed, Volcker's Fate Is Seen Hinging on Two Men New to Reserve Board," *The Wall Street Journal*, March 20, 1986, p. 1. Also see "A Rebellion in the Money Palace," *Newsweek*, March 31, 1986, pp. 36, 38.

16. This quotation can be found in Alan Murray, "Sprinkel Concern About Fed Policy Is Made Public," *The Wall Street Journal*, September 11, 1985, p. 47.

17. *The Wall Street Journal*, January 13, 1987, p. 30.

18. Henry C. Simons, "Rules Versus Authorities in Monetary Policy," *Journal of Political Economy*, Vol. 44, 1936, reprinted in *Readings in Monetary Theory* (Homewood, Ill.: Richard D. Irwin, 1951), pp. 337–368. See also Henry C. Simons, "A Positive Program for Laissez Faire: Some Proposals for a Liberal Economic Policy," Public Policy Pamphlet No. 15 (Chicago: University of Chicago Press, 1934).

19. Milton Friedman, "A Monetary and Fiscal Framework for Economic Stability," *American Economic Review*, Vol. 38, 1948; reprinted in *Readings in Monetary Theory*, pp. 369–393.

20. See Milton Friedman, *A Program for Monetary Stability* (New York: Fordham University Press, 1960).

21. Friedman is reported to have advised, in a speech at the June 1980 International Monetary Conference of bankers from large private banks and central bankers, that there was no need for the Federal Reserve System. He said the economy would work better without the central bank, by maintaining a steady monetary growth (*The New York Times*, June 1980, pp. F6–7). The Neal amendment was added to a proposal that would have ended the FOMC and placed its powers with the Board of Governors.

22. This argument is formally stated in Milton Friedman, "The Effects of a Full-Employment Policy on Economic Stability: A Formal Analysis," in *Essays in Positive Economics* (Chicago: University of Chicago Press, 1953), pp. 117–132. Also see Haskell Benishay, "A Framework for the Evaluation of Short-Term Fiscal and Monetary Policy," *Journal of Money, Credit and Banking*, November 1972, pp. 779–810. Benishay showed that the more variable the lag in monetary policy is, the less likely it is to be destabilizing. This may look like an argument for discretionary monetary policy; however, it can also be an argument against the use of discretionary policy intended to affect a particular variable in a particular future time period. The chance of success is reduced; the chance of great harm is also reduced. In the extreme, if the lag were completely random, a policy of fine tuning would have a series of impacts randomly distributed, and so would a monetary rule policy of constant money growth.

CHAPTER 30

FEDERAL RESERVE POLICYMAKING AND CONGRESSIONAL OVERSIGHT

INTRODUCTION

The chapter begins with a description of a meeting at a regional Federal Reserve bank around 1976, which exemplifies the monetary policy decision-making preparations at the regional Reserve bank level. The choices for short-run monetary policy and an interesting method for determining desired money growth are explained. Then the preparations at the Board of Governors for the Federal Open Market Committee are discussed. Some aspects of FOMC decisions and the dominant influence on policy in the Federal Reserve are described.

Congressional monetary policy oversight hearings are discussed, followed by a section entitled "Who Cares?" in which the role of economists, interest groups, and the public in influencing legislation on banking and financial subjects are described.

A PREWASH MEETING AT A FEDERAL RESERVE BANK

There are approximately 500 economists in the research departments of the Board of Governors of the Federal Reserve and the twelve regional Federal Reserve banks. It is an impressive group, not only in size, but also in quality. Some of the country's finest economists and statisticians (econometricians) are on those staffs.

Directly or indirectly, most of those economists and their supporting personnel have as their primary function the provision of information and advice on monetary policy. This function reaches its moment of greatest application at the regional level before each of the Federal Open Market Committee (FOMC) meetings. Then the efforts of hundreds of economists are incorporated into a meaningful, coherent statement of action regarding monetary policy, a process that has its elements of ritual and façade.

It began (circa 1976 at one Reserve bank) with the "prewash meeting." This was a meeting with the president of the bank, his chief economist (senior vice-president in charge of the research department), and the staff of economists. It took place on the Thursday or Friday before the Tuesday FOMC meeting in Washington, D.C. (Most Federal Reserve banks have only part of the economics staff present.)

Thirteen economists filed into the conference room and took their places around a table. The meeting began as soon as the president of the bank arrived. There would be an extra sense of importance if the president had a vote that year on the FOMC.

Two reports were given, one on financial developments and one on macroeconomic conditions in the economy. There was little interaction in the writing of those reports. The authors of these reports and most of the economists present were usually *not* given up-to-date estimates of the targets

TABLE 30-1   Hypothetical Short-Run Policy Options for the Prewash Meeting, Circa 1976*

This table was constructed to show the wide M-1 targets and narrow federal funds targets before the October 1979 change in policy. However, the 1983 M-1 target range is again exactly a 4 to 8 percent growth rate range.

	Policy A	Policy B	Policy C
Old M-1	4–8%	4.5–8.5%	5–9%
Old M-2	8–12	8.5–12.5	5–13
Federal funds rate	4–5	3.75–4.75	3.5–4.5

* Annual growth rates for aggregates, interest rates for federal funds rate.

adopted at the last FOMC meeting. These targets were a closely guarded secret that only two or three officials in the bank knew. Therefore, the reports were written without knowledge of current monetary policy.

After some discussion, the "go-around" began. Each economist was allowed to register his or her view within some very narrow constraints. There were three choices of sets of monetary aggregate growth rates and corresponding federal funds rates sent from the Board of Governors, as shown in Table 30-1.

There was no evidence presented that the aggregate growth rates and federal funds rate targets were consistent. The casual evidence and inquiry indicated that, at best, the correspondence was rough. It was understood— though discussion was diverted from this avenue of inquiry—that whatever policy was chosen, a decision to focus on money market conditions would mean that the major attempt would be to achieve the federal funds rate target, not the monetary aggregates target. In some cases, as shown in Table 30-1, the monetary target ranges were wide and the federal funds rate ranges were narrow, so that the monetary aggregate target ranges were more likely to be hit if the federal funds rate target ranges were hit.

There seemed to be some tendency in the go-around to select policy B, as it was not an "extreme position" and was frequently thought to be a continuation of existing policy. There were some acrimony and some admonitions from the president to "join the team" when several recalcitrant economists failed to select policies A, B, or C. Instead, they invented policy D.

After several hours of discussion, the president of the bank said a few words that gave little indication of his reaction to the discussion or how he was likely to vote. Then the prewash meeting ended.

Frequently at these meetings, analysis of the correct monetary target went along the following lines: A forecast of nominal GNP from the Board of Governors was combined with a judgmental estimate of the rate of the growth of income velocity. Then a consistent rate of growth for the money supply was selected from the monetary identity.

$$\dot{M} = \dot{Y} - \dot{V} \tag{1}$$

where $\dot{M}$ is the rate of change of old M-1, $\dot{Y}$ is the rate of change of nominal GNP, and $\dot{V}$ is the rate of change of velocity. Insofar as the GNP estimate was based on the Board of Governors' projections, which took into account the effect of a desired M-1 growth, the analysis was partly circular. The monetary assumption of the GNP estimate would appear to the users of the analysis as their own projection, deviating only by their different estimates of the rate of change in velocity.

The approach of starting with a GNP estimate was in keeping with an accommodative method of determining the quantity of money needed to support a given GNP. (Remember that nominal income is the price level times real income.) With the price level assumed to be built in from past influences, including past money growth, a failure to accommodate that level of GNP would force real income to slow down to an undesirable extent.

Those who opposed this approach argued that accommodation induces a higher and higher price level, that it puts too much weight on short-term real adjustments. This argument is illustrated in the stagflation dilemma presented in Chapter 27.

The day before the FOMC meeting, the presidents of the twelve Reserve banks and their chief economists fly to Washington, D.C.

FOMC SELECTION OF TARGETS

Approximately 150 economists at the Board of Governors in Washington, D.C., directly or indirectly (such as through briefing papers) advise the FOMC.

The FOMC selects short-term two- to six-month targets, such as those given in Table 30-2. Twice a year (February and July), twelve-month targets are selected, as is required under the Humphrey–Hawkins Act for presentation to the banking committees of the Congress.

The staff prepares "consensus" forecasts of GNP, inflation, unemployment, and so on, based on a large econometric model and their judgment. Forecasts are based on present monetary and fiscal policy and alternative monetary and fiscal policy assumptions. The staff's "consensus" forecast is placed in the supersecret Green Book. Meanwhile, the staffs at the Board and the New York Federal Reserve Bank develop estimates of recent changes in the monetary aggregates and the federal funds rate and make projections about the future values of these variables. All this is put in the supersecret Blue Book.

Simultaneously, personnel at each of the regional Federal Reserve banks conduct a phone survey of private commercial bankers throughout their district and write short summaries of the survey results. Episodic experience at one bank indicates that an effort is made by officials at the Federal Reserve banks to avoid reporting troubling survey information in their district. (This is in keeping with the tendency of all regulators who find it in their interest to avoid reporting problems in their constituency.) The information is collected

TABLE 30-2 FOMC Short-Term Operating Specifications

Meeting Date	Target Period	Expected Growth Rates			Intermeeting Federal Funds Range
		M-1	M-2	M-3	
December 17–18, 1984*	November 1984–March 1985	around 7%	around 9%	around 9%	6–10%
February 12–13, 1985	December 1984–March 1985	around 8	around 10–11	around 10–11	6–10
March 26, 1985	March–June 1985	around 6	around 7	around 8	6–10
May 21, 1985†	March–June 1985	around 6 or a little higher	less than 7	less than 8	6–10
July 9–10, 1985‡	June–September 1985	5 to 6	around 7.7	around 7.5	6–10
August 20, 1985§	June–September 1985	8 to 9	around 8.5	around 6.5	6–10
October 1, 1985‖	September–December 1985	around 6–7	about 6–7	about 6–7	6–10
November 4–5, 1985¶	September–December 1985	around 6	about 6	about 6	6–10
December 16–17, 1985**	November 1985–March 1986	7 to 9	about 6–8	about 6–8	6–10

* Mr. Solomon dissented from this action because, although he thought some further easing would be appropriate over the coming period, he believed such action should be relatively gradual. In particular, he was concerned that the provision of reserves sought by the Committee risked an excessive decline in short-term rates and an overreaction in the financial markets. He therefore preferred a more cautious probing toward reserve conditions.

Mr. Gramley dissented because he could not accept a directive that called for further easing of reserve conditions. In his view the underlying strength of the economy together with the ongoing effects of earlier declines in interest rates provided the basis for a likely rebound in economic growth during 1985. He also believed that the Committee needed to take greater account of the broader monetary aggregates whose expansion appeared to be exceeding the Committee's expectations by a substantial margin in the fourth quarter. Under current circumstances he was concerned that significant further easing of reserve conditions would foster additional declines in interest rates that would have to be reversed later as economic growth picked up again.

† Mr. Black dissented because he preferred to direct policy implementation in the weeks immediately ahead toward achieving somewhat slower expansion in M-1. In his view, bringing M-1 growth more promptly within the Committee's range for the year would help guard against a possible worsening of inflationary expectations and would limit the risk of a potentially unsettling movement in interest rates later in the year.

‡ Mr. Black dissented because he believed some increase in the degree of reserved pressure was needed to help assure an adequate slowing of M-1 growth over the months ahead. Ms. Seger dissented because she favored some easing of reserve conditions to help reduce current financial strains, moderate the strength of the dollar in foreign exchange markets, and promote faster economic expansion.

§ Mr. Black dissented because he preferred to direct open market operations promptly toward a somewhat greater degree of reserve restraint and thereby improve the prospects of moderating M-1 growth to within the Committee's range for the second half of the year. Ms. Seger dissented because she favored some reduction in the degree of reserve restraint in the light of the financial vulnerability of some sectors of the economy and in order to encourage sustained economic expansion.

‖ Mr. Black dissented because he believed some increase in the degree of reserve pressure was needed at this time to ensure adequate slowing of M-1 growth in the period ahead.

¶ Ms. Seger dissented because she believed that some reduction in the degree of reserve restraint was needed to help relieve financial strains in the economy, and to promote a more acceptable rate of economic expansion closer to the faster growth expected by Committee members early this year.

** Mr. Black dissented because he was concerned about the rapid growth of M-1 and he did not think a decrease in the degree of pressure on reserve positions was desirable under present circumstances.

Source: R. W. Hafer, "The FOMC in 1985: Reacting to Declining M-1 Velocity," *Review*, Federal Reserve Bank of St. Louis, February 1986, p. 11.

through the Federal Reserve wire system and appears for FOMC members in the supersecret Red Book.

Frequently (before 1979) the chairman of the Federal Reserve was asked in congressional hearings to present those staff estimates to explain the reasons for the Federal Reserve monetary policies. What did a particular long-run monetary policy mean for unemployment, inflation, interest rates, and so on?

The Federal Reserve chairman from 1970 to 1977, Arthur Burns, refused to supply a systematic report of this kind, though many of his own estimates were brought out during his testimony. At the monetary policy oversight hearings before the House Banking Committee on February 3, 1977, Chairman Burns gave a reply to Congressman James J. Blanchard (who later became the Governor of Michigan) that indicated the chairman's view of those staff reports and reaffirmed their secrecy.

Mr. Blanchard: ... I understand that the Fed, in its member banks and then here in Washington, has about 500 economists, and I'm wondering if the collective judgment of those people is that your target of $4\frac{1}{2}$ to $6\frac{1}{2}$ percent, for example, for M-1 takes into account the goal of 6 percent GNP and 6.7 to 6.9 percent unemployment, and additionally whether you would be willing to make judgments of those economic thinkers available to the Secretary of Treasury and to Members of Congress?

Dr. Burns: To make available what?

Mr. Blanchard: Their judgments. Do their judgments on the monetary aggregates—

Dr. Burns: We have several hundred economists; you're quite right. They work on a great variety of subjects—they are experts on industrial prices or agricultural prices or foreign trade or other specialities. Few of them have any special ability to judge questions of the sort you raise.

Our staff analyses are regularly made available, and have been over the years, to the secretary of the Treasury on a confidential basis.

As for making them available to the Congress—which, with great respect, means making them available to the general public—I would have to oppose that. And I will tell you why.

Decisions are made by the Federal Open Market Committee. Our staff is an independent staff. I want our staff to remain independent. If the staff's estimates, which are revised from month to month, were made public, I am afraid our staff might lose its objectivity.

Our staff changes its judgments and its forecasts and its projections month by month, and I think they do a thoroughly workmanlike and honest job. However, the result, I must say, is not always good. I don't want to do anything that on the one hand may confuse the public and on the other hand may diminish the scholarly quality, the objectivity of our staff work.

Our staff now revises its projections month by month. The staff members are human; they would not want to be shown to believe one thing today and another thing a few days later or a month later. If the figures become public the staff would tend to stabilize its judgments and forecasts. Their work would then be of less value than it is now.

So, I see no advantage in making our staff analyses public. And let me say this. You in the Congress are not short of projections or forecasts by economists. They are eager to throw projections at you. How much good the projections do you, I don't know. But you get plenty of them.

... Do your advisers at the Fed believe that your monetary targets will lead to the goals of the Carter administration as you know them and as I have stated?

I find that very difficult to answer, because I don't talk to all of our economists. If there were some strong feeling to the contrary, I assume that it would come my way, that I would hear about it. That is as good an answer as I can give you.

I must say to you, I frequently disagree with our economists. I've had a little training in this field myself. [*Conduct of Monetary Policy*, Hearings Before the Committee on Banking, Finance, and Urban Affairs of the U.S. House of Representatives, pp. 106–107]

The Humphrey–Hawkins Act of 1978 required public reports on Federal Reserve projections of important economic variables (except for interest rates). The Federal Reserve now supplies them at the February and July oversight hearings of the two banking committees.

THE FOMC POLICY DECISIONS

The twelve members of the FOMC gather, with supporting staff personnel, at the FOMC meeting. Staff summaries of domestic and international economic conditions are presented. Votes are taken on policy. A summary of the reasons for FOMC actions and the policy directive are released to the public 30 days after the FOMC meeting.

The FOMC normally meets nine or ten times a year. It holds occasional telephone and wire consultations. Normally, the chairman has the most power, and the presidents of the Federal Reserve banks do not vote against the chairman of the Federal Reserve System.

Consider that the Board of Governors approves the appointments of the presidents of the regional Reserve banks every five years and must approve the regional Reserve banks' budgets, plus most important Reserve bank actions. Therefore, there is reason to suspect that Reserve bank presidents cannot exert dominating influence. With notable exceptions, they may only occasionally voice their disapproval. It also appears that Board members do not have nearly the influence of the chairman. After all, the chairman meets with the president and the secretary of the Treasury and appears before Congress as the spokesperson for the Federal Reserve. The chairman represents the primary contact with the government. He conducts the FOMC and Board of Governors meetings. Most of the FOMC's decisions are probably dominated by his views, with primary input from several of the top staff members. Those staff members often appear with the chairman in negotiations with Congress and during hearings, occasionally joining in part of the testimony.

EXCERPTS FROM THE JULY 11, 1986, POLICY DIRECTIVE

In the implementation of policy for the immediate future, the Committee seeks to maintain the existing degree of pressure on reserve positions. This action is expected to be consistent with a deceleration in money growth over the balance of the quarter. However, in view of the rapid money growth thus far in the quarter and the apparent weakness in velocity, the Committee anticipates faster growth for the monetary aggregates, particularly M-1, than expected at the last meeting. M-2 and M-3 are expected to expand over the period from March to June at annual rates of about 8 to 10 percent. While the behavior of M-1 continues to be subject to unusual uncertainty, growth at an annual rate of about 12 to 14 percent over the period is now anticipated. If the anticipated slowing in monetary growth does not develop, somewhat greater reserve restraint would be acceptable in the context of a pickup in growth of the economy, taking account of conditions in domestic and international financial markets. Somewhat lesser reserve restraint might be acceptable in the context of a marked slowing in money growth and pronounced sluggishness in economic performance. The Chairman may call for Committee consultation if it appears to the Manager for Domestic Operations that reserve conditions during the period before the next meeting are likely to be associated with a federal funds rate persistently outside a range of 5 to 9 percent.

Votes for this action: Messrs. Volcker, Corrigan, Angell, Guffey, Mrs. Horn, Messrs. Johnson, Melzer, Morris, Rice, and Ms. Seger. Vote against this action: Mr. Wallich. Absent and not voting: None.

Mr. Wallich dissented because he preferred to direct open market operations toward somewhat greater restraint. He was concerned about the implications of rapid monetary expansion for inflation and wanted to take action promptly to help assure slower monetary growth.

FORMAL CONGRESSIONAL OVERSIGHT OF THE FEDERAL RESERVE BEGINS IN 1975

The mere mention of this title causes passions to rise in Congress, in the financial community, and in segments of the general population. On one side, it is asserted that the Federal Reserve is the creation of the Congress, which voted it into law in December 1913. This view holds that in a democracy the representatives of the people have the right to oversee the federal government, including the central bank. Furthermore, the argument is sometimes made (as in the last chapter) that the Federal Reserve has been a highly political animal, responding in large measure to the desires of the president of the United States. Whether there was fast or slow money growth may have depended more on the president than on the chairman of the Federal Reserve. It is very difficult to fend off pressures from the president of the United States, whatever the legal separation may be.

On the other side, there is the argument for independence—an independent Federal Reserve, "Keep the politicians' hands off the money supply." This argument has its origin deep in the history of money and banking.

Some of those views arose with unusual fury in the early history of the United States. President Andrew Jackson, buttressed by widespread public support, ordered all payments to the government to be in the form of specie, and he withdrew the federal funds from the Second Bank of the United States. These actions were the major causes of a severe depression that began in the late 1830s; they left the United States without a separate central bank (separate from the Treasury) until the Federal Reserve went into operation in the last quarter of 1914. "Moneychangers" or those "manipulating" the money supply were, and still frequently are, looked upon with great distrust by some.

As the structure of the Federal Reserve in 1914 so well exemplifies, there was a design for diffusion of power, primarily in the hands of individuals outside the federal government. Before the reorganization in the 1930s, the presidents of the twelve Federal Reserve banks dominated much of the decision-making process at the Federal Reserve.

The hands-off policy of Congress in the post–World War II period changed following the postwar recession of 1974 and 1975. It was felt that the Federal Reserve had acted improperly, that it had failed to provide enough money, thus intensifying the recession and impairing the recovery. There were suggestions at that time that Congress legislate a minimum rate of growth for the money supply. Those attempts failed, but a different tactic succeeded.

Senator William Proxmire, former chairman of the Senate Banking Committee, and Congressman Henry Reuss, former chairman of the House Banking Committee, were instrumental in the passage in 1975 of a congressional resolution, House Concurrent Resolution 133 (H. Con 133). This resolution called on the Federal Reserve to report formally to the banking committees of the U.S. Congress four times a year, alternating between the House and the Senate. The Federal Reserve was to make target ranges for the monetary aggregates that it wanted to follow during the subsequent twelve-month periods. It was excused from hitting those target ranges if special circumstances arose.

The language of the congressional resolution is especially interesting and is due in large part to the late Robert Weintraub, then a staff member who worked on both the Senate and House banking committees and who in 1980 was staff director of the subcommittee on monetary policy of the House Banking Committee. His staff report presented to the House Banking Committee in 1974 called for formal congressional oversight, but no action was taken until 1975. The Federal Reserve was directed, as a long-range policy, to manage the monetary and credit aggregates so that they grew at a rate "commensurate with the economy's long-run potential to increase production, so as to promote effectively the goals of maximum employment, stable prices, and moderate long-term interest rates." The "long-run potential to increase production" or long-run growth in full employment output or capacity output has been approximately 3 percent. It could grow considerably faster from the trough of a recession when growth is much slower or negative.

Hearings pursuant to House Concurrent Resolution 133 began in March 1975. At that time the chairman of the Federal Reserve was Arthur Burns, formerly a professor of economics at Columbia University, director of the National Bureau of Economic Research in New York (a respected private economic research organization), chairman of the Council of Economic Advisers (appointed in 1952), and a consultant to Presidents Eisenhower and Nixon. Burns was followed in 1978 in the chairmanship by G. William Miller, a successful business executive, whose great bargaining ability was a major factor in the passage of the Depository Institutions Deregulation and Monetary Control Act in 1980, shortly after he had left the Federal Reserve. Miller was succeeded in 1979 by Paul Volcker, a seasoned financial expert who had worked at a large private bank, at the U.S. Treasury, and as president of the New York Federal Reserve Bank. He was an especially knowledgeable and adept witness in explaining Federal Reserve policy.

The quarterly reporting to the Congress by the Federal Reserve ended at the end of 1978, with the passage of the Humphrey–Hawkins Act (the Full Employment and Balanced Growth Act of 1978). The Humphrey–Hawkins Act required the Federal Reserve to present detailed reports to Congress on the conduct of monetary policy twice a year, on February 20 and July 20. The reports were, among other things, to explain how monetary policy was coordinated with fiscal policy and how the Federal Reserve's monetary policy would help achieve full employment and price stability. Both the House and Senate banking committees would then be required to write their own reports on monetary policy. This would require the members of the banking committees to endorse, reject, or pointedly take no stand on the Federal Reserve's monetary policy. Whereas before, under the reporting requirement, members of the House and Senate banking committees might only appear and question the chairman of the Federal Reserve, now their committees issued a report to which they could dissent.

With all this reporting to Congress, on top of frequent consultations with the administration, what is the meaning of independence? Is it possible or desirable for a central bank to pursue policies different from those of the rest of the central government? If the Weintraub hypothesis, developed in the last chapter, is roughly correct, the answer is strictly academic.

GOOD MORNING, CHAIRMAN

Before the monetary policy oversight hearings in February and July, the chairmen of the banking committees of Congress may notify the chairman of the Federal Reserve of special subjects of interest. The Federal Reserve is often asked to have particular information available.

Although House Banking Committee rules require that the testimony of witnesses be received several days in advance, the Federal Reserve has waited until 5 P.M. the night before the hearing to send its testimoney for the February and July monetary policy oversight hearings. This practice provides more assurance that the new long-run target ranges will not leak out before the chairman's appearance the following day. However, it poses serious problems. The 44 members of the House banking committee do not have much time to study the report—which may run over 50 pages. Staff personnnel of both Democratic and Republican members work that night to analyze it and prepare questions for the following day's hearings.

Attendance of members of the House Banking Committee at the hearings varies, but they are usually well attended. The hearings usually begin at 9:30 or 10:00 A.M. By informal agreement, the House and Senate banking committees take turns in having the first day of hearings at the February and July reporting times. If it is a first-day hearing, TV cameras and batteries of bright lights are more likely to be set up. Sometimes an approximately 20-second clip of hearings will back up the dialogue of an approximately 1-minute summary, given by an announcer posed in front of the Capitol on a prime-time news program. The TV cameras sometimes grind away continually for the first hours of the hearing. The monetary policy targets are rarely reported on TV; they are too esoteric. Ten to twenty reporters from the financial press are always in attendance, and they provide more detailed coverage. (The financial press consists of reporters for the wire services and financial and business sections of magazines, newspapers, and newsletters.)

After the chairman of the House Banking Committee and the chairman of the Federal Reserve read their statements, each of the 44 members is allowed 5 minutes for questions and answers under the "5-minute rule." If the House is in session, buzzers and lights on the clock and pager-intercoms carried by some members frequently go off in unison. Members are called in this manner to the floor of the House of Representatives for a vote or a quorum call. The hearings are recessed for 5 to as much as 20 minutes.

Members are called by the chairman to ask questions in order of their length of service in Congress. They sit in this order also, from the top row center (with Democrats to the right and Republicans to the left of the Banking Committee chairman) down through the second and third rows. The TV cameras and the financial press are often gone by the time the junior members' turns come, and sometimes the hearings are adjourned before their turns come because of other appointments of the chairman of the Federal Reserve.

In the Senate hearings there are fewer committee members, which allows more backup questions by the same individuals on a particular subject.

In both the House and Senate hearings, the staff seated behind the members assists in preparing backup questions and providing information as the hearings proceed. Whatever its faults, and there are many, this hearing is an important part of a democracy in action, wherein representatives of the public from many different geographic areas are able to question the basis for the country's monetary policies.

WHO CARES?

WASHINGTON, D.C.—Summer of 1979. Nearly 5,000 protestors jammed the steps on the east side of the Capitol just below the dome. They waved banners, pennants, and signs; some wore imprinted T-shirts; and one had a 30-foot blowup of *Wall Street Journal* writer Lindley H. Clark Jr.'s April 25, 1978, article, which for the second time had revealed the importance of their cause. [Little else had appeared except in trade publications.] They had marched from the White House and were about to swing across Independence Avenue to the Rayburn House Office Building. Police lined the streets; police cars blocked the traffic; several mounted police stood by at the west side of the Capitol on the Mall.

As they crossed Independence Avenue and turned down South Capitol Street toward the horsehoe drive—the main entrance to the Rayburn Building—they became deadly serious and broke into their chant. As clearly as a single voice magnified 5,000 times, they yelled "Down with lagged reserve requirements! Down with lagged reserve requirements! One, two, three, four; do you know what we're for? Five, six, seven, eight; not for requirements that are two weeks late! Nine and ten; for synchronous requirements we do yen!"

Henry Reuss, former chairman of the House Banking Committee, appeared at the door of the Rayburn Building and the crowd broke into enthusiastic applause. Chairman Reuss was leading the fight on this issue. He told them that lagged reserve requirements, in effect since 1968, caused unstable interest rates and unstable monetary aggregates. "Since 1976 I have tried again and again to persuade Chairman Burns, Chairman Miller, and Chairman Volcker with the overwhelming view of experts that lagged reserve requirements seriously interfere with control of the money supply."

Six television cameras swung toward the leader of the antilagged reserve requirement protesters—hitting one or two antiabortion demonstrators in the head. With tears in her eyes the antilagged reserve requirements leader told the crowd, "Go home now and stir the electorate into action."

None of this happened—except that Representative Reuss did work to eliminate lagged reserve requirements—nor is it likely to happen. Reuss also tried to end the "Wednesday scramble," in which all 5,600 member banks were required to come up with their reserve requirements at the close of business on Wednesday—but with even fewer demonstrators lending their support, although Lindley Clark also wrote an article in *The Wall Street Journal* on this issue. In other words, the arcane matters of money and banking are generally of little interest. There are no mass or miniature movements among the public (although there have been demonstrations against higher interest rates and unemployment).

In a June 4, 1980, press release, the Federal Reserve circulated the following statement for public comment:

The Board has been considering a return to contemporaneous reserve accounting as a means of improving monetary control by strengthening the linkage between the reserves of the depositor system and the money supply. Instead of basing required reserves on deposits held two weeks earlier, required reserves would be based on deposits in a current statement week.

This press release indicated that a return to synchronous (or contemporaneous) reserve requirements might be adopted in September 1980. The proposal was rejected with an announcement of the possible adoption of synchronous reserve requirements in September 1981 if further study showed it to be feasible. It was finally implemented on February 2, 1984 (see Exhibit 27-1). The economists at the Federal Reserve, with the congressional committees, with academic situations, and in the financial industry played an important part in advising about and discussing the aspects of this issue. They also constituted the primary force outside the industries affected that presented views on the Depository Institutions Deregulation and Monetary Control Act of 1980. Nearly all other interested parties were trade groups. Former Chairman Henry Reuss of the House Banking Committee was the primary congressional force behind this important legislation, fighting a two-and-one-half-year battle.

Sometimes economists take an interest with letters and testimony before various committees, but their efforts are usually not covered by the press to any great extent except in some trade publications, because the public is not interested. Adding to their feeling of impotence and anticharisma—in a town in which the opposite abilities are constantly honed by the successful—the economists sometimes clear a hearing room more rapidly than one can say, "The Hicksian solution to macroeconomic equilibrium." Partly this is a result of the economists' style of presentation, which is often geared to an academic audience that is mesmerized by an *IS–LM* diagram rather than to a national audience. Their efforts, however, are *extremely important*, as economists are often the only individuals who may be speaking on behalf of the general public. Legislators and economists on their staffs often listen carefully and *are* influenced by what they hear.

Only the trade groups make an ardent effort to voice their interests on banking and finance issues. Some of the leading trade groups in the banking and thrift industries are the American Bankers Association, Securities Industry Association, Independent Bankers Association of America, Conference of State Bank Supervisors, New York Clearing House Association, Credit Union National Association, New York Stock Exchange, Bankers Association for Foreign Trade, Institute of Foreign Bankers, National Savings and Loan League, U.S. League of Savings Associations, National Association of Mutual

Savings Banks, National Bankers Association, and the Chicago Clearing House Association.

The *Bank Letter* of October 11, 1982 (p. 9) reported that the American Bankers Association was the leader among banking group contributors to campaigns of Congress members, with donations of $685,675. The Citicorp voluntary political fund was second, with $163,164. These funds were for congressional campaigns. A massive campaign was mounted by the banking and thrift industries in 1983 to repeal the section of the 1982 tax law that required the withholding of interest by banks and thrifts.

Legislators are often faced with the decision of whether or not to vote for some banking and financial legislation that either alienates or wins applause from the interest groups without arousing their constituency, which is uninterested in the issues involved. A decision to fight the interest groups is often a courageous one, with little reward and sometimes severe penalties, such as defeat at the next election. Remember that members of the House of Representatives run for reelection every two years, so that election battles are always just around the corner.

This does not mean that the interest groups are frequently wrong. Much of the time, they may be correct, and their views may well serve the public interest. That is not the point. The point is that the public must become better educated in these areas. Inflation, unemployment, and economic stability are the major issues at stake, and legislation and congressional oversight in this area should be matters of wide public interest.

STUDY QUESTIONS

1. Does wider public interest in money, banking, financial policy, and legislation ensure policy and legislation that better benefit the economy as a whole? Explain. Are there other reasons for advocating wider public interest?
2. What is congressional oversight of monetary policy, how does it work, and what benefits or harm does it entail?
3. Is it true that the monetary policy decisions of the Federal Reserve are the product of nearly equal inputs from the regional Reserve bank presidents and the governors in Washington? Who is likely to dominate, and why is this so?
4. What does independence for the Federal Reserve mean? Is it desirable?
5. Paraphrased minutes for the FOMC meetings were released five years after the meetings. Then after the sunshine laws were passed, opening most government records to public scrutiny, the FOMC received an exemption, and no minutes were kept. Congress may again pass a bill to restore the minutes. Is this desirable? Why?
6. What effect does Congress have on monetary policy? Will its influence grow, recede, or stay the same?

CHAPTER 31

INTEREST RATES VERSUS MONETARY AGGREGATES

CHAPTER PREVIEW

Introduction. This chapter uses the *IS–LM* analysis to discuss some of the issues in using a monetary aggregates target of a money market target.

Analysis. The analysis assumes that either the *IS* or the *LM* is unstable and then seeks to show whether a monetary aggregates or money market target is more suitable under these alternative conditions.

No Conclusion. The results do not provide a conclusion without taking into account other factors that return to the issue of fine-tuning or a monetary rule.

INTRODUCTION

The Federal Reserve has used both the money supply and the federal funds rate as intermediate targets. These intermediate targets are also called a *monetary aggregates target* and a *money market target*, respectively. In this chapter some of the issues in choosing one or both of these alternatives are discussed with the help of the *IS–LM* analysis.[1]

ANALYSIS

The *IS–LM* analysis is a convenient tool for illustrating some of the issues involved. This is because in its form in Chapter 23, the model may be solved by treating either the money supply or interest rates as a policy variable determined outside the model. Then the model can be solved for the other variables. For simplicity, assume that the price level is fixed and there is no expectation of price level changes. Those assumptions make all real and nominal variables equal, and then the two alterntive intermediate targets can easily be pictured.

The monetary aggregates target is defined in Figure 31-1 as holding the money supply at M_1, a real money balance of M_1/P_0. If the map of the demand-for-money curves at each income is constant, this will translate into a fixed *LM* curve, as shown in Figure 31-2.

The federal funds target is pictured in Figures 31-1 through 31-3 at a level of r_0.

Suppose that the map of the demand-for-money curves shifts, so that at a given real income the demand-for-money curve will move from DD to $D'D'$ in Figure 31-1. Then the interest rate will move from the target rate of r_0 to r_1. If the Federal Reserve is on a money markets target, pegging the federal funds rate at r_0, it will increase the money supply to M_2, which will bring down interest rates to the target level, r_0.

Suppose that the Federal Reserve knew the source of every disturbance. Disturbances might take the form of a shift in the demand for money or some change in a variable affecting the *IS* curve. If the Federal Reserve's objective were to offset short-run changes in real income, it could increase or decrease the money supply just enough to move the *LM* curve and keep real income constant. However, disturbances, especially short-run disturbances, are difficult to predict or diagnose. In practice, there is much uncertainty.

Suppose that in such an environment it is known that the uncertainty pertains mostly to the factors underlying the *IS* curve, so that the *IS* curve is *unstable*. (Unstable means unpredictable.) The *IS* bounces around from *IS* to *I'S'* in Figure 31-2. If the Federal Reserve were on an interest rate target, a shift of the investment-saving curve to *IS* in Figure 31-2 would cause interest rates to fall below the target. Income would fall to y_2. In response, the Federal Reserve would decrease the money supply to drive up interest rates to the target. Then income would fall farther to y_1, as the *LM* curve shifted to *L'M'*.

FIGURE 31-1   The Demand and Supply of Real Money Balances with No Inflationary Expectations and a Fixed Price Level

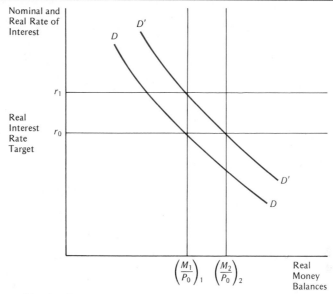

A shift upward in the demand for real money balances moves the equilibrium interest rate from r_0 to r_1.

FIGURE 31-2   Interest Rate Target with an Unstable *IS*, Leading to Wider Income Variations

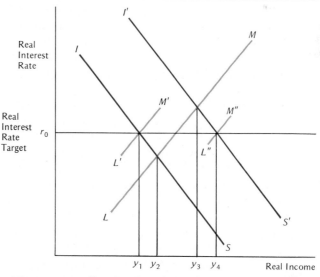

Shifts in the *IS* curve are offset by changes in the money supply that shift *LM* to maintain a target interest rate. Income would fluctuate between y_1 and y_4. If money were kept on target so that *LM* remained constant, shifts in *IS* of the same magnitude would cause smaller income shifts, from y_2 to y_3.

FIGURE 31-3 Money Supply Target with an Unstable *LM*, Leading to Wider Income Variation

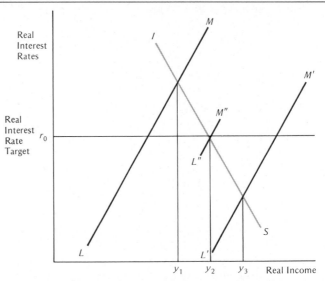

If the demand for money is unstable, *LM* will fluctuate so that income will fluctuate between y_1 and y_3 even if the money supply is on target (in this case, constant). With an interest rate target, the money supply is changed so as to keep the money market locus at $L'M''$, and income does not change.

Thus, the interest rate target strategy would cause income to fluctuate between y_1 and y_4 in Figure 31-2. There would be shifts of the investment-saving function between *IS* and *I'S'*. Reactions by the Federal Reserve would cause the *LM* curve to shift between $L'M'$ and $L''M''$. If a monetary aggregates target were followed, the *LM* would remain constant, and income fluctuations would be smaller, from y_2 to y_3.

If the demand-for-money function were unstable, the liquidity–money curve might fluctuate between *LM* and $L'M'$ in Figure 31-3. Real income would fluctuate between y_1 and y_3 if the money supply were constant.

An interest rate target would cause the Federal Reserve to increase or decrease the money supply so that the *LM* curve would stay at $L''M''$ in Figure 31-3. Income variation would be substantially reduced.

NO CONCLUSION

One cannot conclude from this demonstration that either (or both) a monetary aggregates or a federal funds interest rate target is desirable.

First, one must decide whether it is desirable to offset short-run disturbances, because such actions may produce increased long-run disturbances. For example, an attempt to offset every short-run disturbance may produce a very erratic monetary growth, which will heighten uncertainty, raise real interest rates, and depress economic activity. Also, changes in Federal Reserve policy have income effects and price level effects in the two or three years following their implementation. Therefore, the cumulative effects from trying to offset every short-run disturbance can introduce instability in the future.

Second, problems in short-run monetary control may make it difficult to manipulate the money supply over a month or two so that it will change by the proper amount.

Third, the rational expectations proponents discussed in Chapter 20 would say it is unlikely to work for real income. If the public were able to react rapidly to monetary changes by changing wages and prices, the price level, not real income, would change from these short-run changes in monetary policy.

Nevertheless, the underlying point is valid. If the demand for money is very unstable, an attempt to keep the money supply on a constant target will not produce stable real income or a stable price level. Of course, if the demand for money is only slightly unstable or changes very slowly over time (equivalent to a long-run trend in velocity), then changes in the money supply will produce more predictable effects on income and prices.

The eclectic approach is to try to control both interest rates and monetary aggregates within certain target ranges, as the Federal Reserve has done. If disturbances appear to be greater in the real sector, the interest rate target range can be broadened. If disturbances appear greater in the money market sector, the monetary aggregates target can be broadened. Monetary growth can be guided as a response to a great number of variables. And there it is again: a return to the argument of fine-tuning, or countercyclical monetary policy, versus some form of a long-run monetary rule.

STUDY QUESTIONS

1. Trace through the appropriate intermediate target—interest rates or monetary aggregates—if uncertain movements appear to be prevalent in each of these variables, taken one at a time: (a) real investment, (b) the demand for currency and coin, (c) real consumption.
2. Is the stabilization of short-run changes in real income and prices a desirable target?
3. How would the analysis in this chapter using the *IS–LM* curve change if the initial equilibrium were at full employment income?
4. How would the analysis change if real consumption also depended on real money balances?

NOTE

1. This analysis is based on William Poole's "Rules of Thumb for Guiding Monetary Policy," in *Open Market Policies and Operating Procedures— Staff Studies* (Washington, D.C.: Board of Governors of the Federal

Reserve System, 1971), pp. 135–189. Also see Benjamin Friedman, "The Inefficiency of Short-Run Monetary Targets for Monetary Policy," in Arthur M. Okun and George L. Perry, eds., *Brookings Papers on Economic Activity*, Vol. 2 (Washington, D.C.: Brookings Institution, 1977), pp. 293–335. Also see the discussion by James Duesenberry of Friedman's article in the same book, pp. 336–339; the discussion by William Poole, pp. 339–343; and the general discussion by the participants, pp. 343–346.

PART NINE

THE INTERNATIONAL FINANCIAL SYSTEM

CHAPTER 32

THE BALANCE OF PAYMENTS AND INTERNATIONAL EXCHANGE RATES

CHAPTER PREVIEW

Introduction. New ways for some individuals of thinking about international trade include an idea from 1776 that a higher standard of living, rather than vaults containing gold, may be better related to the wealth of nations.

Exchange Rates. The demand and supply of different currencies can determine their exchange rates.

The Balance of Payments. An accounting statement for international trade and investment of a country includes merchandise trade and capital flows.

Balance-of-Payments Relationships. Saving minus investment equals exports minus imports in an open economy.

Income Changes and the Trade Balance. Income affects aggregate demand, as described in Chapter 22, now extended to international trade.

Devaluation. One way to achieve equilibrium in the trade sector, when there is a deficit in the trade balance, is through a decline in the international value of the country's currency.

Does Devaluation Make Things Worse? Two conditions that are based on opposite characteristics of traded goods can cause the balance of trade to become more in deficit, with a devaluation.

Capital Flows. An important part of the balance-of-payments picture depends on real interest rates and other hard-to-analyze factors that affect capital flows. Of central importance to all of macroeconomic policy is whether or not capital flows change rapidly to equalize real interest rate differentials.

The Value of the U.S. Dollar Is Too High; the Value of the U.S. Dollar Is Too Low. U.S. government policies alternatively favored raising and lowering the exchange value of the U.S. dollar at different times during the 1970s and 1980s. Large trade deficits led to calls for protection from foreign imports and for export subsidies. These policies had some detrimental effects and inconsistencies as well as benefits to particular groups.

INTRODUCTION

This chapter first discusses the accounting classifications for international transactions and their financing, and then the determination of the international value of money—the exchange value of a unit of one country's money in terms of another. The chapter ends with some analysis of how equilibrium in the balance of payments is achieved.

Residents of more than one country, who must use different domestic currencies in international transactions, do not arrange for payments in the same manner as they would for internal transactions, in which a single domestic currency is the medium of exchange. International monetary economics focuses on the characteristics of these international payment arrangements, including the exchange of different types of financial assets and their relationships with other important economic variables, such as international trade and capital flows, domestic price levels, outputs, and interest rates. As in the study of internal monetary analysis, the international monetary relationships cannot easily be separated from the relationships that determine the demands and supply of the real goods and services that are traded.

The student often comes to the subject with entrenched notions that reduce objectivity. Perhaps the most misleading belief is that the inhabitants of a country *must* be better off if they sell more to inhabitants of foreign countries than foreigners sell to them.[1] Adam Smith called attention to this error in 1776, when his *An Inquiry into the Nature and Cause of the Wealth of Nations* was published. True, the inhabitants of a country with a payments surplus due them from other countries may fill their vaults with currency, or even precious metals such as gold, but this should not be the primary objective of a population that desires a high standard of living. Rather, the wealth of nations is measured by the quantity and quality of the goods and services that the inhabitants can obtain for their own use, rather than by the currency or gold they can accumulate for storage in exchange for their own goods and services. Of course, a favorable balance of payments and a lovely hoard of gold will provide the means to buy more goods and services in the future. In addition, misers get their kicks, not from hedonism, but rather from standing in the middle of their cache of gold bullion. However, if foreign imports that would support more productive investments are bypassed in favor of accumulating gold, future domestic output is likely to be reduced.

EXCHANGE RATES

Many things of value are exchanged in international trade, such as goods, services, equities, bonds (used here as a general name for debt instruments), and domestic and international currencies. How are arrangements for the exchange of these assets made?

If, for example, Sarah Martin from South Bend, Indiana, U.S.A., wants to buy a hat in London, she will need British currency. The basic unit of account is the British pound, with the symbol £ (just as the symbol $ indicates dollars). The pound's price was $1.48 on January 9, 1987, when Sarah Martin was in London (see Table 32-1). On that day, suppose that £10 billion cleared the market at a price of $1.48 per pound, as shown in Figure 32-1. Suppose that Sarah Martin had come two weeks later, when a jump in income in the United States had caused an increased demand for British imports (foreign goods shipped into the United States) at every price along *DD* in Figure 32-1. Then *DD* would shift to *D'D'*, and the market price of pounds would be $1.50. There thus would be an increase in demand for British pounds and an increase in the quantity of British pounds supplied, so that the market would settle down at an exchange of £12 billion.

T A B L E 3 2 - 1   Monetary Unit and Exchange Rates for U.S. Currency on January 9, 1987, for Selected Countries

Country	Monetary Unit	Value (U.S. cents)
Australia	Dollar	66.77
Austria	Schilling	7.71
Belgium	Franc	2.506
Canada	Dollar	73.05
Denmark	Krone	13.77
Finland	Markka	21.02
France	Franc	15.63
W. Germany	D. mark	52.14
India	Rupee	7.66
Italy	Lira	.0738
Japan	Yen	.6327
Mexico	Peso	.1072
Netherlands	Guilder	46.22
New Zealand	Dollar	54.70
Norway	Krone	13.61
Portugal	Escudo	.6863
South Africa	Rand	46.60
Spain	Peseta	.7590
Sweden	Krona	14.81
Switzerland	Franc	62.36
United Kingdom	Pound	147.70

FIGURE 32-1   Hypothetical Demand and Supply Curves for British Pounds (U.S. dollar prices for January 9, 1987, per pound)

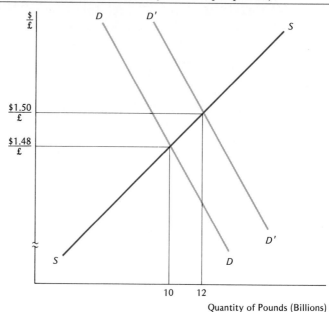

An increase in demand for British pounds increases their price to $1.50 in U.S. money. The quantity of British pounds supplied increases also.

Notice that two equivalent things have happened. The price of pounds went up by $.02 and the price of U.S. dollars fell (from £.677 to £.666).

For a general summary statistic of the international value of a U.S. dollar from 1967 to 1986 see Figure 32-2.

THE BALANCE OF PAYMENTS

One way to arrange international transactions when analyzing their relationships to a number of variables is in a balance-of-payments accounting statement, as shown in Table 32-2. In accounting terminology it is an income statement for a single country.

The two major accounts are the current account and the capital account. The current account records transactions in goods, services, and transfer payments. Gifts and grants are called **transfer payments**. The capital accounts record the transfer of assets such as bonds and stocks.

In these two accounts, any transaction that gives rise to a payment to a foreigner is entered as a debit, whereas a transaction giving rise to a receipt from a foreigner is entered as a credit. Double-entry bookkeeping is followed,

FIGURE 32-2   Weighted Average Exchange Value of the U.S. Dollar, 1967–1986

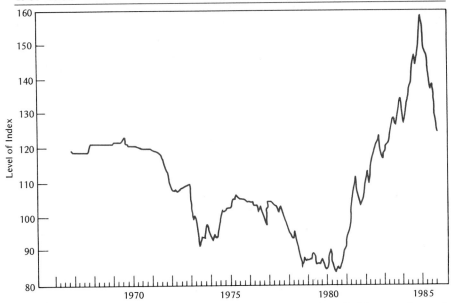

The international value of the dollar rose sharply beginning in 1980. The rate of growth in the money supply fell in the United States in 1981 and the first part of 1982. The money supply grew rapidly in 1985 and 1986, and the value of the dollar declined. The secretary of the Treasury in the second four-year term of the Reagan administration, James Baker, changed the administration's policy from one of nonintervention to one of intervention so as to depress the value of the dollar so that U.S. exports would have a lower international price. Then the dollar fell farther than anticipated in 1986.

Source: Cambridge Planning and Analytics, Inc., Boston.

so that every transaction must be recorded twice. That is, if $100 is recorded as the expenditure on a cup of imported crude oil, there must be another entry showing either an offsetting transaction or the form of payment.

The **trade balance** or **merchandise balance** is part of the current account. It equals exports (goods sold to foreigners outside the country) minus imports (goods purchased from foreigners outside the country). (See Figures 32-3 and 32-4.) A broader **goods and services balance** adds to the trade balance such goods and services as military expenditures and tourist spending.

The **current account balance** is a broader aggregate that adds government and private transfer payments to the goods and services balance.

The **capital account balance** is said to be in surplus if there is a **net capital inflow**. This will occur if the receipts from foreigners from the sale of assets exceed the domestic country's payments for assets purchased from foreigners. If payments exceed receipts, there will be a deficit on the capital accounts, which is called a **net capital outflow**.

TABLE 32-2   The Balance of Payments

The means of payment under a liquidity balance or an official settlements balance are the items under the line that underscores those titles.

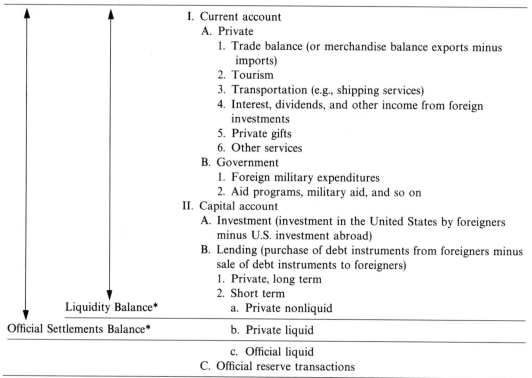

	I. Current account
	A. Private
	1. Trade balance (or merchandise balance exports minus imports)
	2. Tourism
	3. Transportation (e.g., shipping services)
	4. Interest, dividends, and other income from foreign investments
	5. Private gifts
	6. Other services
	B. Government
	1. Foreign military expenditures
	2. Aid programs, military aid, and so on
	II. Capital account
	A. Investment (investment in the United States by foreigners minus U.S. investment abroad)
	B. Lending (purchase of debt instruments from foreigners minus sale of debt instruments to foreigners)
	1. Private, long term
	2. Short term
Liquidity Balance*	a. Private nonliquid
Official Settlements Balance*	b. Private liquid
	c. Official liquid
	C. Official reserve transactions

* Under a liquidity balance, the last three entries are the means of payment. Under an official settlements balance, the last two entries are a means of payment.

Errors and omissions are simply goofs that are recorded under the heading "Discrepancy" in Table 32-3. They arise because the balance of payments is an accounting identity in which total payments must equal total receipts. When the records do not reflect this equality, the remainder is put in *discrepancy* (sometimes called *errors and omissions*). The balance of payments can be changed by putting the discrepancy in different places.

The whole balance of payments consists of the current account, the capital account, and the means of payment. The sum of the current account plus the capital account plus the means of payment is zero. That is easy to understand if you remember that the means of payment is the method for settling (paying out or collecting) for the goods, services, and capital flows recorded in the current and capital accounts. If the sum of the current account plus the capital account is positive, the payments will be from foreign to domestic sources. That is, the payments will be negative, a negative payment being a receipt, and the balance of payments is said to be in *surplus*. But if the sum of the current

FIGURE 32-3   Merchandise Exports and Imports, 1946–1985

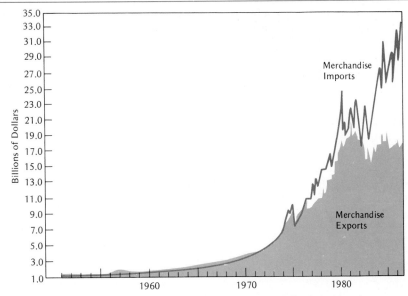

Merchandise imports were close to merchandise exports until 1976, when imports grew faster than exports.

Source: Cambridge Planning and Analytics Inc., Boston.

FIGURE 32-4   Merchandise Deficit, 1966–1985

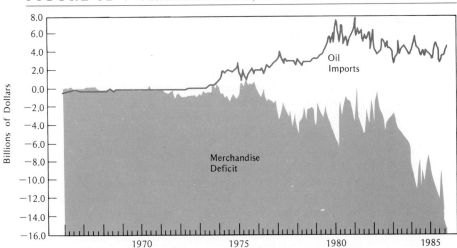

The merchandise defict changed from positive to negative in 1976 as oil imports—a significant part of imports—rose.

Source: Cambridge Planning and Analytics Inc., Boston.

TABLE 32-3   U.S. International Transactions, 1985 (millions of dollars)

This is the way the balance-of-payments statement was presented in 1985. Note the $124.4 billion merchandise deficit and the $128.4 billion increase of foreign assets in the United States, a capital inflow.

Item Credits or Debits[1]	
1 Balance on current account	−117,677
2 Not seasonally adjusted	—
3 Merchandise trade balance[2]	−124,439
4 Merchandise exports	214,424
5 Merchandise imports	−338,863
6 Military transactions, net	−2,917
7 Investment income, net[3]	25,188
8 Other service transactions, net	−525
9 Remittances, pensions, and other transfers	−3,787
10 U.S. government grants (excluding military)	−11,196
11 Change in U.S. government assets, other than official reserve assets, net (increase, −)	−2,824
12 Change in U.S. official reserve assets (increase, −)	−3,858
13 Gold	0
14 Special drawing rights (SDRs)	−897
15 Reserve position in International Monetary Fund	908
16 Foreign currencies	−3,869
17 Change in U.S. private assets abroad (increase, −)[3]	−25,754
18 Bank-reported claims	−691
19 Nonbank-reported claims	1,665
20 U.S. purchase of foreign securities, net	−7,977
21 U.S. direct investments abroad, net	−18,752
22 Change in foreign official assets in the United States (increase, +)	−1,324
23 U.S. Treasury securities	−546
24 Other U.S. government obligations	−295
25 Other U.S. government liabilities[4]	483
26 Other U.S. liabilities reported by U.S. banks	522
27 Other foreign official assets[5]	−1,488
28 Change in foreign private assets in the United States (increase, +)[3]	128,430
29 U.S. bank-reported liabilities	40,387
30 U.S. nonbank-reported liabilities	−1,172
31 Foreign private purchases of U.S. Treasury securities, net	20,500
32 Foreign purchases of other U.S. securities, net	50,859
33 Foreign direct investments in the United States, net[3]	17,856
34 Allocation of SDRs	0
35 Discrepancy	23,006
36 Owing to seasonal adjustments	—
37 Statistical discrepancy in recorded data before seasonal adjustment	23,006

TABLE 32-3 *(continued)*

	MEMO	
	Changes in official assets	
38	U.S. official reserve assets (increase, −)	−3,858
39	Foreign official assets in the United States (increase, +)	−1,807
40	Changes in Organization of Petroleum Exporting Countries official assets in the United States (part of line 22 above)	−6,599
41	Transfers under military grant programs (excluded from lines 4, 6, and 10 above)	64

1. Seasonal factors are not calculated for lines 6, 10, 12–16, 18–20, 22–34, and 38–41.
2. Data are on an international accounts (IA) basis. Differs from the Census basis data, shown in Table 3-11, for reasons of coverage and timing; military exports are excluded from merchandise data and are included in line 6.
3. Includes reinvested earnings.
4. Primarily associated with military sales contracts and other transactions arranged with or through foreign official agencies.
5. Consists of investments in U.S. corporate stocks and in debt securities of private corporations and state and local governments.
Note: Data are from Bureau of Economic Analysis, *Survey of Current Business* (Department of Commerce).
Source: Bulletin, Board of Governors, May 1986, p. A53.

account plus the capitals account is negative, the payments will be from the domestic to foreign sources. That is, the payments will be positive, and the balance of payments is said to be in *deficit.*

There is a problem in defining what is considered to be a payment and what is considered to be a capital flow and, therefore, part of the capital accounts. We will consider three concepts of payments.

The **official reserve transactions,** item IIC in Table 32-2, is one measure of the overall balance of payments. It shows the amount of payments and the means of financing the deficit or collecting the funds from a surplus in the balance of payments. When the balance of payments is in deficit, U.S. residents need foreign currency to pay their bills. The government may sell the foreign currency from its own holdings, the official reserves. The amount supplied represents a change in the official reserve transactions. Similarly, when there is a surplus in the balance of payments, the government may try to buy foreign currencies, again causing a change in the official reserve transactions. This is a narrow definition of the balance of payments.

Sometimes a broader class of transactions is defined to be payments. The **liquidity balance** shown in Table 32-2 separates transactions involving liquid from those involving nonliquid, private short-term debt instruments. For example, a sale of a Treasury bill by a private U.S. resident to a foreigner is then considered a means of payment.

The **official settlements balance** can be described by the following classifications: (1) current account, (2) private capital flows, and (3) transfers to and from official government holdings of liquid assets, where (1) + (2) is the balance of payments and (3) is the financing of the official settlement balance. Items 12 through 16 in Table 32-3 are estimates of the official settlement balance in 1950.

The official settlements balance excludes transactions in the private sector of short-term liquid debt instruments from the definition of the means of payment. Changes in SDRs and errors and omissions can be added into the balance of payments; in that case they are not considered financing transactions. Estimates of these for 1985 are shown in Table 32-3 as items 34 and 35. Special drawing rights (SDRs—international money discussed in the next chapter) and discrepancies (on the grounds that many payments are unrecorded)—can be included in the official means of payment.

BALANCE-OF-PAYMENTS RELATIONSHIPS

The components of the balance of payments may be classified into groups that show some important relationships between internal and external expenditure flows.[2] These relationships are useful in organizing some of the macro-economic variables in an economy that is assumed to engage in international transactions (an **open economy**) rather than the **closed economy** assumed for the model in Chapter 22.

In an open economy, the demand for a country's output is increased by the foreign demand for exports and decreased by the domestic demand for imports. The components of the demand for a country's domestic output are as follows:

$$
\begin{aligned}
\text{total domestic output} = \ &\text{domestic consumption} \\
&+ \text{domestic investment} \\
&+ \text{exports} \\
&- \text{imports}
\end{aligned} \tag{1}
$$

Note in equation (1) that some of the domestic consumption and the domestic investment and even some of the exports consist of goods imported from abroad. Therefore, if one wants to examine domestic output, one must subtract imports from domestic consumption and investment and from exports.

Rearranging the terms, equation (1) can also be written as follows:

$$
\begin{aligned}
\text{total domestic output} \ &- \text{domestic consumption} \\
&- \text{domestic investment} \\
&= \text{exports} - \text{imports}
\end{aligned} \tag{2}
$$

Saving was defined in Chapter 4 as output (which equals income) minus domestic consumption. Therefore, the equality between savings and investment for a closed economy must be amended by substituting saving in equation (2):

$$
\text{domestic saving} - \text{domestic investment} = \text{exports} - \text{imports} \tag{3}
$$

Equation (3) is an equilibrium statement for the domestic economy if it is written in terms of the *desired levels* of each variable, except exports, which depend on foreigners. If desired domestic saving exceeds desired domestic investment, a country need not have a deflation, as described in Chapter 23. Foreign demand for its products (exports) may exceed domestic demand for foreign products (imports), to bring about equilibrium in the expenditure sector (described in Chapters 4, 22, and 23).

Not all the increase in domestic wealth caused by domestic investment will be owned by the residents. Foreigners may demand some of the new securities, thereby causing **capital inflow**, a foreign purchase of new domestic securities. Likewise, some domestic savers may buy foreign securities, reducing the demand for new domestic securities and thereby causing a **capital outflow**, a domestic purchase of foreign securities. The net capital outflow is the difference between capital outflows and capital inflows. Domestic saving can exceed domestic investment by the net capital outflow.[3]

$$\text{domestic saving} - \text{domestic investment} = \text{net capital outflow} \qquad (4)$$

In other words, domestic saving can exceed domestic investment by the value of the purchase of foreign securities minus the purchase of new domestic securities. Equation (4) is the equilibrium condition in the capital market if domestic saving and investment are written in terms of desired levels.

Because the right-hand sides of equations (3) and (4) both equal the same quantity, they may be set equal to each other, to form a third relationship, the overall equilibrium condition for the balance of payments:

$$\text{exports} - \text{imports} = \text{net capital outflow} \qquad (5)$$

This is the identity for equilibrium in the balace-of-payments statement in Table 32-2.

Suppose that desired imports exceed exports and the net capital outflow is zero. The conditions in equation (5) are thus not met, and something must change. The country may lose reserves, paying for the imports until the reserves run so short that the country must borrow from abroad. At some point, if the deficit in the merchandise balance is chronic, the exchange rate of the currency must fall.

How is the rest of the world paid for this deficit in the balance of payments? The deficit country may use its international reserves (say U.S. dollars and gold) until they are exhausted. It may raise the price of imports to domestic residents by imposing **tariffs**—taxes on imports (though there is still the question of how the government spends the proceeds from the tariffs). The country may contract its money supply and/or run a fiscal surplus to induce a lower domestic income and a consequent lower domestic demand for foreign imports. Part, and sometimes most, of the adjustment may come through a devaluation of the country's currency. This can occur through market forces under floating exchange rates, described in the next chapter.

The United States was able to maintain a deficit in its balance of payments under fixed exchange rates (constant exchange value) in the 1960s because the central bankers of many countries agreed to hold U.S. dollar assets. But most countries are not so fortunate. They cannot buy more from the rest of the world than the rest of the world sells to them and have capital outflows for prolonged periods. They run short of reserves and credit, and so they must eventually have some underlying adjustment, such as a change in the international price of their currency. Similarly, a country with a chronic balance-of-payments surplus may not wish to sell to the rest of the world more than it receives for an indefinite period. Rather, it may wish to revalue its currency at a higher level, a process that many economists believe would be automatic under floating exchange rates (exchange rates that fluctuate in free markets).

INCOME CHANGES AND THE TRADE BALANCE

Economic models of international trade are frequently formulated so that (1) the trade balance (exports minus imports) depends primarily on changes in income and (2) capital flows depend primarily on differences in real interest rates between the domestic economy and foreign economies.

Consider first the balance of trade; assume there are no capital flows. Let B be the trade balance, X be exports, M be imports, and P be the price of imports, all in terms of domestic currency.[4] Then

$$B = X - PM \tag{6}$$

Suppose that huge imports (say, of oil) cause imports to exceed exports, so that B is negative. This trade balance is shown along QQ in Figure 32-5, drawn on the assumption that expenditures depend only on real income. The hypothetical size of different trade balances at each level of income before huge imports of foreign oil were demanded is given along QQ. Because the demand at a given *real* income is for a real amount of goods, line QQ is drawn on the basis of a given set of prices in equation (6). After huge imports of oil are demanded, the trade balance is shown along $Q'Q'$. The higher real income is, the greater will be the demand for goods and services, including imports. Both QQ and $Q'Q'$, therefore, slope upward. At a real income of OA, the trade balance is zero before huge oil imports are demanded. After they are demanded, the trade deficit is AF at that level of income.

The assumption underlying the shift in the curves in Figure 32-5 is that the increased demand for imported oil does not depend on real income. Instead, it depends on a reduction in oil production in the United States, causing a switch to imported oil. At each level of real income there is a greater demand for imports. A rise in the price of imports (changed in equation (6) to units of domestic currency) also means that the same quantity of imports demanded will cost more.[5]

FIGURE 32-5   The Trade Deficit and Surplus As a Function of Income*

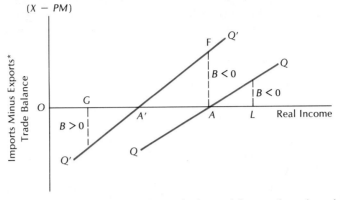

Curve QQ shows that the higher the domestic demand for goods and services is, the greater will be the demand for imports. If the demand increases, the curve will shift to $Q'Q'$. These curves correspond to the aggregate demand curves in Chapter 2 in the sense of excess demand for domestic goods and services that is reflected in the demand for foreign goods and services.

* B is exports minus imports for equation (6), in which both are measured in domestic prices.

One way to achieve equilibrium in the trade balance is to reduce real income. An engineered recession will reduce the demand for imports. In Figure 32-5 a real income level of OG will produce a positive balance in the trade account, and a level of real income of OA will reduce the trade balance to zero. This approach can be costly in terms of unemployment and substantially reduced real incomes.

Taxes on imports (tariffs) and subsidies on exports are direct ways to improve the trade balance if it is in deficit. But they can also be costly, as they change the allocation of goods available in the economy from what is desired for efficient production. In addition, these steps invite retaliatory measures from other countries, resulting in a reduction in world trade. Consequently, world income and, in many cases, the income of the domestic country will fall.

DEVALUATION

Devaluation, a decline in the foreign exchange value of the domestic currency, is another approach to achieving equilibrium in the trade balance if it is in deficit. It can be achieved by market forces or government actions.

Figure 32-6 depicts the demand and supply for imports. The demand curve $D_{yo}D_{yo}$ slopes downward on the usual assumption that a greater quantity is demanded at a lower price. An increase in income will shift the demand curve to the right. The supply curve SS is upward sloping on the assumption that more will be supplied at a higher price.[6]

FIGURE 32-6   The Demand and Supply of Imports

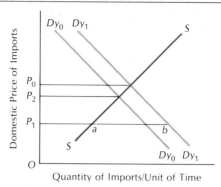

An increase in demand for imports raises their prices.

Suppose the trade deficit is the excess demand for imports, depicted as *ab* in Figure 32-6. Then the price of imports will be OP_1. Market forces will then cause the international exchange price of the domestic currency to fall, making imports more expensive. Remember that the import price is the foreign price times the exchange rate for foreign currency. That exchange rate will rise. The import price—measured in domestic currency—will rise to P_0.

The higher price of imports means that a one-dollar bill buys fewer goods and services. That is, its purchasing power or real value has declined. If real expenditures depend on the level of real money balances, M/P, in individuals' portfolios, real income will decline because of the rise in the price of imports. This decline in the value of M/P is called a *negative real balance effect*. It will cause the demand for imports to shift to $D_{y_0}D_{y_0}$ in Figure 32-6. The price of imports will then rise by less than before, to P_0. The real balance effect will, therefore, cause a more rapid adjustment and require a smaller price change.

DOES DEVALUATION MAKE THINGS WORSE?

Two views hold that the devaluation of a currency will not lead to equilibrium in the trade balance. Instead, devaluation either will have no effect on the trade balance or will make things worse. One of these views holds that goods traded have very imperfect substitutes, and the other holds that goods traded have perfect substitutes.

Suppose that there are a few substitutes for the imported goods and that there is also a trade balance deficit.[7] This causes an excess supply of the domestic currency, which falls in value on international markets. Imports then become more expensive for residents. Because there are no substitutes for the imports, the demand curve will be nearly vertical. This means that a rise in the price of imports is associated with a smaller percentage fall in the quantity of imports demanded. Because the price rises without substantially reducing the quantity demanded, domestic residents end up spending more, not less, on imports. The trade balance is then in greater deficit.

This worsening effect on the trade balance could be offset if foreigners began spending more for exports after the devaluation made the exports cheaper to them. Suppose, however, that the quantiy of exports demanded is not very responsive to changes in the price of these exports on the international markets. Rather than offsetting the preceding effects, therefore, this condition reinforces them.

The quantity of imports demanded and the quantity of exports demanded from the domestic country can, therefore, respond so slowly to price changes that the devaluation of the currency worsens the trade balance.

The devaluation may still work to improve the trade balance. If the devaluation sufficiently reduces either domestic *income*, a *flow* variable (by making imports more expensive), or the purchasing power of the domestic *money supply*, a *stock* variable (including its power to buy imported goods), or both, the demand for imports will be reduced. These two effects of devaluation are called the **income effect** and the **real balance effect**, respectively.

Fortunately, the preceding conditions that cause a devaluation to worsen the trade balance probably do not apply in general. They may apply to limited price ranges for the demand for imports by residents and for the demand for the country's exports by foreigners.

The second view holds that devaluation will have little or no effect on the trade balance, that it will result in an offsetting upward movement in internal prices. Devaluation will lead only to internal inflation. It is in one respect opposite to the first view, as it holds that traded goods have many nearly perfect substitutes. For example, Arthur Laffer pointed out that raw materials are the same everywhere.[8]

This view holds, under the **law of one price**, that identical goods tend not to differ in price from one place to another except in transportation costs. That is, if devaluation raises the price of imports relative to domestic goods, domestic goods will rise in price just enough to make their price relative to that of imports the same as before the devaluation. There is no incentive to switch away from imports, and the trade balance is not affected.

To see this, suppose that the exchange value of the U.S. dollar falls by 10 percent relative to British pounds. Imported silver thus rises in price in the United States. U.S. residents would immediately switch from the more expensive imported silver to the cheaper domestic silver, which is a perfect substitute. This would drive up the price of domestic silver, and the result of devaluation would thus be an offsetting internal rise in prices.

The problem in going from this observation to a statement about the effect of devaluation is that not all individual goods and services are everywhere identical, available, and internationally traded.[9] Many economists would refute this second view of exchange rate changes by pointing out that international trade can be explained in part in terms of these differences. Because of differences among goods, differences in their availability in different places, and differences in the goods that are traded, international trade does improve world real income. That is, there are real effects, not just price level changes, from shifts in trade, and these shifts in trade can result from changes in the international prices of currencies. A devaluation can cause an increase in the price of imports for which there are no perfect domestic substitutes. This price increase is similar to a tax on a group of products, a tax that is not returned to the public. The tax thus changes the internal allocation of goods and services and lowers real income. And this income acts to improve the trade balance.

CAPITAL FLOWS

Sometimes, as in the preceding discussion, it is easier to limit analysis to the trade balance. However, one should always keep in mind that it is only part of the story. That is, a large deficit in the trade balance can be more than offset by capital inflows.

It is more difficult to predict the direction of capital inflows.[10] Capital is attracted by higher real interest rates—the nominal yield minus the expected change in the value of currency used for interest and repayment. Real interest rate differentials can be closed very rapidly in international trade with modern communications, though whether or not they are is still being debated. The problem is that many other factors that are difficult to measure affect capital flows. These factors include various forms of risk premiums (for the stability of the government and the safety of funds) as well as preferences for places of investment.

Even more difficult to predict are portfolio changes in which investors in international companies rearrange their foreign stocks and bonds. If the capital markets are functioning well, small real interest rate changes caused by these portfolio shifts will be rapidly arbitraged out, causing small interest rate and exchange rate disturbances. In crises, however, interest rates and exchange rates fluctuate widely, and governments, for better or worse, step in to attempt to bring about more "orderly" movements.

Arnold C. Harberger eloquently described the major problems in understanding international capital flows, making the following two points:

> We (the economics profession) seem to be genuinely schizophrenic in the ways we build models—many of them are closed-economy models in which the rest of the world does not even appear, yet others of them are models of the "small, open economy" in which hardly any degree of freedom is left for economic policy to influence events. Lying behind the schizophrenia is, I believe, a genuine ignorance on our collective part of how the world capital market works.[11]

And referring to the evidence he assembled,

> The evidence presented above tends to bolster the "capital market" as against the "quasi-closed economy" interpretation, but I must confess that I am not particularly at ease with all the implications of a real well-functioning world capital market. In particular, my own intuition does not want to accept the notion that increments of investment activity are in all or nearly all countries effectively 100 percent "financed" by funds flowing in from abroad and that increments in saving simply spill out into the world capital markets.[12]

If capital flows are rapid enough to close real interest rate differentials, then the fixed interest case presented in Chapter 26 may apply. In that case, real interest rates are determined abroad. Review the case to see that such a condition makes fiscal policy impotent and increases the potency of monetary policy in the *IS–LM* model developed in Chapter 23.

That analysis shows that if government deficits affect real income primarily because of the effect they have on the real interest rate, there will be no effects on real income when the real interest rate is constant. The real interest rate can be constant if it is tied to the real interest rate in the international capital markets, which are very competitive with free capital flows. Money supply changes, by putting more real balances in the public's hands, can change spending. As described in Chapters 18 and 19, these changes affect real income at first. But this effect tends to be washed out over time, and the major effect then becomes a change in the price level.

THE VALUE OF THE U.S. DOLLAR IS TOO HIGH; THE VALUE OF THE U.S. DOLLAR IS TOO LOW

During the 1970s the exchange value of the U.S. dollar fell, as shown in Figure 32-2, and the U.S. government intervened in the foreign exchange market to halt the decline. When the Reagan administration took office in 1981, its initial policy was to end such intervention. Then as the growth of the money supply slowed and the rate of inflation fell in the United States after the 1982 recession, the exchange rate of the U.S. dollar rose. There were cries—from exporters, from unions representing workers in export industries, and from farmers who wanted to sell farm products abroad—that the rise in the price of the dollar was severely injuring employment and profits, both in export industries and from imports such as automobiles. This all was because the international price of U.S. exports rose and the domestic price of imports fell as the exchange value of the U.S. dollar rose. Congress clamored for protectionist measures (tariffs and quotas) against imports, as well as export subsidies. The labor unions also demanded relief:

America's trade problems have reached crisis proportions. . . .

While other nations are maintaining or increasing their barriers to imports, subsidizing their exports, and directing investment flows to benefit their own economies, the Reagan Administration clings to a belief in "free trade" and mythical forces.

In terms of the overvalued dollar, there must be a major effort to readjust currency values to more realistic levels and to bring some measure of stability to the exchange rate system.[13]

The administration, led primarily by Secretary of the Treasury James Baker, responded, proposing a plan to bring down the value of the dollar and lower the international price of U.S. exports. This would be done with the help of other central banks, which would join the United States in intervening in international markets. The central banks could intervene in the foreign exchange markets by selling U.S. dollars. Accordingly, on September 22, 1985, the G-5 countries (the United States, West Germany, Japan, France, and the United Kingdom) announced support for a reduction in the exchange value of the U.S. dollar. At a May 1986 meeting, the G-7 countries (the G-5 countries plus Canada and Italy) agreed on more formal "cooperation."

To buttress this policy, M-1 in the United States continued to grow rapidly in 1985 and 1986. The U.S. dollar began to fall in 1985, not primarily because of the intervention but because of more basic underlying factors, including the increase in the supply of U.S. dollars. The intervention—or even the announcement of the intention to intervene—may have hastened the dollar's decline or, at least, caused additional turbulence in the foreign exchange market. The exchange value of the dollar continued to fall, and in early 1987 newspapers carried stories about the "plunge in the value of the dollar."

What conclusions can be drawn from the U.S. government's policies with respect to the exchange value of the dollar since 1970? First, the government attempted to stop the dollar's exchange value from falling in the 1970s, but it continued to fall until 1980. Second, there was a period of nonintervention in the early 1980s when the dollar's exchange value rose rapidly. Third, there was an attempt to cause the dollar's exchange value to fall in 1985 and 1986, only to have it fall too far. Our conclusion from this record is the following: Intervention had no long-run effect in achieving the policy's desired goal, and it even may have introduced additional turbulence in the foreign exchange market.

Another important part of the policies is the emphasis placed on the trade account and the lack of attention paid to the benefits of a capital inflow of equal size. This raises the question, What are the effects on consumer welfare of foreign financing of domestic investment in the U.S. economy?

There also are inconsistencies in the protectionist policies and export subsidies. Higher tariffs and more important restrictions reduce the supply of U.S. dollars to foreigners that can be used to buy U.S. exports, and thus these protectionist policies hurt the export industries. Furthermore, export subsidies increase the demand for U.S. exports and for the U.S. dollars to buy them, thereby raising the dollar's exchange value and lowering import prices to U.S. residents. Thus export subsidies hurt the firms competing with imports.

All of these government policies were beneficial to particular groups, even if there were harmful effects to the economy in general. For example, protectionist policies that help a domestic industry benefit those connected with that industry. But there is no good way to compare these benefits with the harm that may have been done by restricting the supply of less expensive competing foreign imports. This is one reason that protectionist legislation is popular. The group that benefits is well aware of the issues and forms a powerful lobby. But the individuals that are hurt are from all parts of the society and are largely unaware of protectionism's deleterious effects.

One side effect of the policies in the 1980s came from the dramatic rise in the trade balance when the exchange value of the U.S. dollar was rising. The policies intended to lower its exchange value were partially rationalized by the view that a lower exchange value would cause the trade balance to fall. But the trade balance remained large in 1986 as the dollar's exchange value climbed. Some observers thus saw the failure of the lower exchange value of the U.S. dollar to improve the trade balance as new support for protectionist measures and export subsidies.

The Largest Debtor Nation

The trade balance is only part of the balance of payments. The capital accounts showed an equally large capital inflow, part of which was spent on U.S. government securities. The amount of these purchases was large enough by 1985 to make the United States the world's largest debtor nation, and the amount of U.S. government securities held by foreigners was expected to reach $150 billion by the end of 1986.

These capital inflows produced the following effects:

1. More savings could be invested in the United States.
2. Foreign purchases of U.S. government securities helped finance large U.S. government budget deficits.
3. The present value of future income streams that must be paid to foreigners on the public and private U.S. debt that they hold increased.
4. The effect on future U.S. consumption is uncertain. The future stream of interest payments that will be paid to foreigners will be a tax on future generations in the United States. The additional investment in the current period from the current capital inflow will increase the future supply of goods and services. If the markets were perfect (and a few other assumptions are made concerning individuals' preferences for providing future income streams), these effects should be roughly offsetting. No investor would borrow from abroad unless he or she assumed that the present value of the investment covered the present value of the debt liability. But no such choice is made for government debt. The present value of services from government expenditures financed by borrowing may not equal the

present value of the liability. It is therefore in the interest of elected representatives and government officials who control spending programs to reap the benefits from such expenditures while postponing the ungenerous policy of increased tax payments as long as the public separates the two activities. In addition, government expenditures may be used for investment projects or consumption that has a lower present value than do the same expenditures made by the private sector.

STUDY QUESTIONS

1. What is the balance of payments? Explain the differences among the balance of payments, the balance of trade, the current account, the capital account, and three different concepts of financing the balance of payments.
2. What is a devaluation?
3. What is the difference between the internal and the international value of a currency?
4. How are the values of different currencies determined in international trade? What are the effects on the international value of the U.S. dollar of a deficit and a surplus in the balance of payments? What is the effect of a deficit in the balance of trade?
5. How are real income and real money balances related to the trade balance?
6. Under what conditions will a devaluation fail to improve the trade balance?
7. Assume that from an equilibrium position, U.S. tourism in Italy increases. What effect will this have on the international value of U.S. currency and the U.S. balance of payments?
8. How is the savings = investment identity changed for an open economy?
9. If foreign investments in the U.S. economy increased, causing a net capital inflow, what would happen to U.S. exports and imports? Explain.
10. If there is a large trade deficit as a result of oil imports, does a low level of domestic saving necessarily indicate a change of saving habits? Could it be said that the oil exporters are doing the saving if they buy Treasury bills with the dollars they earn?

GLOSSARY

Capital account balance. The balance of those accounts in the balance-of-payments statement that record capital flows.

Capital inflow. A foreign purchase of domestic securities.

Capital outflow. A domestic purchase of foreign securities.

Closed economy. An economy that is viewed without considering international trade or capital flows.

Current account balance. The

balance in that part of the balance-of-payments statement that includes goods and services and private transfer payment records.

Devaluation. A decline in the foreign exchange value of the domestic currency.

Goods and services balance. A balance that adds to the trade balance such goods and services as military expenditures and tourist spending.

Income effect. The effect of changes in real income, a flow variable, on the demand for real imports.

Law of one price. The law that holds that identical goods tend not to differ in price from one place to another except in transportation costs.

Liquidity balance. The balance in the balance-of-payments statement when private and official liquid short-term debt instruments and official reserve transactions are considered the means of payment.

Net capital outflow (or its opposite, **net capital inflow).** The net flow of investment and loan funds into a country from abroad (an inflow) minus the flow of these funds out of the country (an outflow).

Official reserve transactions. A transaction by the government, including the central bank, that adds to or depletes its own holdings of foreign currencies, international money, or gold.

Official settlements balance. The balance in the balance-of-payments statement in which official short-term liquid debt instruments and official reserve transactions are considered the means of payment.

Open economy. An economy that is viewed together with its international trade and investment and other international economic relationships.

Real balance effect. The effect on real wealth and spending of a change in real money balances, a stock variable, in individual portfolios. In an open economy, the price level includes the price of imports so that a change in the exchange rate causes a real balance effect.

Tariffs. Taxes on imports. They have different effects on income than does a rise in the price of imports because the tariffs are an internal transfer—to the government that disposes of these taxes to the domestic economy. The effects on the beneficiaries of the tariffs must also be considered.

Trade balance (or **merchandise balance).** Exports minus imports.

Transfer payments. Payments not associated with the current production of goods and services. Interest payments and gifts are examples of transfers of wealth, as distinguished from the payment for new goods and services included in national income estimates.

NOTES

1. The objective of a favorable balance of payments is a component of the *mercantilist* view of the objectives of international trade. Adam Smith attacked the logic of mercantilism but did not always relate wealth to the

value of per-capita real income. See Edwin Cannan's editorial note in *An Inquiry into the Nature and Causes of the Wealth of Nations* (New York: Modern Library, 1937), p. ix, footnote 15.

2. For an excellent analysis of these relationships and a model of international adjustment, see Lloyd A. Metzler, "The Process of International Adjustment Under Conditions of Full Employment: A Keynesian View," in his *Collected Papers* (Cambridge, Mass.: Harvard University Press, 1973), pp. 209–233. This section is based on that article.

3. This relationship is defined for the demand for new domestic securities and the demand for foreign securities to conform to saving and investment, which are *flows* in the current period. Changes in the ownership of existing financial wealth—portfolio changes—are not considered.

4. Domestic prices of imports are foreign prices times the currencies' exchange rate.

5. The expenditures on oil and even on all imports may be greater at each level of real income if the price of oil rises. The elasticity of demand for imported oil and imports in general is then said to be inelastic. This means that the percentage change in quantity demanded is less than the percentage change in price at each level of real income. Conversely, the demand for oil and for imports may be elastic. The schedule QQ in Figure 32-5 would then shift (to the left if the demand is inelastic and the right if it is elastic) from a change in the price of oil alone. This change is in addition to a movement along the curve from a decline in real income caused by a rise in the price of imported oil.

6. The position of the supply curve is uncertain. As the quantity of exports demanded from the exporting country rises, the price level in the exporting country may be driven up, causing the supply curve SS in Figure 32-6 to shift to the left.

7. This argument can be put in mathematical form. With the price of exports fixed at unity, the change in the trade balance B with a change in the price of imports becomes, through differentiation of equation (6), M $(X/PM\ N_x + N_m - 1)$, where N_x and M_m are *elasticities of demand for imports* (by residents) and *demand for the country's exports* (by foreigners), respectively. The elasticity to import is the percentage change in imports divided by the percentage change in price. The elasticity to export is the percentage change in exports divided by the percentage change in price. If the preceding expression for the change in the trade balance is positive, devaluation will improve the balance of trade. That is, the value of B will approach equilibrium—which is zero—on the assumption that there are no net capital flows. The condition that $N_x + N_m$ must exceed unity for the preceding expression to be positive and for the devaluation to improve the equilibrium balance of trade is known as the *Marshall–Lerner condition*.

8. Arthur B. Laffer, "The Phenomenon of Worldwide Inflation," in David I. Meiselman and Arthur B. Laffer, eds., *The Phenomenon of Worldwide*

Inflation (Washington, D.C.: American Enterprise Institute, 1975), pp. 27–57.

9. See Thomas D. Willet, *Floating Exchange Rates and International Reform* (Washington, D.C.: American Enterprise Institute, 1977), p. 50.

10. Arnold Harberger, "Vignettes of the World Capital Market," *American Economic Review*, Papers and Proceedings of the Ninety-Second Annual Meeting, December 28–30, 1979, in Atlanta, Georgia, pp. 331–339.

11. Ibid., p. 331.

12. Ibid., p. 336.

13. American Federation of Labor and Congress of Industrial Organizations, *The National Economy and Trade, AFL–CIO Policy Recommendations for 1986* (Washington, D.C.: American Federation of Labor, 1986), pp. 23, 31.

CHAPTER 33

METHODS OF INTERNATIONAL PAYMENTS

CHAPTER PREVIEW

Introduction.   The mechanisms for international payments, the arrangements for determining exchange rate values, and the costs and benefits from the use of single currency, versus different currencies in different areas, are discussed in this chapter.

Methods of Payments.   Methods range from freely floating exchange rates to fixed exchange rates.

The Gold Standard.   Control the price of gold, a system still being advocated.

Commodity Standards.   Stabilize the price of a commodity or a bundle of commodities to achieve price stability.

International Currency and the International Monetary Fund.   Up to 1973, it supervised a system of fairly constant exchange rates.

Flexible Exchange Rates.   Market-determined exchange rates perform part of the functions of internal price-level adjustments.

Optimum Currency Areas.   What is the optimum size area for a single currency?

Key Currency and the Gold Exchange Standard.   This is the current system using gold and U.S. dollars in international trade.

INTRODUCTION

This chapter discusses the institutional characteristics of international arrangements for payments and the relative value of different currencies. A good question to start with is, What are the mechanisms for making payments between parties to a transaction who each use money issued by different countries? The second question is, What arrangements are made for determining the relative value of these two kinds of money? Finally, it is useful to ask, What costs and benefits would follow from the use of a single form of money, not just to the participants in international transactions, but also to the economies of two areas?

METHODS OF PAYMENT

If a U.S. citizen buys a hat in London, the proprietor of the London hat store may insist on payment in the form of British money (£, pounds). The U.S. citizen only has U.S. money ($, U.S. dollars). How can the transaction be completed? There are numerous arrangements made for obtaining the foreign currency needed in international trade, which are summarized here and described further in the following sections (refer to Table 33-1 for current exchange rate policies).

1. Fixed rates of exchange between domestic currencies.
   a. There may be a **fixed** or **pegged exchange rate** between each country's money, arranged by the central banks of each country. That is, the central banks must maintain a supply of the foreign money to buy their own currency if it falls in price. The fixed rates may be changed according to some prearranged system.
   b. A special variant of the fixed exchange rate arrangements is the **gold standard**, whereby each government agrees to exchange a fixed nominal quantity of its money for gold.
   c. Commodities other than gold—such as silver—have been used as a means of international payment. Any group of commodities could theoretically be used, such as bricks or a large collection of different commodities.
   d. **Currency unions** are formed in which a group of countries pegs the exchange rate between their currencies but is flexible with other currencies.
2. Flexible or floating rates of exchange between domestic currencies.
   a. **Flexible** or **floating exchange rates** are determined by market conditions. This is sometimes called a **clean float**. Currencies are traded by foreign exchange dealers for themselves and for customers.
   b. **Limited flexible exchange rates**, whereby the central banks step in and buy or sell currencies to prevent them from falling or rising in value beyond predetermined limits, have also been used. Such rates are identi-

cal to a pegged exchange rate with a narrow tolerance range. When the exchange rate goes outside the tolerance range, the central bank intervenes to restore the exchange rate to a position inside the tolerance range. However, if the tolerance range is fairly wide, this policy can be close to a system of flexible exchange rates, provided that there is little expectation that the limits of the tolerance range will be exceeded.

c. Intermittent intervention by a central bank that attempts to control the value of its currency is sometimes called a **dirty float** or a **managed float**. This method of influencing exchange rates is not always easy to detect, for the central bank may have parties in the private sector to intervene for it.

Countries may directly buy or trade their currencies in international exchanges to obtain the means of payment. They may also trade key currencies or international money.

1. **International money** produced by an international organization has been used in international trade.
2. Under a **key currency** arrangement, all participating countries agree to settle their foreign transactions with the currency of a particular country, the **key currency nation**. U.S. dollars have been a key currency in the free world.
3. Gold has been used, along with U.S. dollars, since World War II in an international payment system called a **gold–dollar** or **dollar–gold exchange standard**.

These arrangements for making payments in international trade involve both the exchange of reserves (commodities used in international payments) and a change in the relative prices of the currencies utilized. The relative price or value of a unit of domestic currency may be stated with respect to a

1. Market basket of domestic goods and services.
2. Unit of foreign currency.
3. Fixed amount of a particular commodity (or group of commodities) such as gold.

Relative prices 1, 2, and 3 are sometimes confused. For instance, the dollar price of gold can rise at the same time that the internal domestic U.S. price level falls and the dollar price of another foreign currency, say British pounds, also falls. There cannot be a worldwide inflation of all relative prices of type 2, the relative prices between currencies. If the relative price of U.S. dollars to British pounds (U.S.\$/£) rises, the relative price of British pounds to U.S. dollars (£/U.S.\$) will fall by the same proportion.

It also follows that if there are N countries with N currencies and $N - 1$ exchange rates are given, all N rates will be determined. For example, if there are only two countries, with two currencies, dollars and pounds, and the dollar price of pounds is given, then the pound price of dollars will also be determined.

TABLE 33-1 Exchange Rate Policies

The 140 members of the IMF are grouped in the table according to the exchange rate policies they followed as of December 31, 1979. On that date, 94 members reported that their exchange rates were pegged, and 45 reported that their exchange rates were governed by other policies (floating).*

The pegged group includes all currencies whose exchange rates were maintained within a well-defined range relative to a single foreign currency or a basket of foreign currencies. Sixty of the pegged currencies were tied to a single currency. Forty-two nations pegged to the U.S. dollar, 14 to the French franc, and 1 to the pound sterling. The currencies of Lesotho and Swaziland were pegged to the South African rand, and the currency of Equatorial Guinea was pegged to the Spanish peseta. Fourteen of the members that pegged maintained the value of their currencies in terms of a basket defined by the SDR, and 20 adopted other basket definitions.

Thirty-four of the 45 members that did not peg intervened at their own discretion to limit fluctuations in their otherwise floating exchange rates. Three members used economic indicators to determine the target levels of their exchange rates. And 8 participated in a cooperative exchange arrangement (the European monetary system).

		Pegs			
	Single Currency	Currency Pegged to		Basket	
U.S. Dollar	£ Sterling	French Franc	Other	SDR	Other Composite
Bahamas	Gambia	Benin	Equatorial	Burma	Algeria
Barbados		Cameroon	Guinea	Guinea	Austria
Botswana		Central African	Lesotho	Guinea-Bissau	Bangladesh
Burundi		Republic	Swaziland	Jordan	Cape Verde
Chile		Chad		Kenya	Cyprus
Costa Rica		Comoros		Malawi	Fiji
Djibouti		Congo		Mauritius	Finland
Dominica		Gabon		Sao Tome	Kuwait
Dominican		Ivory Coast		& Principe	Malaysia
Republic		Madagascar		Seychelles	Malta
Ecuador		Mali		Sierra Leone	Mauritania
Egypt		Niger		Uganda	Morocco
El Salvador		Senegal		Viet Nam	Norway
Nepal					
Nicaragua					
Oman					
Pakistan					
Panama					
Paraguay					
Republic of					
South Korea					
Romania					
Rwanda					
St. Lucia					
St. Vincent					
Somalia					

Pegged currencies (continued):

Ethiopia	Sudan	Togo		Papua New Guinea	Zaire
Grenada	Surinam	Upper Volta		Singapore	Zambia
Guatemala	Syrian Arab			Solomon Is.	
Guyana	Republic			Sweden	
Haiti	Trinidad			Tanzania	
Honduras	& Tobago			Thailand	
Iraq	Venezuela			Tunisia	
Jamaica	Yemen Arab				
Lao People's	Republic				
Dem. Rep.	Yemen People's				
Liberia	Dem. Rep.				
Libya					

Indicators	Cooperative Exchange Arrangements	Floats Float Governed by	Other
Brazil	Belgium	Afghanistan	Israel
Colombia	Denmark	Argentina	Japan
Portugal	Federal Republic	Australia	Lebanon
	of Germany	Bahrain	Maldives
	France	Bolivia	Mexico
	Ireland	Canada	New Zealand
	Italy	Ghana	Nigeria
	Luxembourg	Greece	Peru
	Netherlands	Iceland	Philippines
		India	Qatar
		Indonesia	Saudi Arabia
		Iran	South Africa
			Spain
			Sri Lanka
			Taiwan
			Turkey
			United Arab Emirates
			United Kingdom
			United States
			Uruguay
			Western Samoa
			Yugoslavia

* As reported by the IMF Treasurer's and Exchange and Trade Relations departments. Information concerning the exchange arrangements of Democratic Kampuchea (Cambodia) is not available.
Source: Nicholas Carlozzi, "Pegs and Floats–The Changing Face of the Foreign Exchange Market," *Business Review*, Federal Reserve Bank of Philadelphia, May–June 1980, pp. 22–23.

Forward and Spot Markets

Besides a current or spot relative price for currencies (or monies) and spot markets, there are future markets, where future (or forward) prices are determined by buying and selling futures contracts, as described in Chapter 12. Also, a large volume of forward contracts is made directly between the participants in the foreign exchange markets. **Spot transactions** require the exchange of deposits by two days after the date of the contract. **Forward transactions** require an exchange of deposits at longer maturities specified on the forward contract. There are standardized maturities of three months, six months, and one year, and on major currencies, longer contracts are sometimes available. Banks, acting as financial intermediaries, make available forward contracts tailored exactly to their customers' needs, such as 46-day maturity.

If the spot price is below the forward price, the currency is said to be at a **forward premium**. If the spot price is above the forward price, the currency is said to be at a **forward discount**.

Both spot and forward markets for currencies are subject to control and intervention by governments. The governments may step in to support their domestic currency by buying it, or they may impose exchange controls on the repatriation of profits or interest payments. The risk of loss in forward contracts because of these latter controls can be called **sovereign risk**. Thus spot and forward markets can suffer from imperfections.

The evidence, however, generally tends to support the hypothesis that these markets are approximately efficient, especially the offshore foreign exchange markets (such as is found on Caribbean Island nations) that are free of government controls.[1]

Types of Government Intervention Policies

The government may directly affect the balance of payments not only by directly intervening in the markets for foreign exchange but also by directly intervening in the markets for foreign trade of commodities, services, and financial assets. Direct forms of intervention include import taxes (tariffs) or subsidies, export taxes or subsidies, taxes on foreign investment by domestic residents or on domestic investment by foreigners, and taxes on transfer payments such as repatriated (funds brought back into the country) dividends or interest earned abroad. Indirect effects of monetary and fiscal policy affect the balance of payments by changing domestic income levels, interest rates, and price levels.

THE GOLD STANDARD

A country may adopt a gold standard for its money by means of either of the following equivalent policies:

1. The central government agrees to buy and sell an unlimited amount of gold at a fixed price, such as $800 per ounce of gold.

2. The central government intervenes in the world market for gold by buying and selling gold in exchange for its domestic currency, so as to maintain a fixed price, such as $800 per ounce of gold.

The official government price of $35 per ounce of gold was in effect in the United States from 1934 until 1971. Before that, the official government price of $20.67 per ounce was in effect from 1879 until 1933 (with the exception of World War I). Both prices seem like fossils considering that the price of gold reached a high of $835 per ounce in January 1980 (see Figure 33-1).

If two or more countries adopt a system in which a fixed nominal quantity of their domestic currency is pegged to a given weight of gold, the relative

FIGURE 33-1   Wholesale Prices, Two Gold Standard Periods and the Bretton Woods Period, 1800–1979

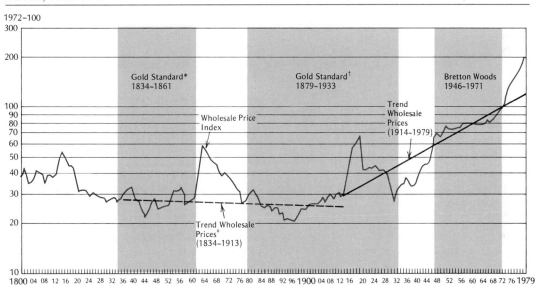

This figure shows the periods when the United States was on a gold standard and the period when the members of the International Monetary Fund (over 100 countries in the free world) agreed to a system of fairly fixed exchange rates under an agreement called the *Bretton Woods agreement*. On judging the record of the gold standard, Michael Bordo made the following conclusion from the record of the gold standard in Great Britain and the United States:

"The gold standard provided us with greater *long-run* price stability, but at the expense of both *short-run* real output and price stability. The higher rates of inflation and lower variability of real output (and lower unemployment) in the two countries in the recent period likely reflect changing policy preferences away from long-run price stability and toward full employment. Indeed, the strong commitment to full employment in both countries likely explains the worsening of inflation in the post-war period."

* Excludes 1838–1843, when specie payments were suspended.
† United States imposed gold export embargo from September 1917 to June 1919.
‡ Broken line indicates years excluded in computing trend.
Source: Michael David Bordo, "The Classical Gold Standard: Some Lessons for Today," *Review*, Federal Reserve Bank of St. Louis, May 1981, p. 9. The quotation is from p. 15.

prices between all their currencies will also be fixed. The countries are then said to be on the gold standard. Suppose that the United States and Great Britain are on a gold standard. One U.S. dollar is pegged at 1 ounce of gold, and 1 British pound is pegged at 2 ounces of gold. Then 2 ounces of gold can be traded for £1 or $2. It follows that £1 is fixed at $2 in international exchange at current spot prices, ignoring transactions costs. The relative pound price of dollars is $2/£1, and the dollar price of pounds is £1/$2.

Suppose that a U.S. citizen buys a hat in London for £5. Most U.S. banks will sell him or her £5 for $10, ignoring the transactions costs. Alternatively, the U.S. citizen in the hypothetical example could buy 10 ounces of gold from the U.S. Treasury and ship the gold to Great Britain, where the British central bank would exchange it for £5. The £5 could then be paid to the London hat store.

THE DIFFERENCE BETWEEN FORWARD AND FUTURES CONTRACTS AND THE USE OF FORWARD CONTRACTS TO EARN PROFITS ON EXPECTED GOVERNMENT INTERVENTION

The futures contracts described in Chapter 12 stipulate a striking price at which the underlying asset, say a stock, can be bought and sold, depending on whether it is a buy or sell contract, respectively. The current price of the futures contract rises or falls depending on expectations of how that striking price is related to the expected future spot price. This relationship is illuminated in the example in that chapter.

A forward contract calls for the future delivery of an asset, such as a given amount of currency, in which the future price is negotiated by the market participants so that the current price of the forward contract is zero (plus transactions costs). Complicated though that explanation sounds, a few words will show its simplicity. Suppose that you want to buy British pounds for delivery in 90 days. The immediate price of the forward contract is zero (plus transactions costs, a small brokerage fee).

However, the negotiation sets the price you will have to pay in 90 days based on what you and the seller expect the future spot price to be.

If, for example, the government is known to have a tolerance range for exchange rates and it is expected that in 90 days the exchange rate will exceed the upper limit of that tolerance range, speculators will step in. They will try to negotiate forward contracts for the currency that allow them to sell it at the currently expected future spot price above the tolerance range. They expect the government to step in and push the rate back into the tolerance range. Then the speculator can buy it at the lower price and sell it at the contracted forward price and make a profit.

One possibility is that the attempt to cover these forward contracts in 90 days will cause a temporary excess demand for the currency, driving its exchange value even higher. The government will have to have even greater sales of the currency to try to drive its price down. Speculators will again "buy forward," anticipating the government's actions. The tolerance range limits can, therefore, make the exchange rate less stable than it otherwise would be under flexible exchange rates.

Scenarios can be developed that show that market conditions can lead to destabilizing prices when market participants believe that rising prices indicate higher future prices, thereby creating excess demands to buy a commodity that, in turn, makes prices rise more rapidly. Such bubbles tend to break as speculators step in with expectations of what they consider to be a more normal price that will eventually prevail.

The costs of transporting the gold back and forth across the Atlantic Ocean cause an increase in the price of the hat or, equivalently, a decrease in the value of dollars traded for pounds. These costs are reduced by keeping much of the free world's supply of gold deep underground in New York City, in the gold vault under the Federal Reserve Bank, where it can be inexpensively moved from one country's compartment to another (see Chapter 15).

Suppose that under a gold standard, the United States has a negative balance of payments with Great Britain. U.S. dollars are given to the inhabitants of Great Britain, who turn them in to the U.S. Treasury in exchange for gold. Gold flows out of the United States to Great Britain, where it is turned in to the British central bank for pounds. The monetary base in the United States declines, whereas the monetary base in Great Britain rises. Through fractional reserve banking, the money supplies in the two countries change by multiples of the changes in their respective monetary bases. In the United States, prices and real incomes fall, while in Great Britain, prices and real incomes rise. (There is a time lag that may be a number of years for all of those effects). The demand for British goods by U.S. residents, who have declining real incomes and must pay higher prices for British goods, declines. The reverse occurs in Great Britain, so that the foreign demand for U.S. goods rises. The deficit in the U.S. balance of payments is eventually automatically corrected. This example illustrates the kind of adjustment that can occur under a gold standard to bring about automatically a balance in the balance of payments, without the "feeble hands and vacillating minds of men" who may take improper action.

Unfortunately, the adjustment period may be too long to be tolerated. No country is likely to completely give up control of its domestic money supply for very long if a severe depression or inflation occurs. The government is likely to change the proportion of the monetary base that is *fiduciary issue* (fiat money—see Chapter 2) or to completely abandon the gold standard. Perverse adjustments can also occur under a gold standard, in which the world supply of gold for monetary uses changes or in which the proportion of the money supply created by private banks or other financial intermediaries—through fractional reserve banking—is altered.

In the 1870s, many countries adopted a gold standard. The gold standard era lasted until the great depressions of the 1930s, with time out for World War I. Both Great Britain in 1931 and the United States in 1933 went off the gold standard. During the heyday of the gold standard, there was a decline in many domestic price levels. Depressions and bank panics occurred during the 1890s in the United States. Output was increasing faster than gold was produced and the monetary base was tied to gold. Then with the intervention of the cyanide process (a less expensive method of extracting gold from gold ore) and with new discoveries of gold in the Yukon and South Africa, gold flowed into the treasuries of countries such as the United States. Internal inflation followed. The value of money fell in terms of the goods and services it could buy, as more and more gold was buried in the vaults of central banks. In an age when humankind has placed a man on the moon, we persist in digging deep into the earth to find gold, which we bury again 76 feet under the Federal Reserve in New York City or underground at Fort Knox, from one hole to another. Why not bury bricks, as is suggested subsequently?

When there is a loss of confidence in fiat money, investments in commodities such as gold look attractive. Gold is a shiny, durable commodity that is limited in supply, as long as the big gold mining countries—South Africa and Russia—do not dig too much up and the United States does not precipitously spend its hoard.

World gold output in 1980 was estimated to be 42.5 million ounces by the Gold Institute, a trade association representing more than 200 companies that mine or refine gold.[2] South Africa, the largest producer, was estimated to have produced 48 percent of the world's gold output and the Soviet Union, the second largest producer, produced roughly 23 percent. The U.S. government had approximately 265 million ounces of gold in 1980, which, valued at $350 per ounce, would be worth $92,750 million. It was an appealing way to store wealth, especially as world tensions flared after November 1979 when U.S. hostages were taken in Iran. There was a rapid rise in the price of gold.

The proponents of the gold standard argue that however wasteful it may be to bury valuable resources in holes in the ground, people perceive utility from such activity, especially when the resources are shiny objects like gold. Therefore, they would say, "Set an appropriate price for gold so that there will be enough for purposes of world trade and let people do what they will do anyway!" The proponents of the gold standard also hold that the automatic adjustments of the gold standard are preferable to some of the manipulations of the money supply of governments that have poor monetary policies. In many countries where the currency has poor medium-of-exchange characteristics in the domestic country and/or is pegged at official rates at which it cannot be exchanged in international trade, the public may have confidence only in a commodity money such as what exists under a gold standard.

There is even an **automatic countercyclical mechanism** under a gold standard. Assume that prices and real income fall as the economy is thrown into a depression. One nominal price is fixed, the price of an ounce of gold. Assume that this price is $800 per ounce of gold. Suppose that there are domestic gold mines and that the cost of gold mining declines during the depression, so that there is an incentive to increase gold production. The gold is sold to the Treasury for $800 per ounce. The equilibrium (marginal) cost of producing $800 of currency is equal to $800. When the (marginal) cost of producing gold falls below $800 an ounce, gold output will be expanded until equilibrium is restored. Also, some gold that was stored for other uses (such as gold jewelry and gold dental inlays) is now worth less for industrial purposes and will be diverted to the monetary authority. That is, the (marginal) return on the nonmonetary uses of gold will be smaller relative to the (marginal) return from selling it to the Treasury. All this will cause the money supply to increase, which will induce increases in real income and prices.

DEFLATION AND INFLATION UNDER THE GOLD STANDARD

The money supply, defined as currency, coin, and bank deposits held by the public, fell slightly from 1865 to 1879, whereas there was a rapid rise in output. The price level declined by one half. After 1879, when the United States went onto the gold standard, the money supply grew at a slower rate than output and the price level tended to fall. This was a period of repeated bank panics, with bank runs (in 1873, 1884, 1890, and 1893) combined with agitation to expand the precious metal base to include silver.

The invention of the cyanide process for inexpensively extracting gold from low-quality ore and the discovery of gold in Alaska, Africa, and Colorado in the 1890s created a large increase in the gold base for the money supply. In the period up to World War I (1897–1914), wholesale prices rose by 50 percent, chiefly as the result of the large amounts of gold sold to the U.S. Treasury. (This average rate of rise of 2.4 percent per year looked very mild from the vantage point of 1982, but its persistence for 17 years was unprecedented for inflation until the post–World War II period.) Remember that the Treasury was obliged, under the gold standard, to buy all gold offered to it at $20.67 an ounce, thus increasing the money supply.

Banking panics had occurred in the previous period of general falling prices; a new banking panic occurred in 1907, during a period of rising prices.

A similar explanation can show how an inflation would be automatically stopped. The effectiveness of the response depends on the responsiveness of the supply of gold (i.e., how much gold is diverted from—or returned to—other uses and how rapidly gold production is changed with a change in the price of mining an ounce of gold, compared with the monetary value of gold). The more responsive the supply of gold is to changes in the price level, the more effective will be the automatic mechanism for restoring equilibrium. Unfortunately, the supply of gold appeared to be rather unresponsive in some of the periods (especially around 1890) when falling prices failed to induce a rapidly increasing supply of gold for monetary purposes.

The most important argument in favor of such an automatic countercyclical mechanism is that it prevents government authorities from having a worse monetary policy. However, if a government is confronted with a five-year adjustment period and the possibilities of other conditions changing the outcome, the government may choose to go off the gold standard. Many factors can significantly alter the period of adjustment, such as new discoveries of gold and less expensive methods for mining gold. These are the kinds of things that a member of Congress would have trouble explaining to the folks back home, and for good reasons. "Don't worry, unemployed workers; you will get a job within five years, when gold mining picks up—barring unforeseen problems in the adjustment process." The historical record of the gold standard in the United States indicates that it was abandoned whenever major events, such as wars or depressions, occurred.

If one country suffers a depression, other countries may also be thrown into a depression as the demand for their exports declines. Each country may prefer an independent monetary policy, so as to maintain internal price stability and to insulate itself partially from conditions in foreign countries, rather than being tied to an international gold standard.

Gold standard countries sometimes **sterilize the effect of gold inflows or outflows** by arbitrarily adjusting the internal money supply in an offsetting direction. This practice bypasses the automatic adjustment process of the gold standard, and from the perspective of a pure gold standard, it violates the "rules."

The Gold Commission

Jesse Helms, a Republican senator from North Carolina, would not agree to an IMF (International Monetary Fund) quota enlargement in 1980. To obtain his approval for the consideration of this action, he was allowed to introduce an amendment that established the U.S. Gold Commission (Public Law 96-389). It was to contain three members of the Board of Governors, six members of the Congress, and four distinguished private citizens.

Although the bill authorizing it was passed during the Carter administration, Carter agreed to wait until after the election before making any appointments. Because Carter lost the election, the new president, Ronald Reagan, made the appointments. Anna J. Schwartz, a well-known monetarist and coauthor of many distinguished books with Milton Friedman, was appointed executive director of the commission. As Schwartz reported, only three of the members that were appointed were proponents of the gold standard, and they did not share the same view on how the gold standard should be organized.[3]

Senator Helms said in setting up the Gold Commission,

> I would expect that the commission would report to the Congress that there is little unanimity among the experts. I would expect, however, that the Keynesian view, the monetarist view, and the neoclassical view will be examined fully; the implications of each will be analyzed and recommendations will be made on the basis of the best judgment of the commission members.[4]

Senator Helms referred to Arther Laffer as one of the leaders of the neoclassical view, and as it happened, Laffer had published a plan on February 20, 1980, to return to the gold standard. (It was an economic study by his consulting firm, A. B. Laffer Associates, "Reinstatement of the Dollar: The Blueprint.")

Laffer was a witness before the commission and presented his plan for a gold standard. It allowed an emergency exit from the gold standard rules if the monetary base changed too rapidly. Congressman Ron Paul, a Gold Commission member who strongly advocated a pure gold standard that would "repeal the privilege of banks to create money," called this part of Laffer's plan "the weakest part." Paul explained,

> It introduces the fact that you plan not to have a stable currency and credit supply. That means you expect and anticipate that we will continue with our Federal Reserve System, with the Congress able to abuse the monetary system, and, therefore, you have to have a hedge and this hedge is the gold holiday system. This may be worse than what we had before.[5]

Congressman Paul's point was well made. One of the worst parts of the gold standard is that it falls apart when there is a large crisis and, some would say, "when it is needed most." The advent of war or a depression causes countries to leave the gold standard. The adjustment period is then probably much worse than if there had been no gold standard in the first place. But Congressman Paul would not like this interpretation of his point; he would insist that the only correct system is to preserve continually the gold standard in its purest form.

Laffer defended his plan with a safety exit:

> It is trying to protect from that situation that occurs infrequently but every 10, 15 years when you have a brand new discovery of gold, if the quantity of gold triples, I would hate to say that the price level rises. . . . When there is a disturbance in the gold market, I don't want to see the whole economy suffer inflation or deflation because of some change in that market.[6]

Laffer thus developed his gold standard plan to take account of the important problem of disturbances in the supply of gold. For example, if the U.S.

money supply becomes erratic, such as during the announced monetary control experiment by the Federal Reserve from 1979 to 1983, many people will look to automatic systems such as Laffer proposed. Yet Laffer's argument about the need to guard against large disturbances, which he defined as greater than very wide boundaries on the permitted change in the monetary base, leaves open the similar problems of smaller disturbances. Should a drop in the monetary base that does not quite reach his limits but does cause a massive recession be ignored?

Once it is admitted that it will not be ignored, then the system becomes an uncertain mixture of price control of gold in some time periods and a monetary aggregate rule in others. Still, such a system *may* produce better results than the current system does if the current system produces extremely unstable monetary growth.

However, the current system or even a monetary rule maintains domestic control over monetary policy. Would the following kind of disturbances be politically tolerable under Laffer's plan?

If the Soviet Union, for example, placed significant portions of its gold on the market in any period, threatening some instability in the domestic price level in the United States from any of this gold that the Treasury must buy under the gold standard rules, no sterilization policies would be undertaken. That is, no offsetting policies could be taken under the Laffer plan if the arbitrary limits on changes in the monetary base he suggested were not reached.

In 1982, the commission voted against suggesting that every country adopt a gold standard. Instead, a weakly worded suggestion (the strongly worded suggestion resulted in a tie vote) for a monetary rule limiting the rate of money growth was proposed. It was also proposed that a gold coin, which would not be legal tender, be minted and sold to the public.

COMMODITY STANDARDS

Gold is only one of the commodities that have been used or suggested for **commodity standards**, sometimes called **commodity reserve standards** (because warehouse receipts rather than the actual commodities would be traded).[7] Gold and silver have been used together in monetary standards, each bought and sold by the government at a different fixed nominal price. This is called a **bimetallic standard**. Under **symmetalism**, on the other hand, the government agrees to buy and sell a combined unit of gold and silver, in a specified proportion and at a fixed nominal price.

Charles Hardy is credited with suggesting that bricks be used in a commodity standard:

> Bricks possess the minor virtues required of a commodity to be used as a currency—they can be reasonably well defined and checked for quality, they can be stored, etc. And they have the major virtue of an exceedingly elastic supply.[8]

As foolish as the brick standard may seem to those who cannot conceive of the bricks as money or of tearing down brick houses and selling the bricks to the Treasury to halt a deflation, the example is useful. It illuminates the operation of a commodity standard, such as a gold standard, with a substance that is superior in many ways to gold for monetary uses. At the same time, it illustrates the bizarre aspects of a commodity standard. The most important of these bizarre characteristics is the burying of valuable commodities.

One type of commodity standard would extend symmetalism much farther than would merely using gold and silver.[9] The government would agree to buy a specified bundle of goods at a fixed nominal price. The selling price could be slightly higher to pay the costs and to earn a profit for printing money. This additional fee is called **seigniorage**. The physical amount of each commodity in the bundle would be fixed, as would the total nominal price of the entire bundle. Many goods could be included in this bundle, such as nonperishable agricultural products and standardized manufactured goods. Agricultural goods might be ruled out because their short-run supply is relatively unresponsive to price changes.

The government must store large quantities of these bundles. This may be especially undesirable if some commodity in the bundle (say, a basic foodstuff) is in short supply. Benjamin Graham suggested that futures contracts on the commodity be used to replace the actual commodity under these conditions.[10] But this may be a poor suggestion, because a higher future price may induce more private storage, worsening the current supply problems.

Notice that each of the commodities in the bundle can fluctuate in price, so long as the total price of the bundle does not fluctuate from the price set by the government and the government does not exhaust its supply of the commodities in the bundle. This plan would stabilize the price level more rapidly than would a brick or gold standard. Still, changes in the costs of producing the commodities in the bundle, caused by changes in technology, changes in tastes and preferences for these commodities in nonmonetary uses, and many other factors could cause substantial oscillations in the price level and real income. The chance of many countries' adopting the same commodity bundle for an international commodity standard would be small. If the same bundle were not adopted, countries would be on different standards, and there would not be fixed rates of exchange between their currencies. The automatic countercyclical feature of the plan would still be operable in each country. Compared with the single-commodity gold standard, this commodity standard could produce more rapid countercyclical adjustments. However, the alternative cost of the resources that might have to be stored by the government and the costs of storage are probably too large to make the idea more than an example to indicate the waste involved in commodity standards.

INTERNATIONAL CURRENCY AND THE
INTERNATIONAL MONETARY FUND

The Bretton Woods Agreement of 1944 led to the establishment of the International Monetary Fund (IMF), an organization affiliated with the United Nations. The IMF began with 35 national government members and had 140 in 1979. Most noncommunist nations are members. Switzerland is a notable exception.

The IMF was created on December 18, 1946, by the Articles of Agreement formulated at the United Nations Monetary and Financial Conference held in Bretton Woods, New Hampshire, in July 1944. The International Bank for Reconstruction and Development, known as the World Bank, was also concurrently created. All IMF members must also be members of this bank. The World Bank makes long-term loans for economic development.

The IMF originally negotiated the relative prices of all members' currencies in terms of gold or U.S. dollars, and members attempted to maintain their currency prices within 1 percent of these fixed exchange prices. Countries could vary the price between 90 and 110 percent of the fixed price after consultation, but such limited changes did not require permission from the IMF.

Each country was required to place funds at the IMF consisting of one fourth gold or U.S. dollars and three fourths its own currency. The IMF lent these funds, under certain conditions, to member countries that ran short of foreign exchange. The IMF was unable to provide sufficient credit to cover chronic balance of payments deficits or, in some cases to restrain government policies to the maintenance within limits of the fixed exchange prices.

The exchange rate system, but not the IMF, fell apart when the United States closed its gold window in 1971 and generalized floating began in 1973. To supplement or replace this system, plans have been suggested to create an international money, managed by the IMF. Robert Triffin suggested a comprehensive plan that would require member countries to hold a fraction of their reserves with the IMF.[11] The IMF could engage in open market operations to acquire dollars in exchange for IMF deposits. The deposits would be "guaranteed" by the reserves from members. The IMF would then be creating international bank money that all member countries would agree to exchange for their goods and services.

A plan was adopted by the IMF for issuing **special drawing rights (SDRs)**. SDRs were created on July 28, 1969, to be used as reserve assets that could be used by member central banks to settle accounts among themselves. The value of the SDR was at first tied to gold and then, on July 1, 1976, to a basket of 16 currencies (see Table 33-2). On January 1, 1981, the basket was reduced to 5 currencies. The U.S. dollar was given a 42 percent weight; the German mark a 19 percent weight; and the French franc, Japanese yen, and British pound each were given a 13 percent weight. The SDR is an official international currency.

Since 1975 there have been some international transactions in SDR units.

TABLE 33-2   Units of Currencies in the Special Drawing Rights Basket, Selected Years, 1974–1981*

The IMF—which daily publishes the official value or exchange rate and the commercial rate for the SDR—and the commercial banks use the same method to calculate the value of the SDR in U.S. dollar terms. But the result varies, depending on the spot exchange rates used. For example, on November 2, 1981, the IMF reported that the exchange value for the official SDR was $1.1596. This was based on the noon middle market rates in London provided by the Bank of England. (If the London markets are closed, the IMF obtains its exchange rates from the Federal Reserve Bank of New York; if the New York markets are closed, the Deutsche Bundesbank in Frankfurt provides the rates.) If the commercial banks had used the 10 A.M. middle market interbank rates in New York for the same date, the dollar value of the SDR would have been $1.1613.

Currency	Effective July 1, 1974		Effective July 1, 1978		Effective January 1, 1981	
U.S. dollar	0.40	(33.0)	0.40	(33.0)	0.54	(42.0)
German mark	0.38	(12.5)	0.32	(12.5)	0.46	(19.0)
Japanese yen	26.00	(7.5)	21.00	(7.5)	34.00	(13.0)
French franc	0.44	(7.5)	0.42	(7.5)	0.74	(13.0)
British pound sterling	0.045	(9.0)	0.05	(7.5)	0.071	(13.0)
Italian lira	47.00	(6.0)	52.00	(5.0)	—	
Dutch guilder	0.14	(4.5)	0.14	(5.0)	—	
Canadian dollar	0.071	(6.0)	0.07	(5.0)	—	
Belgian franc	1.60	(3.5)	1.60	(4.0)	—	
Saudi Arabian riyal	—		0.13	(3.0)	—	
Swedish krona	0.13	(2.5)	0.11	(2.0)	—	
Iranian rial	—		1.70	(2.0)	—	
Australian dollar	0.012	(1.5)	0.017	(1.5)	—	
Danish krone	0.11	(1.5)	—		—	
Spanish peseta	1.10	(1.5)	1.50	(1.5)	—	
Norwegian krone	0.099	(1.5)	0.10	(1.5)	—	
Austrian schilling	0.22	(1.0)	0.28	(1.5)	—	
South African rand	0.0082	(1.0)	—		—	

* Percentage weight in basket at base period in parentheses.
Source: Dorothy Meadow Sobol, "The SDR in Private International Finance," *Quarterly Review*, Federal Reserve Bank of New York, Winter 1981–1982, p. 32.

That is, transactors agree to pay in terms of the currency composition of the SDR's official value. This practice accelerated in 1981. Loans are said to be SDR denominated if they are recorded on the basis of SDR units. Chemical Bank issued SDR-denominated CDs in 1980 through its London branch. The market in private SDRs was estimated to be roughly SDR 3 billion at the beginning of 1981 and SDR 5 to 7 billion by the end of 1981.[12]

There are three important stumbling blocks to the wide implementation by an international organization of an international money. First, it is difficult to work out a plan for the initial distribution of the international money between countries. Second, governments will be hesitant to allow international organizations to issue significant quantities of money that can be exchanged for goods and services in the country. Third, most countries can offer more substantial guarantees for their currencies. These guarantees are in the form of their total marketable stock of wealth and their current output of goods and services, for which their currency can be exchanged. An international organization with relatively small reserves of convertible currencies and precious metals and with virtually no power to force its large members to maintain their agreements may offer a less appealing guarantee than most larger countries provide.

FLEXIBLE EXCHANGE RATES

If the internal price level of a country were perfectly flexible, the most important arguments for a flexible exchange rate would collapse. Assume that the balance of payments is initially in equilibrium at a full employment level of output. There is then an increased demand for imports and a decreased demand for domestic goods and services by residents. This causes a balance-of-payments deficit. If the domestic price level rapidly falls, the internal demand for domestic output and the foreign demand for exports will normally increase to restore balance-of-payments equilibrium at a full employment level. This solution corresponds to the conditions of price flexibility in the *IS–LM* model of Chapter 23. An important condition for unemployment equilibrium, downward rigidity in wages and prices, is removed.

Balance-of-payments equilibrium can be attained under fixed exchange rates if the internal price level adjusts to the new equilibrium level. However, if a fall in prices is necessary to attain equilibrium and if prices are slow to fall, the adjustment period may be exceedingly long. In the meantime, the demand for domestic output will decline, and domestic unemployment will rise.

This situation is somewhat analogous to that of a shoe store owner who demands $10 a pair for shoes that are currently thought by most customers to be worth $5. He sells very few shoes at $10 a pair and is driven into a depressed state, in which he must dramatically reduce his standard of living to a starvation level. "By gosh," he can assert, "no one can say my shoes are worth a cent less than $10." But if the volume of shoes he sells is small relative to the total market (as is true of the international trade of a small country), he may have to change his "fixed" rate of exchange for shoes. If the volume of shoes he sells is large or if his shoes have few substitutes, he may take much longer to adjust to the underlying equilibrium price.

The proponents of flexible exchange rates argue that a large part of the internal price level adjustments and real income adjustments could be avoided by a small change in the exchange rates.[13] For example, an increased demand by U.S. citizens for British goods could be partially absorbed by a change in the relative price of the two currencies. Instead of a prolonged adjustment in the United States, which may include a substantial income adjustment—a recession—the relative international exchange price of U.S. dollars would fall to a lower equilibrium level.

Proponents of flexible exchange rates argue that fixed exchange rates only camouflage the underlying adjustments in real variables. Fixed rates obscure the adjustment process by indicating that the relative prices of currency have not changed. Instead of uncertainties about future spot exchange rates, fixed rates produce increased uncertainties about future real income, other internal economic variables, and the supply of foreign reserves and credit that will be available to support the currency. Although a system of flexible rates does make future exchange rates uncertain, a forward market in currencies removes much of this uncertainty. The uncertainty about future exchange rates is borne by traders who stand willing to sell a contract for the delivery of foreign currency in the future at a fixed price.

Many economists (at least in the United States) are probably in favor of flexible exchange rates between some areas of the world. Many, perhaps the majority, advocate flexible exchange rates between all countries with different currencies. But there are influential economists who disagree with the majority view. Jacques Rueff, for example, argued for a return to the gold standard because it alone has commanded confidence through the centuries.[14]

OPTIMUM CURRENCY AREAS

If flexible exchange rates eliminate much of the costly changes in internal variables, such as domestic real income and internal prices, why not have different currencies for Indiana and Illinois, adjacent states in the United States? An increased demand by Illinois residents for goods in Indiana would not cause much unemployment in Illinois or inflation in Indiana. The relative value of Illinois currency would simply fall. This benefit from a single currency brings up the analysis developed by Robert Mundell on the optimum size of a currency area.[15] The more flexible wages and prices are and the more mobile labor is (between Indiana and Illinois), the less need there will be for separate currencies. The adjustment to an increased demand for Indiana goods could be rapidly resolved without a recession in Illinois or an exchange adjustment in the relative price of their separate currencies. Workers would move to Indiana, and the prices of goods and labor would temporarily rise in Indiana and fall in Illinois.

Suppose that wages and prices are farily rigid in each state and that the mobility of labor between the states is negligible. The increased demand for Indiana goods may cause a prolonged recession in Illinois if the two states have the same currency (as at present) and therefore have a fixed rate of exchange between their currencies.

On the other hand, separate currencies with flexible exchange rates reduce the services of money. The separate state currencies can be used only in a limited area. Costly arrangements must be made to maintain reserves of "foreign" currency and to trade the currency. If many of the goods consumed in each state are imported, frequent and large changes in exchange rates can cause frequent and large changes in the internal cost of goods. The increased variation in the internal cost of goods from flexible exchange rates may impose larger real costs than would be imposed by changes in real output under fixed exchange rates.

The balance of payments may be affected by capital flows, which are likely to be more rapid and more mobile than is the migration of labor. The optimum currency area may be larger than would be indicated from a study of labor migration, once capital flows are considered.

Very few people would argue for a different currency in Illinois than in Indiana. The loss in the services performed by money and the mobility of capital and labor between these states are the bases of strong arguments for a single currency, a fixed exchange rate. The analogy leads to the more relevant question: What is the optimum size of a currency area? Or, equivalently, what is the size of an area (or group of countries in different geographical areas) that should have fixed exchange rates? The difficulty in answering this question led Harry Johnson to make the following observations, given the present state of knowledge: "Specifically, it seems to me that the optimum currency area problem has proved to be something of a dead-end problem."[16] It may parallel problems such as determining the optimum size of firms or countries. Often these problems tend to be answered in an ad hoc way, according to the size of firms and countries that survive for a long enough period in a given (equilibrium) healthy condition. The world is split into national divisions that are taken as given in the immediate future. Each major country wishes to have control over its internal money supply. However, the attempt to form optimum currency areas, such as the European monetary system, does transcend national boundaries. Mundell's insightful analysis provides a useful vehicle for evaluating the optimum size of a currency area and is not, for this purpose, a dead end.

KEY CURRENCY AND THE GOLD EXCHANGE STANDARD

The U.S. dollar has been a key currency in the post–World War II period, just as was the British currency before the 1930s. A key currency is a form of international currency that is created by a single country. Most of the free-world countries have agreed (in meetings of their central bankers) to use either U.S. dollars or gold in international transactions. This is called a gold exchange standard or, more specifically in its post–World War II form, a dollar–gold standard.

The key currency country has certain advantages. For a negligible cost, it can print money and trade it for the output of foreign countries. A U.S. grant in aid of $100 to a less developed country does not necessarily cost the U.S. $100 in goods and services. Suppose that the donee (recipient) country uses $50 to buy U.S. goods and $50 to buy Volkswagens in West Germany. The

West German government keeps the $50 to use in world trade and, in effect, pays approximately half of the cost of the U.S. grant-in-aid, as long as the $50 is not exchanged for U.S. goods and services. For this reason, countries that use the key currency usually want the key currency country to run a surplus, or at least to achieve a balance in its balance of payments. At the same time, there is sometimes the inconsistent desire to have an expanding international currency to accommodate the needs of world trade. The United States has run deficits almost constantly since 1959. By August 1971, the U.S. gold stock, valued at $35 per ounce, had been reduced through exchanges for U.S. dollars to $10.5 billion from its 1949 peak of $24 billion. The United States had over $60 billion in dollar liabilities held by foreigners that was convertible into gold at $35 an ounce at the U.S. Treasury.

Leland Yaeger described the drama leading to President Richard Nixon's announcement that the United States was "going off gold." The final spark that put the plan in motion was provided by John Connally, secretary of the Treasury, in a meeting of high officials with the president at Camp David on Friday, August 13, 1971: "What is our immediate problem? We are meeting here because we are in trouble overseas. The British came in today to ask us to cover $3 billion of their dollar reserves [against loss]. Anybody can topple us—anytime they want—we have left ourselves completely exposed."[17]

When President Nixon closed the gold window in August 1971 (eliminating all transactions in gold by the U.S. Treasury except for an occasional sale of gold), U.S. dollars continued to be used, along with gold, as international money. U.S. dollars were then on a flexible rate with respect to gold and other currencies, with some intervention by the U.S. government to control the price of dollars.[18] U.S. dollars held by foreigners could still be exchanged for goods and services produced in the United States, even though they could not be traded for gold owned by the U.S. Treasury.

Proponents of flexible exchange rates praised the U.S. action. Some were concerned about U.S. intervention in the foreign exchange market to manipulate the exchange rate of dollars (a dirty float) at levels that were inconsistent with long-run equilibrium in the balance of payments.

The U.S. monetary authorities (the Federal Reserve and the U.S. Treasury) were (according to proponents of flexible exchange rates) relieved of the task of maintaining a monetary policy with the often inconsistent external (balance-of-payments equilibrium) and internal (such as price stability) policy targets. The flexible exchange rate could be left alone. However, some observers believed that under a system of flexible exchange rates, devaluations and increases in the exchange value of the domestic currency sufficiently affect the price level to warrant a dirty float or even a return to fixed exchange rates.

Although some observers predicted dire consequences from floating, including the elimination of the U.S. dollar as a key currency, such consequences did not come to pass. However, it is not clear that the flexible exchange rate achieved all the objectives that its proponents envisioned. One of the reasons for this is that the period since 1973 has been marked by a number of problems and crises, which produced gyrations in many economic variables, including the exchange rate of the U.S. dollar. Those crises included in 1973, the self-destruction of wage–price controls in the United States; an oil boycott against the United States by the OPEC countries; and rapid inflation in the 1970s and from 1978 through at least 1987. The United States has run a persistently large deficit. The U.S. dollar fell in value from April 1978 until November 1978. Was this a fall to a new equilibrium level for the U.S. dollar or a short-run fluctuation that should be offset by government action?

On November 1, 1978, President Jimmy Carter unveiled a series of measures to bolster the dollar, including his plan for massive intervention to buy U.S. dollars. There seemed to be general support in the United States, among government officials and members of the U.S. Congress, for this intervention. Some economists pointed out that this intervention would entail a high cost for a temporary lull in the fall of the dollar to its equilibrium level. From October 1977 to October 31, 1978, the dollar had depreciated by more than 12 percent (on a bilateral trade-weighted basis and by about 19 percent using multilateral trade weights). For a year after Carter's November speech, the dollar remained fairly stable. The value of the dollar may have been helped by other countries' policies of more rapid money growth, which tended to reduce the international value of their currencies; but more important, the intervention appeared to have been successful.

Opponents of a freely floating exchange rate can point to 1978 and to a similar decline in the 1986–1987 period as periods in which the dollar fell so rapidly that it produced extreme uncertainty in domestic and foreign financial markets, not only about the future value of the dollar, but also about the general health of the U.S. economy. Those who favor flexible exchange rates would not, in many cases, disagree with this statement. They would add, however, that the basic cause of the problem was not falling exchange rates; it was merely a symptom of other problems, such as surging monetary growth and the resulting inflation.

It is very likely that a system of fixed exchange rates could not have been held in place in the period since 1973. If this is the case, the argument for or against flexible exchange rates should really be posed in terms of those who believe in freely fluctuating exchange rates and those who believe that exchange rates should be controlled for short periods.

Despite all these problems, the U.S. dollar has continued to serve as the key currency.[19] In periodic meetings central bankers sometimes produced proposals for changes in the international payments system. Although it was becoming apparent that a return to a fixed-rate system was impossible, some meetings of central bankers and heads of state emphasized closer cooperation and even outlined the steps necessary to return to a fixed-rate system. However, at the meetings of the heads of state at Rambouillet, France, in 1975 and the Interim Committee of Governors of the International Monetary Fund in Jamaica in 1976, there was a realization of the need for a flexible exchange system. There was disagreement over how much flexibility should be allowed. As Table 33-1 shows, intervention and pegging are prevalent.

TABLE 33-3   Federal Reserve Reciprocal Currency Arrangements, July 31, 1981 (millions of dollars)

On July 31, 1981, the reciprocal currency arrangements, known as the SWAP facility, were authorized to be a maximum of $30.1 billion. The authorization for this limit was given by the Federal Reserve.

Institution	Amount of Facility, July 31, 1981 (millions)
Austrian National Bank	$ 250
National Bank of Belgium	1,000
Bank of Canada	2,000
National Bank of Denmark	250
Bank of England	3,000
Bank of France	2,000
German Federal Bank	6,000
Bank of Italy	3,000
Bank of Japan	5,000
Bank of Mexico	700
Netherlands Bank	500
Bank of Norway	250
Bank of Sweden	300
Swiss National Bank	4,000
Bank for International Settlements	
Swiss francs (dollars)	600
Other authorized European currencies (dollars)	1,250
Total	$30,100

Source: Quarterly Review, Federal Reserve Bank of New York, Autumn 1981, p. 47.

Intervention in the United States has been carried out primarily by the Federal Reserve in consultation with the Treasury. Money used for intervention is often split between Federal Reserve and Treasury balances.

The Federal Reserve, without clear authority—as evidenced by the Federal Open Market Committee meeting minutes for 1962—supervises a huge reciprocal currency arrangement program. These so-called SWAP arrangements allow countries to swap currencies (such as dollars for pesos), ostensibly to support various currencies. On July 31, 1981, the Federal Reserve authorized $30.1 billion for SWAP lines of exchange (see Table 33-3). Not the Congress or the president of the United States or the secretary of the Treasury apparently officially authorized this huge reciprocal currency facility.

STUDY QUESTIONS

1.   How are international payments made? Describe the different types of arrangements.
2.   What kind of arrangements can be made for determining the international price of a currency?

3. How does the gold standard work, and what automatic mechanisms does it provide?
4. What are SDRs and the European currency unit?
5. From the standpoint of optimum currency areas, should every country adopt flexible exchange rates? Under what conditions would it be desirable for a small country to peg the value of its currency to the value of the currency of a large country?
6. Why do countries still use U.S. dollars as a key currency? What circumstances would cause a shift to another key currency? Is it likely that an international currency such as SDRs will take the place of U.S. dollars as international money?
7. Describe the current system for the determination of the values of money in international trade.

GLOSSARY

Automatic countercyclical mechanism. A mechanism occurring under a gold standard, characterized by automatic changes in variables such as the money supply that tend to offset and correct business cycle fluctuations.

Bimetalic standard. A commodity standard in which the prices of two precious metals (such as gold and silver) are pegged at separate levels.

Clean float. A system of flexible exchange rates with no government intervention.

Commodity reserve standard. See **Commodity standard.**

Commodity standard. A system under which a country pegs the price of a commodity such as gold by offering to buy or sell it at a fixed price in unlimited amounts, as a mechanism for controlling the money supply so as to stabilize the price level.

Currency union. An arrangement among a group of countries to peg the exchange rate among their currencies while maintaining flexible exchange rates with other countries.

Dirty float. An exchange rate policy of intermittent intervention by a central bank to control the exchange rate of its currency.

Fixed or **pegged exchange rates.** A policy that keeps an exchange rate constant.

Flexible or **floating exchange rates.** A system for determining the international price of a currency that relies on market conditions.

Forward premium or **discount.** A positive or negative difference between the forward and spot prices, respectively.

Forward transactions. Transactions that require an exchange of funds at a future date specified on the forward contract.

Gold–dollar or **dollar–gold/exchange standard.** The international payment system used since World War II, whereby gold and U.S. dollars are international media of exchange.

Gold standard. A monetary system under which a central bank agrees to buy and sell unlimited amounts of gold for a fixed exchange price of the domestic currency. Under a pure gold standard, the monetary base is changed only by this method.

International money. Money accepted in trade by many countries that can be produced by an international organization such as the International Monetary Fund. It produces special drawing rights (SDRs) that are used only by central banks.

Key currency. An arrangement in international trade whereby many countries agree to settle foreign transactions with the currency of a particular country. Currently, the key currency is U.S. dollars.

Key currency nation. The country issuing the key currency.

Limited flexible exchange rate. An exchange rate policy in which one or more central banks intervenes whenever the exchange rate (or rates) move outside a given tolerance range. It is identical to a pegged rate with a tolerance range if the tolerance range is narrow.

Managed float. See **Dirty float.**

Sovereign risk. The risk of losses on forward contracts in foreign currencies due to the imposition of exchange controls on the currency.

Seigniorage. Narrowly defined, the charge for issuing currency (collected by the sovereign or central bank) when a precious metal, such as gold, is sold to a government. Originally, it was the charge for minting bullion into coins. When no profit is made and only costs are covered, it is called *brassage.*

Special drawing rights (SDRs). Reserve assets that can be used by IMF-member central banks to settle accounts among themselves.

Spot transactions. Transactions that require the exchange of deposits by two days after the date of the contract.

Sterilization of the effects of gold inflows and outflows. A government policy in which the effects of gold flows in and out of the country on the money supply or monetary base are offset through monetary policies such as those carried out at the open market desk of the Federal Reserve.

Symmetalism. An arrangement in which a government agrees to buy and sell a combined unit of gold and silver, in a specified proportion and at a fixed nominal price.

NOTES

1. An excellent review of the extensive tests on the efficiency of the foreign exchange markets was presented by Richard M. Levich, "On the Efficiency of Markets for Foreign Exchange," in Rudiger Dornbusch and Jacob A. Frankel, eds., *International Economic Policy: Theory and Evidence* (Baltimore: Johns Hopkins University Press, 1979), pp. 246–267.
2. *International Letter*, Federal Reserve Bank of Chicago, February 12, 1982, p. 3.
3. Anna J. Schwartz, "Reflections on the Gold Commission Report," *Journal of Money, Credit and Banking*, November 1982, pt. 1, pp. 538–551, 554.

4. Ibid., p. 540.

5. Ibid., p. 542.

6. Ibid.

7. See Milton Friedman, "Commodity-Reserve Currency," reprinted in Milton Friedman, *Essays in Positive Economics* (Chicago: University of Chicago Press, 1953), pp. 204–250.

8. Ibid., p. 212.

9. This was advocated by Benjamin Graham in *Storage and Stability* (New York: McGraw-Hill, 1937) and *World Commodities and World Currency* (New York: McGraw-Hill, 1944); and by Frank Graham (not related), *Social Goals and Economic Institutions* (Princeton, N.J.: Princeton University Press, 1942).

10. See Friedman's discussion, "Commodity-Reserve Currency," p. 225, footnote 15, and F. A. Hayek's support of this idea in "A Commodity-Reserve Currency," *Economic Journal*, June–September 1943, pp. 176–184.

11. Robert Triffin, *Gold and the Dollar Crisis* (New Haven, Conn.: Yale University Press, 1960).

12. Dorothy Meadow Sobol, "The SDR in Private International Finance," *Quarterly Review*, Federal Reserve Bank of New York, Winter 1981–1982, p. 35.

13. The classic statement in support of flexible exchange rates is Milton Friedman's "The Case for Flexible Exchange Rates," in Friedman, *Essays in Positive Economics*, pp. 157–203. Henry C. Wallich presented an opposing view in a widely reprinted statement, " A Defense of Fixed Exchange Rates," from United States Balance of Payments Hearings Before the Joint Economic Committee, 88th Cong., 1st sess., Pt. 3. For a defense of the pure gold standard (and fixed exchange rates), see Jacques Rueff, *The Monetary Sin of the West* (New York: Macmillan, 1972).

14. Rueff, *The Monetary Sin of the West*. See also Robert Mundell, "The Monetary Consequences of Jacques Rueff—Review Article," *Journal of Business*, July 1973, pp. 384–395.

15. For an excellent discussion of optimum currency areas and many other aspects of the argument for and against flexible exchange rates, see Robert A. Mundell and Alexander K. Swoboda, eds., *Monetary Problems of the International Economy* (Chicago: University of Chicago Press, 1969).

16. Harry Johnson believed that once the domain of capital mobility is introduced, the determinant of the optimum currency area "becomes too complex for its statement to be very illuminating." For his comments, see Mundell and Swoboda, *Monetary Problems of the International Economy*, p. 396.

17. Leland B. Yaeger, *The Night We Floated*, International Institute for Economic Research (Ottawa, Ill.: Green-Hill Publishers, 1977), p. 6.

18. Before August 1971, the U.S. Treasury bought and sold gold at $35 per

ounce, whereas the gold traded in free markets was sold at a higher price. This *two-tier system* of separate official and market prices for gold was followed by many governments. After 1971, the U.S. government raised its official price of gold to $42.44 per ounce, but still did not buy or sell any gold. On November 13, 1973, the United States, together with six European countries, agreed to recognize the "true price" of gold at $100 an ounce. Gold was to be officially valued at its market price. The purpose of this agreement appeared to be to end the two-tier system and to enable governments to sell gold at the market price. The dollar exchange price was generally pegged by foreign central bankers until March 1973, when there was generalized floating of exchange rates.

19. Rueff argued in *The Monetary Sin of the West* that the gold exchange standard in the post–World War II period would collapse after 1971 as it did in 1931. Mundell attempted to analyze why he was wrong in his elegant review, "The Monetary Consequences of Jacques Rueff."

CHAPTER 34

THE EURODOLLAR MARKET

CHAPTER PREVIEW

Introduction. There is a huge market for bank deposits denominated in the currency of a country other than the one in which the deposit is made.

Answers to Six Questions. Questions including "What is it?" "How did it come about?" and "What effect does it have on inflation and the U.S. money supply?" are discussed.

Eurobonds. These are long-term instruments of the Eurocurrency market.

Domestic Deregulated International Banking Facilities. Special banking facilities in the United States authorized in 1981 by the Federal Reserve to be free of many domestic banking regulations are discussed.

INTRODUCTION

A huge market for bank deposits, including U.S. dollars, has grown up in many parts of the world. The market is called the *Eurocurrency market* when reference is made to all currency and the *Eurodollar market* when reference is made only to the U.S. dollar part of the market. In March 1986, the estimated (gross) size of the Eurocurrency market was nearly $3 trillion, of which 73 percent was Eurodollars (Table 34-1). The Eurocurrency market is not, however, confined to Europe, although it had 70 percent of the deposits (based on rough estimates) in 1978. The emergence of this huge market suggests a

TABLE 34-1.   Eurocurrency Market, 1979–1986

Eurocurrency Market Size

Based on foreign liabilities of banks in major European countries, the Bahamas, Bahrain, Cayman Islands, Panama, Canada, Japan, Hong Kong, and Singapore (billions of dollars at end of period).

	1979	*1980*	*1981*	*1982*	*1983*	*1984*	*June*	*1985 Sept.*	*Dec.*	*1986 Mar.*
Gross liabilities to:										
Nonbanks	$219	$278	$372	$432	$479	$497	$520	$546	$585	$610
Central banks	112	128	112	91	88	96	106	109	112	106
Other banks	904	1,172	1,470	1,645	1,711	1,793	1,845	1,986	2.149	2,248
Total	1,245	1,578	1,954	2.168	2,278	2,386	2,471	2,641	2,846	2,964
Eurodollars as percentage of total gross liabilities in all Eurocurrencies	72%	76%	79%	80%	81%	82%	80%	77%	75%	73%
Dollar liabilities of foreign branches of U.S. banks as percentage of total gross liabilities in all Eurocurrencies	22%	20%	19%	18%	17%	15%	15%	13%	12%	11%

Eurodollar Deposit Rates

Eurodollar deposits are deposits denominated and payable in U.S. dollars held by banks located outside the United States. Rates are those bid in London at or near the end of the month.

	1982 Dec.	*1983 Dec.*	*1984 Dec.*	*1985 Dec.*	*1986 Mar.*	*June*	*Sept.*
Overnight	8.75%	9.08%	7.81%	8.13%	7.26%	6.93%	5.80%
Seven-day	9.60	11.38	8.52	8.34	7.71	6.98	6.14
One-month	9.26	10.00	8.34	8.17	7.50	6.96	6.04
Three-month	9.36	10.00	8.61	7.95	7.43	6.91	6.00
Six-month	9.64	10.19	9.11	7.94	7.38	6.91	5.99
Twelve-month	9.76	10.38	9.86	7.98	7.43	7.04	6.19

Sources: International Economic Conditions, Federal Reserve Bank of St. Louis, October 1986, p. 8, from the Board of Governors of the Federal Reserve System and Morgan Guaranty Trust Company.

number of questions:

1. What is it?
2. Why did it happen?
3. What does it do?
4. Is it unstable?
5. Is it inflationary?
6. Does it interfere with control of the U.S. money supply?

We will discuss the answers to those questions and then the Eurobond market.

ANSWERS TO SIX QUESTIONS

What Is It?

What is the Eurocurrency market?[1] Any bank deposit in any country that is denominated in another country's currency is a Eurocurrency deposit. For example, a deposit in a French bank denominated in Dutch guilders qualifies as such a deposit. Most of these foreign deposits are denominated in U.S. dollars, so that the Eurodollar market is a substantial portion of the Eurocurrency market. These deposits are not subject to the same stringent regulations as they would be if they were in their domestic country. Together with U.S. dollar–denominated securities, they are the financial assets of the Eurodollar market.

One of the first participants was the Soviet-controlled Banque Commerciale pour l'Europe, which had the code name Eurobank, from which the market took its name. In the 1950s, the bank began holding U.S. dollar–denominated deposits. The U.S. dollar was the key currency and therefore useful in international trade, but there was a preference for holding the funds outside the United States. This preference can be based on many factors, such as privacy and freedom from U.S. government regulations. An important factor is the avoidance of a freeze or an expropriation such as the U.S. freeze on Iranian government bank deposits in 1979. (Although Eurodollar deposits in foreign branches of U.S. banks were ordered frozen by the U.S. government, the legality of this order under foreign laws is probably very questionable.)

Eurodollars are found in Europe, Canada, Hong Kong, Panama, Singapore, and Japan. Roughly 80 percent of gross (total liabilities without any offsetting adjustments) Eurodollar deposits were interbank deposits, and 20 percent were nonbank deposits, according to estimates in mid-1980. Of the 20 percent nonbank deposits, approximately 5 percent were held by U.S. nonbank residents.

Overnight Eurodollars deposits of nonbank U.S. residents are included in the M-2 definition of money. In October 1983 they amounted to $10.5 billion, or 0.5 percent of M-2. Eurodollar deposits of nonbank U.S. residents with maturities greater than one day are included in M-3. They amounted to $91.3

billion, or 3.6 percent of M-3. (See Chapter 2 for a description of these monetary aggregates.) These data are Federal estimates,[2] and the overnight estimates are from the Caribbean branches of U.S. banks. The overnight Eurodollar deposits are officially added into M-2, although an argument could be made to include them in M-1.

Eurodollar certificates of deposit (CDs), first introduced in 1966, amounted to roughly $50 billion at the beginning of 1980. There is an active secondary market in these CDs. Eurodollar floating-rate CDs and Eurodollar floating-rate notes were used in the variable interest rate period in the early 1980s. The coupon rate is typically reset every three or six months between one-eighth and one-fourth percentage point over the interbank lending rate, the London Interbank borrowing rate, or LIBOR.[3]

Why Did It Happen?

The Eurodollar market is in part an extension of the services provided by U.S. dollars, which serve as the key currency in international trade. What caused the rapid growth of the Eurocurrency market beginning in the 1960s? The answer is stringent regulations placed on banking and currencies by domestic countries that are generally not in the Eurocurrency market. For example, in the United States, reserve requirements for large banks were, until 1981, as high as 16.25 percent of any additions to demand deposits. Reserve requirements are generally not applicable to the deposits of banks in the Eurodollar market. In addition, ceilings on interest payments on savings deposits and the prohibition against the payment of interest on domestic demand deposits were not applicable in the Eurodollar market. Domestic banks in the United States have kept only a portion of their deposits in the United States. Thus a large part of their deposits are free of reserve requirements or requirements affecting the maximum amount of interest that can be paid on deposits.

The Eurodollar market was greatly stimulated by the restraints on capital movements imposed by President John F. Kennedy in 1963. A tax was placed on the sales of foreign bonds and equities in the United States. Guidelines were placed on American banks in 1965 that limited their acquisition of foreign assets. In 1968, a reinvestment requirement was placed on American multinational corporations, requiring them to raise funds for new direct foreign investments outside the United States.

Primarily because of the competition from the Eurodollar market, in 1970 the Federal Reserve allowed the sale by banks of certificates of deposit with no ceiling rates (in a minimum size of $100,000). Those CDs are similar to most Eurocurrency deposits, which resemble short-term time deposits rather than demand deposits. However, until 1980, U.S. member banks could not write domestic CDs with maturities of 30 days or less. The Eurodollar market captured the short-term CD business. In 1980, the Federal Reserve announced that it would consider allowing CDs to be written for 15 days or more.

The Depository Institution Deregulation and Monetary Control Act of

1980 removed many of the regulations that induced the export of the U.S. banking business to the Eurodollar market. Reserve requirements were substantially lowered, and the slow removal of interest rate ceilings was authorized. The phase-in for the provision of this law will not be complete until 1988 (1993 in Hawaii).

One way to view the controls placed on domestic U.S. banks is that they were the stimulus for exporting a large portion of American banking activity into the Eurocurrency market, where the regulations are more lax. The reader may ask, Why not impose the same requirements on branches of domestic banks operating offshore? One answer is that if such regulations were imposed only on U.S. banks, they would be at a competitive disadvantage in international markets. Regulations would have to be applied to the entire Eurocurrency market, and that appears to be unlikely. The reason is that some countries—from small Caribbean islands to England, with London being the center of the Eurocurrency market—where regulations are lax will probably refrain from participating in group action that would impede their profitable banking activities. In addition, capital is fungible, and new ways will be found to avoid the regulations. The regulations will therefore impose costs and inefficiencies without being equitable. Alternative solutions include the removal of onerous regulations that apply to domestic banks or to set aside an area in the domestic country that would be free of such regulations—a "free trade area."

It is interesting to note that cities in West Germany have not become major Eurocurrency centers because West Germany does apply the same reserve requirements and interest ceilings to foreign deposits in West Germany as it does to its domestic deposits, Deutsche mark deposits.

What Does It Do?

What does the Eurocurrency market do? First, it is a convenient and profitable way to conduct international trade-financing transactions. Under flexible exchange rates, transactors in international markets often want to buy forward contracts on currencies so that they can avoid the risk of unexpected currency fluctuations, which would raise the price of the commodities they have ordered for future delivery. The Eurocurrency market is used to cover these forward contracts, that is, to hold currency for a future delivery. Because there are no regulations on the payment of interest, this currency can earn market rates of interest. Second, the Eurocurrency market provides a convenient place for U.S. banks to transfer deposits so that these deposits earn market rates of interest. Third, profits from foreign branches of U.S. banks often enjoy local tax rates that are lower than those of the state where their main office is located.

The Eurocurrency market can be looked upon as a group of depository intermediaries with few regulatory constraints. Borrowers and lenders, primarily commercial banks, can use the services of those financial intermediaries to exchange financial assets more efficiently and profitably.

Is It Unstable?

Is the Eurocurrency market unstable? Will such instability cause a wave of bank failures? There is controversy surrounding the answers to these questions. Perhaps the Eurocurrency market reaches some kind of an equilibrium level of growth, depending on the cost of restrictive regulations for domestic financial assets relative to those in the Eurocurrency market. If there is some change in this differential, funds will flow rapidly into or out of the Eurocurrency market. Thus, in 1969, when interest rates on Eurodollar deposits rose much higher than did the ceiling rates on domestic U.S. bank deposits, there was a large shift of deposits from U.S. banks into the Eurocurrency market, deposits that could be "borrowed back" by domestic U.S. banks. In 1970, when ceiling rate limitations on CDs were lifted, the Eurodollar deposits were reduced. During such adjustment periods, the size of the Eurocurrency market may be unstable, that is, unpredictable.

However, because about 80 percent of the deposits are interbank deposits, they can be thought of as representing no liquidity additional to the amounts already included in the money supply of the domestic country. Remember that to avoid double counting, interbank deposits are deducted from a bank's deposits in calculating the money supply held by the nonbank public.

Perhaps the greatest misapprehensions are that the Eurodollars represent either a claim on U.S. dollars that the U.S. government must satisfy or deposits of U.S. residents and that both would suffer a huge loss of wealth in case of default. First, it must be understood that banks operating outside the United States can denominate their deposits in U.S. dollars, whether or not they have U.S. dollar reserves. If the depositor demands U.S. dollars as promised by a bank, the bank must borrow or buy U.S. dollars. This action, taken by itself, can increase the demand for U.S. dollars. But the analysis is incomplete without considering what the depositor does with the U.S. dollar. If a bill is paid or a loan payment is made, the dollars will ordinarily be redeposited in a bank. The U.S. dollar reserves are then reinvested, and the supply of dollars can increase to offset the effect of the increased demand.

The question of extreme instability resulting in the collapse of many banks is broader than the question of instability in the Eurocurrency market. It is a question of whether or not a collapse of one or more large banks would severely injure other banks and other financial institutions, causing a major international banking collapse. It is presumed that governments would rapidly supply needed reserves to their own banks and thereby maintain their solvency. This may allow for a more orderly adjustment.

Instability can be caused by a number of sources. For example, economic sanctions were imposed by Britain and some other European countries against Argentina on April 3, 1982, following Argentina's seizure of the Falkland/Malvina Islands, a British possession. The freeze immobilized $1.4 billion of Argentine deposits in London banks, making it difficult for Argentina to service its $34 billion external debt. Although this did not seem to be a serious problem at that time, the solvency of particular banks could be affected by unexpected problems such as these, in which the banks have a significant part of their portfolio invested in loans that are in, or are subject to, default. While the problems for banks with Argentine debts persisted, the banking industry was also burdened by the problems of the Mexican government in paying its debts, beginning in the summer of 1982, when world oil prices reduced Mexican oil revenues and caused a significant decline in the international value of the peso. These problems and the safety of interbank deposits in the face of such international events would be much the same under a number of plausible alternative relationships other than those in the Eurodollar market.

Is It Inflationary?

In a speech at the American Economic Association's annual meeting (1977), Robert Mundell, a leading international trade theorist, took exception to the argument that the Eurocurrency market is not inflationary. He held that even these interbank deposits could be conceived of as additions to the world's money supply. He presented rough statistical test results showing that world commodity prices had risen at about the same rate as had the growth in the Eurocurrency market. He acknowledged that many of the deposits in the Eurocurrency market would be netted out under the conventional accounting procedures of deducting interbank deposits from gross deposits; however, he found no persuasive argument for following this conventional practice.

Many other experts view the Eurodollar market in the way that financial intermediaries are viewed in the United States. That is, they make the velocity of money higher than it otherwise would be.

There is also rough evidence that the Eurodollar market is not very inflationary. If it were inflationary, it would be expected that the domestic counterpart to Eurodollars in the United States, old M-2, would have had a rising income velocity. In other words, one would expect inflation to have pushed up prices, regardless of the size of M-2. (For precision one might add, "regardless of the size of interest rates also," because interest rates affect velocity.) Recall that M-2 velocity is defined as real income, y, times the price level, P, divided by M-2:

$$V = \frac{yP}{\text{M-2}} \tag{1}$$

The velocity of old M-2 remained fairly constant during the 1960s and 1970s, indicating that Eurodollars probably did not drive up domestic prices.

Does It Interfere with the Control of the U.S. Money Supply?

The argument about the effect of the Eurocurrency market often settles on the issue of whether or not it interferes with the control of the domestic money supply. Insofar as the Eurocurrency market is fairly stable, it appears to have

TABLE 34-2 T-Accounts Showing a Conversion of Demand Deposits into Eurodollars

In the following transaction, a holder of demand deposits at a U.S. bank transfers $100 million into Eurodollar deposits at a Eurobank.* On the public's balance sheet, demand deposits (DDP) decline, and Eurodollar deposits (ED) rise by the same amount. At the Eurobank, the individual's account is credited, and the bank's Eurodollar liabilities rise by $100 million. When the check clears, the U.S. bank's demand deposit liability to the public (DPP) declines, and the demand deposit liability to the Eurobank (DDE) increases. The Eurobank's balance sheet will record this transaction as an increase in assets.

The impact of this transaction on the U.S. money stock depends on how money is measured. Using the old definition of money (M-1), which includes foreign commercial bank demand deposits at U.S. banks, the money supply will not be affected, as DDP declined and DDE rose by the same amount. Because DDP and DDE have the same reserve requirements, excess reserves are not affected, and no further contraction or expansion of loans and deposits in the United States is possible.

On the other hand, if money is measured by either M-1A or M-1B (which *exclude* foreign bank demand deposits at U.S. banks), then the money supply will decrease by the amount of the transaction, as DDP declines while the increase in DDE is not counted. Because excess reserves are still not affected, there will be no further change in the money stock. Thus, the initial effect of deposit outflows into the Eurodollar market lowers the money stock, as currently measured, by an amount equivalent to the size of the transaction.

It is important to note that in this transaction the Eurobanks collectively are assumed to hold total reserves (in the form of demand deposit balances at U.S. banks) equal to the initial dollar outflow from the U.S. banks. If, in the extreme, Eurobanks hold *no* reserves at all, the U.S. money stock, however defined, will be *unaffected.*† However, to the extent that Eurobanks hold some precautionary reserves in the form of demand deposits at U.S. banks, the qualitative effect of the Eurodollar transactions will be the same as outlined above.

Public		U.S. Banks		Eurobanks	
Assets	Liabilities	Assets	Liabilities	Assets	Liabilities
DDP − $100			DDE + $100	DDE + $100	ED + $100
ED + $100			DDP − $100		

* This Eurobank may be a foreign branch of some U.S. bank or an unaffiliated foreign bank.

† The Eurobank could create a new loan equal to the full amount of DDE, thereby drawing down such balances. The borrower would have to acquire a U.S. demand deposit before he or she could spend the proceeds of this loan. This transaction then restores the balance sheet of the U.S. bank to its original position. Note that this intermediation through the Eurodollar market generates a greater extension of credit than would have occurred if generated through the U.S. banking system only.

Source: Anatol B. Balbach and David H. Resler, "Eurodollars and the U.S. Money Supply," *Review*, Federal Reserve Bank of St. Louis, June–July 1980, pp. 6–7.

minimal impact on control of the U.S. money supply. The problem of monetary control arises if there is a technical problem, such as estimating the float between domestic banks and their foreign branches. In addition, the transfer of money in and out of the Eurodollar market has been found to produce "minimal" changes in the U.S. money supply.[4] An example of one of these changes is depicted and described in Table 34-2.

EUROBONDS

Eurobonds are the counterpart of Eurocurrency, with long maturities. International bonds, also known as Eurobonds, are underwritten by an international syndicate and are sold principally in countries other than the country of the currency in which the bond is denominated.[5] Medium-maturity lending is called *Eurocredits*. Foreign bonds are underwritten by a syndicate from one country; they are denominated in the currency of that country, and they are sold in that country—typically to nonresidents.

A novel "Euro-Swiss franc-dollar" bond was offered by the World Bank in 1982. Investors pay for the bond in U.S. dollars. The interest and return of principal payments were calculated in terms of the Swiss franc/U.S. dollar exchange rate on April 19, 1982. Thus the bonds have a constant Swiss franc value. If the Swiss franc falls in value relative to the dollar, the World Bank will guarantee the stated dollar value. The World Bank set a $6\frac{5}{8}$ percent coupon rate that was far below the 14-percent rate on dollar-denominated bonds. The World Bank was hoping that the dollar/franc rate will not change significantly. However, the lower market yield on these bonds may accurately reflect the cost of this risk, so that there will be little benefit, except the appearance of low financing costs.

DOMESTIC DEREGULATED INTERNATIONAL BANKING FACILITIES

The Board of Governors authorized the establishment of *domestic international banking facilities*, *IBFs*, by U.S. banks, effective on December 3, 1981. The IBFs are, like Eurodollar banks, largely exempt from regulatory constraints. There are no reserve requirements or interest rate ceilings. However, deposits may generally be accepted only from non-U.S. residents and other IBFs and must have a minimum maturity of two days. In addition, all deposit transactions must be in minimum amounts of $100,000. IBFs are exempted by statute from insurance requirements of the Federal Deposit Insurance Corporation. A number of states (including New York, California, Illinois, and Florida) have encouraged banking institutions to establish IBFs, by granting favorable tax treatment to IBF operations. By 1983, the IBFs held a significant percentage of the assets of the U.S. banks' foreign offices (plus IBFs), as

FIGURE 34-1. Total Assets at Foreign Offices and IBFs of U.S.–chartered Banks, Level and Percentage of Worldwide Assets of U.S.–chartered Banks, December 1973 and December 1983*

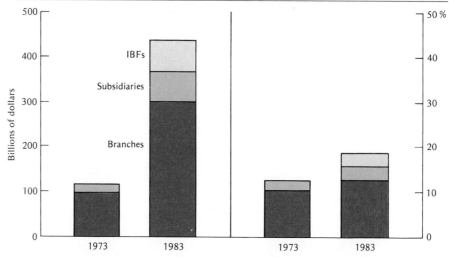

IBFs grew rapidly in the two years after their authorization in December 1981.

* Total assets at foreign offices and IBFs exclude claims on related offices—that is, claims on the parent bank and its foreign branches and subsidiaries.
Source: Federal Reserve System, *Purposes & Functions*, Board of Governors, 1984, p. 82.

shown in Figure 34-1. This popularity attests to the inducement to evade reserve requirements.

To avoid the use of IBFs for domestic business, the Board of Governors required the customers of IBFs to sign a statement of intent. If a U.S.-controlled business makes an IBF deposit or negotiates a loan, a statement must be signed to ensure that IBFs are not used via their foreign subsidiaries for domestic business. It is doubtful—more precisely, impossible—to earmark and monitor funds so that they do not return to the domestic economy after being borrowed from an IBF. Therefore, IBFs should be beneficial to firms with access to them, in much the same way as Eurodollar banks are. However, they are not perfect substitutes for Eurodollar banks. They still have regulatory constraints of the type mentioned, as well as state taxes. Nevertheless, they are a haven from the costs of much regulation for businesses with foreign business.

The exclusiveness of this haven should change by 1988. By 1988, depository institutions will have their Federal Reserve requirements on regular consumer savings accounts reduced to zero; business time accounts will be at a 3 percent reserve requirement, with authority to reduce to zero; and the ceiling rate on interest payments on consumer NOW accounts was removed in 1986. Logical additional steps would be to remove ceiling rates on business demand and savings deposits. The Eurodollar market has forcibly taught the partial ineffec-tiveness of onerous restrictions on financial institutions and on income from financial assets. Innovations to circumvent these regulations stimulated the giant financial markets abroad.

STUDY QUESTIONS

1. What is the Eurodollar market?
2. Why did it happen?
3. What functions does it perform?
4. Is it a source of instability?
5. Does it cause inflation?
6. Does it interfere with the control of the U.S. money supply? Using T-accounts, show the effect on M-1, if any, of a transfer of funds from a domestic demand deposit in a U.S. bank to a foreign Eurodollar bank deposit. How is the effect on M-1 changed by the level of reserves held in the Eurodollar bank?
7. What is an IBF? How can the Federal Reserve ensure that domestic deposits will not be rerouted through foreign banks into IBFs?

NOTES

1. For a general description of the Eurocurrency market, see Ronald I. McKinnon "The Eurocurrency Market," in *Essays in International Finance*, December 1977, International Finance Section, Department of Economics, Princeton University (Princeton, N.J.: Princeton University Press, 1977) pp. 1–40. Basic, but incomplete, data on the Eurocurrency market are calculated by the Bank for International Settlements, BIS. The estimates in the text were taken from *World Financial Markets*, Morgan Guaranty Trust Company of New York, February 1979, p. 15. A summary of some of the issues is found in Ann-Marie Meulendyke, "Causes and Consequences of the Eurodollar Expansion," Research Paper No. 7503, New York Federal Reserve Bank, March 1975. The development of the view that the Eurodollar market is analogous to credit creation in the U.S. fractional reserve banking system was presented by Milton Friedman, "The Eurodollar Market: Some First Principles," *The Morgan Guaranty Survey*, October 1969, pp. 4–15. See also Richard James Sweeney and Thomas D. Willett, "Eurodollars, Petrodollars, and World Liquidity and Inflation," in Karl Brunner and Allan Meltzer, eds., *Stabilization of the Domestic and International Economy*, a supplement to the *Journal of Monetary Economics*, Carnegie-Rochester Conference Series on Public Policy, Vol. 5, 1977, pp. 277–310.

2. Board of Governors of the Federal Reserve System, *Federal Reserve Statistical Release*, February 19, 1982, pp. 4, 8.

3. Marvin Goodfriend, "Eurodollars," *Economic Review*, Federal Reserve Bank of Richmond, May–June 1981, p. 14.

4. Anatol B. Balbach and David H. Resler, "Eurodollars and the U.S. Money Supply," *Review*, Federal Reserve Bank of St. Louis, June–July 1980, pp. 2–12.

5. Federal Reserve Bank of Chicago, *International Letter*, No. 422, May 23, 1980, p. 1.

INDEX*

*Boldface page numbers indicate definitions of key terms in the end-of-chapter glossaries.

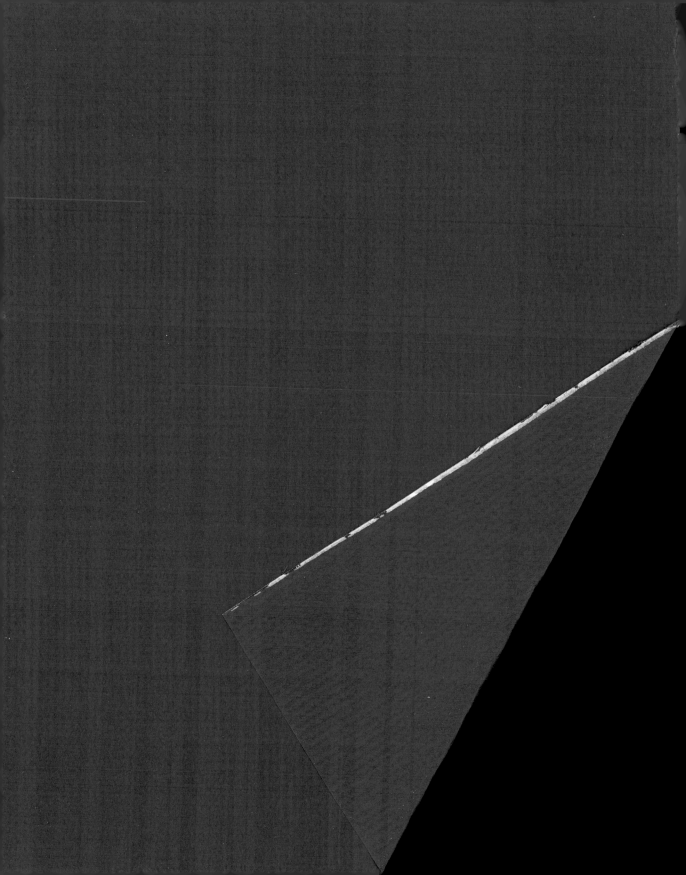